Lecture Notes in Computer Science　　11036

Commenced Publication in 1973
Founding and Former Series Editors:
Gerhard Goos, Juris Hartmanis, and Jan van Leeuwen

More information about this series at http://www.springer.com/series/7408

Thelma Elita Colanzi · Phil McMinn (Eds.)

Search-Based Software Engineering

10th International Symposium, SSBSE 2018
Montpellier, France, September 8–9, 2018
Proceedings

Springer

Editors
Thelma Elita Colanzi (iD)
State University of Maringá
Maringá
Brazil

Phil McMinn (iD)
University of Sheffield
Sheffield
UK

ISSN 0302-9743   ISSN 1611-3349   (electronic)
Lecture Notes in Computer Science
ISBN 978-3-319-99240-2   ISBN 978-3-319-99241-9   (eBook)
https://doi.org/10.1007/978-3-319-99241-9

Library of Congress Control Number: 2018951245

LNCS Sublibrary: SL2 – Programming and Software Engineering

This Springer imprint is published by the registered company Springer Nature Switzerland AG
The registered company address is: Gewerbestrasse 11, 6330 Cham, Switzerland

Foreword

Message from the General Chair

I welcome all readers to these proceedings of the 10th edition of the Symposium on Search-Based Software Engineering (SSBSE). Over the past 10 years, SSBSE has nurtured the blooming field of search-based software engineering, which has explored the exploitation of various automatic search techniques to solve all sorts of hard software engineering issues, ranging from requirements analysis to test generation and performance optimization. For this 10th edition, we designed a program that mixes significant contributions of the past decade (most influential papers, keynote and tutorial) with the current progress in the field. We also wished to open and inspire the next decade of research with a keynote that addresses the exploitation of SBSE in industry and a second one that opens the field of bio-inspired search to runtime software evolution.

Here, I wish to thank the great organizing team of SSBSE 2018 that worked hard to host this event in beautiful Montpellier. I thank Phil and Thelma, with whom I have worked very closely to set the program, plan the special events for the 10th anniversary, and synchronize all tracks. I thank Aldeida and Annibale for their engagement in the Hot-Off-the-Press Track and Wesley and José for designing the challenge track. I thank Mat for the professional interactions between Springer and the whole committee, Erik for spreading the word about SSBSE 2018, and Oscar for the Web design.

Very special thanks go to our sponsors for their great contribution to keep SSBSE an accessible scientific event: Facebook, SAAB, and Université de Montpellier. And final thanks go to the local organizing team, led by Djamel, who arranged all the logistics, interactions, with ASE and social events.

July 2018   Benoit Baudry

Message from the Program Chairs

Welcome to the proceedings of the 2018 International Symposium on Search-Based Software Engineering. It has been a privilege to be program chairs for this, the tenth edition of the symposium. We have several people to thank for their help and support in putting on a strong program for the event, which included special talks to celebrate the ten years of the symposium, all of which we hope to have captured as faithfully as possible as a permanent record in the form of these proceedings.

Firstly, we would like to thank the authors of papers submitted to the main technical track. Over the past decade, SBSE has experienced a great increase in popularity, has seen guided search techniques being applied to a wider variety of problems, and has been employed in a number of industrial applications and contexts. As a result of the great prior efforts of the community in organizing events such as SSBSE and others, research in search-based software engineering has matured to the point that is now strongly and proudly represented at the very top conferences and journals in our field. One downside to this, perhaps, is that SSBSE itself has been starting to receive fewer submissions. In organizing SSBSE 2018 then, our aim was very much to go back to and be cognizant of the original goal of the symposium — that being to "nurture and develop the SBSE research community."[1] As such, one change we made this year was to adjust the review process to build in support for authors to help them improve their work for publication and presentation at the event, through the inclusion of an explicit shepherding phase. We initially received 19 abstracts, of which 12 matured into papers for the full-paper deadline. These were then reviewed by three expert reviewers from our Program Committee. Following the reviews and discussions, six papers were accepted. The remaining six papers were given an additional three weeks to address the comments of the reviewers, under the guidance of a shepherd. Ultimately, all of these papers were also accepted. We would like to thank all of our Program Committee members for their reviews, especially those who worked extra hard in their additional role as shepherds; namely, Shaukat Ali, Andrea Arcuri, Marcio Barros, Erik Fredericks, Gregory Kapfhammer, and Marouane Kessentini.

We would also like to thank our keynote speakers. At SSBSE 2018, we continued the tradition of inviting a keynote from the software engineering community, and one from the search community. We were therefore delighted to announce our two esteemed keynote speakers. Mark Harman, the general chair of the first SSBSE in 2009, gave an industrial keynote on the use of SBSE for software testing at Facebook. Our search speaker was Guillaume Beslon, who gave a keynote on closing the gap between evolutionary biology and engineering through in silico experimentation. Big thanks are also due to our tutorial speakers, Marouane Kessentini and Matias Martinez, for their respective tutorials on search-based refactoring and repair, and for relating

---

[1] Message from the General Chair, Mark Harman, First International Symposium on Search-Based Software Engineering, 2009.

their expertise on these topics. Many keynote and tutorial speakers have written papers that appear in these proceedings to accompany their talk. We hope that the ideas for future work and industrial applications in Mark's keynote, coupled with new ideas for search techniques in Guillaume's talks, supported by the practical advice in the form of the tutorials will help inspire researchers develop new, interesting, and ground-breaking future work in SSBSE.

As the tenth edition of the symposium, SSBSE 2018 was a special event that we decided to celebrate by inviting back one keynote speaker, one tutorial speaker, and one technical paper author regarded as the "best" from the last nine symposiums. This was decided through an online vote, in which the entire SSBSE community was invited to partake. We therefore congratulate and thank Enrique Alba, for being voted best keynote, and giving an updated version of his talk from 2009 entitled "How Can Metaheuristics Help Software Engineers?"; as well as Gordon Fraser, who was voted as giving the best tutorial, originally at last year's event, on his EvoSuite search-based test generation tool for Java. We also thank Jefferson Souza for presenting his 2010 paper a second time, entitled "The Human Competitiveness of Search-Based Software Engineering," which included a perspective of the work eight years later. We congratulate him and his co-authors for being voted the best paper of SSBSE to date. All specially invited "tenth edition of SSBSE" speakers provided papers to accompany their talks, which appear in a dedicated section of these proceedings.

We have a number of people to thank for helping to coordinate this event with us. Firstly, we wish to thank our general chair, Benoit Baudry, for his organization and oversight of all aspects of the symposium. In addition to our main track, SSBSE 2018 featured a popular Hot-off-the-Press Track for late breaking work. We thank Aldeida Aleti and Annibale Panichella for organizing this, along with Wesley K. G. Assunção and José Miguel Rojas for managing the Challenge Track. Finally, a big thanks to Mathew Hall for managing the proceedings, collecting all the camera-ready versions of the papers, and ensuring everything was ready for publication; and to Oscar Luis Vera Pérez for constructing the symposium website and tirelessly handling all of our updates.

These proceedings feature work from industry and on a wide variety of research topics; from software testing to automated program repair, from optimizing an application's energy efficiency to model transformation to cloud-based resource provisioning. We hope you will enjoy reading the papers contained within them, and that you will find them stimulating and thought-provoking. Please do continue to support the event by submitting a paper and participating in next year's and future events of SSBSE. We very much hope to see you there.

July 2018   Thelma Elita Colanzi
                                                                                      Phil McMinn

Organization

Organizers

General Chair

Benoit Baudry   KTH Royal Institute of Technology, Sweden

Program Chairs

Thelma Elita Colanzi   Universidade Estadual de Maringá, Brazil
Phil McMinn   University of Sheffield, UK

Hot-off-the-Press Track Chairs

Aldeida Aleti   Monash University, Australia
Annibale Panichella   Université du Luxembourg, Luxembourg

Challenge Track Chairs

Wesley K. G. Assunção   Federal University of Technology Paraná, Brazil
José Miguel Rojas   University of Leicester, UK

Local Arrangements Chair

Djamel Seriai   University of Montpellier, France

Publicity Chair

Erik Fredericks   Oakland University, USA

Web Chair

Oscar Luis Vera Pérez   Inria, France

Proceedings Chair

Mathew Hall   University of Sheffield, UK

SSBSE Steering Committee

Andrea Arcuri   Westerdals, Norway, and University of Luxembourg
Gordon Fraser   University of Passau, Germany
Gregory Gay   University of South Carolina, USA
Lars Grunske   Humboldt University Berlin, Germany
Marouane Kessentini   University of Michigan, USA
Tim Menzies   North Carolina State University, USA
Mohamed Wiem Mkaouer   Rochester Institute of Technology, USA

Annibale Panichella   University of Luxembourg
Federica Sarro   University College London, UK
Shin Yoo   KAIST, South Korea

Technical Program Committee

Shaukat Ali   Simula Research Laboratory, Norway
Giuliano Antoniol   École Polytechnique de Montréal, Canada
Andrea Arcuri   Westerdals, Norway, and University of Luxembourg
Marcio Barros   UNIRIO, Brazil
Francisco Chicano   University of Málaga, Spain
Robert Feldt   Blekinge Institute of Technology, Sweden
Erik Fredericks   Oakland University, USA
Juan Pablo Galeotti   University of Buenos Aires, Argentina
Gregory Gay   University of South Carolina, USA
Lars Grunske   Humboldt University Berlin, Germany
Hadi Hemmati   University of Calgary, Canada
Muhammad Zohaib Iqbal   FAST-NUCES, Pakistan
Gregory Kapfhammer   Allegheny College, USA
Marouane Kessentini   University of Michigan, USA
Anne Koziolek   Karlsruhe Institute of Technology, Germany
Claire Le Goues   Carnegie Mellon University, USA
Alessandro Marchetto   Independent Researcher, Italy
Tim Menzies   North Carolina State University, USA
Leandro Minku   University of Leicester, UK
Justyna Petke   University College London, UK
Pasqualina Potena   RISE SICS Västerås AB, Sweden
Federica Sarro   University College London, UK
Christopher Simons   University of the West of England, UK
Paolo Tonella   Fondazione Bruno Kessler, Italy
Silvia Vergilio   UFPR, Brazil
Tanja Vos   Open Universiteit, The Netherlands,
                                  and Universitat Politècnica de València, Spain
David White   University of Sheffield, UK
Shin Yoo   KAIST, South Korea

Challenge Track Program Committee

Wasif Afzal   Mälardalen University, Västerås, Sweden
Jonathan M. Aitken   University of Sheffield, UK
Shaukat Ali   Simula Research Laboratory, Norway
Gordon Fraser   University of Passau, Germany
Erik Fredericks   Oakland University, USA
Gregory Gay   University of South Carolina, USA
Roberto E. Lopez-Herrejon   École de technologie superieuré, Montreal, Canada
Inmaculada Medina-Bulo   University of Cadiz, Spain

Héctor Menéndez   University College London, UK
José Raúl Romero   University of Cordoba, Spain
Sevil Sen   Hacettepe University, Turkey
Christopher Simons   University of West England, UK
Tanja Vos   Open Universiteit, The Netherlands,
                                  and Universitat Politècnica de València, Spain

Hot-off-the-Press Track Program Committee

Xavier Devroey   Delft University of Technology, The Netherlands
Fitsum M. Kifetew   Fondazione Bruno Kessler, Italy
Anne Koziolek   Karlsruhe Institute of Technology, Germany
Shiva Nejati   SnT Centre, University of Luxembourg
Sebastiano Panichella   University of Zurich, Switzerland
Outi Sievi-Korte   Tampere University of Technology, Finland
Markus Wagner   The University of Adelaide, Australia

Sponsoring Institutions

Contents

Hot off the Press Papers

Challenge Paper

Keynotes

Deploying Search Based Software Engineering with Sapienz at Facebook

Nadia Alshahwan, Xinbo Gao, Mark Harman$^{(\boxtimes)}$, Yue Jia, Ke Mao, Alexander Mols, Taijin Tei, and Ilya Zorin

Facebook, London, UK
{markharman,kemao}@fb.com

Abstract. We describe the deployment of the Sapienz Search Based Software Engineering (SBSE) testing system. Sapienz has been deployed in production at Facebook since September 2017 to design test cases, localise and triage crashes to developers and to monitor their fixes. Since then, running in fully continuous integration within Facebook's production development process, Sapienz has been testing Facebook's Android app, which consists of millions of lines of code and is used daily by hundreds of millions of people around the globe.

We continue to build on the Sapienz infrastructure, extending it to provide other software engineering services, applying it to other apps and platforms, and hope this will yield further industrial interest in and uptake of SBSE (and hybridisations of SBSE) as a result.

1 Introduction and Background

Sapienz uses multi-objective Search Based Software Engineering (SBSE) to automatically design system level test cases for mobile apps [49]. We explain how Sapienz has been deployed into Facebook's central production continuous integration system, Phabricator, how it collaborates with other Facebook tools and technologies: the FBLearner Machine Learning Infrastructure [38], the One World Mobile Platform [20] and Infer, the Facebook Static Analysis tooling [13]. We also outline some open problems and challenges for the SBSE community, based on our experience.

Our primary focus for this paper is the deployment of the SBSE technology, rather than the SBSE aspects themselves. We believe the deployment throws up interesting new challenges that we would like to surface and share with the SBSE community as one potential source of stimulus for on-going and future

---

This paper was written to accompany the keynote by Mark Harman at the 10th Symposium on Search-Based Software Engineering (SSBSE 2018), Montpellier September 8–10, 2018. The paper represents the work of all the authors in realising the deployment of search based approaches to large-scale software engineering at Facebook. Author name order is alphabetical; the order is thus not intended to denote any information about the relative contribution of each author.

© The Author(s) 2018
T. E. Colanzi and P. McMinn (Eds.): SSBSE 2018, LNCS 11036, pp. 3–45, 2018.
https://doi.org/10.1007/978-3-319-99241-9_1

work on deployable SBSE. The details of the SBSE algorithms, the SBSE approach adopted by Sapienz and its evaluation against state-of-the-art and state-of-practice automated mobile test techniques can be found elsewhere [49].

Sapienz augments traditional Search Based Software Testing (SBST) [33,55], with systematic testing. It is also designed to support crowd-based testing [48] to enhance the search with 'motif genes' (patterns of behaviour pre-defined by the tester and/or harvested from user journeys through a system under test [50]).

Many SBSE testing tools, both more and less recent instances [26,45,71], tend to focus on unit level testing. By contrast, Sapienz is a system-level testing tool, in which the representation over which we design a test is the event sequence at GUI level, making Sapienz approach more similar to the Exsyst[1] approach [30] than it is to other more unit-testing orientated approaches. Such system-level SBSE testing has been found to reduce the false positives that plague automated test data generation at the unit level [30]. However, it does pose other challenges to deployment, particularly on a mobile platform at scale, as we shall discuss.

In September 2017 the Sapienz system first went live at Facebook, deployed on top of Facebook's FBLearner machine learning infrastructure [38] and drawing on its One World Platform which is used to supply mobile devices and emulators [20]. Since then, Sapienz has run continuously within Facebook's Continuous Integration platform, testing every diff that lands into the Facebook Android app's code base. A 'diff' refers to a code commit submitted to the repository by an engineer. Since February 2018, Sapienz has additionally been continuously testing every smoke build of diffs, as they are submitted for review.

The Facebook Android app is one of the largest Android apps available and is one of the most widely used apps in production at the time of writing. It supports social networking and community building for hundreds of millions of users world wide. Since April 2018, we extended Sapienz to test the Messenger app for Android, another large and popular app, with hundreds of millions of users world wide, who use it to connect and communicate with people and organisations that matter to them.

These two apps are not the only communications products available, nor the only large apps for which testing is needed. Nevertheless, the challenges of scale and deployment are likely to be similar for other apps, and so lessons learned will hopefully generalise to other apps and also to the issues associated with SBSE deployment into many other Continuous Integration scenarios.

We are currently extending Sapienz to iOS and to other apps in the Facebook app family. With these extensions we aim to widen the benefits of automated test design from the hundreds of millions who currently use the Android Facebook social media app to the entire Facebook community. At the time of writing, this community numbers more than 2.2 billion monthly active users world wide, thereby representing a significant route to research impact for software engineering scientific research communities.

The 'debug payload' delivered to the engineer by Sapienz, when it detects a crashing input sequence, includes a stack trace, various reporting and

---

[1] http://exsyst.org/.

cross-correlation information and a crash-witness video (which can be walked through under developer control and correlated to activities covered), all of which combine to ensure a high fix rate, an approximate lower-bound on which is 75% at the time of writing.

Determining a guaranteed true fix is a challenging problem in itself, so we use a conservative mechanism to give a lower bound, as explained in Sect. 3.2. The true fix rate is likely higher, with remaining crashes reported being believed to be either unimportant to users or false positives (See Sect. 7.8).

A video presentation, by Ke Mao and Mark Harman from the Sapienz team, recorded at Facebook's F8 developer conference on 1st May 2018 is available[2]. There is also a video of Ke Mao's presentation at the conference FaceTAV 2017[3], on the Sapienz deployment at Facebook[4].

SBSE is now starting to achieve significant uptake in the industrial and practitioner sectors and consequent real world impact. This impact is being felt, not only at Facebook, but elsewhere, such as Ericsson [2], Google [77], and Microsoft [70] as well as the earlier pioneering work of Wegener and his colleagues at Daimler [72]. SBSE has been applied to test embedded systems software in the Automotive domain, for example with industrial case studies involving the Ford Motor Company, Delphi Technologies and IEE S.A. [1, 54, 61], and the space domain at SES S.A. [69]. It has also been deployed in the financial services sector for security testing [42] and in the maritime sector at Kongsberg Gruppen for stress testing [3].

Such industrial applications allow us to evaluate in both laboratory and in industrial/practitioner settings [52]. As has been argued previously [32], both forms of evaluation are important in their own right and each tends to bring to light complementary evaluation findings. That is, laboratory evaluations tend to be more controlled, but less realistic, while industrial/practice evaluations tend to be more realistic, but less controlled.

However, despite the widespread uptake of SBSE, indeed arguably because of it, we now have an even richer set of exciting scientific problems and intellectual challenges to tackle. In our own deployment work in the Sapienz Team at Facebook, we encountered many open problems, some of which are currently the subject of some scientific study, but some of which appeared to be largely overlooked in the literature.

As we moved from the research prototype of Sapienz to a fully scaled-up version, deployed in continuous production, we took the conscious decision to document-but-not-solve these research challenges. Our goal was to focus on deployment first, and only once we had a fully scaled and deployed automated test design platform, did we propose to try to address any open research problems.

---

[2] developers.facebook.com/videos/f8-2018/friction-free-fault-finding-with-sapienz/.
[3] facetavlondon2017.splashthat.com/.
[4] Sapienz presentation starts at 46.45 in this video: www.facebook.com/andre.steed.1/videos/160774057852147/.

We were not surprised to discover that, after 15 months of intensive deployment focus, we had already accrued more exciting and interesting research challenges than we could hope to solve in reasonable time. In this paper we set out some of these challenges and open problems in the hope of stimulating interest and uptake in the scientific research community. We would be interested to partner and collaborate with the academic community to tackle them.

2 Sapienz at Facebook: Overview

Sapienz is deployed using FBLearner, Facebook's Machine Learning Infrastructure. In particular, Sapienz uses the FBLearner flow operators and workflows for continuous deployment and availability. The Sapienz infrastructure also supports sophisticated and extensive facilitates for experimentation, statistical analysis and graphic reporting (see Sect. 5). This section outlines the principal components of the deployment.

2.1 Top Level Deployment Mode

The overall top level depiction of the deployment of Sapienz at Facebook is presented in Fig. 1.

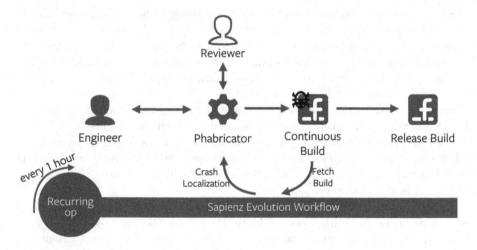

Fig. 1. Overall deployment mode for Sapienz at Facebook

2.2 Phabricator

Phabricator is the backbone Facebook's Continuous Integration system[5]. It is used for modern code review, through which developers submit changes (diffs)

---

[5] http://phabricator.org.

and comment on each others' diffs, before they ultimately become accepted into the code base (or are discarded). More than 100,000 diffs are committed to the central repository every week at Facebook, using Phabricator as a central gatekeeper, reporting, curating and testing system [37]. In 2011 Facebook released Phabricator as open source.

Sapienz reports the test signals it generates directly into the Phabricator code review process. It has been found with earlier tool deployment, such as the previous Infer deployment [13,37], that the code review system is an ideal carrier for the signals that originate in testing and verification technologies. The Sapienz deployment therefore followed a similar pattern to the Infer static analysis tool, which also deployed through Phabricator, commenting on developers' diffs. Infer also originated in the research community via a London-based start up Monoidics [13] in 2013, while Sapienz came from the London-based start up Majicke [24] in 2017.

2.3   Diff Time and Land Time Testing

Sapienz comments on diffs at two different points in the code review process: diff submit time, and post land time. A diff is first submitted by a developer, to be reviewed by other developers, and cannot land into the code base until it has passed this review stage, so diff submit time always occurs strictly earlier in the code development life cycle than land time. The post-land stage is the point at which diffs may be encountered by dogfooding, allowing Sapienz to cross-check whether crashes it has found have also been witnessed in pre-production dogfooding of release candidates.

At diff submit time, Sapienz receives smoke builds from Facebook's 'Sandcastle' test infrastructure, using these to test individual diffs as they are submitted by developers (and batches of such diffs where possible, for efficiency reasons). The aim of diff time testing is to run a selection of tests at least once per diff, selected from those previously-generated by Sapienz. This selection is run as soon as possible after the diff is submitted, in order to give early signal to the developers as they submit their changes to be reviewed. Often, through this mode, Sapienz is able to comment on a crashing diff before a human reviewer has had time to comment, thereby saving precious human reviewer effort. Furthermore, as has been widely-observed in the software testing literature [10,11], the earlier we can detect faults, the cheaper and quicker they can be corrected.

In order to comment at diff time, it is necessary for Sapienz to be able to test the diff quickly. This requires a scheduling system that prioritises recently-submitted diffs, and fast selection of a likely fault-revealing subset of test sequences. We are continuing to work on both the scheduling process, and smarter sampling of appropriate tests; a problem well-studied in the research community [5,16,22,59,67,74] for over two decades. At this stage we use information retrieval approaches, popular elsewhere in software engineering, such as Term Frequency–Inverse Document Frequency (TF*IDF) [68] to promote diversity and relevance of test sequences to diff under test.

When Sapienz executes on diffs that have been landed into the debug build of the code base, the primary role, here, is to *generate* a good set of test sequences, rather than to test the app (although testing does occur, and any crashes found and triaged, will be reported and their fixes tracked). More importantly, by using the debug build as a representative cut of the current user interface of the app, Sapienz is able to maintain, update and curate the Activity Transition Graph (ATG), that captures Sapienz's inferred representation of the GUI structure of the app. This testing phase is where the SBSE algorithms are used to generate new test sequences.

2.4   FBLearner

FBLearner is a Machine Learning (ML) platform through which most of Facebook's ML work is conducted [38]. Sapienz is one many tools and services that is built on top of the FBLearner framework. Facebook uses FBLearner for many other problems, including search queries for videos, photos, people and events, anomaly detection, image understanding, language translation, and speech and face recognition.

Tens of trillions of ML operations are executed per day; a scale that allows Facebook to deploy the benefits of machine learning in real time. For example, Facebook performs natural language translation between approximately 2000 language pairs, serving approximately 4.5 billion translated post impressions every day, thereby allowing 600 million people to read translated posts in their mother tongue [38]. This considerably lowers linguistic barriers to international communication.

Sapienz currently uses the FBLearner Flow components to deploy detection of crashing behaviour directly into the work flow of engineers, integrated with Phabricator for reporting and actioning fixes to correct the failures detected by Sapienz. The current deployment does not yet exploit the other two phases of the FBLearner infrastructure, namely the FBLearner Feature Store and the FBLearner Predictor. Nevertheless, there are many exciting possibilities for predictive modelling in software testing at scale, and this infrastructure will naturally support investigation of these possibilities and potential future research directions. The team at Facebook would be very interested to explore collaboration possibilities with those in the research community who would like to tackle these challenges.

3   The Sapienz FBLearner Workflows

Three of the more important Sapienz FBLearner workflows are depicted in Fig. 2. Each of these three workflows is explained in more detail below.

The Evolution Workflow: The evolution workflow is used to generate test inputs and record information about them and, where they crash, to report this to developers. The evolution workflow has six principal operators, which execute cyclically. At the time of writing, the periodicity is every 30 min for test

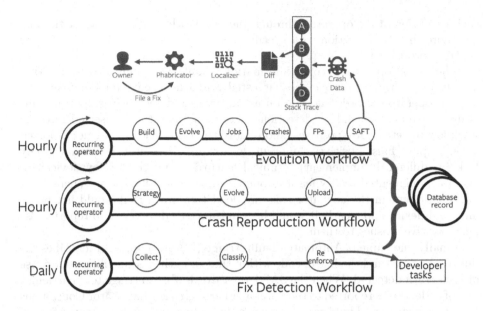

Fig. 2. The three principal Sapienz FBLearner flow workflows and their operators

generation and, for diff time test selection, every 10 min to process the queue of scheduled diff-tine requests. These repeat cycle periodicities are, of course, control parameters that remain under review and are subject to analysis and tuning.

The purpose of these operators is to test the debug build of the application file that contains all of the submitted diffs that have landed into the master build. The overall workflow is broken into 6 separate FBLearner Flow operators. The build operator builds an APK file.

The database of servers, maintained on the emulator by the APK file is updated by Sapienz with a redirection that uses a proxy server to taint the Sapienz requests so that these can be identified in production, when they hit back-end servers, and thereby diverted where they might otherwise affect production. Other than this ability to taint requests via the proxy server, the APK file has the same functionality as that downloaded onto phones by dogfooders, and ultimately, by real users, once the next cut of the debug build has been rendered into one of many release candidates.

The 'Evolve' operator runs the Sapienz evolutionary workflow, executing the Sapienz multi objective evolutionary algorithm to generate new test input sequences from the master build. The details of the evolutionary algorithm are relatively similar to those described in the previous ISSTA paper about the Sapienz research prototype [49]. The primary difference lies the additional technology required to lease and communicate with the emulators used by the MotifCore component, which executes test cases and records, *inter alia*, coverage and crashes. Many 100 s of emulators per app-under-test can be leased for each execution of the operator, through the OneWorld platform, rather than by the more direct connection to a specific device or devices implemented in the research prototype.

The 'Jobs' operator records information about the evolutionary algorithm executions so that these can be harvested and examined later on, while the 'Crash' operator records information about crashes detected in each run. This is used in reporting and fix detection. The 'FPs' operator is inserted into the workflow to detect false positives, and remove these so that they are not reported to developers. False positives can occur, for example, because the emulator may lack (or differently implement) technical features compared to any device, for example, augmented reality features offered in advanced handsets. Where these are not present in the emulator this may lead to a crash that would not occur on a real device and clearly it would be a nuisance to developers to report these false positive crashes to them.

Finally, the Sapienz Automated Fault Triage ('SAFT') operator identifies the diff responsible (and the line of code within that diff) that is the likely root cause of each crash detected. When the SAFT operator is able to triage to a particular line of code, this is reported to the developer through the Phabricator Continuous Integration system. The developer receives a 'Debugging payload', consisting of information about the crash, the stack trace, video(s) showing steps to reproduce the crash, and pointers to collections of information about potentially related crashing behaviour, and debugging support technology.

3.1   Crash Reproduction Workflow

The problem of flaky tests means that many failing test cases will not reliably fail on every test execution, even in apparently identical circumstances. The crash reproduction workflow assesses and records information about the degree of flakiness for each crashing test sequence, using repeated execution.

Several authors have commented on the reasons for this flakiness [28,37,46, 56,62], finding that one of the most common causes lies in the prevalent use of asynchronous waits; functions make asynchronous calls to services, but may not wait sufficient time for those services to respond, producing a different result to that had they waited slightly longer.

The result of this async wait issue is that different pauses between test events can significantly affect the behaviour of the app under test. Sapienz runs a crash reproduction workflow in order to determine the level of repeatability for the failing test cases it discovers. Those found to have higher repeatability are archived and logged as such.

For diff submit time deployment of Sapienz, test flakiness is less of a pernicious problem. This is because any crash, on any occasion, even if not repeatable, has two properties that tend to promote a quick fix:

1. The crash is reported early, at diff submit time, so the developer concerned has the full context in his or her head and is able to act immediately to remediate.

2. The crash serves as a proof of existence; it is possible that this diff *can* cause the app to crash, in *some* circumstance, and this is typically sufficient signal to occasion a change at this stage in the development process.

On the other hand, when Sapienz discovers a crash that relates to a longer-standing problem, and cannot triage the crash to a recent diff submitted or landed into the code base by developer, then repeatability of tests becomes more important. A single flaky test will likely fail to give the developer sufficient signal that he or she will want to invest time effort on a fix attempt.

However, as we have argued elsewhere [37], this does not necessarily mean that flaky tests cannot be useful. Indeed, we believe that more research is needed on *combinations* of flaky tests, such that the combined signal they produce can be highly actionable.

We believe that promising research avenues may exist, for example using techniques such as information theory and other probabilistic interpretations of test outcomes [6,17,73,75]. This is important because, in many situations, particularly with automated test data generation, we may have to work in a world where it is safer to assume that All Tests Are Flaky (ATAF) [37].

3.2 Fix Detection Workflow

It turns out that detecting whether a crash is fixed or not is an interesting challenge, and one that would benefit from further scientific investigation by the research community. This is a problem to which the Search Based Software Engineering community could contribute. The problem consists of two parts:

1. Determining when two or more crashes likely originate from the same cause. This involves grouping crashes and their likely causes.
2. The problem of 'proving a negative'. That is, how long should we wait, while continually observing no re-occurrence of a failure (in testing or production) before we claim that the root causes(s) have been fixed? Since absence of proof is not proof of absence, we can really only more precisely speak of 'apparent fixes' or 'failure symptom non-reoccurrence'. Addressing this question requires a fix detection protocol.

Grouping Crashes and Their Likely Causes. The starting point for this problem is the difference between faults and failures, a problem well-known to the testing literature [10]. While a single fault may lead to multiple failures, a particular failure may also be caused by multiple faults. Therefore, there is a many-to-many mapping between faults and failures. An automated dynamic test design technology such as Sapienz is only able to directly detect a failure (not a fault), and has to use further reasoning to indirectly identify the likely candidate fault (or faults) that may have caused the failure.

In order to identify a particular failure, and distinguish it from others, we need some kind of 'failure hash', or ID, that uniquely identifies each individual failure. However, what we are really interested in, is the fault(s) that lead to these failures. The failure hash ID is thus an attempt to capture fault(s), through these symptoms observed as a failure.

Inevitably, how ever we choose this 'failure hash ID', we are effectively grouping failures that we believe, ultimately, may share a similar cause. This 'failure signal grouping problem' is one that has been known for some time [66]. If the grouping is too coarse grained, then we over approximate, with the result that we falsely group together multiple distinct failures with distinct (unrelated) causes. Conversely, if the granularity is too fine, we separate two or more different failure observations that originate in the same root cause (false splitting).

Whatever approach we choose, there will likely be some false grouping and also some false splitting. We can bias in favour of one or the other, but it is unlikely that we shall find an approach that guarantees freedom from both, since it is a challenge to be sure of root causes. Indeed, even the very concept of causality itself, can become somewhat 'philosophical' and, thereby, open to interpretation.

Hedging in favour of finer granularity, we could consider the identity of a failure to be the precise stack trace that is returned when the failure occurs. However, different executions may follow slightly different paths, leading to slightly different stack traces, while ultimately denoting the same failure and, more importantly, the same root cause (in a fault or set faults). Therefore, using the precise sequence of calls in a stack trace for a failing execution is too fine-grained for our purpose.

Instead, we use a 'message identifier', or mid, which identifies the principal method call in a stack trace that is used as the 'hash' for the failure. In so-doing we err on the side of a coarser granularity, though we cannot guarantee that there is no false splitting. Nevertheless, the use of mids does tend to reduce the cognitive burden on developers who might otherwise be spammed by hundreds (or perhaps thousands) of messages concerning ultimately the same fault.

However, it does raise the problem of false grouping, in which two entirely independent faults can become grouped together by the same mid, and thereby appear to contribute to the same failure. False grouping poses problems for fix detection, because the developer may respond to a signal from the tool, and fix the fault that leads to failure, yet the false grouping of this failure with another, otherwise independent fault, leads to the testing tool apparently re-witnessing the failure. As a result of this apparent re-witness of the failure, the test tool will inadvertently infer that the bug has not yet been fixed, when in fact it has.

Our motivation for adopting the more coarse-grained failure hashing approach derives from the trade off in dis-benefits: We did not wish to over-claim the fix rate for our technology, preferring to be conservative, giving a lower bound to the claimed fix rate. We also cannot afford to spam developers or we risk losing their trust in, and consequent engagement with, our technology. We therefore chose to suffer this false grouping problem rather than the more pernicious problem of giving developea of spammy signal.

Although we use a mid at Facebook, similar problems would occur in any real-world testing system in which we need to identify and distinguish different failures. There is always a trade-off between the fine-grained representation and the risk of a spammy signal, contrasted to more coarse-grained representation which may suffer from the false grouping problem. We continue to refine and optimise for this trade-off, but it is likely to remain a trade-off, and therefore the challenge is to find ways to balance the two competing constraints of not spamming developers, and not falsely grouping; a problem well-fitted to the SBSE research community.

This crash ID problem is compounded by the nature of the continuous integration system and Internet deployment. Continuous integration results in high levels of code churn, in which the particular identity of the method may change. This further fuzzes the information available to the testing technology in stack traces, over time, since code changes may introduce apparent differences in two otherwise identical stack traces. The deployment of Internet-based systems also tends to elevate the degree of flakiness of test cases, since productionised tests will tend to rely on external services, that lie outside the testers' control.

Fix Detection Protocol. Figure 3 depicts an example Fix Detection Protocol with which we have recently been experimenting within the Sapienz Team at Facebook. We do not claim it is the only possible protocol, nor that it is best among alternatives. Rather, we present it here to illustrate the subtleties that arise when one attempts to automate the process of detecting whether a fix can be said to have occurred in a Continuous Integration and Deployment environment.

We are not aware of any research work on the problem of automated fix detection for Continuous Integration and Deployment in the presence of flaky tests. We would like to suggest this as an important open problem for the research community and hope that this section adequately motivates this as an interesting open research problem.

In Fig. 3, when printed in colour, green edges represent the absence of a failure observation, denoted by mid M, within a given time window, while the red edges denote the observation of mid M, within a given observation window. We distinguish two observation windows; the cooling window and the resurrection window. When printed in black and white, these colour-augmentations may be lost, but this should not unduly affect readability.

The cooling window is the period we require the protocol to wait before we initially claim that the mid M is dead. When it is not observed for this cooling window duration, we claim that the bug is 'α-fixed'; it initially appears to be fixed. We mark the mid M as dead and increase our count of α-fixes, but the mid is not yet 'buried'.

If a dead mid is re-observed during the resurrection window, then the mid is said to be 'undead', whereas those mids that remain undetected during the cooling window and the subsequent resurrection window are claimed to be 'dead and buried', and we call this a 'β-fix'. A mid, M which is dead and buried is one for which we have high confidence that, should M subsequently be re-observed after the resurrection window, then this is a 'recycled' mid; one that has reentered our protocol as a result of new, previously unwitnessed, failure and its corresponding cause(s). A recycled mid is a special instance of false grouping in which the resurrection window allows us to accrue evidence that the mid is, indeed, falsely grouped.

We count the overall number of α and β fixes. The aim in choosing the window durations is to have a reasonable chance of the true fix count lying between these two numbers, without making them so wide as to become impractical.

The five nodes along to top of the state machine protocol follow the a relatively simple path from initialisation of the protocol through detection of the first observation of a brand new (never before observed) mid M, its subsequent non-observation during both cooling and resurrection window periods and the ultimate declaration of our claim that M is dead and buried, with consequent increments to both the α and β fix counters along the way. This path through the state machine represents the ideal scenario that we would *like* to witness for *all* failures, in which we detect them, they get fixed, and that is all there is to be said about them.

The remainder of the state machine denotes the complexities involved in fix detection, arising from the problems of flaky tests, false grouping/splitting, and the inevitable attempt to 'prove a negative' inherent in fix detection. Moving from left to right, when we first encounter a mid M after some period, it may turn out to be one that we previously believed was dead and buried, in which case we claim a false grouping (of faults and their failures) has occurred because, by definition (of buried), M has not been observed for, at least, the duration of the cooling and resurrection windows combined. The combination of these two windows can be thought of as the duration after which we believe any mid to be 'recycled' should it re-occur. The duration denoted by these two windows in sequence therefore represents that time after which we believe it is sufficiently safe to assume that any new mid M observation arises due to some newly-introduced root cause.

Another possibility is that the mid M is observed for a new revision, R in which case the mid M is already at some stage in the protocol (prior to being dead and buried). This observation also occasions a false grouping claim, because we know the mid arises from a different code change to the previous observation of the same mid through testing a different revision. For this reason, our protocol effectively treats the 'crash hash' for Sapienz-detected crashes as the combination of the failure hash identifier M (the mid), and the revision, R (the testing of which encounters M). For mids observed in production we may do not always know the corresponding revision, but for mids reported to developers by Sapienz we only report those that we can triage to a specific diff, so this pair is well-defined for all Sapienz crashes reported.

When we detect a (mid, revision) pair (M, R), we initialise a count of the number of occasions on which M has cycled from being dead to undead, MUD_M. Mid UNdead (MUD) is an appropriate acronym for this counter since the status of mids that cycle between dead and undead statuses is somewhat muddy itself, and denotes a primary source of uncertainty in our protocol.

If M was previously buried, we 'dig it up' and note that M has been recycled whereas, if it was not buried previously, we do not treat it as recycled. In either case we believe a false grouping has occurred and claim it. Of course, we cannot be *sure*, so this false grouping claim, like our other claims, is just that; a claim.

Once we have determined whether a newly-observed mid is a brand-new (never before seen) mid, or one of these two categories of falsely-grouped mids, we enter the main sequence of the protocol for the mid M and corresponding revision R. At this stage, we wait for a duration determined by the cooling window. This is a potentially infinite wait, since the cooling window is a sliding window protocol. A mid therefore remains unfixed until it passes the cooling window non-observation criterion.

If it does survive unobserved through the cooling window, we claim it is dead and increment the α-fix count. We then start waiting again, to see if the mid re-occurs. If the mid re-occurs within the (re-initialised) cooling window, it becomes undead, from which status it can either return to being dead (if it does not become re-observed during the cooling window), can remain undead, can oscillate between dead and undead states, or may finally exit the protocol as a 'dead and buried' mid.

Overall, the protocol ensures that no mid can be claimed to be dead and buried unless it has undergone both the cooling window and subsequent resurrection window. The undead status is recorded for subsequent analysis, since it may have a bearing on the false grouping problem, the test flakiness problem, and the determination of suitable durations for the cooling window and resurrection window. However, the undead status plays little role in the external claims made by Sapienz about fixes; it is merely recorded as an aid to further 'healthiness' analysis for our window duration, mid groupings, and test flakiness.

The external claims made by the protocol concern the number of α- and β-fixes, and the claims concerning the dead, and the dead and buried statuses of the mids observed by the fix detection protocol.

3.3   The Evolve FBLearner Flow Operator

The 'Evolve' operator in the evolution workflow, is the core Sapienz FBLearner operator. It is depicted in Fig. 4. This architecture of the Sapienz operator remains similar to that envisaged for the Sapienz Research prototype [49], as can be seen.

The Evolve operator is used to generate test inputs. These are used for testing; if they find a failure then it is reported through the evolution workflow. However, perhaps more importantly, the test inputs are archived and curated into an Activity Transition Graph (ATG). This pool of tests is then used as a source of pre-computed test inputs for diff time testing, so that Sapienz can quickly find a set of pre-vvovled test sequences to apply to each diff as it is submitted, using its smoke build, or a batch of such builds combined.

The Sapienz operator workflow starts by instrumenting the app under test, and extracting statically-defined string constants by reverse engineering the APK. These strings are used as inputs for seeding realistic strings into the app, a

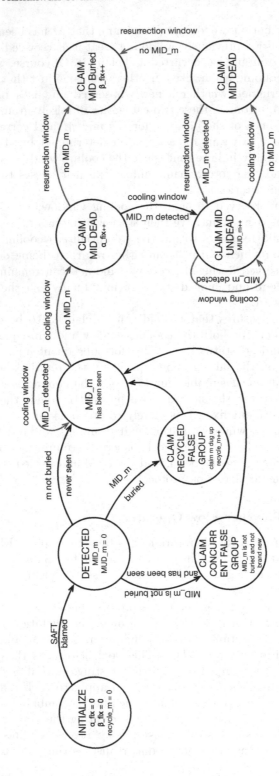

Fig. 3. An example of an FDP (Fix Detection Protocol) with which we are experimenting. In general, much more research is needed on the problem of automated fix detection; a largely overlooked, yet highly intellectually stimulating problem. (Color figure online)

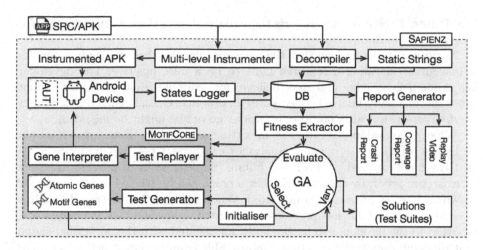

Fig. 4. Sapienz evolution operator workflow (Taken from the ISSTA 2016 paper [49])

technique that has been found to improve the performance of other search based software testing techniques too [4, 27].

Sapienz's multi-objective search algorithm initialises the first population via the *MotifCore* component which runs on the device or emulator. On android, when evaluating individual fitnesses, Sapienz communicates with the *App Exerciser* via the Android Debugging Bridge (ADB) and monitors the execution states, returning measurement data, such as Android activities covered to the fitness evaluator.

Sapienz uses a Search Based Software Engineering (SBSE) approach to optimise for three objectives: code coverage, sequence length and the number of crashes found. Its computational search is a pareto-optimal approach, based on NSGA-II, a widely-used multi-objective evolutionary search algorithm, popular in SBSE research [35], but hybridised with other search techniques, such as localised systematic search on devices/emulators. More details on the Sapienz algorithms and their evaluation against the state of the art and the state of practice can be found in the ISSTA paper [49] and in Ke Mao's PhD dissertation [47].

4   Integration with Other Facebook Tools and Systems

In this section we briefly explain some of the ways in which the Sapienz infrastructure inter-operates with other tools, systems and services at Facebook.

4.1   Collaboration Between Static and Dynamic Analysis: Infer and Sapienz

Facebook has a static analysis technology, Infer [13], for scalable compositional static analysis. Infer reviews potential faults, pinpointing the line of code concerned, and reporting the fault candidate to the developer with a suitable message. For example, Infer statically analyses program flows to highlight potential

Null Pointer Exceptions and reports these to developers through the Phabricator code review interface.

Naturally, it can happen that the developer decides that this fault reporting is inaccurate, deeming a reported fault to be a false positive. The developer has domain knowledge and may believe, for example, that execution cannot cause this statically-inferred issue to arise in practice. Occasionally, the developer maybe correct, but also, on other occasions he or she might be mistaken.

When the developer is incorrect in setting aside advice from Infer, it would be highly useful to use dynamic analysis to provide a positive existence proof that the fault can, indeed, lead to a failure. Sapienz seeks to provide just such an existence proof, by checking whether a crash can be triaged to a line of code on which Infer as previously commented. When such a failure is traced to a line of code on which Infer has previous commented, a specific task is created and reported to the developer to fix the fault, augmented with the additional signal that this fault does really lead to a demonstrable failure (a constructive existence proof), including a witness video, stack trace and line at which the crash occurs.

At the time of writing, the fix detection workflow has detected an almost 100% fixed rate for such Sapienz-Infer ('SapInf') faults. This is evidence that, when static and dynamic analysis techniques can *collaborate* to provide a combined (and thereby strengthened) signal to developers, it is highly likely that such faults are likely to be true positives, and also that they are actionable and, thereby, tend to get fixed. We believe are many more ways in which static and dynamic analysis could collaborate and so we set out this collaboration as a remaining open problem that requires further research work (see Sect. 7.7).

4.2   Combining with Feedback from Field Trials

It can happen that a crash hits real world users of the app, who experience the crash in production. Clearly we try to avoid this where possible. In fact, the 'real world' user may well, in the first instance, be a Facebook dogfooder who is running the app on their own device. We use such dogfooding as a line of defence in preventing crashes hitting our end users.

When any user, dogfooder or end user, experiences a crash, the crash can be logged and used to help improve testing and fault remedy. Sapienz has a continuously running workflow which tracks the crashes it has reported to developers against the real world crashes found in production. Sapienz files a task for the developer when this happens. Once again, this production-firing evidence provides a stronger signal to the developer that a crash really is a true positive.

4.3   Bug Severity Prediction

Sapienz uses a simple tree-based machine learning classification technique (C4.5) to predict whether the crashes it detects are likely to have a high number of real world affected users. This is a measure of bug severity. After some experimentation, we determined that the simple C4.5 classifier produced a high prediction accuracy (of approximately 75%), and therefore adopted for this approach.

The classification algorithm takes as input, drivers of bug severity, such as:

1. **Crash Metadata Features:** e.g., new mid, number of hits, has the mid been seen in prod;
2. **Crash Stack Trace Features:** e.g., crash type, stack depth;
3. **Diff Features:** duration to find crash, code churn metrics, reviewer comment metrics, location in file tree.

5   Automated Scientific Experimental Reporting (ASER) Workflow

The Automated Scientific Experimental Reporting (ASER) seeks to achieve automated empirical software engineering, at scale, and fully in production, using best-practice recommended inferential statistical evaluation and reporting for empirical SBSE [7,36]. The ASER is an example of a broader company-wide (and increasingly sector-wide) approach to evidence-based decision making. For all the challenges of Continuous Integration and Deployment, such demanding modes of deployment do also have the exciting potential to facilitate such evidence-based decision making, through support for automated experimentation.

As well as ensuring the team retains its scientific roots and culture, the ASER also allows the team to collaborate efficiently and effectively with other researchers from the academic and scientific community; new ideas, concerning SBSE algorithms and more general automated Software Testing techniques, originating from outside the team, can be empirically evaluated quickly and systematically on a level playing field.

The ASER has four phases, starting with an initial proof of concept experiment, through to full evaluation in parallel with (and evaluated against) the production release of Sapienz. The motivation for these four phases is to allow the experimenter to devote increasingly larger levels of resource to evaluating a proposed new approach to test generation. As a result, promising techniques are placed under increasingly strong scrutiny in order to evaluate them against ever-increasingly demanding criteria, while less promising approaches can be quickly identified as such and discarded.

Our aim is to explore and experiment, but also to 'fail fast' with those less promising approaches, so that we can divert human and machine resources to the most promising avenues of research and development. At each phase of the ASER, metrics reporting on the performance of the approach are collected and used as the inputs to inferential statistical analyses. These analyses are performed automatically and the results of confidence intervals, significance tests, effect sizes and the corresponding box plots and other visualisations are automatically computed and returned to the experimenter and the overall team, for inspection and assessment.

The overall flows through the four phases from initial proof of concept to full deployment are depicted in Fig. 5. The migration through each of the four phases of evaluation is placed under human control. Movement through the ASER is informed by inferential statistical analysis; should the newly-proposed approach significantly outperform a baseline benchmark version of the deployed technology, the newly-proposed technique moves from the initial proof of concept to a more thorough evaluation against the production deployment.

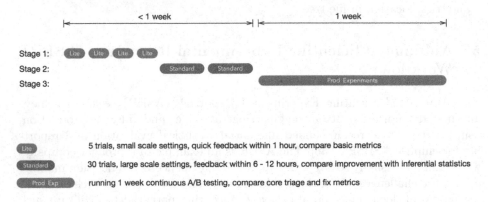

Fig. 5. Experimental workflow into production

The first three phases are christened 'Lite', 'Standard' and 'ProdExp'. The fourth phase is a deployment into production for up to one month alongside production deployment so that we can fully assess the number of faults triaged and fixed by the newly-proposed technique. The Lite phase is designed to give proof-of-concept feedback within an hour. It uses only five emulators on a choice of search based parameter settings that ensures the algorithms terminate quickly.

Ideally, for any testing or verification technique, we should evaluate the signal-to-noise ratio of the technique, rather than give an arbitrary time limit, or we may fall in to the Cherry-Picked Budget (CTB) trap [37]. Using our Lite experiment, it is possible that the reliance on CTB for the Lite phase can cause techniques with a long startup time to be prematurely discarded.

Fortunately, at this stage of the deployment of Sapienz, we are blessed by the large number of potentially promising ideas to explore. Therefore, it is more important that we are able to quickly dismiss those that appear unpromising (albeit initially with a CTB that favours early-stage effectiveness). As the technology matures, we will revisit these assumptions that underpin the ASER.

Newly proposed techniques that pass the initial Lite phase move into the 'Standard' ASER experimental phase. The Standard phase of the ASER deploys best practice [7,36] (thus 'standard') inferential statistical experimental assessment of effectiveness using 30 emulators. This number balances the efficiency of time and computational resources against statistical test reliability.

We believe it sufficient to yield meaningful inferential statistical feedback on the relative performance of the newly-proposed technique against a productionised alternative. We tend balance in favour of avoiding Type I errors (incorrectly rejecting the Null Hypothesis) at the expense of risking Type II errors (incorrectly accepting the Null Hypothesis), reflecting the current opportunity-rich environment in which we seek large effect sizes to motivate further investigations. In terms of resource bounds, our aim is to obtain results within less than a week, so that a decision can be made relatively quickly about whether to move the newly proposed technique to the 'ProdExp' phase.

In the 'ProdExp' phase, the ASER deploys A/B testing, over a period of a week, comparing the number of crashes triaged against the production deployment. The final phase is a longer A/B test, against production, for a period of up to one month before the new technique is finally allowed to become part of the new production deployment. This is necessary because Fix Detection has a natural window (the cooling window; see Sect. 3.2) within which it is not possible to reliably compute a fix rate for any newly-proposed technique. As a result, we can compute the fault reporting rate (the number of crashes triaged) during ProdExp phase, but not the rate at which these crashes are fixed.

The ASER is fully parallelised for scalability, so multiple experiments can be run at any given time, each of which resides at a different stage of the ASER process. Overall, this ensures that less promising techniques are dismissed within a week and that, after one week, we have sufficient evidence to put those techniques that pass standard empirical SBSE evaluation into full A/B testing, yielding their benefit in terms of triages and fixes.

For inferential testing we use a paired Wilcoxon (non Parametric) test, and highlight, for follow up, those results with p values lower than 0.05. We do not perform any p value corrections for multiple statistical testing, since the number of tests is essentially unbounded and unknowable. This choice poses few practical problems, because the final A/B testing phase would allow us to dismiss any Type I errors before their effects hit production. The effect of Type I error is thus an opportunity lost (in terms of time that would have been better spent on other approaches), but it is not a computational cost in terms of the performance of the deployed Sapienz technology.

In the following subsections we give 3 examples of the applications of the ASER framework to evaluate new generation and selection algorithms and techniques we considered for improving fitness computation, the motif core interface and solution representations. Within the first 3 months of deployment of the ASER, we had conducted tens of different high level experimental investigations to answer our research questions, with (overall) hundreds of specific low level experimental algorithm comparisons (thousands of experimental runs), each with different parameter settings and choices.

In the subsections that follow, we chose one example that allowed us to fail fast, one that initially seemed promising, yet failed subsequent more demanding phases of the ASER, and one that made it through the full ASER process to production deployment. Each example also illustrates different aspects of the automated reporting: box plots, scatter-plots and inferential statistical analysis. We show the completely unvarnished output from ASER, exactly as it is automatically rendered to the engineer in these three examples.

5.1   ASER Example: Fail Fast Speed up Experiment

Sapienz communicates with the device or emulator using the Android Debug Bridge (ADB). We had available to us, a modified `ADB` for which others had previously reported *prima facae* evidence for high performance. Naturally, we wanted to investigate whether it could reduce the time Sapienz required for each test case.

RQ: New adb: Can the new `adb` version increase performance of the Sapienz MotifCore and thereby the overall test execution time?

We used the ASER to run an experiment comparing execution time for the modified `ADB` with the original ADB. Figure 6 illustrates the output from ASER's initial 'Lite' phase.

This Lite experiment immediately revealed that the modified `ADB` was, in fact, *slower*, for our use-case, not faster so it was discarded, quickly and without our engineers investing time building a full implementation. This example illustrates the way in which ASER allows us to move fast and fail fast, with those ideas that appear promising yet which, for a myriad of practical reasons, fail to deliver benefits in practice.

5.2   ASER Example: Longer Test Sequences

We considered dropping the test sequence length constraint of Sapienz, to allow it to search for longer test sequences that might achieve higher coverage. This challenged a core assumption in our earlier work. That is, we had initially assumed that shorter test sequences would be inherently good for efficiency and effectiveness of debugging. As a result, length formed part of the original multi objective optimisation approach.

We used a pareto optimal multi objective approach, so length could only be reduced if such reduction could be achieved without sacrificing coverage.

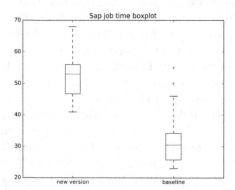

Fig. 6. Answer to RQ: New adb: 'No. The new `adb` is not faster for Sapienz test design'. An example of a box plot outcome that enabled us to Fail fast box plot. Vertical axis shows execution time per overall run, in minutes.

To challenge the assumption that length should be an objective, we created a bi-objective version (crashes and coverage only) of our original tri-objective algorithm, as formulated in the 2016 ISSTA paper [49].

RQ: Length: What is the efficiency and effectiveness of a bi-objective SBSE algorithm compared to the production tri-objective algorithm?

Initial results from ASER's 'Lite' phase were promising, as were inferential statistical results from ASER's subsequent 'Standard' phase; maybe our test sequence length objective should be dropped. The results, as obtained directly and automatically by ASER, are presented in Fig. 7. The figure shows the bi-objective runs (red plots with data points marked as '+') maintaining and slightly improving the activity coverage as the population evolves.

The bi-objective version found 90 mids, while production found 57 with 40 overlaps). The bi-objective version also covered 130 Android activities, while prod covered fewer (114, with 107 overlaps). Inferential statistical analysis from ASER's 'Standard' phase also gave cause for optimism: The unique crash count improved by 109% ($p = 0.003$), while the unique activity coverage count improved 31% ($p < 0.001$). However, set against this, run time slowed down by 21% ($p < 0.001$), largely because the bi-objective version's mean test sequence length was longer.

Based on the inferential statistical analysis from ASER's 'Standard' phase, we were highly optimistic for the bi-objective version of our algorithm: surely a modest test system slow down of 21% was a small price to pay for extra coverage. However, when we deployed the bi-objective version alongside production Sapienz in a full A/B test, we found that the bi-objective version found relatively few extra crashes in practice compared to production and reported fewer per unit time.

This illustrates the importance of the final A/B testing phase, rather than merely relying on (purely) laboratory-condition experimental results alone. The result also underscored, for us, the importance of time-to-signal; bugs-per-minute, being more practically important than coverage or total bugs found, in terms of their immediate impact on our developers, something that has been noted elsewhere [37].

5.3 ASER Example: ATG Test Selection

As described in Sect. 2.3 we use a generate-and-select approach in which we generate a set of tests from the debug build of the app (reporting any errors this uncovers) and use the generated tests as a pool from which we subsequently select tests to be run against each submitted diff. The generate and select approach was first trialed using the ASER against the then production version (which solely used generation). The research question we addressed using the ASER was thus:

RG: ATG: What is the efficiency and effectiveness of an Activity Transition Graph (ATG) generate-and-select algorithm compared to a purely generation-based algorithm?

Figure 8 presents the results obtained from ASER for an experiment on the Activity Transition Graph (ATG) approach, selecting from the ATG, the top activity-covering sequences, rather than simply running in production to generate tests on each and every occasion.

The results were very promising for ASER's 'Standard' phase, as can be seen from Fig. 8. In this case, when we deployed the ATG selection approach alongside prod, in A/B testing the optimism derived from the inferential statistical analysis was fully borne out in practice. As a result of the successful final A/B phase, we moved from purely generation-based testing to a generate-and-select approach.

6   DevOps Results Monitoring

The results obtained from deployment of Sapienz include many of those that we would typically wish to collect for scientific evaluation. That is, in common with any scientific evaluation of a research prototype, we collect information about the key performance indicators of the Sapienz deployment. These include the number of crashes triaged to developers, and breakouts of this data, by Android API level, application under test, and so on. These data are plotted, typically, as timeseries data, and are available on dashboards.

In essence, this can be thought of as a continuous empirical software engineering experiment of efficiency and effectiveness of the production deployment against a sequence of recent debug builds and submitted diffs. The comparatively rapid rate at which diffs are submitted ensures that regressions are detected quickly.

In addition to the continuous monitoring of efficiency and effectiveness, the Sapienz infrastructure also needs to collect a large number of DevOps infrastructural 'health' monitoring metrics. These health metrics help engineers to detect any issues in continuous deployment.

Facebook provides much infrastructural support to make it easy to mash up such dashboards, data analysis, and inferential statistical analysis. This provides the deployment of Sapienz with detailed and continuous empirical evaluation feedback. We developed the Automated Scientific Experimental Reporting (ASER) framework, described in Sect. 5, to allow us to use these data science infrastructure features to quickly prototype new experiments and ideas. We use the same infrastructural support to monitor the ongoing performance and health of the Sapienz fault triage and reporting system and its fault detection protocols and workflows.

Many continuous integration and deployment organisations use a so-called 'DevOps' approach such as this, in which system deployment is continuously monitored by engineers. This DevOps process is supported by key 'health metrics' reporting, which we briefly describe in this section. We also briefly illustrate the kind of performance indicators that we continually monitor to understand the signal that the Sapienz deployment gives to our user community of developers.

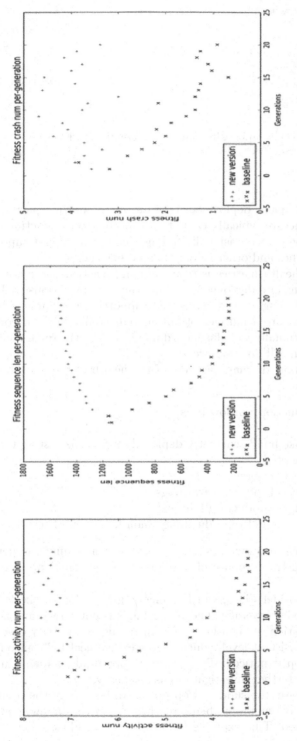

Fig. 7. Sample ASER output: Scatter plots. The upper (red) scatter plot (smaller '+' points) shows the result of Bi-Objective Algorithms. The lower plot (larger 'X' points) is the original tri-objective algorithm. The bi-Objective algorithm appears to be superior to the tri-objective algorithm; an observation re-enforced by the inferential statistical analysis of effectiveness (but not efficiency). In subsequent A/B testing, the tri-objective algorithm's faster execution proved pivotal for bug detection *rate*. This demonstrated that the modest efficiency hit suffered by the bi-objective approach proved to be pivotal in practice, when A/B tested against the tri-objective version. (Color figure online)

Name	Baseline	New Version	%Diff (p_value)
mid_count	2	11	+450.00% (p = 0.000)
nonunique_crash_count	22	68	+209.09% (p = 0.000)
sap_job_time	81	90	-11.11% (p = 0.201)
unique_activity_count	38	58	+52.63% (p = 0.000)
unique_crash_count	22	48	+118.18% (p = 0.002)

Fig. 8. RG: ATG: sample ASER output: inferential statistics

6.1 Health

As explained in Sect. 3, Sapienz deployment contains many 'moving parts', and such large-scale infrastructure typically cannot be expected to run continuously without individual components occasionally failing, due to timeouts, temporary interoperability mismatches and other resource-based exigencies.

The role of Sapienz health metrics is to understand whether these are routine, temporary incursions into deployment, or whether a more serious problem has occurred which needs engineer intervention. Supporting the Sapienz team in making these decisions are a number of automated monitoring and control systems, that report continually to a dashboard monitored by the team member who is the designated 'on-call' for each week.

These dashboards report on many aspects of the health of the deployment, including the

1. number of failed production worflow runs,
2. activity coverage,
3. number of tested smoke builds currently deployed on Sapienz testing tasks,
4. number of crashes detected,
5. number of requests sent to server,
6. logging of various internal soft error warnings,
7. numbers of replication of production failures,
8. the number and proportion of reproducibility (non flakiness) of test cases.

The DevOps reporting also includes a suite of data concerning the performance of the triage, and the response of developers to the signal provided to them.

As an illustration, consider Fig. 9, which depicts a graph plot for six days in April 2018, showing activity coverage. The vertical axis is not shown and is not necessary for this illustration. As can be seen from the figure, activity coverage retains an apparently consistent level, which we regard as 'healthy', but on the 29th April a sudden drop is noticed. This points to potential problems in the deployment, occasioning further investigation, as necessary.

Fortunately, in this case, the sudden drop proved to be merely the result of a temporary quota limit on emulators being reached and within a few minutes, normal behaviour resumed. This example is included as an illustration of the

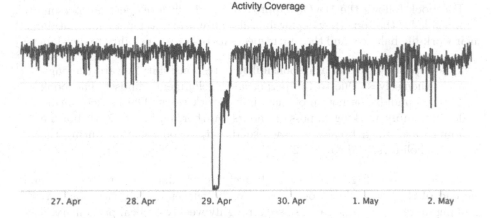

Fig. 9. Example DevOps monitoring: activity coverage over three days' worth of production runs in April 2018 (vertical axis deliberately occluded).

way in which a DevOps approach is used to tackle availability and resilience of the Sapienz infrastructure. Naturally, an interesting challenge is to automate, to the greatest extent possible, this resilience, so that little human intervention is required to maintain healthy operation.

6.2 Key Performance Indicators

Figure 10 shows the two key performance indicators of crashes triaged to developers by Sapienz, and fixes detected by the automated fix detection protocol described in Sect. 3.2. We are interested in fixes detected as a proxy for assessing a bound on the likely false positive rate (more precisely, the signal-to-noise ratio [37]) from Sapienz. Currently Sapienz enjoys a fix rate of approximately 75%, indicating that the signal carries low noise. As explained in Sect. 3.2, this is both an estimate on fix rate and a likely lower bound.

The figure covers the period from the first minimal viable product, in the summer of 2017, through deployment, in full production, at the end of September 2017, to the end of May 2018. Up to the end of September 2017, all crashes triaged to developers (and consequent fixes detected), were implemented by hand, as a result of experiments with the initial minimal viable product. Since the end of September 2017, after successful experimentation, the Sapienz automated fault triage system went live, and Sapienz started commenting, automatically, on diffs that had landed into the debug build of the Facebook android app.

In February 2018, the Activity Transition Graph (ATG) diff time generate-and-select approach, described in Sect. 2.3, was deployed, following successful experimentation with the ASER scientific experimentation framework (described in Sect. 5.3). As can be seen from the figure, this produced a significant uptick in the number of crashes detected and fixed.

Facebook follows the DevOps approach, in which developers are personally responsible for the code they deploy, but also supports developers in maintaining their work-life balance, and thereby respects its own responsibility to developers:

"The flip side of personal responsibility is responsibility toward the engineers themselves. Due to the perpetual development mindset, Facebook culture upholds the notion of sustainable work rates. The hacker culture doesn't imply working impossible hours. Rather, engineers work normal hours, take lunch breaks, take weekends off, go on vacation during the winter holidays, and so on" [25].

As can be seen, Fig. 10 reveals a relatively 'quiet time' for developers around the end of the year, which corresponds to the winter holiday vacation period. Looking more closely, one can also see a roughly weekly cyclical periodicity, post February (when Sapienz was deployed at diff submit time) which is accounted for by weekends off.

7   Open Problems and Challenges

In this section, we outline a few interesting research challenges we have encountered during our attempts to improve the deployment of Sapienz at Facebook. Some of these problems have been partially tackled, but we believe all of them would benefit from further research work.

We eagerly anticipate results from the scientific research community on these open research challenges and problems. We believe that progress will likely impact, not only the Sapienz deployment, but also other automated test design initiatives elsewhere in the software engineering sector.

7.1   Flaky Tests

As previously observed [37], it is better for research to start from the assumption that all tests are flaky, and optimise research techniques for a world in which failing tests may not fail reliably on every execution, even when all controllable variables are held constant. This raises a number of research challenges, and provides rich opportunities for probabilistic formulations of software testing, as discussed in more detail elsewhere [37].

7.2   Fix Detection

As we described in Sect. 3.2, it remains challenging to determine whether a fix has occurred, based solely on the symptoms of a fault, witnessed/experienced as a failure. More research is needed to construct techniques for root cause analysis, allowing researchers and practitioners to make more definite statements about fix detection. Given the assumption that tests are flaky (described in the previous section), it seems likely that statistical inferences about causal effects are likely

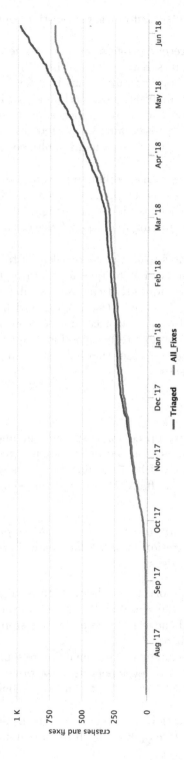

Fig. 10. Example Key Performance Indicators: the first 1k crashes triaged and (detected as) fixed by Sapienz since deployment for the Facebook Android App. The upper curve depicts crashes triaged to a developer; lower line depicts those detected as fixed. As with scientific evaluation and reporting, a key concern is the rate of detection of failures and the proportion that get fixed (a proxy indicator of true positives). The period before the end of September 2017 involved only initial experiments on (by-hand) triage. The effect of deploying, in full production mode, at the end of September 2017 can clearly be seen from the figure. The quieter period around the end of the year can also be seen in the data. The tapering of the fix rate is a consequence of the need for a cooling window, during which no fix can be detected, and also recency effects; crashes take some non-zero time to fix, so older crashes are more likely to be detected as fixed. Finally, the noticeable step change in performance in February 2018 resulted from the successful deployment of the Activity Transition Graph Approach at diff submit time (See Sect. 2.3).

to play a role in this work, due to the probabilistic nature of testing continuously deployed Internet-based systems.

Fortunately, there has been much recent progress on causal inference [63], which has seen applications elsewhere in software engineering [53], as well as in defect prediction [14]. Therefore, the opportunity seems ripe for the further development and exploitation of causal analysis as one technique for informing and understanding fix detection. Empirical software engineering research is also needed to understand whether different classes of fault have different fix detection characteristics, and whether different approaches to fixing faults could lead to different fix detection characteristics.

In general, the problem of fix detection can shed light on a collection of inter-related software testing problems, such as the mapping between faults and failures, the flaky test problem, the cost benefit trade-offs in testing, fault severity, debugging and social aspects of software testing and repair (whether automated or otherwise).

Part of the fix detection problem arises from the subproblem of tackling the mapping between faults and failures. We need techniques for inferring this mapping from observed failures. We need techniques that can use plausible reasoning and inference to identify likely groupings of failures that originate with the same cause, minimizing false grouping and false splitting according to their likely root causing fault(s). Research might also develop techniques for adaptive testing that could be used to drive the search for test cases that help to distinguish such falsely grouped and/or falsely split crashes.

7.3   Automated Oracle

In our work on Sapienz deployment, we opted for a simple and unequivocal implicit oracle [9]; any test which exposes crashing behaviour is a test that is deemed to lead to a failure. Furthermore, if it is possible for a test to witness a crash only *once*, and even if this test is flaky, this is a strong signal to the developer that action is needed:

> A Sapienz-detected crash is, essentially, a constructive existence proof; it proves that there does exist a configuration in which the app can crash on the input sequence constructed by Sapienz.

This use of an implicit oracle was important, both for us to be able to fully automate deployment and to increase the actionability of the signal Sapienz provided the developers. However, we believe it is merely a first step, with an obvious starting point, using an implicit oracle.

Much more work is needed to find techniques to automate more sophisticated and nuanced test oracles. Naturally, if the developers use assertions or exception handling, then these can lead to soft errors that can be exploited by an automated search-based testing technique.

Nevertheless, it remains an open question how to either augment or improve the existing test oracles provided by developers [41]. It is also important to find techniques that generate, from scratch, likely test oracles using techniques such as assertion inference [23]. As test input generation becomes more mature, and more widely-deployed in industry, we can expect a natural migration of the research challenges from the problems of automatically generating test inputs, to the problems of automatically generating test oracles.

Ultimately, if we can automate the generation of oracles *and* the generation of repairs, then we are very close to the grand challenge of FiFiVerify [34]; automatically finding, fixing and verifying software. By tackling the FiFiVerify challenge, we would have practical deployed approaches that would take an existing software system (which may be buggy), and return a new version of the software, guaranteed to be free of certain classes of bugs, *entirely automatically*.

7.4   Fitness Evaluation Resource Requirements

One of the practical problems in deploying search-based software testing lies in the resources required for fitness evaluation. This problem falls inbetween engineering detail and research question. Undoubtedly, some of the solution involves specific platforms and their characteristics and therefore is more a matter of engineering implementation excellence than it is for scientific research.

Nevertheless, there is insufficient guidance in the research literature, and insufficient evaluation in the empirical software engineering literature, of techniques for *reducing* time spent on fitness evaluation. Fitness evaluation reduction techniques essentially trade the computing resources needed for individual fitness evaluation, against the quality of signal returned by fitness evaluation. The ultimate efficacy of fitness evaluation optimisation depends upon the observed impact on higher-level system-wide metrics, such as fault detection rate.

A fast-but-imprecise fitness computation may significantly reduce correctness and thereby guidance provided by an individual fitness evaluation. Nevertheless, such an apparently suboptimal individual fitness evaluation, when executed many millions of times over the lifetime of an evolutionary process, may have a profound effect in reducing the execution time for the overall technique.

As a result, a relatively imperfect fitness evaluation that is fast may be preferable to a much more precise fitness evaluation. These questions naturally centre on cost-benefit trade-offs, which are at the very heart of *any* engineering discipline. In taking scientific ideas from the evolutionary computation community and turning these into practical engineering techniques for the software engineering research community, much more work is needed on the question of reducing fitness evaluation resource consumption.

7.5   Wider Search Spaces

In common with most system-level approaches to search based testing in particular, and automated test data generation in general, Sapienz considers the input to the program to consist solely of user interactions. Other approaches to search-based testing, at the unit level, typically consider a vector of values that can be presented to the unit under test.

However, there has been little work on extending the test data generation search space to include the app's user state and environment. User state and the users' device environment can play a critical role in both elevating coverage of the application under test, and in revealing faults. Some of the faults revealed through different state/environment settings may occur only in certain specific user state and environment settings.

These observations are not peculiar to Facebook, but apply to any software system in which the history of interactions of the user and other state variables and configurations can play a role in determining which path is executed. More research is needed in order to define general approaches to tackling this wider search space.

In our particular situation, we are concerned, naturally, with the 'social state' of the user. For example, a fault may not be witnessed by a test input sequence, unless the user has already responded to at least one post by another user, or has at least one connection in their social network. The user state is thus a part of the wider space in which we search for test cases using SBSE. Characterising the circumstances under which a crash occurs, in terms of this state, would yield highly actionable signal to the developer. It may also prove pivotal in helping to debug otherwise very subtle bugs.

For other apps, and other organisations, the details of the user state will clearly differ, but the general problem of characterising the user state, and the search space it denotes, and defining fitness functions on that representation remains an important, generic, and open research problem. Scientific progress on this open problem is highly likely to yield impactful and actionable research.

We distinguish the user state from the user environment. The environment is general to all applications, while the state is particular to a particular application under test. The environment will, nevertheless, have different impact on different applications. For example, for a photo sharing app, it will likely be important that the user has photos in their photo library on the device. For a map or travel application, GPS settings may prove to be important, although both apps will have access to photos and GPS settings and may use both. In most applications, the network environment will also play an important role.

As devices become more sophisticated, the environment will become ever richer, offering interesting opportunities for SBSE-based characterisations of the search space. More work is needed to characterise this environment in which users execute applications, particularly on mobile devices, to tease out notations for eloquently and succinctly defining this environment. Once characterised, techniques such as Combinatorial Interaction Testing (CIT) [43,60,64] can be used to explore interaction faults, for example.

For the SBSE community, we also need to consider different representations for those environments that promote efficient and effective search. Such work will enrich the search space and tackle several practical problems, such as device fragmentation and context-aware test case generation.

More work is also needed to provide general notations for describing the user state, such that the generic properties of state-based testing can be explored scientifically and empirically. Such work will shed light on the nature of state-based testing for Internet-deployed, device-executed, applications. This notation may also use and benefit from work on CIT.

Research on user state and environment will have multiple benefits to the research community and to practitioners. For researchers, this work will provide a rich avenue of untapped research questions, with potential insights that may help the research community to understand different kinds of deployment mode, applications, environments and properties of states. For practitioners, this research may help us to better understand the applications we are testing, may help us to go beyond merely revealing faults, and also help us to characterise salient properties that yield deep insights into app performance, usability, and different use-case scenarios for different sub-communities of users.

7.6   Smarter, Unobtrusive and Controllable White Box Coverage

After so many years of software testing, in which instrumentation of the system under test has often played a central role, the reader could be forgiven for believing that the problem of white box coverage assessment is entirely solved. However, while it may be true that white box coverage techniques exist for most languages, platforms and systems, for search based software testing there are more stringent requirements than simply the ability to collect coverage information.

Instrumentation of a system under test changes the behaviour of the system, and these changes can impact on the test data generation technique. Search-based software testing, in particular, may be vulnerable to such influences, where the instrumentation changes timing properties, possibly occluding or revealing race conditions, and other time-based behaviours, differently in the app under the test, when compared to the app in the field.

We need smarter control of white box coverage information, that is minimally obtrusive on the execution characteristics of the app under test. Such techniques need to be smarter. That is, for effective SBSE we need a greater level of control over the parameters that affect the trade-offs between quality of white box coverage information and the impact of collecting this signal.

Some of this work is necessary engineering and implementation detail, but there are also interesting high-level scientific problems. The challenge is to tease out and empirically investigate these trade-offs between quality of signal from white box coverage, and impact of collecting any signal on the system under test.

7.7   Combining Static and Dynamic Analysis and Hybrids of SBSE

Although there has been a great deal of research on static analysis techniques, and dynamic analysis techniques, there has been comparatively less work on the combination of static and dynamic analysis. This 'blended' analysis (as it has been called [19]), has the potential for practical impact, since we can leverage the strengths of both techniques to overcome some of the weaknesses of the other.

Equally importantly, such combinations of static and dynamic analysis may yield insights into fundamental questions of computation, touching on the limits imposed by decidability constraints and the connections between statistical and logical inferences.

7.8   False Positives and Pseudo False Positives

It is sometimes claimed, partly as an aphorism [18], that static analysis uses a conservative over approximation, thereby avoiding false negatives (at the expense of some false positives), while dynamic analysis suffers many false negatives, but does not suffer from false positives because it is an under approximation.

This claim is based on an attractive (but misplaced) assumption that the symmetries of over and under approximation, inherent in the theoretical char-acterisation of static and dynamic analysis, carry over into practice. They do not [37]. Both static *and* dynamic analysis, whether over or under approximat-ing their respective models of computation in production, suffer from both false positives *and* false negatives.

It is well known that static analysis yields false positives when it seeks to offer a conservative over-approximation. However, static analysis, even when con-strued as a conservative (i.e., 'safe') approach, can also yield false negatives. For example, a static slicing algorithm is only conservative with respect to a set of assumptions, and these assumptions always allow *some* false negatives; depen-dencies that exist between elements of real systems, yet which go undetected by the slicing algorithm [12].

Dynamic analysis is well-known to suffer from false negatives, due to the inability to exhaustively test (apart from in special circumstances and with respect to strong assumptions, such as integration testing with stream X-machines [39, 40]).

At the unit level, dynamic analysis has also been shown to suffer from false positives [30]. However, *even* at the system level, dynamic analysis also suffers from false positives. System level false positives occur in dynamic analyses, such as the testing deployed by Sapienz. We generate tests on a version of the system as close to production as possible. Nevertheless, since the testing tool is not the real end user, there can be differences in behaviour that will cause the testing tool to detect crashes that no real user will ever encounter.

This occurs, for example, due to differences in the device used for testing, and devices used by end users. False positives are also caused by differences in the abilities of the automated testing tool compared to real user abilities; the test tool has an arbitrary number of 'fingers' at its disposal. Finally, due to differences in the deployment environment for the test infrastructure and the production infrastructure used by the end users can also cause false positives.

Sapienz uses emulators to perform test execution. We have found that, because Facebook has 2.2 billion monthly active users (at the time of writing), this means that almost *any* crash we can find with an emulator can be found on *some* device in the real world. Therefore, we have *not* experienced a large number of false positives, simply due to our use of emulators, rather than real devices.

Nevertheless, we have witnessed a kind of pseudo false positive due to implementation details concerning emulators, such as inadequate emulation of Augmented Reality (AR) features in earlier instances of the Android emulator API (e.g., API 19, which lacks the relevant AR library support). This leads to crashes which are 'true' positives, strictly speaking (since the system should not crash if the AR library is not present). However, we need to treat such a crash like a 'pseudo false positive', since it instantly crashes the app and thereby prohibits further testing, yet it is unlikely to be a priority for fixing (since such a crash tends not to fire in the field, although it *could* in *theory*).

This observation of 'pseudo' false positives suggests a spectrum in which a completely false positive lies at one extreme, but for which a pseudo false positive, that is exceptionally unlikely to occur in practice, lies close to the 'fully false' positives; it shares many of the practical characteristics of 'fully false' positives.

In deployment scenarios where there are only relatively few end users, and these end users only use a strict subset of the available Android devices available, deployment of automated testing techniques, like Sapienz, may also yield further pseudo false positives (which we do not tend to witness at Facebook) due to the differences in test devices and end-user devices.

The degree of 'pseudo falseness' of a crash signal is, effectively, a function of the number of likely end users, since this is a determinant of the probability that a test-time crash will be found in production. As testers at Facebook, we are thus blessed by the relatively large number of end users we serve, because of the way in which this number tends to reduce pseudo false positiveness to a minimum; almost any signal concerning crashes is treated as a true positive by our developer community.

End user abilities may also differ from those of the automated testing system. The primary difference we have noticed lies in the speed with which the automated test sequence can be executed on an emulator; potentially far faster than that achieved by any human. Once again, this has led to fewer false positives than we initially expected. The wide variety of different Android devices in circulation means that test sequences executed by a user on a slower device may have similar characteristics to a faster-executed test sequence on a higher-end device. Nevertheless, some false positives can occur due to speed of test sequence execution.

A further source of difference between test user ability and real user ability, lies in the exceptionally dextrous nature with which an automated test technique can interact with the device or emulator. Effectively, the test user is not hampered by physical constraints imposed by the number fingers and thumbs on a typical human hand, and their varying degrees of freedom to articulate. Previously, it was proposed to use robotic testing to achieve fully black box testing, thereby avoiding this potential source of false positives [51]. This is not something we have currently deployed, but it remains an option, should the false positive problem ever become more pernicious.

7.9   Unit Tests from System Tests

Sapienz generates system-level tests, that test the application, end to end, imitating as closely as possible the behaviour of real users. This system-level approach significantly reduces the propensity of automated test design to produce false positives, that have been widely reported to occur for more lower-level, unit level, testing [30]. However, an interesting research problem lies in converting system level test sequences into corresponding unit level test information, thereby circumventing the unit level false positive problem, while simultaneously facilitating unit testing through automated test design.

One possibility lies in generating a set of system-level tests [21], instrumented to witness the pre- and post-condition state for some unit under test, and the subsequent use of likely invariant inference, such as Daikon [23], to infer the constraints that apply at the unit level. With these inferred constraints in hand, automated test design (at the unit level) can now proceed within the constrained search space, thereby reducing the incidence of unit-level false positives.

7.10   Combining Human- and Machine- Designed Tests

Humans have designed tests for many years. Automated test design techniques, like Sapienz, might reduce human effort and thereby minimize the 'friction' of the test design process, but they are unlikely to fully replace humans. After all, humans have domain knowledge and engineers can link this domain knowledge to specific aspects of code. There is a productive benefit in finding hybrids that can combine human- and machine-designed tests, but this remains an open research challenge.

One possibility is to extract assertions from human-designed tests and re-use them as partial oracles for machine-designed test cases. Humans' domain knowledge is an important resource, while automating the test oracle design process is non-trivial. Perhaps human-written tests can be mined for re-usable test oracle information in the form of assertions extracted from human-designed test cases.

Another possibility would be for the human test to act as a prefix to the machine-designed test. Perhaps the human test might move the system into a state that is hard to reach, but important, or it may simply do so more efficiently than a machine-designed test. Perhaps a human-designed test prefix might establish a state of interest or set up a particular environmental configuration that enables machine-designed tests. For all these reasons, it makes sense to use a human-designed test as a prefix for a Sapienz (or other automatically designed) test. More research is needed on techniques to best combine human-designed and machine-designed test cases.

7.11   Enhancing the Debug Payload

Far too little research is undertaken on the important problem of debugging [37]. Many problems in software debugging can be characterised in terms of multi-objective search. Therefore, we believe the SBSE community has a role to play in tackling this important and under-researched set of challenges.

In some cases, as much as 50% of engineers' time spent on programming may be devoted to the problem of debugging in its various forms. It is therefore surprising (and disappointing) that there is not a single dedicated annual international academic conference, nor any scientific journal dedicated to the perennially important problem of automated support for debugging.

We would like to encourage the software engineering community, more generally, and the Search Based Software Engineering community, in particular, to renew research interest and activity on debugging. Even if automated software repair were ultimately able to remove the need for human debugging effort, the problem of automated debugging would remain a pressing one. That is, techniques that supply additional context and guidance to a human concerned with complex debugging tasks, would also be likely to provide useful input to improve the efficiency and effectiveness of automated program repair. This potential dual use of debugging support, for both human-based debugging activity and automated program repair, makes it all the more important that we should see significant attention and energy devoted to techniques to support debugging activity, whether that activity be by machine or by human hand.

7.12 Search in the Presence of Inherent Flakiness

Search-based software engineering is well-adapted to tackle the problems of test flakiness [37,46,57,62]. We envisage a bright future for probabilistic approaches to testing, and believe that the SBSE community has an important role to play here. By making flakiness of first class property of test cases, and test suites, we can optimise for this property. Furthermore, by measuring the signal and signal-to-noise ratio [37] produced by automated testing tools, we can define these evaluation criteria, and potentially also surface them as fitness functions.

Addressing the Assume Tests Are Flakey (ATAFistic) world [37], we may construct a fully probabilistic formulation of software testing and verification. We hope to formulate and investigate new concepts of correctness, better-fitted to Internet-based deployment than their precursors that were generally initially constructed in the era of mainframes and stand alone desk tops with low numbers of inter-connections.

Probabilistic testing and verification is nascent in the work in information theory for testing [73,75] and probabilistic model checking [15,44], but more work is required on theoretical foundations to unify testing and verification within a fully probabilistic framework. More work is also required to develop the fruits of such foundations in practical, scalable and deployable techniques for probabilistic testing and verification.

7.13 New Search Algorithms that Fully Realize Efficiently Deployable Parallelism at Scale

Search-based software testing systems have rested on evolutionary computing as one of the primary search techniques to explore the space of all candidate inputs to the system under test [33,55]. While there has been some work on parallelisation to achieve the, oft-stated but seldom witnessed, 'embarrassing parallelism' of SBSE [8,58,76], there has been little work on the formulation of SBSE algorithms to better fit modern distributed computational resources.

The bottleneck for most search based testing (and much of SBSE, more generally), lies in the computation of fitness for a candidate test input sequence (more generally, of a software engineering artefact). The distribution of computation times for SBSE fitness inherently involves a high degree of variance, due to the highly stochastic nature of software deployment for Internet-based computing.

Therefore, any approach based on iterative generations of the population is inherently inefficient when we require that all members of the population have to be evaluated in lockstep. We believe there is further work to be done on extending, rethinking, and redefining the underlying evolutionary algorithms. We need to fully decouple unnecessary interdependence between fitness computations, so that maximal parallelism can be achieved; algorithms that can fully exploit asynchronous fitness evaluation will scale well with available parallel computation resources.

Furthermore, closer integration of evolutionary algorithm technology with predictive modelling and machine learning is required in order to better use computational resources for static fitness estimation. For example, predicting likely fitness outcomes and maximising the quantity of information derived from each fitness outcome are both important concerns to maximise the impact of Search Based Software Engineering.

7.14   Automated Fixing

Automated software repair remains an active topic in the research community [29]. At Facebook we find ourselves in an excellent position to act as both a producer and consumer of research and development on deployable automated program repair; as this paper explains we have infrastructure in place for automated testing and for fix detection. We would be particularly interested to collaborate with the academic research community on this topic.

7.15   Automated Performance Improvement

Generalising from automated repair to genetic improvement [65], and related topics in program synthesis [31], we also see great potential for research in automating program improvement, particularly for non-functional properties, such as performance-related behaviours and resource consumption characteristics [34].

We would also be very interested to collaborate with the academic community on scalable and deployable automated program improvement techniques. With Sapienz now deployed at Facebook, we are in a good position to provide the automated test input generation infrastructure that would be a natural prerequisite for the deployment of test-based program improvement and synthesis techniques such as genetic improvement.

Facebook also has static analysis and verification technology in the form of Infer [13], as well as dynamic test design infrastructure (Sapienz) and manually-designed automated execution frameworks (such as the Buddy end-to-end testing system). We are therefore also in an excellent position to offer collaborative support to academics seeking to tackle the FiGiVerify challenge; Finding issues (bugs, performance, resource-related), Genetically Improving them (to synthesize improvements), and Verifying the improvements' correctness [37].

8 The History of Sapienz Deployment to Date

Sapienz was developed as a research prototype, which was initially proposed by Ke Mao and grew out of his PhD work [47]. The first version of Sapienz was described in the Ke's thesis [47] and at ISSTA 2016 [49], the International Symposium on Software Testing and Analysis (ISSTA 2016). This version was made publicly available as a research prototype[6]. The research prototype found 558 unique crashes among the top 1,000 Android apps, several of which were reported and fixed [49].

The three authors of the ISSTA 2016 paper (Ke Mao and his two PhD supervisors, Mark Harman and Yue Jia) launched an Android testing start-up, called Majicke Ltd., in September 2016, with Ke at the CTO, Yue as CEO and Mark as scientific advisor. Majicke's technical offering was based on Sapienz. The three subsequently moved to Facebook[7] on February 6th 2017, where they founded the Sapienz team at Facebook London, with Ke moving into the role of technical lead, Yue focusing on long term technical issues (the vital 'important but not urgent') and Mark taking up the role of team manager.

The Facebook Sapienz Team's role is to deploy, develop and research SBSE-related techniques for automated test case design so that we can have Friction-Free Fault Finding and Fixing. The team has been strongly supported by Facebook's Developer Infrastructure team (DevInfra).

The Sapienz team has grown significantly since then and now includes (or has included) the authors of this paper. Taijin Tei subsequently moved to work for another team, while Alexander Mols has worked and continues to work part time on Sapienz and other projects. The remaining authors of this paper have worked full time, continuously, on Sapienz since starting work at Facebook. Many others at Facebook have helped with support, advice and other contributions and we thank them in the acknowledgements of this paper.

The Sapienz team's many partners, collaborators and supporters in the Facebook developer community have also provided a wealth of support, advice and collaboration. Their willingness to try new technologies and to explore and experiment was evident from the very outset. Facebook's open engineering culture has greatly accelerated the deployment of SBSE at Facebook.

---

[6] https://github.com/Rhapsod/sapienz.
[7] http://www.engineering.ucl.ac.uk/news/bug-finding-majicke-finds-home-facebook/.

9 Conclusions

We have outlined the primary features of the deployment of the Sapienz Search Based Testing system at Facebook, where it is currently testing Facebook's Android social media and messaging apps. These are two of the largest and most widely-used apps in the overall international Android ecosystem. Work is under way to extend to other apps and platforms and to improve the algorithms and technology on which Sapienz relies.

To achieve rapid development of research into production, we use an Automated Scientific Experimental Reporting (ASER) framework, which automates experiments from proof of concept, through inferential statistical testing to full experiment-to-prod A/B testing.

We also outline some of the challenges and open problems that we believe are suitable for tackling by the automated testing and SBSE research communities, based on our experience from this Search Based Software Testing deployment work.

Acknowledgement. Thanks to all our colleagues at Facebook and in the scientific research, open source and developer communities for their support, both technical and non-technical, that has allowed us to so-rapidly deploy search based system-level testing into regular production. Many people at Facebook have helped with the deployment work reported on here in this keynote paper. We would like to thank these colleagues who gave of their time and support while at Facebook, including Sharon Ayalde, Michelle Bell, Josh Berdine, Kelly Berschauer, Andras Biczo, Megan Brogan, Andrea Ciancone, Satish Chandra, Marek Cirkos, Priti Choksi, Wojtek Chmiel, Dulma Churchill, Dino Distefano, Zsolt Dollenstein, Jeremy Dubreil, Jeffrey Dunn, David Erb, Graham French, Daron Green, Lunwen He, Lawrence Lomax, Martino Luca, Joanna Lynch, Dmitry Lyubarskiy, Alex Marginean, Phyllipe Medeiros, Devon Meeker, Kristina Milian, Peter O'Hearn, Bryan O'Sullivan, Lauren Rugani, Evan Snyder, Don Stewart, Gabrielle Van Aacken, Pawel Wanat, and Monica Wik. We sincerely apologise to any who we omitted to mention here.

References

1. Abdessalem, R., Nejati, S., Briand, L., Stifter, T.: Testing vision-based control systems using learnable evolutionary algorithms. In: 40th International Conference on Software Engineering (ICSE 2018) (to appear)
2. Afzal, W., Torkar, R., Feldt, R., Wikstrand, G.: Search-based prediction of fault-slip-through in large software projects. In: Second International Symposium on Search Based Software Engineering (SSBSE 2010), Benevento, Italy 7–9 September 2010, pp. 79–88 (2010)
3. Alesio, S.D., Briand, L.C., Nejati, S., Gotlieb, A.: Combining genetic algorithms and constraint programming to support stress testing of task deadlines. ACM Trans. Softw. Eng. Methodol. **25**(1), 4:1–4:37 (2015)
4. Alshahwan, N., Harman, M.: Automated web application testing using search based software engineering. In: 26th IEEE/ACM International Conference on Automated Software Engineering (ASE 2011), Lawrence, Kansas, USA, 6th–10th November 2011, pp. 3–12 (2011)

5. Alshahwan, N., Harman, M.: Coverage and fault detection of the output-uniqueness test selection criteria. In: International Symposium on Software Testing and Analysis (ISSTA 2014), pp. 181–192. ACM (2014)
6. Androutsopoulos, K., Clark, D., Dan, H., Harman, M., Hierons, R.: An analysis of the relationship between conditional entropy and failed error propagation in software testing. In: 36th International Conference on Software Engineering (ICSE 2014), Hyderabad, India, pp. 573–583, June 2014
7. Arcuri, A., Briand, L.: A practical guide for using statistical tests to assess randomized algorithms in software engineering. In: 33rd International Conference on Software Engineering (ICSE 2011), pp. 1–10. ACM, New York (2011)
8. Asadi, F., Antoniol, G., Guéhéneuc, Y.: Concept location with genetic algorithms: a comparison of four distributed architectures. In: 2nd International Symposium on Search based Software Engineering (SSBSE 2010), pp. 153–162. IEEE Computer Society Press, Benevento (2010)
9. Barr, E.T., Harman, M., McMinn, P., Shahbaz, M., Yoo, S.: The oracle problem in software testing: a survey. IEEE Trans. Softw. Eng. **41**(5), 507–525 (2015)
10. Beizer, B.: Software Testing Techniques. Van Nostrand Reinhold (1990)
11. Bertolino, A.: Software testing research: achievements, challenges, dreams. In: Briand, L., Wolf, A. (eds.) Future of Software Engineering 2007. IEEE Computer Society Press, Los Alamitos (2007)
12. Binkley, D., Gold, N.E., Harman, M., Islam, S.S., Krinke, J., Yoo, S.: ORBS and the limits of static slicing. In: 15th IEEE International Working Conference on Source Code Analysis and Manipulation (SCAM 2015), pp. 1–10. IEEE, Bremen, September 2015
13. Calcagno, C., et al.: Moving fast with software verification. In: Havelund, K., Holzmann, G., Joshi, R. (eds.) NFM 2015. LNCS, vol. 9058, pp. 3–11. Springer, Cham (2015). https://doi.org/10.1007/978-3-319-17524-9_1
14. Ceccarelli, M., Cerulo, L., Canfora, G., Penta, M.D.: An eclectic approach for change impact analysis. In: Kramer, J., Bishop, J., Devanbum, P.T., Uchitel, S. (eds.) 32nd ACM/IEEE International Conference on Software Engineering (ICSE), vol. 2, pp. 163–166. ACM (2010)
15. Chechik, M., Gurfinkel, A., Devereux, B.: ξChek: a multi-valued model-checker. In: Brinksma, E., Larsen, K.G. (eds.) CAV 2002. LNCS, vol. 2404, pp. 505–509. Springer, Heidelberg (2002). https://doi.org/10.1007/3-540-45657-0_41
16. Chen, Y.F., Rosenblum, D.S., Vo, K.P.: TestTube: a system for selective regression testing. In: 16th International Conference on Software Engineering (ICSE 1994), pp. 211–220. IEEE Computer Society Press (1994)
17. Clark, D., Hierons, R.M.: Squeeziness: an information theoretic measure for avoiding fault masking. Inf. Process. Lett. **112**(8–9), 335–340 (2012)
18. Dijkstra, E.W.: Structured programming (1969). http://www.cs.utexas.edu/users/EWD/ewd02xx/EWD268.PDF, circulated privately
19. Dufour, B., Ryder, B.G., Sevitsky, G.: Blended analysis for performance understanding of framework-based applications. In: International Symposium on Software Testing and Analysis, ISSTA 2007, 9–12 July, London, UK, pp. 118–128. ACM (2007)
20. Dunn, J., Mols, A., Lomax, L., Medeiros, P.: Managing resources for large-scale testing, 24 May 2017. https://code.facebook.com/posts/1708075792818517/managing-resources-for-large-scale-testing/
21. Elbaum, S.G., Chin, H.N., Dwyer, M.B., Jorde, M.: Carving and replaying differential unit test cases from system test cases. IEEE Trans. Softw. Eng. **35**(1), 29–45 (2009)

22. Engström, E., Runeson, P., Skoglund, M.: A systematic review on regression test selection techniques. Inf. Softw. Technol. **52**(1), 14–30 (2010)
23. Ernst, M.D., Cockrell, J., Griswold, W.G., Notkin, D.: Dynamically discovering likely program invariants to support program evolution. IEEE Trans. Softw. Eng. **27**(2), 1–25 (2001)
24. Facebook Research: Facebook Research post describing the move of Majicke to Facebook (2017). https://facebook.com/academics/posts/1326609954057075
25. Feitelson, D.G., Frachtenberg, E., Beck, K.L.: Development and deployment at Facebook. IEEE Internet Comput. **17**(4), 8–17 (2013)
26. Fraser, G., Arcuri, A.: EvoSuite: automatic test suite generation for object-oriented software. In: 8th European Software Engineering Conference and the ACM SIG-SOFT Symposium on the Foundations of Software Engineering (ESEC/FSE 2011), pp. 416–419. ACM, 5th–9th September 2011
27. Fraser, G., Arcuri, A.: The seed is strong: seeding strategies in search-based software testing. In: Antoniol, G., Bertolino, A., Labiche, Y. (eds.) 5th International Conference on Software Testing, Verification and Validation (ICST 2012), pp. 121–130. IEEE, Montreal, April 2012. http://ieeexplore.ieee.org/xpl/mostRecentIssue.jsp?punumber=6200016
28. Gao, Z., Liang, Y., Cohen, M.B., Memon, A.M., Wang, Z.: Making system user interactive tests repeatable: when and what should we control? In: Bertolino, A., Canfora, G., Elbaum, S.G. (eds.) 37th International Conference on Software Engineering (ICSE 2015), pp. 55–65. IEEE Computer Society, Florence, 16–24 May 2015
29. Goues, C.L., Forrest, S., Weimer, W.: Current challenges in automatic software repair. Softw. Qual. J. **21**(3), 421–443 (2013)
30. Gross, F., Fraser, G., Zeller, A.: Search-based system testing: high coverage, no false alarms. In: International Symposium on Software Testing and Analysis (ISSTA 2012), pp. 67–77 (2012)
31. Gulwani, S., Harris, W.R., Singh, R.: Spreadsheet data manipulation using examples. Commun. ACM **55**(8), 97–105 (2012)
32. Harman, M., Burke, E., Clark, J.A., Yao, X.: Dynamic adaptive search based software engineering (keynote paper). In: 6th IEEE International Symposium on Empirical Software Engineering and Measurement (ESEM 2012), Lund, Sweden, pp. 1–8, September 2012
33. Harman, M., Jia, Y., Zhang, Y.: Achievements, open problems and challenges for search based software testing (keynote paper). In: 8th IEEE International Conference on Software Testing, Verification and Validation (ICST 2015), Graz, Austria, April 2015
34. Harman, M., Langdon, W.B., Jia, Y., White, D.R., Arcuri, A., Clark, J.A.: The GISMOE challenge: constructing the Pareto program surface using genetic programming to find better programs (keynote paper). In: 27th IEEE/ACM International Conference on Automated Software Engineering (ASE 2012), Essen, Germany, pp. 1–14, September 2012
35. Harman, M., Mansouri, A., Zhang, Y.: Search based software engineering: trends, techniques and applications. ACM Comput. Surv. **45**(1), 11:1–11:61 (2012)
36. Harman, M., McMinn, P., de Souza, J.T., Yoo, S.: Search based software engineering: techniques, taxonomy, tutorial. In: Meyer, B., Nordio, M. (eds.) LASER 2008-2010. LNCS, vol. 7007, pp. 1–59. Springer, Heidelberg (2012). https://doi.org/10.1007/978-3-642-25231-0_1

37. Harman, M., O'Hearn, P.: From start-ups to scale-ups: opportunities and open problems for static and dynamic program analysis (keynote paper). In: 18th IEEE International Working Conference on Source Code Analysis and Manipulation (SCAM 2018), Madrid, Spain, 23rd–24th September 2018, to appear
38. Hazelwood, K., et al.: Applied machine learning at Facebook: a datacenter infrastructure perspective. In: 24th International Symposium on High-Performance Computer Architecture (HPCA 2018), Vienna, Austria, 24–28 February 2018
39. Hierons, R.M., Harman, M.: Testing against non-deterministic stream X-machines. Formal Aspects Comput. **12**, 423–442 (2000)
40. Ipate, F., Holcombe, M.: Generating test sequences from non-deterministic X-machines. Formal Aspects Comput. **12**(6), 443–458 (2000)
41. Jahangirova, G., Clark, D., Harman, M., Tonella, P.: Test oracle assessment and improvement. In: International Symposium on Software Testing and Analysis (ISSTA 2016), pp. 247–258 (2016)
42. Jan, S., Panichella, A., Arcuri, A., Briand, L.: Automatic generation of tests to exploit XML injection vulnerabilities in web applications. IEEE Transactions on Software Engineering (2018, to appear)
43. Jia, Y., Cohen, M.B., Harman, M., Petke, J.: Learning combinatorial interaction test generation strategies using hyperheuristic search. In: 37th International Conference on Software Engineering (ICSE 2015), Florence, Italy, pp. 540–550 (2015)
44. Kwiatkowska, M., Norman, G., Parker, D.: PRISM: probabilistic symbolic model checker. In: Field, T., Harrison, P.G., Bradley, J., Harder, U. (eds.) TOOLS 2002. LNCS, vol. 2324, pp. 200–204. Springer, Heidelberg (2002). https://doi.org/10.1007/3-540-46029-2_13
45. Lakhotia, K., Harman, M., Gross, H.: AUSTIN: an open source tool for search based software testing of C programs. J. Inf. Softw. Technol. **55**(1), 112–125 (2013)
46. Luo, Q., Hariri, F., Eloussi, L., Marinov, D.: An empirical analysis of flaky tests. In: Cheung, S.C., Orso, A., Storey, M.A. (eds.) 22nd International Symposium on Foundations of Software Engineering (FSE 2014), pp. 643–653. ACM, Hong Kong, 16–22 November 2014
47. Mao, K.: Multi-objective Search-based Mobile Testing. Ph.D. thesis, University College London, Department of Computer Science, CREST centre (2017)
48. Mao, K., Capra, L., Harman, M., Jia, Y.: A survey of the use of crowdsourcing in software engineering. J. Syst. Softw. **126**, 57–84 (2017)
49. Mao, K., Harman, M., Jia, Y.: Sapienz: multi-objective automated testing for Android applications. In: International Symposium on Software Testing and Analysis (ISSTA 2016), pp. 94–105 (2016)
50. Mao, K., Harman, M., Jia, Y.: Crowd intelligence enhances automated mobile testing. In: Proceedings of the 32nd IEEE/ACM International Conference on Automated Software Engineering, ASE 2017, pp. 16–26 (2017)
51. Mao, K., Harman, M., Jia, Y.: Robotic testing of mobile apps for truly black-box automation. IEEE Softw. **34**(2), 11–16 (2017)
52. Marculescu, B., Feldt, R., Torkar, R., Poulding, S.: Transferring interactive search-based software testing to industry. J. Syst. Softw. **142**, 156–170 (2018)
53. Martin, W., Sarro, F., Harman, M.: Causal impact analysis for app releases in Google Play. In: 24th ACM SIGSOFT International Symposium on the Foundations of Software Engineering (FSE 2016), Seattle, WA, USA, pp. 435–446 November 2016
54. Matinnejad, R., Nejati, S., Briand, L., Bruckmann, T.: Test generation and test prioritization for simulink models with dynamic behavior. IEEE Trans. Softw. Eng. (2018, to appear)

55. McMinn, P.: Search-based software test data generation: a survey. Softw. Test. Verif. Reliab. **14**(2), 105–156 (2004)
56. Memon, A.M., Cohen, M.B.: Automated testing of GUI applications: models, tools, and controlling flakiness. In: Notkin, D., Cheng, B.H.C., Pohl, K. (eds.) 35th International Conference on Software Engineering (ICSE 2013), pp. 1479–1480. IEEE Computer Society, San Francisco, 18–26 May 2013
57. Memon, A.M., et al.: Taming Google-scale continuous testing. In: 39th International Conference on Software Engineering, Software Engineering in Practice Track (ICSE-SEIP), pp. 233–242. IEEE, Buenos Aires, 20–28 May 2017
58. Mitchell, B.S., Traverso, M., Mancoridis, S.: An architecture for distributing the computation of software clustering algorithms. In: IEEE/IFIP Working Conference on Software Architecture (WICSA 2001), pp. 181–190. IEEE Computer Society, Amsterdam (2001)
59. Mansour, N., Bahsoon, R., Baradhi, G.: Empirical comparison of regression test selection algorithms. Syst. Softw. **57**(1), 79–90 (2001)
60. Nie, C., Leung, H.: A survey of combinatorial testing. ACM Comput. Surv. **43**(2), 11:1–11:29 (2011)
61. Ouni, A., Kessentini, M., Sahraoui, H.A., Inoue, K., Deb, K.: Multi-criteria code refactoring using search-based software engineering: an industrial case study. ACM Trans. Softw. Eng. Methodol. **25**(3), 23:1–23:53 (2016)
62. Palomba, F., Zaidman, A.: Does refactoring of test smells induce fixing flakey tests? In: International Conference on Software Maintenance and Evolution (ICSME 2017), pp. 1–12. IEEE Computer Society (2017)
63. Pearl, J.: Causality. Cambridge University Press, Cambridge (2000)
64. Petke, J., Cohen, M.B., Harman, M., Yoo, S.: Efficiency and early fault detection with lower and higher strength combinatorial interaction testing. In: European Software Engineering Conference and the ACM SIGSOFT Symposium on the Foundations of Software Engineering, ESEC/FSE 2013, pp. 26–36. ACM, Saint Petersburg, August 2013
65. Petke, J., Haraldsson, S.O., Harman, M., Langdon, W.B., White, D.R., Woodward, J.R.: Genetic improvement of software: a comprehensive survey. IEEE Trans. Evol. Comput. (2018, to appear)
66. Podgurski, A., et al.: Automated support for classifying software failure reports. In: 25th International Conference on Software Engineering (ICSE 2003), pp. 465–477. IEEE Computer Society, Piscataway, 3–10 May 2003
67. Rothermel, G., Harrold, M.J.: Analyzing regression test selection techniques. IEEE Trans. Softw. Eng. **22**(8), 529–551 (1996)
68. Salton, G., Buckley, C.: Term-weighting approaches in automatic text retrieval. Inf. Process. Manag. **24**(5), 513–523 (1988)
69. Shin, S.Y., Nejati, S., Sabetzadeh, M., Briand, L., Zimmer, F.: Test case prioritization for acceptance testing of cyber physical systems: a multi-objective search-based approach. In: International Symposium on Software Testing and Analysis (ISSTA 2018) (to appear)
70. Tillmann, N., de Halleux, J., Xie, T.: Transferring an automated test generation tool to practice: from Pex to Fakes and Code Digger. In: 29th ACM/IEEE International Conference on Automated Software Engineering (ASE), pp. 385–396 (2014)
71. Tracey, N., Clark, J., Mander, K.: The way forward for unifying dynamic test-case generation: the optimisation-based approach. In: International Workshop on Dependable Computing and Its Applications (DCIA), IFIP, pp. 169–180, January 1998

72. Wegener, J., Baresel, A., Sthamer, H.: Evolutionary test environment for automatic structural testing. Inf. Softw. Technol. **43**(14), 841–854 (2001)
73. Yang, L., Dang, Z., Fischer, T.R., Kim, M.S., Tan, L.: Entropy and software systems: towards an information-theoretic foundation of software testing. In: 2010 FSE/SDP Workshop on the Future of Software Engineering Research, pp. 427–432, November 2010
74. Yoo, S., Harman, M.: Regression testing minimisation, selection and prioritisation: a survey. J. Softw. Testing Verif. Reliab. **22**(2), 67–120 (2012)
75. Yoo, S., Harman, M., Clark, D.: Fault localization prioritization: comparing information theoretic and coverage based approaches. ACM Trans. Softw. Eng. Methodol. **22**(3), Article no. 19 (2013)
76. Yoo, S., Harman, M., Ur, S.: GPGPU test suite minimisation: search based software engineering performance improvement using graphics cards. J. Empir. Softw. Eng. **18**(3), 550–593 (2013)
77. Yoo, S., Nilsson, R., Harman, M.: Faster fault finding at Google using multi objective regression test optimisation. In: 8th European Software Engineering Conference and the ACM SIGSOFT Symposium on the Foundations of Software Engineering (ESEC/FSE 2011), Szeged, Hungary, 5th–9th September 2011. Industry Track

Evolving Living Technologies—Insights from the EvoEvo Project

Guillaume Beslon[1](✉), Santiago F. Elena[2,3,4], Paulien Hogeweg[5],
Dominique Schneider[6], and Susan Stepney[7]

[1] Université de Lyon, INSA-Lyon, INRIA, LIRIS UMR5205, Beagle Team,
Villeurbanne, France
guillaume.beslon@inria.fr
[2] Instituto de Biología Molecular y Celular de Plantas
(CSIC-Universitat Politècnica de València), Valencia, Spain
sfelena@ibmcp.upv.es
[3] Instituto de Biología Integrativa de Sistemas (CSIC-Universitat de València),
Paterna, Valencia, Spain
[4] Santa Fe Institute, Santa Fe, USA
[5] Theoretical Biology and Bioinformatics Group, Utrecht University,
Utrecht, The Netherlands
p.hogeweg@uu.nl
[6] Univ. Grenoble Alpes, CNRS, Grenoble INP, TIMC-IMAG, Grenoble, France
dominique.schneider@univ-grenoble-alpes.fr
[7] Department of Computer Science, and York Cross-disciplinary Centre for Systems
Analysis, University of York, Heslington, York, UK
susan.stepney@york.ac.uk

Abstract. The EvoEvo project was a 2013–2017 FP7 European project
aiming at developing new evolutionary approaches in information science
and producing novel algorithms based on the current understanding of
molecular and evolutionary biology, with the ultimate goals of addressing open-ended problems in which the specifications are either unknown
or too complicated to express, and of producing software able to operate even in unpredictable, varying conditions. Here we present the main
rationals of the EvoEvo project and propose a set of design rules to evolve
adaptive software systems.

1 Introduction

Evolution by natural selection is the major source of biological complexity on
earth, the origin of all the species we can observe, interact with, or breed. On a
smaller scale, evolution is at the heart of the adaptation process for many species,
in particular microorganisms (*e.g.* viruses, bacteria or unicellular eukaryotes).
Microbial evolution not only results in the emergence of the species itself but also
contributes to real-time adaptation of the organisms when facing perturbations
or environmental changes. These organisms are not only built up *by* evolution,
they are also organized *to* evolve.

© Springer Nature Switzerland AG 2018
T. E. Colanzi and P. McMinn (Eds.): SSBSE 2018, LNCS 11036, pp. 46–62, 2018.
https://doi.org/10.1007/978-3-319-99241-9_2

As far as information science is concerned, evolution has inspired generations of researchers since the pioneers of the 1950s and 1960s. Nevertheless, most evolutionary algorithms do not take into account the fact that all the molecular systems involved in the evolutionary process are themselves shaped by past evolution. This implies that evolution can influence its own course. This evolution of evolution ("EvoEvo") is at the heart of many phenomena overlooked by evolutionary algorithms, like second-order evolution, evolution of robustness, of evolvability, of mutation operators and rates, co-evolution... Yet, all these processes are at work in living organisms from viruses to whales. Particularly in the case of microorganisms, possibly accelerating their evolution and enabling them to quickly adapt in response to environmental changes like new drugs, pollution, response of their host immune system, or emergence of new ecological niches.

The EvoEvo project was a 2013–2017 FP7 European project aiming at developing new evolutionary approaches in information science and producing novel algorithms based on the current understanding of molecular and evolutionary biology, with the ultimate goals of addressing open-ended problems in which the specifications are either unknown or too complicated to express, and of producing software able to operate even in unpredictable, varying conditions. To do so, the project consortium proposed to start from experimental observations of the evolution of microorganisms under laboratory conditions and to use these observations to reproduce EvoEvo, first in computational models, and then in application software. Our aim was to observe EvoEvo in action, model EvoEvo, understand EvoEvo and, ultimately, reproduce EvoEvo to exploit it in software and computational systems.

In this article we briefly present the rationale of the EvoEvo project. We then focus on the main outcomes of the project, with specific emphasis on those that are likely to have an influence on evolutionary computation and evolutionary software development, as detailed in the project deliverables[1].

2   Overview of the EvoEvo Project

2.1   Introduction

One ultimate goal of Information and Communications Technologies (ICT) is to improve human life through the extension of human capacities, abilities or communications. Yet, one of the profound movements that traverse modern social and human sciences is that the world cannot be described as a stable system. Humans and societies continuously change due to the many interactions that lead to instability, to the emergence of new social groups, ideas, modes, media. But today's ICT can barely tackle such highly unstable situations: Every encountered situation needs to be foreseen long before it occurs, at the time the software is

---

[1] The following text is massively derived from the EvoEvo project documents. In particular, many paragraphs are derived from the EvoEvo Description of Work (DoW) and from the project Final Report (EvoEvo Deliverable 6.8), available at www.evoevo.eu.

designed; and the development cycle of ICT systems is so long that its environment is likely to have changed before the first release of a system. A consequence of this necessary stability of today's ICT systems is that users – individuals and society – must adapt to the ICT systems that are supposed to serve them. Inside the ICT world, the same difficulties are at work since software systems cannot efficiently adapt to the emergence of other pieces of software (or new releases of existing ones) in their environment. Thus, one of the challenges of modern ICT is to develop technologies that are able to adapt dynamically to the evolution of their context, of their user, of the data they receive, and of other systems they interact with – in a single word, of their environment.

The situation in completely different when looking at biology: Evolution, the process that created (and still creates) all the diversity of life, is a process by which generations of organisms continually adapt to their environment. Moreover, the environment of an organism is never stable as it also depends on the evolution of other organisms. Higher eukaryotes have evolved complex sensori-motor systems to adapt their behavior to their changing environment. Microorganisms are less sophisticated systems that lack complex sensori-motor abilities, yet they efficiently use mutation and selection to dynamically adapt to new conditions. Recent experimental evolution results have shown that they are able to evolve at an amazing speed: in virtually all experimental studies that have used bacteria or viruses, important phenotypic innovations have emerged in only a few tens of generations [16]. These results show that, more than being adapted to a specific condition, microorganisms are adapted to evolve: evolution has optimized their own ability to evolve, as a primary means to react to environmental changes. The central idea of the EvoEvo project is that this "evolution of evolution" could offer ICT new paradigms to enable computational systems to dynamically adapt to their environment, *i.e.* to their users, domain of use or condition of use.

2.2 How Can Evolution Evolve?

Variation and selection are the two core engines of Darwinian Evolution. Yet, both are directly regulated by many processes that are themselves products of evolution (*e.g.* DNA repair, mutator genes, transposable elements, horizontal transfer, stochasticity of gene expression, sex, network modularity, niche construction...). Moreover, in a biological system, variation and selection do not act at the same organization level. While variation modifies organisms at the genetic level (by modification of their DNA content), selection acts at the phenotypic level (on the whole organism). The genotype-to-phenotype mapping summarizes in a single conceptual entity (the "mapping") the complex molecular processes by which information flows from the genetic sequence to the organism's phenotype. It captures in a single abstract process different phenomena such as mRNA transcription, gene translation, protein folding, biochemistry and cell dynamics. Again, all these process are themselves dependent on the genetic material that encodes the decoding machinery. Hence the genotype-to-phenotype mapping is itself evolving. Since this mapping directly influences the phenotypic consequences of a DNA modification, the evolution of the genotype-to-phenotype mapping is likely to change the evolutionary dynamics, *e.g.* by buffering the effect of mutations.

"Evolution of Evolution", or "EvoEvo", encompasses all the processes by which evolution is (or may be) able to influence its own dynamics and to accelerate (or slow down) its own course depending on the environmental conditions. EvoEvo is thus a very general concept that can be difficult to study as a whole, given the wide diversity of mechanisms at stake. That is why, in the context of the EvoEvo project, we decided to focus on four simpler concepts, directly linked to EvoEvo but easier to define, hence to measure *in vivo*, to model *in silico* and, ultimately, to exploit in evolutionary software.

Variability. Variability is the ability to generate new phenotypes, by genetic or epigenetic mutations or by stochastic fluctuations. It is a necessary condition for any evolutionary process to take place. In biological organisms, the amount of variability is controlled by complex pathways that *e.g.* correct DNA mismatches or double strand-breaks. In an ICT context, evolution of variability could help the evolving system to quickly discover new solutions either on a transient or on a stable way through efficient exploration of the functional space. Moreover, in real biological systems, mutational operators are highly diversified: they include not only point mutations, but also large chromosomal rearrangements that can rapidly reshuffle the chromosome organization, extend or reduce the gene repertoire of an organism, or even duplicate its entire genome through whole genome duplication. Current evolutionary algorithms exploit only a tiny part of this complex mutation repertoire.

Robustness. Although necessary, variation is a dangerous process since it produces deleterious mutations that lead to maladapted individuals. Robustness may evolve to correct these deleterious effects. It enables evolving systems to support mutational events without losing fitness, through *e.g.* canalization or the selection of structures that create neutral landscapes. In an ICT context, selection of robustness may favor the emergence of an "organism" structured such that its service will not be perturbed by the random occurrence of mutational events.

Evolvability. Depending on the genotype-to-phenotype mapping, the proportion of deleterious/neutral/favorable mutational events may vary. Evolvability is the ability of a specific genotype-to-phenotype mapping to increase the proportion of favorable events. This can be done by the selection of specific genome structures or by the selection of specific networks structures. In an ICT context, evolvability would enable evolution to exploit past events to increase the system's ability to adapt to new users or conditions.

Open-Endedness. Biological evolution is not directed towards a specific target. On the contrary, evolution has the ability to generate new challenges while evolving, *e.g.* by exploiting new niches created by the evolution of other species. In an ICT context, open-endedness [2] can be exploited when an application is made from an ecosystem of evolving individuals. In such a structure, new functions would arise continuously by emergence of new species in the ecosystem and/or the extinction of maladapted ones.

2.3   A Route from Biological Evolution to Artificial Evolution

The idea of using a bio-inspired evolutionary metaphor in ICT has led to many powerful developments such as genetic algorithms, evolutionary strategies, and genetic programming. However, most of these developments stay far from current knowledge in evolutionary and molecular biology. The EvoEvo project aimed at creating a true interdisciplinary consortium gathering experimental and computational biologists as well as computer scientists. This gives rise to a difficult question: how can one guarantee that the biological foundations of EvoEvo – which we aimed to observe *in vivo* – are effectively and efficiently transfered to the ICT world and to the computational application? To tackle this issue, we proposed a particular route from evolutionary biology to artificial evolution through modeling. The project was organized to benefit from the pivotal role of computational modeling of evolution, aka *in silico* experimental evolution [3,16]. These models are computational artifacts that mimic the phenomenon observed *in vivo*. They thus constitute an intermediate step between life science and ICT. Now, models must not be mistaken for application code. Their objectives are – and must stay – clearly different. That is why the transition from life science to application code was organized in two steps. The *in vivo* experiments were modeled *in silico*, and those models were then reinterpreted to develop a computational framework that benefited from them but enabled the introduction of simplification and/or generalization of the full model's bio-like structures.

2.4   EvoEvo... What For?

As explained above, the EvoEvo project covered a large range of research domains, from experimental biology to software development. To ensure that EvoEvo would produce results that fulfill the target of the EVLIT European program[2] (designing "empirical, theoretical and synthetic approaches that define the key bio-inspired principles that can drive future living technologies and the environment to use them in a controlled way"), we proposed to develop proof-of-concept applications aiming to demonstrate the power of EvoEvo. This opened a difficult discussion within the consortium on which kind of application were (1) doable in a reasonable time and (2) likely to benefit from the EvoEvo principles. We finally decided to develop "personal evolutionary companions": software systems that continuously evolve through the interaction with their user by means of sensor networks. To keep the system's complexity low enough, we focused on a very specific situation: the interaction between a dancer and the music. This led to the development of the EvoMove system, a personal companion that learned to play music while the dancer is dancing through continuous adaptation to the dancer's moves. EvoMove is briefly described in Sect. 4.2.

---

[2] ICT-2013.9.6 – FET Proactive: Evolving Living Technologies (EVLIT).

3   Results: EvoEvo Insights from Biological and *in Silico* Evolutionary Experiments

3.1   What Is Evolution?

After Darwin and "The Origin of Species" (1859), evolution can be basically defined by the process of species emergence through the simultaneous action of variation and selection. Given that evolution takes place in the context of populations, a third mechanism was later added by Kimura [20]: Neutral genetic drift, which accounts for the unavoidable effect of sampling in finite populations. This mechanistic definition of evolution can easily be shared by different disciplines, from evolutionary biology to computer sciences, even though the underlying mechanisms can be very different. However, the disciplines are much less in agreement when defining evolution by its consequences on the organisms and on the species. While computer scientists and mathematicians tends to consider that evolution is an optimization process, this notion of optimization is not clearly defined in biology, not least because there is no universal definition of an "optimum" and of what must be considered as the "fitness" of the organisms (*i.e.* their reproductive success). When dealing with a "simple" artificial system, the fitness can often be easily computed though a predefined algorithm. But this is not the case for a real organism in which the fitness encompass many different effects (*e.g.* number of offspring, offspring viability, sexual selection...). If Darwinian evolution is an optimization process, we are completely blind to what it optimizes.

During the EvoEvo project, we developed many computational models of evolution with different formalisms [9,28,31]. Hence, the definition of fitness in these different models also varied. However, a strong point of convergence of all these models is that the measured fitness is generally different from the specified fitness (*i.e.* from the coded criteria of success at the individual level). In these models, which all encoded an optimization process through selection at the individual level, the evolutionary outcome was a much more complicated process that involved different levels of organization: the interaction between the multiple levels of organization encoded in the models (genotype, phenotype, population...) blurred the optimization criterion that acted at a single level (the phenotype). Hence, we were facing the same kind of problem biologists face when measuring the evolutionary success of an organism. On the one hand, this is an interesting result for biology (as it enabled us to identify new evolutionary mechanisms) but on the other hand, it makes it difficult to transfer our models and results to the computational world since the outcome of evolution is no longer clearly defined.

To overcome this difficulty, we propose an alternative definition of the evolutionary outcome. Even if evolution is not optimization, it can still be defined as the process by which an organism (or a species) accumulates information about its environment while thriving in it. This definition opens interesting issues. Information is evidently accumulated in the inherited material (the genome), but it can also be accumulated in other characteristics of the organisms, providing these characteristics can be transmitted to the next generation. An example of this process is the spatial or temporal organization of the population (Sect. 3.2). The information accumulation in the genome depends on many parameters that are likely to vary during evolution (the genome size, the coding proportion, the genome structure, the epigeneetic methylation patterns) and this opens a clear path to EvoEvo mechanisms (Sect. 3.3). Viewing evolution as information accumulation also poses the question of information stability: information can accumulate to the extent that the organisms are able to transmit it efficiently to the next generation. This directly links the notion of fitness to the notion of robustness and evolvability (Sect. 3.4).

3.2   Long-Term Information Integration

Long-term information integration – the capacity of evolving systems to accumulate information over long time scales, possibly overriding immediate disadvantages – has long been taboo for explaining what has evolved, because without explicit modeling it invites just-so stories. Moreover, classical evolutionary models and algorithms in which evolution is limited to modifying allele frequencies, or few parameters, do not allow long-term information integration.

All the models we designed or used during the EvoEvo project included not only a genetic information level but also many additional degrees of freedom. These degrees of freedom were different in the various models, but included: the spatial position of the organisms (and subsequently the spatial interaction between the organisms); non-coding sequences and relative position of the genes along the genomic sequence; waste production and release in a shared environment... In virtually all *in silico* experiments we conducted with these models, evolution found ways to use these degrees of freedom to accumulate information about its environment. This information was then empowered to regulate evolution (*e.g.* in the case of additional degrees of freedom at the genomic sequence level, see next section) or led to transitions from individual levels of selection to higher level selection of composite entities, one of the "major evolutionary transition" [30] and a clear stepping-stone for open-ended evolution [2].

One example is the *in silico* experiments of Colizzi at Utrecht University [9], which shows how such higher level selection can overcome the well known tragedy of the commons problem. When the production of an essential "common good" is costly, individual level selection will reduce its production leading to eventual extinction of the whole population. However when the population is embedded in space this is no more the case. Instead, when the cost of production is high enough, the population splits in a subpopulation of cheaters, not producing the common good, and a subpopulation that produces much of it. But space enables both subpopulations to self-organize, hence evolving stable higher-level entities: both subpopulations together form traveling waves, the producers in front, and the cheaters in the tail (Fig. 1). It is this robust spatial organization which overcomes individual level selection to avoid the cost, and thus prevents the tragedy of the commons. Strikingly the system as a whole will produce more common good the higher the cost! Interestingly, the structure of the traveling waves is not encoded in the genome of the organisms. It is rather encoded in the dynamic eco-evolutionary interactions between producers and cheaters, *i.e.* at a higher organization level.

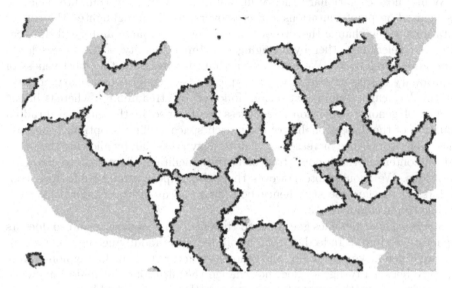

Fig. 1. Example of the high-level structures (traveling waves) created by the interaction between producers (gray) and cheaters (black). The producers form an expanding front that colonizes free space. The cheaters follow common good gradient, hence the front, thereby leading to the extinction of the wave. This frees space that hence become available for another wave. This interaction between front expansion and space freeing results in a stable high-level spatial temporal dynamics which enables evolution of high production common good despite high cost to individuals (reproduced from [9]).

The "real world" (in our case, the biotic world) contains many of such degrees of freedom (*e.g.* spatial interactions, non-specific interactions between molecular compounds, non-genetic inheritance) and evolution can empower them to accumulate information. Our results suggest that including similar "messy" interactions between all levels and components could be a way to increase the innovation power (the "open-endedness") of evolutionary algorithms, although maybe not their optimization efficiency. A first, easy, step would be to embed populations in space (providing individuals can spatially interact with each others), as it improves even simple evolutionary search. Similarly, exploiting long term information integration by using sparse fitness evaluation, in which subproblems co-evolve with solutions, could improve evolutionary search [11, 22].

3.3 Evolution of Genetic Architecture and the Role of Non-coding Sequences

One fundamental mechanism we identified is the evolution of the size and the structure of the genome. The size and structure determines the dimensionality

of the evolutionary search space and the overall mutation pressure; it also determines the relative pressure due to the different mutational operators and the
kind of genomic changes these mutational operators can achieve.

While most evolutionary theory in biology, as well as in computer science,
has focused on point mutations and crossovers, we have highlighted the role of
mutations which change the size of the genome – *e.g.* large and small duplications and deletions – thereby changing the dimensionality of the fitness landscape and search space. We have shown that this increases the effectiveness of
evolutionary search in several ways. Typically, successful evolutionary adaptation involves early genome expansion, followed by streamlining, whereas in the
absence of genome expansion less fitness is obtained in the end: the gradual
reduction of the dimensionality of the search space facilitates optimization [10].
These operators hence increase the evolutionary potential: by allowing the information content of the genome to evolve, they facilitate adaptation to changing
conditions. We should note however they also impose strong robustness constraints on the genome size, hence bounding the quantity of information the
genome can accumulate [13].

Structuring of genomes goes beyond the effect on genome size and so does its
impact on evolution. Indeed, the variation operators modifying the genetic content are differently impacted by the genome structure (*e.g.* including non-coding
sequence between two genes does not change the effect of point mutations while
it strongly changes the effect of duplications). Hence, an evolvable genetic structure enables evolution to fine tune the distribution of offspring fitness, selecting
for robustness and/or evolvability when needed. This fine tuning can even allow
for simultaneous selection of robustness *and* evolvability, as exemplified by the
results of Rutten [29]. His experiments show that organisms in which the point
mutation rate is raised by a factor of 100 react by reorganizing their genome.
While theoretical results with simpler models predict a fitness loss due to the
loss of robustness, genome reorganization enables the organisms to change the
distribution of offspring fitness, and so to increase evolvability. Although the
high mutation rate occasionally leads to fitness loss through loss of the master
sequence, the increased evolvability enables the population to quickly recover,
hence keeping the fitness of the best individuals at the same level (and sometimes at a higher level) than that of the wild-type individuals that evolved under
a constant mutation rate. Similar results have been obtained in another class of
model studied in the course of the project: by evolving RNA sequences, Colizzi
[8] has shown that the RNA structure (the equivalent of the genome structure
in the RNA model) is selected such that the population contains an efficient
proportion of mutated sequences and such that the mutants help the master
sequence to thrive.

In conclusion, genome structuring, mediated by a plethora of mutational
operators, is a powerful mechanism for EvoEvo. It helps explain recent observations of very fast adaptation to novel environments in experimental evolution
[27], and may help regulate evolutionary dynamics by changing the impact of
the different kinds of mutation, hence the distribution of sequences/fitnesses in
the population.

3.4   On the Importance of Long Jumps

One of the difficult open questions in evolutionary biology (and so far an unsolved issue in artificial evolution) is the question of evolutionary innovation: When trapped on a local optimum, how does a population escape to find a new, higher, peak in the fitness landscape? Different hypotheses have been proposed in the literature, one of the most popular being exploration of the so-called "neutral landscape". In this view, a local optimum can be changed into a plateau when the number of dimensions increases, and this plateau is likely to be connected to higher peaks, whereas in lower dimensions (a shorter genome), it would have been surrounded by fitness valleys. Though this theory has many advocates, it suffers from a major drawback: the curse of dimensionality. When the number of dimensions increases, the time needed to explore the plateau increases exponentially [6], making it very unlikely to find an escape route in a reasonable time. Moreover, as we explain above, increasing the size of the genome may have a strong effect on robustness [13], hence limiting the interest of this strategy.

We studied evolutionary innovation in the Aevol *in silico* experimental evolution platform (www.aevol.fr) by evolving populations for a very long time. Once these populations get stuck on local fitness optima, we cloned them and resumed the evolution of the clones. This procedure enabled us to isolate the clones that innovate from those that stay stuck on the initial optimum, and so to analyze the route to innovation [4]. The results emphasize again the role of large scale modifications of the genome structure: In a large majority of the "innovator clones" innovation was triggered by a specific mutational event that strongly increased the evolvability of the clone by increasing the size of its genome, generally through duplication of a small sequence. This result sheds new light on the innovation dynamics: rather than randomly diffusing on a neutral landscape or accumulating deleterious mutations to cross a fitness valley, the innovator clones stay on the top of their local fitness peak but try "long jumps": mutations that directly connect them to a distant part of the fitness landscape. Of course, the vast majority of these jumps are deleterious, but their combinatorics is much larger than the one of point mutations: the number of possible point mutations in a genome is proportional to N, the size of the genome, while the number of possible sequence duplications is proportional to N^3. Hence, a population can quickly explore the whole set of available point mutations (if the population is large enough), ending stuck on a local optimum. Exploring the whole set of chromosomal duplications does takes time, but leads to innovation.

Following this result, a strong recommendation for evolutionary algorithms is to include a set of mutations with a very high combinatorics, that enables long jumps in the fitness landscape. In our experiments this role is played by chromosomal duplications, but other operators could play the same role. One could for instance consider Horizontal Gene Transfer (HGT), providing the source and destination of the gene are different enough (this is not the case in the classical crossover operators used in evolutionary computation) or large scale modification of the genome conformation and folding.

4   Results: EvoEvo Algorithms and Applications for Living Technologies

4.1   EvoEvo Algorithms and Computational Concepts

Based on the insights gained from studying various evolutionary phenomena (Sect. 3), the EvoEvo project developed several novel evo-evolutionary algorithms and architectures.

EvoMachina. EvoMachina [19] is a novel meta-evolutionary algorithm that incorporates several of key findings: that *genomic reorganization* is an important factor in the evolution of evolvability; that the machinery of evolution (expression, replication, etc.) is implemented by *machines* that are themselves encoded on the genome, and hence are themselves subject to evolution; that spatial organization of replicating entities provides an extra level of information integration.

EvoMachina allows multiple different types of genomes, allowing appropriate representations and machinery to be used for different parts of the application. For example, the mutation machinery can be encoded in a separate genome, allowing the mutation operators to evolve in a different manner, and at a different rate, from the application's candidate solutions.

An implementation of EvoMachina is available as an open-source Java framework at github/evoevo-york/evomachina. The framework includes a variety of evolutionary variants such as classic EA and microbial GA, as well as the EvoMachina specific operators, and a variety of spatial options, including a well-mixed option and a 2D toroidal grid.

Bio-reflective Architecture. We have argued that computational reflection is an essential component of computational novelty generation [2]. Based on this, we developed a new *bio-reflective architecture* [14]. It is a synthesis of concepts from: von Neumann's Universal Constructor Architecture; procedural computational reflection; evolutionary algorithms; computational open-ended novelty mechanisms; the EvoMachina architecture of evolvable active machines and passive genomic structures.

Parts of this architecture were realised in the stringmol automata chemistry and used to demonstrates a form of semantic closure [7]. Parts were realised in a stand-alone evolutionary music application [15], and also informed the "commensual architecture" of the dance application [1] (Sect. 4.1).

The Commensal Architecture. One of the core universal properties of living beings is their autonomy. Even if some forms of cooperation or altruism can be observed in nature, every biological system is fundamentally selfish and cooperation can emerge only when multiple levels co-evolve, the selfishness of some constraining the cooperativeness to others. On the opposite, one of the core universal properties of technology is its controllability.

These two antagonistic properties immediately conflict when one wants to design "living technologies". They also conflict when one wants to design open-ended technologies: if open-ended systems are to continuously produce novelty [2], how can they be designed? So when designing living technologies, one of the central problems is to design a system that is autonomous enough to surprise its user (by producing novelties) and, at the same time, is constrained enough to serve the goals it has been built for (as a technology). Since the very beginning of this project, this tension has been at the heart of EvoEvo: if autonomy is one of the core properties of life, how can a technology be simultaneously alive and controllable?

As said above, biological systems can be cooperative or altruistic provided they are embedded in higher/lower levels of evolution that constrain them. We propose here a bio-inspired approach to resolve the autonomy vs. controllability conundrum. We called this approach "commensal computation" [1]. In biology a commensal (from the Latin cum mensa, at the same table) interaction is a form of mutualism between two organisms where the association is not detrimental but not obviously beneficial to the partners [17]. Indeed, the idea of commensal computation is based on one of the main functions of the gut microbiota: nutrient processing. Gut microbes degrade ingested substances that would otherwise be non-digestible or even harmful to the gut [18]. This role enables the organism to uptake nutrients originating from a wider variety of sources than would otherwise be the case: microbes preprocess the complex flow of nutrients and transfer the results to the host, helping it to regulate its feeding and to extract specific nutrients. While doing so, the microbiota live their own lives, and change and evolve according to their environment: what the host eats: The commensal association of the microbiota and the host contains a part of autonomy (the microbes) and a part of control (the host).

We propose to organize living computational system following the manner in which host and microbiota are engaged in a mutualistic association. In commensal computation, the complex data (e.g., data generated by the sensor networks) are pre-processed by a virtual microbiome that transforms them in digestible data that the processing system can use. Such an architecture differs from classical pre-processing in that here the pre-processing is performed by an evolving community of virtual bacteria that uptake data, transform them in recognizable objects (symbols, clusters, classes, . . .) and feed them to the main processing system. In the context of the EvoEvo project, we used a subspace-clustering layer to implement the commensal level[3]: virtual bacteria evolve subspace classifiers and send the result to the processing layer. The interest of subspace classification

---

[3] Clustering is a data-mining task that aims to group objects sharing similar characteristics into a same cluster over the whole data space. Subspace clustering similarly aims at identifying groups of similar objects, but it also aims at detecting the subspaces where similarity occurs. Hence it can be conceived as "similarity examined under different representations" [23]. Subspace clustering is recognized as a more complicated and general task than standard clustering. Moreover, retrieving meaningful subspaces is particularly useful when dealing with high dimensional data [21].

here is that it enables a sensor network (or more generally the source of data) to change its dimensionality (*e.g.*, adding/removing sensors) without causing a complete failure of the classification: new dimensions can be dynamically added to the system and will (or will not) be integrated to the clustering depending on their pertinence with regards to the existing clusters and to the data.

We designed an evolutionary subspace clustering algorithm using the evolutionary principles detailed in the previous sections. In particular, we tried to empower the principle of an evolvable genomic structure (variable number of genes, regulation of coding proportion...) and the principle of using a large variety of mutational operators (point mutations, gene duplication and deletion...). Simultaneously we tried to simplify as much as possible the models that were used as a source of inspiration in order to reduce the computational load and to enable real-time execution of the algorithm, a mandatory property for its use in an evolving personal companion.

These principles led to a series of algorithms from "Chameleoclust" [24] to "SubCMedian" [26]. All these algorithms have been tested on public benchmarks and have shown state-of-the-art levels of performances.

4.2   Proof of Concept: Evolving a Living Personal Companion

One of the objectives of EvoEvo was to produce not only concepts but to test these concepts in proof-of-concept applications. This has been done in two steps corresponding to the commensal architecture described previously. In a first step, we designed the "commensals": artificial entities able to evolve in an environment composed of static and dynamic data (the evolutionart subspace clustering algorithms described above). Then, in a second step, we used these algorithms as a commensal pre-treatment layer in a musical personal companion: EvoMove.

The ultimate proof-of-concept of our EvoEvo approach of evolving software was to evolve a real application and to have it used by a real "naive" user. That is why we choose to implement a personal companion, software able to continuously evolve through interaction with its user. Then, in order both to address naive users and to test the software in short training sessions, we decided to design a musical personal companion: a system that would be able to evolve music depending on the performance of a dancer and that would evolve in real time while the performance is ongoing. This resulted in the EvoMove System [25].

The principles of EvoMove are detailed in Fig. 2. The system leverages the evolutionary subspace clustering algorithm described above, by embedding it into a commensal architecture: the moves of the dancer are captured through Inertial Measurement Units (IMU) and transmitted to the subspace clustering algorithm that identifies moves similar to those it has seen before. The subspace clustering is then computed in complete autonomy, intentionless and without any need for calibration. The identified clusters are then transmitted to the "host", here a sound generating system that triggers new sounds each time a new cluster is identified and that repeats this sound each time this cluster is activated again. The commensal architecture hence results in a host fed by motion data and producing music, and a bacterial community that processes the motion data, helping the host to interpret the moves. Both organisms thus "eat at the same table" (the motion) and co-evolve. The music produced by the host depends on the command objects produced by the virtual bacteria. The motion fed to the bacteria depends on the movements the users make in reaction to the music they hear.

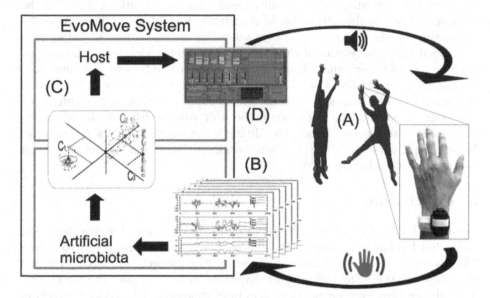

Fig. 2. The EvoMove feed-back loop. (A) Dancer moves are captured by Inertial Measurement Unit (IMU). (B) The sensors produce a high-dimensional data-stream. (C) This data-stream is clustered by SubCMedian algorithm that outputs a set of clusters. (D) The sound system outputs sounds that are immediately perceived by the dancers who can adapt their dance, leading to reciprocal adaptation of the clusters, hence of the music. This feedback loop produces coherent music due to the close integration of dancers and clustering algorithm: the duration of the loop is less than 1 second, enabling real-time response of the system.

Thus, this system creates a feedback loop including the human user. One iteration of the loop is run approximately every second. This timing is short enough to allow interaction. Contrary to most software where the human is acting on a system, here the users are acting *in* the system. They do not have full freedom about what sounds will be produced, but they can influence them. They have to decide how they react to what could be called "sound proposals" from the system, and this decision changes the shape of what the system produces next. And contrary to most of music software, the output of the system is not only the sound produced, but what is produced at each step of the loop and especially what is visible: music and moves.

[12] presents a short video of an EvoMove test with a EvoMove-naive dancer (an experienced dancer who had not used the system before and who did not know its mechanisms). EvoMove has also been used during the "Meute" dance

performance, which has been publicly presented at several dance festivals in Lyon (France). It is difficult to claim that such a system "works" or not since it is strongly dependent on the sensations of the user. But in all these situations, EvoMove has convinced the dancers by stimulating them in such a way that they were all eager to use it again and interact with it on other occasions. Our supposition about what produces this, besides the possibilities offered by the commensal layer, is the integration of the human user in the feedback loop. As a consequence, the dancers are always adapting their own moves and actions to fit what they understand of the state of the system. Thus, even though the machine part of the system is deviating from what would be seen as interaction, the human is able to follow it so as to keep this interaction alive. This process does not have to be conscious from the user perspective. Just by investing effort into being understood by the system, the user adapts their actions alongside the system state changes. Hence, the "living technology" is not (or not only) in the system; it is rather in the close interaction of the system and its user, both reacting to each other's proposal.

5   Conclusion

As the 2011 FET Consultation Report "Living Technology, Artificial Systems, Embodied Evolution" shows, many approaches have been proposed to create living technologies. Now at the end of the EvoEvo project, and having created what we think is a living technology ("EvoMove"), one can draw the big picture of the design principles we identified and briefly exposed here. Indeed, we claim that the key insight into building evolutionary living technologies is to go back to a fundamental property of living systems. Living systems are in essence strongly integrated systems, while technological systems are, by construction, strongly modular systems. Evolutionary living technologies will only be efficient if they are strongly integrated within the systems (in order to enable the system to innovate) and with their users, be it a real person (as in EvoMove), or a software entity (as in commensal architecture).

In some sense, this proposal is not a total surprise, since it is a similar mind shift as the one that happened at the end of the 1980s in robotics. The development of Behavior-Based Robotics under the impulsion of Rodney Brooks was nothing else than the close integration of robots with their environments and of robots' components one with the others [5]. We now propose that software systems themselves, although they are not physical entities, follow the same path in order to be able to leverage Darwinian evolution to dynamically react and adapt to their users. This will enable living software systems to co-construct their behavior with a user who, in that same moment, will become a partner of this behavior.

Acknowledgments. This work was supported by the European Commission 7th Framework Program (FP7-ICT-2013.9.6 FET Proactive: Evolving Living Technologies) EvoEvo project (ICT- 610427, http://www.evovo.eu/). The authors thank all the partners of the EvoEvo project for fruitful discussions.

References

1. Abernot, J., Beslon, G., Hickinbotham, S., Peignier, S., Rigotti, C.: Evolving instrument based on symbiont-host metaphor: a commensal computation. J. Creative Music Syst. **2**(1), 1–10 (2017)
2. Banzhaf, W., et al.: Defining and simulating open-ended novelty: requirements, guidelines, and challenges. Theory Biosci. **135**(3), 131–161 (2016)
3. Batut, B., Parsons, D.P., Fischer, S., Beslon, G., Knibbe, C.: In silico experimental evolution: a tool to test evolutionary scenarios. In: BMC Bioinformatics, vol. 14, no. 15, p. S11 (2013)
4. Beslon, G., Liard, V., Elena, S.F.: Evolvability drives innovation in viral genomes. In: 2nd EvoEvo Workshop, Satellite Workshop of CCS2016, Amsterdam, September 2016, 6 p. (2016)
5. Brooks, R.A.: Elephants don't play chess. Rob. Auton. Syst. **6**(1–2), 3–15 (1990)
6. Chatterjee, K., Pavlogiannis, A., Adlam, B., Nowak, M.A.: The time scale of evolutionary innovation. PLoS Comput. Biol. **10**(9), e1003818 (2014)
7. Clark, E.B., Hickinbotham, S.J., Stepney, S.: Semantic closure demonstrated by the evolution of a universal constructor architecture in an artificial chemistry. J. R. Soc. Interface **14**, 20161033 (2017)
8. Colizzi, E.S., Hogeweg, P.: Evolution of functional diversification within quasispecies. Genome Biol. Evol. **6**(8), 1990–2007 (2014)
9. Colizzi, E.S., Hogeweg, P.: High cost enhances cooperation through the interplay between evolution and self-organisation. BMC Evol. Biol. **16**(1), 31 (2016)
10. Cuypers, T.D., Hogeweg, P.: Virtual genomes in flux: an interplay of neutrality and adaptability explains genome expansion and streamlining. Genome Biol. Evol. **4**(3), 212–229 (2012)
11. de Boer, F.K., Hogeweg, P.: Co-evolution and ecosystem based problem solving. Ecol. Inform. **9**, 47–58 (2012)
12. https://youtu.be/p_eJFiQfW1E
13. Fischer, S., Bernard, S., Beslon, G., Knibbe, C.: A model for genome size evolution. Bull. Math. Biol. **76**(9), 2249–2291 (2014)
14. Hickinbotham, S., Stepney, S.: Bio-reflective architectures for evolutionary innovation. In: A Life 2016, Cancun, Mexico, pp. 192–199. MIT Press (2016)
15. Hickinbotham, S., Stepney, S.: Augmenting live coding with evolved patterns. In: Johnson, C., Ciesielski, V., Correia, J., Machado, P. (eds.) EvoMUSART 2016. LNCS, vol. 9596, pp. 31–46. Springer, Cham (2016). https://doi.org/10.1007/978-3-319-31008-4_3
16. Hindré, T., Knibbe, C., Beslon, G., Schneider, D.: New insights into bacterial adaptation through in vivo and in silico experimental evolution. Nat. Rev. Microbiol. **10**, 352–365 (2012)
17. Hooper, L.V., Gordon, J.I.: Commensal host-bacterial relationships in the gut. Science **292**, 1115–1118 (2001)
18. Hooper, L.V., Midtvedt, T., Gordon, J.I.: How host-microbial interactions shape the nutrient environment of the mammalian intestine. Ann. Rev. Nutr. **22**(1), 283–307 (2002)
19. Hoverd, T., Stepney, S.: EvoMachina: a novel evolutionary algorithm inspired by bacterial genome reorganisation. In: 2nd EvoEvo Workshop, CCS 2016, Amsterdam, Netherlands (2016)
20. Kimura, M.: Evolutionary rate at the molecular level. Nature **217**, 624–626 (1968)

21. Kriegel, H.-P., Kröger, P., Zimek, A.: Clustering highdimensional data: a survey on subspace clustering, pattern-based clustering, and correlation clustering. ACM Trans. Knowl. Discov. Data **3**(1), 1–58 (2009)

22. Pagie, L., Hogeweg, P.: Evolutionary consequences of coevolving targets. Evol. Comput. **5**(4), 401–418 (1997)

23. Patrikainen, A., Meila, M.: Comparing subspace clusterings. IEEE Trans. Knowl. Data Eng. **18**(7), 902–916 (2006)

24. Peignier, S., Rigotti, C., Beslon, G.: Subspace clustering using evolvable genome structure. In: Proceedings of the 2015 Annual Conference on Genetic and Evolutionary Computation, pp. 575–582 (2015)

25. Peignier, S., Abernot, J., Rigotti, C., Beslon, G.: EvoMove: evolutionary-based living musical companion. In European Conference on Artificial Life (ECAL), pp. 340–347 (2017)

26. Peignier, S., Rigotti, C., Rossi, A., Beslon, G.: Weight-based search to find clusters around medians in subspaces. In: ACM Symposium on Applied Computing, p. 10 (2018)

27. Plucain, J., et al.: Epistasis and allele specificity in the emergence of a stable polymorphism in Escherichia coli. Science **343**, 1366–1369 (2014)

28. Rocabert, C., Knibbe, C., Consuegra, J., Schneider, D., Beslon, G.: Beware batch culture: seasonality and niche construction predicted to favor bacterial adaptive diversification. PLoS Comput. Biol. **13**(3), e1005459 (2017)

29. Rutten, J., Hogeweg, P., Beslon, G.: (in prep) Adapting the engine to the fuel: mutator populations can reduce the mutational load by reorganizing their genome structure. in prep

30. Szathmáry, E., Maynard-Smith, J.: The major evolutionary transitions. Nature **374**(6519), 227–232 (1997)

31. van Dijk, B., Hogeweg, P.: In silico gene-level evolution explains microbial population diversity through differential gene mobility. Genome Biol. Evol. **8**(1), 176–188 (2016)

Tutorials

Ultra-Large Repair Search Space
with Automatically Mined Templates:
The Cardumen Mode of Astor

Matias Martinez[1]([⊠]) and Martin Monperrus[2]

[1] University of Valenciennes, Valenciennes, France
matias.martinez@univ-valenciennes.fr
[2] KTH Royal Institute of Technology, Stockholm, Sweden
martin.monperrus@csc.kth.se

Abstract. Astor is a program repair library which has different modes. In this paper, we present the Cardumen mode of Astor, a repair approach based mined templates that has an ultra-large search space. We evaluate the capacity of Cardumen to discover test-suite adequate patches (aka plausible patches) over the 356 real bugs from Defects4J [11]. Cardumen finds 8935 patches over 77 bugs of Defects4J. This is the largest number of automatically synthesized patches ever reported, all patches being available in an open-science repository. Moreover, Cardumen identifies 8 unique patches, that are patches for Defects4J bugs that were never repaired in the whole history of program repair.

Keywords: Automated program repair
Test-suite based repair approaches · Code templates · Patch dataset

1 Introduction

There have been major contributions in the field of automatic program repair in recent years. The program repair community explores different directions, most notably *Generate and Validate (G&V)* repair approaches [9] as well as synthesis-based approaches [25,39].

In this paper, we aim at creating an ultra-large search space, possibly the largest repair search space ever. To maximize the number of synthesized test-suite adequate patches, we design a new program repair algorithm. This algorithm is called Cardumen. Cardumen extracts code templates from the code under repair. Those templates contain placeholders to be bound to available variables at a potential repair location. Moreover, in order to speed up exploration of the search space, Cardumen uses a probability model for prioritizing candidates patches.

We evaluate the capacity of Cardumen for discovering *test-suite adequate patches* over the 356 real bugs from Defects4J [11]. The results go beyond our initial vision. First, Cardumen finds 8935 patches over 77 bugs of Defects4J.

T. E. Colanzi and P. McMinn (Eds.): SSBSE 2018, LNCS 11036, pp. 65–86, 2018.
https://doi.org/10.1007/978-3-319-99241-9_3

This is the largest number of automatically synthesized patches ever reported for Defects4J. It demonstrates the width of Cardumen's search space. Second, Cardumen identifies 8 unique patches, i.e., patches for Defects4J bugs that were never handled by any system in the whole history of program repair. This shows that Cardumen's search space is unique, it explores completely uncharted territories of the repair search space.

To sum up, our contributions are:

1. Cardumen: a novel program repair algorithm that is designed to maximize the number of test-suite adequate patches. It is based on mining repair templates. It uses a novel probabilistic heuristic for prioritizing candidate patches.
2. An analysis of the execution of Cardumen over 356 real bugs from Defects4J. Cardumen is capable of finding test-suite adequate patches for 77 bugs from Defects4J, including 8 uniquely fixed bugs that no other program repair system has ever fixed. For those uniquely fixed bugs, we discuss the unicity of Cardumen's search space.
3. A publicly available list of 8935 test-suite adequate patches for 77 bugs from Defects4J. We envision that this list will support future research in program repair, for instance to improve synthesis of patches, ranking of patches, and dynamic analysis of patches.

The paper is organized as follows: Sect. 2 presents the approach Cardumen. Section 3 evaluates Cardumen over bugs from Defects4J. Section 4 presents the related works. Section 5 presents a discussion about the experiment and the threats of validity. Section 6 concludes the paper.

2   Program Repair with Automatically Mined Templates

We now present the design and the main algorithms of Cardumen.

2.1   Cardumen in a Nutshell

Cardumen is a repair system designed for discovering the maximum number of test-adequate patches. It takes as input: (a) the source code of a buggy program, and (b) the test-suite of that program with at least one failing test case that exposes the bug.

Cardumen first applies a spectra fault localization [29] to detect suspicious buggy pieces of code. For a given source code location, Cardumen introduces a novel patch synthesis. The repair always consists of a replacement of the suspicious code element by an instance of a code template. The code templates are mined and instantiated in a unique two-step process. The first step is the *Automated Code Template Mining*, which mines code templates from the code of the application under repair for creating a template-based search space (explained in Sect. 2.4). The second step is *Probabilistic-based Template Space Navigation*, which uses a probabilistic model for navigating the space of candidate patches, each synthesized from template mined from the application under repair (explained in Sect. 2.5).

Once a candidate patch is synthesized from a template instantiation, the patched version of the buggy program is executed first on the originally failing test cases and then, if all of them pass, on the remaining test cases (i.e., regression test, which originally pass over the buggy version).

Example of Patch Generated by Cardumen. Cardumen is able to find test-suite adequate patches for bug Math-73 from the bug dataset Defects4J [11]. One of them, presented in Listing 1.1, modifies the expression of a **return** statement at line 138 from class **BrentSolver**.

Listing 1.1. Patch for bug Math-73 by Cardumen at BrentSolver class

```
138 − return solve(f, min, yMin, max, yMax, initial, yInitial);
138 + return solve(f, yMin, yMax);
```

The template used by Cardumen for synthesizing that patch is presented in Listing 1.2 and it was mined from the statement **return solve(f, min, max)** written at line 68 of the same class.

Listing 1.2. Template used for synthesize a patch for bug Math-73

```
solve(_UnivariateRealFunction_0, _double_1, _double_2)
```

The template has 3 placeholders: the first one **_UnivariateRealFunction_0** of type UnivariateRealFunction, the other two **_double_1** and **_double_2** of type Double. Cardumen creates candidate patches by binding those placeholders with variables available at the repair location. There, it synthesized 196 patches using the 14 variables of type double and the unique variable of type UnivariateReal-Function available at the line 138. Cardumen then selected one of them using a probability model which prioritized those patches according to the frequency of the variable names used by each patch. For example, the patch from Listing 1.1, which uses variables **f, yMin, yMax**, is prioritized before than another patch which uses variables **f, initial, functionValue**, due to the variables of the former patch are used more frequently together in the code than those from the latter patch. Finally Cardumen evaluated the selected patch using the test-suite of the buggy program.

2.2 Cardumen Repair Algorithm

Algorithm 1 presents the main workflow of Cardumen. Cardumen first executes a fault localization approach for obtaining the suspicious line (Line 1) and it then creates a list of modification points from the suspicious code elements (Line 2). Cardumen proceeds to mine code templates from the application code under repair (Line 4) and to create the probability model of variables names (Line 5). After that, Cardumen starts navigating the search space during an amount of time (Line 7). On each step, Cardumen carries out the following steps. It first randomly selects a modification point mp_i (Line 8) and a template (Line 9). Then, from mp_i and t_i, it creates a list of template instances $tinstances_i$ (Line 10), and from that list, it selects one template instance (ti_i) using the

---

Algorithm 1. Cardumen's main algorithm

Input: A buggy program P
Input: A Test suite TS for P
Output: A list of patches $tsa\_patches$ to the buggy program P
1: $suspicious \leftarrow runFaulLocalization(P, TS)$
2: $mpl \leftarrow createModifPoint(suspicious)$
3: $tsa\_patches \leftarrow \emptyset$
4: $templates \leftarrow mineTemplates(P)$
5: $varNameProbModel \leftarrow createVarNameProbModel(P)$
6: $t \leftarrow 0$
7: **while** t to MAX_TIME **do**
8:     $mp_i \leftarrow chooseMPRandom(mpl)$
9:     $t_i \leftarrow chooseTemplateRandom(mp_i)$
10:     $tinstances_i \leftarrow createInstances(mp_i, t_i)$
11:     $ti_i \leftarrow chooseInstance(tinstances_i, varNameProbModel)$
12:     $pc_i \leftarrow createPatchCode(ti_i)$
13:     $nbFT_i \leftarrow getNbOfFailingTests(TS, P, pc_i)$
14:     **if** $nbFT_i = 0$ **then**
15:         $tsa\_patches \leftarrow tsa\_patches \cup pc_i$
16:     **end if**
17: **end while**
18: **return** $tsa\_patches$

---

probabilistic model (Line 11). Finally, it synthesizes the patch code from the selected instance (Line 12), and runs the test-suite over the patched application (Line 13). If there is not any failing test case (Line 14), Cardumen adds the patch to a list of test-suite adequate patches (Line 15). At the end, Cardumen returns that list (Line 18).

Now, let us describe in detail each step from the mentioned algorithm.

2.3 Identifying Potential Modification Points

The first step carried out by Cardumen is the creation of a representation of the buggy program, which only includes buggy suspicious code elements. This allows to reduce the search space. Then, Cardumen generates patches by modifying only those elements, ignoring the rest of the code not included in that representation.

Reducing Search Space Using Fault Localization. For calculating the suspiciouness of code elements, Cardumen uses a spectrum based fault localization called GZoltar [2] which produces as output a suspicious value (between 0 and 1) for each statement and method of the program. Cardumen first orders decreasing statements according to suspiciousness value and takes the first X statement with suspicious greater than a given threshold γ.

Creation of Modification Points. We call *Modification Point.* a code element from the program under repair that could be transformed to synthesize a candidate repair. Cardumen creates modification points from the filtered suspicious statement returned by the fault localization approach.

Previous approaches on automated work at the level of statements. For example, the original GenProg [33] and its Java implementation contained in the Astor framework [23] work at that level. For instance, Astor framework represents each suspicious element with a modification point. In GenProg, program statements are labeled with the suspicious values and later manipulated by applying operator over them (i.e., replacing, removing or adding statements).

In Cardumen, a Modification point is related to fine-grained code elements rather than statements. Our approach has two main differences w.r.t previous works. First, it is flexible with respect to the kind of code element that it can manipulate. Cardumen receives as input a *set of kinds of code element* to consider as modification points. We call them *Target code types.* For a code c, its *Target code type* is the *type* of the AST node root corresponding to c. For example, the target type of code **a + b** is binary operator.

Second, Cardumen considers the *type* of the object returned by the evaluation of a code element. For example, the *Return code type* of the expression (**a or b**), where **a** and **b** are Boolean variables, is a Boolean, whereas the return type of (**c − d**), where **c** and **d** are Integer variables, is Integer.

For creating modification points, Cardumen receives as input the Target code types *tct* and the Return type *ert*, then it parses the AST of suspicious code elements, filtering those AST nodes of types according to sets *tct* and *ert*, and finally creates one modification point *mp* for each filtered AST node. By default, the implementation of Cardumen considers expressions as *target code type*, and every kind of object as *return type*.

As we will see later, the *Target code types* and the *Return type* are also used for navigating the search space.

Note that, as Cardumen considers fine-grained elements as modification points, it could exist the case that multiples modification points refer to different code elements included in a single statement. For example, for the code (**a > b**) **&&** ((**d − e**) **> 3**), Cardumen creates four modification points: one for reference to the whole Boolean expression, the other for the Boolean expression (**a > b**), a third one for a Boolean expression (**d − e**) **> 3**, and the last one for the Integer expression (**d − e**).

2.4 Definition of Cardumen's Template-Based Search Space

Once Cardumen has created a list of potential modification points, it then creates a pool of code templates that are later used to synthesize candidate patches.

Intuition Behind the Use of Code Templates. Cardumen redefines the idea presented by [33] and empirically validated by [24] and [1] which states that the code of a patch have been already written in the program under repair, they are called the "repair ingredients" or "patch ingredients". In GenProg, a candidate patch $c = s_1, s_2, .., s_n$ is synthesized from statements taken as-is from somewhere else in the application.

The core idea of Cardumen is to *reuse code templates* rather than reusing raw, unmodified code elements (such as raw statements in GenProg). Contrary to previous works such as PAR [13] or SPR [18], where candidate patches are synthesized from predefined manually written templates, Cardumen parses the source code of the buggy program and automatically creates the code templates.

Mining Code Templates from Source Code. For mining templates, Cardumen parses the AST of the program under repair. For each AST node, Cardumen replaces all variable names by a placeholder composed of the variable type and one numeric identifier. For example, the code element ((a > b) && (c > a)), where a, b and c are Integer variables, now becomes ((_int_1 > _int_2) && (_int_3 > _int_1)), where, for instance, _int_1 is a placeholder. After the variable renaming, Cardumen obtains a template which is stored in a template pool. Note that Cardumen also stores for a template the *Target code type* and the *return type* (as described in Sect. 2.3): those types take the same value than the *Target code type* and the *Return type* of the code where template was mined.

Cardumen stores each mined template in a structure called *Templates pool*, which is later used when navigating the search space.

2.5   Probabilistic-Based Navigation of the Code Template Search Space

Once Cardumen has created a list of potential modification points and a template pool, it proceeds to navigate the search space for finding test-suite adequate patches. For synthesizing a patch, Cardumen applies different steps explained in the rest of this section.

Selecting a Modification Point. Cardumen starts the navigation of the search space by selecting one modification point using weighted random selection. The weight of a modification point mp corresponds to the suspicious value that the fault localization approach assigned to the code pointed by mp.

Selecting a Code Template. Once a modification point mp_i is selected, Cardumen proceeds to select a template that is used for synthesizing candidates patches at mp_i. For that, Cardumen first queries the template pool (defined in Sect. 2.4) which returns a list of templates compatible with the suspicious code to be replaced at mp_i. Then, Cardumen selects one of of the templates.

Let us dwell on those steps: template pool querying and template selection. When templates are searched for, the template pool of Cardumen applies two filters: *Compatibility* filter and *Location* filter.

Filtering Templates Based on Compatible Types. When selecting a template from the pool, Cardumen must guarantee that the *Return types* of the replacement and of the replaced code *are compatible*. For example, suppose that a modification point is the expression (**a** > **b**). The *Return type* of (**a** > **b**) is Boolean. Cardumen can only replace this expression by an expression whose return type is also Boolean. Otherwise, the patch will produce an incorrect, uncompilable AST.

In this example, Cardumen would replace the modification point (**a** > **b**) by, for example, a template (**isGreater(_int_1, _int_2)**) with two placeholders _int_1 and _int_2, whose method invocation **isGreater** returns a Boolean value.

Filtering Templates Based on Code Location. Cardumen also proposes a mechanism to reduce the number of potential templates that is based on code location. It filters the candidate templates for mp_i according to the location where the template was extracted. We call to this filter, the location filter.

Cardumen handles three template location filters, configured by the user: *local*, *package* and *global*. If the scope filter is set to *local*, Cardumen keeps in the pool all templates mined from code contained in the same file f as the one from where the selected modification point mp_i is located (i.e., $mp_i \in f$). For the *package* scope filter, it keeps all templates deduced from all files of the package containing mp_i, whereas for the *global* scope filter, Cardumen considers templates deduced from all statements of the program under repair.

Selecting a Code Template. For selecting a template from the list of filtered templates, Cardumen carries out a weighted random selection, where the probability of selecting a template t_i corresponds to the proportion of code elements that can be represented by t_i (i.e., whose placeholders correspond to the actual values of the expression under consideration).

Instantiating a Code Template. Given a template t_i and a modification point mp, a *template instance* is a binding of each placeholder from t_i to a particular variable that are in the scope of mp.

The process of *instantiating* a template t_i at one location mp consists on finding all template instances, product of the binding of placeholders of the template and variables on the scope of mp. For example, the instantiation of a template with one placeholder *ph* of type long at a mp with two variables long in scope, *v1* and *v2*, produces two instances: one bound *v1* to *ph*, the other *v2* to *ph*. Then, from each instance, Cardumen is able of synthesizing a candidate patch.

Creating Template Instances for a Modification Point. Given a modification point mp and a template t_i, the template instantiation process has the following steps:

1. for each placeholder ph_i from the template, Cardumen finds all variables with compatible types from the scope of mp, obtaining the set $cv_i = mv_1, mv_2, ..., mv_n$.

2. if there is no compatible variable for at least one placeholder from the template t, i.e., $\exists ph_i | cv_i = \emptyset$, it means that the template cannot be instantiated at mp. Thus, the template is discarded and Cardumen continues by selecting another template. We say that t is *sterile* for mp.
3. if all placeholders from the template have compatibles variables, i.e., $\forall ph_i | cv_i \neq \emptyset$, Cardumen creates a template instance by choosing, for each placeholder ph_i, a compatible variable mv_i from cv_i. Hence, a template instance ti_i binds each placeholders to a variable: $ti_i = \{(ph_1, mv_{11}), ..., (ph_n, mv_{n1})\}$, where n is the number of placeholders from template t and mv_{ij} is a variable that belongs to cv_i.

Prioritizing Template Instances Based on Variable Names. The number of template instances for a modification point mp_i and a template t_j is : $\prod_{i=1}^{|v|} |cv_i|$. In practice, this number of instances can be large. For example, the instantiation of template $((\_int\_1 > \_int\_2) \&\& (\_int\_3 > \_int\_4))$ at the place of mp_i with ten integer variables in the scope of mp_i, produces 10000 instances (i.e., 10^4).

With the goal of reducing the search spaces, Cardumen prioritizes the template instances based on variable names as we explain now.

Defining a Probabilistic Model Based on Variable Name Occurrences. For prioritizing instances, Cardumen automatically creates a binomial distribution model pml (Eq. 1) to capture the probability mp of n variable names $\{v_1, ..., v_n\}$ to appear together in a statement.

$$pml_n(\{v_1, ..., v_n\}) = \frac{(number\_statements\_containing\{v_1, ..., v_n\})}{all\_statements\_with\_n\_names}, \qquad (1)$$
$$pml_n \in [0, 1].$$

In turn, Cardumen defines different models, $pml_i(v_1, ..., v_i)$, where each of one captures the probability of occurrence of a set of i variables in a statement with *at least* i variables. Note that $i \in [1, n]$ where n is the maximum number of variables that a statement (from the program under repair) has.

For creating the model pml_n, Cardumen scans all the statements of the program under repair. For each statement s_i, it collects all variable names: $vs = \{v_{i1}, ..., v_{in}\}$. Then, it updates the model as follows: it first creates subsets of variables of size i, $(i \in [1, n])$, corresponding to all combinations[1] of size i that can be created from vs. Finally, Cardumen updates the model according to each subset.

As example, suppose a model build pml from three statements s_1, s_2 and s_3 composed by the variables $v_1 = a, b, c, x$, $v_2 = a, b, d$ and $v_3 = a, d, f$, respectively. In that model, the probability of having a variable named "a" together with another named "b" is $pml_2(a, b) = 2/3$, and is larger than the probability of having "a" together with "f" ($pml_2(a, f) = 1/3$) . As consequence, using that

---

[1] Cardumen does not takes in account the order of variable names inside a statement.

model, for instantiating a template with two placeholders, Cardumen prioritizes an instance with bindings to variables "a" and "b", over another instance with bindings to "a" and "f".

Adding Localness to the Probability Model. Inspired on the work by Tu et al. [31] about the localness of code, which proposes an extended version of n-gram model to capture local regularities, Cardumen creates two sub-models, which conform the probability model pml: one, called 'Global' pml_g, which consider all statements from the program under repair, the other, called 'Cache' pml_c, that only considers the statements from one file (called Local) or from one package (called Package). With the same spirit that [31], the Global model aims at capturing large global and static model of variable names, whereas the cache model aims at modeling a small local (dynamic) name model estimated from the proximate local context (File or Package). Consequently, pml (Eq. 2) is a linear combination of the two models:

$$pml(\{v_1, ..., v_n\}) = \lambda \cdot pm_g(\{v_1, ..., v_n\})$$
$$+ \quad (1 - \lambda) \cdot pm_c(\{v_1, ..., v_n\}) \tag{2}$$

Finally, Cardumen uses the model pml to obtain the probability of each template instance. Then, it selects the ϱ instances with higher probability.

Selecting an Instance Template. Cardumen selects one instance from the list of instances by applying weighted random selection, where the weight of an instance is given by the probability of its variables' names, calculated using the probability model presented in Sect. 2.5.

Synthesizing Candidate Patch Code. For synthesizing the code of a candidate patch from a template instance, Cardumen first takes the template, creates a clone of it, and replaces each placeholder by the variable bound to it, according to the template instance. After that, the patch is ready to be applied in the place related to the modification point. Then, the patched version of the buggy program can be evaluating using the test-suite of the original program.

2.6   Example: Synthesizing Candidate Patches for Math-70

In this section, we show how Cardumen creates multiple candidate patches for a real-world Java bug included in the bug dataset Defects4J by [11]. The subject under study, identified as Math-70, has a bug in class 'BisectionSolverImpl'.

Cardumen first identifies 12 modification points (Sect. 2.3), 10 of them reference statements located on the buggy class 'BisectionSolver', the other two reference statements from class 'UnivariateRealSolverImpl'.

Then, Cardumen creates a pool of templates (Sect. 2.4) mined from the application code under repair. For instance, from the code element:

if (abs(max − min) <= absoluteAccuracy) located at line 100 of class **BisectionSolverImpl**, Cardumen mined three templates:

Table 1. Top-5 most frequent var names used in file BisectionSolver (Local) and in the entire buggy application code (Global) from buggy revision Math-70.

Model	#Vars	Variable Names	#	Frequency
Local	1	min	9	0.069
		upper	8	0.062
		max	8	0.062
		f	8	0.062
	2	lower, upper	7	0.097
		max, min	7	0.097
		function, lower	3	0.0417
		m, min	3	0.0417
	..	..	..	..
Global	1	i	2137	0.058
		length	1591	0.043
		j	841	0.022
		n	699	0.019
	2	i, length	365	0.011
		i, j	244	0.007
		data, i	219	0.006
		data, length	199	0.0043
	..	..	..	..

(1) 'abs((_double_0 − _double_1))) <= (_double_2)', of type "Binary Operator" (<=) and return type "Boolean";

(2) 'abs((_double_0 − _double_1)))', of type "Method Invocation" and Return type "Double"(mined from left-most term of the − operator);

(3) '(_double_0 − _double_1)', of type "Binary Operator" (−), and Return type "Double" (mined from argument of method abs).

For creating a candidate patch, Cardumen first chooses a modification point and a template. In this example, we suppose that Cardumen first selects: (a) the modification point mp corresponding to the Boolean condition (i < maximalIterationCount) from line 87, which has a suspicious value of 0.5 (see Sect. 2.3), and (b) the template (_double_0 * _double_1) > 0.0, which is a Boolean binary operator mined from line 92 if (fm * fmin > 0.0) (see Sect. 2.5).

Instantiating a Template. In the next step, Cardumen tries to instantiate the selected template by replacing each of its placeholders (_double_0 and _double_1) by compatible variables that are in the scope at the place of the selected modification point (line 87 of BisectionSolverImpl). Cardumen found 13 variables of type Double in scope of line 87: 4 fields on class **UnivariateRealSolverImpl** (parent class of BisectionSolver), other 4 fields on **ConvergingAlgorithmImpl** (parent class of UnivariateRealSolverImpl), 2 parameters for the method **solves** (which includes line 87), and 3 local variables from that method declared before the line 87. Using those variables, Cardumen then creates 169 instances of the template obtained from the combination of those variables i.e., $13^2 = 169$. For example, a mapping relates the placeholder _double_0 with variable "max" and _double_1 with "min", both variables are parameters of method **solver**. After that, Cardumen prioritizes those 169 instances, using a probability model based on variable name frequency (Sect. 2.5). A portion of this model for subject Math-70 is presented in Table 1. It shows the probabilities of the variable names according to the number of variables per statements (column '#Vars'). For example, the first row shows that the probability of having a variable named "min" in statements (a) with only one variable, and (b) from class BisectionSolver (i.e., local model) is 6.9%.

Synthesizing the Patch. Cardumen selects one instance using the probability model. For example, suppose that Cardumen selects the instance with the mapping between placeholders and variables: (_double_0= max) and (_double_1= min). Then, Cardumen proceeds to synthesize the candidate patch by replacing the placeholders from the template (_double_0 * _double_1) > 0 by the bound variables given by the instance: _double_0 by "max" and placeholder double_0 by "min". This step gives as result the candidate patch (max * min) > 0.0, which can be applied at line 87 of BisectionSolverImpl class.

2.7 Implementation

Cardumen is a new mode in the Astor framework [23] for repairing Java code. Cardumen's implementation uses Spoon [26] to create the code model of the application under repair. For sake of open-science, the source code of Cardumen is publicly available at https://github.com/SpoonLabs/astor.

3 Evaluation

The research questions that guide the Cardumen evaluation are:

RQ 1: To what extent does Cardumen generate test-suite adequate patches?
RQ 2: (a) Is Cardumen able to identify multiple test-suite adequate patches, i.e., does it have a rich search space? (b) How many bugs can be repaired by a high number of test-suite adequate patches (6 or more patches)? (c) Does the presence of multiple patches happen often, in several projects?
RQ 3: To what extent is Cardumen able to generate (a) patches located in different locations, and (b) different kind of patches for a bug?

3.1 Methodology

We run Cardumen over the Defects4J bug benchmark [11]. Each execution trial is configured as follows. Maximum execution time: 3 h, maximum number of modification points: 1000 (Sect. 2.3), scope of template ingredients: 'package' (Sect. 2.5), and maximum number of tried template instances: 1000 (Sect. 2.5). Since Cardumen is randomized algorithm, we executed 10 trials for each bug from Defects4J. Note that we do not evaluate Cardumen over bugs from Mockito project included in Defects4J due to a technical issue when parsing the Mockito's

Table 2. Identifiers of the 77 bugs from Defects4J repaired by Cardumen, together with the number of different test-suite adequate patches found for each bug (Column #Patches). Column #Loc displays the number of different locations the patches are applied. Column #KindP displays the number of different kind of expression involved on the patches.

Group	Id	#Patches	#Loc	#KindP
Closure	Cl7	2	2	2
	Cl10	4	2	3
	Cl12	2	1	1
	Cl13	2	1	2
	Cl21	135	3	5
	Cl22	141	4	5
	Cl33	2	2	1
	Cl40	4	1	1
	Cl45	10	1	3
	Cl46	25	3	4
	Cl55	1	1	1
	Cl133	1	1	1
	12/65	**329**		
Time	T4	7	1	3
	T7	1	1	1
	T9	1	1	1
	T11	288	11	7
	T17	14	1	3
	T18	1	1	1
	6/27	**312**		
Lang	L7	8	1	2
	L10	4	2	2
	L14	8	2	2
	L22	21	1	3
	L24	2	2	2
	L27	164	3	8
	L39	617	2	12
	7/65	**824**		
Chart	Ch1	780	1	6
	Ch3	19	3	3
	Ch4	2	1	1
	Ch5	700	6	11
	Ch6	2	1	1
	Ch7	396	8	5
	Ch9	23	4	4
	Ch11	2	2	1
	Ch12	1	1	1
	Ch13	1227	7	14
	Ch15	24	1	1
	Ch17	1	1	1

Group	Id	#Patches	#Loc	#KindP
Chart	Ch24	3	1	1
	Ch25	454	32	25
	Ch26	138	15	11
	15/26	**3772**		
Math	M2	28	5	5
	M5	28	2	3
	M6	2	1	1
	M8	82	3	4
	M18	4	3	3
	M20	67	17	12
	M28	203	13	14
	M30	45	1	2
	M32	2	1	2
	M33	1	1	1
	M40	12	4	5
	M41	46	4	2
	M46	15	1	1
	M49	9	3	3
	M50	722	3	10
	M57	5	1	1
	M58	1	1	1
	M60	17	1	2
	M62	2	2	2
	M63	33	2	4
	M69	2	1	1
	M70	8	1	1
	M73	554	3	3
	M74	2	2	2
	M78	13	4	5
	M79	6	1	1
	M80	585	6	12
	M81	676	23	16
	M82	39	3	3
	M84	149	1	4
	M85	109	2	5
	M88	5	1	1
	M95	134	3	11
	M97	86	2	3
	M101	1	1	1
	M104	2	1	1
	M105	3	1	1
	37/105	**3698**		
	TOTAL: 77	**8935**		

code. Bugs from that project were also discarded by the automated repair literature (e.g., [3,15,21,35,37]). All the experimental results, including the patches found by Cardumen, are publicly available at https://github.com/SpoonLabs/astor-experiments/tree/master/cardumen-patches.

3.2   RQ 1: To What Extent Does Cardumen Generate Test-Suite Adequate Patches?

Table 2 shows the results of our experiment. It displays the identifier of the bugs from Defects4 repaired by Cardumen (column Id), and the number of unique patches for each bug (column #Patches). The other columns will be explained later.

In total, Cardumen discovers 8935 different test-suite adequate patches for 77 bugs of Defects4J. Cardumen found one patch (at least) for 15 out of 27 bugs from Chart project, 37 out of 105 for Math, 6 out of 27 for Time, 7 out of 65 for Lang, and 12 out of 135 for Closure.

Response to RQ1: Cardumen finds **8935** test-suite adequate patches for **77** bugs of Defects4J.

Implication for program repair research: So far program repair research has neglected the exploration of the complete search space: most papers report a single patch. However, this experiment shows that the search space is much richer than that. This represents a mine of information on the behavior of the program under repair.

Additionally, we found that, between those 77 bugs, Cardumen is the first repair system to find test-suite adequate patches for **8** new bugs of Defects4J, for which no system ever has managed to find a single one. Those 8 uniquely repaired bugs are: 1 bug from Chart (id 11), 3 from Math (ids 62, 101 and 104), 1 from Lang (id 14), 2 from Closure (ids 13 and 46), and 1 from Time (id 9). For the other 69 bugs repaired by Cardumen, there is at least one other approach that also proposes a test-suite adequate patch. The repair system that we analyzed where those that: (1) the evaluation was done over the dataset Defects4J; (2) the identifiers of the repaired bugs from Defect4J are given on the respective paper or included in the appendix. They are: ACS [38], Nopol [6,39], jGenProg [21], DynaMoth [7], DeepRepair [35], GP-FS [34], JAID [3], ssFix [37] and HDRepair [15] (for this approach, as neither the identifiers of the repaired bugs nor the actual patches were reported, we considered the results reported by ssFix's authors [37]).

3.3 Is Cardumen Able to Identify Multiple Test-Suite Adequate Patches per Bug?

Now, let us study the number of patches per bug. Between the 77 patches, 67 of them (87%) have 2 or more test-suite adequate patches. We observe that for 32 out of 77 (41.5%) the number of patches that Cardumen finds is smaller than 5, whereas 10 (13%) has a single patch. On the contrary, 19 bugs (24.7%) can be repaired by more than 100 test-suite adequate patches, and even one bug (Chart-13) has 1227 patches.

Response to RQ 2: The results show that: **(a)** for 67 out of 77 bugs Cardumen found 2+ patches; **(b)** a high abundance of patches occurs frequently (e.g., 45 bugs (58%) with 6+ patches); and **(c)** a high abundance of patches is not project-specific, it is valid to all projects from Defects4J.

3.4 RQ 3 (a): To What Extent Is Cardumen Able to Generate Patches Located in Different Locations for a Bug?

Each test-suite adequate patch is applied at a specific location (i.e., file name and line). For each bug, we study the locations of Cardumen's patches. Column #Loc from Table 2 displays the number of different locations where the patches are applied. For instance, bug Chart-11 has two patches, one is applied to class ShapeUtilities at line 274 and the other one is applied to in the same class at line 275.

For 36 out of 77 (46.7%) bugs, the patch are all applied in a single location. For 41 (53.3%) bugs, the Cardumen test-adequate patches are applied to different locations of the buggy application (2+), whereas for 11 out of 77 (14%) bugs, the number of locations is 5+. For them, the number of patches is always high (+50). However, abundance does not depend on number of locations: there are bugs with low number of locations (i.e., 3 or less) but with a large number of patches (Closure-21, Lang-39, Chart-1 and Math-73).

Response to RQ 3: (a) The results show that Cardumen has the ability to discover patches applied at different locations of the buggy application. This happens for 53% of the repaired bugs.

Implication for program repair research: The program repair search space is a combination of the location space and the modification space at a given location. This is known, but nobody has ever reported on the actual number of different locations, and we are the first to do so at this scale. Comparing the behavior of patches happening at different locations seems very promising: we envision that the patches would have different execution traces that could be compared one against the other.

3.5   RQ 3 (b): To What Extent Is Cardumen Able to Generate Different Kind of Patches for a Bug?

Cardumen has the ability to synthesize patches at the level of expression. We now study the kinds of expressions involved in each patch to know whether Cardumen is able to synthesize patches that are fundamentally different.

We define the *kind of a patch* as the concatenation of (a) the kind of expression of the patch, with (b) the kind of the parent element where that expression is applied. For example, Math-32 has two test-adequate patches, both replacing the right size of a variable initialization. The first one, replaces it by a method invocation (**FastMath.max**), the second one by a binary expression (**x * x**). The kind of expression introduced by the patch are different: the first patch replaces the buggy code by an expression of kind "Method invocation", the second one by another kind of expression: Binary Operator (***, i.e., multiplication**). Then, the parent element of both method invocation (first patch) and binary operator (second patch) is a variable declaration. Consequently, the kinds of patches of Math-32 are "Method_Invocation|LocalVariableDeclaration" and "BinaryOperator|LocalVariableDeclaration".

Column #KindP from Table 2 gives the number of different kinds of patches per bug. For 50 out of 77 bugs (65%), Cardumen found patches with different kinds. Math-18 is one of those bugs. Cardumen found 4 patches: 2 correspond to a change in a **for** condition, one a change in a **if** condition, and the last a change in right side of an assignment. For 11 bugs (14%), the number of different kinds involved in the patch is 10 or more.

The remaining 27 out of 77 bugs (35%) have patches that all involve the same kind of patch. For instance, Math-6 has 2 patches, both applied to the same location, which replace a buggy method invocation inside a return statement, but those invocations are different (be the message or the called object).

Response to RQ 3: (b) For the majority of the repaired bugs (65%), Cardumen found test-suite adequate patches whose kinds are different, the patches are made over different kinds of code elements. This shows the richness and variety of Cardumen's repair search space.

Implication for program repair research: So far, program repair has mostly focused a handful of specific kind of patches (e.g., conditions or RHS of assignments). The open-ended search space of Cardumen enables the community to identify novel kinds of patches for which dedicated repair algorithms will eventually be devised in the future.

4   Related Work

4.1   Repair Approaches

Test-Suite Based Repair Approaches. One of the most popular families of automated program repair recently proposed are *Generate-and-validate repair techniques*. Those kind of techniques first search within a search space to generate a set of patches, and then validate the generated patches. The *Test-suite based repair approach* family uses test-suites for validating the generated patches. GenProg [9,33], one of the earliest generate-and-validate techniques, uses genetic programming to search the repair space and generates patches created from existing code from elsewhere in the same program. It has three repair operators: add, replace or remove statements. Other approaches have extended GenProg: for example, AE [32] employs a novel deterministic search strategy and uses program equivalence relation to reduce the patch search space. RSRepair [27] has the same search space as GenProg but uses random search instead, and the empirical evaluation shows that random search can be as effective as genetic programming. The original implementation of GenProg [33] targets C code and was evaluated against dataset with C bugs such as ManyBugs and IntroClass [8]. It exists other implementations of GenProg for targeting other code languages, for example, jGenProg, built over the framework Astor [23], is an implementation of the approach in Java language that targets Java bugs. Wen et al. [34] presented a systematic empirical study that explores the influence of fault space on search-based repair techniques. For the experiment, they created GP-FS, a modified GenProg (i.e., the java implementation jGenProg [23]) which receives as input a faulty space. In their experiment, the authors generated several fault spaces with different accuracy, and then they feed GenProg with those spaces, finding that GP-FS is capable of fixing more bugs correctly when fault spaces with high accuracy are fed.

Cardumen has two main differences with respect to those approaches. The first one is it works at a fine-grained level rather than statements: Cardumen is able to repair expressions insides a statement. The second is the use of templates derived from the program under repair, rather than the reuse of statements without applying any modification.

The approach ACS (Automated Condition Synthesis) [38], targets to insert or modify an "if" condition to repair defects. ACS combines three heuristic ranking techniques that exploit (1) the structure of the buggy program, (2) the document of the buggy program (i.e., Javadoc comments embedded in the source code), and (3) the conditional expressions in existing projects. NpeFix [5] focuses on repairing null-pointer exceptions.

Contrary to them, Cardumen targets to any kind of code elements (due to its works at the expression level) rather than to a particular defect case (such as "If" conditions for ACS).

Template Based Repair Approaches. Other approaches have proposed new set of repair operators. PAR [13], which shares the same search strategy with

GenProg, uses patch templates derived from human-written patches to construct the search space. SPR [18] uses a set of predefined transformation schemas to construct the search space, and patches are generated by instantiating the schemas with condition synthesis techniques. JAID [3] is a state-based dynamic program analyses which synthesizes patches based on schemas (5 in total). Each schema triggers a fix action when a suspicious state in the system is reached during a computation. JAID has 4 types of fix actions, such as modify the state directly by assignment, and affects the state that is used in an expression. Contrary to them, Cardumen does not have neither any predefined transformation schema nor template: it automatically mines them from the application under repair.

Approaches Guided by Examples. There are approaches that leverage on human written bug fixes. For example, Genesis [17] automatically infers code transforms for automatic patch generation. The code transformation used Genesis are automatically infer from previous successful patches. HRD [15] leverages on the development history to effectively guide and drive a program repair process. The approach first mines bug fix patterns from the history of many projects and then employs existing mutation operators to generate fix candidates for a given buggy program. Both approaches need as input, in addition to the buggy program and its test suite, a set of bug fixes. Two approaches leveraged on semantics-based examples. SearchRepair [12] uses a large database of human-written code fragments encore as satisfiability modulo theories (SMT) constraints on their input-output behavior for synthesizing candidates repairs. S3 (Syntax- and Semantic-Guided Repair Synthesis) [14], a repair synthesis engine that leverages programming-by-examples methodology to synthesize repairs. Contrary to them, Cardumen does not use any extra information rather than the buggy program code and its test-suite: it deduces the templates *on-the-fly*, (i.e., during the repair of a give buggy program) from the code of the application under repair.

The approach ssFix [37] performs syntactic code search to find existing code from a code database (composed by the application under repair and external applications) that is syntax-related to the context of a bug statement. The approach applies code transformation to adapt the selected code existing code into the buggy location, leveraging the candidate patch. Contrary or it, Cardumen leverages on templates mined from the application under repair and does not transform the template code: it binds template placeholders with variables from the context of the buggy statement.

Probabilistic Models Based Repair Approaches. As Cardumen, there are other approaches that leverage on probabilistic model. An extension of SPR, Prophet [20] applies probabilistic models of correct code learned from successful human patches to prioritize candidate patches so that the correct patches could have higher rankings. DeepRepair [35], an extension of jGenProg, which navigates the patch search space guided by method and class similarity measures inferred deep unsupervised learning. Martinez et Monperrus [22] proposed to probabilistic model built from bug fixes to guide the navigation of the search space. Contrary to those works, Cardumen builds the probability model from the code under repair, without leverage on provided human bug fixes.

4.2 Patches Analysis

Recent studies have analyzed the patches generated by some of the approaches we listed before. The results of those studies show that generated patches may just overfit the available test cases, meaning that they will break untested but desired functionality. For example, Qi et al. [28] find that the vast majority of patches produced by GenProg, RSRepair, and AE avoid bugs simply by functionality deletion. A subsequent study by Smith et al. [30] further confirms that the patches generated by of GenProg and RSRepair fail to generalize. An empirical study [21] reveals that among the 47 bugs fixed by jGenProg, jKali, and Nopol, only 9 bugs are correctly fixed, the rest being overfitting. Jiang et al. [10] analyzed the Defects4J dataset for finding bugs with weak test cases. They results shows that 42 (84%) of the 50 defects could be fixed with weak test suites, indicating that, beyond the current techniques have a lot of rooms for improvement, weak test suites may not be the key limiting factor for current techniques.

4.3 Analysis of Repair Search Spaces

Long et al. [19] presented a systematic analysis of the SPR and Prophet search spaces. The analysis focused on the density of correct and plausible patches in the search spaces, on the ability of those approaches to prioritize correct patches. Some of the finding were: the relatively abundant plausible (i.e., overfitted test-adequate) patches in the search space compare to the correct, sparse correct patches, and the effectiveness of both SPR and Prophet at isolating correct patches within the explored plausible patches.

Weimer et al. [32] presented an study of the size of the search space considered by AE and GenProg approaches. Their goal was to compare the improvement introduced by AE (such as program equivalence) over GenProg. Their results shows and that AE dramatically reduces the search space by 88%, when compared with GenProg and, at the same time, keeps the same repair effectiveness than GenProg.

4.4 Repair Approaches Extension for Avoiding Overfitted Patches

Due to the problematic of test overfitting, recent works [16,41] propose to extend existing automated repair approach such as Nopol, ACS and jGenProg. Those extended approaches generate new test inputs to enhance the test suites and use their behavior similarity to determine patch correctness. For example, Lui et al. [16] reported that their approach, based on patch and test similarity analysis, successfully prevented 56.3% of the incorrect patches to be generated, without blocking any correct patches. Yang et al. [40] presented a framework named

Opad (Overfitted PAtch Detection) to detect overfilled patches by enhancing existing test cases using fuzz testing and employing two new test oracles. Opad filters out 75.2% (321/427) overfitted patches generated by GenProg/AE, Kali, and SPR.

5 Discussion

5.1 Threats to Validity

Internal Threats: Due to Cardumen being stochastic, we executed Cardumen over each bugs 10 times for 3 h, each trial with a different seed. In total, our evaluation took approximately 10710 h of execution equivalent to 446 days.[2] Running more executions will involve that Cardumen navigates places from the search space not yet visited and thus potentially discovers new patches. Moreover, the experimental setup could impact on the repairability, for instance, we decide to consider the 1000 most suspicious modification points. Between the excluded modification points it could exist one or more places where Cardumen could generate a test-suite adequate patch.

External Threats: We run Cardumen over 356 bugs from 5 open-source Java projects. More bugs from other kind of applications (all evaluated are libraries) could help to validate the efficacy of Cardumen. As studied by [21,28], test-suite based repair approaches can generate plausible patches, yet incorrect. That means, they pass all the test cases from a suite but they are incorrect due to the limitation of the bug oracle: when using test suite as oracle, this limitation is the missing of inputs and outputs for correctly exercising the patch. Currently, approaches by [36,41] aim at improving the quality of test suite for avoiding accepting incorrect patches. However, in this work, we do not focus on the correctness of patches, which demands another correctness oracle, yet manual or automated: our goal is Cardumen finds the most quantity of code changes that produce a buggy version of a program passing a test-suite (either the original test suite or one augmented).

5.2 Limitations

As described previously in Sect. 2.1, Cardumen synthesizes patches that only modify expressions. Thus, Cardumen is not able to synthesize patches that add new statement or remove code. However, we believe that each repair approach focuses on particular defect classes. We envision that the general process of repair a bug automatically is composed by the execution of different approaches, each targeting on particular set of defect classes. We aim at implement that vision in our repair framework Astor, which already includes different repair approaches such as jGenProg, jKali, jMutRepair (an implementation of approached proposed by [4]), DeepRepair and, from now, Cardumen.

---

[2] Total execution time: 10710 = 357 *bugs* X 10 *trials* X 3 h.

6   Conclusion

In this paper, we take an original approach to program repair: we aim at finding as many test-suite adequate patches as possible for a given bug. For that, we created an automated repair approach named Cardumen. Cardumen found in total 8935 test-suite adequate patches, repairing 77 bugs from Defects4J, 8 of them not previously repaired by any other repair system. This result shows the richness of Cardumen's search space. Furthermore, 53% of repaired bugs have patches applied on different locations; and 65% of the repaired bugs have different kinds of patches.

As future work, we envision a new repair system that would perform: (*1*) a first reduction of the complete search space to a subspace only composed of *test-adequate patches*; and (*2*) a second reduction of that space to a subspace with only *correct* patches. For implementing this approach, our future plan is to study and compare the 8935 patches generated by Cardumen.

References

1. Barr, E.T., Brun, Y., Devanbu, P., Harman, M., Sarro, F.: The plastic surgery hypothesis. In: Proceedings of the 22Nd ACM SIGSOFT International Symposium on Foundations of Software Engineering, FSE 2014, pp. 306–317. ACM, New York (2014)
2. Campos, J., Riboira, A., Perez, A., Abreu, R.: GZoltar: an eclipse plug-in for testing and debugging. In: 2012 Proceedings of the 27th IEEE/ACM International Conference on Automated Software Engineering, pp. 378–381, September 2012
3. Chen, L., Pei, Y., Furia, C.A.: Contract-based program repair without the contracts. In: Proceedings of the 32nd IEEE/ACM International Conference on Automated Software Engineering, ASE 2017, pp. 637–647. IEEE Press, Piscataway (2017)
4. Debroy, V., Wong, W.E.: Using mutation to automatically suggest fixes for faulty programs. In: Proceedings of the 2010 Third International Conference on Software Testing, Verification and Validation, ICST 2010, pp. 65–74 (2010)
5. Durieux, T., Cornu, B., Seinturier, L., Monperrus, M.: Dynamic patch generation for null pointer exceptions using metaprogramming. In: 2017 IEEE 24th International Conference on Software Analysis, Evolution and Reengineering (SANER), pp. 349–358, February 2017
6. Durieux, T., Danglot, B., Yu, Z., Martinez, M., Urli, S., Monperrus, M.: The patches of the Nopol automatic repair system on the bugs of Defects4J version 1.1.0. Research Report hal-01480084, Université Lille 1 - Sciences et Technologies (2017)
7. Durieux, T., Monperrus, M.: DynaMoth: dynamic code synthesis for automatic program repair. In: Proceedings of the 11th International Workshop on Automation of Software Test, AST 2016, pp. 85–91. ACM, New York 2016
8. Le Goues, C., et al.: The ManyBugs and introclass benchmarks for automated repair of C programs. IEEE Trans. Softw. Eng. **41**(12), 1236–1256 (2015)
9. Le Goues, C., Nguyen, T., Forrest, S., Weimer, W.: GenProg: a generic method for automatic software repair. IEEE Trans. Softw. Eng. **38**(1), 54–72 (2012)

10. Jiang, J., Xiong, Y.: Can defects be fixed with weak test suites? An analysis of 50 defects from defects4j. arXiv preprint arXiv:1705.04149 (2017)
11. Just, R., Jalali, D., Ernst, M.D.: Defects4J: a database of existing faults to enable controlled testing studies for Java programs. In: Proceedings of the International Symposium on Software Testing and Analysis (ISSTA), San Jose, CA, USA, 23–25 July 2014, pp. 437–440 (2014)
12. Ke, Y., Stolee, K.T., Le Goues, C., Brun, Y.: Repairing programs with semantic code search (t). In: Proceedings of the 2015 30th IEEE/ACM International Conference on Automated Software Engineering (ASE), ASE 2015, pp. 295–306. IEEE Computer Society, Washington, D.C. (2015)
13. Kim, D., Nam, J., Song, J., Kim, S.: Automatic patch generation learned from human-written patches. In: Proceedings of the 2013 International Conference on Software Engineering, ICSE 2013, pp. 802–811. IEEE Press, Piscataway (2013)
14. Le, X.-B.D., Chu, D.-H., Lo, D., Le Goues, C., Visser, W.: S3: syntax- and semantic-guided repair synthesis via programming by examples. In Proceedings of the 2017 11th Joint Meeting on Foundations of Software Engineering, ESEC/FSE 2017, pp. 593–604. ACM, New York (2017)
15. Le, X.B.D., Lo, D., Le Goues, C.: History driven program repair. In: 2016 IEEE 23rd International Conference on Software Analysis, Evolution, and Reengineering (SANER), vol. 1, pp. 213–224. IEEE (2016)
16. Liu, X., Zeng, M., Xiong, Y., Zhang, L., Huang, G.: Identifying patch correctness in test-based automatic program repair (2017)
17. Long, F., Amidon, P., Rinard, M.: Automatic inference of code transforms for patch generation. In: Proceedings of the 2017 11th Joint Meeting on Foundations of Software Engineering, ESEC/FSE 2017, pp. 727–739. ACM, New York (2017)
18. Long, F., Rinard, M.: Staged program repair with condition synthesis. In: Proceedings of the 2015 10th Joint Meeting on Foundations of Software Engineering, ESEC/FSE 2015, pp. 166–178. ACM, New York (2015)
19. Long, F., Rinard, M.: An analysis of the search spaces for generate and validate patch generation systems. In: Proceedings of the 38th International Conference on Software Engineering, ICSE 2016, pp. 702–713. ACM, New York (2016)
20. Long, F., Rinard, M.: Automatic patch generation by learning correct code. SIGPLAN Not. **51**(1), 298–312 (2016)
21. Martinez, M., Durieux, T., Sommerard, R., Xuan, J., Monperrus, M.: Automatic repair of real bugs in Java: a large-scale experiment on the Defects4J dataset. Empirical Softw. Eng. **22**, 1–29 (2016)
22. Martinez, M., Monperrus, M.: Mining software repair models for reasoning on the search space of automated program fixing. Empirical Softw. Eng. **20**, 1–30 (2013)
23. Martinez, M., Monperrus, M.: ASTOR: a program repair library for Java (demo). In: Proceedings of the 25th International Symposium on Software Testing and Analysis, ISSTA 2016, pp. 441–444. ACM, New York (2016)
24. Martinez, M., Weimer, W., Monperrus, M.: Do the fix ingredients already exist? An empirical inquiry into the redundancy assumptions of program repair approaches. In: Companion Proceedings of the 36th International Conference on Software Engineering, ICSE Companion 2014, pp. 492–495 (2014)
25. Nguyen, H.D.T., Qi, D., Roychoudhury, A., Chandra, S.: SemFix: program repair via semantic analysis. In Proceedings of the 2013 International Conference on Software Engineering, ICSE 2013, pp. 772–781. IEEE Press, Piscataway (2013)
26. Pawlak, R., Monperrus, M., Petitprez, N., Noguera, C., Seinturier, L.: Spoon: a library for implementing analyses and transformations of java source code. Softw.: Pract. Exp. **49**, 1155–1179 (2015)

27. Qi, Y., Mao, X., Lei, Y., Dai, Z., Wang, C.: Does genetic programming work well on automated program repair? In: 2013 Fifth International Conference on Computational and Information Sciences (ICCIS), pp. 1875–1878. IEEE (2013)

28. Qi, Z., Long, F., Achour, S., Rinard, M.: An analysis of patch plausibility and correctness for generate-and-validate patch generation systems. In: Proceedings of the 2015 International Symposium on Software Testing and Analysis, ISSTA 2015, pp. 24–36. ACM, New York (2015)

29. Reps, T., Ball, T., Das, M., Larus, J.: The use of program profiling for software maintenance with applications to the year 2000 problem. In: Jazayeri, M., Schauer, H. (eds.) ESEC/SIGSOFT FSE - 1997. LNCS, vol. 1301, pp. 432–449. Springer, Heidelberg (1997). https://doi.org/10.1007/3-540-63531-9_29

30. Smith, E.K., Barr, E.T., Le Goues, C., Brun, Y.: Is the cure worse than the disease? Overfitting in automated program repair. In: Proceedings of the 2015 10th Joint Meeting on Foundations of Software Engineering, pp. 532–543. ACM (2015)

31. Tu, Z., Su, Z., Devanbu, P.: On the localness of software. In: Proceedings of the 22nd ACM SIGSOFT International Symposium on Foundations of Software Engineering, FSE 2014, pp. 269–280. ACM, New York (2014)

32. Weimer, W., Fry, Z.P., Forrest, S.: Leveraging program equivalence for adaptive program repair: models and first results. In: 2013 IEEE/ACM 28th International Conference on Automated Software Engineering (ASE), pp. 356–366, November 2013

33. Weimer, W., Nguyen, T., Le Goues, C., Forrest, S.: Automatically finding patches using genetic programming. In: Proceedings of the 31st International Conference on Software Engineering, ICSE 2009, pp. 364–374 (2009)

34. Wen, M., Chen, J., Wu, R., Hao, D., Cheung, S.-C.: An empirical analysis of the influence of fault space on search-based automated program repair (2017)

35. White, M., Tufano, M., Martinez, M., Monperrus, M., Poshyvanyk, D.: Sorting and transforming program repair ingredients via deep learning code similarities (2017)

36. Xin, Q., Reiss, S.P.: Identifying test-suite-overfitted patches through test case generation. In: Proceedings of the 26th ACM SIGSOFT International Symposium on Software Testing and Analysis, ISSTA 2017, pp. 226–236. ACM, New York (2017)

37. Xin, Q., Reiss, S.P.: Leveraging syntax-related code for automated program repair. In: Proceedings of the 32nd IEEE/ACM International Conference on Automated Software Engineering (ASE), pp. 660–670. IEEE (2017)

38. Xiong, Y., et al.: Precise condition synthesis for program repair. In: Proceedings of the 39th International Conference on Software Engineering, ICSE 2017, pp. 416–426. IEEE Press, Piscataway (2017)

39. Xuan, J., et al.: Nopol: automatic repair of conditional statement bugs in Java programs. IEEE Trans. Softw. Eng. **43**, 34–55 (2016)

40. Yang, J., Zhikhartsev, A., Liu, Y., Tan, L.: Better test cases for better automated program repair. In: Proceedings of the 2017 11th Joint Meeting on Foundations of Software Engineering, ESEC/FSE 2017, pp. 831–841. ACM, New York (2017)

41. Yu, Z., Martinez, M., Danglot, B., Durieux, T., Monperrus, M.: Alleviating patch overfitting with automatic test generation: a study of feasibility and effectiveness for the Nopol repair system. Empirical Softw. Eng., 1–35 (2018)

Special Tenth SSBSE papers – "Best of Previous SSBSEs"

How Can Metaheuristics Help Software Engineers?

Enrique Alba[✉]

Universidad de Málaga, Málaga, Spain
eat@lcc.uma.es
http://www.lcc.uma.es/~eat

Abstract. This paper is a brief description of the revamped presentation based in the original one I had the honor to deliver back in 2009 during the very first SSBSE in London. At this time, the many international forces dealing with search, optimization, and learning (SOL) met software engineering (SE) researchers in person, all of them looking for a quantified manner of modeling and solving problems in software. The contents of this work, as in the original one, will develop on the bases of metaheuristics to highlight the many good ways in which they can help to create a well-grounded domain where the construction, assessment, and exploitation of software are not just based in human expertise, but enhanced with intelligent automatic tools. Since the whole story started well before the first SSBSE in 2009, we will mention a few previous applications in software engineering faced with intelligent algorithms, as well as will discuss on the present interest and future challenges of the domain, structured in both short and long term goals. If we understand this as a cross-fertilization task between research fields, then we could learn a wider and more useful lesson for innovative research. In short, we will have here a semantic perspective of the old times (before SBSE), the recent years on SBSE, and the many avenues for future research and development spinning around this exciting clash of stars. A new galaxy has been born out of the body of knowledge in SOL and SE, creating forever a new class of researchers able of building unparalleled tools and delivering scientific results for the benefit of software, that is, of modern societies.

Keywords: Search · Optimization · Learning · Metaheuristic
Software engineering · Computational intelligence

1 Converging Trajectories

Software engineering (SE) and complex search/optimization/learning (SOL) are two important and historical knowledge areas in Computer Science (CS), and

Supported by the Spanish-FEDER projects TIN2017-88213-R and TIN2016-81766-REDT.

T. E. Colanzi and P. McMinn (Eds.): SSBSE 2018, LNCS 11036, pp. 89–105, 2018.
https://doi.org/10.1007/978-3-319-99241-9_4

the bases for the vast majority of applications of IT in today's world. But, with a few exceptions, separate research fields.

As to SE, its history is linked to the very nature of computers, with a deep relation to programming and the art/engineering task of planning, executing, and delivering products and services. Since its first conception, it was clear in SE that building, using, extending, and maintaining software is a very complex task, where we would need the help of computer tools to complement human experience and even creativity.

As to SOL, the landscape is still larger and older: optimization is embedded in most activities of life, and computer procedures aim for maximizing benefits, reducing costs, and searching in innovative ways, all playing a major role in every subfield of CS and IT. Indeed, optimization has greatly grown in the company of machine learning, and both admit a point of view in which the procedure for searching/learning (or the found result itself) is the focus of the study.

It was just a matter of time that the two areas got together, enriching each other and merging into a new domain where SE is understood as a real/normal engineering work, with artifacts that can be numerically modeled, and the management of the process and product has a quantitative flavor, that however has been largely dismissed in the SE community (with some important exceptions!).

From seminal works like [2,20] it was clear that SOL could transform the way in which SE deals with products and services, by measuring software quality in a numerical manner (performance, but also usability, security, ...), what would allow *automatic and intelligent* (both!) decision making and guidance. In this context, the search for better software solutions has finally converged to the so called *Search-Based Software Engineering*, a term coined by Harman [16] and popularized by an active community of practitioners across the world. Search and also optimization are there paramount to solve traditional problems of software (like program testing) and support new ones (like automatic repair or identification of potential defects), and thus there is a natural interest in knowing more on the techniques that would allow such an enhanced management of software tools.

Among the many techniques for SOL, metaheuristics [15,27] represent a para-mount field feeding algorithms and operations that would allow numerical modeling of SE problems, and will ease an important boosting in quality of the software we all are building nowadays. Metaheuristics exhibit a short list of requirements to be applied and a long list of benefits. On the requirements, they need **(a)** to be able of encoding a solution to the problem (*phenotype*) in a kind of vector of symbols (*genotype*) with no loss of generality (remember that the memory of a computer is a big vector) and **(b)** to be able of assessing the relative quality of two vectors as potential problem solutions. With only this, an iterative improvement of tentative solutions by means of some (non deterministic) operators is able of reaching solutions for problems out of the reach of classical methods. This is true because metaheuristics can deal with a list of handy real settlements: no need for differentiation, able to manage arbitrary constraints, no need of analytical description of the problem (!), facility to deal with continuous and discrete representations... all of them wanted in any field where problems are frequently ill-defined, very large, and of course NP-hard.

This article contains a brief discussion on what, how, and when these techniques can help SE researchers and practitioners.

In the next section, we will describe the main types of metaheuristics and the many useful extensions to cover virtually any problem that SE wants to throw to them. In Sect. 3 we will present some issues on SBSE and a somewhat new twist, going beyond SBSE to suggest how SE can have an impact in metaheuristics also, a bit on the contrary of what the reader can expect. Then, in Sect. 4 we will define some interesting and new open challenges to the community, just to end in Sect. 5 with conclusions and several of the many future works ahead.

2   A High Level Glimpse on Metaheuristics

Most of works where metaheuristics are used nowadays fit in some manner the resolution of a global optimization problem. An optimization problem is defined as a pair (S, f), where $S \neq \emptyset$ is called the *solution space* (or search space), and f is a function named *objective* function or *fitness* function, defined as $f : S \to \mathbb{R}$ solving an optimization problem consisting in finding a solution $i^* \in S$ such that: $f(i^*) \leqslant f(i), \forall i \in S$. Note that assuming either maximization or minimization does not restrict the generality of the problem. Depending on the domain which S belongs to, we can speak of binary ($S \subseteq \mathbb{B}^*$), integer ($S \subseteq \mathbb{N}^*$), continuous ($S \subseteq \mathbb{R}^*$), or heterogeneous optimization problems ($S \subseteq (\mathbb{B} \cup \mathbb{N} \cup \mathbb{R})^*$).

A simple classification of the optimization methods used throughout the history of CS is shown in Fig. 1. In a first approach, the techniques can be classified into *exact* versus *approximate* (and *others* as a category for difficult to classify procedures). Exact techniques are based on the mathematical finding of the optimal solution, what can also be described as an exhaustive search until the optimum is found, guaranteeing the optimality of the obtained solution. However, these techniques present many practical drawbacks. The time they require, though bounded, may be very large, especially for NP-hard problems. Furthermore, it is not always possible to find such an exact technique for every problem. Indeed, exact techniques often require from the solved problem to exhibit special types of constraints or features (e.g., derivability, continuity, and having an analytical expression -not that usual!-). This makes exact techniques not to be a good choice in many occasions, either because their time and memory requirements can become unpractical or because the real problem does not really show the expected requirements to admit a solution with an exact technique. For this reason, approximate techniques have been widely used by the international research community in the last few decades. These methods (sometimes) sacrifice the guarantee of finding the optimum in favor of providing a satisfactory solution within reasonable times an real resource consumption.

Among approximate algorithms, we can find two types: *ad hoc* heuristics, and *metaheuristics*. Ad hoc heuristics can be further divided into *constructive* heuristics and *local search* methods. Constructive heuristics are usually the swiftest methods. They construct a solution from scratch by iteratively incorporating components until a complete solution is obtained, which is returned as

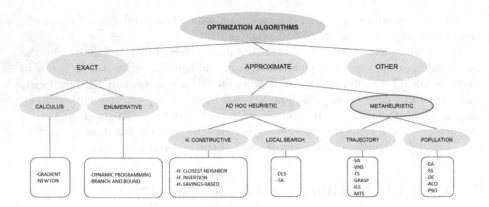

Fig. 1. Taxonomy of search algorithms.

the algorithm output. Finding a constructive heuristic that actually produces high quality solutions is a nontrivial task, since it mainly depends on the problem, and requires a thorough understanding of it. For example, in problems with many constraints, it could happen that many partial solutions do not lead to any feasible solution.

Local search or gradient descent methods start from a complete solution. They rely on the concept of *neighborhood* to explore a part of the search space defined for the current solution until they find a local optimum. The neighborhood of a given solution s, denoted as $N(s)$, is the set of solutions (neighbors) that can be reached from s through the use of a specific modification operator (generally referred to as a *movement*). A *local optimum* is a solution having equal or better objective function value than any other solution in its own neighborhood. The process of exploring the neighborhood, finding and keeping the best neighbor in the way, is repeated until the local optimum is found (or a maximum search budget has been exhausted). Complete exploration of a neighborhood is often unapproachable, therefore some modification of this generic scheme has to be adopted. Depending on the movement operator, the neighborhood varies and so does the manner of exploring the search space, simplifying or complicating the search process as a result.

During the 70's, a new class of approximate algorithms appeared whose basic idea was to combine operations in a *structured* (family-like) way in a higher level to achieve an efficient and effective search of the problem landscape. These techniques are called *metaheuristics*. The term was first introduced by Glover [14], and until it was ultimately adopted by the scientific community, these techniques were named modern heuristics [28]. This class of algorithms includes many diverse techniques such as ant colony, evolutionary algorithms, iterated local search, simulated annealing, and tabu search. A survey of metaheuristics can be found in [4,15]. Out of the many descriptions of metaheuristics that can be found in the literature, the following fundamental features can be highlighted:

- They are general strategies or templates that guide the search process.
- Their goal is to provide an efficient exploration of the search space to find (near) optimal solutions.
- They are not exact algorithms and their behavior is generally non deterministic (stochastic).
- They may incorporate mechanisms to avoid visiting non promising (or already visited) regions of the search space.
- Their basic scheme has a predefined structure.
- They may use specific problem knowledge for the problem at hand, by including some specific heuristic controlled by the high level strategy.

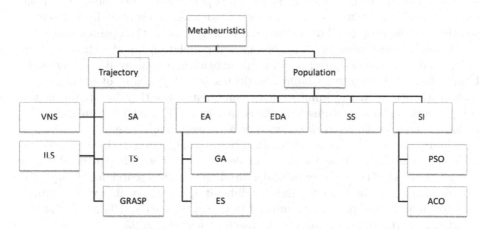

Fig. 2. Taxonomy of metaheuristics [13].

In other words, a metaheuristic is a general template for a non deterministic process that has to be filled with specific data from the problem to be solved (solution representation, specific operators to manipulate them, etc.), and that can tackle problems with high dimensional search spaces. In these techniques, the success depends on the correct balance between *diversification* and *intensification*. The term diversification refers to the evaluation of solutions in distant regions of the search space (with some distance function previously defined for the solution space); it is also known as *exploration* of the search space. The term intensification refers to the evaluation of solutions in small bounded regions, or within a neighborhood (*exploitation* in the search space).

The balance between these two opposed aspects is of the utmost importance, since the algorithm has to quickly find the most promising regions (exploration), but also those promising regions have to be thoroughly searched (exploitation). We can distinguish two kinds of search strategies in metaheuristics [4]. First, there are "intelligent" extensions of local search methods (*trajectory-based* metaheuristics in Fig. 2). These techniques add to the basic local search method some mechanism to escape from local optima (which would otherwise stuck in it).

Tabu search (TS) [14], iterated local search (ILS) [15], variable neighborhood search (VNS) [24] or simulated annealing (SA) [21] are some techniques of this kind. These metaheuristics operate with a single solution at a time, and one (or more) neighborhood structures. They are usually fast in converging to a solution (high exploitation), though suboptimal solutions are frequently found.

A different strategy is followed in ant colony optimization (ACO) [11], particle swarm optimization (PSO) [9] or evolutionary algorithms (EA) [3]. These techniques operate with a set of solutions at any time (called colony, swarm or population, respect.), and use a learning factor as they, implicitly or explicitly, try to grasp the correlation between design variables in order to identify the regions of the search space with high-quality solutions (*population-based techniques* in Fig. 2). In this sense, these methods perform a biased sampling of the search space. They tend to make a good exploration of the search of potential solutions to the problem, but a slow final tuning towards the optimal one.

Of course, a combination of trajectory and population-based techniques is in order, and thus the design of new metaheuristics is a healthy line of research. Using theoretical results to build algorithms is today a way of avoiding any useless wandering in the infinite set of combinations, either by analyzing the components of the algorithms [29], the search space [7] or the way in which the technique is expected to work versus how it actually works [22].

Finally, metaheuristics are not black boxes nor general recipes to success. Researchers need to know them, go in deep on their working principles and extract the most of their power by understanding how they search for the optima. In order to extend the basic families for difficult applications, it is very common that researchers need to learn on multiobjective optimization [10], parallel structured models [1], and combinations to machine learning [6,23].

3   Search for Software and Software for Search: SBSE and SAAL

In this section we briefly describe some existing ways of profiting from metaheuristics to face a variety of problems in SE. In all cases, the first step consists in describing the problem in a precise and quantitative way, as expected in any engineering domain. This usually means to define a global optimization problem in terms of objective functions and some type of constraints [8,18].

From the seminal work introducing the name for this field [17] the leading "S" has been read as "Search". We however think that, as of today, this term should be broaden, so as to talk on search, optimization, and learning. As a consequence, we propose here the term "SOL" as the modern meaning for the leading "S" in the term SBSE. Indeed, machine learning tools (like clustering, predicting, data science, probability analysis...) are ready normal in the field, as well as many applications put the stress in the optimization process instead of in the search technique used. Whether "SOL-Based Search Engineering" will become popular or not depends on the community of researchers in next years.

The first obvious goal, and the base for SBSE, is then solve problems in SE by using SOL algorithms. In addition, at the end of this section, we will give a twist on a different perspective were software knowledge is used to improve SOL algorithms, a not so well-known task that we here dare to name for the first time here as *Software Aware ALgorithms* (SAAL).

To finish this initial introduction to the section we will quickly review the field at an international level. To this end, we have computed the world questions on this topic from 2004 to now (according to Google Trends). In Fig. 3 we show the results (percentage of representative queries on the term SBSE). It can be seen that in years 2006–2007 a few important peaks of interest existed, that where later repeated in 2008–2009, and with a lower intensity from 2010–2011 and later years. As of today, the term and domain seems to attract a moderate attraction, though here we cannot judge because these are just percentages.

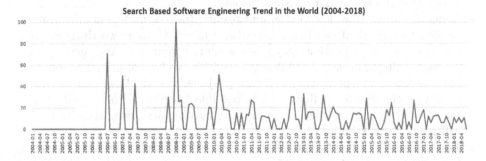

Fig. 3. Search-based Software Engineering in the world: interest between 2004 and 2018 according to Google Trends.

In Fig. 4 we include the relative interest raised from 2004 to 2018 but this time including metaheuristics to have a comparative picture. It seems that the algorithmic domain is far more developed, since the trend is always well above SBSE. This is just to say that there is more to be gained in SBSE by taking algorithms and solutions to SBSE till this field is fully developed at international level. In a (non shown here) comparison of SBSE to the whole domain of software engineering the picture shows a much larger interest for software engineering and SBSE is almost not noticeable (visually it is a plain zero-like line on axis X), a trend that we all should have to change by providing breakthrough results and a more intense dissemination in the SE community.

3.1 SOL-Based Software Engineering

Let us begin with the benefits of using SOL in general, and metaheuristics in particular for software engineering. We can list them here:

- SE Problems will be precisely defined and thus quantification and numerical comparisons are possible. Though it might look as a minor benefit, it is a paramount one, since SE has been playing around for its whole life (and still now, in many parts of the world) with fuzzy ideas of "flexibility", "power", and other supposedly attractive features that have never been quantified nor compared in a fair way between products and services in the field.

- Software artifacts, like instructions, variables, objects, classes, functions, and many others get now a precise numerical definition and manipulation. Metrics can be defined, and advances can be objectively stated. This is in the base of the very definition of Science and Engineering, and metaheuristics give the intelligent and automatic manner of evolving, testing, designing, and understanding them.
- Scalability is another important benefit here. No more solving problems of one page of code, since actual software systems have millions of lines of code. The use of parallelism, cloud computing, and the fundamentals like numerical efficiency, robustness, and SOL theory work together to offer a unique domain of tools for the researcher and practitioner.
- Generality of studies, knowledge, and results. Indeed, metaheuristics can be applied to any SBSE problem. Investing time in them is worth, since you learn for future applications as you solve your current one. Also, getting surprising results on apparently different activities like how to prioritize software tests/tasks, assign persons to software projects, and dealing with the complexity of the execution flow, is only possible because of them, and offer a unique unified point of view. Your time in learning and using metaheuristics will pay you back for sure.
- The understanding on the problem and its context, and the solutions you get (e.g., by using genetic programming or constructive algorithms like ACO) allows knowledge accumulation. While other techniques are obscure in the solutions they provide (notably neural networks) metaheuristics offer you a white box access to solutions and even to the process by which you got them, an appreciated feature for any tool in Science.

The following sensible question is now: where can we use and find these benefits in software engineering? Well, the list will never be comprehensive, but

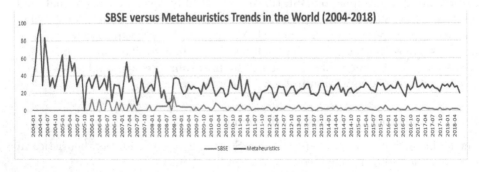

Fig. 4. SBSE and metaheuristics in the world: interest between 2004 and 2018 according to Google Trends.

here we have some of the major fields endorsed because of the utilization of SOL techniques:

- Software Planning
- Requirement Analysis and Design
- Coding Tools and Techniques
- Testing, Validation, Verification, and Debugging
- Distribution, Maintenance, Enhancement
- General Management of Software Products and Services
- Concurrent Systems
- Networks and Critical Systems
- Human Decision Making
- Evolution of Interfaces
- Web Services
- Web Ontologies
- Evolution of Architectures

There are applications of difficult classification, like the domain of *quantitative quality* [5], that usually touches many sub-fields. Also, the list does not inform on the relative importance in terms of attention received in research, and thus, e.g. the reader should be aware of the massive number of scientific articles on the different flavors of testing compared to the rest of research lines.

Before we close this first SBSE section, let us mention some high level hints for researchers. Of course, this is an informal exercise, so others could think differently. The first key factor in a good design of metaheuristics for SE is the decision on whether or not we need non-traditional representations (trees, graphs, Petri nets, automata...) that could suit the problem much better than a simple vector of symbols. The second key factor is the definition of a smart fitness function: we are not forced to use any particular function, so let us select (devise!) one with nice properties for the induced landscape, so as to ease the location of the optima. And finally, the third key factor is to use specialized operators in the algorithms, since the basic ones (one point crossover, immediate neighborhood search, arithmetical operations) are far from being good to find a solution for complex problems, where efficiency and efficacy are mandatory. The more the problem knowledge used, the better.

There are of course more hints, but this could become and endless list, so let us summarize in a brief manner some guidelines in a nutshell, organized according to what you need:

- According to the **representation**, some advices are those: if it is binary then try SA, GA, CHC, EDA or ILS. If it is a tree, go for GP. If you have a float representation go for ES, PSO, DE or CMAES. If it is a permutation representation, try to use GAs with special operators for permutations, or VNS and specialized algorithms for your problem.
- If your search problem has an underlying **graph** structure, go for ACO.
- If you face a very **expensive fitness function**, then use parallel metaheuristics. Also, use theory to lean the algorithm. Finally, try to use a kind of surrogates (like e.g. neuronal networks) for the fitness calculation.

- If your environment/function is **dynamic**, go for cellular GAs, PSO, ES or SA. Distributed versions of metaheuristics also pay off. In all cases, using an explicit memory on past experiences and a strong exploration component (e.g. hypermutation) is in place.
- If your problem is **multimodal** then go for structured EAs like cellular EAs or distributed EAs (nothing to do with parallelism, this is on structuring the population).
- If **constraints** are the hard part of your problem, then try to build hybrids (memetic algorithms?) and use specific operators considering them; search in the contour of the feasible regions defined by the constraints, optimal solutions often live there.

We stop here, though we could go on in talking on the means for a proper *initial population* (seeding with latin squares, Voronoi initialization, ad hoc sets of representative individuals merged with random ones...), the way in which the *random numbers* are generated (beyond `random`, `random48` standard methods, like using white noise from atmosphere or at least using Meresenne twister), and details like whether a new solution is accepted if its fitness is *equal* to the best existing one (yes, do accept it to scape from plateaus!).

3.2   Software Aware Algorithms (SAAL)

We now will discuss in a brief manner a kind of very related topic, but a non well-known one. The very nature of algorithms describes them as procedures to solve a problem, and then no mention to computer programs is often done. In this sense, algorithms are developed by mathematicians and other researchers whose goal is to develop the abstract technique and think in their *theoretical* behavior and complexity. However, for the vast majority of situations in modern research, algorithms need to be implemented in a computer, and thus they will enter the realm of *programming artifacts*. As any other software, algorithms running on a computer use data structures, flow-control sentences, and have a wide variety of details on how to best implement them.

The research questions here are many: are SOL algorithms well/correctly implemented? Is there a best way to do so? What data structures should we use? If using object orientation, what is the best way to define the system of classes? Are we paying attention to compiler directives and operating systems? ...and a long etcetera.

It may seem that these questions are marginal, but think in the following problems if we dismiss them:

Implementing the idea. Like for any software, we will always have a reasonable doubt that the implemented algorithm is the designed abstract algorithm. In fact, SOL algorithms are seldom having a specification for guiding a later implementation. Errors and defects might appear, taking the actual runs far from their expected behavior. Since metaheuristics are non deterministic techniques, it can be hard to know whether a bad or unexpected results is due to the actual behavior of the correct algorithm or to the wrong implementation of the correct algorithm.

Representation of vectors. Since we will have thousands and millions of temporary variables containing the bits/integer/float variables, using high level data structures could lead to an unaffordable management of memory, either using too much of it and thus preventing it from running, or making the algorithm very slow. Some applications could even need to pack variables into basic data types like integers, with an additional time cost of packing/unpacking for their interpretation.

Object orientation. Many important issues appear when using OO for implementing metaheuristics: should we explicitly call the garbage collector? Static objects are managed far more efficiently than normal ones, so should we define static data structures as often as possible? Are operators part of the class of the individual or part of the algorithm?

Compiler directives. Different languages compile (or interpret) according to explicit directives that the researcher can use to improve efficiency. Should we use -O3 in gcc? What is the best way to optimize a compiled Java program? Should we compile for the processor architecture? When making one run becomes a task of one week (or we aim real time response), this is relevant.

Variables. Many guidelines on programming exist, and most are up when implementing metaheuristics. A first question is whether researchers are following them or not...A paramount issue is for example on using global variables, something not good for the quality (understanding, error analysis, extensibility) of a program, but at the same time often more efficient than using local variables. Finding the right balance is difficult in most languages, do we even care about this? If not, then why to bother on not using goto jumps, raising/catching exceptions or giving meaningful names to variables? Why should we only take arbitrary best practices? Let us take them "all".

Toolboxes versus languages. Many researchers select their implementation tools so as to only focus on the application, and this means going into *closed* packages like MATLAB, SPSS and similar ones. The many advantages (all is inside, the researcher already knew them, no need of advanced programming skills) sometimes do not compensate for the long running times, the many unknown internal calls to intermediate procedures, and the lack of extensions available in them (parallelism, for example). General purpose programing languages (Java, C, C++, Python, R, Javascript...) allow much more freedom (and problems) for implementation. Of course, every language also has a baseline speed that needs to be considered when starting a new project.

After reading the previous list, any sensible researcher should be now concerned on whether he/she is actually able of getting much more from his/her present implementation. Here an intriguing question: what is the actual quality of the many libraries we all are using with no formal proof that they are implementing the actual expected algorithms and (at least) show a reasonable efficiency? We take software as a black box and apply it, take correctness for granted, and then try to explain results that could be unexplainable due to software errors. Also, we might be missing tons of new research lines in not making our algorithms aware of the operating system, not to mention being aware of the energy consumption (for running algorithms e.g. in smartphones) or the underlying hardware (processor power, available memory, network communications).

In summary, it seems weird that the entire world is developing software for search, optimization and learning while not using for this the well-known SE tools and knowledge to do so. In the domain of SBSE, it is especially weird that researchers are dismissing this in their papers and public libraries. The reader might think that this is just a personal tick or some kind of luxury task, however research results show how you can save 30% or more time with a good implementation [25]. This time can be used for additional runs, a deeper understanding, or to write more scientific papers per year. Indeed, efficiency is just part of the quality of any software package; other factors like maintainability, reliability, extensibility, usability, also apply to public SOL software, and thus should be relevant in future studies.

4   Open Challenges and Ideas for the Future

In this section we will find an analysis of the potential challenges and good directions for the interplay between SE and metaheuristics in the future. They will be presented in two parts: a first set of challenges for SBSE (short and long term), and some final challenges for SAAL. Of course, mentioning challenges is not a formal scientific task, so this is clearly subject to debate. Indeed, since the whole existing community, plus the newcomers to arrive, will be deciding on how and what is important as a future challenge, this is just an exercise of good guessing to help interested readers.

Let us start with potentially interesting SBSE challenges. We can there define the following ones in the short term:

- Stopping Criteria
    Analyze the techniques both under a predefined effort (to later evaluate the resulting fitness), solution quality (to later evaluate the needed fitness effort), study the algorithm convergence (phenotype and genotype ones), and explore combined stopping condition and their effect on the results. Limited budget, for example, are of great interest to set the interest of any new technique. Also, what is the meaning of the results for the SBSE problem?
- Landscape Visualization
    Knowing the problem you are solving is very important to design a good algorithm. Visualization of search landscapes, of the work of search operators, or of the contents of the resulting solution is very important. Looking for new tools like *parallel coordinates* [19] or *local optima networks* [26] could be worth.
- Landscape Characterization
    We really need to know, visualize and use the properties of the search landscape of our problem: multimodality, epistasis, discontinuities, pla-teaus, etc. Metrics encoding this, such as the number of suboptimal

solutions, or the fitness-distance correlation, are of much interest to allow the designer to arrive to a good algorithm design.

- Human Competitive Results

  Having an intelligent technique to beat a human is difficult, we indeed should go for specialized sub-domains and very concrete tasks, and then computer aided software management would become universal. To this end, programming interfaces, testing GUIs, and web services to assess software packages, are interesting and expected for all of us.

Let us now shift to a short discussion on potential long term challenges:

- Multiobjective Optimization

  There is a rich set of information in the metaheuristic field: goals, algorithms, metrics, statistics are available to study and use for SE. Decision making (versus optimization) is a growing field also here, and higher level tools are wanted to help innovation in SBSE. It seems that this is presently happening, but when going to the details of existing articles, they can be classified as out of the main stream in multiobjective optimization, because of their lack of basic contents in the paper in this sense.

- Interactive Optimization

  Humans work better with visual concepts, and then a better relation to GUIs is expected to appear, so that we approach the industry of software with usable tools embedding our SBSE solutions inside.

- Prediction

  The software industry (well, we all) need an assisted prediction of what is going to happen, so that we can react in advance and have a global better management of product and services. Predicting how and why we need a next release of software packages, where will be hidden the next defect, error or failure (not the same!) in software, the future status of a project, etc. are all very welcomed SBSE outputs.

- Hybrid SOL Algorithms

  SBSE is a field where a natural handshaking between exact and approximate algorithms is happening. Also in a natural way, researchers should build hybrid techniques with existing knowledge, wherever it is coming from. In this sense, personal preferences for a technique just create an unwanted bias: let us use the best techniques for the (sub)problem at hands and combine them to make more powerful ones.

- On Line (Dynamic) Optimization

  Up to now, most SBSE problems are static, that is, the target function to optimize behaves the same along the whole run of the algorithm. However, for more complex problems in databases, shared programming environments, testing, etc. could need to rely on the existing knowledge on *dynamic optimization problems* (DOP), like adding memory to our algorithm, use hypermutation for a enhanced exploration, and relying to self-adaptation for improved performance.

- Applying New Models of Search

  SBSE researchers know a great deal of SOL algorithms, but this last domain is so large and evolves so quickly that they should be continuously looking for new trends, like running algorithms on GPUs, programming for smartphones to execute solvers on them, using cloud computing to deal with real-size software testing, or refactoring/repairing big software projects found in Github.

We now finish this section with some open challenges for SAAL research, where our solvers are seen as software programs to be understood and improved:

- Software Libraries

  Here, we should start designing libraries with (e.g.) extended UML tools, discuss on the best class architecture for complex algorithms, find errors in them by testing the source code, and analyze quality metrics (from specification/requirements to real usability). Taking the correctness and quality of optimization, search and learning libraries for granted is a risk that we cannot take in the domain, if we think in ourselves as good scientists and engineers.
- Data Structures

  Since there are so many variables and objects in a complex SBSE solver, we should care on how a population or an individual should be better implemented in any population-based technique. The more a data structure is used in our solver, the deeper the analysis on its memory and CPU consumption should be addressed.
- Profiling

  Once our solver is programmed, or while it is being improved, profiling is a must. Gathering information on the solver components, on how executions are done, and proposing a better implementation, all come handy to make better and more efficient research. Of course, after the profiling analysis we should act, and thus review the design and the implementation of our software before putting it to solve a SBSE problem.
- Program Complexity

  It is very common that papers lack of any information on the computational complexity of their solutions. As so, many solvers published today have a low impact in research. Characterizing program complexity of well-known techniques is a must, to know whether we should lose our time in learning them or not, because they would not work even in similar slightly larger conditions of problem size. Something similar happens with the parameterization used to solve a problem: the robustness (sensitivity) of the parameters as implemented in the solver has to be assessed by researchers in every research paper.
- New Frontiers

  There are many goals that researchers need to consider if aiming a wide impact: deal with programs having million of lines, going for complete Github repositories as a routine task, create SBSE tools for software companies, etc. Besides, lots of specialized information are needed in SBSE before going to implement parallel solvers, properly analyzing multiobjective approaches (yes, this can not be done in one month), target drivers and operating systems as the goal of research, apply data science to software, and a plethora of points of view to come.

5   One Conclusion, Many Future Works

This article is a summary of the talk delivered at SSBSE 2018, what in turns is a fresh view of the talk offered in the very first SSBSE 2009 in London. The topic is a perspective on how metaheuristics can help researchers and practitioners in software engineering. In this sense, this is not a normal research paper, but a position paper showing a filtered vision on the last years in this domain, according to the opinion to the author. Of course, others can think differently.

Our main conclusion here is a positive one: SBSE is a healthy domain and getting more specialized every day. There is much to find in metaheuristics to help SBSE researchers define SOL problems in the domain of software engineering, so as to quantify and give fair numerical analyses in a field where industry and even academia have neglected a bit the engineering part: quantify, understand, manage, optimize. That should be normal in any engineering activity [12], and thanks (in part) to SBSE, this is happening.

We have summarized many types of metaheuristics to help readers, as well as gave some hints to guide newcomers. We have introduced the idea of changing "search" by "search, optimization, and learning" as a new meaning for the first "S" in "SOL-Based Software Engineering". We do think that more than search is happening, so such a re-interpretation of the leading "S" comes in place. We even dared to introduce for the first time the concept of going on the other way, and using software engineering concepts, tools and research for building algorithms: SAAL. Much can be gained if we all consider going that way in a structured manner, and some existing works point to the right direction.

A big deal of cross-fertilization is needed between SOL and SE. Challenges are many in scientific areas like the algorithm types (many-objective, dynamic, uncertain problems) as well as on the new definition of problems (complex modeling of real world SE tasks) and the overall needed set of best practices for researchers, something that should come as soon as possible to avoid meaningless studies showing, sometimes, minor/incremental contributions to the community. Being able of understanding and reading results in the two domains will lead sooner than later to a completely new/separate body of knowledge for this field, with a potential huge impact in today's economy and science.

References

1. Alba, E.: Parallel Metaheuristics: A New Class of Algorithms. Wiley, Hoboken (2005)
2. Alba, E., Troya, J.M.: Genetic algorithms for protocol validation. In: Voigt, H.-M., Ebeling, W., Rechenberg, I., Schwefel, H.-P. (eds.) PPSN 1996. LNCS, vol. 1141, pp. 870–879. Springer, Heidelberg (1996). https://doi.org/10.1007/3-540-61723-X_1050

3. Bäck, T., Fogel, D.B., Michalewicz, Z. (eds.): Handbook of Evolutionary Computation. Institute of Physics Publishing Ltd., Bristol (1997)
4. Blum, C., Roli, A.: Metaheuristics in combinatorial optimization: overview and conceptual comparison. ACM Comput. Surv. **35**(3), 268–308 (2003)
5. Boehm, B.W., Brown, J.R., Lipow, M.: Quantitative Evaluation of Software Quality. In: Proceedings of the 2nd International Conference on Software Engineering (ICSE 1976), pp. 592–605. IEEE Computer Society Press (1976)
6. Calvet, L., De Armas, J., Masip, D., Juan, A.A.: Learnheuristics: hybridizing metaheuristics with machine learning for optimization with dynamic inputs. Open Math. **15**, 261–280 (2017). https://doi.org/10.1515/math-2017-0029
7. Chicano, F., Ferrer, J., Alba, E.: Elementary landscape decomposition of the test suite minimization problem. In: Cohen, M.B., Ó Cinnéide, M. (eds.) SSBSE 2011. LNCS, vol. 6956, pp. 48–63. Springer, Heidelberg (2011). https://doi.org/10.1007/978-3-642-23716-4_7
8. Clark, J.A., et al.: Formulating software engineering as a search problem. IEE Proc. Softw. **150**(3), 161–175 (2003)
9. Clerc, M.: Particle Swarm Optimization. Wiley, Hoboken (2010)
10. Coello Coello, C., Lamont, G.B., Van Veldhuizen, D.A.: Evolutionary Algorithms for Solving Multi-Objective Problems. Springer, New York (2007). https://doi.org/10.1007/978-0-387-36797-2
11. Dorigo, M.: Optimization, learning and natural algorithms. Ph.D. thesis, Politecnico di Milano (1992)
12. Fenton, N.E.: Software measurement: a necessary scientific basis. IEEE Trans. Softw. Eng. **20**(3), 199–206 (1994)
13. Ferrer, F. J.: Optimization techniques for automated software test data generation. Ph.D. thesis, Universidad de Málaga (2016). https://riuma.uma.es/xmlui/handle/10630/13056. Accessed 25 June 2018
14. Glover, F.: Future paths for integer programming and links to artificial intelligence. Comput. Oper. Res. **13**(5), 533–549 (1986)
15. Glover, F.: Handbook of Metaheuristics. Kluwer, Dordrecht (2003)
16. Harman, M., Afshin Mansouri, S., Zhang, Y.: Search-based software engineering: trends, techniques and applications. ACM Comput. Surv. **451**, 1–64 (2012)
17. Harman, M., Jones, B.F.: Search-based software engineering. Inf. Softw. Technol. **43**(14), 833–839 (2001)
18. Harman, M., Jones, B.F.: Software engineering using metaheuristic innovative algorithms: workshop report. Inf. Softw. Technol. **43**(14), 905–907 (2001)
19. Inselberg, A.: Parallel Coordinates: Visual Multidimensional Geometry and Its Applications. Springer, New York (2009). https://doi.org/10.1007/978-0-387-68628-8
20. Jones, B.J., Sthamer, II.-H., Eyres, D.: Automatic structural testing using genetic algorithms. Softw. Eng. J. **11**, 299–306 (1996)
21. Kirkpatrick, K., Gelatt, G.D., Vecchi, M.P.: Optimization by simulated annealing. Science **220**(4598), 671–680 (1983)
22. Luque, G., Alba, E.: Math oracles: a new day of designing efficient self-adaptive algorithms. In: Proceedings of GECCO (Companion), pp. 217–218 (2013)
23. Memeti, S., Pllana, S. Binotto, A., Kolodziej, J., Brandic, I.: Using Metaheuristics and Machine Learning for Software Optimization of Parallel Computing Systems: A Systematic Literature Review. arXiv:1801.09444v3 [cs.DC], https://doi.org/10.1007/s00607-018-0614-9 (2018)
24. Mladenovic, N., Hansen, P.: Variable neighborhood search. Comput. Oper. Res. **24**(11), 1097–1100 (1997)

25. Nesmachnow, S., Luna, F., Alba, E.: An empirical time analysis of evolutionary algorithms as C programs. Softw. Pract. Exp. **45**(1), 111–142 (2015)
26. Ochoa, G., Veerapen, N.: Mapping the global structure of TSP fitness landscapes. J. Heuristics **24**(3), 265–294 (2018)
27. Osman, I.H., Laporte, G.: Metaheuristics: a bibliography. Ann. Oper. Res. **63**, 513–623 (1996)
28. Reeves, C.R. (ed.): Modern Heuristic Techniques for Combinatorial Problems. Wiley, Hoboken (1993)
29. Villagra, A., Alba, E., Leguizamósn, G.: A methodology for the hybridization based in active components: the case of cGA and scatter search. Comput. Int. Neurosci. **2016**, 8289237:1–8289237:11 (2016)

A Tutorial on Using and Extending the EvoSuite Search-Based Test Generator

Gordon Fraser[✉]

University of Passau, Passau, Germany
`gordon.fraser@uni-passau.de`

Abstract. EvoSuite is an automated unit test generation tool for Java. It takes as input a Java class under test, and produces JUnit tests optimised for code coverage, and enhanced with regression assertions, as output. This paper is a tutorial on how to use EvoSuite to generate tests, on how to build and extend EvoSuite, and how to use EvoSuite to run experiments on search-based testing.

1 Introduction

EvoSuite [6] is a tool that automatically generates JUnit test cases for Java classes. It applies search-based techniques, such as genetic algorithms, to generate these tests. Besides various optimisations at the algorithmic level proposed over time (e.g., [3,9,11]), EvoSuite also implements many different Java-specific optimisations (e.g., mocking of interactions with the filesystem [4] or network [5]) and has reached a good level of maturity (read: it does not crash *too* often). While the principle techniques underlying EvoSuite and their empirical evaluations have been published (e.g., [7]), the aim of this article is to provide an introduction to the tool from a user and researcher point of view.

The tutorial is structured in three parts: First, we describe how to generate tests with EvoSuite from the command line. Second, we show how to build and extend EvoSuite. Finally, in the third part we provide an example of how EvoSuite can be used to run experiments, for example to evaluate different configurations or extensions to EvoSuite. This tutorial covers a subset of the online tutorial available at http://www.evosuite.org.

2 Using EvoSuite

There are plugins [2] to use EvoSuite within different IDEs (e.g., IntelliJ and Eclipse), and there is a Maven plugin that simplifies the usage in larger projects. In this tutorial, however, we will focus on the basic use case as a standalone application, on the command line. For this, EvoSuite is available as an executable `jar` (Java Archive) file. The latest release of EvoSuite is always available at http://www.evosuite.org/downloads/, or in the release section on EvoSuite's GitHub page at http://github.com/EvoSuite/evosuite/. At the time of this writing, the

T. E. Colanzi and P. McMinn (Eds.): SSBSE 2018, LNCS 11036, pp. 106–130, 2018.
https://doi.org/10.1007/978-3-319-99241-9_5

latest release version was 1.0.6; the filenames stated in this article refer to this version number, but obviously new releases will lead to changed filenames. There are two different `jar` files:

- `evosuite-1.0.6.jar` is the main file used to generate tests, including all its dependencies.
- `evosuite-standalone-runtime-1.0.6.jar` is an archive containing only those parts of EvoSuite and its dependencies that are necessary in order to execute tests generated by EvoSuite.

In this tutorial, we will assume that you have these `jar`-files. Furthermore, for several parts of the tutorial you will need Apache Maven[1].

2.1   Invoking EvoSuite

As the name suggests, the executable jar file can be executed. To do so, call EvoSuite like this:

```
java -jar evosuite-1.0.6.jar
```

You should see the following output:

```
* EvoSuite 1.0.6
usage: EvoSuite
...
```

This output is EvoSuite listing all the possible command-line options, as we haven't told EvoSuite what to do yet. To make the rest of this tutorial easier to read, we will create an environment variable to point to EvoSuite, e.g.:

```
export EVOSUITE="java -jar $(pwd)/evosuite-1.0.6.jar"
```

Now we can simply invoke EvoSuite by typing:

```
$EVOSUITE
```

(If you are not using the Bash shell, the commands to create an alias `$EVOSUITE` might differ.)

2.2   Generating Tests

As a running example in this tutorial, we will use the `tutorial.Stack` class shown in Fig. 1. We will assume that this file is part of a standard Java project structure, where the source code of the `Stack` class is kept in the file `src/main/java/tutorial/Stack.java`, and the compiled bytecode is placed in the directory `target/classes`. You can find a project set up like this as a Maven project in our online tutorial[2].

To generate tests with EvoSuite, there are two essential pieces of information that EvoSuite needs: (1) What is the class under test, and (2) what is the classpath where it can find the bytecode of the class under test and its dependencies.

---

[1] https://maven.apache.org/.

[2] http://evosuite.org/files/tutorial/Tutorial_Stack.zip.

```
package tutorial;

import java.util.EmptyStackException;

public class Stack<T> {
    private int capacity = 10;
    private int pointer = 0;
    private T[] objects = (T[]) new Object[capacity];

    public void push(T o) {
        if(pointer >= capacity)
            throw new RuntimeException("Stack exceeded capacity!");
        objects[pointer++] = o;
    }

    public T pop() {
        if(pointer <= 0)
            throw new EmptyStackException();
        return objects[--pointer];
    }

  public boolean isEmpty() {
        return pointer <= 0;
    }
}
```

Fig. 1. Example Java class `tutorial.Stack` used in the tutorial.

The class under test is specified using the `-class` argument (assuming we are targeting a single class). Note that we need to use the fully qualified class name; that is, we need to include the package name. Thus, in our example, we need to use `-class tutorial.Stack`.

The classpath is specified using the `-projectCP` argument. This takes a regular classpath entry, like you would specify when using `java -cp` or by setting `export CLASSPATH=....` As we assumed that compiled bytecode is placed in `target/classes` (as is, for example, done by Maven), this is the classpath which we specify using `-projectCP target/classes`. Thus, we can now run EvoSuite as follows:

```
$EVOSUITE -class tutorial.Stack -projectCP target/classes
```

Note that this assumes that the `Stack` class has been compiled, and there exists a resulting file `target/classes/tutorial/Stack.class`. If you don't have this and don't know how to produce it, consider getting the example project set up[2]. If everything worked correctly, then EvoSuite has now produced two files:

```
evosuite-tests/tutorial/Stack_ESTest.java
evosuite-tests/tutorial/Stack_ESTest_scaffolding.java
```

Let's take a closer look at these two files. If we look into the scaffolding file, we'll see lots of things happening in methods annotated with `@Before` and `@After`. These are JUnit annotations which ensure that these methods are executed before/after execution of each individual test. The reason for all this is that EvoSuite avoids flaky tests by controlling everything that might be nondeterministic. The scaffolding ensures that tests are always executed in the same consistent state, so they should really only fail if they reveal a bug, not because they are flaky. The scaffolding may look a bit scary, but the good news is that you'll probably never need to look at it.

The tests are in the main `Stack_ESTest.java` file. The test class inherits from the scaffolding, such that all the setup/pulldown happens without showing all the overhead to ensure tests are not flaky:

```
@RunWith(EvoRunner.class) @EvoRunnerParameters(mockJVMNonDeterminism
    = true, useVFS = true, useVNET = true, resetStaticState = true,
    separateClassLoader = true)
public class Stack_ESTest extends Stack_ESTest_scaffolding {
    // ...
```

Besides inheriting from the scaffolding, we also see some annotation that is specific to EvoSuite. The test class declares that it will be executed with the EvoRunner, rather than a default JUnit runner. The test runner takes a couple of parameters that tell it which parts of the execution environment are controlled. You can safely ignore these for now – the values for these parameters are set automatically by EvoSuite.

The rest of the file consists of the actual tests. The tests use JUnit 4 and are annotated with `@Test`. Because automatically generated tests sometimes do silly things causing infinite loops, all tests have a specified timeout, with a default value of 4 seconds.

2.3   Running Tests

Let's compile the tests. The compiler will need several things on the classpath:

- `target/classes`: This is the classpath directory containing the compiled bytecode, which we need for the `tutorial.Stack` class.
- `evosuite-standalone-runtime-1.0.6.jar`: This is the EvoSuite runtime library (you can also use the full EvoSuite jar file instead of this, although that will lead to more output since it uses EvoSuite's logger configuration).
- `evosuite-tests`: This is the root directory where EvoSuite put the test class files.
- `junit-4.12.jar` and `hamcrest-core-1.3.jar`: We need JUnit to execute JUnit tests.

To automatically resolve the JUnit and Hamcrest dependencies, an easy way is to use the Maven-version of our example project[2] and use Maven to retrieve the dependencies:

```
mvn dependency:copy-dependencies
```

This will download the two jar files and put them into `target/dependency`.

Now we need to tell the Java compiler where to find all these things, for which we set the CLASSPATH environment variable:[3]

```
export CLASSPATH=target/classes:evosuite-runtime-1.0.6.jar:\
        evosuite-tests:target/dependency/junit-4.12.jar:\
        target/dependency/hamcrest-core-1.3.jar
```

For now, we will simply compile the tests in place. Check the online tutorial[4] if you want to see how to integrate EvoSuite into the Maven project properly, such that Maven takes care of compiling the tests. Type the following command:

```
javac evosuite-tests/tutorial/*.java
```

Check that there are the two .class files in `evosuite-tests/tutorial`. If they are not there, then check what error messages the Java compiler gave you – most likely some part of the classpath is not set correctly. If they were compiled correctly, we can now run the tests on the commandline:

```
java org.junit.runner.JUnitCore tutorial.Stack_ESTest
```

If you followed all the steps so far correctly, you should see the following output:

```
JUnit version 4.12
.....
Time: 2.021

OK (5 tests)
```

Congratulations! You just generated and executed an EvoSuite test suite!

2.4   Configuring EvoSuite

Now let's take a closer look at how we can influence what EvoSuite does. First, we had to wait quite a while until test generation completed – even though this is such a simple class. A simple way to tell EvoSuite that we've waited long enough for test generation is to simply hit Ctrl+C while it is generating tests. EvoSuite will stop the search, and write the test cases generated up to that point. If you hit Ctrl+C a second time, this will kill EvoSuite completely. To try this out, generate some more tests:

```
$EVOSUITE -class tutorial.Stack -projectCP target/classes
```

After a couple of seconds, when you think coverage is sufficient, hit Ctrl+C and wait for the tests to be written. If you wait 10–20 s, you will notice that the tests we got still cover all the lines in the Stack class. So why does EvoSuite

---

[3] Note that, as is common, wrapped lines at the commandline are indicated with a backslash "\" in this paper. These lines are only wrapped to fit the text in the paper, you can also type these commands on a single line.

[4] http://www.evosuite.org/documentation/tutorial-part-2/.

take so long? The reason is that EvoSuite by default targets not only lines of code, but attempts to satisfy a range of different testing criteria, including things like mutation testing. Some of the testing goals described by these criteria are infeasible, which means that there exist no tests that satisfy; some other goals are just so difficult to cover that EvoSuite cannot easily produce the tests. This is a well-known aspect of test generation, and to deal with it, EvoSuite uses a fixed amount of time for test generation, and stops generating tests once this time has been used up. By default, this is 60 s. If we want to change this, then besides manually stopping EvoSuite, we have two options: Either we change the testing criteria to avoid the stronger criteria that may not be satisfiable, or we set the timeout explicitly.

Let's start by generating tests for a weaker criterion. We'll use branch coverage, which requires that all if-conditions evaluate to true and false, and all lines of code are covered. We can set the criterion using the -criterion argument. To generate branch coverage tests, type:

```
$EVOSUITE -class tutorial.Stack -projectCP target/classes \
          -criterion branch
```

EvoSuite will work for a couple of seconds, but once it has reached 100% branch coverage it will terminate and give us a branch coverage test suite.

Alternatively, we can tell EvoSuite how much time to spend on test generation. EvoSuite uses search-based techniques, so the time it spends on test generation is called the search budget. Unlike the target criterion, the search budget is not a command line argument, but one of many properties that configure how EvoSuite behaves. To set properties, we can use the -Dproperty=value command line argument. For example, to specify the search budget to 20 s, we would use the following command:

```
$EVOSUITE -class tutorial.Stack -projectCP target/classes \
          -Dsearch_budget=20
```

EvoSuite has many properties that can all be set using the -Dproperty=value syntax. To get an overview of the available properties, type the following command:

```
$EVOSUITE -listParameters
```

For example, by default EvoSuite will apply minimization to test cases, which means that it removes all statements that are not strictly needed to satisfy the coverage goals; this can be deactivated using -Dminimize=false. EvoSuite also minimizes the assertions it adds, and this can be changed by switching the assertion generation strategy, e.g. to -Dassertion_strategy=all. Thus, to generate long tests with loads of assertions we could use the following command:

```
$EVOSUITE -class tutorial.Stack -projectCP target/classes \
          -Dsearch_budget=20 -Dminimize=false -Dassertion_strategy=all
```

```
package tutorial;

import org.junit.Test;
import org.junit.Assert;

public class StackTest {
  @Test
  public void test() {
    Stack<Object> stack = new Stack<Object>();
    stack.push(new Object());
    Assert.assertFalse(stack.isEmpty());
  }
}
```

Fig. 2. Manually written test class for the Stack class.

2.5 Working with Existing Tests

Let's assume we have previously written some tests for our Stack class manually. For example, suppose the file src/test/java/tutorial/StackTest.java contains a test suite consisting of a single test shown in Fig. 2. This is not a very exciting test, and also one that EvoSuite could easily generate. However, in practice you might have already written some tests at the point you invoke EvoSuite, and so maybe you don't want to see generated tests for code you have already covered.

We can tell EvoSuite to only output tests that are not already covered using the junit property. For example, to tell EvoSuite to only give us tests that are not already covered by tutorial.StackTest, we would set the property using -Djunit=tutorial.StackTest. If we have multiple test classes, we can use a colon-separated list for the property.

We also need to tell EvoSuite where to find this test, as it needs to execute the test. So let's first make sure that the test is compiled and passes. If we have set up our project as a Maven project, we can simply run the following command:

```
mvn test
```

(If you are not using Maven or the example project provided online, you can also invoke JUnitCore as described above, but with the corresponding classname). This should give you the following output (among some other messages):

```
-------------------------------------------------------
 T E S T S
-------------------------------------------------------
Running tutorial.StackTest
Tests run: 1, Failures: 0, Errors: 0, Skipped: 0, Time elapsed:
    0.091 sec

Results :

Tests run: 1, Failures: 0, Errors: 0, Skipped: 0
```

If the test doesn't pass then most likely you have edited (and broken?) the `Stack` class and should fix it.

If you are using Maven to run tests, then for EvoSuite the interesting part is that Maven placed the bytecode of this test into the directory `target/test-classes`. If we want to know how great this test suite is, we can ask EvoSuite to measure the coverage for us. EvoSuite supports the command `-measureCoverage`, and we need to specify the class under test (`-class tutorial.Stack`), the tests we are interested in (`-Djunit=tutorial.StackTest`), the classpath containing the class under test and the tests (`-projectCP target/classes:target/test-classes`), and optionally, which criteria we are interested (e.g., `-criterion branch`):

```
$EVOSUITE -measureCoverage -class tutorial.Stack \
          -Djunit=tutorial.StackTest -criterion branch\
          -projectCP target/classes:target/test-classes
```

This should give you the following output (among other messages):

```
* Total number of covered goals: 3 / 7
* Total coverage: 43%
```

If we now only want to have tests that cover the remaining 4 branch coverage goals, we would invoke EvoSuite as follows:

```
$EVOSUITE -class tutorial.Stack -Djunit=tutorial.StackTest \
          -projectCP target/classes:target/test-classes \
          -criterion branch
```

Take a look at the file `evosuite-tests/tutorial/Stack_ESTest.java` to check that it worked.

2.6   Running EvoSuite on Multiple Classes

Our example project only has a single class, so all calls to EvoSuite so far used the argument `-class`. However, sometimes we might want to target more than just a single class, for example when generating a regression test suite. In this case, we can replace the `-class` argument with either `-prefix` or `-target`.

The `-target` argument specifies a classpath entry (e.g., directory or jar file). EvoSuite will then be invoked sequentially on every testable class it can find in that classpath entry. If you want to know which classes EvoSuite thinks are testable (e.g., public), then type the following command:

```
$EVOSUITE -listClasses -target target/classes
```

Since our example project only contains one class, the output should be just our example class:

```
tutorial.Stack
```

To invoke EvoSuite on all the classes in a classpath entry, type the following:

```
$EVOSUITE -target target/classes
```

EvoSuite will now go and test each class it finds, one at a time. Alternatively, we might want to test all classes in a certain package. To test all classes in the tutorial package, type the following command:

```
$EVOSUITE -prefix tutorial
```

As our project has only one class this will again just test the Stack.

The arguments -target and -prefix will run EvoSuite sequentially on each class they find. If your project is large, this might not be the ideal strategy. In fact, if your project is large and you want to use EvoSuite repeatedly, you will probably not want to run things manually on the command line, but instead use Maven to automate and parallelise things. This is not covered in this paper, but you can find a tutorial for this online[4].

3   Extending EvoSuite

EvoSuite is not only intended to serve as a test generator for developers, but also as a platform to support experimentation in search-based software testing. Often, this involves modifying or extending EvoSuite. In this section, we take a look at how one can build EvoSuite from sources, and how one can extend it.

3.1   Obtaining the EvoSuite Source Code

The source code of EvoSuite is available on GitHub in a public Git repository. The first step of this part of the tutorial thus consists of checking out the source code. How to do this will differ depending on which IDE you prefer to use. On the command line, we would check out the repository with Git directly:

```
git clone https://github.com/EvoSuite/evosuite.git
```

The source code is organised into several Maven sub-modules. That is, there is one parent pom.xml in the main directory of the source code you just checked out, and then there are several separate sub-projects in subdirectories. Let's have a closer look at the main sub-modules:

- master: EvoSuite uses a master-client architecture because things can go wrong when executing randomly generated tests (e.g., we could run out of memory). The client sends the current search result to the master process every now and then, so that even if things go wrong, we still get some tests in the end. The master module handles the user input on the command line (e.g., parsing of command line options), and then spawns client processes to do the actual test generation.
- client: The client contains all the heavy lifting. The genetic algorithm is in here, the internal representation of test cases and test suites used by the algorithm, the search operators, mechanisms to execute the test cases, all the bytecode instrumentation that is needed to produce trace information from which to calculate fitness values.

- `runtime`: This is the runtime library, i.e., all the instrumentation that is needed to make test execution deterministic, the mocked Java API, etc.
- `plugins`: There are several sub-projects in here that are plugins for various third-party tools, such as Maven, IntelliJ, Eclipse, or Jenkins.

Besides these, there are several other modules or sub-directories. You will not usually need to access any of these, but in case you are curious what they are:

- `standalone_runtime`: There is no source code in this library, this is simply a Maven sub-module that produces a standalone jar file, i.e., one that includes all the dependencies of the runtime library.
- `shaded`: There is no source code in here either; this is a Maven module that produces a version of EvoSuite where the package name is renamed from `org.evosuite` to something else. This is to allow EvoSuite to be applied to itself (which otherwise wouldn't work, as EvoSuite refuses to instrument its own code).
- `generated`: This is a sub-module in which we are putting tests generated by EvoSuite to test EvoSuite. This is still work in progress.
- `release_results`: This is not a Maven sub-module, it is just a collection of data that represents the results of the experiment on the SF110 dataset we conduct every time we perform a release.
- `src`: No Java source code in here, only some Maven-related meta-data.
- `removed`: Some source code files that are not used in the main source tree but have been useful to keep as a reference.

3.2   Building EvoSuite

If you know Maven, then it will probably not come as a surprise to you that, using Maven, Evosuite can be compiled using:

```
mvn compile
```

Most likely, your IDE will do this for you automatically. However, it is important that your IDE supports Maven, and that you have configured the project as a Maven project. If you haven't done this, what you will get are error message complaining that the compiler cannot find classes in the package `org.evosuite.xsd`. These classes are generated automatically by jaxb based on an XML schema – and this is only done if you properly compile the project with Maven.

Recall that the EvoSuite distribution consists of two jar files – one with the standalone runtime dependencies, and one for test generation. You can generate these by invoking:

```
mvn package
```

The main EvoSuite jar file is generated in the master sub-module: `master/target`. You can validate that this is the case by invoking the executable with Java:

```
java -jar master/target/evosuite-master-1.0.7-SNAPSHOT.jar
```

You should now see the help text with the usage instructions. The standalone runtime library is in directory `standalone_runtime/target/`.

Building EvoSuite can take a while, but a lot of that time is spent executing unit tests. Although we don't recommend doing that, if you do need to build a jar file quickly and can't wait for the unit tests to complete, you can add `-DskipTests` to the Maven command line.

3.3   Testing EvoSuite

As with any Maven project, you will find the source code in `src/main/java` for every sub-module, and the tests in `src/test/java`.

EvoSuite has a fair number of unit tests, but it has a lot more system and integration tests (executing all system tests takes somewhere between 1–2 h, depending on your machine). You can distinguish between the two types of tests based on the classname: all system tests have the suffix `SystemTest` in their name. Most of these system tests consist of a class under test that captures a specific testing challenge, and then invoke EvoSuite to check that it is able to cover the class fully, using a specific configuration.

In the test directories of the various sub-packages, you will find two main packages of classes: Everything with a package name starting with `org.evosuite` are the actual tests; the package `com.examples.with.different.packagename` package contains example classes under test used in the tests.

Let's take a closer look at one of the system tests. For example, open the class `org.evosuite.basic.NullStringSystemTest`, which you can find in the file `master/src/test/java/org/evosuite/basic/NullStringSystemTest.java` (Fig. 3).

The first thing worth noting is that this system test extends `SystemTestBase`. This is important for system tests, as it resets the state of EvoSuite (e.g., properties) and prepares everything for test execution (e.g., classpath). It also sets a couple of important properties for tests - if you are interested to see which ones they are, check out method `setDefaultPropertiesForTestCases` in the `SystemTestBase` class. In particular, it sets this property:

```
Properties.CLIENT_ON_THREAD = true;
```

This tells EvoSuite not to spawn a new process for the client (i.e., the part that runs the search and executes the tests). The reason for this is that a standard Java debugger will only allow you to work in the process it is attached to, not in any child processes spawned. So, if you want to, for example, set some breakpoints, it is essential that `Properties.CLIENT_ON_THREAD` is set to true, otherwise the debugger will not be involved when the breakpoint is passed.

The `testNullString` test starts by creating a new instance of EvoSuite (Line 5); then, it tells EvoSuite what the class under test is, by setting the property `Properties.TARGET_CLASS` to the fully qualified name of the class under test. As you can see, if you want to set any specific properties of EvoSuite for your test, you can simply set them in the test. The SystemTestBase will ensure

```
1   public class NullStringSystemTest extends SystemTestBase {
2
3     @Test
4     public void testNullString() {
5       EvoSuite evosuite = new EvoSuite();
6
7       String targetClass = NullString.class.getCanonicalName();
8
9       Properties.TARGET_CLASS = targetClass;
10
11      String[] command = new String[] { "-generateSuite", "-class",
           targetClass };
12
13      Object result = evosuite.parseCommandLine(command);
14      GeneticAlgorithm<?> ga = getGAFromResult(result);
15      TestSuiteChromosome best =
16          (TestSuiteChromosome) ga.getBestIndividual();
17      System.out.println("EvolvedTestSuite:\n" + best);
18
19      int goals = TestGenerationStrategy.getFitnessFactories().get(0)
20          .getCoverageGoals().size(); // assuming single fitness
               function
21      Assert.assertEquals("Wrong number of goals: ", 3, goals);
22      Assert.assertEquals("Non-optimal coverage: ", 1d,
23                          best.getCoverage(), 0.001);
24    }
25  }
```

Fig. 3. Example system test checking that EvoSuite can assign `null` values to parameters of type `String`.

that these properties are reset to their defaults after test execution. In our example, the class under test is `NullString`, which the class shown in Fig. 4. On this class, we can only achieve 100% branch coverage if EvoSuite is able to provide a null and a non-null value for String parameters. Thus, this class serves to test whether EvoSuite properly supplies null values for strings.

The test next invokes EvoSuite for the target class in Line 13. This essentially is the same as calling EvoSuite on the command line and passing in some arguments, which are captured in the `command` array here. EvoSuite will then generate some tests, and return an object that summarizes the test generation. `SystemTestBase` provides a helper function `getGAFromResult` to extract the genetic algorithm instance from this result object, called in Line 14. This GA object can be queried about various things, and most importantly, we can ask it for the best individual, i.e., the result of the test generation; this is done in Line 16. Given this test suite, we can do what we want with it – for example print it to stdout, like done in Line 17. Or, more importantly, we can write some assertions to check that the result is as expected. In this particular test, there are two assertions. The first assertion (Line 21) checks if the number of coverage goals for the class under test is 3. The second assertion (Line 23) checks

```
package com.examples.with.different.packagename; .

public class NullString {

  public boolean isNull(String s){
    if(s==null){
      return true;
    } else {
      return false;
    }
  }
}
```

Fig. 4. NullString example class that is used as a target to check if EvoSuite can produce null values as parameters for methods that expect Strings.

that we have achieved 100% coverage. Checking the number of coverage goals has proven quite useful over time, as a change in the number of coverage goals (for whatever reason) will usually have implications on the coverage that can be achieved. Debugging this case is much easier if we know explicitly that this has happened, rather than when trying to guess why the coverage percentage is not as expected.

Try to execute the test and see if it passes. Then, insert the following line before the call to evosuite.parseCommandLine:

```
Properties.NULL_PROBABILITY = 1.0;
```

Re-run the test again – EvoSuite is now configured to only generate null objects (i.e., with a probability of 1.0), so it should only achieve 67% branch coverage (it covers the default constructor and the true branch in the target method 'isNull').

Now let's remove that line again from the test to make sure we don't have a broken test! (Re-run the test after removing the line to make sure it passes again.)

3.4   Extending the Search Algorithm

Now let's make some changes to EvoSuite. As you might know, EvoSuite uses a Genetic Algorithm to drive the test generation. In a nutshell, this means that there is a population of candidate solutions (chromosomes, which are test suites in this case), and these test suites are evolved using search operators that are intended to simulate natural evolution. A fitness function estimates how good each candidate solution is. The fittest individuals have the highest likelihood of reproducing, and if they are selected for reproduction, then two parent individuals are combined to produce two new offspring individuals using a crossover operator, and then mutation makes smaller changes to these offspring.

All this is implemented in the client module, in the org.evosuite.ga package. For the abstract superclass org.evosuite.ga.metaheuristics. GeneticAlgorithm there are several concrete implementations, such as

StandardGA (a default textbook genetic algorithm), a SteadyStateGA, or Evo-
Suite's default, the MonotonicGA. If you look at the GeneticAlgorithm class
you will see that the search algorithm has plenty of members, such as a selection operator selectionFunction, the crossover operator crossoverFunction,
and a population (population). The population is a list because individuals are
ranked by their fitness value; this value is calculated by the fitnessFunctions.
This, in turn, is a list because EvoSuite typically is used with several fitness
functions at the same time, and there is a fitness value for every fitness function.

The GeneticAlgorithm class is configured with a SinglePointCrossOver
by default. Let's have a closer look at how this class looks like – open up the
class org.evosuite.ga.operators.crossover.SinglePointCrossover in an
editor. The class extends the abstract class CrossOverFunction, and implements
the method crossOver. The method receives two individuals as parents and
chooses two crossover points point1 and point2 randomly, one for each of the
two individuals. Then, it clones the parents, and on the resulting individuals
it invokes the crossover method to do the actual work. This is the beauty
of meta-heuristic search algorithms: The algorithm is independent of what the
chromosomes represent.

Let's assume that we would like to implement an alternative crossover
operator, which always cuts chromosomes in the middle, unlike the existing
crossover operators which all choose random crossover points. Let's create a
new Java class org.evosuite.ga.operators.crossover.MiddleCrossOver in
the client module (in the directory client/src/main/java/org/evosuite/
ga/operators/crossover). The class should extend the abstract class
CrossOverFunction, which means it has to implement the method crossOver.
The skeleton thus looks like this:

```
package org.evosuite.ga.operators.crossover;

import org.evosuite.ga.Chromosome;
import org.evosuite.ga.ConstructionFailedException;

public class MiddleCrossOver extends CrossOverFunction {

    @Override
    public void crossOver(Chromosome parent1, Chromosome parent2)
        throws ConstructionFailedException {
        // TODO
    }
}
```

In order to implement this crossover function, we need to understand one
important aspect: Textbook examples on genetic algorithms will usually assume
a fixed number of genes in a chromosome. However, unlike many other standard
applications of genetic algorithms, the size of individuals in EvoSuite can vary,
as we cannot know the right number of test cases before we even start the search.
Consequently, what is the "middle" is different for every individual.

Thus, the first thing we need to check is whether our individuals even have more than one test case. If they don't there's no way we can do any crossover:

```
if (parent1.size() < 2 || parent2.size() < 2) {
    return;
}
```

After this, we can assume that both parent chromosomes have at least 2 tests, and so we can calculate the middle of each of them:

```
int middle1 = (int) Math.round(parent1.size() / 2.0);
int middle2 = (int) Math.round(parent2.size() / 2.0);
```

The crossover operator in EvoSuite changes a chromosome in place. That means we first need to create the offspring as direct copies of the parents:

```
Chromosome t1 = parent1.clone();
Chromosome t2 = parent2.clone();
```

Now we can change the offspring using the `crossOver` method, which takes as parameters (1) the other chromosome with which to cross over, (2) the crossover point in the chromosome the method is invoked on, and (3) the crossover point in the other chromosome:

```
parent1.crossOver(t2, middle1, middle2);
parent2.crossOver(t1, middle2, middle1);
```

That's it! Let's write a test case `MiddleCrossOverTest.java` to find out if it works. Add the new file in the appropriate directory in the `client` module (`client/src/test/java/org/evosuite/ga/operators/crossover/`).

The tests in the client module have a `DummyChromosome` implementation that we use for the test. A `DummyChromosome` takes a list of integers, and does mutation and crossover. For example, we could create to parents with different sizes (e.g., 4 and 2), and then check if the resulting individuals have the right genes. For example, the test could look like this:

```
@Test
public void testSinglePointCrossOver() throws
    ConstructionFailedException {

    DummyChromosome parent1 = new DummyChromosome(1, 2, 3, 4);
    DummyChromosome parent2 = new DummyChromosome(5, 6);

    MiddleCrossOver xover = new MiddleCrossOver();

    DummyChromosome offspring1 = new DummyChromosome(parent1);
    DummyChromosome offspring2 = new DummyChromosome(parent2);

    xover.crossOver(offspring1, offspring2);

    assertEquals(Arrays.asList(1, 2, 6), offspring1.getGenes());
    assertEquals(Arrays.asList(5, 3, 4), offspring2.getGenes());
}
```

If you did everything correctly, then this test should pass. Does it?

Now that we've got this wonderful new crossover operator, the next big question is: How do we make EvoSuite use it? EvoSuite is highly configurable, and the configuration is controlled by the class `org.evosuite.Properties` in the client module. In this class, you'll find all the different properties that EvoSuite supports – there are a lot of them. Each property consists of a public static field in all caps, which is how the properties are accessed from within code. In addition, each property has `@Parameter` annotation, in which we define a key – this is the key we use on the command line, if we set properties using the `-Dkey=value` syntax. If we look for crossover, we will find the following relevant code:

```
public enum CrossoverFunction {
    SINGLEPOINTRELATIVE, SINGLEPOINTFIXED, SINGLEPOINT, COVERAGE
}

@Parameter(key = "crossover_function", group = "Search Algorithm",
    description = "Crossover function during search")
public static CrossoverFunction CROSSOVER_FUNCTION =
    CrossoverFunction.SINGLEPOINTRELATIVE;
```

Thus, there is a property `Properties.CROSSOVER_FUNCTION`, and it is of type of the enum class `CrossoverFunction`, which contains all the possible crossover functions. In the future maybe EvoSuite will see some way to make it extensible at runtime, but for now we need to add our new crossover operator to the enum:

```
public enum CrossoverFunction {
    SINGLEPOINTRELATIVE, SINGLEPOINTFIXED, SINGLEPOINT,
    COVERAGE, MIDDLE
}
```

The final thing we need to change is the place where this property is read and the crossover function is instantiated. If we look up where in the source code the property `Properties.CROSSOVER_FUNCTION` field is used, we see that it is used in `org.evosuite.strategy.PropertiesSuiteGAFactory` and `PropertiesTestGAFactory`. These are two factory classes that create and configure a genetic algorithm object based on the values in the Properties class. As we are doing whole test suite generation (it's EvoSuite's default), let's edit `PropertiesSuiteGAFactory`. Find the method `getCrossoverFunction()`. It contains a switch over the value of our property, and calls the corresponding constructor. Thus, we need to add a new case:

```
case MIDDLE:
    return new MiddleCrossOver();
```

That's it! Now we're ready to generate a jar file and use EvoSuite with our new crossover function. Recall that you can generate the jar file (which will be located in `master/target`) using:

```
mvn package
```

When we now run EvoSuite with this jar file, we can specify to use our new crossover function using `-Dcrossover_function=Middle`. Likely this operator will not make a difference – it's just an example for illustration purposes.

However, in the next section we will look at how to run experiments with Evo-Suite in general, and you could investigate this crossover operator with some similar experiments.

4   Running Experiments with EvoSuite

4.1   Preparing the Experiment

For the third part of the tutorial, we will be looking at how one can collect data about the test generation. We will use a simple example scenario: EvoSuite by default uses a combination of different coverage criteria [10]. What are the effects of this combination over using just branch coverage as target criterion? A reasonable hypothesis would be that the combination leads to more tests, and better test suites. But is that actually true? Let's run an experiment to find out!

The experiment will involve running EvoSuite on a number of classes with its default configuration and configured to only use branch coverage, and then to take different measurements of the resulting test suites. When doing experiments of this kind, the selection of classes has implications on how much our results generalize: If we use a very specific and small selection of classes, then whatever our findings, they may only be relevant to that particular type of classes. Therefore, we generally would want to select as many as possible, as diverse as possible, and as representative as possible classes in order to get results that generalize. However, this is not the aim of this tutorial, so let's just use a selection of classes we've prepared for this tutorial. The tutorial assumes that you download and extract the archive containing the selection of example classes (but note you can, in principle, use any collection of Java classes instead):

```
wget http://evosuite.org/files/tutorial/Tutorial_Experiments.zip
unzip Tutorial_Experiments.zip
```

Change into the main directory again, and compile the example project with Maven:

```
cd Tutorial_Experiments
mvn compile
```

We will be invoking EvoSuite directly in this part of the tutorial. To avoid having to set the classpath repeatedly, let's set up EvoSuite. First, we need to download all dependency jar files of the example project. To make things slightly more challenging, the class `tutorial.Bank` has a (quite artificial) dependency on the Apache Commons Collections library. When running EvoSuite from Maven, then Maven downloads all dependencies and sets up the classpath for us automatically – but when we run EvoSuite directly it is our responsibility to set up a correct classpath. Fortunately, this is easy enough: To download all dependencies, type the following Maven command:

```
mvn dependency:copy-dependencies -DincludeScope=runtime
```

This command downloads all dependency jar files, and puts them into the `target/dependency` directory. The reason for specifying the scope to be run-time using `-DincludeScope=runtime` is that the project has test dependencies on JUnit and EvoSuite – but neither of these dependencies are necessary in order to generate some tests for the classe under test, we really just need the compile and runtime dependencies. Thus, the full project classpath consists of the classes in `target/classes` and the jar file `target/dependency/commons-collections-3.2.2.jar`. We can store this information by creating an `evosuite.properties` file that saves this classpath, by use the following command:

```
$EVOSUITE -setup target/classes
    target/dependency/commons-collections-3.2.2.jar
```

Check that the resulting evosuite-files/evosuite.properties at the top has the correct classpath set:

```
CP=target/classes:target/dependency/commons-collections-3.2.2.jar
```

4.2   Collecting Data with EvoSuite

Let's start by invoking EvoSuite on the `Stack` class in our project, targeting only branch coverage:

```
$EVOSUITE -class tutorial.Person -criterion branch
```

We have already had a closer look at the test suites that EvoSuite produces. However, EvoSuite also produces data to document what happened. This is stored in the following file:

```
evosuite-report/statistics.csv
```

Use your favourite editor to have a closer look at this file. You should see something like this:

```
TARGET_CLASS,criterion,Coverage,Total_Goals,Covered_Goals
tutorial.Person,BRANCH,1.0,3,3
```

This file is in comma-separated value format. The first row contains headers showing what the individual columns contain, and then the rows contain the actual data. The first column contains the name of the class we tested (`tutorial.Person`). The second column shows us the coverage criteria that we used – in this case we see the full list of criteria that EvoSuite uses by default, separated by semicolons. The third column tells us the achieved coverage – 1.0 in this case, which means we have 100% coverage (yay!). This is calculated based on the ratio of coverage goals covered to total goals (last two columns).

Let's test the same class again, but this time using line and branch coverage:

```
$EVOSUITE -class tutorial.Person -criterion line:branch
```

If we look at evosuite-report/statistics.csv again we'll see a new row:

```
TARGET_CLASS,criterion,Coverage,Total_Goals,Covered_Goals
tutorial.Person,BRANCH,1.0,3,3
tutorial.Person,LINE;BRANCH,1.0,9,9
```

As you can see, we now have a new entry for our second call to EvoSuite, where we specified branch and line coverage as target criteria.

Let's try another class and criterion:

```
$EVOSUITE -class tutorial.Company -criterion line
```

Again, the `evosuite-report/statistics.csv` file will now contain a new line:

```
TARGET_CLASS,criterion,Coverage,Total_Goals,Covered_Goals
tutorial.Person,BRANCH,1.0,3,3
tutorial.Person,LINE;BRANCH,1.0,9,9
tutorial.Company,LINE,1.0,4,4
```

The `tutorial.Company` class has four lines of code, and the generated tests cover all of them. Great!

4.3   Setting Output Variables

We now know where to find data about the test generation. However, the data we have seen does not help us to answer the questions we would like to investigate. Recall that our scenario was that we wanted to know if the default combination of criteria leads to more tests, and better test suites. We cannot answer this with the data in the statistics.csv files currently—the coverage values cannot be compared (they refer to different criteria), and neither can the numbers of goals.

Fortunately, we can generate more data than just the columns our data file has shown us so far. EvoSuite has a property `output_variables` which determines which values should be written to the `statistics.csv` file. Before we do that, let's remove the old statistics.csv file:

```
rm evosuite-report/statistics.csv
```

This is important if we decide to change the columns of the data files – our data file currently has a header row and three data rows that assume there are five columns; if we change the columns, and additional rows will not match the existing data.

Now, let's include some new values. There are two main types of output variables: *runtime variables*, which are the result of computation (e.g., the coverage), whereas *properties* are the input properties we can set. For example, `TARGET_CLASS` and `criterion` are properties, whereas `Total_Goals` and `Covered_Goals` are runtime variables. There are some inconsistencies in terms of which variables are capitalised – this is for historic reasons, as changing the runtime variable names may break existing experimental infrastructure. However, in a future major release we may decide to change the variable names to a consistent format.

Let's think about what values we would like to include. Our first question is whether the combination of criteria leads to more tests. The corresponding output variable is `Size`, which reports the number of tests. However, let's not forget that these are unit tests, where a single test can consist of several statements. Thus, we can also use the `Length` variable to count the total number of statements, which is maybe a better representation of the size of a test suite.

Our second question is whether the combination of criteria leads to better tests. A standard way to evaluate test suites is by measuring coverage – but which criterion would we use to measure this? A better way might be to compare the test suites in terms of their mutation scores. The mutation score is a metric based on the idea of Mutation Analysis, and quantifies how many artificial faults a test suite can find. There are several mutation analysis frameworks for Java available, but EvoSuite also has a basic mutation functionality integrated [8], as it can aim to generate tests that kill mutants directly. The output variable for this is MutationScore.

To summarize, for our experiment we would like to have the following data:

- Class under test (TARGET_CLASS)
- Criteria (criterion)
- Size (Size)
- Length (Length)
- Mutation score (MutationScore)

The list of variables is passed as a comma separated list to the output_variables property. Let's try this out:

```
$EVOSUITE -class tutorial.Company -criterion branch
    -Doutput_variables=TARGET_CLASS,criterion,Size,Length,MutationScore
```

If you look at the resulting evosuite-report/statistics.csv file, you should see something like this:

```
TARGET_CLASS,criterion,Size,Length,MutationScore
tutorial.Company,BRANCH,1,2,1.0
```

Thus, we have just generated one test consisting of two statements, and this test killed all the mutants EvoSuite generated for the class.

If we look at the test suite in evosuite-tests/tutorial/Company_ESTest.java you should see something like this:

```
@Test(timeout = 4000)
public void test0() throws Throwable {
    Company company0 = new Company("");
    String string0 = company0.getName();
    assertEquals("", string0);
}
```

Note that the assertion is not included in EvoSuite's statement count. This is because assertions are not generated as part of the search-based test generation, but are added in a post-processing step.

4.4   Running an Experiment

Now let's run an actual experiment and gather some data. We would like to get information on all classes in our project, so we need to run EvoSuite on all of them. Furthermore, let's not forget that EvoSuite is randomized: If you run it twice in sequence, you will get different results. That also means that if you get a very large test suite in one run, you may get a test suite with a different size in the next run. In general, when we have randomized algorithms, we need to run repetitions, and statistically analyze our data. Therefore, we'll generate tests on all our classes, and repeat this 10 times. Furthermore, we need to do all this twice, once with only branch coverage, and once with the default criteria. Before we start the experiment, let's remove the old statistics.csv file again:

```
rm evosuite-report/statistics.csv
```

Now, let's run the experiment. We will tell EvoSuite to test all classes in the tutorial package using the -prefix argument, and pass in the target criterion (branch) as well as our output variables.

```
$EVOSUITE -criterion branch -prefix tutorial -Dshow_progress=false \
    -Doutput_variables==TARGET_CLASS,criterion,Size,Length,MutationScore
```

We added -Dshow_progress=false; this isn't essential, but the progress bar does tend to clutter up log files if we perform larger numbers of runs, so we deactivated it here. If you look at the data file, you should see something like this:

```
TARGET_CLASS,criterion,Size,Length,MutationScore
tutorial.ATM,BRANCH,10,75,0.3888888888888889
tutorial.ATMCard,BRANCH,8,40,1.0
tutorial.Bank,BRANCH,4,15,0.8
tutorial.BankAccount,BRANCH,2,6,0.8
tutorial.Owner,BRANCH,1,1,1.0
tutorial.CurrentAccount,BRANCH,2,7,0.6521739130434783
tutorial.SavingsAccount,BRANCH,2,7,0.8529411764705882
tutorial.Company,BRANCH,1,2,1.0
tutorial.Person,BRANCH,2,4,0.0
```

We now have data for all classes, for the first configuration we are interested in (branch coverage). If we re-run this command without the -criterion branch argument, we'll get some more data for all classes for the other configuration (default coverage criteria). When analysing this data, we need to distinguish between the two configurations; we can either use the criterion column we have already added, or we can also label our configurations, using the -Dconfiguration_id=name syntax, and then including this property in the output variables. Thus, to run our experiment, we will need the following two commands, one for branch coverage, one for the default combination:

```
$EVOSUITE -Dconfiguration_id=Default \
    -prefix tutorial -Doutput_variables=configuration_id,\
    TARGET_CLASS,criterion,Size,Length,MutationScore
$EVOSUITE -Dconfiguration_id=Branch -criterion branch \
    -prefix tutorial -Doutput_variables=configuration_id,\
    TARGET_CLASS,criterion,Size,Length,MutationScore
```

This will result in something like the following in `statistics.csv`:

```
configuration_id,TARGET_CLASS,criterion,Size,Length,MutationScore
Default,tutorial.ATM,[...],14,109,0.3611111111111111
Default,tutorial.ATMCard,[...],13,65,1.0
Default,tutorial.Bank,[...],6,22,0.8
Default,tutorial.BankAccount,[...],8,24,1.0
Default,tutorial.Owner,[...],1,1,1.0
Default,tutorial.CurrentAccount,[...],4,12,0.7608695652173914
Default,tutorial.SavingsAccount,[...],4,12,0.8823529411764706
Default,tutorial.Company,[...],3,6,1.0
Default,tutorial.Person,[...],6,12,1.0
Branch,tutorial.ATM,BRANCH,10,77,0.4166666666666667
Branch,tutorial.ATMCard,BRANCH,8,40,1.0
Branch,tutorial.Bank,BRANCH,4,15,0.8
Branch,tutorial.BankAccount,BRANCH,2,6,0.8
Branch,tutorial.Owner,BRANCH,1,1,1.0
Branch,tutorial.CurrentAccount,BRANCH,2,7,0.6739130434782609
Branch,tutorial.SavingsAccount,BRANCH,3,8,0.6470588235294118
Branch,tutorial.Company,BRANCH,1,2,1.0
Branch,tutorial.Person,BRANCH,2,4,0.0
```

(In this example, we replaced the list of criteria (`LINE;BRANCH;...`) with `[...]` to make it fit into this article.)

Just by eyeballing the results, we can see that the default configuration leads to more tests in all classes except `tutorial.Owner`. Your specific data will look different – in the data down above, the mutation score is higher for `tutorial.Person`, `tutorial.SavingsAccount`, `tutorial.CurrentAccount`, but surprisingly, lower for `tutorial.ATM`. How can that be the case? Recall that EvoSuite is randomized—sometimes test generation will be lucky to hit a specific value that is good at killing some mutants, sometimes it isn't. What we need to establish, then, is not whether one configuration is better than the other in one particular run, but on average. Thus, we need to repeat our experiment several times, and do some more rigorous analysis.

A simple way to do the repetitions would be to simply wrap the call in a bash-loop to run it, for example, 5 times:

```
for I in {1..5}; do $EVOSUITE -Dconfiguration_id=Default [...] ; done
for I in {1..5}; do $EVOSUITE -Dconfiguration_id=Branch [...] ; done
```

This is going to take quite a while. In fact, 5 repetitions is not even a suitably large number for serious experiments, ideally you'd want 30 repetitions or more to get representative results.

4.5 Analyzing Results

Now we have some data – from at least one run, and if you were patient enough, maybe from 5 or more additional runs. What are we going to do with that data? The best thing to do now is to use statistical analysis package to process and analyze the data. For example, using Python's Matplotlib[5] we can produce the boxplots shown in Fig. 5. Besides visualizing the data, you will also need to statistically analyze it [1]. If we consider the data of our experiment, you will find that, with statistical significance, we can say that test suites generated for branch coverage have different sizes, numbers of statements, and mutation scores than those generated for the default criteria. The effect size tells us that for all three of these properties there is a medium increase when using the default configuration over the branch configuration. So all in all, it sounds like a good idea to use the default configuration! (After all, that is why it is the default configuration...)

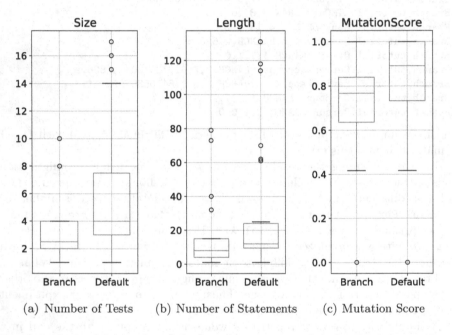

(a) Number of Tests   (b) Number of Statements   (c) Mutation Score

Fig. 5. Analysis of the results on the branch coverage vs. default criteria comparison.

4.6 Other Useful Variables

To get a full overview of the available output variables, the best place is currently the source code, in particular the file `RuntimeVariable.java` in the `client` module (package `org.evosuite.statistics`). For example, if you want to know how certain values evolved over time, there are timeline variables that capture this data for you. Assume we would like to see how branch coverage evolves over the first 30 s of the search, and we want to sample once every second. To do this, we would add an output variable `CoverageTimeline`, and specify the sampling interval using `-Dtimeline_interval=1000`:

---

[5] https://matplotlib.org/.

```
$EVOSUITE -class tutorial.ATM -criterion branch \
-Doutput_variables=TARGET_CLASS,BranchCoverage,CoverageTimeline \
-Dtimeline_interval=1000 -Dsearch_budget=30
```

As we specified a time budget of 30 s in total (-Dsearch_budget=30), the
statistics.csv file will now have 30 columns labeled CoverageTimeline_T1
up to CoverageTimeline_T30, with the individual values for each second of the
search.

As another interesting example, the BranchCoverageBitString variable will
produce a string of 0 and 1 digits, where each digit represents one branch in the
program, and 1 indicates that the branch was covered. This bitstring allows us
to compare whether specific branches were covered by specific configurations.

5   Conclusions

In this tutorial, we covered basic usage of EvoSuite on the command-line, some
simple changes to EvoSuite's source code, and some basic experiments. If you
want to learn more about EvoSuite, here are some pointers:

- http://www.evosuite.org: The main EvoSuite website contains many papers
  related to EvoSuite, experimental data to reproduce past experiments, and
  documentation. The documentation includes a more elaborate version of this
  tutorial, and instructions on how to use the different plugins (e.g., Maven).
- https://github.com/EvoSuite/evosuite: EvoSuite is open source, licensed
  with the GNU Lesser General Public License version 3. The source code
  repository is on GitHub, as is an issue tracker. Since EvoSuite is an open
  source project, its continued maintenance depends on contributions. If you
  produce work or improvements to EvoSuite, please do consider to feed them
  back to the project!

References

1. Arcuri, A., Briand, L.: A Hitchhiker's guide to statistical tests for assessing randomized algorithms in software engineering. Softw. Test. Verif. Reliab. (STVR)
   24(3) (2012)
2. Arcuri, A., Campos, J., Fraser, G.: Unit test generation during software development: EvoSuite plugins for Maven, IntelliJ and Jenkins. In: IEEE International
   Conference on Software Testing, Verification, and Validation (ICST) (2016)
3. Arcuri, A., Fraser, G.: Parameter tuning or default values? An empirical investigation in search-based software engineering. Empir. Softw. Eng. (EMSE) **18**(3),
   594–623 (2013)
4. Arcuri, A., Fraser, G., Galeotti, J.P.: Automated unit test generation for classes
   with environment dependencies. In: ACM/IEEE International Conference on Automated Software Engineering (ASE), pp. 79–90. ACM (2014)
5. Arcuri, A., Fraser, G., Galeotti, J.P.: Generating TCP/UDP network data for automated unit test generation. In: ACM SIGSOFT Symposium on the Foundations
   of Software Engineering (FSE), pp. 155–165 (2015)

6. Fraser, G., Arcuri, A.: Whole test suite generation. IEEE Trans. Softw. Eng. (TSE) **39**(2), 276–291 (2013)
7. Fraser, G., Arcuri, A.: A large-scale evaluation of automated unit test generation using EvoSuite. ACM Trans. Softw. Eng. Methodol. (TOSEM) **24**(2), 8 (2014)
8. Fraser, G., Arcuri, A.: Achieving scalable mutation-based generation of whole test suites. Empir. Softw. Eng. **20**(3), 783–812 (2015)
9. Panichella, A., Kifetew, F.M., Tonella, P.: Reformulating branch coverage as a many-objective optimization problem. In: IEEE International Conference on Software Testing, Verification and Validation (ICST), pp. 1–10. IEEE (2015)
10. Rojas, J.M., Campos, J., Vivanti, M., Fraser, G., Arcuri, A.: Combining multiple coverage criteria in search-based unit test generation. In: Barros, M., Labiche, Y. (eds.) SSBSE 2015. LNCS, vol. 9275, pp. 93–108. Springer, Cham (2015). https://doi.org/10.1007/978-3-319-22183-0_7
11. Rojas, J.M., Fraser, G., Arcuri, A.: Seeding strategies in search-based unit test generation. Softw. Test. Verif. Reliab. **26**(5), 366–401 (2016)

A Preliminary Systematic Mapping Study of Human Competitiveness of SBSE

Jerffeson Souza[1]([✉]), Allysson Allex Araújo[2], Raphael Saraiva[1],
Pamella Soares[1], and Camila Maia[3]

[1] Optimization in Software Engineering Group, State University of Ceará,
Fortaleza, Brazil
jerffeson.souza@uece.br
[2] Optimization in Software Engineering Group, Federal University of Ceará,
Crateús, Brazil
[3] Optimization in Software Engineering Group, Federal Data Processing Service,
Fortaleza, Brazil
http://goes.uece.br

Abstract. Search Based Software Engineering (SBSE) seeks to reformulate Software Engineering complex problems as search problems to be, hereafter, optimized through the usage of artificial intelligence techniques. As pointed out by Harman in 2007, in his seminal paper about the current state and future of SBSE, it would be very attractive to have convincing examples of human competitive results in order to champion the field. A landmark effort in this direction was made by Souza and others, in the paper titled "The Human Competitiveness of Search Based Software Engineering", published at SSBSE'2010, voted by the SBSE community as the most influential paper of the past editions in the 10th anniversary of the SSBSE, in 2018. This paper presents a preliminary systematic mapping study to provide an overview of the current state of human competitiveness of SBSE, carried out via a snowball reading of Souza's paper. The analyses of the 29 selected papers showed a growing interest in this topic, especially since 2010. Seven of those papers presented relevant experimental results, thus demonstrating the human competitiveness of results produced by SBSE approaches.

Keywords: Human competitiveness
Search based software engineering · SBSE · Systematic mapping study

1 Introduction

Search Based Software Engineering (SBSE) seeks to reformulate Software Engineering (SE) complex problems as "search problems" to be, hereafter, optimized through the usage of artificial intelligence techniques [1]. This approach to optimization is natural, since several SE problems are characterized by many complex and competing objectives in large search spaces [2]. In these scenarios, automated optimization techniques pose as natural candidates [3].

© Springer Nature Switzerland AG 2018
T. E. Colanzi and P. McMinn (Eds.): SSBSE 2018, LNCS 11036, pp. 131–146, 2018.
https://doi.org/10.1007/978-3-319-99241-9_6

It has been argued that comparisons with results produced by humans are often couched as a criterion for success for the field of machine intelligence [4]. As stated by Samuel, the aim is to get machines to exhibit behavior, which if done by humans, would be assumed to involve the use of intelligence [5]. This assumption has attracted great interest in results that can be said to be human competitive. A result obtained by automatic computation is said to be human competitive if it meets any of the eight criteria proposed by Koza *et al.* [6]. As we can see in Table 1, many of these criteria refer to patents and existing results.

Table 1. Eight criteria for saying that an automatically created result is human-competitive [6].

	Criterion
A	The result was patented as an invention in the past, is an improvement over a patented invention, or would qualify today as a patent able new invention
B	The result is equal to or better than a result that was accepted as a new scientific result at the time when it was published in a peer-reviewed scientific journal
C	The result is equal to or better than a result that was placed into a database or archiveof results maintained by an internationally recognized panel of scientific experts
D	The result is publish able in its own right as a new scientific result—independent ofthe fact that the result was mechanically created
E	The result is equal to or better than the most recent human-created solution to along-standing problem for which there has been a succession of increasingly better human-created solutions
F	The result is equal to or better than a result that was considered an achievement in its field at the time it was first discovered
G	The result solves a problem of indisputable difficulty in its field
H	The result holds its own or wins a regulated competition involving human contestants (in the form of either live human players or human-written computer programs)

As stated 11 years ago by Harman in his seminal paper about the future of SBSE, it would be very attractive to have convincing examples of human competitive results in order to champion the field of SBSE [2]. Throughout these years, a few works have addressed and proved the human competitiveness of SBSE (e.g. [7–9]). A landmark effort in this direction was made by Souza *et al.* in the paper titled "The Human Competitiveness of Search Based Software Engineering" [10]. This work sparked the interest in discussing the human competitiveness of SBSE, which can be seen through the increasing number of articles addressing this issue. In addition, this paper was honored by the SBSE community as the most influential paper of the past editions in the 10th anniversary of the Symposium on Search Based Software Engineering (SSBSE'18).

Therefore, motivated by this ongoing interest, the relevance of this particular subject to the SBSE community and the distinguished award, we performed a preliminary systematic mapping study to provide an overview of the current state of human competitiveness of SBSE. We refer to this as a preliminary study because we make no claim for completeness, since we have solely focused in carrying out a snowball reading of Souza's *et al.* paper. Aligned with this goal, our purpose is three-fold: (1) to discuss when, how many times and in which context human competitiveness has been addressed in SBSE; (2) to bring up new results, from other researchers, related to the human competitiveness of SBSE; and finally, (3) to point out to some open questions and remaining challenges to be addressed on that issue.

2   Systematic Mapping Study

We have opted for conducting a systematic mapping study instead of a systematic literature review due to the type of question that each one answers. While a systematic literature review asks a fairly specific set of questions, a systematic mapping study asks more general questions [11]. The main goal of a systematic mapping study is to provide an overview of a research area and identify the quantity and type of research and results available within it [12]. To achieve this goal, we adopted the mapping process proposed by Petersen *et al.* [13] which is described along the next three subsections.

2.1   Definition of Research Questions

As we previously discussed, our general goal is to provide an overview of the research that addresses human competitiveness in SBSE. In order to accomplish this goal, we formulated the following research questions:

- **RQ$_1$**: How have the publications addressing human competitiveness in SBSE evolved over the years? *Rationale*: this question was formulated aiming at investigating the number, constancy, publication fora and, finally, which SE areas the human competitiveness have been covered in SBSE.
- **RQ$_2$**: In which context the human competitiveness has been discussed by the SBSE community? *Rationale*: through this question, we are interested in analysing whether and how many of the papers empirically evaluated human competitiveness or merely mentioned it as baseline argument.

2.2   Conduct Search for Primary Sources and Screening of Papers

In this step of the systematic mapping, the list of papers to be further analyzed is defined. To perform our search, we followed the work of Webster and Watson [14], which advocate the use of snowballing as the main method for finding relevant literature. Snowballing refers to using the reference list of a paper or the citations to the paper to identify additional papers [12]. Thus, we carried out a snowball reading of Souza's *et al.* work as a start paper, by considering both forward and backward procedures. It is worth to note that human competitive studies in automatic computation have been widely investigated before (e.g., [4,6]), however, we are interested solely in the works in the context of SBSE.

According to Wohlin [15], snowballing could benefit from not only looking at the reference lists and citations, but to complement it with a systematic way of looking at where papers are actually referenced and where papers are cited. Using the references and the citations is referred to as backward and forward snowballing, respectively. In our research, the citations were obtained through the list provided by Google Scholar[1]. As depicted in Fig. 1, we identified a set of 53 and 37 papers as to backward and forward, respectively.

Fig. 1. Backward and forward snowballing.

In addition, Fig. 2 summarizes our three-stage approach to search and select the primary sources. As we previously discussed, we initially defined the article of Souza's *et al.* as a start paper. In Stage 2, we identified a set of 90 papers through backward and forward snowball readings. Then, we performed the following inclusion/exclusion procedures. We looked for the title, abstract, keywords, introduction, conclusion and the entire paper whenever necessary. Our inclusion criteria was solely the clear mention of human competitiveness related to SBSE. Regarding exclusion, we removed duplicated papers and those who were not available online. Finally, after the inclusion/exclusion processes were performed, we have selected 29 papers in Stage 3 to form the primary sources of our mapping study.

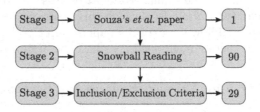

Fig. 2. Three-stage approach to search and select the primary sources.

2.3   Classification Scheme and Data Extraction

After analysing all selected papers, we classified them into three major dimensions: (i) Publication forum (journal, conference or thesis/dissertation) where

---

[1] https://scholar.google.com/scholar?cites=12366459541329916171&as_sdt=2005.

Table 2. Mapping primary sources.

ID	Reference	Year	SE areas						Type of publication				Context	
			Requirements/ specifications	Theory of SBSE	Management	Software/ program verification	Distribution, maintenance and enhancement	Software properties	Conference paper	Journal paper	Master thesis	PhD dissertation	Empirical Evaluation	Baseline argument
[S1]	[7]	2006	✓		.				✓				✓	
[S2]	[2]	2007		✓					✓					✓
[S3]	[16]	2009	✓						✓				✓	
[S4]	[10]	2010	✓		✓	✓			✓					✓
[S5]	[17]	2010		✓	✓				✓					✓
[S6]	[18]	2011							✓					✓
[S7]	[19]	2011	✓							✓				✓
[S8]	[20]	2011	✓						✓					✓
[S9]	[21]	2011	✓							✓			✓	
[S10]	[22]	2011		✓					✓					✓
[S11]	[23]	2012		✓					✓				✓	
[S12]	[24]	2012	✓			✓			✓					✓
[S13]	[25]	2012				✓				✓			✓	
[S14]	[26]	2012				✓				✓				✓
[S15]	[27]	2013				✓			✓				✓	
[S16]	[9]	2013					✓		✓				✓	
[S17]	[28]	2013				✓				✓				✓
[S18]	[29]	2013								✓				✓
[S19]	[30]	2013	✓					✓		✓				✓
[S20]	[31]	2014	✓								✓			✓
[S21]	[32]	2014	✓			✓				✓				✓
[S22]	[33]	2015	✓							✓				✓
[S23]	[34]	2016					✓		✓					✓
[S24]	[35]	2016				✓				✓				✓
[S25]	[36]	2017								✓				✓
[S26]	[37]	2017				✓				✓				✓
[S27]	[38]	2017				✓						✓		✓
[S28]	[39]	2017					✓		✓					✓
[S29]	[40]	2017			✓							✓		✓

the publication appeared; (ii) SE area according to the 2012 ACM Computing Classification System and, finally, (iii) Context of discussion to which the categories were (a) works that empirically evaluate the human competitiveness or (b) works which only mention it as part of their fundamental background.

For gathering the data we created a Google Sheets file to collect the required information about all papers. In addition to the dimensions previous defined, the spreadsheet contained the following standard data fields: primary study ID, reference, title of the paper, name of the authors and year of publication. Hence, a meeting with the authors was organized in order to classify each single paper for each criterion. Table 2 lists the details of the 29 papers that form the primary sources of our mapping study. We have omitted the title of the paper and the name of the authors. However, by interlinking the ID and Reference, it is possible to identify these information, if intended.

3   Results and Analyses

In this section we present and analyse the outcomes obtained by our mapping study. Initially, we discuss the results related to the research question concerned to the analysis of the publications throughout the years and, then, in which context they have been discussed by the community.

3.1   RQ$_1$: Number and Frequency of Publications

We can observe by analysing Fig. 3 that human competitiveness is a frequent topic in SBSE research. Since 2009, it has at least one work dealing with this subject. In particular, 2007 can be considered a significant year, since it was the year in which Harman clarified and pointed out the necessity of having convincing examples of human competitive results in SBSE [S2]. In addition, we can see that the number of works on this topic considerably increased after Souza's *et al.* paper, published in 2010. Another aspect to be emphasized is the continuous engagement and interest of the community up to date. For instance, in 2017, seven years after Souza's *et al.* paper, we identified another peak of works (5) as higher as 2011 and 2013 (5).

Moreover, we have investigated in which publication fora the human competitiveness has been addressed more frequently. As we can see in Fig. 4, the Symposium on Search Based Software Engineering poses as the most frequent venue for publications, with 5 primary sources [S4, S6, S12, S16, S23]. Considering only the conference venues, the SSBSE was followed by the Brazilian Symposium on Software Engineering, with 2 publications [S3, S10]. Among journal publications, the International Journal of Computer Applications [S9, S13], Journal of Empirical Software Engineering [S18, S24] and the ACM Transactions on Software Engineering and Methodology [S19, S21] were the most frequent ones, with 2 publications each.

Complementing the previous analyses, we examined how many of the papers correspond to conference fora, journal publications or final course assignments.

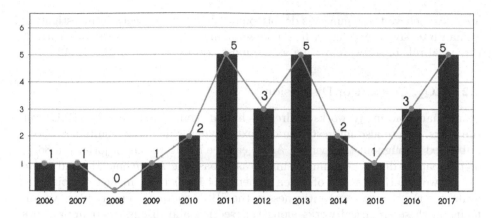

Fig. 3. Publication per year since 2006.

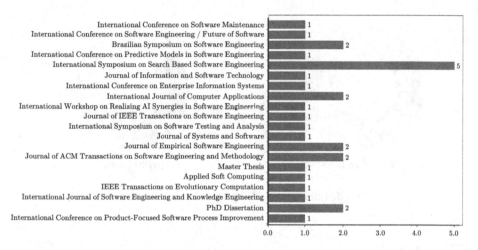

Fig. 4. Publication for a summary.

As depicted by the Fig. 5a, there is a certain similarity between the conference (48.3%) and journal (41.4%) publications. In addition to these results, we identified 1 Master Thesis [S20] and 2 PhD Dissertations [S27, S29], respectively representing 3.4% and 6.9% of the total.

Furthermore, we investigated in which SE area the human competitiveness has been addressed. Figure 5b shows the number of publications classified according to the 2012 ACM Computing Classification System. Additionally to this classification, we included a category named "Theory of SBSE" which reflects those papers which are focused on discussing the role of SBSE as research field [S2, S5, S10, S11, S17]. As we can see, human competitiveness was addressed in 5 different SE areas, with Requirements/Specification [S1, S3, S4, S7-S9, S12, S19, S20, S22] and Software/Product verification [S4, S13-S15, S18, S21, S24, S26, S27, S29] being the ones with more papers with 32.3% of the total, each area. We believe these numbers denote on one hand the concern in investigating human-intensive processes such as release planning [41] and, on the other hand, the usual role of software testing as the most addressed area in SBSE [42].

3.2   RQ₂: Context of Discussion

More than how many works addressed human competitiveness in SBSE over the years, we are also interested in contextualizing which new results have been published throughout this period. As we can see in Fig. 6, the majority (75.86%) of the papers discussed human simply as a baseline argument. Beyond these works, we identified a set of seven papers (24.14%) that, in fact, empirically evaluated the human competitiveness in the SBSE context. In particular, we will focus on these empirical works along this section and discuss their approaches and contributions.

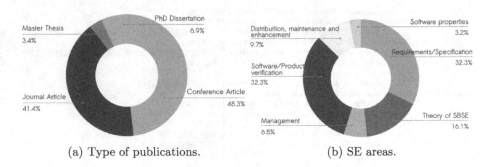

(a) Type of publications.   (b) SE areas.

Fig. 5. Information about the primary sources.

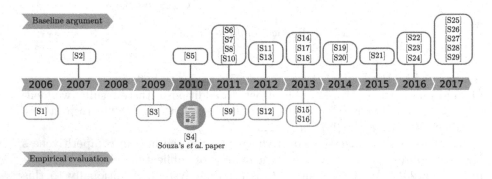

Fig. 6. Context of discussion of the primary sources.

As exposed in Fig. 6, two papers with human competitiveness contributions were published before Souza's *et al.* work, respectively in 2006 and 2009. The first one was conducted by Baker *et al.* [S1]. They presented results of automated approaches to solve two requirements engineering problems: Component Selection and Component Prioritisation. These problems require optimisation of more than one objective aiming to minimize risk and maximize fiscal return while respecting a given bound of total cost. The authors evaluated a real world dataset from a large telecommunications organisation.

For the experiment, 40 components were used and ordered according to an expert ranking. Five of these components were considered as basic and essential and were not included in the list of candidates for the experiment, remaining 35 components. An analysis was performed to compare the results from Greedy Algorithm, Simulated Annealing, and human experts. The results showed that both search algorithms produced significantly better sets of components than those selected by expert judgment. For example, by considering a more restrictive bound, the fitness of the Greedy Algorithm was around 136% better when compared to the human evaluation. The fitness for the Simulated Annealing was even better, with a 158% increase. The authors pointed out that the high fitness values obtained by the algorithms are due to the fact that them can add many more features in each run.

The second empirical work was the multiobjective formulation proposed by Colares *et al.* to the Software Release Planning [S3]. In this approach, the objectives were to maximize the stakeholders' satisfaction and to minimize the project risks by respecting the available resources and the interdependencies among requirements. The authors picked NSGA-II as search algorithm and the problem instance was artificially generated, being composed of 19 requirements to be implemented in 5 releases. Each release had a limited amount of resources and interdependencies of the requirements were established. It was defined a total of 5 stakeholders where each one has an importance to the company as well as some requirements priorities.

In order to prove the applicability in real projects, the authors compared the outcomes of the proposed approach with the results achieved by a random search algorithm, by the multiobjective approach proposed by Zhang *et al.* [43] and human-based solutions. In this last case, five experienced software engineering practitioners were required to make a release plan with the same data of the configured instance. The conclusions indicated that the human subjects results were outperformed by the proposed approach using NSGA-II.

In 2010, Souza *et al.* conducted a comprehensive experimental study specifically focused on evaluating the human competitiveness of SBSE [S4]. They addressed four different SE problem formulations, two instances for each problem, four search algorithms and a total of 63 SE practitioners. Their evaluation have focused in one of the eight human competitiveness criteria, more specifically: "the result holds its own or wins a regulated competition involving human contestants". All experimental results supported the capability of SBSE to generate precise solutions with very little computational effort relative to the results produced by humans. In other words, it was possible to conclude that SBSE can, indeed, be said to be human competitive.

Hereafter, all other works were published after Souza's *et al.* publication. In 2011, Freitas, Coutinho and Souza proposed and evaluated the usage of

Branch-and-Bound to the Next Release Problem (NRP) under the presence of dependent requirements [S9]. They performed a comparative study between the exact technique, metaheuristics and solutions provided by experts. For the evaluation, the authors artificially generated five instances of different sizes, namely NRP-A, NRP-B, NRP-C, NRP-D and NRP-E. As search techniques, Simulated Annealing and Genetic Algorithms were chosen as well as a random search algorithm as sanity test. In relation to the solutions of the experts, they were collected on forms specifically designed for the task. In total, 21 people solved NRP-A and 13 NRP-B. The results for NRP-A and NRP-B showed that the exact optimization approach performed, as expected, better than the metaheuristics. The Genetic Algorithm performed 2.03% worse than exact technique in NRP-A, and 0.61% for NRP-B. The Simulated Annealing was 4.67% and 5.76% worse in NRP-A and NRP-B, respectively. However, when comparing the exact approach to the human evaluation, the results pointed out a significant difference. For NRP-A, the exact optimization technique obtained overall superiority. The average solution of specialists was 40.74% worse when compared to the optimal solution found by the exact technique. Regarding the NRP-B, the average for the experts was 18.90% worse.

Ramirez *et al.* introduced AutoRELAX, an approach that generates relaxed goal models in a fuzzy logic-based specification language (RELAX) for assisting Dynamically Adaptive Systems (DAS) that must cope with changing system and environmental conditions [S12]. A Genetic Algorithm was used in AutoRELAX as a search heuristic for exploring the solution space encompassing all possible RELAXed goal models. Throughout the search process, AutoRELAX uses an executable specification of DAS to measure how candidate RELAXed goal models handle the effects of system and environmental uncertainties. In the proposed approach, a set of fitness subfunctions reward candidate RELAXed goal models that enable a DAS to satisfy its functional requirements while also reducing the number of adaptations the DAS performs and, consequently, the impact of a dynamic reconfiguration at run time.

The authors validated the approach in an application that handles the dynamic reconfiguration of a remote data mirroring (RDM) provided by industry collaborators. In their experiment, the AutoRELAX goal models were compared to unRELAXed goal models and a model developed by a requirement engineer that consists of five goal RELAXations. The results demonstrated that AutoRELAX generated RELAXed goal models that perform better than unRELAXed goal models and manually RELAXed goal models. According to the authors, there are two reasons for this difference in fitness values. The first one, while the manually RELAXed goal model introduced RELAXations to five goals, AutoRELAX mostly introduced RELAX operators only to three goals, thereby slightly boosting its fitness value in comparison. Secondly, the manually RELAXed goal model contained some goal RELAXations that were too constrained. For instance, AutoRELAX was able to extend the goal satisfaction boundary of a goal beyond the bounds applied in the manually RELAXed goal model. Although the authors did not intend to study human efficacy, AutoRELAX was able to generate relaxed goal models that perform better than manually.

Under the context of software testing, Fraser *et al.* evaluated the use of automation techniques in the generation of white box tests [S15]. The authors assumed that automatically generation of tests facilitates the task of the developer, which may be reduced to just checking the test results. In their empirical study, two experiments were carried out comparing a total of 97 individuals divided into two groups: those who would write tests manually and those who would write the tests with the help of an evolutionary tool to derive test suites, named EvoSuite [44]. For each test suite produced, the authors computed several metrics, such as statement, branch, method coverage and others. The results showed that sets of automatically generated tests obtained improvements in the evaluated quality metrics. For instance, the automatic test suites obtained a higher structural coverage (increase of up to 300%) when compared to manually made test suites. However, not all the results were satisfactory. There is no case in which the ability of subjects to detect faults was improved by using EvoSuite and, in fact, detection was often slightly decreased. In an illustrative case, the results showed a slight benefit when using manual testing, with average fault detection of 0.89 mutants killed compared to 0.38 of EvoSuite. Furthermore, the paper also underlined there are some questions to be answered in future works, such as the influence of code ownership and how automated test generation influences software maintenance.

Finally, Xie *et al.* proposed a Genetic Programming (GP) approach to resolve the fault localisation problem [S16]. They applied the GP-evolved risk evaluation formulae developed by Yoo [8]. Their purpose was not only to demonstrate that the SBSE results are human competitive, but also to reach provably optimal and human competitive results is fault localisation.

The authors focused in comparing formulas for risk assessment generated by GP with formulas manually developed for programs with single fault. Among the 30 GP-evolved formulae evaluated, four formulae, namely GP02, GP03, GP13, and GP19 were optimal. GP13 is proved to be equivalent to the human-discovered optima, while the remaining three formulae form three distinct and entirely new groups of optima. They justified the achieved results by highlighting that human beings are more likely to be confined to their intuition and previous experiences. Thus, it is possible that some maximal formulae may be overlooked by humans. However, GP does not suffer from this problem and has the advantage of being unbiased. GP not only can deliver maximal formulae having the same features as some maximal formulae designed by humans, but also can help to provide novel insights and intuitions about effective formulae that humans may overlook.

Interestingly, the authors also described some of the optimal GP-evolved formulae display characteristics as "unintuitive". This is, once that results are both optimal, yet counter-intuitive, they are not only human competitive with respect to the past decade of human efforts, but also unlikely to have been discovered by a further decade of human efforts.

As we can notice, there is a minority of works that, in fact, evaluate the human competitiveness of SBSE. Additionally, from the seven empirical works interested in empirically evaluating human competitiveness, more than a half (71.43%) are related to Requirements/Specifications, while the other ones addressed Software/Program verification (14.29%) and Distribution, maintenance and enhancement (14.29%). Another strong result to be emphasized is that in all evaluations the SBSE approaches were able to outperform the human-based solutions.

4   Threats to Validity

In this section we followed the guidelines suggested by Wohlin *et al.* to discuss the threats to the validity of our study [45].

A major threat to the Internal validity of our mapping study is that we have only focused on the Souza's *et al.* article as start paper and, consequently, we did not conduct an in-depth search in scientific databases such as IEEE Xplore, ACM Digital Library and Scopus, for example. As stated in the definition of our study, we have focused on carrying out a snowball reading as main method to find relevant literature [14]. Therefore, those works that do not cite or were not cited by Souza's *et al.* paper were not considered in our analysis. In addition, it may occur that some works have, indeed, cited Souza's *et al.* paper, but Google Scholar has not accounted it.

A possible threat to the Conclusion validity is the data extraction process as well as the criteria for inclusion and exclusion. We established the following steps to mitigate these threats: (i) we initially defined the classification, the inclusion/exclusion criteria and the standard data fields to be captured; (ii) we created a Google Sheets file to collect the required information about all papers and, finally, (iii) we organized a meeting with the authors to perform the classification based on the papers obtained by the backward and forward snowball readings.

5   Conclusions

Human competitiveness is a widely investigated subject in the machine intelligence field, in particular by the optimization, genetic and evolutionary computation communities. In this sense, Harman highlighted more than 10 years ago about the importance of having convincing examples of human competitive results in order to champion SBSE [2]. From that point, SBSE has evolved and different works showed its ability to produce human competitive results. An important effort into this direction was made by Souza *et al.* in the paper titled "The Human Competitiveness of Search Based Software Engineering", published at SSBSE'10, which raised awareness to this issue and motivated additional works.

Despite the fact that human competitiveness seems to be of growing interest to the SBSE community, we have not identified any systematic study on this issue up to date. Therefore, given this research gap and ongoing interest, we aimed at providing an overview of the current state of human competitiveness in SBSE, through a mapping study by carrying out a snowball reading of Souza's *et al.* paper.

Overall, this study confirms the increasing interest in discussing human competitiveness in SBSE, specially after 2010. We also identified the Symposium on Search Based Software Engineering as the publication forum with most papers. Furthermore, there is some similarity between the number of papers published in conferences (48.3%) and journals (41.4%). In addition, Requirements/Specification and Software/Product Verification were identified as the most common software engineering areas addressed by our primary sources. Our study also revealed the need for increasing empirical evaluations involving human competitiveness. Of all the papers that compose our primary sources (29), 75.86% of them only discussed human competitiveness as baseline argument. On the other hand, of the seven empirical works identified by our study that, indeed, produced human competitiveness results, the majority was concerned to the Requirements/Specification area.

Given those results, some open questions and remaining challenges may be pointed out as motivation for new researches. Firstly, considering the huge spectrum where SBSE can be applied, more work could be done in different SBSE tasks. Moreover, it would be important to produce such results over more realistic settings, considering real-world datasets and environments. To produce more reliable and acceptable conclusions, studies should involve more human subjects, with practical experiences dealing with the SE task of interest. Other than that, different optimization approaches should be evaluated, including human-in-the-loop approaches. Finally, the SBSE field would benefit if researchers incorporate the culture of evaluating the human competitiveness of their optimization results in a regular basis, even over simplified experimental settings, with a handful of software engineering practitioners and toy datasets, but which could create a body of results that, together, would increase SBSE acceptance outside its research community.

References

1. Harman, M., McMinn, P., de Souza, J.T., Yoo, S.: Search based software engineering: techniques, taxonomy, tutorial. In: Meyer, B., Nordio, M. (eds.) LASER 2008-2010. LNCS, vol. 7007, pp. 1–59. Springer, Heidelberg (2012). https://doi.org/10.1007/978-3-642-25231-0_1
2. Harman, M.: The current state and future of search based software engineering. In: 2007 Future of Software Engineering, pp. 342–357. IEEE Computer Society (2007)
3. Harman, M.: Search based software engineering for program comprehension. In: 15th IEEE International Conference on Program Comprehension, ICPC 2007, pp. 3–13. IEEE (2007)
4. Koza, J.R.: Human-competitive results produced by genetic programming. Genet. Program. Evolvable Mach. **11**(3–4), 251–284 (2010)
5. Samuel, A.L.: AI, where it has been and where it is going. In: International Joint Conference on Artificial Intelligence (IJCAI), pp. 1152–1157 (1983)

6. Koza, J.R., Keane, M.A., Streeter, M.J., Mydlowec, W., Yu, J., Lanza, G.: Genetic Programming IV: Routine Human-Competitive Machine Intelligence, vol. 5. Springer, Heidelberg (2006). https://doi.org/10.1007/b137549
7. Baker, P., Harman, M., Steinhofel, K., Skaliotis, A.: Search based approaches to component selection and prioritization for the next release problem. In: 22nd IEEE International Conference on Software Maintenance, ICSM 2006, pp. 176–185. IEEE (2006)
8. Yoo, S.: Evolving human competitive spectra-based fault localisation techniques. In: Fraser, G., Teixeira de Souza, J. (eds.) SSBSE 2012. LNCS, vol. 7515, pp. 244–258. Springer, Heidelberg (2012). https://doi.org/10.1007/978-3-642-33119-0_18
9. Xie, X., Kuo, F.-C., Chen, T.Y., Yoo, S., Harman, M.: Provably optimal and human-competitive results in SBSE for spectrum based fault localisation. In: Ruhe, G., Zhang, Y. (eds.) SSBSE 2013. LNCS, vol. 8084, pp. 224–238. Springer, Heidelberg (2013). https://doi.org/10.1007/978-3-642-39742-4_17
10. de Souza, J.T., Maia, C.L., de Freitas, F.G., Coutinho, D.P.: The human competitiveness of search based software engineering. In: Second International Symposium on Search Based Software Engineering, SSBSE 2010, pp. 143–152. IEEE (2010)
11. Kitchenham, B.: What's up with software metrics?–a preliminary mapping study. J. Syst. Softw. **83**(1), 37–51 (2010)
12. Budgen, D., Turner, M., Brereton, P., Kitchenham, B.: Using mapping studies in software engineering. In: Proceedings of Psychology of Programming Interest Group (PPIG), vol. 8, pp. 195–204. Lancaster University (2008)
13. Petersen, K., Feldt, R., Mujtaba, S., Mattsson, M.: Systematic mapping studies in software engineering. In: International Conference on Evaluation and Assessment in Software Engineering, EASE 2008, vol. 8, pp. 68–77 (2008)
14. Webster, J., Watson, R.T.: Analyzing the past to prepare for the future: writing a literature review. MIS Q. xiii-xxiii (2002)
15. Wohlin, C.: Guidelines for snowballing in systematic literature studies and a replication in software engineering. In: Proceedings of the 18th International Conference on Evaluation and Assessment in Software Engineering, EASE 2014, p. 38. ACM (2014)
16. Colares, F., Souza, J., Carmo, R., Pádua, C., Mateus, G.R.: A new approach to the software release planning. In: XXIII Brazilian Symposium on Software Engineering, SBES 2009, pp. 207–215. IEEE (2009)
17. Harman, M.: The relationship between search based software engineering and predictive modeling. In: Proceedings of the 6th International Conference on Predictive Models in Software Engineering, PROMISE 2010, p. 1. ACM (2010)
18. Ren, J., Harman, M., Di Penta, M.: Cooperative co-evolutionary optimization of software project staff assignments and job scheduling. In: Cohen, M.B., Ó Cinnéide, M. (eds.) SSBSE 2011. LNCS, vol. 6956, pp. 127–141. Springer, Heidelberg (2011). https://doi.org/10.1007/978-3-642-23716-4_14
19. Zhang, Y., Harman, M., Finkelstein, A., Afshin Mansouri, S.: Comparing the performance of metaheuristics for the analysis of multi-stakeholder tradeoffs in requirements optimisation. Inf. Soft. Technol. **53**(7), 761–773 (2011)
20. Brasil, M.M.A., da Silva, T.G.N., de Freitas, F.G., de Souza, J.T., Cortés, M.I.: A multiobjective optimization approach to the software release planning with undefined number of releases and interdependent requirements. In: Zhang, R., Zhang, J., Zhang, Z., Filipe, J., Cordeiro, J. (eds.) ICEIS 2011. LNBIP, vol. 102, pp. 300–314. Springer, Heidelberg (2012). https://doi.org/10.1007/978-3-642-29958-2_20
21. Freitas, F.G., Coutinho, D.P., Souza, J.T.: Software next release planning approach through exact optimization. Int. J. Comput. Appl. (IJCA) **22**(8), 1–8 (2011)

22. Vergilio, S.R., Colanzi, T.E., Pozo, A.T.R., Assunção, W.K.G.: Search based software engineering: a review from the Brazilian symposium on software engineering. In: 25th Brazilian Symposium on Software Engineering, SBES 2011, pp. 50–55. IEEE (2011)

23. Harman, M.: The role of artificial intelligence in software engineering. In: Proceedings of the First International Workshop on Realizing AI Synergies in Software Engineering, RAISE 2012, pp. 1–6. IEEE Press (2012)

24. Ramirez, A.J., Fredericks, E.M., Jensen, A.C., Cheng, B.H.C.: Automatically RELAXing a goal model to cope with uncertainty. In: Fraser, G., Teixeira de Souza, J. (eds.) SSBSE 2012. LNCS, vol. 7515, pp. 198–212. Springer, Heidelberg (2012). https://doi.org/10.1007/978-3-642-33119-0_15

25. Roshan, R., Porwal, R., Sharma, C.M.: Review of search based techniques in software testing. Int. J. Comput. Appl. (IJCA), **51**(6) (2012)

26. Ali, S., Iqbal, M.Z., Arcuri, A., Briand, L.C.: Generating test data from ocl constraints with search techniques. IEEE Trans. Softw. Eng. **39**(10), 1376–1402 (2013)

27. Fraser, G., Staats, M., McMinn, P., Arcuri, A., Padberg, F.: Does automated whitebox test generation really help software testers? In: International Symposium on Software Testing and Analysis, ISSTA 2013, pp. 291–301. ACM (2013)

28. Colanzi, T.E., Vergilio, S.R., Assunção, W.K.G., Pozo, A.: Search based software engineering: review and analysis of the field in Brazil. J. Syst. Softw. **86**(4), 970–984 (2013)

29. Yoo, S., Harman, M., Ur, S.: Gpgpu test suite minimisation: search based software engineering performance improvement using graphics cards. Empir. Softw. Eng. (ESE) **18**(3), 550–593 (2013)

30. Harman, M., Krinke, J., Medina-Bulo, I., Palomo-Lozano, F., Ren, J., Yoo, S.: Exact scalable sensitivity analysis for the next release problem. ACM Trans. Softw. Eng. Methodol. (TOSEM) **23**(2), 19 (2014)

31. Paixao, M.: A robust optimization approach to the next release problem in the presence of uncertainties (written in portuguese). Master's thesis, Mestrado Acadêmico em Ciências da Computacão, Fortaleza (2014)

32. Fraser, G., Staats, M., McMinn, P., Arcuri, A., Padberg, F.: Does automated unit test generation really help software testers? A controlled empirical study. ACM Trans. Softw. Eng. Methodol. (TOSEM) **24**(4), 23 (2015)

33. do Nascimento Ferreira, T., Araújo, A.A., Neto, A.D.B., de Souza, J.T.: Incorporating user preferences in ant colony optimization for the next release problem. Appl. Soft Comput. **49**, 1283–1296 (2016)

34. Langdon, W.B., White, D.R., Harman, M., Jia, Y., Petke, J.: API-constrained genetic improvement. In: Sarro, F., Deb, K. (eds.) SSBSE 2016. LNCS, vol. 9962, pp. 224–230. Springer, Cham (2016). https://doi.org/10.1007/978-3-319-47106-8_16

35. Ali, S., Iqbal, M.Z., Khalid, M., Arcuri, A.: Improving the performance of OCL constraint solving with novel heuristics for logical operations: a search-based approach. Empir. Softw. Eng. (ESE) **21**(6), 2459–2502 (2016)

36. Paixao, M., Harman, M., Zhang, Y., Yu, Y.: An empirical study of cohesion and coupling: balancing optimisation and disruption. IEEE Trans. Evol. Comput. (TEC) (2017)

37. Saeed, A., Hamid, S.H.A., Sani, A.A.: Cost and effectiveness of search-based techniques for model-based testing: an empirical analysis. Int. J. Softw. Eng. Knowl. Eng. (IJSEKE) **27**(04), 601–622 (2017)

38. Wu, F.: Mutation-based genetic improvement of software. Ph.D. thesis, UCL (University College London) (2017)

39. Mohan, M., Greer, D.: MultiRefactor: automated refactoring to improve software quality. In: Felderer, M., Méndez Fernández, D., Turhan, B., Kalinowski, M., Sarro, F., Winkler, D. (eds.) PROFES 2017. LNCS, vol. 10611, pp. 556–572. Springer, Cham (2017). https://doi.org/10.1007/978-3-319-69926-4_46

40. Ali, A., Saeed, A.: Test case generation from state machine with OCL constraints using search-based techniques. Ph.D. thesis, University of Malaya (2017)

41. Ruhe, G., Wohlin, C.: Software project management: setting the context. In: Ruhe, G., Wohlin, C. (eds.) Software Project Management in a Changing World, pp. 1–24. Springer, Heidelberg (2014). https://doi.org/10.1007/978-3-642-55035-5_1

42. Harman, M., Afshin Mansouri, S., Zhang, Y.: Search based software engineering: a comprehensive analysis and review of trends techniques and applications. Department of Computer Science, King's College London, Technical report TR-09-03 (2009)

43. Zhang, Y., Harman, M., Afshin Mansouri, S.: The multi-objective next release problem. In: Proceedings of the 9th Annual Conference on Genetic and Evolutionary Computation, GECCO 2007, pp. 1129–1137. ACM (2007)

44. Fraser, G., Arcuri, A.: EvoSuite: automatic test suite generation for object-oriented software. In: Proceedings of the 19th ACM SIGSOFT Symposium and the 13th European Conference on Foundations of Software Engineering, pp. 416–419. ACM (2011)

45. Wohlin, C., Runeson, P., Höst, M., Ohlsson, M.C., Regnell, B., Wesslén, A.: Experimentation in Software Engineering. Springer, Heidelberg (2012). https://doi.org/10.1007/978-3-642-29044-2

Main Track Papers

Search-Based Stress Testing the Elastic Resource Provisioning for Cloud-Based Applications

Abdullah Alourani$^{(\boxtimes)}$, Md. Abu Naser Bikas$^{(\boxtimes)}$, and Mark Grechanik$^{(\boxtimes)}$

University of Illinois at Chicago, Chicago, IL 60607, USA
{aalour2,mbikas2,drmark}@uic.edu

Abstract. One of the main benefits of cloud computing is to enable customers to deploy their applications on a cloud infrastructure that provisions resources (e.g., memory) to these applications on as-needed basis. Unfortunately, certain workloads can cause customers to pay for resources that are provisioned to, but not fully used by their applications, and as a result their performances then deteriorate beyond some acceptable thresholds and the benefits of cloud computing may be significantly reduced or even completely obliterated. We propose a novel approach to automatically discover these workloads to stress test elastic resource provisioning for cloud-based applications. We experimented with four non-trivial applications on the Microsoft Azure cloud to determine how effectively and efficiently our approach explores a very large space of the workload parameters' values. The results show that our approach discovers the first irregular workload faster in the search space of over 10^{40} input combinations compared to the random approach, and it discovers more irregular workloads that result in much higher costs and performance degradations for applications in the cloud.

Keywords: Cloud computing · Performance testing
Cloud elasticity · Genetic algorithms · Multi-objective optimization
Irregular workloads · Stress testing

1 Introduction

One of the main benefits of cloud computing is to enable customers to deploy their applications on a cloud infrastructure that provisions resources (e.g., *virtual machines (VMs)*) to these applications on as-needed basis [26]. That is, instead of buying and hosting expensive hardware, customers pay for renting resources for running these applications from cloud computing facilities [22]. A fundamental problem of cloud computing is to provision resources according to the application's runtime needs in order to ensure that its performance does not worsen below a predefined threshold, and it affects the technology spending in the excess of $1 trillion by 2020 [29].

© Springer Nature Switzerland AG 2018
T. E. Colanzi and P. McMinn (Eds.): SSBSE 2018, LNCS 11036, pp. 149–165, 2018.
https://doi.org/10.1007/978-3-319-99241-9_7

The decisions to provision certain resources are typically made by engineers who create and maintain cloud-based applications, and they express their decisions in rules. A common and frequently used rule recommended by the Amazon and Google Cloud documentations is to provision one more VM when the CPU's utilization increases above 80% [3,13,24]. There are many different rules like that for controlling cloud *elasticity*, a term that designates on-demand resource provisioning to an application [5,14]. Unfortunately, the behaviours of the nontrivial applications are very complex, so some rules may be far from optimal in terms of allocating best possible resources for maximizing the applications' performance.

In performance testing, input workloads are often created that resemble typical usages of applications and their performance characteristics are analyzed for regular workloads. In this paper, we are interested in *irregular workloads*, whose occurrences are rare and deviate beyond what is normally expected and they are extremely difficult to predict. Whereas test input workload generation techniques concentrate on finding patterns in the existing past workloads [20], there is no approach for finding new irregular workloads for *stress testing*, where applications are used beyond the normal operational capacity to a breaking point [4]. Unfortunately, when irregular workloads happen, customers pay for resources that are provisioned to, but not fully used by their applications [18], and the benefits of cloud computing may be significantly reduced or even completely obliterated [2].

We propose a novel approach for automatically discovering irregular workloads that result in situations when customers pay for resources that are not fully used by their applications while at the same time, some performance characteristics of these applications are not met, i.e., the *Cost-Utility Violations of Elasticity (CUVE)*. We implemented our approach for *Testing for Infractions of CLoud Elasticity (TICLE)* that combined a search-based heuristic with rule-guided resource provisioning to discover irregular workloads that led to CUVEs. These irregular workloads and rules can be reviewed by developers and performance engineers, who optimize the rules to improve the performance of the corresponding application. To the best of our knowledge, TICLE is the first fully automatic CUVE approach for discovering irregular workloads for applications deployed on the cloud. We TICLEd four nontrivial open-source applications in the Microsoft Azure cloud to determine how automatically and accurately TICLE explored a large search space of over 10^{40} input combinations while discovering CUVEs. The results show that TICLE finds the first irregular workload faster thus enabling stakeholders to investigate its impact sooner, and it finds more irregular workloads that lead to much higher costs and performance degradations for applications in the cloud compared to the random approach. TICLE's source code and all the experimental data are publicly available [1].

2   Problem Statement

In this section, we provide a background on workloads and rules for elastic resource provisioning, discuss sources of CUVE, and formulate the problem statement.

2.1   Rules and Workloads

In general, `if-then` elasticity rules contain antecedents that describe the level of resource utilization (e.g., CPU utilization $\geq 80\%$), and the consequents that specify (de)provisioning actions (e.g., to (de)provision a VM). Unfortunately, rule creation is an error-prone manual activity, and provisioning certain resources using manually created rules does not often improve the application's performance. For example, when the CPU utilization reaches some threshold due to a lot of page swapping or a lack of the storage space, provisioning more CPUs does not fix the underlying cause that requires giving more memory and storage to the application. That is, often rules are not optimal in terms of allocating required resources based on projected applications' needs [18].

It is very difficult to create rules that provision resources optimally to maximize the performance of the application while minimizing the cost of its deployment. Doing so requires the application's owners to understand which resources to (de)provision at what points in execution, how the cost of the provisioned resources varies, and how to make trade-offs between the application's performance and these costs [16]. Optimal provisioning is difficult even for five basic resource types (i.e., CPU, RAM, storage, VM, and network connections), where each type has many different attributes (e.g., the Microsoft Azure documentation mentions 30 attributes [24], which result in tens of millions of combinations).

Definition 1. *An application workload is a time-dependent collection of request tuples as shown in Fig. 1 that contains a function of time that maps a time interval to the subset of input requests and its input data.*

The *application workload* includes not only the static part of the input to the application (i.e., combinations of HTTP requests with their parameter values) but also the dynamic part that comprises the number of HTTP requests submitted to the application per time unit and how this number changes as a function of time [23]. For example, a workload specifies how the number of requests to the application fluctuates periodically according to a circular function $y_t = \alpha \sin \omega t$, where α is the amplitude of the workloads that designates the maximum number of HTTP requests, t is the discrete time of the execution, and ω is the periodicity coefficient.

Application workloads are often characterized by *fast fluctuations* and *burstiness*, where the former designates a fast irregular growth and then a decline in the number of requests over a short period of time, and the latter means that many inputs occur together in bursts separated by lulls in which they do not occur [25]. By changing the coefficients of the function, irregular workloads can be generated for stress testing in varying degrees of burstiness and fluctuation.

2.2   Sources of Cost-Utility Violations of Elasticity

There are two main sources of CUVE. First, there is a problem of provisioning resources to an application that are not optimal for achieving the application's best performance. For example, the application may not perform better with additionally provisioned many CPUs instead of some more RAM [18]. Recall that cloud providers recommend some generic rules for resource provisioning [3,13,24]. Often, during stress testing, applications are run under regular heavy workloads that reflect the expected pattern of usage (e.g., loads peak during evening hours when people shop online), and they are unable to find CUVEs that result from irregular workloads. As a result, when these workloads occur during deployment, resources that are provisioned to an application may not improve its performance; however, its owner still has to pay the cloud provider for these needlessly provisioned resources.

Second, when the cloud infrastructure allocates resources, there is a delay between the moment when the cloud assigns a resource to an application and the moment when this application takes control of this resource. There are at least a couple of reasons for this delay: the startup time for a VM that hosts the application or its components includes the VM's loading and initialization time by the underlying infrastructure; assigning a new CPU to the existing VM requires its hosted operating system to recognize this CPU, which takes from seconds to tens of minutes [21]. Of course, the cloud infrastructure starts charging the customer for the resources at the moment it provisions them rather than when the application can control these resources [18]. However, all these may be done in vain – if the application rapidly changes its runtime behavior during a resource initialization time, this resource may not be needed any more by the time it is initialized to maintain the desired performance of the application. As a result, during irregular workloads, customers pay for resources that are not used by their applications for some period of time resulting in performance degradations.

2.3   The Problem Statement

Software engineers make performance enhancements routinely during perfective maintenance [19] when they use mostly exploratory random performance testing to identify when the performance of the *Application Under Test (AUT)* worsens. In this paper, we address a fundamental problem of performance testing in the cloud – *how to increase the effectiveness and efficiency of obtaining irregular workloads for software applications deployed on the cloud that lead to instances of the CUVE*. The root of this fundamental problem is that using only regular workloads for applications as part of random exploratory performance testing results in a large number of executions, many of which are not effective in determining CUVE instances. Selecting randomly a subset of workloads often results in a complete absence of the CUVE instances. To the best of our knowledge, there is no automatic approach to obtain irregular workloads that can produce instances of the CUVE.

Specifically, we want to construct irregular workloads automatically using combinations of inputs to which some functions are applied to cause fluctuations and burstiness to detect situations where the cost increases significantly while the average throughput (i.e., a measure inverse to the response time) of the application decreases beyond a certain threshold defined in a *service level agreement (SLA)* that indicates a desired performance level and the provisioned resources remain under-utilized or even completely unused at the same time. This is an instance of the *multiobjective optimization problem (MOOP)*. Automatically discovering irregular workloads is very difficult in general, especially when trying to satisfy multiple conflicting constraints.

3   Our Approach

In this section, we state our key ideas for our approach for *Testing for Infractions of CLoud Elasticity (TICLE)*, explain the *genetic algorithm (GA)* with MOOP (*GAMOOP*), and describe the algorithm for TICLE.

3.1   Key Ideas

A goal of our approach is to automatically obtain irregular workloads for the AUT using GAMOOP. In general, GAs are based on natural selection techniques where solutions to optimization problems are obtained using a stochastic search [17]. The advantage of a GA is in evolving multiple candidate solutions in parallel thus allowing it to explore efficiently a large search space of possible solutions. Thus, TICLE is likely to scale well to modern AUTs with enormous search space.

In TICLE, a workload is represented by a *chromosome* that contains a sequence of *genes* divided into three parts as it is shown in Fig. 1. The first part refers to the types of periodic circular functions (e.g., sinusoidal) that represent changes in the number of HTTP requests in the workload, the second part refers to the functions' parameters (e.g., amplitudes), and the third part refers to a set of HTTP requests, where each HTTP request is assigned to a unique ID, i.e., a HTTP request that includes various parameters is assigned to various IDs. For each application, we used a spider tool [8] to traverse the web interface of the application, log all unique HTTP requests sent to the backend of the application, and ensure these HTTP requests are valid. Each chromosome contains one function of time, two function parameters (e.g., amplitude and periodicity), and a set of HTTP requests, where each function of time uses only two function parameters. Therefore, modifying the values of these parameters in the second part of the chromosome by the GA is independent of changing the function of time in the first part of the chromosome. Once chromosomes are constructed, they are modified by GAs iteratively to find solutions that satisfy multiple objectives. That is, TICLE generates the combination of inputs (i.e., HTTP requests) plus the parameters of workloads for formulae that describe them.

We use GAs for finding CUVEs that result from irregular workloads. In GAs, new solutions, or *offsprings* are generated using existing solutions, or *parents*. New solutions are often "fitter" to meet the objectives of the desired solution. A predefined *fitness function* is used to evaluate how close each solution is to being the optimal solution and fitter solutions have a better chance to "survive" multiple iterations [17]. In order to create a new generation of workload solutions, the operator selection, mutation, and crossover are applied to workloads, where

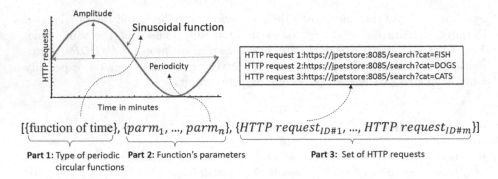

Fig. 1. The representation of the workload and the chromosome.

a selection operator selects parents based on their fitness, a crossover operator recombines a pair of selected parents and generates new offspring workloads, and a mutation operator produces a mutant of one workload solution by randomly altering its gene. It is our hypothesis that GAMOOP can efficiently generate close to optimal workloads using the properties of their parents.

Our other key idea is to include user-defined rules for SLA violations as objective constraint functions for TICLE. For example, the Amazon's SLA rule limits the response time to 300 ms for its web-based application [10]. Finding workloads that violate SLA thresholds is one of the main goals of performance testing. However, if finding workloads that break the SLA rules was the only objective, simply exponentially increasing the amplitude of the workloads with a very large burstiness would likely result in a sudden increase of the response time. Unfortunately, doing so results in ignoring the other two objectives (i.e., increasing the cost of the provisioned resources and decreasing the utilization of resources), since the cost is likely to remain the same if the cloud does not rapidly provision resources and the utilization will keep increasing with the increasing workloads. Thus, workload parameters should be chosen in such a way that delays between resource provisioning and resource availability are exploited by changing the fluctuations and the burstiness of the workloads in addition to differences in how applications use resources based on the workload content that includes HTTP requests, which trigger different execution paths in AUTs.

3.2 TICLE Algorithm

TICLE is shown in Algorithm 1 that includes the following major steps: (i) randomly generate an initial set of workloads, (ii) use these workloads to execute the cloud-deployed AUT and measure its performance, such as the utilization of the provisioned resources and the average response time, and (iii) use fitness functions, as described by Eq. 2 [31] to evaluate the objectives and to select workload solutions using *the quality indicator* described by Eq. 1 [31] to select solutions using GAMOOP. The fitness function is Pareto dominance compliant since it uses the quality indicator to rank solutions based on their usefulness regarding multiple objectives, amplifying the influence of dominating solutions over dominated solutions. A Pareto optimal solution dominates some other one if the dominating solution is better in some objectives and it is not worse in all the other objectives. Each solution can be represented as a point in a multidimensional space of orthogonal objectives. A curve can be drawn to connect non-dominated solutions that can be selected as optimal when no objective could be improved without sacrificing the other objectives. The curve is named a *Pareto optimal front* and is used by GAMOOP to choose winning workloads that result in CUVEs.

$$I(S, S') = \max \left\{ \forall w' \in S' \, \exists w \in S : g_j(w) \geq g_j(w') \quad \text{for} \quad j \in \{1, \ldots, n\} \right\},$$
$$S, S' \in \Omega, \quad w, w' \in P \tag{1}$$

$$F(w) = \Sigma_{w' \in P \setminus \{w\}} - e^{-I(\{w'\}, \{w\})/k}, \quad k > 0 \tag{2}$$

Where Ω indicates the entirety of all Pareto sets, S is a Pareto set and S' is another Pareto set in all Pareto set approximations. P indicates the initial population P of workloads, w is a workload (i.e., solution), and w' is another workload in the population. I is the quality indicator function that compares the quality of two Pareto set approximations or solutions with respects to n objective functions $g_1, \ldots, g_n$ that are described below, k is a fitness scaling factor and is set to 0.05 experimentally.

We chose *Non-dominated Sorting Genetic Algorithm II (NSGA-II)* because previous evaluations showed that it finds a much better spread of solutions and it converges near the true Pareto optimal front. NSGA-II does not require the user to prioritize, scale, or weigh objectives like many other algorithms, which would be a major manual effort in TICLE. Finally, NSGA-II can generate new non-dominated solutions in unexplored parts of the Pareto front by applying the crossover operator to take advantage of good solutions with respect to multiple conflicting objectives [9].

That is, the space of workload parameters (e.g., the amplitude, periodicity) is explored to optimize three objectives in parallel by evaluating a fitness function (Eq. 2) that maps workloads to the unused resources of provisioned VMs (objective 1), the cost of provisioned resources (objective 2), and the average response time (objective 3). An ideal solution is a workload that maximizes these objectives, as described by Eq. 1, i.e., to achieve the maximum cost of the deployment with the minimum resource utilization and the application throughput that violates predefined SLA constraints. These objectives cannot be formally defined, since their values are obtained from the Microsoft Azure cloud. Since no solution exists to address this important problem, using NSGA-II to find a better solution and to compare it with a random performance testing approach is our major contribution.

The algorithm for TICLE takes in the complete set of input ranges for the subject AUT and the GAMOOP configurations Ω, including the crossover and mutation rates, fitness functions for their respective objectives, an SLA threshold, and the termination criterion. In Step 2, the algorithm generates an initial

Algorithm 1. TICLE's algorithm for automating workload search for instances of the CUVE problem.

1: **Inputs:** GAMOOP Configuration Ω, Input Set $\mathcal{I}$
2: $\mathcal{P} \leftarrow$ InitializePopulation($\mathcal{I}$)
3: **while** $\neg$ Terminate **do**
4:     EvalFitnessObjectiveFunctions($\mathcal{P}$, Ω)
5:     EvalConstraintsFunctions($\mathcal{P}$, Ω)
6:     $\mathcal{F} \leftarrow$ FastNondominatedSort($\mathcal{P}$)
7:     CrowdingDistanceAssignment($\mathcal{F}$)
8:     $\mathcal{S} \leftarrow$ SelectParentsByRankDistance($\mathcal{F}$, $|\mathcal{P}|$)
9:     $\mathcal{R} \leftarrow$ RemoveLowerRankedSolutions($\mathcal{S}$)
10:     $\mathcal{C} \leftarrow$ CrossoverMutation($\mathcal{R}$, Ω)
11:     $\mathcal{P} \leftarrow \mathcal{P} \cup$ Merge($\mathcal{P}$, $\mathcal{C}$)
12: **end while**
13: **return** $\mathcal{P}$

---

population of workloads by combining randomly selected HTTP requests. In TICLE, we create four types of workload fluctuation functions: sinusoidal, where the workload changes with periodicity, as described by the equation $y_t = \alpha \sin t$, where α is the amplitude of the workloads that designates the maximum number of HTTP requests, and t is the discrete time of the execution; linear, where the workload increases or decreases linearly, as described by the equation $y_t = \alpha \times t$; exponential, with a rapid rise or drop of the workload $y_t = \alpha^t$; and random, where a random number generator is used to define the amplitude and the HTTP requests for the workloads. In the RANDOM approach, a workload contains AUT's HTTP requests, the types of periodic circular functions that represent changes in the number of HTTP requests in the workload, and the functions' parameters (e.g., amplitudes and periodicities). Once workloads are constructed, their parameters are modified randomly to find solutions. Based on previous research, these functions represent a majority of workload shapes [23].

Starting from Step 3, the evolution process begins by evaluating if the termination condition is satisfied. In Step 4, fitness functions are applied to evaluate each individual workload and in Step 5 constraint functions are evaluated to determine if the SLA holds. After the evaluation, in Step 6 the population is sorted and in Step 7 the distances of the solutions on the Pareto front are estimated. Using those closest to the Pareto front, in Step 8 the solutions are ranked into a hierarchy of sub-populations based on the ordering of the Pareto dominance. In Step 9, lower ranked solutions are removed from the population. In Step 10, for each part of the chromosome, the mutation operator replaces the value of one random gene with another value within the specified range, thus creating a new (updated) individual.

All newly generated individual workloads are evaluated using the defined fitness functions, and the fittest workloads are selected for the next generation that is formed first by the order of dominating precedence of the Pareto front and then by using the distance within the front. Finally, the new workload solutions are added to the population. The cycle of Steps 3–12 repeats until the termination criterion is satisfied, and the final population is returned in Step 13 as the algorithm terminates.

4   Empirical Evaluation

In this section, we describe the design of the empirical study to evaluate TICLE and state threats to its validity. We pose the following three *Research Questions (RQs)*:

RQ_1: How effective is TICLE in finding irregular workloads that lead to the greater cost of the AUT's deployment?

RQ_2: How fast is TICLE in finding the first irregular workload that infracts the elasticity rules for the AUT?

RQ_3: Is TICLE more effective than the random approach in finding more CUVEs for different elasticity rules?

Table 1. Characteristics of the subject AUTs: their names followed by their versions, the number of lines of code (LOC), the number of classes, the number of methods and the approximate size of the search space of the input requests for the AUT.

AUT	Version	LOC	Classes	Methods	Space
JPetStore	$v4.0.5$	2,762	42	400	10^{31}
JForum	$v2.1.9$	36,401	397	3,487	10^{49}
PhotoV	$v2.1.0$	10,549	81	931	10^{36}
RUBiS	$v1.4.3$	83,640	641	4,396	10^{14}

4.1   Subject Applications

We evaluated TICLE on four web-based, open-source subject applications written in Java: JPetStore, JForum, PhotoV, and RUBiS. Their basic characteristics are shown in Table 1. These applications are written by different programmers, come from different domains, and have high popularity indexes. Choosing up to 50 input requests from 100+ HTTP requests results in over 10^{40} combinations.

All subject AUTs have a three-tier architecture. Response time is measured between the moment when a sent request is received by the AUT and the moment when a response to the request is issued from the AUT, and the network latency time is not included. All components of the same AUT are deployed on the same VM. When the cloud provisions VMs to the AUT, each VM will have a replica of these three tiers to ensure full horizontal scalability of the AUT.

4.2   Methodology

We use the definition a *workload* from Sect. 2.1 to specify the set of input requests and how their quantities change over time. For example, the HTTP request https://jpetstore:8085/search?cat=FISH is an input to JPetStore, where **search** is the path component of the HTTP request, `cat` is the name of its parameter, and `FISH` is the value of this parameter. TICLE generates workloads and uses JMeter [15] that simulates users sending the workload requests to web servers of the AUT and collects performance measurements of the provisioned VMs that host AUT's components that execute the workload requests. In our experiments, we set the number of HTTP requests in a workload between 10 and 50 to observe a wide range of the AUT's behaviors.

Table 2. The set of predefined `if-then` elasticity rules.

Rule	Provisioning action	
	Scale in	Scale out
R_1	$CPU_{utilization} < 20\%$	$CPU_{utilization} > 50\%$
R_2	$CPU_{utilization} < 40\%$	$CPU_{utilization} > 60\%$
R_3	$CPU_{utilization} < 20\%$	$CPU_{utilization} > 80\%$

Also, we defined three elasticity rules with different ranges for VM (de)provisioning that are shown in Table 2 to determine how effectively TICLE finds irregular workloads that infract these elasticity rules for the AUTs. Since our goal is to find irregular workloads that lead to CUVEs, violating the predefined SLA threshold is an important objective of the experiments. We use the AUT's response time as the SLA. To determine the SLA threshold, we first run each subject AUT under heavy workloads in a single VM to determine the longest possible response time. Then, we repeat our experiments with 20%, 40%, and 60% of this longest response time as the SLA threshold.

The experiments for the AUTs were carried out using 10 small VMs/servers from the A-series in the Microsoft Azure cloud called Standard A1 with 1 GHz CPU and 1.75 GB of memory. We wrote a client for JMeter [15] that applied generated workloads to the subject AUTs, and JMeter clients were run externally on laptops. All experiments were conducted on the same experimental platform.

We implemented TICLE using `jMetal`, which is an open-source framework for multi-objective optimization with various evolutionary algorithms [11]. We used the following GAMOOP settings for TICLE: the crossover rate of 0.9, the mutation rate of 0.3, the population of 100 individuals, and the tournament selection of size two. The evolution was terminated if the workload solutions did not improve after 10 generations. The maximum number of generations was set to 30. We chose these values experimentally for the platform based on the limitations of the hardware.

4.3   Threats to Validity

A threat to the validity of our empirical study is that our experiments were performed on only four open-source, web-based applications, which makes it difficult to generalize the results to other types of applications that may have different logic, structure, or input types. However, the subject AUTs were used in other empirical studies on performance testing [27]. Therefore, we expect our results to be generalizable.

Our current implementation of TICLE deals with simple types of inputs, HTTP requests with basic parameter types (e.g., integer), whereas other programs may have complex input types (e.g., JSON or XML structures). While this is a threat, TICLE can be adapted to encode inputs of other types. In order to apply TICLE to other applications, the user needs to modify only the gene representation approach so that TICLE recognizes other types of inputs.

One threat to validity is that we deployed an AUT fully in a single VM. Indeed, deploying an AUT's components in multiple VMs may lead to performance bottlenecks since many shared resources are used in the application layer. This situation may result in more CUVEs, thus making it easier for TICLE to find them. However, deploying these layers on the same VM (i.e., it is scaled horizontally) puts TICLE at a disadvantage to find CUVEs since many bottlenecks do not show up easily, thus making our experiments robust.

We experimented with only three generic elasticity rules using the recommendations from Amazon, Azure, and Google Cloud documentations. This is a threat for two reasons. First, users may create much more sophisticated rules that would make it difficult for TICLE to find CUVEs. Second, our rules provision only VMs, whereas real-world rules could also provision storage, RAM, network connections, and other virtual hardware. However, understanding the effect of various resources is currently out of scope for this paper and will be addressed in future work.

5   Empirical Results

In this section, we describe and analyze the results of the experiments to answer the three RQs stated in Sect. 4.

5.1   Finding Workloads that Lead to Higher Costs

The results of the experiments are shown in the box-and-whisker plots in Fig. 2a and b that summarize the deployment costs and the time it takes to find the first CUVE for the subject AUTs using the TICLE and RANDOM approaches for three different SLA threshold values of the longest response time. We observe that the average costs for the found CUVEs using TICLE are consistently higher than the average costs of the CUVEs found by RANDOM among all SLA threshold values. The costs for CUVEs have the highest difference between TICLE and RANDOM at 60% of the SLA threshold, then at 40%, followed by 20%. This result suggests that the higher threshold values require more sophisticated workloads to break the threshold and to lead to a higher cost of deployment, because it is more difficult to construct workloads when longer response times are permitted. The cost variance for CUVEs computed by TICLE is significantly lower when

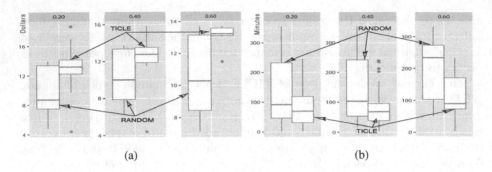

Fig. 2. Box-and-whisker plots compare (a) the deployment costs and (b) the time to the first CUVE discovery for detected CUVEs that are computed using the TICLE and RANDOM approaches for the subject AUTs for three SLA thresholds (i.e., 0.2, 0.4, and 0.6) of the longest response time. The cost is measured in dollars and the time is measured in minutes.

Table 3. The comparison of the results of Mann-Whitney-Wilcoxon U-Tests for TICLE and RANDOM using three SLA thresholds. The first column designates the null hypothesis followed by the column for SLA thresholds, and the cells contain the p-values.

Null hypothesis	SLA threshold		
	20%	40%	60%
Cost	9.7×10^{-15}	8.2×10^{-3}	0.03
Detection time	1.4×10^{-4}	5.5×10^{-4}	0.02

compared to the RANDOM approach, which suggests that TICLE favors workloads that have the highest impact on increasing the cost of deployment.

Similarly, it is shown in the box-and-whisker plot in Fig. 2b that TICLE is consistently faster than RANDOM in finding the first CUVE. This result is important not only to answer RQ_2, but also to show that TICLE is efficient in practice, since taking less time to find the first CUVE shows that TICLE beats the RANDOM approach in notifying stakeholders faster that there is a workload that results in a CUVE. We expect that TICLE will be used by performance testers, and it is important for them to find CUVEs faster to report them to developers who will start looking for fixes to the detected CUVEs. Thus, a faster-to-find-CUVE approach is also more efficient in using fewer computer resources and stakeholders' time.

In our case, the data cannot be guaranteed to follow the normal distribution, therefore, we applied Mann-Whitney-Wilcoxon U-Tests to evaluate the statistical significance of the difference in the median value of deployment cost between TICLE and RANDOM for the subject AUTs. The results of Mann-Whitney-Wilcoxon U-Tests for TICLE and RANDOM are shown in Table 3. The results confirm that the values for the differences between TICLE and RANDOM are always statistically significant according to the Mann-Whitney-Wilcoxon U-Test, thus **positively addressing** RQ_1.

5.2   Finding Workloads Faster

We applied Mann-Whitney-Wilcoxon U-Tests to evaluate the statistical significance of the difference in the median value of detection time, which indicates
the execution time to find irregular workloads that lead to the CUVE, between
TICLE and RANDOM for the subject AUTs. The results of Mann-Whitney-Wilcoxon
U-Tests for TICLE and RANDOM are shown in Table 3. The results confirm that
the values for the differences between TICLE and RANDOM are always statistically
significant according to the Mann-Whitney-Wilcoxon U-Test, thus **positively
addressing** RQ_2, which states that TICLE is more efficient in finding CUVE
using significantly fewer computational resources compared to the RANDOM approach.

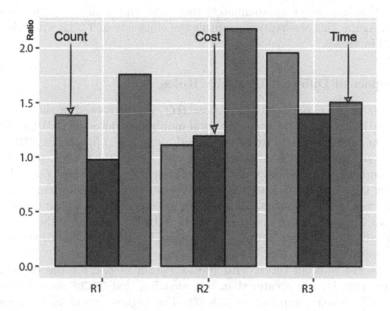

Fig. 3. Comparing TICLE and RANDOM for detecting CUVEs for the subject AUTs with
different elastic rules that are shown in Table 2. The X-axis designates elasticity rules.
The leftmost red bar represents the ratio of the total number of detected CUVEs using
the approaches TICLE and RANDOM, $\frac{count_{TICLE}}{count_{RANDOM}}$. The middle green bar represents the
ratio of the average costs for CUVEs, $\frac{cost_{TICLE}}{cost_{RANDOM}}$. The rightmost blue bar represents
the ratio of detection times for the first found CUVE, $\frac{time_{RANDOM}}{time_{TICLE}}$. (Color figure
online)

5.3   The Impact of the SLA Threshold

An interesting question is how an SLA threshold affects the process of finding
CUVEs. As discussed in Sect. 4.2, a higher percentage of the SLA threshold
means that longer response times are acceptable. Since one of the objectives is
to find CUVEs where the SLA threshold is violated, the higher the percentage

at which the SLA threshold is chosen, the more difficult it is to obtain CUVEs. Consider the box-and-whisker plots that are shown in Fig. 2a and b – the visual inspection clearly identifies the rise of the average cost and the detection time with the increase of the SLA threshold. However, our analysis shows that the cost of the application deployment increases robustly when using TICLE whereas for RANDOM, the average cost stays approximately the same, but it shows a much wider variance. Our explanation is that TICLE is more effective in finding workloads for CUVEs with much higher SLA thresholds, since it systematically chooses workloads with a higher cost using the fitness functions.

Alternatively, the detection time to the first occurrence of the CUVE shows almost an opposite pattern. The detection time increases steadily when using RANDOM with a large variance of the measurements whereas for TICLE, the average detection time stays approximately the same, and it shows a much smaller variance. Again, this observation confirms the efficiency of TICLE when the SLA threshold increases.

5.4 Impact of Different Elasticity Rules

The results of the experiments to answer RQ_3 are presented in the histogram plot in Fig. 3 that shows ratios for the total numbers of detected CUVEs, deployment costs, and detection times computed using the approaches TICLE and RANDOM over subject AUTs for three elasticity rules, which allocate and deallocate resources in consonance with the user-specific conditions (i.e., the utilization of CPUs increases above 80%). We used three elasticity rules that are recommended by the Amazon, Microsoft Azure, and Google Cloud documentations [3,13,24], and these rules are shown in Table 2. The higher the ratios, the more effective and efficient TICLE is in finding CUVEs compared to the RANDOM baseline approach.

We observe that all ratios with the exception of one for the deployment cost of the rule R_1 are greater than one meaning that TICLE finds faster and more CUVEs when compared to RANDOM. The highest count ratio is for R_3 and R_1, followed by R_2, which suggests that a higher range value between the lower threshold that triggers the scale-in operation and the upper threshold that triggers the scale-out operation for elasticity rules results in more detected CUVEs. In summary, these experimental results demonstrate that TICLE is more effective and efficient in finding CUVEs for all elasticity rules than the RANDOM baseline approach, thus **positively addressing RQ_3**.

6 Related Work

Gambi et al. developed a tool that uses predefined workloads to test the automation of cloud-based elastic systems [12]. Bodik et al. proposed a workload model that characterizes volume and data spikes to test the robustness of stateful systems [6]. Chen et al. developed a tool that uses user-defined workloads to analyze performance and energy consumption for cloud applications [7]. Snellman et al.

developed a tool that uses user-defined test scripts to evaluate the performance and scalability of rich internet applications in the cloud [28]. Shen *et al.* presented an approach that uses genetic algorithms to find the combinations of inputs that lead to performance problems [27]. Xiao *et al.* presented an approach that uses complexity models to predict workload-dependent performance bottlenecks [30]. However, TICLE is the first fully automatic approach that finds irregular workloads that lead to the CUVEs for stress-testing applications deployed on the cloud.

7   Conclusion

We presented a novel approach for automating the discovery of situations when customers pay for resources that are not fully used by their applications while at the same time, some performance characteristics of these applications are not met, i.e., the cost-utility violations. We implemented our approach for *Testing for Infractions of CLoud Elasticity* (TICLE) and we TICLEd four nontrivial open-source applications in the Microsoft Azure cloud. The results show that TICLE is effective for automatic stress testing of elastic resource provisioning for applications deployed on the cloud to determine infractions of elastic rules. With TICLE, experts can analyze the discovered workloads to determine their impact on applications. To the best of our knowledge, TICLE is the first fully automatic approach for discovering irregular workloads that are very difficult to create using other approaches.

Acknowledgments. We warmly thank Prof. Márcio Barros and anonymous reviewers for their comments and suggestions that helped us to improve the quality of this paper. This work is supported by NSF EAGER-1650000, NSF CCF-1615563, NSF I-Corps-1547597, Microsoft, and Grammatech. Any opinions, findings and conclusions expressed herein are the authors' and do not necessarily reflect those of the sponsors.

References

1. TICLE source code and experimental data (2018). https://www.dropbox.com/s/c2rs5afh5g4icdl/TICLEProject.zip?dl=0
2. Albonico, M., Mottu, J.M., Sunyé, G.: Controlling the elasticity of web applications on cloud computing. In: Proceedings of the 31st Annual ACM Symposium on Applied Computing, SAC 2016, pp. 816–819. ACM, New York (2016)
3. AWS: What is auto scaling? (2018). http://docs.aws.amazon.com
4. Beizer, B.: Software Testing Techniques. Dreamtech Press, New Delhi (2003)
5. Bikas, M.A.N., Alourani, A., Grechanik, M.: How elasticity property plays an important role in the cloud: a survey. Adv. Comput. **103**, 1–30 (2016). https://doi.org/10.1016/bs.adcom.2016.04.001
6. Bodik, P., Fox, A., Franklin, M.J., Jordan, M.I., Patterson, D.A.: Characterizing, modeling, and generating workload spikes for stateful services. In: Proceedings of the 1st ACM Symposium on Cloud Computing, pp. 241–252. ACM (2010)

7. Chen, F., Grundy, J., Schneider, J.G., Yang, Y., He, Q.: StressCloud: a tool for analysing performance and energy consumption of cloud applications. In: Proceedings of the 37th International Conference on Software Engineering, vol. 2, pp. 721–724. IEEE Press (2015)

8. crawler4j: Open source web crawler for Java (2018). https://github.com/yasserg/crawler4j

9. Deb, K., Pratap, A., Agarwal, S., Meyarivan, T.: A fast and elitist multiobjective genetic algorithm: NSGA-II. Trans. Evol. Comput. **6**(2), 182–197 (2002)

10. DeCandia, G., et al.: Dynamo: Amazon's highly available key-value store. In: ACM SIGOPS Operating Systems Review, vol. 41, pp. 205–220. ACM (2007)

11. Durillo, J.J., Nebro, A.J.: jMetal: a Java framework for multi-objective optimization. Adv. Eng. Softw. **42**(10), 760–771 (2011)

12. Gambi, A., Hummer, W., Dustdar, S.: Automated testing of cloud-based elastic systems with AUToCLES. In: 2013 IEEE/ACM 28th International Conference on Automated Software Engineering, ASE, pp. 714–717. IEEE (2013)

13. Google: Autoscaling groups of instances (2018). https://cloud.google.com

14. Grechanik, M., Luo, Q., Poshyvanyk, D., Porter, A.: Enhancing rules for cloud resource provisioning via learned software performance models. In: Proceedings of the 7th ACM/SPEC International Conference on Performance Engineering, ICPE 2016, Delft, The Netherlands, 12–16 March 2016, pp. 209–214 (2016). https://doi.org/10.1145/2851553.2851568

15. Halili, E.: Apache JMeter. Packt Publishing, Birmingham (2008)

16. Herbst, N.R., Kounev, S., Reussner, R.: Elasticity in cloud computing: what it is, and what it is not. In: Proceedings of the 10th International Conference on Autonomic Computing, ICAC 2013, pp. 23–27. USENIX, San Jose (2013)

17. Holland, J.H.: Adaptation in Natural and Artificial Systems: An Introductory Analysis with Applications to Biology, Control, and Artificial Intelligence. U Michigan Press, Ann Arbor (1975)

18. Islam, S., Lee, K., Fekete, A., Liu, A.: How a consumer can measure elasticity for cloud platforms. In: Proceedings of the 3rd ACM/SPEC International Conference on Performance Engineering, ICPE 2012, pp. 85–96. ACM, New York (2012)

19. Lientz, B.P., Swanson, E.B.: Software Maintenance Management. Addison-Wesley, Boston (1980)

20. Liu, Z., Cho, S.: Characterizing machines and workloads on a Google cluster. In: Proceedings of the 2012 41st International Conference on Parallel Processing Workshops, ICPPW 2012, pp. 397–403. IEEE Computer Society, Washington (2012)

21. Mao, M., Humphrey, M.: A performance study on the VM startup time in the cloud. In: Proceedings of the 2012 IEEE Fifth International Conference on Cloud Computing, CLOUD 2012, pp. 423–430. IEEE Computer Society, Washington (2012)

22. Mendelson, H.: Economies of scale in computing: Grosch's law revisited. Commun. ACM **30**(12), 1066–1072 (1987)

23. Mian, R., Martin, P., Zulkernine, F., Vazquez-Poletti, J.L.: Towards building performance models for data-intensive workloads in public clouds. In: Proceedings of the 4th ACM/SPEC International Conference on Performance Engineering, ICPE 2013, pp. 259–270. ACM, New York (2013)

24. MSAzure: Autoscaling (2018). https://docs.microsoft.com

25. Perez-Palacin, D., Mirandola, R., Scoppetta, M.: Simulation of techniques to improve the utilization of cloud elasticity in workload-aware adaptive software. In: Companion Publication for ACM/SPEC on International Conference on Performance Engineering, ICPE 2016 Companion, pp. 51–56. ACM, New York (2016)

26. Mell, P., Grance, T.: The NIST Definition of Cloud Computing (2009). http://csrc.nist.gov/groups/SNS/cloud-computing/cloud-def-v15.doc

27. Shen, D., Luo, Q., Poshyvanyk, D., Grechanik, M.: Automating performance bottleneck detection using search-based application profiling. In: Proceedings of the 2015 International Symposium on Software Testing and Analysis, pp. 270–281. ACM (2015)

28. Snellman, N., Ashraf, A., Porres, I.: Towards automatic performance and scalability testing of rich internet applications in the cloud. In: SEAA 2011, pp. 161–169. IEEE (2011)

29. van der Meulen, R.: Gartner says by 2020 "cloud shift" will affect more than $1 trillion in it spending (2018). http://www.gartner.com/newsroom/id/3384720

30. Xiao, X., Han, S., Zhang, D., Xie, T.: Context-sensitive delta inference for identifying workload-dependent performance bottlenecks. In: ISSTA 2013, pp. 90–100 (2013)

31. Zitzler, E., Künzli, S.: Indicator-based selection in multiobjective search. In: Yao, X. (ed.) PPSN 2004. LNCS, vol. 3242, pp. 832–842. Springer, Heidelberg (2004). https://doi.org/10.1007/978-3-540-30217-9_84

Injecting Social Diversity in Multi-objective Genetic Programming: The Case of Model Well-Formedness Rule Learning

Edouard Batot[(⊠)] and Houari Sahraoui[(⊠)]

GEODES, DIRO, Université de Montréal, Montreal, Canada
{batotedo,sahraouh}@iro.umontreal.ca

Abstract. Software modelling activities typically involve a tedious and time-consuming effort by specially trained personnel. This lack of automation hampers the adoption of the Model Driven Engineering (MDE) paradigm. Nevertheless, in the recent years, much research work has been dedicated to learn MDE artifacts instead of writing them manually. In this context, mono- and multi-objective Genetic Programming (GP) has proven being an efficient and reliable method to derive automation knowledge by using, as training data, a set of examples representing the expected behavior of an artifact. Generally, the conformance to the training example set is the main objective to lead the search for a solution. Yet, single fitness peak, or local optima deadlock, one of the major drawbacks of GP, remains when adapted to MDE and hinders the results of the learning. We aim at showing in this paper that an improvement in populations' social diversity carried out during the evolutionary computation will lead to more efficient search, faster convergence, and more generalizable results. We ascertain improvements are due to our changes on the search strategy with an empirical evaluation featuring the case of learning well-formedness rules in MDE with a multi-objective genetic algorithm. The obtained results are striking, and show that semantic diversity allows a rapid convergence toward the near-optimal solutions. Moreover, when the semantic diversity is used as for crowding distance, this convergence is uniform through a hundred of runs.

1 Introduction

Model Driven Engineering (MDE) aims at raising the level of abstraction of programming languages. MDE advocates the use of models as first-class artifacts. It combines domain-specific modeling languages to capture specific aspects of the solution, and transformation engines and generators in order to move back and forth between models while ensuring their coherence, or to produce from these models low level artifacts such as source code, documentation, and test suites [1]. Still, designing and developing artifacts able to perform automated

© Springer Nature Switzerland AG 2018
T. E. Colanzi and P. McMinn (Eds.): SSBSE 2018, LNCS 11036, pp. 166–181, 2018.
https://doi.org/10.1007/978-3-319-99241-9_8

tasks in MDE (ensuring the well-formedness of models, transforming models, etc.) requires one to have both knowledge in the targeted domain as well as in the design and development tools. If done manually, these activities typically involve a tedious and time-consuming effort by specially trained personnel. Such a lack of automation is considered by many MDE specialists as a threat to MDE adoption [2,3].

Yet, in recent years, many research contributions have shown that it is feasible to automatically learn how to perform a task through examples, or by analogy to similar, previously-solved tasks. More precisely, many of the proposed learning methods are based on Genetic Programming (GP) algorithms, and thereby promise to ease the burden of hand-programming growing volumes of increasingly complex information. As a matter of fact, empirical studies have shown a strong potential in learning automatically model transformations [4–6] and model well-formedness rules [7,8] from examples of tasks input/outputs. An *example* here must be understood as a couple <*input model*; *expected output*> defining the constraints that bind artifacts' output to input. The set of training examples represents the expected behavior of the artifact to learn and thus constitutes a convenient objective to lead the search of a solution.

Genetic programming and more generally multi-objective evolutionary computation has received increasing attention in the last decades. From early works [9–12], authors have formulated the idea that optimizing for multi-objective is to search for multiple solutions, each of which satisfy the different objectives to different degrees. The selection of the final solution with a particular combination of objectives' values is thus postponed until a time when it is known what combinations exist [13]. Studies have shown the value of such technics and their suitability to real problems. However, from the very beginning, authors pointed out two major drawbacks to the application of genetic programming (GP): (i) diversity of populations is difficult to maintain during evolution, and populations tend to gather around a *single fitness peak*; and, (ii) individuals tend to grow unnecessarily in size – also called *bloating* effect.

Both bloating and single fitness peak symptoms have been well investigated by researchers since early works, and valuable research directions were proposed [14–16]. Nevertheless, while adapting GP as an automatic process to learn well-formedness rules from examples, we encountered these same scenarios in a great amount of runs. Solutions agree on finding the correct outputs for a large number of examples, but fail all on a few same examples – a *single fitness peak* is reached. The approach seems to favor solutions with a high fitness, i.e., a high percentage of correct output found, at the expense of the diversity of the solutions.

On promoting diversity, Vanneshi *et al.* showed in their work the superior importance of research on indirect semantic methods that *"act on the syntax of the individuals and rely on survival criteria to indirectly promote a semantic behavior"* [17]. In as much as semantics are considered in GP as a vector of examples, MDE learning from examples methodology offers an auspicious support for such investigations. In the present study, we introduce a new Social Semantic Diversity Measure of individuals (inspired from Natural Language Processing) operating indirectly during the execution of a well-established multi-objective genetic algorithm [18]. We illustrate our work and assess its value in an empirical study featuring the problem of automatic learning of well-formedness rules from examples and counter examples.

The following section draws a map of the two main drawbacks of genetic programming and how researchers tackle them. Section 3 details how employing our Social Semantic Diversity Measure foster efficiency and accuracy of a GP run. We illustrate our approach in a case study depicted in Sect. 4. We assess our assumption through an empirical evaluation in Sect. 5. Section 6 concludes briefly.

2   Background, Related Work, and Problem Statement

Genetic Programming (GP) execution is best understood using Fig. 1. At the beginning, an initial population of programs must be created (1). Then, every program of the population is executed on the example inputs, and fitness is evaluated by comparing outputs with the expected ones (2). If a termination criterion is reach (3), the solution program (or a set of near-optimal solutions, in case of multi-objective) is returned (6). Otherwise, a new population of programs is created by genetic operations (crossover and mutation) applied on selected potential reproducers (4). The new population replaces the previous one (5), and a new iteration starts (2). The loop is repeated until a termination criterion is reach (commonly, a perfect fitness, or an arbitrary large number of iterations). Although this process allows to find good solutions for many problems, it is known to suffer from two issues, *bloating* and *single fitness peak*. In the remainder of this section, we briefly discuss the *bloating* issue, and then focus more of the *single fitness peak* issue and its relation to diversity, which is the main object of this paper.

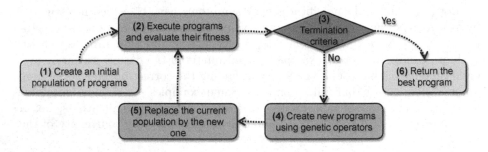

Fig. 1. A typical genetic programming cycle

2.1   Bloating

Luke *et al.* suggest that, from a high level perspective, *bloating* (or *code growth*) happens because adding genetic material to individuals is *more* positively correlated to the fitness than removing material. They define it as the "uncontrolled growth of the average size of an individual in the population" [16]. Nonetheless, much work has been done to reduce the effect of bloating, offering to present readers a few options to choose from [15]. More precisely, in a multi-objective context, Pareto-based Multi-objective Parsimony Pressure (*i.e.*, using an objective devoted to constraining size of individuals) has been found very effective – with limited side effects [13, 19]. We use this technique in our experiments.

2.2   Single Fitness Peak

The second problem with GP is the risk of a *single fitness peak* [13], consisting in a premature convergence together with a loss of diversity. Candidate solutions get stuck in a local optima and often no further improvement in fitness is noticed [20]. To tackle this issue, the level of diversity a population conveys must be given due consideration during a GP run [21]. More precisely, two phases of such a run are appropriate: at the initial population creation, to ensure a broad genetic material base; and/or during the evolution itself, to ensure that diversity does not fall from one generation to the next. In both cases, diversity exists in two kinds: genotypic diversity considers the level of variability in individuals' structure, whereas phenotypic diversity focuses on the behavior of individuals.

Genotypic Diversity. Genotypic diversity is the variety of individuals among a population with regards to their structure. It's a measure of the distance between individuals' syntax [22, 23]. MDE though, since the syntax of artifacts is (very) complex, does not bare a single consensual definition of genotypic (or structural) diversity [24, 25]. Nonetheless, to bestow a sufficiently diverse genetic material to start an evolutionary computation with, teams have used different metrics based on coverage estimations and showed interesting results. Works vary in nature and offer automatic generation of *diverse* models [8, 26], or a user visual assistance helping when eliciting learning inputs data [27–29]. In any case, both techniques can be employed to provide with diverse initial population of solutions as well as with qualified input data.

Phenotypic Diversity. As opposed to genotypic diversity, phenotypic diversity is measured on the behavior of a program – independently to its syntax. A phenotypic (or semantic [17]) measure, refers to the proportion of examples correctly processed by a program (*i.e.*, producing the expected output when executed on a specific input). It is a tangible fact that phenotypic diversity is more efficient than genotypic diversity to avoid the single fitness peak problem [17]. Nonetheless, if some early studies went as far as to expand the Darwinian metaphor and considered preference between individuals during GP run [30], to the best of our knowledge, there exists no study explicitly measuring benefits of phenotypic diversity when learning MDE artifacts.

Indirect Semantic Diversity Methods. Roughly speaking, these methods combine both genotypic and phenotypic diversities. The rationale behind indirect diversity methods lies in their ability to distinguish between the aim of the method: individuals with acute Semantic Fitness, and the mean of its application: genetic modifications performed on their syntax. Understood as such, the heuristic remains agnostic of its mean of achievement and is ready to convey a strong generalization potential [31]. Vanneshi *et al.* [17] have proven the power of indirect diversity methods and call for more research in this field. It is to note here that, in the context of learning artifacts from examples in MDE, Semantic Fitness measure is a built-in feature and comes at no extra cost.

3   Social Semantic Diversity Measure

Notwithstanding that MDE-artifact learning from examples might be perfectly fit to GP adaptation, single fitness peaks yet keep happening during evolution. This leads to a disproportionate number of solutions with a good fitness, at the expense of their diversity. Processing most examples correctly, these *alphas* [14] struggle to solve all examples exhaustively. Meanwhile, unfortunately, solutions able to solve the remaining corner cases reach a (much) lower fitness. Withal, since reproducers are chosen with regard to their fitness, the genetic material these latter *partial solutions* convey is lost and *corner cases* are never solved. A remedy to this deficiency was found using a social diversity measure.

We call *Social Diversity Measure* a measure that does not take into account the only individualistic fitness (*i.e.,* how many examples an individual resolves) but considers as well a social dimension (*i.e.,* what does that individual bring to the general fitness of the population).

Since we use a Semantic fitness, the remaining of this paper will mention Social Semantic Diversity Measure (SSDM). Its computation, based on the *inverse example resolution frequency* (IERF) is inspired from the *term frequency-inverse document frequency* (TF-IDF) numerical statistic [32] from information retrieval research field. In other words, the SSDM of a solution is the sum of IERF of the examples it solves.

Paraphrasing *TFIDF* definition may help the reader to grasp the general idea of SSDM. We formulate it as follows: "SSDM increases proportionally to the number of examples solved and is offset by the frequency of which an example is solved by the population's individuals, which helps to adjust for the fact that some examples are more frequently solved in general."

As a consequence, SSDM favors solutions solving *corner cases* by considering how many solutions in the population solve an example.

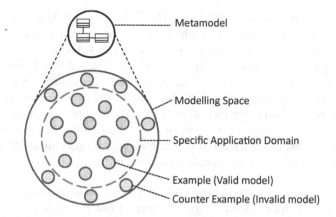

Fig. 2. Metamodel, modelling space and application domain (Color figure online)

4   Learning Well-Formedness Rule

In this section, we illustrate how social semantic diversity can be implemented in a multi-objective genetic-programming algorithm to learn well-formedness rules (WFRs) from examples. As mentioned in the introduction, researchers offer to use GP to learn some of MDE artifacts automatically as a substantial alternative to writing them manually. Indeed, we aim at showing in this paper that, during the process, which scalability remains at stake [33], an improvement in populations' social diversity will lead to more efficient search and more generalizable results. Thus far, the reader is asked to understand the little space left for implementation details.

After a brief overlook at the use and function of well-formedness rules, we will depict how much a tangible support GP, and more precisely multi-objective GP, offers to learn them automatically from examples and counter examples.

4.1   Well-Formedness Rules

In the MDE paradigm, due to their high level of abstraction, metamodels usually define too-large modelling spaces. They must be enriched with constraints, or rules, limiting the scope of their possible instantiations, *i.e.,* well-formed models in contrast to ill-formed models. Figure 2 schematizes the concept of specific application domain: a metamodel defines a modelling space (within blue line); of which a specific application domain is a sub-space (within red dashed line). A set of WFRs allows to automatically differentiate between valid (well-formed) and invalid (ill-formed) models – it formally describes the limit of that targeted specific domain.

Representation. In the context of a GP learning process, a solution to our problem is thus a set of WFRs. More precisely, we represent a WFR as a tree which nodes are logical operators (*AND, OR, IMPLIES,* and *NOT*) and first-order quantifiers (*forAll* and *exists*), and which leaves are learning atomic blocks in the form of *OCL patterns* instances. Consequently, a solution is a tree with as root a vector whose elements are pointers to the individual WFR trees. Figure 3 shows an example of a candidate (not necessarily valid) solution with 3 WFRs for the state-machine metamodel. The first and second rules constrain a *final* state to have respectively one incoming transition and no outgoing transition. The third rule requires that a pseudostate *choice* must have at least one incoming or outgoing transition. As for their execution, we implement WFRs in the *defacto* language Object Constraint Language (OCL[1]).

OCL Patterns. The rationale behind OCL patterns is beyond the scope of this paper. They result from empirical studies carried out on more than 400 meta-models from industry and academe alike [34]. In a nutshell, OCL patterns should be understood here as a minimalistic set of templates which instantiation and composition allows to express all and every *useful* WFR.

Size Concern. Since solutions must be legible by final user (*i.e.,* within human reach), the size of constraints must be kept as small as possible.

4.2   GP Adaptation

Our goal is to find the minimal set (*i.e.,* size) of WFRs that best discriminates between the valid and invalid example models (*i.e.,* fitness). Size and fitness objectives being contradictive in nature, we represent the learning of WFRs as a multi-objective optimization problem, and we solve it using the Non-Sorting Genetic Algorithm NSGA-II [18].

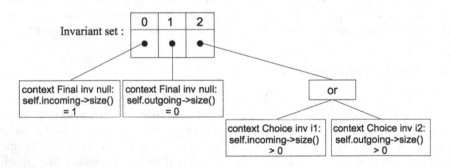

Fig. 3. An example of solution containing 3 WFRs.

The idea of NSGA-II [18] is to make a population of candidate solutions evolve toward the near-optimal solution in order to solve a multi-objective optimization problem. NSGA-II is designed to find a set of optimal solutions, called

---

[1] http://www.omg.org/spec/OCL/.

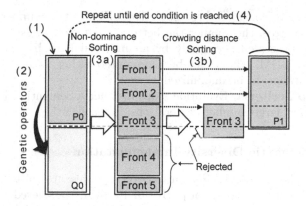

Fig. 4. Non Sorting Genetic Algorithm NSGA-II [18]

non-dominated solutions, also Pareto set. A non-dominated solution is the one which provides a suitable compromise between all objectives without degrading any of them. As described in Fig. 4, the first step in NSGA-II is to create randomly a population P_0 of $N/2$ individuals encoded using a specific representation (1). Then, a child population Q_0, of the same size, is generated from the population of parents P_0 using genetic operators such as crossover and mutation (2). Both populations are merged into an initial population R_0 of size N, which is sorted into dominance fronts according to the dominance principle (3a). A solution s_1 dominates a solution s_2 for a set of objectives $\{O_i\}$ if $\forall i, O_i(s_1) \geqslant O_i(s_2)$ and $\exists j \mid O_j(s_1) > O_j(s_2)$. The first (Pareto) front includes the non-dominated solutions; the second front contains the solutions that are dominated only by the solutions of the first front, and so on and so forth. The fronts are included in the parent population P_1 of the next generation following the dominance order until the size of $N/2$ is reached. If this size coincides with part of a front, the solutions inside this front are sorted, to complete the population, according to a crowding distance which favors "diversity" in the solutions (3b). This process will be repeated until a stop criterion is reached, *e.g.*, a number of iterations or a certain value of the Semantic Fitness.

We adapted NSGA-II to our problem as follows.

- **Solution Representation and Creation.** A solution to our problem is represented as mentioned in Sect. 4.1, *i.e.*, a set of OCL constraints, each implementing a WFR represented as a tree. The initial population is created randomly. For each individual, the average number of nodes in the WFR trees, the maximum depth, and the maximum width are configurable.
- **Reproduction.** As genetic operators, we use a single-point crossover applied to the tree-root vector, and two kinds of mutations. First, a node from a WFR tree is chosen randomly. If it is a leaf, the pattern instance is either replaced with a new randomly created one or, if applicable, the pattern parameters are replaced randomly with applicable values. If the selected node is a logical operator, this is changed randomly.

- **Objectives.** We consider three objectives: *Size* is the number of leaves in the constraint tree, the smaller the better; *Semantic Fitness* is the number of examples processed accurately by an individual, to be maximized; and *Diversity* is SSDM, which can be represented either as an objective or a crowding distance, to be maximized as well.
- **Termination criteria.** Evolution stops if either a Semantic Fitness of 99%, or an arbitrary large number of iterations, is reach.

4.3   Social Semantic Diversity Implementation

We offer to employ the Social Semantic Diversity Measure (SSDM) in two different ways. The first is as an objective of its own, considered together with above-mentioned size and fitness (as promoted by Dejong *et al.* [13]). The other builds on peculiar limitation of NSGA-II [35] and acts as an alternative to the computation of a crowding distance. In both cases, SSDM computation remains the same.

More specifically, implementing SSDM comes to adapting TF-IDF [32] using examples as documents and solutions as words. This is detailed in Listing 1.1. At a given iteration, SSDM is calculated from a binary matrix in which each cell represents the score of an individual against an example of the training set. The frequency of an example is the number of times it is solved by individuals (first *for* loop). Finally, individual's SSDM value is the sum of *inverse example resolution frequencies* of examples that it processes accurately (last *for* loop). More precisely, variables are:

- *example_set*, the vector of training examples;
- *sol_vs_examples*, which contains the result of the comparison between output of individuals and output of the oracle when executed on *example_set*;
- and *fq_ex*, which contains examples frequencies, recording how many solutions solve each example from *example_set*;
- *ierfi*, the vector of *inverse example resolution frequencies* of training examples.

5   Evaluation

To assess the improvement brought by our social semantic diversity in the search strategy, we conducted an empirical evaluation[2]. We formulate our research questions as follows:

- **RQ0:** Are our results a consequence of an efficient exploration of the search space, or are they due to the vast number of individuals we consider during the evolution?

---

[2] All experiment data is available at http://www-ens.iro.umontreal.ca/~batotedo/ssdm_exp/.

Listing 1.1. Excerpt for SSDM weights calculation.

```
\\ Compute frequencies of examples solved
for (int i = 0; i < sol_vs_ex.length; i++)
  for (int j = 0; j < sol_vs_ex[i].length; j++)
    fq_ex[j] += sol_vs_ex[i][j];

\\ Inverse document frequencies
for (int j = 0; j < fq.length; j++)
  ierfi[j] = Math.log10(D/fq_ex[j]);

\\ Weigthing
weight = 0;
for(int j = 0; j < example_set.length; j++)
  if(example_set[j].isAccurate())
    weight += ierfi[j];
```

- **RQ1:** Does the use of Social Semantic Diversity as an objective improves the search strategy, and, if so, how much?
- **RQ2:** Does the use of Social Semantic Diversity as an alternative crowding distance exhibit better efficiency and generalizability than as an objective?

5.1   Setting

In order to mitigate the influence of a metamodel specific structure on the learning process, we selected three metamodels (`FamilyTree`, `Statemachine`, and `Project Manager`) that demonstrate different levels of structure complexity and require diverse OCL WFR sets. We provided with oracle (*i.e.,* expected WFRs) manually. In more details, `FamilyTree` is the most simple case. Yet, it has been used as an illustrative example in various publications in the MDE research literature, such as [36]. `Statemachine` illustrates structural cardinality restrictions and define a common, widely used language. Finally, `Project Manager` is the most complex case and comes from [37].

Learning Examples. To provide with example sets of *quality* (*i.e.,* covering at best the modelling space, yet as small as can be), we used a model generator [8]. Size matters since every generated model example must be, in a real setting, tagged manually as *valid* or *invalid*. For the sake of experiment, we use the WFRs oracles to mimic the manual tagging. To run the experiment, we used two sets of examples for each metamodel. On the one hand, 20 models (10 valid, 10 invalid) were required for the learning (a *training set*). On the other hand, a *test bench* of 100 models (50 valid, 50 invalid) was used to measure solutions' accuracy (or generalizability).

Configurations and Variables. Four configurations were considered to illustrate and answer our research questions (see Sect. 4.2 for implementation details).

RND is a random exploration of the search space that takes the best among a given number of solutions randomly generated; **STD** is a standard run of NSGA-II [18] with two objectives, size and semantic fitness; **OBJ** is a run of NSGA-II with three objectives: size, semantic fitness, and SSDM diversity; and **CD** is a run of NSGA-II with size and semantic fitness as objectives, and SSDM as crowding distance.

We used two dependent variables to quantify experiment results: **#GEN**, the number of generation the evolutionary computation needed to find a solution. A score of 3000 means that there was no solution with perfect fit found during the search, and **ACC**, the proportion of examples from the test bench a solution process accurately.

Evaluation Protocol. For the NSGA-II parameters, we use a maximum number of iterations of 3000 and a population size of 30 solutions. Crossover and mutation probabilities are set to 0.9 and 0.3 respectively. In addition, solutions are created with between 5 to 15 WFRs with each WFR having a maximum depth of 3 and width of 15. We answer RQ0 with a comparison between the results given when using SSDM as an objective (OBJ) in the search strategy and those of a random exploration (RND). Since our strategy explores 3000*30 solutions, the random exploration explores randomly 90000 solutions as well and considers the best individual so created. We answer RQ1 with a comparison between the solutions obtained after an execution with and one without social semantic diversity objective (respectively OBJ and STD). Finally, we answer RQ2 by comparing the configurations with social semantic diversity objective (OBJ) and with social semantic diversity crowding distance (CD). We ran each treatment 100 times to tackle GP indeterminism and we guarantee statistical significance of the findings using the Mann-Whitney test.

5.2   Results and Analysis

RQ0 - Sanity Check. As can be seen in Table 1, the RND configuration gives very poor results in comparison with an OBJ execution for the two most complex metamodels (average accuracy on test bench is 0.5 vs 0.76 for `Project Manager` and 0.53 vs. 0.94 for `Statemachine`). The difference in both cases is statistically significant (p-$value < 0.001$) and the effect size is large ($Cohen's\,d > 5$). For the small metamodel `FamilyTree`, although statistically significant, the difference and the effect size are small. *We can conclude that solutions are significantly more generalizable when using OBJ configuration.*

RQ1 - Social Semantic Diversity Method, an Improvement? Efficiency shows a significant improvement when SSDM is used, as can be seen in odd columns of Fig. 5. The number of generations required to find a solution when employing OBJ is a lot smaller than when employing STD. With `Project Manager` metamodel, an STD run hardly find solutions solving all training examples within 3000 generations, but OBJ do it in an average of 260 generations.

Table 1. Statistical comparison of results between random search and our approach on three WFR learning scenarios.

	Average ACC Value		Mann Witney p-value	Effect Size Cohen's d
	RDN	OBJ		
Project Manager	0.5	0.76	<0.001	7.35
Statemachine	0.53	0.94	<0.001	5.38
FamilyTree	0.93	0.98	<0.001	0.74

More, solutions were found with significantly better accuracy than STD (respectively 0.76 against 0.69) and thus strengthen solutions' generalizability likewise. This success is also noticed, if of lesser magnitude, during executions on the Statemachine metamodel. Here, if solutions are found in both configuration, yet OBJ is significantly faster (with 782 generations, when STD requires more than 1782). As for the FamilyTree metamodel (not shown if the figure), solutions given by OBJ executions output a similar ACC (0.98) but significantly faster with 25 generations (resp. 76 with STD). *We can conclude that injecting the social semantic diversity significantly improves the learning results.*

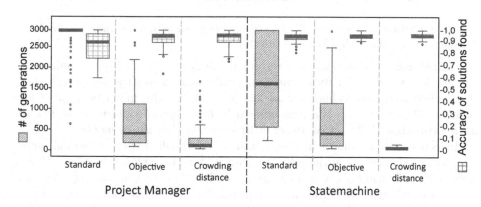

Fig. 5. Number of generations to find solutions and their accuracy on test bench for Project Manager and Statemachine metamodels.

RQ2 - Social Semantic Diversity Method as an Alternative Crowding Distance, Any Better Yet?

Results of RQ2 are flagrant (see the third configuration for both metamodels in Fig. 5). In Fig. 6, a hundred runs show together how using SSDM (Fig. 6c and b) surges the learning curves and fosters solution exploration compared to a standard run (Fig. 6a). As for generalizability, it doesn't seem that choosing between SSDM as an objective (OBJ) or in the crowding distance (CD) has any significant impact on the accuracy of solutions on test bench found (Mann Witney p-value > 0.01; see even columns in Fig. 5 for an illustration). Thence, the main difference lies in the smaller average number of iterations CD needs to converge, compared to OBJ runs. Note that analysis is the strongest with Project Manager and FamilyTree metamodels.

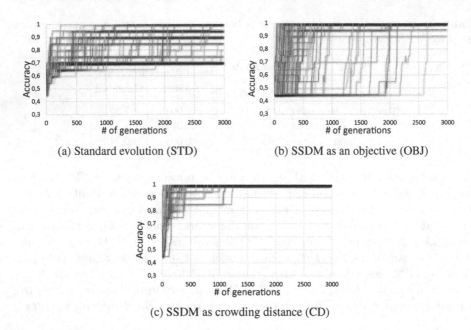

(a) Standard evolution (STD)   (b) SSDM as an objective (OBJ)

(c) SSDM as crowding distance (CD)

Fig. 6. Evolution of individuals' average accuracy value during runs on `Project Manager` metamodel, with a hundred runs a plot.

With `Statemachine` metamodel's results are slightly mitigated but remains significant. In that case, WFRs are more generally focused on structural cardinality than WFRs of the two other metamodels. We conceive this might be a factor for slightly different results. *We can conclude that social semantic diversity as a crowding distance is more efficient than as an objective.*

In conclusion, as shown in Figs. 5 and 6 and certified with statistical analysis, the OBJ strategy surpasses significantly a STD exploration of solutions. Convergence is faster and output more generalizable (*i.e.,* confronting solutions to a test bench gives better results). A reason for these results might come from the way size is controlled. As recognized in the literature, we implemented it as a Pareto-based Multi-objective Parsimony Pressure. We noted, as expected [13], that solutions were skewed toward a 1.0 size, and the Pareto front grew large. Solutions' size was indeed the one expected (*i.e.,* legible by a human), and the search, passed a few generations, relied mainly on Semantic Fitness. As a presumed consequence, when putting SSDM as an alternative to crowding distance, results were breathtaking on the three metamodels. Finally, using Social Semantic Diversity Measure as an alternative crowding distance outperforms its use as an additional objective. Convergence is boosted, and generalizability is kept at its maximum. We hope these results are generalizable and claim the need to explore other applications, with OBJ and CD alike.

5.3   Thread to Validity

Although our approach produced good results on three metamodels, a threat to validity resides in the generalization of our approach to other scenarios. Still, metamodels show different characteristic and origin, and while our sample does not cover all learning scenarios, we believe that it is representative enough of a wide range of metamodels.

Another threat to the validity of our results relates to the use of a single set of (20) models to learn each WFR sets. Characterization of example sets is an ongoing investigation, and different sets might show different results. Yet, to mitigate what specificities the manual design of models can bring and encourage replication of our work, we used a generator [8]. Also, using the same set in every configuration ensures a difference in sets do not interfere in the experiment.

Regarding the applicability to other MDE artifacts, we believe that the idea to consider the social dimension of individuals' characteristics shall apply to the evolutionary computation of model transformation as well. In this case, *inverse example resolution frequency* could be used as well and we prospect, as future work, to replicate this study on model transformation learning.

6   Conclusion

This paper studies the impact of using a social semantic diversity to improve the search process for the multi-objective optimization problem of learning model well-formedness rules from examples and counter examples. The *Social Semantic Diversity* is measured (SSDM) in a way that does not take into account the only individualistic fitness (*i.e.*, how many examples an individual resolves) but considers as well a social dimension (*i.e.*, what does that individual bring to the general fitness of the population). We integrated SSDM in the NSGA-II algorithm as (i) an additional objective, and (ii) as an alternative to the crowding distance.

We evaluated the two options by learning WFRs for three metamodels. Our results are compiling evidence that injecting the social semantic diversity in the search process, especial as an alternative to the crowding distance, improves the convergence and the quality of the learned artifacts. The proposed measure and its integration in the multi-objective optimization algorithm are agnostic with respect to the learned artifact and the input/output examples used to guide the search. This allows to use social semantic diversity for a wide range of problem that can be solved by a multi-objective genetic programming algorithm. This claim must, however, be supported by replication studies. We expect to conduct some of these studies, especially for model transformation learning. Finally, we encourage further replication of our work to determine whether different multi-objective GP algorithms could benefit as well from our discovery.

References

1. Schmidt, D.C.: Model-driven engineering. IEEE Comput. Soc. **39**(2), 25 (2006)
2. Selic, B.: What will it take? A view on adoption of model-based methods in practice. Int. J. Softw. Syst. Model. **11**(4), 513–526 (2012)
3. Whittle, J., Hutchinson, J., Rouncefield, M.: The state of practice in model-driven engineering. IEEE Softw. **31**, 79–85 (2014)

4. Kessentini, M., Kessentini, W., Sahraoui, H., Boukadoum, M., Ouni, A.: Design defects detection and correction by example. In: Proceedings of the International Conference on Program Comprehension, pp. 81–90 (2011)
5. Saada, H., Dolques, X., Huchard, M., Nebut, C., Sahraoui, H.: Generation of operational transformation rules from examples of model transformations. In: France, R.B., Kazmeier, J., Breu, R., Atkinson, C. (eds.) MODELS 2012. LNCS, vol. 7590, pp. 546–561. Springer, Heidelberg (2012). https://doi.org/10.1007/978-3-642-33666-9_35
6. Baki, I., Sahraoui, H.: Multi-step learning and adaptive search for learning complex model transformations from examples. ACM Trans. Softw. Eng. Methodol. **X**, 36 (2015)
7. Faunes, M., Cadavid, J., Baudry, B., Sahraoui, H., Combemale, B.: Automatically searching for metamodel well-formedness rules in examples and counter-examples. In: Moreira, A., Schätz, B., Gray, J., Vallecillo, A., Clarke, P. (eds.) MODELS 2013. LNCS, vol. 8107, pp. 187–202. Springer, Heidelberg (2013). https://doi.org/10.1007/978-3-642-41533-3_12
8. Batot, E., Sahraoui, H.: A generic framework for model-set selection for the unification of testing and learning MDE tasks. In: Proceedings of the International Conference on Model-Driven Engineering Languages and Systems. ACM (2016)
9. Schaffer, J.D.: Multiple objective optimization with vector evaluated genetic algorithms. In: Proceedings of the 1st International Conference on Genetic Algorithms, pp. 93–100. L. Erlbaum Associates Inc., Hillsdale (1985)
10. Goldberg, D.E.: Genetic Algorithms in Search, Optimization and Machine Learning, 1st edn. Addison-Wesley Longman Publishing Co., Inc., Boston (1989)
11. Holland, J.H.: Adaptation in Natural and Artificial Systems: An Introductory Analysis with Applications to Biology, Control and Artificial Intelligence. MIT Press, Cambridge (1992)
12. Koza, J.R.: Genetic Programming: On the Programming of Computers by Means of Natural Selection. MIT Press, Cambridge (1992)
13. de Jong, E.D., Watson, R.A., Pollack, J.B.: Reducing bloat and promoting diversity using multi-objective methods. In: Proceedings of the 3rd Annual Conference on Genetic and Evolutionary Computation, GECCO 2001, pp. 11–18 (2001)
14. Bersano-Begey, T.F.: Controlling exploration, diversity and escaping local optima in GP: adapting weights of training sets to model resource consumption. In: Koza, J.R. (ed.) Late Breaking Papers at the 1997 Genetic Programming Conference, pp. 7–10 (1997)
15. Soule, T., Foster, J.A.: Effects of code growth and parsimony pressure on populations in genetic programming. Evol. Comput. **6**(4), 293–309 (1998)
16. Luke, S., Panait, L.: A comparison of bloat control methods for genetic programming. Evol. Comput. **14**(3), 309–344 (2006)
17. Vanneschi, L., Castelli, M., Silva, S.: A survey of semantic methods in genetic programming. Genet. Programm. Evol. Mach. **15**(2), 195–214 (2014)
18. Deb, K., Agrawal, S., Pratap, A., Meyarivan, T.: A fast elitist non-dominated sorting genetic algorithm for multi-objective optimization: NSGA-II. In: Schoenauer, M., et al. (eds.) PPSN 2000. LNCS, vol. 1917, pp. 849–858. Springer, Heidelberg (2000). https://doi.org/10.1007/3-540-45356-3_83
19. Ekárt, A., Németh, S.Z.: A metric for genetic programs and fitness sharing. In: Poli, R., Banzhaf, W., Langdon, W.B., Miller, J., Nordin, P., Fogarty, T.C. (eds.) EuroGP 2000. LNCS, vol. 1802, pp. 259–270. Springer, Heidelberg (2000). https://doi.org/10.1007/978-3-540-46239-2_19

20. Wyns, B., De Bruyne, P., Boullart, L.: Characterizing diversity in genetic programming. In: Collet, P., Tomassini, M., Ebner, M., Gustafson, S., Ekárt, A. (eds.) EuroGP 2006. LNCS, vol. 3905, pp. 250–259. Springer, Heidelberg (2006). https://doi.org/10.1007/11729976_22
21. Burke, E.K., Gustafson, S., Kendall, G.: Diversity in genetic programming: an analysis of measures and correlation with fitness. IEEE Trans. Evol. Comput. **8**(1), 47–62 (2004)
22. McPhee, N.F., Hopper, N.J.: Analysis of genetic diversity through population history. In: Proceedings of the 1st Annual Conference on Genetic and Evolutionary Computation, vol. 2, pp. 1112–1120. Morgan Kaufmann Publishers Inc. (1999)
23. McPhee, N.F., Ohs, B., Hutchison, T.: Semantic building blocks in genetic programming. In: O'Neill, M., et al. (eds.) EuroGP 2008. LNCS, vol. 4971, pp. 134–145. Springer, Heidelberg (2008). https://doi.org/10.1007/978-3-540-78671-9_12
24. Baudry, B., Monperrus, M.: The multiple facets of software diversity: recent developments in year 2000 and beyond. ACM Comput. Surv. **48**(1), 16:1–16:26 (2015)
25. Giraldo, F.D., EspaÃśa, S., Pastor, O.: Analysing the concept of quality in model-driven engineering literature: a systematic review. In: 2014 IEEE Eighth International Conference on Research Challenges in Information Science, RCIS, pp. 1–12, May 2014
26. Wu, H.: Generating metamodel instances satisfying coverage criteria via SMT solving. In: Proceedings of the International Conference on Model-Driven Engineering and Software Development, pp. 40–51 (2016)
27. Ferdjoukh, A., Galinier, F., Bourreau, E., Chateau, A., Nebut, C.: Measuring differences to compare sets of models and improve diversity in MDE. In: International Conference on Software Engineering Advances, ICSEA, Athens, Greece, October 2017
28. Sánchez-Cuadrado, J., de Lara, J., Guerra, E.: Bottom-up meta-modelling: an interactive approach. In: France, R.B., Kazmeier, J., Breu, R., Atkinson, C. (eds.) MODELS 2012. LNCS, vol. 7590, pp. 3–19. Springer, Heidelberg (2012). https://doi.org/10.1007/978-3-642-33666-9_2
29. López-Fernández, J.J., Guerra, E., de Lara, J.: Example-based validation of domain-specific visual languages. In: Proceedings of the International Conference on Software Language Engineering, SLE 2015, pp. 101–112 (2015)
30. Ryan, C.: Racial harmony in genetic algorithms (1994)
31. Dabhi, V.K., Chaudhary, S.: A survey on techniques of improving generalization ability of genetic programming solutions. CoRR abs/1211.1119 (2012)
32. Sparck Jones, K.: A statistical interpretation of term specificity and its application in retrieval. In: Willett, P. (ed.) Document Retrieval Systems, pp. 132–142 (1988)
33. Harman, M., Jia, Y., Zhang, Y.: Achievements, open problems and challenges for search based software testing. In: Proceedings of the International Conference on Software Testing Verification and Validation, pp. 1–12 (2015)
34. Cadavid, J.J., Combemale, B., Baudry, B.: Ten years of meta-object facility: an analysis of metamodeling practices. AtlanMod, Research Report RR-7882 (2012)
35. Fortin, F.-A., Parizeau, M.: Revisiting the NSGA-II crowding-distance computation. In: Proceedings of International Conference on Genetic and Evolutionary Computation, GECCO. ACM (2013)
36. Gogolla, M., Vallecillo, A., Burgueno, L., Hilken, F.: Employing classifying terms for testing model transformations. In: Proceedings of the International Conference on Model-Driven Engineering Languages and Systems, pp. 312–321 (2015)
37. Hassam, K., Sadou, S., Fleurquin, R.: Adapting OCL constraints after a refactoring of their model using an MDE process. In: 9th Edition of the BElgian-NEtherlands Software eVOLution Seminar, pp. 16–27 (2010)

Automated Optimization of Weighted Non-functional Objectives in Self-adaptive Systems

Kate M. Bowers[1]([✉]), Erik M. Fredericks[1]([✉]), and Betty H. C. Cheng[2]([✉])

[1] Oakland University, Rochester, MI 48309, USA
{kmlabell,fredericks}@oakland.edu
[2] Michigan State University, East Lansing, MI 48824, USA
chengb@cse.msu.edu

Abstract. A self-adaptive system (SAS) can reconfigure at run time in response to adverse combinations of system and environmental conditions in order to continuously satisfy its requirements. Moreover, SASs are subject to cross-cutting non-functional requirements (NFRs), such as performance, security, and usability, that collectively characterize *how* functional requirements (FRs) are to be satisfied. In many cases, the trigger for adapting an SAS may be due to a violation of one or more NFRs. For a given NFR, different combinations of hierarchically-organized FRs may yield varying degrees of satisfaction (i.e., satisficement). This paper presents `Providentia`, a search-based technique to optimize NFR satisficement when subjected to various sources of uncertainty (e.g., environment, interactions between system elements, etc.). `Providentia` searches for optimal combinations of FRs that, when considered with different subgoal decompositions and/or differential weights, provide optimal satisficement of NFR objectives. Experimental results suggest that using an SAS goal model enhanced with search-based optimization significantly improves system performance when compared with manually- and randomly-generated weights and subgoals.

Keywords: Search-based software engineering
Non-functional requirements · Self-adaptive systems
Evolutionary computation

1 Introduction

A self-adaptive system (SAS) provides adaptation strategies for reconfiguration at run time to mitigate unexpected issues that arise as a result of uncertainty (e.g., adverse environmental conditions or unexpected issues in the system itself) [15,19]. The SAS generally will use these adaptation strategies to select an optimal configuration that enables continuous requirements satisficement (i.e., degree of satisfaction) [5]. An SAS is governed by functional requirements (FRs) that can be mathematically quantified to monitor satisficement, as well as by non-functional requirements (NFRs) that tend to be qualitative and may not be

© Springer Nature Switzerland AG 2018
T. E. Colanzi and P. McMinn (Eds.): SSBSE 2018, LNCS 11036, pp. 182–197, 2018.
https://doi.org/10.1007/978-3-319-99241-9_9

easily mathematically quantifiable (e.g., resiliency and efficiency) [17,34]. However, this process relies on domain knowledge and may be sub-optimal given changing environmental conditions. This paper presents Providentia, a search-based technique to be used at design time to automatically determine an optimal set of FRs, including the level of impact of each, to support each NFR in an SAS.

NFRs can be modeled as behavioral goals (e.g., KAOS [17]) or soft goals (i.e., NFR framework [34] and iStar modeling language [36]). Soft goals describe preferences of system behaviors that tend to be qualitative in nature [23], thereby making the determination of an optimal reconfiguration strategy more challenging for SASs. Similar to Providentia, the Analytic Hierarchy Process (AHP) decomposes NFRs into one or more weighted FRs using an automated weighting scheme to prioritize FRs [27]. However, prioritizations in an SAS determined at design time may change drastically as the system experiences various forms of uncertainty due to changing environmental conditions and unexpected system changes, such as unwanted feature interactions.

We introduce Providentia to address the challenges with quantifying and analyzing NFRs at run time via a design-time technique that takes into account environmental and system uncertainty. Providentia uses a utility function that specifies a mathematical expression of goal satisficement for each FR. Each NFR has a linear-weighted expression that specifies the impact that a given FR has in satisficing the NFR objective [27]. For a given set of SAS FRs with corresponding metrics to assess their satisficement, Providentia explores different combinations of weights for a linear-weighted expression of FRs that contribute to the satisficement of their respective NFRs.

To make the overall system robust to adverse conditions, an evolutionary-based search process assesses the system's run-time behavior using an executable specification of the system that is subjected to randomly-generated sources of uncertainty in order to identify optimal goal model configurations for maximizing FR/NFR satisficement. Providentia optimizes the FR selection process using a genetic algorithm as a search heuristic, where the search space is the different goal model configurations that capture varying combinations of FRs. The genetic algorithm determines optimal weight assignments that result in the highest satisficement of the NFR when faced with uncertainty. The Providentia-optimized goal model is then applied to the SAS at run time. The correlated evaluation of NFR and FR satisficement enables traditionally soft goals to be evaluated with FR metrics during execution, thereby enabling online SAS reconfiguration in response to high-level non-functional and functional objectives. Furthermore, optimizing the weighted contributions of FRs to each NFR according to estimated sources of uncertainty enables the system to perform better at run time under actual sources of uncertainty, as a requirements engineer may not be able to foresee the diverse range and scope of cases when deriving their respective weights.

We illustrate the effectiveness of Providentia with an industry-provided application, namely, a remote data mirroring (RDM) network [13,14]. The RDM application must replicate and disseminate messages to each RDM within the network and can experience uncertainty due to dropped or delayed messages, sensor noise, and unexpected server and network link failures. For run-time assessment purposes, we use a network simulator that conforms to the specifications provided by our industrial collaborator. Experimental results suggest that using Providentia to optimize NFRs based on simulated sources of uncertainty significantly improves overall requirement fitness as well as decreases the number of requirement violations of the RDM application when compared to NFRs using human-generated identification of contributing FRs, their weights, as well as those assigned by random search. The remainder of this paper is organized as follows. Section 2 provides relevant background information on the RDM application, goal-oriented requirements engineering (GORE), NFRs, and utility functions for assessing metrics. Section 3 details the implementation of Providentia for automatically determining FR selection and weight assignment for NFRs. Section 4 presents our experimental results and Sect. 5 discusses related work. Section 6 summarizes our results and overviews future directions.

2   Background

This section provides relevant background information on the RDM application, GORE, NFRs, and utility functions.

2.1   Remote Data Mirroring

RDM is a data protection technique for ensuring that data loss is minimized and data availability is maximized in the context of data replicates that are disseminated to other servers (i.e., data mirrors) in physically remote locations [13,15]. An RDM network can be modeled as an SAS [26], enabling reconfiguration in terms of network topology and data propagation parameters to enable continuous requirements satisficement. Uncertainty can impact the RDM in terms of unexpected dropped or delayed messages, random network link or data mirror failures, and noise applied to network links and data mirror sensors. These reconfiguration strategies can be fulfilled by downgrading the status of the affected data mirrors from active (i.e., can send and receive messages) to passive (i.e., can only receive messages) or quiescent (i.e., cannot send or receive messages).

2.2   Goal-Oriented Requirements Engineering

GORE is an approach for graphically specifying a system's key objectives and constraints using both *functional* and *non-functional* goals [8]. A goal is a system behavior achieved through the cooperation of its agents, where an agent is a system component that performs actions based on the behavior specified by goals. A requirement is a goal under the responsibility of a single agent. An expectation is a requirement whose agent is a part of the environment. Functional goals specify a service to be provided and non-functional goals impose a quality constraint on those functional services [17].

GORE enables goal decomposition using a directed acyclic graph, where each node represents a goal and each edge represents a goal refinement [17]. GORE has been extended with additional refinement strategies through KAOS [8,17] and iStar [35]. KAOS introduces AND- and OR-refinements for additional satisficement constraints, where an AND-refined goal is satisfied if *each sub-goal* is also satisfied and an OR-refined goal is satisfied if *at least one sub-goal* is satisfied. KAOS functional goals may be further categorized as *invariant* or *non-invariant*, where invariant goals must always be satisfied and non-invariant goals may be temporarily unsatisfied due to transient conditions. Invariant goals are denoted by the keywords "Maintain" or "Avoid" and non-invariant goals are denoted by the keyword "Achieve."

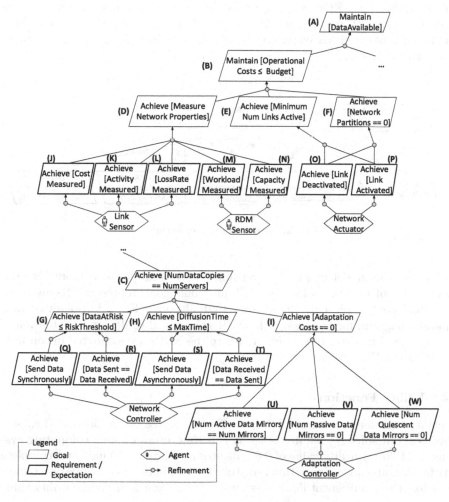

Fig. 1. RDM goal model.

Figure 1 presents the KAOS goal model of the RDM application that describes its hierarchical relationships between goals, requirements/expectations, and agents.[1]

2.3   Non-functional Requirements

NFRs impose a quality constraint on a system [6]. Such goals are often difficult to quantify, given their relative subjectivity. Moreover, cross-cutting concerns may manifest in NFRs, given their broad impacts on the overall system [6]. While rigorous mathematical models have been previously described for calculating requirements satisfaction [10,24], such models generally require a detailed understanding of the real-world environment that is often difficult or impossible to derive for NFRs. A sample NFR for the RDM application in Fig. 1 is `Minimize [Power]`, where many factors (e.g., Goals (A), (E), (I), (V), and (W)) could contribute to either increasing or decreasing power consumption over time, as illustrated in Fig. 2.

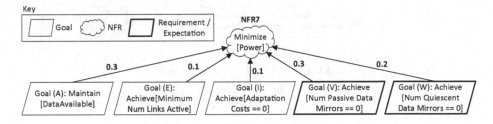

Fig. 2. NFR7: minimize[power].

We use the model in Fig. 2 as an illustrative example to demonstrate the effectiveness of `Providentia`, where all functional goals represent FRs and non-functional goals represent NFRs. Note that although Fig. 2 is presented in a separate diagram, for discussion, the NFR is intended to depict an extension of the input goal model shown in Fig. 1, where the NFRs are evaluated in conjunction with the FRs.

2.4   Utility Functions

A utility function can be used to quantify the degree of satisfaction (i.e., satisficement) of software requirements at run time in autonomic computing systems [9,24,30]. A utility value of 0.0 indicates a violation, 1.0 indicates complete satisfaction, and any value within range of (0.0, 1.0) indicates a degree of satisficement for that requirement [5]. For example, Expression 1 shows the utility value

---

[1] This work does not use the KAOS formal refinement infrastructure.

calculation for Goal (V) to `Achieve` `[Num Passive Data Mirrors == 0]`, as introduced in Fig. 1.

$$util(goal_V) = \begin{cases} 1.0 & \text{if Num Passive Data Mirrors} == 0 \\ x & \text{if } 0 < \text{Num Passive Data Mirrors} < 20\% \text{of total nodes} \\ 0.0 & \text{if Num Passive Data Mirrors} \geq 20\% \text{ of total nodes} \end{cases}$$

(1)

Goal (V) can be quantified by monitoring the state of each RDM within the network. If there are no RDMs in a passive state, then the utility value is 1.0. Otherwise, the utility value linearly decreases until a threshold (e.g., 20% of the total number of nodes for this paper) is met and then the utility value equals 0.0, indicating a requirement violation.

3 Approach

This section introduces `Providentia`, our technique for automatically optimizing the selection of FRs and their corresponding weights for satisficing NFR objectives. We first describe the inputs and outputs of `Providentia` and then present the approach.

3.1 Providentia: Inputs and Outputs

`Providentia` requires the following inputs: a goal model representing both FRs and NFRs of the SAS, a set of utility functions for run-time requirements monitoring, a set of applicable FRs for each NFR, and an executable specification or prototype of the SAS to be used for run-time simulation, including any defined sources of uncertainty (for this experiment, environmental and system uncertainty are used). The output of `Providentia` is a goal model with optimized FR/NFR relationships. Note that the success of `Providentia` relies on the accuracy of the input data. For example, if the set of applicable FRs for each NFR is inaccurate or if any sources of uncertainty are omitted, the effectiveness of the search-based heuristic may not necessarily be optimal. Note that the time to compute an optimal goal model increases as the size of the input goal model and requirements data increases.

Goal Model. A KAOS goal model is required to specify the FRs and NFRs of the SAS.

Utility Functions. A utility function shall be derived for each FR for run-time monitoring of SAS requirements [9,30]. Each utility function comprises a mathematical function that maps monitoring data to a scalar value within [0.0, 1.0], demonstrating how well the FR is satisfied at run time.

Applicable Set of FRs. A requirements engineer shall provide an initial set of applicable FRs that can have an impact on an NFR. For example, a requirements engineer may specify that Goals (A), (E), (I), (V), and (W) most critically impact the NFR for reducing power consumption, however that list may be further expanded at design time (e.g., due to uncertainty factors) to include Goals (B), (K), (M), (O), (P), and (U). Extending the list of possible FRs for each NFR allows a larger search space for Providentia to find an optimal solution that a requirements engineer may not be able to foresee.

Executable Specification. An executable specification, such as a simulation or prototype, of an SAS must also be provided as input. The specification applies the FR utility functions to measure how well SAS requirements are being satisfied at run time. The executable specification also applies different combinations of system and environmental parameters, including possible sources of uncertainty and their impact on the system (e.g., broken links, failed servers, etc.), to enable the SAS to experience a wide range of configuration states.

Output. The output of Providentia is (1) the NFR goal model, with (2) a set of FRs that collectively contribute to the satisficement of each NFR, and (3) an optimized weight value assigned to each FR. A weight value of 0.0 for an FR indicates that the FR does not contribute to the satisfaction of the NFR. For example, for NFR7 (Minimize [Power]), Providentia determined the following weights to be optimal for each Goal: B: 0.237144, E: 0.241000, K: 0.007185, M: 0.373794, O: 0.049442, U: 0.067218, V:0.024216. Although Goal (A) was included in the initial set of applicable FRs, its weight value was 0.0 to indicate that Goal A did not contribute to satisfying the requirements to minimize power.

3.2   Providentia Technique

This section overviews the Providentia technique, comprising a genetic algorithm [12] to search for optimal NFR weighting and requirements combinations. Figure 3 presents a data flow diagram that illustrates the process used by Providentia. Each step is next presented in detail.

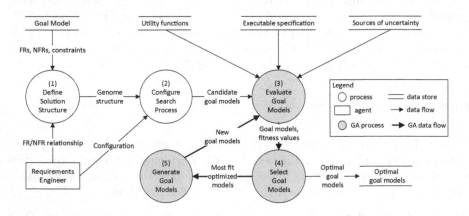

Fig. 3. Data flow diagram of providentia technique.

Goal:	A	B	E	I	K	M	O	P	V	W	
Genome:	0.3	0.0	0.1	0.1	0.0	0.0	0.0	0.0	0.3	0.2	...NFR_n

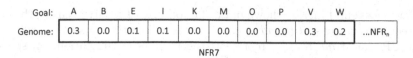

NFR7

Fig. 4. Providentia sample genome.

(1) Define Solution Structure. Each candidate solution in `Providentia` is encoded in a fixed-length genome as shown in Fig. 4, where each gene corresponds to a floating-point weight specified for a supporting FR. Each set of weights that correspond to an NFR (i.e., sub-genome, denoted by bolded line) must sum to a value of 1.0. The entire genome comprises all sub-genomes that can be used to define each NFR, e.g., $[[weights_{nfr_1}],[weights_{nfr_2}],....,[weights_{nfr_n}]]$.

(2) Configure Search Process. The search process must be configured by specifying a population size, number of generations, crossover rate, mutation rate, and selection rate. Based on empirical evidence on convergence rates, this paper specifies a population size of 20, 50 generations, a crossover rate of 25%, and a mutation rate of 50%. For selection, we use the tournament selection approach [12] and set the tournament size to 3. While larger values for population size and generations were tested (e.g., populations of 25–50 and generations of 50–100), an optimal convergence was discovered on average at the specified values.

(3) Evaluate NFR Models. The simulation provided as input applies the goal model to randomized combinations of uncertainty in order to obtain a set of FRs with weights adjusted to be as robust as possible. To guide the search process, we maximize average FR/NFR satisficement as shown in Eqs. 2–4 and minimize the number of SAS adaptations to reduce overall network disruption as shown in Eq. 5. We collect these metrics in a linear weighted sum as shown in Eq. 6. We next describe each equation in turn.

The performance of each NFR as an aggregate utility function is defined as:

$$utility\_value_{nfr_n} = \sum_{i=1}^{|frs_{nfr_n}|} utility_{fr_i} * weight_{fr_i} \qquad (2)$$

where $|frs_{nfr_n}|$ refers to the number of supporting FRs for nfr_n, $utility_{fr_i}$ refers to the calculated utility value for fr_i, and $weight_{fr_i}$ refers to the defined weight (i.e., relative importance) of fr_i. Based on Eq. 2, each NFR has a utility function that can be monitored to quantify performance at run time. If NFR7 (`Minimize [Power]`) becomes violated or satisficed to an unsatisfactory degree,[2] then the RDM application will self-reconfigure to perform an appropriate mitigation strategy.

---

[2] For this paper, we select a threshold of 0.4 to signify requirement non-satisfaction based on empirical evidence.

The fitness sub-function shown in Eq. 3 maximizes FR satisficement throughout execution, where $utility\_value_{functional}$ represents the calculated utility values for FRs and $timesteps_{sim}$ represents the number of simulation timesteps:

$$FF_{fr} = \frac{\sum utility\_value_{functional}}{|utility\_value_{functional}| * timesteps_{sim}} \tag{3}$$

The fitness sub-function shown in Eq. 4 maximizes NFR satisficement throughout execution, where $utility\_value_{non-functional}$ references the calculated utility values from Eq. 2:

$$FF_{nfr} = \frac{\sum utility\_value_{non-functional}}{|utility_v alue_{non-functional}| * timesteps_{sim}} \tag{4}$$

The fitness sub-function shown in Eq. 5 minimizes the number of adaptations performed by the SAS, where $|adaptations|$ reports the total number of reconfigurations performed by the SAS, and $|faults|$ reports the total number of adverse conditions introduced within the simulation.

$$FF_{na} = 1.0 - \frac{|adaptations|}{|faults|} \tag{5}$$

We aggregate FF_{nfr}, FF_{fr}, and FF_{na} into a linear weighted sum as shown in Eq. 6:

$$FF = \begin{cases} \alpha_{nfr} * FF_{nfr} + \alpha_{fr} * FF_{fr} + \alpha_{na} * FF_{na} & \text{iff invariants true} \\ 0.0 & \text{otherwise} \end{cases} \tag{6}$$

where α_{nfr}, α_{fr}, and α_{na} are manually set by a requirements engineer based on domain knowledge/empirical evidence, reflect the relative importance of each sub-FR, and must cumulatively sum to a value of 1.0. While many different approaches exist for combining fitness sub-functions, we find that a linear-weighted sum balances competing concerns adequately for this domain.

(4) Select NFR Models. Providentia selects genomes, using tournament selection, with the highest fitness values calculated from Eq. 6 to guide the search process towards promising areas of the search space. The remainder of the population is removed from consideration.

(5) Generate NFR Models. Providentia uses two-point crossover and single-point mutation to generate new solutions. Two-point crossover selects two indices to be used as crossover points, selects two candidate solutions as parents, and swaps genes between the crossover points to create two new child solutions. Single-point mutation randomly selects a single gene for mutation, where the floating-point weight value can be modified within ±20% of its original value.

Given that each genome comprises sets of weights for each NFR (i.e., sub-genomes), crossover and mutation are applied to internal sub-genomes. Furthermore, a process of normalization follows creation of child solutions. Specifically, each value selected to participate in either crossover or mutation is retained, and the remaining genes for that particular NFR within a sub-genome are normalized to sum to 1.0. Steps (3)–(5) are applied iteratively (i.e., the genetic algorithm loop) until the number of generations is reached. Providentia then outputs a set of optimal weighted FRs for each NFR.

4 Experimental Results

This section describes our experimental setup and presents our experimental results from applying Providentia to the RDM application.

4.1 Experimental Setup

We modeled the RDM network application as a completely-connected graph, where each node represents an RDM and each edge represents a network link. System and environmental parameters were randomized for each trial and based on an operational model previously presented by Keeton et al. [13,14]. For each experimental trial, a given network comprised random number of RDMs (i.e., within [15, 30]), a random number of valid messages (i.e., [100, 200]) were inserted into RDMs throughout the network at random timesteps and were required to be replicated to all other RDMs. We examined seven NFRs specific to the system. The simulation was performed over 300 timesteps.

We compared and evaluated different combinations of supporting FR weights optimized by Providentia. The set of seven NFRs was applied to three types of treatments: (1) FRs and weights generated by random search [1], (2) manually-selected FRs and corresponding weights assigned by a requirements engineer, and (3) Providentia-optimized FRs and weights. We limit our discussion to NFR4 and NFR7 due to space constraints. The manually selected goals and weights for NFR4 are Goals A, B, D, G, H with corresponding weights 0.4, 0.2, 0.2, 0.1, 0.1, and for NFR7 manually selected Goals A, E, I, V, W with corresponding weights 0.3, 0.1, 0.1, 0.3, 0.2. Using the fitness functions defined in Eqs. 3-6, we demonstrate the benefits of using Providentia to both mitigate uncertainty (e.g., environmental and system) and reduce the impact of security threats against the RDM network. For this experiment, we set $\alpha_{fr} = 0.375$, $\alpha_{nfr} = 0.375$, and $\alpha_{na} = 0.25$ to emphasize minimization of network adaptations while considering maximization of FR/NFR satisficement. To demonstrate statistical significance, 50 trials were conducted for each experiment. Moreover, an equal number of experimental evaluations was performed per experiment.

4.2 Experimental Results

For this experiment, we define two null hypotheses. The first, $H1_0$, states that "there is no difference between Providentia-optimized NFRs and those that are unoptimized." The alternate hypothesis, $H1_1$, states that "there is a difference between Providentia-optimized NFRs and those that are unoptimized."

The second null hypothesis, $H2_0$, states that "there is no difference between Providentia-optimized NFRs and those that are optimized by a requirements engineer," with the corresponding alternate hypothesis, $H2_1$, stating that "there is a difference between Providentia-optimized NFRs and those that are optimized by a requirements engineer."

To demonstrate these hypotheses, Fig. 5(a) shows three boxplots with averaged fitness values calculated from Providentia-generated weights, from FR weights optimized by an engineer, and FR weights randomly selected, for NFR4. Similarly, Fig. 5(b) presents the averaged fitness values for NFR7.

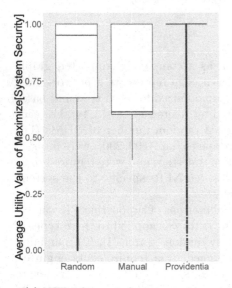
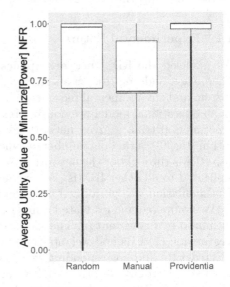

(a) NFR4 fitness value comparison.   (b) NFR7 fitness value comparison.

Fig. 5. NFR fitness experimental results.

As the boxplots in Fig. 5 demonstrate, Providentia-optimized NFRs impact overall fitness significantly more than those set manually by a requirements engineer or randomly selected ($p < 0.05$[3]). The ideal utility value for a given NFR is 1.0 to indicate complete satisfaction and therefore the boxplot closest to 1.0 indicates optimal behavior. Table 1 provides the average utility values (μ) and standard deviation (σ) for each NFR. The genetic algorithm is able to effectively search for optimal FRs and weights when the system is subjected to randomized sources of uncertainty at design time to harden the system against uncertainty at run time, enabling a more robust set of NFRs in comparison to randomly- or manually-defined NFRs.

---

[3] The Wilcoxon-Mann-Whitney U-test was performed for all presented statistics.

Table 1. NFR average utility values and standard deviations.

NFR	Random	Manual	Providentia
NFR1: maximize [Reliability]	μ: 0.654 σ: 0.325	μ: 0.615 σ: 0.191	μ: 0.905 σ: 0.149
NFR2: maximize [Throughput]	μ: 0.655 σ: 0.325	μ: 0.666 σ: 0.262	μ: 0.882 σ: 0.153
NFR3: maximize [Speed]	μ: 0.875 σ: 0.207	μ: 0.743 σ: 0.148	μ: 0.975 σ: 0.085
NFR4: maximize [System security]	μ: 0.802 σ: 0.273	μ: 0.736 σ: 0.177	μ: 0.979 σ: 0.085
NFR5: maximize [Secure communication]	μ: 0.621 σ: 0.273	μ: 0.742 σ: 0.191	μ: 0.925 σ: 0.146
NFR6: maximize [Message security]	μ: 0.921 σ: 0.181	μ: 0.919 σ: 0.072	μ: 0.980 σ: 0.069
NFR7: minimize [Power]	μ: 0.821 σ: 0.270	μ: 0.758 σ: 0.172	μ: 0.926 σ: 0.188

Providentia also significantly decreased the amount of encountered FR violations when compared to manual and random search ($p < 0.05$) of FR combinations and their respective weights as seen in Fig. 6. These results further demonstrate the effectiveness of Providentia. The ideal number of FR violations is 0,
and once again the difference between Providentia and random/manual results
is significant. Providentia is able to not only significantly improve NFR satisficement, but is able to do so while significantly reducing the number of FR
violations rather than creating extra overhead with additional functionality at
run time.

The overall intent of Providentia is to ensure continuing requirements satisficement when faced with both uncertainty and NFR concerns. Given the overall
success of Providentia when optimizing FR selection weights and minimizing
violations, the presented results enable us to reject both $H1_0$ and $H2_0$, accept
$H1_1$ and $H2_1$, and conclude that an optimized weighting scheme can significantly improve overall requirements satisfaction when compared to random
search or manually-derived weighting schemes, given that FF_{fr} and FF_{nfr} (c.f.,
Eqs. 3 and 4) form a major aspect of the overall fitness function.

Threats to Validity. This research has been a proof of concept to demonstrate
how quantifying NFRs, elevating them to first-class entities, and automatically
optimizing them can significantly improve overall requirements satisfaction and
minimize violations. One threat to validity includes the derivation of FRs that
negatively impact the satisfaction of an NFR, as Providentia currently only
focuses on FRs that positively impact NFR satisfaction. Additionally, the manual selection of the FR subset for each NFR could be argued to use better

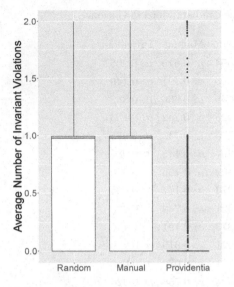
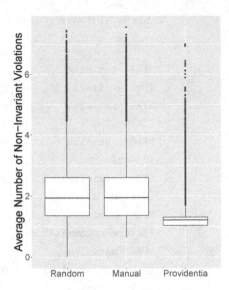

(a) Invariant violation comparison.   (b) Noninvariant violation comparison.

Fig. 6. FR violation experimental results.

selections. The scalability of `Providentia` with respect to large numbers of goals and NFRs is a possible threat to validity as well.

5 Related Work

This section overviews related work in the areas of goal modeling, NFRs, and using functional and non-functional satisficement for guiding the adaptation of SASs.

Goal Modeling. Approaches similar to `Providentia` in goal modeling address dependencies between FRs [21], use probabilistic methods to improve NFR/FR satisficement [4,22] or optimize SAS satisficement [3,18,33], and represent NFRs as soft goals [11,35]. Our technique focuses solely on NFR/FR dependencies, optimizing for run-time performance without prior knowledge of system performance that most probabilistic methods require. We also do not discuss early-phase requirements engineering or high-level abstraction [7,20], but rather focus on a run-time model used by an SAS.

Non-functional Requirements. Other techniques have been introduced to quantify NFRs, generally representing NFRs as soft goals [16,32,34]. Our technique is independent of any framework (e.g., NFR Framework, iStar, and KAOS) and our weighted approach enables greater flexibility that an SAS can use to find an optimal reconfiguration strategy at run time rather than modeling NFRs at design time. Salehie *et al.* use a Goal-Action-Attribute Model (GAAM) and an automated weighting scheme called Analytic Hierarchy Process to prioritize NFRs. Providentia uses a genetic algorithm to optimize goal and weight selection rather than prioritization, as priorities may shift due to uncertainty and requirement interactions. Contributing work has decomposed NFR behaviors into monitored patterns [28] and used quantifiable metrics to separate NFRs from the FR goal model [29]. Providentia monitors requirements at run time and does not separate NFRs from the goal model of FRs, as a separation does not necessarily allow the requirements engineer to identify cross-cutting concerns in NFRs.

6 Conclusion

This paper presented Providentia, a search-based technique for automatically quantifying NFRs at run time by optimizing FR and weight selections at design time. To demonstrate the effectiveness of Providentia, we used an industry-provided RDM application that must distribute messages amongst a network of RDMs that experienced uncertainty. Experimental results suggest that our approach significantly improves overall FR and NFR satisficement and decreases goal violations when compared to NFRs configured manually by a requirements engineer or configured by random search. Future directions for this research include performing the search process at run time while the system is subjected to uncertainty, exploring different search heuristics for Providentia, and applying Providentia to a real-world system. Furthermore, the RELAX language [25, 31] and FLAGS [2] introduce flexibility into the satisfaction of selected requirements via fuzzy logic that can directly be applied to Providentia to better measure NFR satisfaction.

Acknowledgements. This work has been supported in part by grants from the NSF (CNS-1657061, CNS-1305358, and DBI-0939454), the Michigan Space Grant Consortium, the Comcast Innovation Fund, Oakland University, Ford Motor Company, General Motors Research, the Air Force Research Laboratory (AFRL) under agreement number FA8750-16-2-0284, and Michigan State University through the Institute for Cyber-Enabled Research. The U.S. Government is authorized to reproduce and distribute reprints for Governmental purposes notwithstanding any copyright notation thereon. The views and conclusions contained herein are those of the authors and do not necessarily represent the opinions of the sponsors.

References

1. Arcuri, A., Briand, L.: A practical guide for using statistical tests to assess randomized algorithms in software engineering. In: Proceedings of the 33rd International Conference on Software Engineering, ICSE 2011, pp. 1–10. ACM (2011)
2. Baresi, L., Pasquale, L., Spoletini, P.: Fuzzy goals for requirements-driven adaptation. In: 18th IEEE International Requirements Engineering Conference (RE), 27 September 2010-1 October 2010, pp. 125–134 (2010)

3. Bencomo, N., Belaggoun, A.: A world full of surprises: Bayesian theory of surprise to quantify degrees of uncertainty. In: Companion Proceedings of the 36th International Conference on Software Engineering, pp. 460–463. ACM (2014)
4. Cailliau, A., van Lamsweerde, A.: Runtime monitoring and resolution of probabilistic obstacles to system goals. In: Proceedings of the 12th International Symposium on Software Engineering for Adaptive and Self-Managing Systems, pp. 1–11. IEEE Press (2017)
5. Chung, L., Nixon, B., Yu, E., Mylopoulos, J.: Non-functional requirements. Softw. Eng. (2000)
6. Chung, L., Nixon, B.A., Yu, E., Mylopoulos, J.: Non-functional Requirements in Software Engineering. Springer, Heidelberg (2012). https://doi.org/10.1007/978-1-4615-5269-7
7. Dalpiaz, F., Borgida, A., Horkoff, J., Mylopoulos, J.: Runtime goal models: keynote. In: 2013 IEEE Seventh International Conference on Research Challenges in Information Science (RCIS), pp. 1–11. IEEE (2013)
8. Dardenne, A., Van Lamsweerde, A., Fickas, S.: Goal-directed requirements acquisition. Sci. Comput. Program. **20**(1), 3–50 (1993)
9. deGrandis, P., Valetto, G.: Elicitation and utilization of application-level utility functions. In: Proceedings of the 6th International Conference on Autonomic Computing, ICAC 2009, pp. 107–116. ACM (2009)
10. Garlan, D., Cheng, S.W., Huang, A.C., Schmerl, B., Steenkiste, P.: Rainbow: architecture-based self-adaptation with reusable infrastructure. Computer **37**(10), 46–54 (2004)
11. Giorgini, P., Mylopoulos, J., Sebastiani, R.: Goal-oriented requirements analysis and reasoning in the tropos methodology. Eng. Appl. Artif. Intell. **18**(2), 159–171 (2005)
12. Holland, J.H.: Adaptation in Natural and Artificial Systems. MIT Press, Cambridge (1992)
13. Ji, M., Veitch, A., Wilkes, J.: Seneca: Remote mirroring done write. In: USENIX 2003 Annual Technical Conference, pp. 253–268. USENIX Association, Berkeley, June 2003
14. Keeton, K., Santos, C., Beyer, D., Chase, J., Wilkes, J.: Designing for disasters. In: Proceedings of the 3rd USENIX Conference on File and Storage Technologies, pp. 59–62. USENIX Association, Berkeley (2004)
15. Kephart, J., Chess, D.: The vision of autonomic computing. Computer **36**(1), 41–50 (2003)
16. Kobayashi, N., Morisaki, S., Atsumi, N., Yamamoto, S.: Quantitative non functional requirements evaluation using softgoal weight. J. Internet Serv. Inf. Secur. **6**(1), 37–46 (2016)
17. van Lamsweerde, A.: Requirements Engineering: From System Goals to UML Models to Software Specifications. Wiley, Hoboken (2009)
18. Letier, E., van Lamsweerde, A.: Reasoning about partial goal satisfaction for requirements and design engineering. In: Proceedings of the 12th ACM SIGSOFT Twelfth International Symposium on Foundations of Software Engineering, pp. 53–62 (2004)
19. McKinley, P., Sadjadi, S., Kasten, E., Cheng, B.H.C.: Composing adaptive software. Computer **37**(7), 56–64 (2004)
20. Mylopoulos, J., Chung, L., Nixon, B.: Representing and using nonfunctional requirements: a process-oriented approach. IEEE Trans. Softw. Eng. **18**(6), 483–497 (1992)

21. Nagel, B., Gerth, C., Post, J., Engels, G.: Kaos4SOA-extending KAOS models with temporal and logical dependencies. In: CAiSE Forum, pp. 9–16 (2013)
22. Paucar, L.H.G., Bencomo, N.: The reassessment of preferences of non-functional requirements for better informed decision-making in self-adaptation. In: IEEE International Requirements Engineering Conference Workshops (REW), pp. 32–38. IEEE (2016)
23. Qureshi, N.A., Perini, A.: Engineering adaptive requirements. In: 2009 ICSE Workshop on Software Engineering for Adaptive and Self-managing Systems, pp. 126–131, May 2009
24. Ramirez, A.J., Cheng, B.H.C.: Automatically deriving utility functions for monitoring software requirements. In: Proceedings of the 2011 International Conference on Model Driven Engineering Languages and Systems Conference, Wellington , pp. 501–516 (2011)
25. Ramirez, A.J., Fredericks, E.M., Jensen, A.C., Cheng, B.H.C.: Automatically RELAXing a goal model to cope with uncertainty. In: Fraser, G., Teixeira de Souza, J. (eds.) SSBSE 2012. LNCS, vol. 7515, pp. 198–212. Springer, Heidelberg (2012). https://doi.org/10.1007/978-3-642-33119-0_15
26. Ramirez, A.J., Knoester, D.B., Cheng, B.H.C., McKinley, P.K.: Applying genetic algorithms to decision making in autonomic computing systems. In: Proceedings of the 6th International Conference on Autonomic Computing, pp. 97–106 (2009)
27. Salehie, M., Tahvildari, L.: Towards a goal-driven approach to action selection in self-adaptive software. Softw.: Pract. Exp. **42**(2), 211–233 (2012)
28. Supakkul, S., Hill, T., Chung, L., Tun, T.T., do Prado Leite, J.C.S.: An NFR pattern approach to dealing with NFRS. In: 2010 18th IEEE International Requirements Engineering Conference (RE), pp. 179–188. IEEE (2010)
29. Sykes, D., Heaven, W., Magee, J., Kramer, J.: Exploiting non-functional preferences in architectural adaptation for self-managed systems. In: Proceedings of the 2010 ACM Symposium on Applied Computing, pp. 431–438. ACM (2010)
30. Walsh, W.E., Tesauro, G., Kephart, J.O., Das, R.: Utility functions in autonomic systems. In: Proceedings of the First IEEE International Conference on Autonomic Computing, pp. 70–77. IEEE Computer Society (2004)
31. Whittle, J., Sawyer, P., Bencomo, N., Cheng, B.H.C., Bruel, J.: Relax: Incorporating uncertainty into the specification of self-adaptive systems. In: 17th IEEE International Requirements Engineering Conference (RE 2009), pp. 79–88 (2009)
32. Yamamoto, S.: An approach for evaluating softgoals using weight. In: Khalil, I., Neuhold, E., Tjoa, A.M., Da Xu, L., You, I. (eds.) CONFENIS/ICT-EurAsia - 2015. LNCS, vol. 9357, pp. 203–212. Springer, Cham (2015). https://doi.org/10.1007/978-3-319-24315-3_20
33. Yang, Z., Jin, Z., Li, Z.: Achieving adaptation for adaptive systems via runtime verification: a model-driven approach. arXiv preprint arXiv:1704.00869 (2017)
34. Yrjönen, A., Merilinna, J.: Extending the NFR framework with measurable non-functional requirements. In: NFPinDSML@ MoDELS (2009)
35. Yu, E.S.K.: Towards modelling and reasoning support for early-phase requirements engineering. In: Proceedings of the Third IEEE International Symposium on Requirements Engineering, pp. 226–235 (1997)
36. Yu, E.: Social Modeling for Requirements Engineering. MIT, Cambridge (2011)

Comparison of Search-Based Algorithms for Stress-Testing Integrated Circuits

Basil Eljuse$^{(\boxtimes)}$ and Neil Walkinshaw

University of Leicester, Leicester, UK
be38@leicester.ac.uk

Abstract. This paper is concerned with the task of 'stress testing'an integrated circuit in its operational environment with the goal of identifying any circumstances under which the circuit might suffer from performance issues. Previous attempts to use simple hill-climbing algorithms to automate the generation of tests have faltered because the behaviour of the circuits can be subject to non-determinism, with a search space that can give rise to local maxima. In this paper we seek to work around these problems by experimenting with different search algorithms which ought to be better at handling such search-space properties (random-restart hill-climbing and simulated annealing). We evaluate these enhancements by applying the approach to test the Arm Cache Coherent Interconnect Unit (CCI) on a new 64-bit development platform, and show that both simulated annealing and random-restart hill-climbing outperforms simple hill-climbing algorithm.

Keywords: Automated search-based testing
Cache coherent interconnect · Stress testing
Random-restart hill-climbing · Simulated annealing

1 Introduction

When developing Integrated Circuits (ICs), a huge emphasis is placed on optimising performance. Accordingly, it is especially important that any test suites include tests that can probe and stress performance. Such tests commonly take the form of different processing 'pay-loads'that are loaded on to the IC to be executed, whilst the IC is monitored for key performance-indicators, such as data stall cycles resulting from higher memory cache miss rates.

Previous work by Eljuse *et al.* [1] has demonstrated that search-based techniques are appropriate for this non-functional testing of ICs. Obtaining data that can feed directly into fitness functions (e.g. data stall cycles) is straightforward, and can be achieved in a way that does not interfere with the execution of the chip itself. Eljuse *et al.* used a straightforward hill-climbing algorithm to explore the search space, picking inputs in such a way as to maximise the data stall cycles.

© Springer Nature Switzerland AG 2018
T. E. Colanzi and P. McMinn (Eds.): SSBSE 2018, LNCS 11036, pp. 198–212, 2018.
https://doi.org/10.1007/978-3-319-99241-9_10

Although the above approach produced good results (when compared against random baseline tests), our own experience of using simple hill-climbing algorithms on ICs has been mixed. Although it does tend to outperform random testing, simple hill-climbing runs frequently terminate after a low number of iterations because they reach a local maximum, plateau, or a ridge [2]. The data stall cycles generated is affected by a number of factors including the non-determinism due to the underlying hardware complexity and due to the complex set of software stack, which cannot be externally controlled, that affects the underlying functionality making the search space uneven.

The random-restart hill-climbing algorithm is a variant of the conventional hill-climbing algorithm, which restarts the search from a new random seed with the potential to escape from local maxima. Simulated annealing is an advanced search-based algorithm mimicking the principle of 'Annealing'from metallurgy. This algorithm allows tests to select sub-optimal candidates earlier on with the view to arrive at eventual global maxima, and thus avoid being stuck at local maxima.

In this paper we apply these approaches to a similar IC testing scenario as in [1]. The specific contributions are as follows:

- We apply random-restart hill-climbing and simulated annealing to address the problems of local maxima.
- We present an empirical study to show that both random-restart hill-climbing and simulated annealing outperform simple hill-climbing.

The rest of the paper is structured as follows. Section 2 provides essential details about the IC hardware we are testing, the simple hill-climbing approach by Eljuse *et al.* [1], and the alternative search-based algorithms that we will be applying (random-restart hill-climbing and simulated annealing). Section 3 presents the implementation of our approach. Section 4 evaluates the performance of these alternative search-based algorithms. Section 5 outlines the related work that helped shape our approach and finally Sect. 6 outlines the future direction of this research.

2   Background

In this section we start by describing the specific testing scenario. This is followed by a more detailed overview of the Cache Coherent Interconnect (CCI) subject system that is the focus of our experimental work.

2.1   Motivating Scenario

The CCI is a hardware component that provides cache coherency management. It provides multiple levels of configurability, specifically at (a) design time and (b) reset time. There are multiple configuration options available [4], such as transaction tracker size, snoop related configurations, etc. These can have a significant effect on the final system behaviour.

This configurability comes at a cost. Although the CCI is highly configurable for designers who incorporate the CCI into their own devices, it is hard to test. Indeed, this is a common situation with embedded systems; they maximise configurability to facilitate reuse, but this reduces their testability.

Currently, tests are largely developed by hand. In order to cater for specific configurations, separate set of scenarios are developed. The downside of this is that there is limited reuse of such tests; a slight change in configurations can lead to very different behaviours, necessitating very different test sets. Automating an approach to generate these tests would improve the re-usability and reduce the time and effort required.

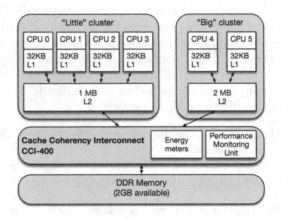

Fig. 1. Juno platform with CCI-400

2.2 The Cache Coherent Interconnect

CCI is an IC component to manage coherent accesses to memory caches from multiple CPUs. It is an "infrastructure component" for Arm based systems, which means that it is used across a variety of hardware platforms. In our work we'll be focussing on the new 64-bit Juno development platform. It has two clusters of CPUs and a GPU, all of which have access to a single multi-level cache, managed by CCI. CCI also has built-in hardware counters allowing to monitor the internal operations of the IC component.

Test Platform: Juno [6] is an Arm development platform (ADP) which is the first 64-bit development board implementing a big.LITTE™ architecture. Similar to the earlier TC2 platform used by Eljuse *et al.* [1], Juno also have a heterogeneous cluster of CPUs with multi-level cache for data access. However there are significant differences between TC2 and Juno platform.

Juno being a 64-bit platform allows 64-bit addressing capability and has a dual cluster topology of 2×4 (two-by-four). There are multiple variants of Juno platform and in this study we chose the R0 variant of Juno platform. The Juno R0 platform has a big cluster made of dual-core Cortex-A57 MPCore™ CPU and a little cluster made of quad-core Cortex-A53 MPCore™CPU. It has both level1 (L1) and level2 (L2) caches, with CCI-400 providing the interconnect and cache coherency across the 2 CPU clusters. Additionally Juno[1] also have a Quad-core Arm Mali™GPU with 128 KB L2 cache.

Figure 1 shows where the CCI cache interconnect sits in the Juno platform. Juno has two processor clusters, where different processors may require access to the same data (hence the need for a cache interconnect). On Juno the little cluster has 1 MB L2 cache compared to that of 512 KB L2 cache in case of TC2 platform as in [7]. The big cluster on Juno platform has 2 MB L2 cache compared to 1 MB in case of TC2 platform as in [7].

One pertinent point from a testing perspective is that the CCI component is necessarily below a mixture of hardware and software layers. A software application sends computational payloads to the CPUs on the clusters via Android. These CPUs in turn carry out memory operations. Each memory operation is modulated by an L1 and an L2 cache. The CCI sits between the L2 caches for the various clusters and the physical memory. The CCI can in other words not be tested directly; in-situ amounts to sending instructions and payloads via the software layer, in the hope that these indirectly stress the CCI.

Performance Monitoring Unit: CCI includes a component called Performance Monitoring Unit (PMU) [4], which has the logic to gather various statistics about the operation of the interconnect at runtime and expose them through counters monitoring certain events. Typically there are multiple counters and different event types that could be monitored using this PMU logic. CCI-400 supports four 32-bit counters allowing one event per counter to be monitored in parallel. This means one can monitor up-to 4 events in parallel without incurring any penalty on accuracy.

As a general rule of thumb, the occurrence of stall cycles do indicate that the CCI component is having to pause some of its operations to cope with the demand for ensuring coherency. This stall cycles can be used as a measure of stress in the system. Larger number of stall cycles observed can be an indication of stress in the platform leading to sub-optimal system performance. This can be used as a means to assess whether the configurations evaluated by the system designer during the design phase is sub-optimal or not.

2.3   Search-Based Software Testing

Search-based software testing techniques re-frame the testing challenge as a search-problem [3]. This can support test automation by leaving the selection and execution of test cases to an algorithm, which selects test inputs with the aim of optimising some objective. Search-based algorithms are ultimately guided by an "objective function" (a function that is used to evaluate a test case); in testing this tends to be a measure of code coverage (or model-coverage if the tests are being derived from a specification). Two of the most basic search-based algorithms are Hill-Climbing and Simulated Annealing:

---

[1] All references of 'Juno' would imply R0 variant of the board in the rest of the paper.

Hill-Climbing. Given a starting-point in a search space (this can be a test-case or a test-set, depending on the objective function), the hill-climbing algorithm will start by evaluating it's 'neighbourhood' - by running and evaluating adjacent test cases. It then simply picks the test case that led to the best improvement in terms of objective-function. This process is repeated until no further improvements can be made (in which case it has hit a maximum/minimum point in the search-space).

The random-restart variant of hill-climbing algorithm provides a means to escape a local maxima by restarting the algorithm from a new random start point in the hope of arriving at a better solution. It retains the simplicity of hill-climbing algorithm but is more suitable for search spaces that have multiple local maxima.

Simulated Annealing. Simulated annealing [8] is a search-based algorithm inspired by the thermodynamic principles involved in the process of 'Annealing' used in metallurgy. It allows the search space exploration to explore paths, occasionally lead by sub-optimal neighbouring candidates, with the increasing chance of escaping local maxima. The probability of the algorithm selecting a sub-optimal neighbouring candidate for exploration is higher at the earlier stages of the execution when the 'temperature' is high and progressively reduces at later stages of execution. Simulated annealing is seen effective in avoiding local maxima in some problem domains as discussed in [9].

The algorithm has a set of parameters (which we will refer to later). These are:

- *tempstart* the start temperature for simulated annealing.
- *tempend* the terminating temperature for simulated annealing.
- *flooringscore* a score to constrain the selection of suboptimal candidates for further exploration.
- *flooringratio* the ratio of the maximum score to be applied as the flooring value to constrain selection of suboptimal candidates.
- *repeatcount* denotes the number of repeats attempted in a given temperature before lowering the temperature.
- *tempstep* the rate at which the temperature is reduced in every step after exhausting the evaluation of a set amount of *repeatcounts*.

3   Improved Stress Testing of the CCI

As is the case with most embedded systems, the CCI is difficult to test (at least in a systems context) because it is difficult to control. It sits at the bottom of a relatively complex stack of hardware and software components (including the Android operating system). It is virtually impossible to reset to a fixed state at runtime. With the operating system continually manipulating the memory and catering for other routine OS processes, the behaviour of the CCI becomes effectively non-deterministic. Advanced features of CCI and the effects of systems with a multi-stage pipeline only exacerbate this problem.

In their attempt to address this problem, Eljuse *et al.* [1] applied search-based testing to the CCI. Specifically, they used the hill-climbing algorithm without restarts, and used the number of data stall cycles to measure the effectiveness of the test cases at 'stressing' the system. They found that the test cases that were generated in this manner significantly outperformed purely random test cases. In this paper we build upon their work by experimenting with the application of two slightly more sophisticated search algorithms: Hill-Climbing with Restarts, and Simulated Annealing.

In the rest of this section we describe how we represent the testing challenge as a search problem, and our selection of the various search algorithm parameters.

3.1 Test Input Representation

We use a similar basic test case representation to that of Eljuse *et al.* [1], who identified the key high level factors that influence the performance of CCI. Test cases $TS = <PS, SP, AC>$ are represented in three dimensions: payload size (PS), sparsity (SP) and actor profile (AC). These are elaborated below:

Payload Size PS: The payload size $PS = (x, y)$ where $0 \leq x \leq 16384$ and $0 \leq y \leq 8192$ represents the amount of test data that is read or written. x and y represent the number of columns and rows in memory that will be required to represent the data, where a basic unit of data is 4-bytes. For our experimental setting the maximum payload size configured is 512 MB considering the overall available system memory and taking into account the L2 cache configuration of the system.

Sparsity SP: The sparsity $SP = [1 : 4]$ is an integer representing four levels of data 'sparsity' that is to be written-to and read-from memory. The behaviour of the cache will differ if all of the data is to be written and read from a single, contiguous zone of memory, as opposed to a range of non-contiguous, widely dispersed regions. This is based on the principle of 'locality of reference' based on which memory systems work efficiently.

The four levels are interpreted as follows: (1) Unconstrained – the payload can be written-to or read-from anywhere from the 1024 MB of available memory, (2) relatively sparse – the operational memory is limited to half of the available memory (512 MB). (3) dense – the operational memory is limited to a tenth of the memory (102.4 MB), or (4) very dense – the operational memory is limited to a hundredth of the total memory (10.24 MB).

Actor Profile AC: The number of actors (or processes) writing-to and reading-from memory can affect cache performance. This factor not only take into account the number of actors but also considers the manner in which they are spread across the clusters. We ensure that a single actor is pinned to a given CPU and same type of actors are assigned to a given cluster. Thus the affinity of the actors of certain type (read or write) to the clusters were fixed for our experiment - read actors pinned to big cluster and write actors pinned to little cluster, to facilitate the stress test conditions on the CCI component providing coherency across clusters. The Table 1 shows the current configurations which are varied during tests and these are determined based on the cpu topology of the selected platform.

Table 1. Actor profile

AC config	Cluster1 (Little)				Cluster2 (Big)	
	cpu0	cpu1	cpu2	cpu3	cpu4	cpu5
Config1	Write	-	-	-	Read	-
Config2	Write	Write	-	-	Read	Read
Config3	Write	Write	Write	Write	Read	Read

3.2   Test Output Representation

Testing non-functional properties of ICs such as the CCI is greatly facilitated by the fact that it can be straightforward to obtain performance data without interfering with the routine behaviour of the IC itself. Since this data is so crucial to performance-tuning, the CCI has several dedicated components to measure performance (see Sect. 2.2).

For our test generation we focus on the outputs provided by the Performance Monitoring Unit (the PMU). We use the PMU to gauge the stress on the memory read-write functionality by recording the number of data stall cycles for a given test. The data stall cycle counts provide us an indication of the stress in the underlying IC.

3.3   The Test Execution Framework

As an overall system we do have an android system similar to the study by Eljuse *et al.* [1]. However we use the newer Juno platform (see Sect. 2.2). We use Android 7.1.2 (Android Nougat) and its corresponding firmware for the Juno platform.

We perform on-target execution of the test suite from android user space. We use the adb (android debug bridge) interface to interact with the target device from a host computer. Juno provides an usb interface for updating the board firmware. The test execution setup includes a host machine facilitating the target image flashing and interactions with the target device under test through the available interfaces. The test suite is executed on the target device with results fetched from target to host for post processing.

As discussed previously, the contents of the memory and cache are routinely affected by many processes within the system that are difficult to control in the context of the test-application. To attenuate this we carry out the following steps for each test to reduce this potential interference:

- We stop as many Android background tasks as is possible (some cannot be stopped).
- We perform an identical memory walk-through sequence between iterations to give better chances for an equivalent initial state.
- We use data barrier instructions - an Arm architecture specific instruction [11] - to ensure all out-of-order data access is cleared before every test data is evaluated.

4   Evaluation

In this section we present an experiment to compare the effectiveness of the random-restart hill-climbing and simulated annealing algorithms. Specifically, the experiment addresses the following research questions:

- RQ1 - Which approach manages to achieve the highest stress-measures?
- RQ2 - How efficient are the approaches - how many tests are required to achieve their best results?

4.1   Methodology

Different search algorithms were compared in terms of the maximum number of data stall cycles produced by their respective test sets. In order to provide a common baseline for the search-based approach, we generated the data stall cycles using simple hill-climbing algorithm which is prone to be stuck at local maxima. We repeated the simple hill-climbing algorithm for 30 experiments and on average it took 1 hour 40 min duration compared to the 2 hour fixed budget given for random-restart hill-climbing and simulated annealing algorithms.

Search Algorithm Parameters. In this section we briefly outline the various parameters selected for each of the algorithm variants outlined in previous section.

Random-restart Hill-Climbing: The random-restart hill-climbing algorithm is allotted a 2 h search budget. During the execution window the random-restart hill-climbing algorithm restarts as many times possible from a new random seed when a maxima is reached during search space exploration. The state space representation defines the neighbouring test candidates by varying PS with a random step size to the parent test candidate while keeping SP and AC same as the parent test candidate. Similarly more neighbouring candidates are generated by varying SP and AC individually while keeping other factors same as parent test candidate.

Simulated Annealing: Similar to random-restart hill-climbing, simulate annealing algorithm is also allotted a 2 hour search budget. The various parameters for simulated annealing algorithm are set as below:

- *tempstart* the algorithm starts with an initial temperature of 1.0.
- *tempend* the algorithm stops when the temperature reaches 0.1.
- *flooringratio* the algorithm uses a flooring ratio of 75% and applies this on the maximum achieved score, to compute the flooring score, that will control the sub-optimal node selection.
- *repeatcount* the algorithm repeats with new neighbouring candidates for 10 times before reducing the temperature.
- *tempstep* the algorithm degrades the temperature by 10% after it has exhausted the number of repeats at a given temperature.

The temperature start, temperature stop and temperature degradation step were selected based on initial experiments as most of the cooling schedules for simulated annealing are problem specific. Some studies as in [10] provide a systematic approach for parameter selection, but most practical cases we did experimentations to arrive at the current selection of these parameters.

We initially had no floor limit, and this frequently led to situations where the algorithm would fail to sustain any improvements in fitness. The floor limit of 75% of the maximum score was achieved by experimentation. This was also in the case for repeatcount.

Criteria for the Evaluation of RQ1: In order to evaluate RQ1 (which approach managed to achieve the highest stress-measures), we measured the mean and maximum data-stall cycles achieved. To accommodate the fact that the algorithm could start from different starting points, we also measured the overall gain achieved over the course of the search. We applied the Wilcoxon signed rank test on the paired measurements for the means computed above, in order to establish whether differences in results produced by search algorithms are significant.

Criteria for the Evaluation of RQ2: The efficiency of a test case is a measure of how rapidly it is able to reach high data stall cycles. To establish this we compute an Area Under the Curve score by summing the highest data stall cycle achieved at any given point (a monotonic value) for all iterations. If tests achieve higher data stall cycles more rapidly, this will lead to a higher 'area under the curve'.

4.2   Results and Discussion

RQ1 - Which approach manages to achieve the highest stress-measures? The results are summarised in Figs. 2 and 3. Looking at the median best scores generated by the approaches we can see that simulate annealing has a marginally

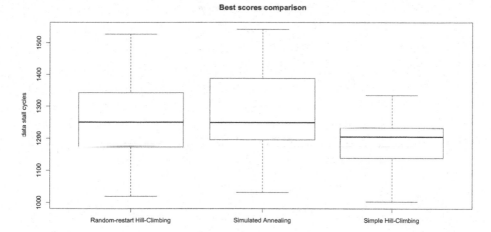

Fig. 2. Data stall cycle comparison *Random-restart Hill-Climbing vs Simulated Annealing vs Simple Hill-Climbing*

better average best score of 1271 (upper quartile 1375 and lower quartile 1197) as opposed to 1258 of random-restart hill-climbing (upper quartile 1343 and lower quartile 1173). Both are better than the common baseline of simple hill-climbing which gave an average best score of 1189 (upper quartile 1233 and lower quartile 1140). It is evident that both random-restart hill-climbing and simulated annealing are better in terms of generating tests that would maximally stress the platform, by virtue of higher average data stall cycles generated, when compared against simple hill-climbing algorithm.

We performed the Wilcoxon signed rank test on the data stall cycle measurements and computed the p-values to establish whether the comparison of the computed means are statistically significant. The p-value of 0.9 for random-restart hill-climbing versus simulated annealing indicates that neither can be considered significantly better than the other. However the p-value of 0.03325 for random-restart hill-climbing versus simple hill-climbing and the p-value of 0.02607 for simulated annealing versus simple hill-climbing do confirm that both these can be considered as better to simple hill-climbing considering the average best scores.

For each algorithm variant we computed the score gain as below:

$$gain = (max\_score - min\_score)/min\_score \qquad (1)$$

Looking at the average score gain achieved in case of random-restart hill-climbing, we get a 37% improvement compared to the initial seed (upper quartile 50% and lower quartile 26%). Analysing the results we can see that there have been some iterations where the random seed yielded a relatively higher score and hill-climbing failed to move any further in the state space (since all the neighbours were evaluated as inferior to that initial seed). So we observe there had been some restarts which failed much earlier in the state space exploration in

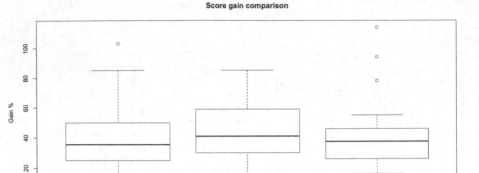

Fig. 3. Gain comparison *Random-restart Hill-Climbing vs Simulated Annealing vs Simple Hill-Climbing*

case of random-restart hill-climbing approach which emphasises the multi-modal nature of the state space.

However looking at the simulated annealing based approach we can see moderately better average score gain of 43% (upper quartile 59% and lower quartile 30%). Analysing the results from the individual experiments of simulated annealing, we observed that some intermediate sub-optimal candidates lead to subsequent better scores.

The simple hill-climbing shows a gain of 41% (upper quartile 46% and lower quartile 27%) during our tests which is better than random-restart hill-climbing but worse than simulated annealing.

We performed the Wilcoxon signed rank test on the score gain measurements and computed the p-values to test the statistical significance of the means for comparison. The computed p-values for the pairs are: 0.2486 (random-restart hill-climbing, simulate annealing), 0.5944 (random-restart hill-climbing, simple hill-climbing), 0.5393 (simulated annealing, simple hill-climbing). These suggest that none of the techniques produces a significantly higher gain than the other.

RQ2 - How efficient are the approaches - how many tests are required to achieve their best results? In order to compare the efficiency of the 2 algorithm variants we plotted the best scores achieved across the test payloads executed over time within the fixed execution budget. We computed the area under the curve for each of the 30 experiments for both random-restart hill-climbing and simulated annealing. Figure 4 shows the area under curve for these 2 algorithm variants.

Simulated Annealing has a higher average computed area under the curve of 25059 (upper quartile of 26272 and lower quartile of 23344) when compared with random-restart hill-climbing with 24769 (upper quartile of 26703 and lower quartile of 22702).

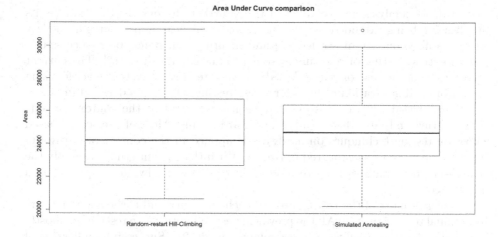

Fig. 4. Area under curve for best scores found across payloads evaluated

We performed the Wilcoxon signed rank test on the area under curve measurements and computed the p-values to test the statistical significance of the means for comparison. The p-value of 0.8073 indicate that we could not treat one method better than the other based on higher computed mean value alone.

4.3   Threats to Validity

Internal Threats: A large variation in the measure of data stall cycles could pose a threat to the validity of the results, unless controlled. We observed in our experimentation a large extent of variation in the PMU counter values even when same test data was executed repeatedly. The potential for additional variability can be introduced by the fact that the test framework is also running on the target. Also in case of Juno platform the GPU also has an L2 cache which can affect the operations of the CCI-400 component. At the moment there is no option to define and use a data agent resident on GPUs during the test execution. This internal threat put the need for measures beyond what is currently applied to ensure the validity of the experimental results.

External Threats: Hardware cache coherency components do provide additional hardware mechanisms like PMU that can be exploited by this methodology as a fitness function. In the absence of such hardware support, other relevant meta-heuristics need to be defined to ensure the applicability of the proposed methodology.

5   Related Work

Application of search-based test techniques are not new at system level testing and in particular targeting non-functional system properties including performance analysis as explained in [12]. Further surveys in [13] confirms its application being extended to other non functional system attributes like safety [14], usability, quality of service [15] and security [16]. It has been successfully used in stress testing of real-time systems too as explained in [17]. The current study extends the use of search-based software testing at system level focusing on automated generation of tests for stress testing which was detailed in [1].

Search-based software testing had been often used in the context of software testing and much lesser in the hardware testing. Most of the search-based software testing techniques on hardware is applied in the context of hardware-in-the-loop systems as captured in [18,19]. With the current study we apply the search-based software testing techniques in testing a hardware component in a system context.

Typically most of the testing around cache memory and cache coherency are functional tests in nature. All the prevalent research into cache testing are mostly focused on hardware self testing as explained in [20,21]. Successful application of search-based software testing methodology in the area of memory system validation can be seen in the work using genetic algorithms with memory consistency model (MCM) verification as per [22]. Further we could see that in the area of testing cache coherency management, again the focus had been mostly on functional testing as explained in [23]. In this current study we do focus on the stress testing of a hardware component providing cache coherency and successfully evaluated the relative benefits of more complex search-based software testing techniques, thus extending the work done by Eljuse *et al.* as outlined in [1].

6   Conclusions and Future Work

In this study we have investigated the use of random-restart hill-climbing and simulated annealing algorithms in generating tests for stress testing systems with hardware cache coherency support. It is evident that, with the current state space representation, simulated annealing provides a marginally better approach as opposed to random-restart hill-climbing.

In the current evaluation we focused on using a single objective fitness function targeting a single PMU event. Juno platform provides the support for on-board energy meters which can provide another fitness function which could be orthogonal to the PMU events in measuring the stress condition of CCI component. This could be utilised in a multi-objective search-based approach. Additionally suitability of further advanced search-based algorithms needs to be evaluated. In current study we arrived at the various parameters for simulated annealing algorithm mostly by experimentation. However studies by [10] do provide a more systematic approach to do parameter selection for simulated annealing algorithm. We could improve parameter tuning for simulated annealing algorithm using these methods as opposed to current selection, which is done by experimentation.

References

1. Eljuse, B., Walkinshaw, N.: A search based approach for stress-testing integrated circuits. In: Sarro, F., Deb, K. (eds.) SSBSE 2016. LNCS, vol. 9962, pp. 80–95. Springer, Cham (2016). https://doi.org/10.1007/978-3-319-47106-8_6
2. Yuret, D., de la Maza, M.: Dynamic hill climbing: overcoming the limitations of optimization techniques. In: The Second Turkish Symposium on Artificial Intelligence and Neural Networks (1993)
3. McMinn, P.: Search-based software test data generation: a survey. Softw. Test. Verif. Reliab. **14**(2), 105–156 (2004)
4. Arm CoreLink CCI-400 Cache Coherent Interconnect - Technical Reference Manual. http://infocenter.arm.com/help/topic/com.arm.doc.ddi0470k/DDI0470K_cci400_r1p5_trm.pdf
5. Linaro - A non-profit organisation working on open source software for Arm based platforms. http://www.linaro.org
6. Juno ADP - part of Arm Versatile Express product family. https://www.arm.com/files/pdf/DDI0515D1a_juno_arm_development_platform_soc_trm.pdf
7. TestChip2 - part of Arm Versatile Express product family. http://www.arm.com/products/tools/development-boards/versatile-express/index.php
8. Nikolaev, A.G., Jacobson, S.H.: Simulated annealing. In: Gendreau, M., Potvin, J.Y. (eds.) Handbook of Metaheuristics. International Series in Operations Research & Management Science, vol. 146. Springer, Boston (2010). https://doi.org/10.1007/978-1-4419-1665-5_1
9. Henderson, D., Jacobson, S.H., Johnson, A.W.: The theory and practice of simulated annealing. In: Glover, F., Kochenberger, G.A. (eds.) Handbook of Metaheuristics. International Series in Operations Research & Management Science, vol. 57, pp. 287–319. Springer, Boston (2003). https://doi.org/10.1007/0-306-48056-5_10
10. Moon-Won, P., Yeong-Dae, K.: A systematic procedure for setting parameters in simulated annealing algorithms. Comput. Oper. Res. **25**(3), 207–217 (1998)
11. When to use Barrier instructions? http://infocenter.arm.com/help/index.jsp?topic=/com.arm.doc.faqs/ka14041.html
12. Shen, D., Luo, Q., Poshyvanyk, D., Grechanik, M.: Automating performance bottleneck detection using search-based application profiling. In: International Symposium on Software Testing and Analysis (2015)
13. Afzal, W., Torkar, R., Feldt, R.: A systematic review of search-based testing for non-functional system properties. Inf. Softw. Technol. **51**, 957–976 (2009)
14. Baresel, A., Pohlheim, H., Sadeghipour, S.: Structural and functional sequence test of dynamic and state-based software with evolutionary algorithms. In: Cantú-Paz, E. (ed.) GECCO 2003. LNCS, vol. 2724, pp. 2428–2441. Springer, Heidelberg (2003). https://doi.org/10.1007/3-540-45110-2_147
15. Canfora, G., Penta, M. D., Esposito, R., Villani, M. L.: An approach for QoS-aware service composition based on genetic algorithms. In: Conference on Genetic and Evolutionary Computation (2005)
16. Grosso, C., Antoniol, G., Penta, M. D., Galinier, P., Merlo, E.: Improving network applications security: a new heuristic to generate stress testing data. In: Annual Conference on Genetic and Evolutionary Computation (2005)
17. Briand, L.C., Labiche, Y., Shousha, M.: Stress testing real-time systems with genetic algorithms. In: 7th Annual Conference on Genetic and Evolutionary Computation (2005)

18. Wegener, J., Kruse, P.M.: Search-based testing with in-the-loop systems. In: First International Symposium on Search Based Software Engineering (2009)
19. Lindlar, F., Windisch, A.: A search-based approach to functional hardware-in-the-loop testing. In: Second International Symposium on Search Based Software Engineering (2010)
20. Theodorou, G., Kranitis, N., Paschalis, A., Gizopoulos, D.: Software-based self test methodology for on-line testing of L1 caches in multithreaded multicore architectures. IEEE Trans. Very Large Scale Integr. Syst. (VLSI) **21**, 786–790 (2013)
21. Theodorou, G., Kranitis, N., Paschalis, A., Gizopoulos, D.: Software-based self-test for small caches in microprocessors. IEEE Trans. Comput. Aided Des. Integr. Circuits Syst. **33**, 1991–2004 (2014)
22. Elver, M., Nagarajan, V.: McVerSi: a test generation framework for fast memory consistency verification in simulation. In: The 22nd Symposium on High Performance Computer Architecture (2016)
23. Acle, J.P., Cantoro, R., Sanchez, E., Reorda, M.S.: On the functional test of the cache coherency logic in multi-core systems. In: 6th Latin American Symposium on Circuits and Systems (2015)

Damage Reduction via White-Box Failure Shaping

Thomas B. Jones(✉) and David H. Ackley

Department of Computer Science, University of New Mexico,
Albuquerque, NM 87131, USA
ThomasBJones2@gmail.com, ackley@cs.unm.edu

Abstract. Emerging hardware that trades reliability guarantees for resource savings presents a challenge to software engineered for deterministic execution. Research areas like approximate computing, however, embrace non-determinism by abandoning strict correctness in favor of maximizing the *probability* and *degree* of correctness. Existing work has used stochastic failure sampling to perform white-box searches along software execution paths, producing *criticality assessments* of which selected operations are likely most damaging if they fail. Here, we apply these assessments to a new domain and employ them using *failure shaping*, an automated method for reducing a computation's expected output damage in a model where failures can be relocated but not eliminated. In two case studies, we demonstrate error reductions of 38% to 63% on Strassen's matrix multiplication algorithm despite a virtually identical failure count. We discuss how our framework helps provide a smooth landscape for performing the search-based software engineering that will be required to apply this technology to larger problems.

Keywords: Criticality assessments · Failure shaping
Failure interfaces

1 Postdeterministic Software Engineering

Architectures built on guaranteed deterministic hardware have powered the computer revolution, but the cost of hardware determinism is rising. Growing systems of shrinking technology now present terrifying reliability issues such as the 'silent data corruption' (SDC) of high-performance computing—when there is no crash or fault detected, but the output is nonetheless wrong [13]. Also, new hardware options are emerging, like processors that can sacrifice determinism to save energy [15, 31, 46]. Unfortunately, because traditional software engineering simply assumes deterministic execution, we know little about *how* a program's output will be damaged when failures occur, and *which* operations in a program are most critical to obtain high-quality results.

The field of *approximate computing* [3, 48] recognizes that software and systems sometimes can, and increasingly must, provide useful results even when

© Springer Nature Switzerland AG 2018
T. E. Colanzi and P. McMinn (Eds.): SSBSE 2018, LNCS 11036, pp. 213–228, 2018.
https://doi.org/10.1007/978-3-319-99241-9_11

strict correctness cannot be guaranteed. Approximate computing differs from *fault tolerance*, (e.g. [8, 26, 39]), which recognizes that failures may occur, but strives to preserve deterministic results nonetheless by suppressing those failures. Instead, approximate computing *begins* by accepting that implementation choices and operational failures *will* damage the final end-user output. This makes it especially useful in applications such as approximate video processing (e.g. [34, 42]), where even large failures may produce only minor output errors.

Approximate computing, however, often requires that technology choices and trade-offs be ultimately evaluated only in a whole-systems context, risking chicken-and-egg problems if actual end-use data is expected to inform the system's computational design. Past energy conservation approximation techniques have relied on detailed hardware knowledge to limit their search space when finding the best economization for a given system application (e.g. [42]).

In modern computer systems, built on large deterministic hardware, functional modules are often designed, deployed, and composed with virtually no knowledge of the overall system behavior. This paper's first contribution is the notion of *method level failure interfaces* that allow the study of approximate computations separate from their underlying hardware stack, freeing us from the need for specialized hardware knowledge.

This paper's second contribution is a generalized framework, embodied in a search tool called *Criticality Explorer* which can be found at https://github.com/ThomasBJones2/CriticalityExplorer. This tool performs a Monte Carlo search through a computation's possible method level failures, producing a statistical characterization of each failure's performance impact. Although at present that search process is fairly naive, terminating after hitting an observation count limit, we suggest possible search procedure improvements in Sect. 4.2.

Unlike traditional approaches that use fault tolerance to reduce or eliminate failures, we have a 'hardware reliability budget' that treats failure rates as an independent variable: *guaranteeing that failures cannot be avoided*. Using this independent variable combined with the results of our criticality search, the tool generates a reliability resource configuration that conforms to the budget and minimizes output error. Finally, the tool reports the degree of loss incurred with the given configuration. Since the amount of approximation is an observable result, rather than a parameter, this approach risks potentially unbounded loss—but it provides one way to proceed in a relatively modular fashion, without presuming a full system upon which to measure resource-accuracy tradeoffs.

1.1   Method-Level Failure Interfaces

Criticality Explorer experiments require an *input generator*, an *error measure*, and a set of *failure interfaces* for each algorithm assessed. Inputs are drawn from the input generator and outputs are assessed with the error measure. Our *failure interfaces* operate at the level of Java methods chosen by the user. In addition to the correct method code, the user provides an alternate *failure method*. This method has the same signature as the original Java method excepting that it

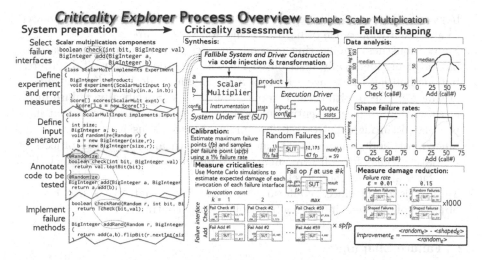

Fig. 1. Criticality Assessment and Failure Shaping Overview. *Criticality Explorer* takes a prepared algorithm with error measures, input generator, and annotated method level failure interfaces shown on the left. After a calibration step to evaluate the maximum failure point count, and samples per failure point, the tool then estimates failure point criticalities through a Monte Carlo simulation. Each sample produces the output of a single run with, and without, a failure injected on the a given failure point and scores the error between the two runs. We present the errorful inputs, outputs, and absolute difference score in the bottom center of the figure. Failures are then shaped using the median criticality and error scores are produced for average i.i.d. as well as shaped failures. See Sect. 1.3 for details.

accepts an added parameter, a random number generator, to be used to simulate underlying failures in the stack beneath the method. See Fig. 1.

The failure interfaces identify a spatiotemporal set of *failure points* bucketed at some space-time granularity. These buckets are locations uniquely defined by their associated failure interface and an invocation count on that failure interface. *Criticality Explorer* assess the *criticality* of a failure point by estimating the expected degree of damage that failure point would cause, assuming all else is equal. Given a set of failure interfaces, we call the criticality distribution produced by the assessment process a *failure shape*.

Failure interfaces could be defined at higher, lower, or just other levels of abstraction but we see five principal advantages to method-level failure interfaces:

1. In a direct hardware realization, the data paths of multiple instances of an object method are likely to pass through similar or even the exact same circuits. Method-level failures may thus provide increased abstraction while still approximating important spatial failures of real hardware.
2. Method-level failure interfaces are flexible. Beyond the SDCs and energy economization failures that inspire this paper, they can also represent software

bugs or failures in distributed computations. *Criticality Explorer* can be used to analyze a wide range of hardware and software failures.

3. Many robustness engineering methods are designed only to compensate for independent, identically distributed failures. We too consider i.i.d. failures, but method-level interfaces can also model higher-order *coordinated failures* arising from deep within the computational stack. Specifically, failure interfaces written on major, central methods, can simulate SDC errors that have percolated through the stack to become visible to the user.

4. Since most modern languages treat methods as (nearly) first class objects, it is relatively easy for software engineers to understand and implement failure interfaces at the method level.

5. Method level interfaces conform to the intuition that SDCs occur when objects uphold their interfaces but violate their contracts.

1.2   Failure Shaping

We define *failure shaping* as the deliberate redistribution of reliability resources from trivial to critical operations in a computation. This process is designed to deal with reliability budgets that are smaller than required for strictly correct execution. We assume a fine-grained reliability management that may be difficult to realize in current technologies, but recent advances offer hope that failure shaping will be a viable error control method in the future.

Dynamic voltage and frequency scaling techniques trade computational accuracy for lower hardware energy use [15, 22, 30, 36]. Conceivably, future chips will present a reliability-efficiency interface for use by economizing software.

Administrators of large, centralized systems are seeking access to energy-efficient methods [18]. Future economizaton middleware is likely to exploit approximation algorithms and methods to save resources on unimportant operations while more critical services run resource-intensive exact algorithms.

Farther in the future, non-silicon-based hardware may emerge. Tradeoffs have been observed between the use of energy intensive materials like mRNA and robust biological latch operation [46]. Biological computation will require new reliability paradigms that accept fallible components.

Together, these issues raise a fundamental question: *How to maximize correctness with a reliability budget insufficient to produce* **strictly** *correct results?*

We address this question by pairing failure interfaces with an *economy of failure* for each fallible method in a computation. This economy makes use of a failure rate $\epsilon \in [0, 1]$ such that roughly ϵ of the failure points generated at runtime will fail. As a baseline *Criticality Explorer* uses an i.i.d. failure model at each failure point. Then, *Criticality Explorer* shapes the failures: the *least* critical failure points—those with a criticality below the median criticality—are adjusted to 2ϵ. Alternatively, the *most* important coordinates are given a failure rate of 0. This keeps the total failure rate over the whole computation at ϵ.

This stylized and simplified economy of failure is oblivious to whatever actual underlying mechanisms are used to shape failures within the system. We explore the effects of failure shaping without proposing a complete, concrete, failure shaping technology. However, relationships between power and failure rate presented in [30], for example, give us hope that economizations like this may be realizable in existing technology.

1.3 *Criticality Explorer*

Criticality Explorer performs criticality assessments and economic analysis on a prepared algorithm. For each assessment an input object and experiment object are required. Input objects must have a **randomize** method that acts as the input generator, while experiment objects require an **experiment** method that accepts input objects. Outputs are assessed via the experiment object's **score** method which accept both an errorful and a correct experiment object. Failure interfaces are annotated with '**@Randomize**' and require two implementations—the correct implementation, and a failure method—to function.

Criticality Explorer automatically records the number of invocations on each method-level failure interface to generate the failure point search space. A small number of exploratory runs at tested input sizes and ϵ failure rate are performed in order to find each failure interfaces maximum invocation count. Using this information *Criticality Explorer* then evaluates each failure point criticality through Monte Carlo simulation. A random input is drawn using **randomize** and an experiment, failed only at the given failure point, is compared with a failure-free (strictly correct) run of the algorithm on the same input. The error in their outputs is evaluated using the **score** method.

Because failed operations can cause unexpected behavior, *Criticality Explorer* automatically catches and records any exceptions produced by experiment code at run time. It also automatically terminates experiments after a hard coded two minute time limit and records the termination as a runtime error.

After criticality assessment, *Criticality Explorer* then performs three additional experiments. The first measures experiment code output error with an i.i.d. failure model with ϵ in $[0, 0.1]$. The experiment code is then failure shaped according to the criticality assessment results. Finally, a proxy economization experiment that uses some failure point's criticalities as stand-ins for others is also available. As we will show, this proxy method has the benefit of shrinking the criticality search space, providing improved performance at a lower cost.

Here, we demonstrate *Criticality Explorer* in two case studies. In Sect. 2.1 we failure shape both naive matrix multiplication and Strassen's algorithm. In Sect. 3 we show that failure shaping can be applied at multiple levels, with scalar multiplication failure interface criticalities standing as proxies for failures on methods internal to the scalar multiplication method.

Finally, in Sect. 4 we discuss how failure shaping can be successfully applied to other computational systems, in Sect. 5 we present related work, and in Sect. 6 we present our final conclusions.

2 Failure Shaping Matrix Multiplication

Here we failure shape two matrix multiplication algorithms. Although our case studies are tiny, matrix operations are a valuable problem domain for approximate computing and robustness studies since many SDC-prone high performance computing algorithms make heavy use of matrices. We consider the $O(N^3)$ 'naive' matrix multiplication algorithm, and Strassen's algorithm as specified at [1]. The latter algorithm runs in $O(N^{2.8})$ and was the first divide-and-conquer matrix multiplication algorithm found to run faster than $O(N^3)$. The input generators used for both algorithms were randomly generated matrices of size $N \times N$ with 10 bit integers for each element. We employed three error measures: the *Frobenius norm* 'FN' (also known as the matrix euclidean distance or ℓ^2 norm), the *infinity norm* 'IN', and the *logarithmic Frobenius norm* 'LFN'.

We defined failure interfaces for check and add methods used by both algorithms. The Boolean check method returns *true* (*false*) if the given bit of a number is 1 (0), and its failure method returns the opposite result. The add method returns the sum of two numbers and its failure method randomly flips one bit on the output when called. Both algorithms used the naive scalar multiplication sub-algorithm, which checks bits in the first multiplicand to decide whether to invoke the add method on the second multiplicand and an accumulator. A failure interface based on naive scalar multiplication was used as a proxy for check and add in Sect. 3.

2.1 Criticality Assessment Results on Matrix Multiplication

Figure 2 presents example criticalities for both algorithms on selected operations and scales, and we see immediately they have significantly different shapes. In general, naive matrix multiplication has lower and flatter criticalities compared to those found in the highly structured Strassen's algorithm. Note also the seemingly scale-free appearance of Strassen's algorithm criticality. At every test scale we see spikes in both add and check operations about 2/7, 3/7 and 5/7 through the algorithm, run on both the infinity and Frobenius norm error measures. In naive multiply, criticalities lie close to both the average and the median criticality. By contrast, in Strassen's algorithm important operations are outliers with criticalities often an order of magnitude greater than the median.

2.2 Failure Shaping Results on Matrix Multiplication

Figure 3 shows the direct failure shaping results on naive and Strassen's matrix multiply algorithms using an i.i.d. failure model, with 1000 samples at each percentile in [0, 0.1]. We can see that direct failure shaping produces roughly 40% error reductions compared to a baseline i.i.d. error model.

Failure shaping, as we have outlined it, can distort the underlying failure rate, ϵ. We believe this is caused by innacuracies in measuring the median failure rate, or by changes in the run time caused when ϵ increases from zero. Therefore, we report results at the *actual observed rate of failure*, ϵ', in our graphs. Nonetheless, ϵ' is generally within 5% of ϵ.

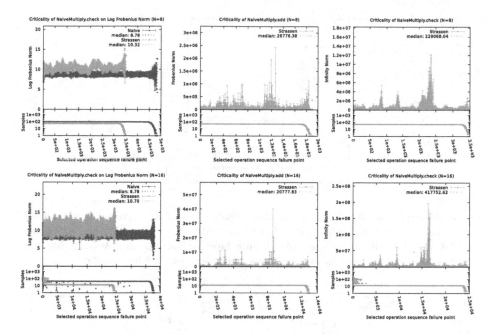

Fig. 2. Matrix Multiplication Criticality Assessment Results. Criticality results for both Naive and Strassen's matrix multiplication, using three different error measures: *(Left)* log Frobenius norm, *(Middle)* Frobenius norm, *(Right)* infinity norm. The top row is matrix input size 8; the bottom is size 16. Similar results for Naive matrix multiply are omitted from the two right columns to emphasize the apparent scale-free structures in the more efficient Strassen's algorithm. Note that x and y axes do not match, and each error measure uses its own units. See Sect. 2.1 for details.

Monte Carlo sampling is a powerful statistics-gathering method, but its simulation costs grow with the number of failure points in the system under test. *Criticality Explorer* can be connected to the AWS Lambda [35] on-demand compute service, allowing investigators to trade money for time by performing massively parallel assessments in the cloud. As an example, the data presented in this paper was produced for under \$320 in cloud costs—with the majority of that consumed by the scale 16 criticality assessments.

Even assuming such a large-scale infrastructure, though, brute force Monte Carlo costs will become prohibitive as the software stack under test grows ever deeper, placing more and more computational levels between the hardware and the end-user error measures. In the next section we introduce 'proxy criticalities'—an approach to assessing such multilevel software that not only slashed assessment costs, but also, we found, even improved performance.

3   Proxy Failure Shaping Matrix Multiplication

We took advantage of method level failure interface flexibility to speed up the failure shaping procedure by using *proxy criticalities*. Rather than measuring

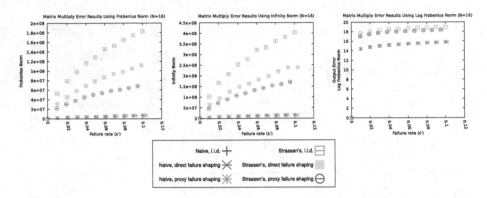

Fig. 3. Matrix Multiplication Proxy Failure Shaping Results. Average error rates for both naive and Strassen's algorithms. Errors are reduced between 38% and 63% from the i.i.d. model to the direct and proxy failure models. Note the graphs have different y axes, and each error measure uses its own units. See Sect. 3.1 for details.

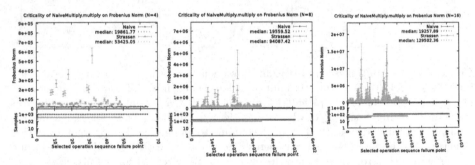

Fig. 4. Matrix Multiplication Proxy Method Criticality Assessment Results. Criticality results for naive and Strassen on the scalar multiplication failure interface, using the FN error measure. Note that x and y axes do not match, and each error measure uses its own units. See Sect. 3 for details.

each failure point's criticality, we instead measured the criticality of a *proxy method*—a method that stands in for those methods originally intended to fail.

In this section experiments continued to make use of fallible `check` and `add` operations. However, each `add` and `check` failure interface was only called as part of a `scalar multiplication` method. We wrote a failure interface that randomly flipped one bit in a `scalar multiplication` invocation's output. Thus, the search space of possible errors was decreased from all `check` and `add` operations to just `scalar multiplication` operations. Using this method, criticality assessment costs on matrices with element size e required only $\approx 1/e$ resources. For example, the size 32 proxy algorithm assessment cost $\approx\$13$ on AWS Lambda.

Using this failure interface we measured each multiplication failure point's criticality. Figure 4 shows criticality assessment results on scalar multiply operations employed by both matrix multiply algorithms.

These criticalities and their median value were then employed to make decisions about the reliability budgeting of every `check` and `add` failure point that occurred *during* each multiplication operation's execution. Note that this means that information collected by failing `scalar multiplication` could be used to failure shape the underlying `check` and `add` operations.

3.1 Criticality and Failure Shaping Results on Proxy Method

Figure 5 shows proxy failure shaping results on size 32 matrices. As with criticality measurements on the `check` and `add` operations, `multiply` operations are flat for naive matrix multiply and structured for Strassen's multiply.

`Scalar multiply` failure shapes in Strassen's matrix multiplication algorithm also appear to exhibit scale-free properties and similar distributions to `check` and `add` operations. At all tested sizes we find criticality spikes roughly 2/7, 3/7 and 5/7 of the way through the algorithm, suggesting they are inherent to Strassen's multiplication algorithm.

Figure 3 shows proxy failure shaping results on `check` and `add` failure interfaces using the `scalar multiply` failure interface as a proxy. These results are compared to the baseline i.i.d. model results, and the results from the simple failure shaping procedure applied in Sect. 2.2. As can be seen, proxy failure shaping can work as well as direct failure shaping.

However, caution must be used: proxy failure shaping only works on `scalar multiplication` applied to `check` and `add` operations because all three failure interface's failure methods produce similar failures.

4   Analysis and Discussion

We have shown that the failure shaping framework can successfully improve the reliability performance of algorithms running on abstracted non-deterministic hardware. To do this, we found criticality assessment search spaces that have low *variance* and high *compactness*. Failure points with high *variance* occur when many different kinds of execution paths overlap, some important and some unimportant while *compact*

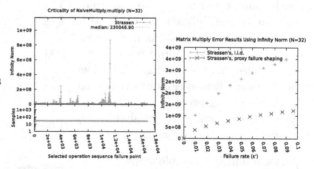

Fig. 5. Proxy Criticality Assessment and Failure Shaping Results on Input Size 32. *(Left)* Criticality assessment for proxy failure interface `scalar multiply` on the *infinity norm* error measure for $N = 32$, though smaller N display similar structures. *(Right)* Proxy failure shaping results for size 32 without direct failure shaping results. See Sect. 3.1 for details.

descriptions grow no more quickly than the algorithm they are describing. There is a necessary tension between these two concepts, but we were able to balance them by using time-bucketed function level failure interfaces. We also showed that it is possible to shrink the error search space by moving the locus of analysis from lower level to higher level methods through the proxy method failure shaping experiment.

In both cases, whether with a proxy method or through direct failure shaping, it was imperative that the algorithm's failure shape have some structure that our budgeting process could bite into. This can easily be seen in the differences observed between failure shaped naive matrix multiply and Strassen's algorithm. Strassen's algorithm simply had more *leverage* than naive matrix multiply.

4.1   The Importance of Leverage

An algorithm's *leverage* is the ratio of the average criticalities of its important and unimportant operations. In this paper we use the median failure point criticality as the dividing line between important and unimportant operations, however this will not be the best line for all algorithms and economizations.

In [28,29] the authors also found computational leverage in sorting algorithms. Specifically, the greater the algorithmic efficiency, the greater the leverage. Further, unleveraged sorting algorithms outperformed leveraged algorithms on baseline i.i.d. failure model experiments.

We see a similar pattern with matrix multiplications. In Fig. 6 the leverage of both naive and Strassen's matrix multiply using the *Frobenius norm* are presented. Strassen's matrix multiply consistently shows a higher leverage than naive matrix multiplication, which also outperforms Strassen's matrix multiplication on baseline i.i.d. failure tests. However, because Strassen's algorithm has higher leverage, it also responds better to the failure shaping procedure.

Overall, economic failure shaping is best suited to computations that

1. perform multiple fallible steps,
2. each of which has a definable cost,
3. at definable failure rates, with
4. high *leverage*, and
5. limited overall resources.

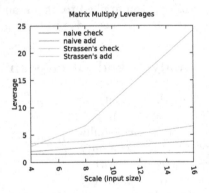

Fig. 6. Selected Leverage Results. *Frobenius norm* leverage results on the matrix multiply algorithms are presented above. Strassen's algorithm leverage on all operations grows faster than naive matrix multiply's leverage on any operation. See Sect. 4.1 for details.

Although satisfying most of these conditions is a matter of framing the question properly, condition 4 largely depends on the underlying algorithms being performed. Fortunately, we find that *high efficiency* algorithms often have high leverage. In prior work, we found this to be true of sorting algorithms in [28], and we have also found it true here, with matrix multiplication algorithms. Intuitively, this makes sense, as efficiency often depends on making high-impact decisions about the output based on examining as little data as possible at the decision point.

To frame the other four conditions, we seek out the operations that are most heavily impacted when increasing algorithmic efficiency. So, for example, comparisons in sorting and scalar multiplications in matrix multiplication are both heavily economized as algorithms become more efficient. Facing a graph algorithm, the critical failures might involve choose which edge to follow.

4.2   Generalization Through Search

Failure shaping currently requires significant human labor. Making it more efficient will require leveraging multiple strategies. One strategy includes a library of standardized input types, error measures, and failure interfaces that can be used to produce automatically annotated programs in the future.

Such a strategy, though, will tend to increase the computational resources required by the method. The spaces we have presented are sufficiently limited that they can be almost completely characterized relatively cheaply, but larger spaces cannot be so completely explored. Our observation of apparently scale-free failure shapes (see Fig. 2) suggests one strategy could be to scale the criticality assessment directly by run time in some programs. For non-trivial software in general, we will need more sophisticated search methods—ones capable of performing significant *generalization* across failure points, rather gathering fully-independent statistics as we have here.

Genetic algorithms, genetic programming, and other adaptive search procedures are often employed to search highly combinatoric spaces, as in [9,12,32]. A common problem in this space is the flag variable problem [23]. In [4], the authors note that GAs work best in search spaces that avoid these "needle-in-the-haystack" spikes. Our use of continuous error measures compared to typical all-or-none test failures may help produce such 'softened' search space gradients, as medium criticality operations tend to cluster around spikes both here and in other algorithms we have explored [28].

This is a new area and we are only at the beginning, but a relatively sparse set of data-points plus a suitable heuristic search procedure may allow us to build imperfect but high-quality *criticality estimators* for the failures of much larger pieces of software than are reachable via Monte Carlo search alone.

5   Related Work

Criticality analysis is a common method for understanding failures in industries working with finite engineered machines. While this analysis is taken to be generalizable, its application is often limited to industries where safety is important, especially in medicine, industrial engineering, cyber-physical systems, and travel [19,47,49]. Other authors have used criticality analysis to track system sensitivity to failure or environmental effects in online services [11,16]. Analysis of code importance and tendency to fail has also been used to aid designers in tracking vulnerabilities when introducing code edits [40,41,43]. Like us, other authors have used aspects to build fault tolerant systems [10].

Some robustness researchers (e.g. [7,24]) consider concrete hardware component failures such as in ALUs and memories, and study their impacts on the *probability* of strict computational correctness. Others (e.g. [14]) assume deterministic hardware execution and focus on the *degree of damage* caused by corrupted inputs. Along with our own work, these join a growing number of research efforts examining algorithmic and systemic *sensitivity* to faults and failures, such as [7,37,44]. The authors of [42], for example, provide a method for discovering a quality-efficiency economization curve for a camera applications that should be fairly generalizable. A paradigm of correctness sensitivity also complements works, such as [20] that seek to use oracles to search for failures in traditional software engineering settings by further softening oracle requirements. As stated in Sect. 4.2, it may further strengthen the field of SBSE by improving the properties of search spaces.

Criticality Explorer extends input/output based software engineering testing suites such as that found in [33] by providing a hardware failure layer that acts as a second level of input to the algorithm.

I.i.d. error models plausibly describe many classes of physical errors [6,15,21]. However, our interfacing framework also allows for coordinated errors below the object function level in keeping with results that show that low level failure coordination can produce greater error rates than uncoordinated failures [2]. Any reasonable error model shows that large computational scales are also paired with an increased SDC risk. Maintaining a computationally deterministic perspective in exascale-class machines is increasingly impossible [13]

This new field is often complemented by research into fault injection and error propagation techniques [5,24,27,38]. Exciting efforts in this direction have also looked at language tools for leveraging programmer reasoning about error propagation across the semantic divide between stack and application in large scale system [17,25,34,45]. *Criticality Explorer* extends these research efforts by providing services that *discover* critical code operations through *space* and *time*.

6   Conclusion

Traditional digital computing presumes deterministic hardware, which simplifies reasoning about software, but leaves us with no guiding principle—except patching failures after we notice them—when such perfection is cost-prohibitive or errors escape from hardware despite all our efforts. We need methods that allow us to reason about failures throughout the computational stack.

But, to reason about damage, we must be able to see it. Failure interfaces are a bridge between idealized computations and the fallible hardware and software upon which those computations must inevitably run. In principle, a failure interface could be defined for an arbitrary failure in a computational stack. However, to employ strategies like those found in *Criticality Explorer*, failure interfaces must somehow be run-time economizable, and the damage created by failures at the interface should have low variance.

Of course we cannot utterly abstract away the physical and expect to reason effectively about error and damage—but limited and carefully-designed abstractions, such as method level failure interfaces, may offer significant opportunities. We view the temporal and spatial abstractions presented here for matrix multiplication as a step in this direction.

References

1. Divide and Conquer — Set 5 (Strassen's Matrix Multiplication). https://www. geeksforgeeks.org/strassens-matrix-multiplication/. Accessed 21 May 2018
2. Ackley, D.H.: Beyond efficiency. Commun. ACM **56**(10), 38–40 (2013)
3. Akram, R., Alam, M.M.U., Muzahid, A.: Approximate lock: trading off accuracy for performance by skipping critical sections. In: 2016 IEEE 27th International Symposium on Software Reliability Engineering (ISSRE), pp. 253–263. IEEE (2016)
4. Arcuri, A., Iqbal, M.Z., Briand, L.: Black-box system testing of real-time embedded systems using random and search-based testing. In: Petrenko, A., Simão, A., Maldonado, J.C. (eds.) ICTSS 2010. LNCS, vol. 6435, pp. 95–110. Springer, Heidelberg (2010). https://doi.org/10.1007/978-3-642-16573-3_8
5. Areias, C., Cunha, J.C., Vieira, M.: Studying the propagation of failures in SOAs. In: 2015 IEEE International Conference on Dependable Systems and Networks Workshops (DSN-W), pp. 81–86. IEEE (2015)
6. Assaf, S., Upfal, E.: Fault tolerant sorting networks. SIAM J. Discret. Math. **4**(4), 472–480 (1991)
7. Atkinson, B., DeBardeleben, N., Guan, Q., Robey, R., Jones, W.M.: Fault injection experiments with the CLAMR hydrodynamics mini-app. In: 2014 IEEE International Symposium on Software Reliability Engineering Workshops (ISSREW), pp. 6–9. IEEE (2014)
8. Avižienis, A.: Fault-tolerance and fault-intolerance: complementary approaches to reliable computing. SIGPLAN Not. **10**(6), 458–464 (1975). https://doi.org/10.1145/390016.808469
9. Baudry, B., Fleurey, F., Jézéquel, J.M., Traon, Y.L.: From genetic to bacteriological algorithms for mutation-based testing: research articles. Verif. Reliab. Softw. Test. **15**(2), 73–96 (2005)
10. Borchert, C., Schirmeier, H., Spinczyk, O.: Protecting the dynamic dispatch in C++ by dependability aspects. In: GI-Jahrestagung, pp. 521–536 (2012)
11. Cámara, J., de Lemos, R.: Evaluation of resilience in self-adaptive systems using probabilistic model-checking. In: Proceedings of the 7th International Symposium on Software Engineering for Adaptive and Self-Managing Systems, pp. 53–62. IEEE Press (2012)
12. Campos, J., Ge, Y., Fraser, G., Eler, M., Arcuri, A.: An empirical evaluation of evolutionary algorithms for test suite generation. In: Menzies, T., Petke, J. (eds.) SSBSE 2017. LNCS, vol. 10452, pp. 33–48. Springer, Cham (2017). https://doi.org/10.1007/978-3-319-66299-2_3

13. Cappello, F., Geist, A., Gropp, B., Kalé, L.V., Kramer, B., Snir, M.: Toward exascale resilience. IJHPCA **23**(4), 374–388 (2009). http://dblp.uni-trier.de/db/journals/ijhpca/ijhpca23.html#CappelloGGKKS09
14. Chaudhuri, S., Gulwani, S., Lublinerman, R.: Continuity and robustness of programs. Commun. ACM **55**(8), 107–115 (2012)
15. Chippa, V.K., Chakradhar, S.T., Roy, K., Raghunathan, A.: Analysis and characterization of inherent application resilience for approximate computing. In: Proceedings of the 50th Annual Design Automation Conference, p. 113. ACM (2013)
16. Dantas, J., Matos, R., Araujo, J., Oliveira, D., Oliveira, A., Maciel, P.: Hierarchical model and sensitivity analysis for a cloud-based VoD streaming service. In: 2016 46th Annual IEEE/IFIP International Conference on Dependable Systems and Networks, Workshop, pp. 10–16. IEEE (2016)
17. De Kruijf, M., Nomura, S., Sankaralingam, K.: Relax: an architectural framework for software recovery of hardware faults. ACM SIGARCH Comput. Archit. News **38**(3), 497–508 (2010)
18. Filiposka, S., Mishev, A., Juiz, C.: Current prospects towards energy-efficient top HPC systems. Comput. Sci. Inf. Syst. **13**(1), 151–171 (2016)
19. Gargama, H., Chaturvedi, S.K.: Criticality assessment models for failure mode effects and criticality analysis using fuzzy logic. IEEE Trans. Reliab. **60**(1), 102–110 (2011)
20. Gay, G., Rayadurgam, S., Heimdahl, M.P.: Automated steering of model-based test oracles to admit real program behaviors. IEEE Trans. Softw. Eng. **43**(6), 531–555 (2017)
21. Guo, S., Huang, H.Z., Wang, Z., Xie, M.: Grid service reliability modeling and optimal task scheduling considering fault recovery. IEEE Trans. Reliab. **60**(1), 263–274 (2011)
22. Han, J., Orshansky, M.: Approximate computing: an emerging paradigm for energy-efficient design. In: 2013 18th IEEE European Test Symposium (ETS), pp. 1–6. IEEE (2013)
23. Harman, M., et al.: Testability transformation. IEEE Trans. Softw. Eng. **30**(1), 3–16 (2004)
24. Holler, A., Macher, G., Rauter, T., Iber, J., Kreiner, C.: A virtual fault injection framework for reliability-aware software development. In: 2015 IEEE International Conference on Dependable Systems and Networks Workshops (DSN-W), pp. 69–74. IEEE (2015)
25. Hukerikar, S., Lucas, R.F.: Rolex: resilience-oriented language extensions for extreme-scale systems. J. Supercomput. **72**(12), 4662–4695 (2016)
26. Ibtesham, D., DeBonis, D., Arnold, D., Ferreira, K.B.: Coarse-grained energy modeling of rollback/recovery mechanisms. In: 2014 44th Annual IEEE/IFIP International Conference on Dependable Systems and Networks (DSN), pp. 708–713. IEEE (2014)
27. Irrera, I., Vieira, M.: Towards assessing representativeness of fault injection-generated failure data for online failure prediction. In: 2015 IEEE International Conference on Dependable Systems and Networks Workshops (DSN-W), pp. 75–80. IEEE (2015)
28. Jones, T.B., Ackley, D.H.: Comparison criticality in sorting algorithms. In: 2014 44th Annual IEEE/IFIP International Conference on Dependable Systems and Networks (DSN), pp. 726–731. IEEE (2014)
29. Jones, T.B., Ackley, D.H.: Scalable robustness. In: 2016 46th Annual IEEE/IFIP International Conference on Dependable Systems and Networks Workshop, pp. 31–38. IEEE (2016)

30. Kahng, A.B., Kang, S., Kumar, R., Sartori, J.: Slack redistribution for graceful degradation under voltage overscaling. In: Proceedings of the 2010 Asia and South Pacific Design Automation Conference, pp. 825–831. IEEE Press (2010)
31. Kim, E.P., Shanbhag, N.R.: Soft N-modular redundancy. IEEE Trans. Comput. **61**(3), 323–336 (2012)
32. Kukunas, J., Cupper, R.D., Kapfhammer, G.M.: A genetic algorithm to improve Linux kernel performance on resource-constrained devices. In: Proceedings of the 12th Annual Conference Companion on Genetic and Evolutionary Computation, pp. 2095–2096. ACM (2010)
33. Larsen, K.G., Mikucionis, M., Nielsen, B.: Online testing of real-time systems using UPPAAL. In: Grabowski, J., Nielsen, B. (eds.) FATES 2004. LNCS, vol. 3395, pp. 79–94. Springer, Heidelberg (2005). https://doi.org/10.1007/978-3-540-31848-4_6
34. Liu, S., Pattabiraman, K., Moscibroda, T., Zorn, B.G.: Flikker: saving dram refresh-power through critical data partitioning. ACM SIGPLAN Not. **47**(4), 213–224 (2012)
35. Mathew, S., Varia, J.: Overview of Amazon Web Services. Amazon Whitepapers (2014)
36. Mohapatra, D., Chippa, V.K., Raghunathan, A., Roy, K.: Design of voltage-scalable meta-functions for approximate computing. In: Design, Automation and Test in Europe Conference and Exhibition (DATE), pp. 1–6. IEEE (2011)
37. Monson, J.S., Wirthlin, M., Hutchings, B.: A fault injection analysis of Linux operating on an FPGA-embedded platform. Int. J. Reconfig. Comput. **2012**, 7 (2012)
38. Natella, R., Cotroneo, D., Duraes, J.A., Madeira, H.S.: On fault representativeness of software fault injection. IEEE Trans. Softw. Eng. **39**(1), 80–96 (2013)
39. Oliveira, D.A., Lunardi, C.B., Pilla, L.L., Rech, P., Navaux, P.O., Carro, L.: Radiation sensitivity of high performance computing applications on Kepler-based GPGPUs. In: 2014 44th Annual IEEE/IFIP International Conference on Dependable Systems and Networks (DSN), pp. 732–737. IEEE (2014)
40. Pai, G.J., Dugan, J.B.: Empirical analysis of software fault content and fault proneness using Bayesian methods. IEEE Trans. Softw. Eng. **33**(10) (2007)
41. Piancó, M., Fonseca, B., Antunes, N.: Code change history and software vulnerabilities. In: 2016 46th Annual IEEE/IFIP International Conference on Dependable Systems and Networks, Workshop, pp. 6–9. IEEE (2016)
42. Raha, A., Raghunathan, V.: Towards full-system energy-accuracy tradeoffs: a case study of an approximate smart camera system. In: Proceedings of the 54th Annual Design Automation Conference 2017, p. 74. ACM (2017)
43. Rodrigues, I., Ribeiro, M., Medeiros, F., Borba, P., Fonseca, B., Gheyi, R.: Assessing fine-grained feature dependencies. Inf. Softw. Technol. **78**, 27–52 (2016)
44. Rudolph, L.: A robust sorting network. IEEE Trans. Comput. **100**(4), 326–335 (1985)
45. Sampson, A., Dietl, W., Fortuna, E., Gnanapragasam, D., Ceze, L., Grossman, D.: EnerJ: approximate data types for safe and general low-power computation. ACM SIGPLAN Not. **46**, 164–174 (2011)
46. Siciliano, V., Garzilli, I., Fracassi, C., Criscuolo, S., Ventre, S., Di Bernardo, D.: MiRNAs confer phenotypic robustness to gene networks by suppressing biological noise. Nat. Commun. **4**, 2364 (2013)
47. Ukkusuri, S.V., Yushimito, W.F.: A methodology to assess the criticality of highway transportation networks. J. Transp. Secur. **2**(1–2), 29–46 (2009)

48. Vazirani, V.V.: Approximation Algorithms. Springer, Heidelberg (2001). https://doi.org/10.1007/978-3-662-04565-7
49. Xiang, J., Ye, L., Vicario, E., Tadano, K., Machida, F.: Analysis of relevance and importance of components in system reliability. In: 2015 2nd International Symposium on Dependable Computing and Internet of Things (DCIT), pp. 146–147. IEEE (2015)

Automated Co-evolution of Metamodels and Transformation Rules: A Search-Based Approach

Wael Kessentini[1(✉)], Houari Sahraoui[1], and Manuel Wimmer[2]

[1] University of Montreal, Montreal, Canada
{kessentw,sahraouh}@iro.umontreal.ca
[2] CDL-MINT, TU Wien, Vienna, Austria
wimmer@big.tuwien.ac.at

Abstract. Metamodels frequently change over time by adding new concepts or changing existing ones to keep track with the evolving problem domain they aim to capture. This evolution process impacts several depending artifacts such as model instances, constraints, as well as transformation rules. As a consequence, these artifacts have to be co-evolved to ensure their conformance with new metamodel versions. While several studies addressed the problem of metamodel/model co-evolution (Please note the potential name clash for the term co-evolution. In this paper, we refer to the problem of having to co-evolve different dependent artifacts in case one of them changes. We are not referring to the application or adaptation of co-evolutionary search algorithms.), the co-evolution of metamodels and transformation rules has been less studied. Currently, programmers have to manually change model transformations to make them consistent with the new metamodel versions which require the detection of which transformations to modify and how to properly change them. In this paper, we propose a novel search-based approach to recommend transformation rule changes to make transformations coherent with the new metamodel versions by finding a trade-off between maximizing the coverage of metamodel changes and minimizing the number of static errors in the transformation and the number of applied changes to the transformation. We implemented our approach for the ATLAS Transformation Language (ATL) and validated the proposed approach on four co-evolution case studies. We demonstrate the outperformance of our approach by comparing the quality of the automatically generated co-evolution solutions by NSGA-II with manually revised transformations, one mono-objective algorithm, and random search.

Keywords: Model transformation evolution
Search-based software engineering · ATL

1 Introduction

Model-driven engineering (MDE) [2] relies on metamodels as first-class entities [21] which evolve to accommodate new features, improve structural and

T. E. Colanzi and P. McMinn (Eds.): SSBSE 2018, LNCS 11036, pp. 229–245, 2018.
https://doi.org/10.1007/978-3-319-99241-9_12

semantical concerns and fix errors [27]. While this evolution process is vital, it impacts several depending artifacts such as model transformations since transformation rules need to be adapted to new metamodels versions as they use the metamodel elements as part of their type system [15]. Thus, a systematic process is needed to guide the co-evolution of the transformations when the involved metamodels evolve [27]. However, currently, this co-evolution process is mostly done manually which leads to significantly increased fault-proneness and cost of maintenance [14,15].

Several studies have been proposed for automated co-evolution within the MDE literature, cf. [14] for a survey. The co-evolution of metamodels and their models have been addressed using various techniques to make model instances consistent with new metamodel versions by translating metamodel changes into model changes using a set of manually defined rules [8] or automatically adapting models towards reducing the number of conformance errors with the metamodels [18]. In addition, the co-evolution of metamodels and constraints written in the Object Constraint Language (OCL) has also been studied to reduce OCL errors when evolving metamodels by localizing the set of constraints to repair, and then, fixing them either manually [19] or automatically [1]. However, the co-evolution of metamodels and transformation rules—although it is considered as a significant problem [15]—is still less studied with only a few studies that identify metamodel changes, then manually define templates to map the metamodel changes into co-changes applied to the transformations, e.g., cf. [9,10,12,20,23,24,26]. None of the existing studies addressed the central question of how to automate the metamodel/transformation co-evolution without the need to manually define higher-order transformations to map metamodel changes into transformation changes. These higher-order transformations are language specific and require the correct identification of metamodel changes which is a challenge on its own. As a result, the co-evolution of metamodels and transformations is still far from being automated.

This paper remedies the gap by proposing, as one of the first studies in the MDE literature, an automated approach to revise transformation rules when metamodels evolve. In particular, we focus on the automated co-evolution of transformations expressed in the ATLAS Transformation Language (ATL) [16]. We leverage the use of search-based software engineering algorithms [13] to deal with the large search space of possible co-evolution solutions to repair the rules based on three main criteria: maximizing the coverage of metamodel changes and minimizing the number of static errors in the transformation and the number of applied changes to the transformation. Since these objectives are intuitively conflicting, we used a multi-objective algorithm, based on NSGA-II [7], to find a trade-off between them when exploring the search space of possible transformation co-evolutions. We considered differently-sized transformations available in the ATL Zoo[1], a public repository of model transformations, to validate our approach by comparing the newly generated ATL rules by our approach and the expected rules that are manually co-evolved. Since it is the first formulation of

---

[1] https://git.eclipse.org/c/gerrit/www.eclipse.org/atl.git/tree/atlTransformations.

the metamodels and transformation rules co-evolution as a search problem, we also compared our results to a mono-objective algorithm, combining the different objectives, and random search. Furthermore, we evaluated the performance of our automated co-evolution approach comparing to the manual correction of co-evolution issues by a total of 6 participants on one of the case studies. On average, for all of our four studied ATL projects, 89% of the proposed edit operations were correct while the random search, mono-objective and manual techniques have a correctness of respectively 41%, 66% and 76%.

2 Background

2.1 Metamodels and Model Transformation

Model transformations are considered as the heart and soul of MDE [31]. Model transformations are not only used for deriving implementations out of models, but also to analyze, compare, merge, and improve models [25]. In this context, metamodels contribute important information for model transformations. In particular, they introduce the type systems which can be used in model transformation programs [6]. The elements contained in a metamodel are accessible through model transformation languages and represent essential information needed to formulate transformations. Figure 1(a) shows the model transformation pattern which illustrates that on the metamodel level the transformation is defined and executed on the model level. Of course, when metamodels change, this has a direct impact on the existing transformations as the referred types and features have to exist in the metamodels. Figure 1(b and c) show the cases of source metamodel evolution and target metamodel evolution and the required transformation co-evolutions, respectively. Please note that both cases may occur simultaneously. The quest is to find the corresponding delta (i.e., changes) to patch the transformation for a given metamodel delta.

ATL [16] is a model transformation language which follows the mentioned model transformation pattern. In particular, ATL transformations are rule-based programs (cf. *rule* keyword in Listing 1.1) which are executed on fixed input models to produce output models. For this process, matches in the input model are computed based on the input patterns (cf. *from* keyword in Listing 1.1) of the transformation rules which trigger the creation of output elements based on the output patterns (cf. *to* keyword in Listing 1.1) of the transformation rules. Please note that ATL transformations are typed by the source and target metamodels, i.e., the input and output pattern elements have to refer to existing elements in the involved metamodels. In addition, OCL expressions may be employed for filter definitions to restrict the matches in the input model as well as for computing values with so-called bindings for setting features of the produced output elements.

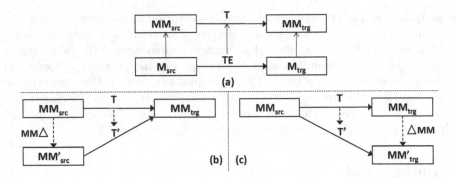

(a)

(b)   (c)

Fig. 1. Metamodel evolution/transformation co-evolution context: (a) model transformation pattern, (b) source metamodel evolution/transformation co-evolution, and (c) target metamodel evolution/transformation co-evolution; (b) and (c) may occur in combination.

2.2   Metamodel/Transformation Co-evolution: A Motivating Example

To further introduce ATL as well as to motivate the need of automatically repairing ATL transformations when metamodels evolve, an excerpt of an example ATL transformation is shown in Listing 1.1. Furthermore, we show in Fig. 2 an evolution scenario for the input metamodel of the given ATL transformation.

The transformation example we are using is a simple transformation for generating documentation from class diagrams. In particular, we focus on transforming the features into list items. The content of the items is derived from the feature names and types–cf. the binding at line 8 of Listing 1.1.

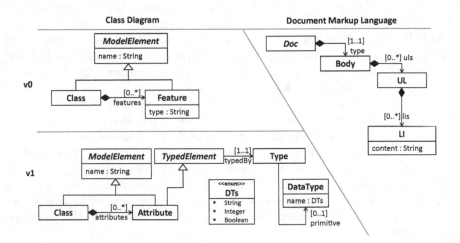

Fig. 2. Motivating example: metamodel evolution

Listing 1.1. Excerpt of the initial and migrated Class2Doc Transformation.

```
1  -- deletions are shown in red, additions in green
2  module Class2Doc;
3  create OUT : Doc from IN : Class;
4  ...
5  rule Attribute2ListItem {
6    from f : Class! Attribute Feature
7    to li : Doc!LI (
8      content <- f.name + '␣:␣' + f.type typedBy.primitive.name
9    )
10 }
11 ...
```

Let us assume that the class diagram language evolves by some rename refactorings as well as by explicating the types of features. This process results in a new metamodel version which now speaks about attributes instead of features. Attributes are typed elements whereas a typed element refers to an explicit type object which may describe the used types in more detail. Given the discussed changes in the source metamodel, the excerpt of the transformation example shown in Listing 1.1 has to be adapted. In particular, the type of the input pattern has to be changed as well as the binding for the *content* feature. The type of an attribute has now to be retrieved by following a navigation path before the required value can be accessed.

While there are already existing approaches for dealing with transformation co-evolution, most of them are based on certain change patterns such as the renaming refactoring in metamodels which may have an associated co-refactoring for the transformation rules. For more complex change patterns, as it is the case for retrieving the type information in our example by following a longer navigation path with several hops is currently not supported by existing approaches. Thus, we motivate our approach by the fact that for more complex evolution scenarios, a sophisticated search process is needed to repair the transformations to get rid of static typing errors in the transformation, but still have as much as possible the same behaviour as for the initial transformation. Furthermore, detecting metamodel changes precisely is still a challenge, especially when it comes to the detection of refactorings as is the case in our example. Our approach does not rely on computing such metamodel changes. Finally, while there are approaches for detecting static type errors in ATL programs [6], there are no approaches which consider this kind of information explicitly in the co-evolution process. Thus, one may end up with co-evolved transformations which have static type errors.

3 Multi-objective Metamodel/Transformation Co-evolution

3.1 Approach Overview

A co-evolution solution to our problem consists of a sequence of rule-level change operations to revise the existing transformation rules to make them conformed to the evolved source or target metamodel. The search space is determined not only by the number of possible rule-level change operations combination but also by the number of existing transformation rules, and the order in which these changes are applied. A heuristic-based optimization method is used to generate co-evolution solutions. The best solution should optimize 3 objectives: (1) minimize the number of errors; (2) minimize the number of recommended change operations to the transformation rules; and (3) maximize the coverage of the evolved source or target metamodel. To handle these conflicting objectives, we formulate this co-evolution problem as a multi-objective one using the Non-Dominated Sorting Genetic Algorithm (NSGA-II) [7].

Our approach takes as inputs a model transformation program and the evolved source and target metamodels. It generates as output a sequence of recommended changes to the initial transformations program. To calculate the fitness functions, we used AnATLyzer [6] to identify the number of static type errors in the transformation rules and the ATL footprint tool [3] to estimate the coverage of the evolved source or target metamodels by the newly revised transformation rules.

3.2 NSGA-II Adaptation for Metamodel/Transformation Co-evolution

Solution Representation. A candidate solution to the problem is a set of revised transformation rules, i.e., a set of change operators applied to the initial transformation rules. A valid solution assigns a set of different rule-level changes to the transformation rules. We used a set of 27 types of operations that are defined in a previous study [5]. A complete description of all change operators for ATL can be found in [17].

We adopt the *vector-based* encoding where a candidate solution is represented as a *vector* of n positions, where n is the number of change operations to be applied to a transformation program. Each position corresponds to specific change operation. For instance, Fig. 3 shows an example of a solution composed of three change operations applied to the transformation rules discussed in the motivating example (Listing 1.1). The generated solution included two types of change operations that were instantiated: NavigationModification(variable, navigationExpression, replacement) and InPatternElementModification(objectToModify, oldFeatureValue, replacement). Thus, the generation of solutions consists of selecting the type of operations and their parameters (objects to modify, rules to revise, etc.). The initial population is completely random where a maximum number of rule-level change operations n is fixed; then the generated changes are randomly assigned to several rules of the transformation.

Solution (i)	InPatternElementModification ("f", "Feature", "Attribute")	NavigationModification ("f","type","typeBy.primitive")	NavigationModification ("f","typeBy.primitive","typedBy.primitive.name")

Fig. 3. Solution encoding.

Fitness Functions. We defined three objective functions in our adaptation.

Minimize the Number of Recommended Rule-Level Changes. The underlying assumption to minimize the number of changes to the transformation is to reduce the effort of understanding the new program after evolution. Thus, this fitness function is defined as:

$$Min f1(S) = |S| \tag{1}$$

Where S is the solution to evaluate. Thus, this fitness function calculates the size of S (number of changes) which corresponds to the number of dimensions in the vector.

Minimize the Number of Transformation Errors. We used AnATLyzer [6] to identify the number of errors in the transformation after applying the solution on the initial transformation. Thus, the second fitness function is defined as follows:

$$Min f2(S) = r \tag{2}$$

Where r is the number of errors identified in the revised transformation program. The errors are mainly the non-conformance between the metamodels and rules that can be statically detected by static semantic constraints for ATL transformations [6].

Maximize the Metamodel Coverage. The footprint tool of Burgueno et al. [3] estimates the coverage of the evolved source or target metamodels by the newly revised transformation after applying the recommended rule-level changes. The third fitness function is as follows:

$$Max f3(S) = |re \cap mme| \tag{3}$$

Where re is the set of covered metamodel elements by the revised transformation rules as identified by the footprint tool and mme is the set of the evolved metamodel elements.

Evolutionary Operators. Population-based search algorithms deploy crossover and mutation operators to improve the fitness functions of the solutions in the population in each iteration. Change operators such as crossover and mutation aim to drive the search towards near-optimal co-evolution solutions. The *crossover* operator is responsible for creating new solutions based on already existing ones, e.g., re-combining solutions. In our adaptation, we use a single random cut-point crossover to construct offspring co-evolution solutions. It starts by selecting and splitting at random two-parent co-evolution solutions. Then crossover creates two child solutions by putting, for the first child, the first part of the first parent with the second part of the second parent, and vice versa for the second child.

The *mutation* operator is used to introduce slight random changes into candidate co-evolution solutions. This operator guides the algorithm into areas of the search space that would not be reachable through recombination alone and avoids the convergence of the population towards a few elite solutions. In our adaptation, we used a mutation operator that picks at random one or more positions (change operation) from their vector and replaces them by either another type of change operator or modifying the parameters of the operation type to apply it for another rule.

When applying crossover and mutation operators, we ensure the validity of the solution using a repair function. This function consists of removing edit operations from the solution when conflicts are detected using a set of constraints (redundancy, inapplicable edit operations after changes, etc.).

4   Validation

4.1   Research Questions and Evaluation Metrics

Our study addresses the following research questions:

- **RQ1 Solution Correctness:** To what extent do the co-evolution solutions generated by our approach compare to manually developed solutions?
- **RQ2 Benefits:** To what extent can our approach reduce the number of changes and manual effort to evolve the rules after a metamodel evolution?
- **RQ3.1 Search Validation:** Do we need a metaheuristic search for the metamodel/transformation co-evolution problem?
- **RQ3.2 Search Quality:** How does the proposed multi-objective approach based on NSGA-II perform compared to a mono-objective one (aggregating the three objectives)?

Our research questions are evaluated using the following four ATL case studies. We selected to use ATL to validate our approach since it is one of the widely used model transformation languages [4,30]. Each case study consists of one model transformation and all the necessary artifacts to execute the transformation, i.e., the input and output metamodels and a sample input model. For replication purposes, the different case studies used in our experiments along with a description of the used ATL change operations, the implementation of our approach, and the detailed 30 runs result of the different approaches can be found in [17].

We have selected these case studies due to their difference in size, structure and number of dependencies among their transformation artifacts, i.e., rules and helpers. Furthermore, the metamodel evolution scenarios used in our experiments were defined in a previous work based on the selected ATL case studies [11]. Table 1 summarizes, for each case study, the number of rules in the transformation (R), the number of rules to co-evolve/modify (CR) and the number of expected operations to fix the rules based on the manually created solutions in [11].

To see whether our approach produces sufficiently good results (RQ1), we compare our generated set of solutions with a set of manually created solutions

Table 1. Selected ATL case studies.

ID	Name	Rules (R)	Coevolved rules (CR)	Edit operations (EOp)
Case study 1 (CS1)	Ecore2Maude	40	12	21
Case study 2 (CS2)	R2ML2RDM	58	16	34
Case study 3 (CS3)	XHTML2XML	31	8	17
Case study 4 (CS4)	XML2Ant	29	7	13

based on a manual correctness measure (MC) defined as the intersection between the recommended changes operations and expected ones then divided by the number of expected operations. Since the number of correct recommendations may not be sufficient to evaluate the correctness, we evaluate the number of rules (FR) fixed by the recommended changes.

To evaluate the benefits of our approach (RQ2), we reported the execution time (T) of the different search algorithms to obtain good co-evolution solutions compared to manually fixing the transformation programs. Furthermore, we evaluate the ability of our approach to recommend the best co-evolution solutions with a minimum number of change operations (NOp).

To validate the problem formulation of our approach (RQ3.1), we compared our multi-objective approach with Random Search (RS), using MC, FR, and NOp, to justify the use of a metaheuristic search. If RS outperforms an intelligent search method, we can conclude that there is no need to use a metaheuristic search. To allow such a comparison, we used the knee-point [28] strategy to select a unique solution from each of the final Pareto sets of RS and NSGA-II. Thus, we identified the solution from the set of non-dominated ones providing the maximum trade-off using the following strategy when comparing between RS and NSGA-II. To find the maximal trade-off solution of the multi-objective algorithm, we use the trade-off worthiness metric proposed by Rachmawati and Srinivasan [28] to evaluate the worthiness of each non-dominated solution in terms of compromise between the objectives. This metric is expressed as follows:

$$\mu(x_i, S) = \underset{x_j \in S, x_i \not\prec x_j, x_j \not\prec x_i}{Min} T(x_i, x_j) \quad where, \quad T(x_i, x_j) = \frac{\sum_{m=1}^{M} max\left[0, \frac{f_m(x_j) - f_m(x_i)}{f_m^{max} - f_m^{min}}\right]}{\sum_{m=1}^{M} max\left[0, \frac{f_m(x_i) - f_m(x_j)}{f_m^{max} - f_m^{min}}\right]}$$

We note that x_j denotes members of the set of non-dominated solutions S that are non-dominated with respect to x_i. The quantity $\mu(x_i, S)$ expresses the least amount of improvement per unit deterioration by substituting any alternative x_j from S with x_i. We note also that $f_m(x_i)$ corresponds to the mth objective value of solution x_i and f_m^{max}/f_m^{min} corresponds to the maximal/minimal value of the mth objective in the population individuals. In the above equations, normalization is performed to prevent some objectives being predominant over others. In the last equation, the numerator expresses the aggregated improvement gained by substituting x_j with x_i. However, the denominator evaluates the deterioration generated by the substitution.

To evaluate the need for a multi-objective approach, we compared the results of our NSGA-II approach with the results retrieved from a mono-objective Genetic Algorithm (GA) aggregating the three fitness functions into one (with equal weights to all the objectives after normalizing them in the range [0,1]).

We limited the investigation of the relevance of our automated approach comparing to manually fixing the co-evolution issues to only CS1. CS1 represents the average case among the four case studies regarding the complexity (rules, expected edit operations and co-evolved rules) since the most complex case study is CS2 and the simplest one is CS4. Thus, the use of CS1 can be a good representative among all the case studies. Our study involved 6 master students in Software Engineering. All the participants are volunteers and familiar with MDE and co-evolution/refactoring since they are part of a graduate course on Software Quality Assurance (SQA). All the graduate students have already taken at least one position as software developer/engineer in industry for at least three years and most of them (5 out of 6 students) participated in similar experiments in the past, either as part of a research project or during the SQA graduate course. Furthermore, 3 out of the 6 students are currently working as full-time or part-time developers in the software industry. Participants were first asked to fill out a pre-study questionnaire containing four questions. The questionnaire helped to collect background information such as their modeling experience, and their familiarity with MDE and co-evolution/refactoring. Also, all the participants attended one lecture about model transformations and ATL, and passed four tests to evaluate their performance in evaluate and suggest co-evolution solutions.

4.2   Parameters Setting and Statistical Tests

The initial population/solution of NSGA-II, GA and RS are completely random. The stopping criterion for all the studied search algorithms is 100,000 evaluations. After several trial runs of the algorithms, the parameter values of the three techniques are fixed to 100 as population size and 20,000 iterations. For the change operators, we set crossover rate to 0.8 and mutation at 0.3 probability. We used a high mutation rate to ensure the diversity of the population and avoid premature convergence to occur. Indeed, there are no general rules to determine these parameters, and thus, we set the combination of parameter values by the trial-and-error method.

Our experimental study is based on 30 independent simulation runs for each problem instance, and the obtained results are statistically analyzed by using the Wilcoxon rank sum test with a 95% confidence level ($\alpha = 5\%$). In fact, for each problem instance, we compute the p-value obtained by comparing the results of the different algorithms with our approach. In this way, we determine whether the performance difference between our technique and one of the other approaches is statistically significant or just a random result. The Wilcoxon rank sum test verifies whether the results are statistically different or not; however, it does not give any idea about the difference in magnitude. Thus, we used the Vargha-Delaney A measure which is a non-parametric effect size measure.

Table 2. Mean manual correctness (MC) based on 30 runs for NSGA-II, RS, and GA.

Manual correctness	Case study 1	Case study 2	Case study 3	Case study 4
NSGA-II	19/21 (90%)	29/34 (85%)	14/17 (82%)	13/13 (100%)
Genetic algorithm	13/21 (61%)	19/34 (55%)	13/17 (76%)	10/13 (74%)
Random search	9/21 (42%)	10/34 (29%)	8/17 (45%)	6/13 (48%)

Table 3. Mean number of fixed rules (FR) based on 30 runs for NSGA-II, RS, and GA.

Fixed rules	Case study 1	Case study 2	Case study 3	Case study 4
NSGA-II	11	14	7	7
Genetic algorithm	6	9	5	4
Random search	5	6	3	3

4.3   Results

Results for RQ1. As reported in Table 2, the majority of the ATL changes recommended by our multi-objective approach were correct and similar to the ones manually applied by developers in [11], for the different evolution scenarios. On average, for all of our four studied projects, 89% of the proposed ATL change operations are correct. We decided to compare our recommendations with the ones manually proposed in another study (rather than manually checking the proposed solutions) to avoid biasing our experiments with our judgments. The highest MC score is 100% where all the changes applied to the ATL program were correct for the XML2Ant program, and the lowest score is 82% for the R2ML2RDM transformation program. Thus, it is clear that the results are independent of the size of the ATL programs and the number of recommended changes. The deviation between the expected and recommended rule-level change operations is limited up-to four which means that the number of recommended changes was similar to the expected ones.

Table 3 shows that the recommended co-evolution solutions fixed most of the ATL transformation rules to make them consistent with the source or target metamodel evolution. The maximum number of rules that were not fixed are two (the case of R2ML2RDM) and for the remaining cases, up-to only one rule remains to be fixed by the designer manually. Some of these rules are hard to fix automatically due to a significant number of non-trivial metamodel changes that renamed several elements.

Results for RQ2. Table 4 shows that our approach requires a reasonable execution time to converge towards good co-evolution solutions within less than 20 min. The highest execution time was reported on the largest case study of Ecore2Maude (19.5 min) and the lowest one on XML2Ant (9 min). The execution time is significantly lower than the average of two hours spent by developers

Table 4. Mean execution time (T) based on 30 runs for NSGA-II, GA, and RS.

Execution time (minutes)	Case study 1	Case study 2	Case study 3	Case study 4
NSGA-II	19.5	17.4	12	9
Genetic algorithm	15.4	14.2	8.2	7.1
Random search	8.3	7.2	2.5	3

Table 5. Number of edit operations (NOp) mean values of NSGA-II, GA, and RS over 30 independent runs.

Recommendation	Case study 1	Case study 2	Case study 3	Case study 4
NSGA-II	18	30	15	13
Genetic Algorithm	24	37	22	15
Random Search	29	42	26	20

to fix the ATL programs manually as reported in [11]. Furthermore, the number of errors detected after applying the recommended changes to the ATL rules was limited up-to two rules which may require low effort from the developers to fix them rather than writing all the co-evolution changes manually.

Table 5 describes the number of changes to be applied on the ATL programs to make them consistent with the new metamodels. It is clear that the number of changes is correlated with the number of rules to evolve and the metamodel changes. However, our multi-objective approach generated the minimum number of changes compared to the two other approaches as detailed later. The highest number of changes is 29 to evolve a total of 16 rules, which is reasonable since our tool enables the automated execution and testing of these changes.

Table 6. Statistical tests summary. A "+" symbol at the ith position means that the evaluation metric value of algorithm A is statistically different from algorithm B on CSi. A "−" symbol at the ith position means the opposite.

	NSGA-II (CS1,CS2,CS3,CS4)				GA (CS1,CS2,CS3,CS4)				RS (CS1,CS2,CS3,CS4)			
	MC	T	Nop	FR	MC	T	Nop	FR	MC	T	Nop	FR
NSGA-II					(++++)	(++++)	(++++)	(++++)	(++++)	(++++)	(++++)	(++++)
GA	(++++)	(++++)	(++++)	(++++)					(-+++)	(++++)	(+++-)	(-++-)
RS	(++++)	(++++)	(++++)	(++++)	(-+++)	(++++)	(+++-)	(-++-)				

Results for RQ3.1 and RQ3.2. The results summarized in Tables 2, 3, 4 and 5 confirm that NSGA-II is better than random search based on the different evaluation metrics of MC, FR, and Nop on all four ATL case studies. The average manual correctness values of random search on the different ATL programs are lower than 41%. RS also proposed the highest number of errors and number of recommendations among all the algorithms with the lowest number of fixed rules. This can be explained by the huge search space to explore to generate relevant rule-level changes.

Tables 2, 3, 4 and 5 confirm the average superior performance of our multi-objective approach compared to a mono-objective GA. Table 2 shows that our approach provides significantly higher manual correctness results (MC) than a mono-objective formulation having MC scores between 55% and 76% on the different ATL programs. The same observation is valid for FR and NOp as described in Tables 3 and 5. Thus, it is clear that all the three different objectives considered in our formulation are conflicting justifying the outperformance of NSGA-II.

Since our proposal is based on multi-objective optimization, it is important to evaluate the execution time (T). It is evident that NSGA-II requires a higher execution time than RS and GA since NSGA-II is considering more objectives and evolutionary operators. All the search-based algorithms under comparison were executed on machines with Intel i7 processors 4 GHz and 8 GB RAM. Overall, RS and GA algorithms were faster than NSGA-II. In fact, the average execution times for NSGA-II, GA and RS were respectively 14.5, 11 and 6 min. However, the execution for NSGA-II is still reasonable because the algorithm is not executed daily by the developers, and the co-evolution of ATL programs is not a real-time problem.

An average of 16 edit operations (mean value among all participants) were correctly identified manually by the subjects, which corresponds to 76% as average manual correctness. Our automated multi-objective approach successfully recommended an average of 19 edit operations out of the expected 21 operations (91% of manual correctness). The minimum number of manually identified correct edit operations is 14 (one participant), and the maximum is 17 (two participants) while three participants correctly identified 16 operations. Our automated approach successfully fixed, on average, a total of 11 out of 12 rules which outperforms the average number of rules fixed manually, which corresponds to 9 rules. A maximum of 10 rules was fixed manually by two participants while one participant was able only to fix 8 rules. The controlled experiment was limited to two hours thus all the results are obtained in two hours, which is significantly higher than the execution time of our approach limited to an average of 19 min. Thus, our automated approach can significantly improve the productivity of developers during the evolution process.

The results of our experiments, on all the case studies, algorithms and the evaluation metrics, were found to be statistically significant on 30 independent runs using the Wilcoxon rank sum test with a 95% confidence level when comparing our multi-objective approach to the remaining techniques (RS, GA and manual) as described in Table 6. In our experiments, we have found the following results as well: (a) on small-scale programs (XHTML2XML and XML2Ant) our approach is better than all the other algorithms based on all the performance metrics with an A effect size higher than 0.92; and (b) on medium and large-scale programs (Ecore2Maude, and R2ML2RDM), our approach is better than all the other algorithms with an A effect size higher than 0.88 using all the evaluation metrics.

4.4 Threats to Validity

Conclusion validity is concerned with the statistical relationship between the treatment and the outcome. The parameters tuning of the different optimization algorithms used in our experiments creates an internal threat that we need to evaluate in our future work. The parameters' values used in our experiments are found by trial-and-error. However, it would be an interesting perspective to design an adaptive parameter tuning strategy for our approach so that parameters are updated during the execution to provide the best possible performance.

Internal validity is concerned with the causal relationship between the treatment and the outcome. We dealt with internal threats to validity by performing 30 independent simulation runs for each problem instance. This makes it highly unlikely that the observed results were caused by anything other than the applied multi-objective approach. However, the comparison between multi-objective and mono-objective approaches is challenging since multiple solutions are generated by NSGA-II while the GA algorithm can generate only one co-evolution solution. We selected, in our experiments, the solution that represents the maximum trade-off between the three objectives (knee-point [7]) to compare with the GA's solution. However, we treated the different objectives with equal weights in our GA adaptation, which can be considered as an internal threat.

External validity refers to the generalizability of our findings. In this study, we performed our experiments on four different ATL programs belonging to different domains and having different sizes. However, we cannot assert that our results can be generalized to other programs. In addition, our study was limited to the use of specific change types related to ATL rules. Furthermore, the manual evaluation was limited to only one case study and a total of 6 participants. Thus, the main threats are the difficulty in generalizing the obtained manual results and the impact of participants expertise on them. To deal with these threats, we selected CS1 that represents the average case among the four case studies regarding the complexity (#rules, #expected edit operations, and #co-evolved rules). Furthermore, the participants are selected based on their experience in MDE, thus they can be representative of the average expertise of developers in practice.

5   Related Work

Co-evolution in the area of MDE has been heavily studied in the last decade [14]. The starting point was the metamodel/model co-evolution challenge [8] which attracted much research interest in dealing with large migration spaces [29]. In this context, search-based approaches have been proposed [18]. However, other co-evolution scenarios are understudied. We now outline work which has been done for co-evolving OCL expressions and model transformations.

Concerning the co-evolution of OCL expressions, dedicated approaches have been presented very recently. Approaches which are based on coupling changes for metamodels with co-changes for OCL expressions are presented in [19,22]. The main goal of these approaches is to repair OCL expressions for a set of provided metamodel change types. A search-based formulation of this problem has been also proposed [1].

Concerning transformation co-evolution, several approaches followed the idea of building on a set of metamodel changes for which co-changes for transformations can be derived [9,10,12,20,23,24,26]. For instance, Levandovsy et al. [23] proposed a higher-order transformation to adapt existing transformations. They classify metamodel changes, with respect to the effect on transformations into three categories [23]: (i) fully automated, i.e., changes affecting existing transformations that can be automatically migrated without user intervention, (ii) partially automated, i.e., changes or modifications that affect existing transformations which can be adapted automatically, even though some manual fine-tuning is required to complete the adaptation, and (iii) fully semantic, i.e., changes that effect transformations that cannot be automatically migrated, and the user has to completely define the adaptation.

All the mentioned approaches require the full correctness of the detected metamodel changes, which is still a challenge, especially when it comes to the intention behind the changes. Furthermore, the co-evolution is only possible for a set of predefined change types. In our work, we do not require the metamodel changes and use a larger set of transformation co-evolution rules and a sophisticated search algorithm which allows migrating a transformation in any promising direction.

6   Conclusion

We propose, in this paper, an automated approach for metamodel/transformation co-evolution that finds a trade-off between different three objectives. Our approach allows developers to benefit from search-based rule-level change recommendations without defining a generic template to map metamodel changes into rule-level changes. To evaluate the effectiveness of our tool, we conducted a study based on four evolution scenarios of the source or target metamodels of ATL programs and compared it with random search, mono-objective formulation and manual technique. Our evaluation results provide evidence that our tool improves the applicability and automation of existing co-evolution techniques between metamodels and transformation rules.

Future work involves validating our technique with additional types of rule-level changes, more multi-objective algorithms and other transformation languages to conclude about the general applicability of our methodology. We focused, in this paper, on checking the correctness of the co-evolution solutions. We will use the quality indicators, such as the Hypervolume, when we compare between intelligent search algorithms such as MOPSO vs. NSGA-II.

Acknowledgements. This work has been partially funded by the Austrian Federal Ministry of Science, Research and Economy, National Foundation for Research, Technology and Development, by the Austrian Science Fund (FWF) P 28519-N31, and by the Canada NSERC grant RGPIN/06702-2014.

References

1. Batot, E., Kessentini, W., Sahraoui, H.A., Famelis, M.: Heuristic-based recommendation for Metamodel - OCL coevolution. In: MODELS, pp. 210–220 (2017)
2. Brambilla, M., Cabot, J., Wimmer, M.: Model-Driven Software Engineering in Practice, 2nd edn. Morgan & Claypool Publishers, San Rafael (2017)
3. Burgueño, L., Troya, J., Wimmer, M., Vallecillo, A.: Static fault localization in model transformations. IEEE Trans. Softw. Eng. **41**(5), 490–506 (2015)
4. Cheng, Z., Monahan, R., Power, J.F.: A sound execution semantics for ATL via translation validation. In: ICMT, pp. 133–148 (2015)
5. Cuadrado, J.S., Guerra, E., de Lara, J.: Quick fixing ATL transformations with speculative analysis. Softw. Syst. Model 1–35 (2016)
6. Cuadrado, J.S., Guerra, E., de Lara, J.: Static analysis of model transformations. IEEE Trans. Softw. Eng. **43**(9), 868–897 (2017)
7. Deb, K., Pratap, A., Agarwal, S., Meyarivan, T.: A fast and elitist multiobjective genetic algorithm: NSGA-II. IEEE Trans. Evol. Comput. **6**(2), 182–197 (2002)
8. Di Ruscio, D., Iovino, L., Pierantonio, A.: What is needed for managing coevolution in MDE? In: Workshop on Model Comparison in Practice, pp. 30–38 (2011)
9. Ehrig, H., Ehrig, K., Ermel, C.: Refactoring of model transformations. In: ECEASST (2009)
10. Etzlstorfer, J., Kapsammer, E., Schwinger, W.: On the evolution of modeling ecosystems: an evaluation of co-evolution approaches. In: MODELSWARD, pp. 90–99 (2017)
11. Fleck, M., Troya, J., Kessentini, M., Wimmer, M., Alkhazi, B.: Model transformation modularization as a many-objective optimization problem. IEEE Trans. Software Eng. **43**(11), 1009–1032 (2017)
12. García, J., Díaz, O., Azanza, M.: Model transformation co-evolution: a semiautomatic approach. In: SLE, pp. 144–163 (2012)
13. Harman, M., Mansouri, S.A., Zhang, Y.: Search-based software engineering: trends, techniques and applications. ACM Comput. Surv. **45**(1), 11:1–11:61 (2012)
14. Hebig, R., Khelladi, D.E., Bendraou, R.: Approaches to co-evolution of metamodels and models: a survey. IEEE Trans. Softw. Eng. **43**(5), 396–414 (2017)
15. Iovino, L., Pierantonio, A., Malavolta, I.: On the impact significance of metamodel evolution in MDE. J. Object Technol. **11**(3), 1–33 (2012)
16. Jouault, F., Allilaire, F., Bézivin, J., Kurtev, I.: ATL: a model transformation tool. Sci. Comput. Program. **72**(1–2), 31–39 (2008)
17. Kessentini, W.: https://sites.google.com/site/coevolutionkessentini/data
18. Kessentini, W., Sahraoui, H.A., Wimmer, M.: Automated metamodel/model coevolution using a multi-objective optimization approach. In: ECMFA, pp. 138–155 (2016)
19. Khelladi, D.E., Bendraou, R., Hebig, R., Gervais, M.: A semi-automatic maintenance and co-evolution of OCL constraints with (meta)model evolution. J. Syst. Softw. **134**, 242–260 (2017)

20. Kruse, S.: On the use of operators for the co-evolution of metamodels and transformations. In: Models and Evolution Workshop (2011)
21. Kühne, T.: Matters of (meta-)modeling. Syst. Softw. Model 5(4), 369–385 (2006)
22. Kusel, A., et al.: Systematic co-evolution of OCL expressions. In: APCCM, pp. 33–42 (2015)
23. Levendovszky, T., Balasubramanian, D., Narayanan, A., Karsai, G.: A novel approach to semi-automated evolution of DSML model transformation. In: SLE, pp. 23–41 (2010)
24. Lohmann, W., Riedewald, G.: Towards automatical migration of transformation rules after grammar extension. In: CSMR, pp. 30–39 (2003)
25. Lúcio, L., et al.: Model transformation intents and their properties. Softw. Syst. Model. 15(3), 647–684 (2016)
26. Mendez, D., Etien, A., Muller, A., Casallas, R.: Towards transformation migration after metamodel evolution. In: Models and Evolution Workshop (2010)
27. Meyers, B., Vangheluwe, H.: A framework for evolution of modelling languages. Sci. Comput. Program. 76(12), 1223–1246 (2011)
28. Rachmawati, L., Srinivasan, D.: Multiobjective evolutionary algorithm with controllable focus on the knees of the pareto front. IEEE Trans. Evol. Comput. 13(4), 810–824 (2009)
29. Ruscio, D.D., Etzlstorfer, J., Iovino, L., Pierantonio, A., Schwinger, W.: Supporting variability exploration and resolution during model migration. In: ECMFA, pp. 231–246 (2016)
30. Selim, G.M.K., Cordy, J.R., Dingel, J.: How is ATL really used? Language feature use in the ATL zoo. In: MODELS, pp. 34–44 (2017)
31. Sendall, S., Kozaczynski, W.: Model transformation: the heart and soul of model-driven software development. IEEE Softw. 20(5), 42–45 (2003)

Learning Without Peeking: Secure Multi-party Computation Genetic Programming

Jinhan Kim[1]([⊠]), Michael G. Epitropakis[2], and Shin Yoo[1]([⊠])

[1] School of Computing, KAIST, Daejeon, Republic of Korea
{jinhankim,shin.yoo}@kaist.ac.kr
[2] Department of Management Science, Lancaster University, Lancaster, UK

Abstract. Genetic Programming is widely used to build predictive models for defect proneness or development efforts. The predictive modelling often depends on the use of sensitive data, related to past faults or internal resources, as training data. We envision a scenario in which revealing the training data constitutes a violation of privacy. To ensure organisational privacy in such a scenario, we propose SMCGP, a method that performs Genetic Programming as Secure Multiparty Computation. In SMCGP, one party uses GP to learn a model of training data provided by another party, without actually knowing each datapoint in the training data. We present an SMCGP approach based on the garbled circuit protocol, which is evaluated using two problem sets: a widely studied symbolic regression benchmark, and a GP-based fault localisation technique with real world fault data from Defects4J benchmark. The results suggest that SMCGP can be equally accurate as the normal GP, but the cost of keeping the training data hidden can be about three orders of magnitude slower execution.

1 Introduction

Genetic Programming is a variant of Genetic Algorithm that evolves programs and expressions instead of solutions [22]. While its recent popularity for Automated Program Repair (APR) [7,32] is closely related to GP's original ambition of automated programming, it has also been widely used by SBSE community to build predictive models for defect prediction [18], development effort prediction [6], and software quality estimation [17]. Recently, GP has also been successfully used to produce ranking models for fault localisation [12,27].

While GP has been successfully applied to various problem domains, its application to each of the above domains requires access to potentially sensitive past data, such as historial defect proneness data, information about internal resources and project cost, quality metrics, and test coverage data. GP uses the past data either to perform symbolic regression to find a model that fits the past results the best or to build ranking model that places the faulty program element as high in a ranking as possible.

© Springer Nature Switzerland AG 2018
T. E. Colanzi and P. McMinn (Eds.): SSBSE 2018, LNCS 11036, pp. 246–261, 2018.
https://doi.org/10.1007/978-3-319-99241-9_13

The requirement on the use of sensitive past data raises a concern for both researchers and practitioners. It is difficult for researchers to study real world data, because data related to defects or internal resources can be regarded as highly sensitive and may not be disclosed to external researchers. For practitioners, this rules out any form of Optimisation-as-a-Service type analysis. Hence we ask the following question: *is it possible to apply GP to learn predictive or ranking models for software engineering, without revealing sensitive data for training?*

This paper proposes a method that allows data to be hidden from GP, using Secure Multiparty Computation (SMC) [4], as an answer to our research question. SMC is a subdomain of cryptography whose goal is to enable multiple parties to jointly compute a function over their inputs while keeping the inputs hidden from each other. We instantiate Secure Multiparty Computation GP (SMCGP) using an SMC protocol called garbled circuits [35], and show that GP can be performed while not revealing the individual datapoints without loss of accuracy. We empirically evaluate the performance of SMCGP using a range of symbolic regression benchmark problems, as well as training of GP-based fault localisation model [27] using a real world fault data from Defects4J benchmark [11].

The technical contributions of this paper are as follows:

- We introduce the concept of SMCGP, the goal of which is to perform GP while remaining oblivious to the training data.
- We present an empirical study of well known symbolic regression benchmark problems, as well as a GP-based fault localisation technique in conjunction with the Defects4J repository. The results show that SMCGP is feasible without loss of accuracy, but requires significantly longer execution time.

Section 2 introduces Oblivious Transfer and Garbled Circuit, which is used to formulate SMCGP described in Sect. 3. Section 4 presents the experimental setup. Section 5 discusses the experimental results. Section 6 presents the threats to validity, and Sect. 7 contains the related work. Section 8 concludes.

2   Background

Secure Multiparty Computation (SMC) aims to perform distributed computation that involves multiple parties in a secure manner. In particular, its aim is to maintain each party's input to the computation process oblivious to other involved parties, while ensuring that the results are correct and uncorrupted.

Perhaps the most widely known example of SMC is the Yao's millionaires' problem, introduced by Yao [35]. Suppose there are two millionaires: both want to know who is richer without revealing the exact amount of one's wealth to the other. More formally, assume that there exist n participants, $p_1, \ldots, p_n$, each of which is holding private data, $d_1, \ldots, d_n$. SMC aims to compute the value of a public function over the set of all private data, i.e., $F(d_1, \ldots, d_n)$, while all participants keep their own data private.

Yao suggested the garbled circuit protocol, also known as Yao's protocol, to achieve secure computation between two parties (2PC). For more than two parties (MPC), secret sharing schemes such as Shamir Secret Sharing [26] are used. We formulate our GP under the 2PC context using garbled circuits, which is explained in the rest of this section.

2.1 Oblivious Transfer

In cryptography, oblivious transfer refers to a scenario in which the sender transfers one out of many possible messages without knowing what message has actually been transferred. Our choice of SMC, garbled circuits, is based on a specific type of oblivious transfer called 1–2 oblivious transfer [5]. Under the 1–2 oblivious transfer protocol, the sender has two strings, S_0 and S_1, and the receiver chooses $i \in \{0, 1\}$. After the transfer, the sender should not know which value of i the receiver chose, and the receiver should not know S_{1-i} (i.e., the string not chosen by the receiver).

The 1–2 oblivious transfer protocol can be implemented over asymmetric cryptography, such as the RSA [23]. The following is a brief description of Oblivious Transfer. Suppose Alice has two messages, m_0 and m_1, and Bob has a bit b. Bob wants to receive m_b without the sender knowing b. Let $N = pq$, where both p and q are large prime numbers; let e be relatively prime to $(p-1)(q-1)$. The encryption of message m is $m^e \mod N$. The transfer takes place as follows:

1. Alice generates an RSA key pair and sends the public exponent e to Bob. The private exponent, d, is secret.
2. Alice also generates and sends two random messages, x_0 and x_1, to Bob.
3. Bob chooses $b \in \{0, 1\}$, and generates a random k. Bob then sends $v = (x_b + k^e) \mod N$ (i.e., encryption of k blind to x_b) to Alice.
4. Alice computes $k_0 = (v - x_0)^d \mod N$ and $k_1 = (v - x_1)^d \mod N$. Alice knows k is one of these values, but does not know which.
5. Alice sends $m'_0 = m_0 + k_0$ and $m'_1 = m_1 + k_1$ to Bob.
6. Bob decrypts m'_b because Bob knows which x_b was chosen earlier.

Alice cannot determine which of x_0 and x_1 Bob chose. Bob cannot know the message he did not choose, as he can only unblind the message m_b with his k.

2.2 Garbled Circuit

The oblivious transfer deals with the secure transfer of messages: let us now turn to computation of functions for SMC. Garbled Circuit is a cryptographic protocol for two party secure computation. Intuitively, it operates by representing the function to be computed as a Boolean circuit and sending the circuit using the 1–2 oblivious transfer. We outline the process of garbled circuit transfer with a simple working example below:

1. Convert the function to be computed into a Boolean circuit with 2-input gates. As an working example, we are going to assume that our function itself is a logical AND. Table 1(a) shows the raw truth table.

2. Alice, the *garbler*, replaces 0s and 1s in the truth table with randomly generated string labels. The result is shown in Table 1(b).
3. Alice encrypts the output column(s) of the truth table with corresponding input labels. Alice also permutes the encrypted output rows so that the values cannot be guessed from the order (hence the name *garbled*).
4. Alice sends the encrypted circuit to Bob, along with her inputs. For example, if Alice's input for a is 1, Alice sends X_0^a. Since Alice generated the labels randomly, Bob does not know what Alice's actual input is.
5. In order to obtain the result, Bob needs the labels for his input. If Bob's input for b is 0, Bob asks for $b = 0$ between X_0^b and X_1^b through 1–2 oblivious transfer, after which Alice does not know which Bob chose between X_0^b and X_1^b and Bob does not know what the other label (in our case X_1^b) is.
6. Bob tries to decrypt each output row: he can only decrypt a single row, which is the output for the input from both Alice and Bob.

Table 1. Garbled circuit operation on $F(a, b) = AND(a, b)$: (a) the raw truth table, (b) Alice assigns random string labels to values in the truth table, (c) the output garbled table that is transferred.

$a\ b\ c$	a	b	c	Garbled Table
0 0 0	X_0^a	X_0^b	X_0^c	$Enc_{X_0^a, X_0^b}(X_0^c)$
0 1 0	X_0^a	X_1^b	X_0^c	$Enc_{X_0^a, X_1^b}(X_0^c)$
1 0 0	X_1^a	X_0^b	X_0^c	$Enc_{X_1^a, X_0^b}(X_0^c)$
1 1 1	X_1^a	X_1^b	X_1^c	$Enc_{X_1^a, X_1^b}(X_1^c)$
(a)	**(b)**			**(c)**

While our small working example only concerns a single logical operator as the function of interest, one can convert an arbitrary function into an optimised Boolean circuit [28] and apply the outlined process to the truth table of each 2-input gate within the circuit. By repeatedly applying the above process, Alice and Bob can securely compute the garbled circuit. The cost of privacy is the runtime overhead that stems from encryption and decryption as well as the conversion and execution of arbitrary functions as Boolean circuits.

2.3   Obliv-C

Obliv-C [37] is both a domain specific extension of C and a gcc wrapper that compiles the extension.[1] It is designed for developers to easily implement 2PC Secure Multiparty Computation: Obliv-C provides high-level interface to SMC via language extension, performs the Boolean circuit conversion, and handles the garbled circuit protocol. It has been applied to various privacy preserving machine learning scenarios [9,29] as well as to email communications [10].

---

[1] It is available from https://oblivc.org.

While we leave the low level implementation details of Obliv-C out in this paper (please refer to the original paper [37] for all the details), let us focus on two core language constructs, obliv qualifier and obliv if statement.

- obliv: this qualifier denotes variables whose values need to remain oblivious. All oblivious variables are declared with the qualifier and assigned with actual values transferred from the garbled circuit protocol.
- obliv if: to prevent information leak from control flow, Obliv-C converts all control dependencies into data dependencies. This means that the body of obliv if will be always executed, regardless of how the branch predicate evaluates. When the predicate is false, the garbled circuit ensures that the values computed inside the block are simply ignored.

Figure 1 shows an example code of Obliv-C for the Yao's millionaires' problem. Variable a and b represent the wealth of two millionaires respectively. Using the function feedOblivInt, a and b are converted into an obliv qualified integers. The following if statement at Line 13 is a obliv if statement, because it makes a comparison between obliv qualified values. The result of comparison between a and b is stored in result, which is also obliv qualified variable. Finally, the call to revealOblivBool ensures that only the result is revealed to each party at the end of computation.

```
1  #include <million.h>
2  #include <obliv.oh>
3
4  void millionaire (void *args) {
5    ProtocolIO *io = args;
6    obliv int a, b;
7    obliv bool result = false;
8    a = feedOblivInt (io->myinput, 1);
9    b = feedOblivInt (io->myinput, 2);
10   obliv if (a < b) result = true;
11   revealOblivBool (&io->result, result, 0);
12 }
```

Fig. 1. An Obliv-C program that implements Yao's Millionaires' problem taken from Zahur et al. [37].

3 Secure Multiparty Computation GP Using Obliv-C

In GP, the majority of the computation takes place during the fitness evaluation. In addition, this is the place where the training dataset is used by GP. This section describes how we can formulate SMC using the fitness evaluation as the function of interest. Our focus in this paper is the scenario in which multiple parties are holding different parts of the training dataset. We call this the multiparty dataholder scenario.

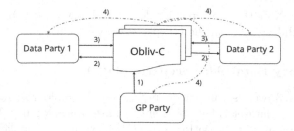

Fig. 2. The multiparty dataholder scenario when there are two data parties and one GP party: (1) GP party generates the SMC program, and (2) sends it to each party. (3) each party enters their input, and (4) the SMC program computes and all parties get the results.

3.1 Multiparty Dataholder Scenario (2PC)

The multiparty dataholder scenario is a natural extension of the original Yao's millionaires' problem, as shown in Fig. 2. We simply replace the function that returns the result of comparison between two numbers with the fitness function that evaluates the given GP candidate solution using the data held by the two participating parties. Let us call the data holders the *data parties*, and the mediator who is running the GP the *GP party*.

- **GP Party**: GP party executes the GP evolutionary loop, and generates Obliv-C based SMC program that contains the garbled circuits of the candidate solution to evaluate.[2] This SMC program is used by data parties to securely commit their inputs.
- **Data Party**: data parties hold the split training dataset. There are two ways a training dataset can be split. Suppose a training dataset contains n datapoints, each with m properties. A *horizontal* split means each data party holds mutually exclusive subset of the n datapoints (the union should be the entire training dataset). A *vertical* split means each data party holds mutually exclusive subset of the m properties of all n datapoints (the union of two property subsets should be the set of all m properties).

Whenever the GP party needs to evaluate a candidate solution, it first generates an Obliv-C source code that corresponds to the solution, builds it, and distributes the executable to data parties. Subsequently, data parties execute the SMC program and provide their parts of the split training dataset. Once all data parties enter their input, the fitness function computes and all data parties get the resulting fitness value. GP party receives the result and continues with the GP iteration until the predefined termination criterion is met. During the process, none of the data parties get to know more than their own shares of

---

[2] In practice, our implementation gathers all candidate solutions in a generation and combines them all into a single Obliv-C program, to save the compilation overhead. This is similar to the approach taken by existing GPGPU based parallelisation approach for GP [14].

training dataset. Note that data parties do get to know what is being computed (i.e., which candidate solution the GP party is evaluating).

3.2 Singleparty Dataholder Scenario (1PC)

As shown in Fig. 3, we also present a singleparty dataholder scenario, in which the entire training dataset is held by a single participating party. We think this can also be a common use case for SMCGP, in which two stakeholders exist, one with the data (data party) and the other with Genetic Programming (GP party). The data party allows the GP party to learn from its data, but does not want to reveal the data. This scenario can be easily implemented by making the GP party to double as a data party with no training data subset to contribute.

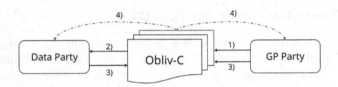

Fig. 3. The singleparty dataholder scenario when there are one data party and one GP party: (1) GP party generates the SMC program, and (2) sends it to the data party. (3) The data party enters its input, whereas GP party enters nothing, and (4) the SMC program computes and all parties get the results.

4   Experimental Setup

This section presents out research questions, and describe experimental subjects and configurations.

4.1   Research Questions

This paper aims to compare our implementations of both single and multiparty data holder SMCGP to the Normal-GP through the following research questions.

- **RQ1. Effectiveness:** how well does the SMCGP perform compared to the Normal-GP?
- **RQ2. Efficiency:** what is the runtime overhead of SMCGP when compared to Normal-GP?

RQ1 is essentially a sanity check for Obliv-C: we should achieve the same level of effectiveness if Obliv-C performs oblivious and correct computation. RQ1 is answered by comparing the Mean Squared Errors (MSEs) for the symbolic regression problems, and by comparing wasted effort (wef) for the GP-based fault localisation dataset: wef means the number of program elements which should be investigated before finding faulty program elements.

We use two-tailed Mann-Whitney U test to compare values from two different types of GP. The null hypothesis is that the mean values of different types of GP are the same. Failing to reject the null hypothesis would show that results from SMCGP cannot be distinguished from those of Normal-GP.

Our primary interest lies with **RQ2**, which investigates whether the runtime overhead of Obliv-C is practical. We expect both the use of garbled circuit protocol and the communication overhead itself will have a negative impact on the execution time of SMCGP. Therefore, we answer **RQ2** by statistically comparing the execution time of Normal-GP and SMCGP.

4.2   Subjects

Table 2 shows the subjects of our experiment. We use four symbolic regression benchmark problems that have been widely studied in the literature [33], and one GP-based fault localisation technique and a real world fault dataset based on Defects4J repository [27].

Table 2. Four symbolic regression benchmark problems and one real world fault localisation data from Defects4J repository studied in this paper.

Subject	Equation	Size of training data	# of variables
Keijzer-6 [13]	$\sum_i^x \frac{1}{i}$	50	1
Nguyen-7 [30]	$\ln(x+1) + \ln(x^2+1)$	20	1
Dow Chemical	Chemical process data	747	57
Vladislavleva-4 [31]	$\frac{10}{5 + \sum_{i=1}^{5}(x_i-3)^2}$	1,024	5
FLUCCS [27]	Real-world fault data	7,280	40

Symbolic regression is a regression analysis that aims to find a mathematical expression that best fits the given dataset [15]. Symbolic regression is usually performed by evolving trees that represent expressions, using the difference between the given data (i.e. the training data) and the data produced by candidate expressions as the fitness. Among the studied symbolic regression benchmark problems, Keijzer-6 [13], Nguyen-7 [30], and Vladislavleva-4 [31], are synthetic problems. On the other hand, the Dow Chemical symbolic regression dataset was the subject of the EvoCompetitions event at the 2010 edition of EvoStar conference and is based on real world industrial application at Dow Chemical.[3]

GP has been used for fault localisation to build ranking models: given various features (including data from both passing and failing test executions) for program elements as input, the aim is to learn a ranking model that places the faulty program element at the top. The expression evolved by GP returns what is called *suspisiousness score* for program elements, which are then sorted

---

[3] http://dces.essex.ac.uk/research/evostar/competitions.html.

according to their scores.[4] For the fault localisation problem, we use the publicly available data from FLUCCS [27], which contains per-method Spectrum Based Fault Localisation (SBFL) scores [34], as well as various code and change metrics [27], for the faulty real world Java programs in the Defects4J benchmark [11].

In our experiment, we select a single target program, Mockito, of which there exist 36 faulty versions in the FLUCCS dataset: each of the faulty version contains 1,040 methods on average. Out of 36 faulty versions, we use 32 for training, and use the remaining four for testing.

Since the 2PC scenario requires two data parties holding split dataset, we divide the original dataset in half. Datasets for the symbolic regression benchmark are split horizontally, whereas GP-based fault localisation dataset is split vertically (i.e., it results in generating two datasets that have 20 variables respectively). We posit that SMCGP will not be significantly slowed down for the 2PC scenario, as long as the network provides sufficient speed.

4.3 Configurations and Environments

We implement the GP party using DEAP [8], a Python library for evolutionary algorithm that includes an implementation of tree-GP. For fitness evaluation of each candidate GP tree, our GP party generates an Obliv-C source file using a template. To reduce the overhead of invoking Obliv-C compiler, we convert and compile the entire population in a single Obliv-C source file.

For symbolic regression benchmarks, we use a population size of 40 individuals, a single point crossover with a rate of 0.6, and a subtree replacement mutation with a rate of 0.2. For the FLUCCS dataset, we use a population of 40 individuals, a single point crossover with the rate of 1.0, and a subtree replacement mutation with the rate of 0.1. Types of non-terminal GP nodes are addition, subtraction, multiplication, and safe division (i.e., $div(a, b) = \frac{a}{b}$ if $b \neq 0$ and 1 if $b = 0$). While parameter values may affect the quality of outcome, our main interest is the efficiency of SMCGP and not the solution quality.

We set the maximum tree depth to three and the stopping criterion to be after ten generations. While these may not be ideal choices for the accuracy, note that our primary aim in this empirical study is to investigate the impact of SMC on GP's efficiency and not to evolve the best possible solution. Note that, for the FLUCCS data, we do not use all 32 faulty versions simultaneously during training: rather, we randomly sample seven programs for every GP generation to lessen the burden of computation and mitigate overfitting.

We repeat each configuration of both types of GP 20 times. The experiments have been performed on machines equipped with Intel i7-6700 CPU and 32 GB of RAM, running Ubuntu 14.04.5 LTS.

---

[4] Note that, while FLUCCS [27] makes a link between defect prediction and fault localisation via shared features, the GP formulations for two problems are different. Defect prediction *classifies* each program element to be fault prone or not: fault localisation *assigns suspiciousness scores* to program elements, aiming to place the faulty element at the top when ranked by them.

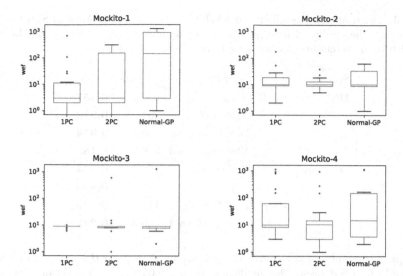

Fig. 4. Boxplots of *wef* by each test program. The y-axis is shown on logarithmic scale.

5   Results

Table 3 shows the results of Mann-Whitney U test on the MSE of SMCGP and Normal-GP, and Table 4 shows the results of Mann-Whitney U test on the *wef* value of SMCGP and Normal-GP. Based on these results, we conclude that there is *no statistically significant difference* between the results from SMCGP and Normal-GP, for both the symbolic regression benchmarks and the fault localisation problem ($\alpha = 0.05$). While this is as expected and should be, the sanity check through RQ1 was not wasted, as it enabled us to report a serious defect in `Obliv-C`, which has been reported and subsequently patched by the developers of `Obliv-C`.

There is one exception, which is the p–values obtained from the case of Mockito-1. The p–values from 1PC and 2PC, 0.01 and 0.04 respectively, suggest statistically significant difference between SMCGP and Normal-GP. Figure 4 provides the possible reason for this: the 20 repeated runs of Normal-GP for Mockito-1 resulted in much higher average *wef* including more outliers. Both 1PC and 2PC SMCGP performed *better* than Normal-GP, hence the statistically significant difference. We attribute the poor performance of Normal-GP for Mockito-1 to two possible reasons: (1) stochastic nature of GP, regardless of whether the fitness evaluation is secure or not, and (2) the possibility that learning to localise the fault Mockito-1 is particularly challenging.[5]

---

[5] It is known that faults exhibit modal behaviours against fault localisation ranking models learnt by FLUCCS [27]: Mockito-1 may be one such a fault that can only be localised well by a small minority of ranking models.

Table 3. The result of two-tailed Mann-Whitney U test on the MSE of SMCGP and Normal-GP. The significant level is 0.05 and the number of sample size is 20. The cases for which the p–values are not significant are typeset in **bold**.

Scenario	Subject	U–value	p–value
1PC, Normal-GP	Keijzer-6	220.5	**0.557**
	Nguyen-7	204.5	**0.910**
	Dow Chemical	204.5	**0.914**
	Vladislavleva-4	248.5	**0.183**
2PC, Normal-GP	Keijzer-6	156.5	**0.184**
	Nguyen-7	192.0	**0.833**
	Dow Chemical	179.0	**0.579**
	Vladislavleva-4	239.5	**0.272**

Table 4. The results of two-tailed Mann-Whitney U test on the wef metric values from the FLUCCS dataset. The significance level is 0.05 and the number of sample size is 20.

Scenario	Test program	U–value	p–value
1PC, Normal-GP	Mockito-1	105.5	0.010
	Mockito-2	205.5	**0.890**
	Mockito-3	210.0	**0.767**
	Mockito-4	205.0	**0.903**
2PC, Normal-GP	Mockito-1	124.5	0.040
	Mockito-2	194.5	**0.890**
	Mockito-3	182.0	**0.612**
	Mockito-4	161.5	**0.302**

In general, we conclude that the two samples of performance metrics from the studied problems are from the same distribution. We thereby answer **RQ1** as follows: there is no loss of accuracy in SMCGP when compared to Normal-GP.

For **RQ2**, we measure the execution time for each GP run. The results are shown in Fig. 5. The differences in the execution time between 1PC and Normal-GP is significant: we observe that SMCGP is, on average, 1,739, 1,590, and 541 times slower than Normal-GP, for the Keijzer-6, Dow Chemical, and FLUCCS, respectively. The trend is similar between 2PC and Normal-GP. The main reason for this overhead is the use of garbled circuits protocol (i.e., generating and building `Obliv-C` SMC programs), as well as the TCP communication (i.e., transferring the encrypted data), as the core GP configuration is the same for SMCGP and Normal-GP. Based on these observations, we answer **RQ2** as follows: the cost of data obliviousness in SMCGP can be up to three orders of magnitude slower execution time.

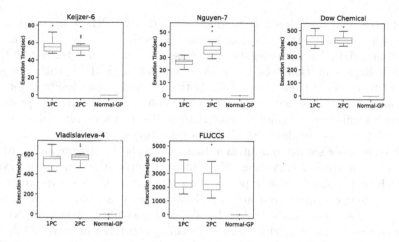

Fig. 5. Boxplots of execution time by each subject.

6   Threats to Validity

Threats to internal validity concern the extent to which the observed results from the empirical evaluation warrants our claims, such as implementation correctness. Both core components of our implementation of SMCGP, DEAP and Obliv-C, have been scrutinised as open source projects and widely applied to various work in the literature [9,10,14,27]. The remaining parts of the implementation written by us have been carefully analysed manually to minimise the risk of implementation errors.

Threats to external validity concern the extent to which our empirical evaluation results generalise. We chose widely studied symbolic regression benchmarks as well as a real world SBSE application to promote generalisation.

Threats to construct validity concern how accurately the measurements we take are actually correlated to what they claim to measure. We assess the level of any threats to construct validity to be low, as our evaluation metric, MSE, is a standard evaluation metric for symbolic regression and based on actually observed errors.

7   Related Work

Genetic Programming evolves programs, often using trees as representation [22]. Its ability to evolve expressions rendered itself as a tool for predictive modelling in domains such as software development effort estimation [6] and defect proneness prediction [18]. It has been used to evolve risk evaluation formulas [36] as well as to learn more complicated ranking models [27] for fault localisation. Many application domain involve potentially sensitive data, which motivates our use of Obliv-C for SMCGP.

Peters et al. maintained the data privacy for cross-company defect prediction in which data from one company is used to train defect predictors for another [21]. The underlying technique is called MORPH: it obfuscates datapoints while ensuring that the obfuscated points do not cross the boundaries between the original and its neighbouring class. Li et al. later extended MORPH to Sparse Representation based Double Obfuscation (SRDO) with the same intention to preserve class labels [16]. Both techniques are designed for classification problems and need labels: SMCGP can be applied to any problems. Also, both techniques are much faster than SMCGP, they only obfuscate and not completely hide the data: SMCGP does not reveal any information.

There are other secure computation frameworks, both software and hardware based. Homomorphic Encryption (HE) allows computation on the encrypted data without the need to decrypt the data first [20], but is known to require inhibitively long execution time and significant memory usage. Hardware assisted secure computation methods, such as Intel's Software Guard Extension (SGX) [1, 19], provide an enclaves in which user code can be securely executed. While SGX is an ideal solution for secure executions of a given specific program [3,25], it does not support multiple parties and requires proprietary hardware.

Data privacy has been extensively studied in relation to machine learning [2, 24] but remains a relatively new topic for SBSE. As far as we know, ours is the first implementation of GP that attempts to completely hide training data while achieving the same computation.

8   Conclusion

We present SMCGP, a Genetic Programming that allows training data to remain private to data holders. We implement our version of SMCGP a Secure Multiparty Computation (SMC) protocol called garbled circuit, through a framework called Obliv-C. Our empirical evaluation of SMCGP using a set of widely studied symbolic benchmark and a fault localisation dataset from Defects4J repository shows that SMCGP is feasible without any loss of precision. However, the cost of hiding the data is about three orders of magnitude longer execution time. Future work will investigate the adversarial scenarios, in which the candidate solutions of GP also need to remain oblivious, as well as the possibility of application of secure multiparty computation model for other types of evolutionary algorithms.

Acknowledgement. This work was supported by the National Research Foundation of Korea (NRF) grant funded by the Korea government (MEST) (Grant No. NRF-2016R1C1B1011042).

References

1. Anati, I., Gueron, S., Johnson, S., Scarlata, V.: Innovative technology for CPU based attestation and sealing. In: Proceedings of the 2nd International Workshop on Hardware and Architectural Support for Security and Privacy, vol. 13 (2013)
2. Balcan, M., Blum, A., Fine, S., Mansour, Y.: Distributed learning, communication complexity and privacy. In: COLT 2012 - The 25th Annual Conference on Learning Theory, pp. 26.1–26.22 (2012)

3. Baumann, A., Peinado, M., Hunt, G.: Shielding applications from an untrusted cloud with haven. In: Proceedings of the 11th USENIX Conference on Operating Systems Design and Implementation OSDI 2014, pp. 267–283. USENIX Association, Berkeley, CA, USA (2014)

4. Du, W., Atallah, M.J.: Secure multi-party computation problems and their applications: a review and open problems. In: Proceedings of the 2001 Workshop on New Security Paradigms, pp. 13–22. ACM (2001)

5. Even, S., Goldreich, O., Lempel, A.: A randomized protocol for signing contracts. Commun. ACM **28**(6), 637–647 (1985)

6. Ferrucci, F., Gravino, C., Oliveto, R., Sarro, F.: Genetic programming for effort estimation: an analysis of the impact of different fitness functions. In: 2010 Second International Symposium on Search Based Software Engineering (SSBSE), pp. 89–98. IEEE (2010)

7. Forrest, S., Nguyen, T., Weimer, W., Le Goues, C.: A genetic programming approach to automated software repair. In: Proceedings of the 11th Annual Conference on Genetic and Evolutionary Computation GECCO 2009, pp. 947–954. ACM (2009)

8. Fortin, F.A., De Rainville, F.M., Gardner, M.A., Parizeau, M., Gagné, C.: DEAP: evolutionary algorithms made easy. J. Mach. Learn. Res. **13**, 2171–2175 (2012)

9. Gascón, A., et al.: Privacy-preserving distributed linear regression on high-dimensional data. In: Proceedings on Privacy Enhancing Technologies PPET 2017, vol. 4, pp. 345–364 (2017)

10. Gupta, T., Fingler, H., Alvisi, L., Walfish, M.: Pretzel: email encryption and provider-supplied functions are compatible. In: Proceedings of the Conference of the ACM Special Interest Group on Data Communication, SIGCOMM 2017, Los Angeles, CA, USA, 21–25 August 2017, pp. 169–182 (2017)

11. Just, R., Jalali, D., Ernst, M.D.: Defects4J: a database of existing faults to enable controlled testing studies for Java programs. In: Proceedings of the 2014 International Symposium on Software Testing and Analysis ISSTA 2014, pp. 437–440. ACM, New York, NY, USA (2014). https://doi.org/10.1145/2610384.2628055

12. Kang, D., Sohn, J., Yoo, S.: Empirical evaluation of conditional operators in GP based fault localization. In: Genetic and Evolutionary Computation GECCO 2017, pp. 1295–1302 (2017)

13. Keijzer, M.: Improving symbolic regression with interval arithmetic and linear scaling. In: Ryan, C., Soule, T., Keijzer, M., Tsang, E., Poli, R., Costa, E. (eds.) EuroGP 2003. LNCS, vol. 2610, pp. 70–82. Springer, Heidelberg (2003). https://doi.org/10.1007/3-540-36599-0_7

14. Kim, J., Kim, J., Yoo, S.: GPGPGPU: evaluation of parallelisation of genetic programming using GPGPU. In: Menzies, T., Petke, J. (eds.) SSBSE 2017. LNCS, vol. 10452, pp. 137–142. Springer, Cham (2017). https://doi.org/10.1007/978-3-319-66299-2_11

15. Koza, J.R.: Genetic Programming: On the Programming of Computers by Means of Natural Selection. MIT Press, Cambridge (1992)

16. Li, Z., Jing, X.Y., Zhu, X., Zhang, H., Xu, B., Ying, S.: On the multiple sources and privacy preservation issues for heterogeneous defect prediction. IEEE Trans. Softw. Eng. 1 (2017)

17. Liu, Y., Khoshgoftaar, T.M.: Genetic programming model for software quality classification. In: Proceedings 6th International Symposium on High Assurance Systems Engineering, Special Topic: Impact of Networking, pp. 127–136 (2001)

18. Maua, G., Galinac Grbac, T.: Co-evolutionary multi-population genetic programming for classification in software defect prediction. Appl. Soft Comput. **55**(C), 331–351 (2017)
19. McKeen, F., et al.: Innovative instructions and software model for isolated execution. In: Proceedings of the 2nd International Workshop on Hardware and Architectural Support for Security and Privacy HASP 2013, p. 10:1. ACM, New York, NY, USA (2013)
20. Moore, C., O'Neill, M., O'Sullivan, E., Doröz, Y., Sunar, B.: Practical homomorphic encryption: a survey. In: IEEE International Symposium on Circuits and Systems ISCAS 2014, pp. 2792–2795, June 2014
21. Peters, F., Menzies, T., Gong, L., Zhang, H.: Balancing privacy and utility in cross-company defect prediction. IEEE Trans. Softw. Eng. **39**(8), 1054–1068 (2013)
22. Poli, R., Langdon, W.B., McPhee, N.F.: A field guide to genetic programming. Published via http://lulu.com, http://www.gp-field-guide.org.uk (2008)
23. Rivest, R.L., Shamir, A., Adleman, L.: A method for obtaining digital signatures and public-key cryptosystems. Commun. ACM **21**(2), 120–126 (1978)
24. Sarwate, A.D., Chaudhuri, K.: Signal processing and machine learning with differential privacy: algorithms and challenges for continuous data. IEEE Signal Process. **30**(5), 86–94 (2013)
25. Schuster, F., et al.: VC3: trustworthy data analytics in the cloud using SGX. In: 2015 IEEE Symposium on Security and Privacy, pp. 38–54, May 2015
26. Shamir, A.: How to share a secret. Commun. ACM **22**(11), 612–613 (1979)
27. Sohn, J., Yoo, S.: FLUCCS: using code and change metrics to improve fault localisation. In: Proceedings of the International Symposium on Software Testing and Analysis ISSTA 2017, pp. 273–283. ACM, July 2017
28. Songhori, E.M., Hussain, S.U., Sadeghi, A.R., Schneider, T., Koushanfar, F.: Tinygarble: highly compressed and scalable sequential garbled circuits. In: IEEE Symposium on Security and Privacy SSP 2015, pp. 411–428, May 2015
29. Tian, L., Jayaraman, B., Gu, Q., Evans, D.: Aggregating private sparse learning models using multi-party computation. In: NIPS Workshop on Private Multi-Party Machine Learning, PMPML 2016 (2016)
30. Uy, N.Q., Hoai, N.X., O'Neill, M., McKay, R.I., Galván-López, E.: Semantically-based crossover in genetic programming: application to real-valued symbolic regression. Genet. Program. Evolvable Mach. **12**(2), 91–119 (2011)
31. Vladislavleva, E.J., Smits, G.F., den Hertog, D.: Order of nonlinearity as a complexity measure for models generated by symbolic regression via pareto genetic programming. IEEE Trans. Evol. Comput. **13**(2), 333–349 (2009)
32. Weimer, W., Nguyen, T., Goues, C.L., Forrest, S.: Automatically finding patches using genetic programming. In: Proceedings of the 31st IEEE International Conference on Software Engineering ICSE 2009, pp. 364–374. IEEE, May 2009
33. White, D.R., et al.: Better GP benchmarks: community survey results and proposals. Genet. Program. Evolvable Mach. **14**(1), 3–29 (2013)
34. Wong, W.E., Gao, R., Li, Y., Abreu, R., Wotawa, F.: A survey on software fault localization. IEEE Trans. Softw.Eng. **42**(8), 707 (2016)
35. Yao, A.C.C.: How to generate and exchange secrets. In: Proceedings of the 27th Annual Symposium on Foundations of Computer Science SFCS 1986, pp. 162–167. IEEE Computer Society, Washington, DC, USA (1986)

36. Yoo, S.: Evolving human competitive spectra-based fault localisation techniques. In: Fraser, G., Teixeira de Souza, J. (eds.) SSBSE 2012. LNCS, vol. 7515, pp. 244–258. Springer, Heidelberg (2012). https://doi.org/10.1007/978-3-642-33119-0_18

37. Zahur, S., Evans, D.: Obliv-C: a language for extensible data-oblivious computation. IACR Cryptol. ePrint Arch. **2015**, 1153 (2015)

Towards Minimizing the Impact of Changes Using Search-Based Approach

Bogdan Korel[1], Nada Almasri[2(✉)], and Luay Tahat[2]

[1] Illinois Institute of Technology, Chicago, IL 60616, USA
korel@iit.edu
[2] Gulf University for Science and Technology, Mishref, Kuwait
{almasri.n, tahat.l}@gust.edu.kw

Abstract. Software maintenance is becoming more challenging with the increased complexity of the software and the frequently applied modifications. To manage this complexity, systems development is headed towards Model-driven engineering (MDE) and search-based software engineering (SBSE). Additionally, prior to applying a change to these complex systems, change impact analysis is usually performed in order to determine the scope of the change, its feasibility, and the time and resources required to implement the change. The bigger the scope, the riskier the change is on the system. In this paper, we introduce a set of transformation rules for Extended Finite State Machine (EFSM) models of state-based systems. These transformation rules can be used as the basis for search-based model optimization in order to reduce the average impact of a potential change applied to an EFSM model. Assuming that Model-driven development is adopted for the implementation of a state-based system, reducing the change impact at the model level will lead to reducing the impact at the system level. An exploratory study is performed to measure the impact reduction for a given EFSM model when the transformation rules are applied by a search-based algorithm. The initial results show a promising usage of the transformation rules which can lead to a reduction of more than 50% of the initial average change impact of the model.

Keywords: Model transformation · Extended finite state machine
Impact analysis · Search-based software engineering

1 Introduction

The demand for large and complex software systems has been steadily increasing over time. The development and maintenance of these systems are difficult and costly due to their increased complexity [5, 6]. To manage this complexity, systems development is headed towards Model-driven engineering (MDE) and search-based software engineering (SBSE) [2, 10]. Additionally, to manage the complexity of a change applied to these complex systems, impact analysis is usually performed in order to determine the scope of the change, its feasibility, and the time and resources required to implement the change [6, 8, 9]. In many cases a single modification applied to the software could propagate to a large proportion of the system. Indeed, several studies indicated that software maintenance consumes 50% to 70% of the total life cycle development cost [1, 3, 5, 6].

T. E. Colanzi and P. McMinn (Eds.): SSBSE 2018, LNCS 11036, pp. 262–277, 2018.
https://doi.org/10.1007/978-3-319-99241-9_14

Consequently, estimating the impact of a requested change prior to its implementation allows the development team to properly plan the implementation process. The higher the estimated change impact, the riskier the implementation process is.

In this paper, we introduce a set of model transformation rules which can be applied to Extended Finite State Machine (EFSM) models to improve their maintenance. We present model transformation-based search algorithm which applies these transformation rules to an EFSM model in order to reduce the average impact of a potential change to the model. Assuming that Model-driven development is adopted, where models are always kept consistent with the underlying system, the reduction of the change impact at the model level is expected to reduce the impact of the change at the system level.

An exploratory study is performed to demonstrate the feasibility and the effectiveness of the proposed transformation-based search approach when applied to a sample EFSM model. The results of this exploratory study demonstrate the potential of the transformation-based search in significantly improving the maintainability of the model (by more than 50%).

The major contributions of this paper are:

- Proposing a set of novel model transformation rules.
- Presenting model-transformation based search approach to improve the model's maintainability.
- Demonstrating the feasibility and effectiveness of transformation rules when applied on EFSM models using search-based approach.

The rest of the paper is organized as follows: Sect. 2 outlines the related work. Section 3 provides an overview of EFSM, model dependence, and model impact analysis. Section 4 presents three model transformation rules. The search algorithm is discussed in Sect. 5, followed by an exploratory study in Sect. 6. In Sect. 7, conclusions and future research are discussed.

2 Literature Review

Model-Driven Engineering (MDE) refers to the systematic use of models as primary engineering artifacts throughout the engineering lifecycle. In recent years, system modeling has expanded beyond its initial scope. Indeed, system models are being increasingly used as the basis to validate the system design, generate system level test suites, estimate the impact of a change, and simulate the system behavior by executing the model and to determine properties of the system [1, 3–6].

Model transformation is an important technique in the field of MDE. It is used to transform one or more models to one or more target models based on set of transformations rules [13, 14, 24]. Generally, model transformation can be categorized into horizontal transformation or vertical transformation. Vertical transformation is a transformation where the source and target models reside at different abstraction levels. A typical example is refinement and abstraction [12, 13]. Furthermore, model-to-code generation can be viewed as a vertical transformation. Horizontal transformation, on the other hand, is a transformation where the source and target models reside at the same abstraction level. Typical examples are refactoring or migration [7, 11].

Refactoring is one of the widely used techniques for evolving software systems. Fowler [15] defines refactoring as "a change made to the internal structure of software to make it easier to understand and cheaper to modify without changing its observable behavior". In early stages, refactoring techniques have focused on the source-code as the primary artifact of the refactoring process [16]. Recently, several model refactoring approaches have been proposed in the literature [18], and many of which use search-based model transformation [17], however, none of them target refactoring models in order to enhance its maintainability. Adenis et al. [21] present two transformation algorithms for state splitting and state merging for probabilistic finite state automata (PFSA), however their work is focused on modeling the behavior of dynamical systems for future predictions. They use these two algorithms to construct the model from the output of the dynamical system. Our approach on the other hand is focused on transforming deterministic EFSMs which are known to be accurately matching the behavior of the system. Within this context, the approach presented in this paper can be viewed as model refactoring approach which uses a set of novel transformation rules that can be applied on an EFSM model using search-based technique in order to enhance its maintainability.

3 Preliminaries

3.1 EFSM Models

An EFSM model M is expressed formally as a 7 tuple: $M = (\Sigma, Q, Start, Exit, V, O, R)$ where: Σ is the set of events, Q is the set of states, Start $\in$ Q is the start state, Exit $\in$ Q is the exit state, V is a finite set of variables, O is the set of actions, R is the set of transitions, where each transition T is represented by the tuple: $T = (E, C, A, S_b, S_e)$ where: $E \in \Sigma$ is an event which may contain a list of arguments $E(arg_1, arg_2, ..., arg_k,)$

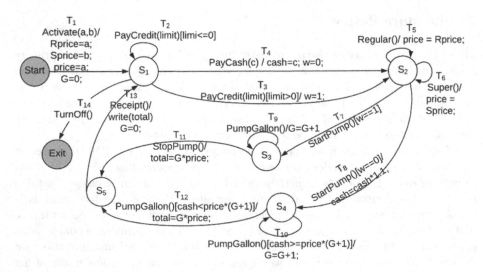

Fig. 1. Fuel pump EFSM model

where the scope of the arguments is the transition T associated with this event. C is an enabling condition defined over V, A is a sequence of actions, $A = <a_1, a_2,...., a_j>$, where $a_i \in O$. The action may manipulate variables, read input or produce output. $S_b \in Q$ is the transition's originating state, $S_e \in Q$ is the transition's terminating state. Figure 1 shows an example of an EFSM model for a Fuel Pump system.

3.2 Model Dependencies

Dependencies capture the notion of potential "interactions" between transitions in the model. There are two types of model dependencies: data and control dependence.

Data Dependence: A data dependence captures the notion that one transition defines a value to a variable and another transition may potentially use this value [1, 6]. There exists *data dependence* between transitions T_i and T_k if transition T_i modifies value of variable v, transition T_k uses v, and there exists a path (transition sequence) in the model from T_i to T_k along which v is not modified. For example, there exists data dependence between transitions T_1 and T_5 in the model of Fig. 1 because transition T_1 assigns a value to variable *Rprice*, transition T_5 uses *Rprice*, and there exists a path (T_1, T_4, T_5) from T_1 to T_5 along which *Rprice* is not modified.

Control Dependence: In [1], the concept of program control dependence was extended to EFSM models. Control dependence in an EFSM exists between transitions and it captures the notion that one transition may affect traversal of another transition. For example, transition T_5 is control dependent on T_4 in the model of Fig. 1 because (1) $S_b(T_4)$ does not post dominate $S_b(T_5)$ (condition 1 of control dependence definition is true) and (2) state $S_b(T_5)$ post dominates transition T_4 (condition 2 is TRUE). Note that $S_b(T_4)$ is S_1 and $S_b(T_5)$ is S_2. The issue of control dependence in EFSMs is discussed in more details in [1, 3–6].

3.3 Measuring Model Change Impact

Impact analysis is the process of identifying the expected impact of a change, and it was formally defined by Bohner and Arnold [8] as "identifying the potential consequences of a change, or estimating what needs to be modified to accomplish a change".

An approach to identifying the impact of a change for EFSM models is proposed in [6], where for any given model modification (MF), two impact sets are identified; the starting impact set (SIS) which comprises the set of transitions identified as directly impacted by the change since they have experienced a change in their dependencies on other transitions in the model, and the extended impact set (EIS) which consists of indirectly impacted transitions which are iteratively dependent on one or more transitions in the SIS. To quantify the impact of the change, the number of transitions in the EIS can be used as a measure.

For any given model, it is possible to estimate the *average change impact* of a potential change applied to the model as a measure of the average propagation of the change within the model. This measure gives a better understanding for the development team about how easy or difficult the model and its underlying system are to maintain. One approach to estimate the average change impact of a potential change applied to a model M with n transitions, is to calculate the size of the extended impact set for each transition in the model assuming that this transition has been modified. Then calculating the average size of the EIS for all transitions. In this paper, we call this measure, the average change impact of the model. When applied to the model of Fig. 1, the average change impact generated will be 5.07 transitions as shown in Table 1.

Table 1. Measuring average change impact.

Transition	Extended impact set	Number of transitions in EIS
T_1	$\{T_5, T_6, T_9, T_{10}, T_{11}, T_{12}, T_{13}\}$	7
T_2	$\{\}$	0
T_3	$\{T_5, T_6, T_7, T_8, T_9, T_{10}, T_{11}, T_{12}, T_{13}\}$	9
T_4	$\{T_5, T_6, T_7, T_8, T_9, T_{10}, T_{11}, T_{12}, T_{13}\}$	9
T_5	$\{T_9, T_{10}, T_{11}, T_{12}, T_{13}\}$	5
T_6	$\{T_9, T_{10}, T_{11}, T_{12}, T_{13}\}$	5
T_7	$\{T_9, T_{10}, T_{11}, T_{12}, T_{13}\}$	5
T_8	$\{T_8, T_9, T_{10}, T_{11}, T_{12}, T_{13}\}$	6
T_9	$\{T_9, T_{10}, T_{11}, T_{12}, T_{13}\}$	5
T_{10}	$\{T_9, T_{10}, T_{11}, T_{12}, T_{13}\}$	5
T_{11}	$\{T_9, T_{10}, T_{11}, T_{12}, T_{13}\}$	5
T_{12}	$\{T_9, T_{10}, T_{11}, T_{12}, T_{13}\}$	5
T_{13}	$\{T_9, T_{10}, T_{11}, T_{12}, T_{13}\}$	5
T_{14}	$\{\}$	0
	Average change impact	**5.07**

4   Transformation Rules

In this section we introduce three transformation rules which can be applied to EFSM models. When applied to an EFSM model, these rules keep the semantics of the model exactly the same, however they may change the structure of the model by changing the number of states or the number of transitions.

To formally define a transformation rule, we will use the following notation:

$M = (\Sigma, Q, Start, Exit, V, O, R)$ *is an EFSM model*
$S \in Q$ *is a state in model M*
$T \in R$ *is a transition in model M, where* $T = (E, C, A, S_b, S_e)$.
$T_{in}(S)$ *is the set of incoming transitions to state S, excluding self-looping transitions*
$T_{out}(S)$ *is the set of outgoing transitions from state S, excluding self-looping transitions*
$T_{self}(S)$ *is the set of self-looping transitions in state S*

4.1   State Splitting

Splitting a state into two or more states could reduce the complexity of the model by distributing the incoming/outgoing transitions into sub-states. One criterion on which a state S can be split into other states is by looking at the flow of execution between the incoming and the outgoing transitions of the state S, as demonstrated in Fig. 2.

In this paper, it is assumed that the original model has been tested using well known model-based testing methods. In particular, All-Transition-Pairs Coverage [19] has been used. According to this test coverage, for each state S, all transition pairs (incoming transition, outgoing transition) must be executed at least once. As a result, during model testing, all executable transition pairs can be easily identified. Since some transition pairs may not be executable, it is assumed that testers/developers used, for example, some test generation methods [22, 23], and carefully verified that these transition pairs are not executable. Therefore, one can assume with a high degree of confidence that these pairs are non-executable. The state splitting transformation, presented in this section, takes advantage of the knowledge of executable and non-executable transition pairs in the model.

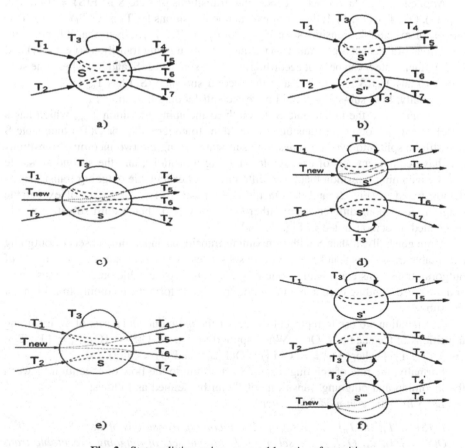

Fig. 2. State splitting using executable pairs of transitions

If the execution of an incoming transition T_i never leads to the execution of an outgoing transition T_o (e.g. T_1 in Fig. 2a doesn't lead to the execution of T_6 or T_7), then T_i and T_o do not need to be linked to the same state. We call the pair of transitions (T_1, T_6) and (T_1, T_7) *non-executable pairs*. Similarly, we call the pairs of (incoming, outgoing) transitions that can be executed successively as the *pairs of executable transitions*. In this case, state S can be split into two states S' and S" as demonstrated in Fig. 2b. More generally, a state can be split into several sub-states where each sub-state has a unique set of outgoing transitions which are all executable for all incoming transitions.

Formally, we use the following notation for the set of all executable pairs of (incoming, outgoing) transitions for a state S:

$E(S) = \{(T_i, T_o)|T_i \in T_{in}(S), T_o \in T_{out}(S)$, *and there is a sequence of events on which a transition pair* (T_i, T_o) *is executed}*.

Additionally, we use the following notation for the set of all outgoing transitions that are executable for a given incoming transitions $T_i \in T_{in}(S)$ for a given state S:

$O(T_i) = \{T_o \in T_{out}(S)|(T_i, T_o) \in E(S)\}$.

Applied to Fig. 2a, the set of executable transitions of state S is: $E(S) = \{(T_1, T_4),$ $(T_1, T_5), (T_2, T_6), (T_2, T_7)\}$; the set of executable transitions for T_1 is: $O(T_1) = \{T_4, T_5\}$; the set of executable transitions for T_2 is: $O(T_2) = \{T_6, T_7\}$. Given that all incoming transitions of the state S generate two unique sets of outgoing transitions (i.e. $O(T_1)$ and $O(T_2)$), then state S can be split accordingly to two sub-states (S' and S") where one sub-state (S') has $T_{out}(S') = O(T_1)$ and the second sub-state (S") has $T_{out}(S") = O(T_2)$. Additionally, both sub-states should have the self-looping transition T_3.

Assuming that the initial state S, has a third incoming transition T_{new} which has a set of executable outgoing transitions equivalent to either $O(T_1)$ or $O(T_2)$ then state S will still be split into two sub-states, one sub-state having the two incoming transitions that have equivalent sets of executable outgoing transitions, and the second sub-state has the incoming transition that has a different set of executable outgoing transitions as demonstrated in (Fig. 2c and d). On the other hand, if T_{new} has a set of executable outgoing transitions different from either $O(T_1)$ or $O(T_2)$, then a third sub-state would be created as demonstrated in Fig. 2e and f.

More generally, a state S with n incoming transitions and m unique sets of outgoing executable transitions, can be split into m sub-states; where each sub-state has its set of outgoing transitions equivalent to one of the m sets of executable outgoing transitions, and the corresponding executable incoming transitions form the incoming transitions of the sub-state.

The notation we use to represent the set of the m unique $O(T_i)$ sets of all incoming transitions of the state S is: $O(S)$. When applied to Fig. 2c, $O(S) = \{O_{1,new} = \{T_4, T_5\},$ $O_2 = \{T_6, T_7\}\}$ where $O_{1,new} = O(T_1) = O(T_{new})$, and $O_2 = O(T_2)$.

Formally, the rule of splitting a state S according to the flow of execution between the incoming and outgoing transitions of S can be defined as follows:

Let S be a state in model M, where:

$T_{in}(S) = \{T_1, ..., T_n\}$, *is the set of all n incoming transitions of state S.*
$O(S) = \{O_1, ..., O_m\}$, *is the set of all m unique sets of outgoing executable transitions for all transition* $T_i \in T_{in}(S)$ *where* $1 \leq m \leq n$.

Then, state S can be split into m sub-states, S_1 to S_m, where each sub-state S_k $(1 \leq k \leq m)$ has:

$$T_{out}(S_k) = O_k$$
$$T_{in}(S_k) = \{T_i | T_i \in T_{in}(S), O(T_i) = O_k\}$$
$$T_{self}(S_k) = T_{self}(S)$$

Applying the above rule to state S_2 of the EFSM model in Fig. 1 we notice that:

$T_{in}(S_2) = \{T_3, T_4\}, T_{out}(S_2) = \{T_7, T_8\}, T_{self}(S_2) = \{T_5, T_6\}, E(S) = \{(T_4, T_8), (T_3, T_7)\}$
$O(T_3) = \{T_7\}, O(T_4) = \{T_8\}, O(S_2) = \{\{T_7\}, \{T_8\}\}$

Since O(S) contains two elements representing the unique sets of executable outgoing transitions, then state S_2 can be split into two sub-states S_2' and S_2'' where:

$$T_{out}(S_2') = \{T_7\}, T_{in}(S_2') = \{T_3\}, \text{ and } T_{self}(S_2') = \{T_5, T_6\}$$

$$T_{out}(S_2'') = \{T_8\}, T_{in}(S_2'') = \{T_4\}, \text{ and } T_{self}(S_2'') = \{T_5', T_6'\}$$

The resulting model after splitting state S_2 is shown in Fig. 3.

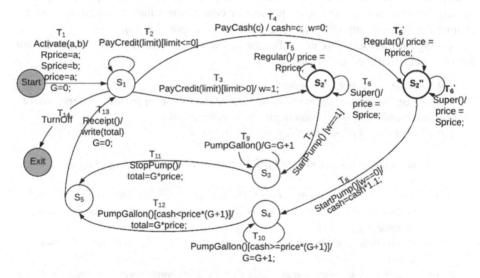

Fig. 3. EFSM fuel model after splitting state S_2

4.2 Moving Assignment Actions Forward

For a given state S in an EFSM model M, an assignment action defined in one or more incoming transitions can be moved to one or more outgoing transitions if certain conditions are met.

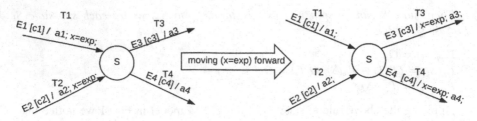

Fig. 4. Moving assignment action forward

In its simplest form, this rule states that for a given state S, if all incoming transitions define the same action a ($x = expr$) as the last action in their sequence of actions, then it is possible to move the action a to be the first action in the sequence of actions associated with the outgoing transitions of the state S. This rule assumes that none of the outgoing transitions use the variable x in their enabling condition, and it also assumes that if self-looping transitions are present at state S, then they do not use or change variable x or any other variable used in the expression *expr*.

In a more general context, an incoming transition, T_i, may have a sequence of n actions $A(T_i) = <a_1, a_2, ..., a_j, a_{j+1}, ..., a_n>$ as demonstrated in Fig. 4. In this case, an action a_j defining the variable x could be anywhere in the middle of this sequence. Consequently, moving the action to the outgoing transitions can take place only if all subsequent actions (a_{j+1} to a_n), do not use or change the value of x, and they do not change the value of any other variable used in the expression *expr*.

Taking into account this general context, the rule of moving assignment actions forward can be defined as follows:

Let S be a state in an EFSM model

*Let **a** be an assignment action of variable x of the following format: x=expr, where x and all variables in expr are not arguments of any event.*

*Let U(**a**) be the set of all variables used by action a*

if

    (1)   *all incoming transitions T_I in $T_{in}(S)$ contain the action **a**, i.e., $A(T_I)=<a_1, a_2, ..., **a**, a_i, ..., a_n>$, and*

    (2)   *in every incoming transition T_I in $T_{in}(S)$, a subsequence of actions $<a_i, ..., a_n>$ that follows action **a** in T_I does not use or change variable x and it does not change any variable in U(a), and*

    (3)   *the enabling conditions of all outgoing transitions T_O in $T_{out}(S)$ do not use variable x, and*

    (4)   *all self-looping transitions in $T_{self}(S)$ do not use or change variable x, and they do not change any variable in U(a),*

then

        Action a can be moved forward from all incoming transitions T_I in $T_{in}(S)$ to all outgoing transitions T_O in $T_{out}(S)$ by placing action a as the first action in $A(T_O)$.

For example, when applying this rule to action a: *(total = G * price)* and state S_5 of the EFSM model in Fig. 1, where $U(a) = \{G,\ price\}$, $T_{in}(S_5) = \{T_{11},\ T_{12}\}$, $T_{out}(S_5) = \{T_{13}\}$, $T_{self}(S_5) = \{\ \}$, we notice that all of the four conditions of the above rule are met. The first condition is met since all incoming transitions; namely T_{11} and T_{12}, contain the action *(total = G * price)*. The second condition is also satisfied, since there are no actions following *(total = G * price)* in $A(T_{11})$ or in $A(T_{12})$. The third condition is also met, since the only outgoing transition (T_{12}) has no enabling condition. Similarly, the fourth condition is also met since state S_5 has no self-looping transitions. Consequently, the action *(total = G * price)* can be removed from T_{11} and T_{12} and placed as the first action in T_{13}.

4.3   Moving Assignment Actions Backward

This rule attempts to move an action defining a variable x backwards in the model. For a given state S in an EFSM model M, an assignment action defined in one or more outgoing transitions can be moved to one or more incoming transitions of the same state if certain conditions are met.

In its simplest form, this rule states that for a given state S, if all outgoing transitions define the same action a $(x = expr)$ as the first action in their sequence of actions, then the action can be moved backward to be placed as the last action of all incoming transitions of the same state.

Of course in a more general context, the state S may have self-looping transitions, the outgoing transitions may have enabling conditions, and the action defining the variable x could be anywhere in the middle of the sequence of actions (Fig. 5).

Taking into consideration this general context, the rule of moving assignment actions backward can be generalized as follows:

Let S be a state in an EFSM model
*Let **a** be an assignment action of variable x of the following format: x=expr, where x and all variables in expr are not arguments of any event.*
*Let U(**a**) be the set of all variables used by action a*
if

(1)   *every outgoing transition T_O in $T_{out}(S)$ contains the action **a**, i.e., $A(T_O)=<a_1, a_2,...,$ $a_i, a,\ ...,\ a_n>$, and*

(2)   *in every outgoing transition T_O in $T_{out}(S)$, a subsequence of actions $<a_1,\ ...,\ a_i>$ that precedes action **a** in T_O does not use or change variable x and it does not change any variable in U(a), and*

(3)   *the enabling conditions of all outgoing transitions T_O in $T_{out}(S)$ do not use variable x, and*

(4)   *all self-looping transitions in $T_{self}(S)$ do not use or change variable x, and they do not change any variable in U(a),*

then

Action a can be moved backward from all outgoing transitions T_O in $T_{out}(S)$ to all incoming transitions T_I in $T_{in}(S)$ by placing action a as the last action in $A(T_I)$.

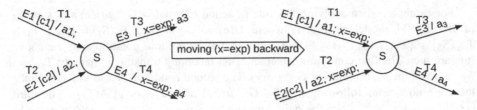

Fig. 5. Moving assignment action backward

Since this rule acts in the opposite direction of rule 4.2, then any action moved forward using rule 4.2 can be moved backward using rule 4.3. For example, we notice that all of the four conditions of this rule are met for action (total = G * price) at T_{13}. Consequently, applying rule 4.3 will allow moving the action backward to T_{11} and T_{12}.

5 Search Algorithm

5.1 Fitness Function

Using a search algorithm, the transformation rules introduced in the previous section can be applied on a given EFSM model in order to minimize the average change impact of a potential change applied to the model. In this case the fitness function f of the search algorithm can be expressed as the average change impact of the model as calculated in Sect. 3.3.

This measure gives an estimation of the average number of transitions impacted by a potential single change applied to the model. Given that when calculating this measure, each transition T_i in the model is only assumed to be changed, but there is no actual change applied to the variables defined or used in this transition, or in the source or target state of the transition, then the generated EIS set will be equivalent to the set of transitions that are directly or transitively dependent on T_i (i.e. no new or removed dependency edge(T_e, T_e) as expressed in cases 9.a and 9.b in [6]). Consequently, the fitness function f (M) can be expressed using the transitive closure of the dependency graph of the model M.

More formally,

Let $M = (\Sigma, Q, Start, Exit, V, O, R)$ be an EFSM model, and
Let $G = (R, E)$ be the dependence graph of M where
R is the set of transitions in M (represented as nodes in the dependency graph), and
E is a binary relation on R, $E \subseteq R \times R$, referred to a set of directed edges where:
edge $(T_i, T_k) \in E$, if T_k has either control or data dependency on T_i.
Let E^+ be a binary relation representing the transitive closure of E
Let $|E^+|$ be the number of edges in E^+

then

$$f(M) = |E^+| / |R|$$

Notice that the number of states in the model doesn't need to be included as part of the fitness function because data and control dependence are based on the relationships between transitions which are the active components of the system, while states are passive components of the model where a state represents a snapshot of the system at a particular point in time.

It is worth noting here that the average change impact calculated for the fuel pump EFSM model in Table 1 is equivalent to the fitness function of that model, i.e., f (M) = 5.07. Indeed, the sum of the number of transitions in all of the EIS sets of the 14 transitions in the model is the same as $|E^+|$ = 71. Since the model has 14 transitions, then $|R|$ = 14, and consequently: $|E^+|/|R|$ = 5.07.

5.2   Algorithm

Given the original model M_O, the goal of the search is to find the semantically equivalent transformed model, M_T, for which the impact of the potential change is minimized. The change impact fitness function $f(M)$ is used to guide the search. The algorithm strives to find the transformed model for which the value of the fitness function is minimal. The search algorithm is shown in Fig. 6.

The presented algorithm is a heuristic algorithm that is based on the "greedy" search paradigm [20] that makes the locally optimal choices at each stage of the search with the hope of finding the global minimum of the fitness function. However, the algorithm does not guarantee identifying a transformed model with the global minimum of the fitness function. In step 2, the fitness function is evaluated for the original model. In step 3, a set of all possible transformations that can be applied to the model are identified. In steps 5–13, every transformation is tried to determine if it leads to the decrease of the fitness function. At the end of these steps, a transformed model M_m with the minimal value of the fitness function is identified. Such a model is chosen as the best candidate to continue with the search in steps 14–16 and a new set of potential transformations is identified for this candidate model in step 17. This process continues in steps 4–19, until a transformed model M_T is identified for which no more decrease of the fitness function can be achieved using model transformations.

It is worth mentioning here that the complexity of the algorithm depends on the number of possible transformations that can be applied to the model. Assuming that this number is K, the complexity in the best case scenario when no improvement can be found is K, while it can reach $O(|R|^3)$ when f(M) has the maximum possible starting value of $|R|$ and it ends with the minimum possible value of 0. Note that this estimation doesn't account for the complexity of the calculation of the fitness function.

Input: **M₀**   original model
Output: **Mᴛ**   transformed model
1:      Mᴛ=M₀
2:      F₀=f(Mᴛ)
3:      Identify a set TS(Mᴛ) of all possible transformations that can be applied to model Mᴛ
4:      **while** (TS(Mᴛ) is not empty) **do**
5:              F₁=F₀
6:                  **for** every transformation Tr in TS(Mᴛ) **do**
7:                          Apply transformation Tr to model Mᴛ resulting in a transformed model M
8:                          F=f(M)
9:                          **if** (F<F₀) **then**
10:                             Mₘ=M
11:                             F₀=F
12:                 **endif**
13:         **endfor**
14:         TS(Mᴛ)=∅
15:         **if** (F₀<F₁) **then**
16:             Mᴛ=Mₘ
17:             Identify a set TS(Mᴛ) of all possible transformations that can be applied to model Mᴛ
18:         **endif**
19: **endwhile**
20: return Mᴛ

Fig. 6. Search algorithm

6   Exploratory Study

This study is conducted as a proof of concept. Its main objective is to demonstrate the feasibility and effectiveness of the presented model transformations by applying the search algorithm presented in 5.2 on the model presented in Fig. 1.

Table 2. Sequence of transformations applied to the EFSM model in Fig. 1

	Transformations applied to fuel pump model	$f(M_T)$	Percentage of impact reduction
0	Original fuel pump model M_O	5.07	–
1	Tr_1: (moving $G = 0$ forward from T_{13} and T_1 to T_3, T_4, and T_{14})	3.36	34%
2	Tr_2: (moving $total = G * price$ forward from T_{11} and T_{12} to T_{13})	3	41%
3	Tr_3: (splitting S_2 into two states)	2.63	48%
4	Tr_4: (moving $cash = cash * 1.1$ backward from T_8 to T_4)	2.44	52%

When applied to the fuel pump model, the search algorithm finds and applies the sequence of transformations presented in Table 2, where each of the transformations is identified in one iteration of the algorithm as having the least value of the fitness function compared to other candidate transformations. It is worth noting that when the third transformation (splitting state S_2) is applied, the transformed model generated after has a different structure where the number of states has increased to by one, and the number of transitions has increased by two, similar the model presented in Fig. 3.

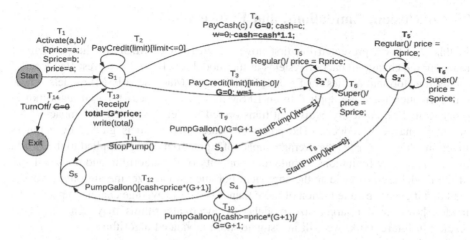

Fig. 7. Transformed EFSM model after applying transformation sequence in Table 2

After this transformation, a new transformation was discovered, Tr_4, which had not been identified as a possible transformation in any of the previous iterations of the algorithm. Indeed, before the split of state S_2, $T_{out}(S_2)$ had two outgoing transitions T_7 and T_8, and only one of them had the action (cash = cash * 1.1), so the action was not identified as a possible candidate as the first condition of the rule of moving an action backward was not satisfied. After the split, however, $T_{out}(S_2'')$ has only T_8, consequently, all of the four conditions of the rule of moving actions backward become true, and moving (cash = cash * 1.1) becomes a possible transformation. The final transformed model is shown in Fig. 7. The figure shows all actions that have been moved backward or forward in bold.

The results of this exploratory experiment show that the search algorithm can find an EFSM model that is semantically equivalent to the original model, while it has a lower average change impact compared to the original model. For the particular EFSM model investigated in this experiment, the original model had an estimated average of 5.07 transitions impacted by a potential change applied to the model, while the final transformed model has an average change impact of only 2.44 transitions. This reduction of 52% of the average change impact can be highly effective in the maintenance of larger systems with hundreds of transitions and states.

Finally, after applying the four transformations on the model, some actions and conditions can be cleaned up as they become unnecessary. These actions and conditions are shown in the Fig. 7 with strikethrough text. Clearly, after the split of state S_2, the condition $[x == 0]$ at T_8 can be safely removed since it always evaluates to true given that the only incoming transition of S_2'' sets the value of w to zero. Similarly, the condition $[x == 1]$ can be safely removed since x is set to one by the only incoming transition of the state S_2'. Having removed both enabling conditions $[x == 0]$ and $[x == 1]$, the variable x is no longer used in the EFSM model, hence the assignment actions $(x = 0)$ at T_4 and $(x = 1)$ at T_3 can be safely removed. Finally, action $(G = 0)$ can be safely removed from transition T_{14} as variable G will not be used after transition T_{14} is executed.

7 Conclusion, Limitations, and Future Work

In this paper, we presented the first novel application of SBSE to the problem of reducing the change impact of systems at the model level. We have presented a set of model transformation rules for Extended Finite State Machine (EFSM) models. These transformation rules are applied to an EFSM model using search-based algorithm in order to find semantically equivalent transformed model, for which the impact of the potential change is reduced. The presented search algorithm is guided by a fitness function which estimates the average impact of a potential change applied to the EFSM model. The study limitations include the simplicity of the algorithm and the small size of the model used to validate the approach. For such small size, the algorithm worked well and it generated a reduction of more than 50% of the average change impact of the model, however, for larger size models, advanced algorithms may generate better results. In future work, we will investigate more advanced algorithms.

In addition, in a future research, we plan to introduce further refined model transformation rules that can be used to improve the system maintainability. In addition, we will develop enhanced model-transformation search algorithms that are based on genetic algorithms and we will investigate their properties. Finally, we plan to perform an expanded empirical study for several larger models of varying characteristics.

Acknowledgments. This work is supported by Kuwait Foundation for Advancement of Science (KFAS), Project number: P116-18QS-01.

References

1. Tahat, L., Korel, B., Koutsogiannakis, G., Almasri, N.: State-based models in regression test suite prioritization. Soft. Qual. J. **25**(3), 703–742 (2016)
2. Boussaïd, I., Siarry, P., Ahmed-Nacer, M.: A survey on search-based model-driven engineering. Autom. Softw. Eng. **24**(1), 233–294 (2017)
3. Korel, B., Tahat, L., Vaysburg, B.: Model based regression test reduction using dependence analysis. In: Proceedings of the International IEEE Conference on Software Maintenance, pp. 214–223 (2002)
4. Korel, B., Tahat, L.: Understanding modification in state-based system. In: Proceeding of the 12th IEEE International Conference on Program Comprehension London, UK, pp. 246–250 (2004)
5. Tahat, L., Korel, B., Hartman, M., Ural, H.: Regression test suite prioritization using system models. Soft. Test. Ver. Rel. (STRV) **22**(7), 481–506 (2011)
6. Almasri, N., Tahat, L.: Towards automatically quantifying the impact of a change in systems. Softw. Qual. J. **25**(3), 601–640 (2016)
7. Williams, J.R., Paige, R.F., Polack, F.A.C.: Searching for model migration strategies. In: Proceedings of the 6th International Workshop Models and Evolution, pp. 39–44. ACM, New York (2012)
8. Bohner, S.A., Arnold, R.S.: Software Change Impact Analysis. IEEE Computer Society Press (1996)

9. Lehnert, S.: A review of software change impact analysis. Ilmenau University of Technology, Technical report (2011)
10. Harman, M., Jones, B.F.: Search-based soft. Eng. Inf. Soft. Tech. **43**(14), 833–839 (2001)
11. O'Keeffe, M., Cinnéide, M.Ó.: Search-based refactoring: an empirical study. J. Softw. Maint. Evol. **20**(5), 345–364 (2008)
12. Favre, J.: Towards a basic theory to model driven engineering. In: Proceedings of the UML 2004 International Workshop on Software Model Engineering (2004)
13. Mens, T., Van Gorp, P.: A taxonomy of model transformation. Electron. Notes Theory Comput. Sci. **152**(1), 125–142 (2006)
14. Czarnecki, K., Helsen, S.: Classification of model transformation approaches. In: Proceedings of the 2nd OOPSLA Workshop on Generative Techniques in the Context of MDA (2003)
15. Fowler, M.: Refactoring: Improving the Design of Existing Code. Addison-Wesley, Boston (1999)
16. Mkaouer, M.W., Kessentini, M., Bechikh, S., Ó Cinnéide, M.: A robust multi-objective approach for software refactoring under uncertainty. In: Le Goues, C., Yoo, S. (eds.) SSBSE 2014. LNCS, vol. 8636, pp. 168–183. Springer, Cham (2014). https://doi.org/10.1007/978-3-319-09940-8_12
17. Räihä, O.: A survey on search-based software design. Comput. Sci. Rev. **4**(4), 203–249 (2010)
18. Misbhauddin, M., Alshayeb, M.: UML model refactoring: a systematic literature reviews. Empir. Softw. Eng. **20**(1), 206–251 (2015)
19. Devroey, X., Perrouin, G., Legay, A., Cordy, M., Schobbens, P.-Y., Heymans, P.: Coverage criteria for behavioural testing of software product lines. In: Margaria, T., Steffen, B. (eds.) ISoLA 2014. LNCS, vol. 8802, pp. 336–350. Springer, Heidelberg (2014). https://doi.org/10.1007/978-3-662-45234-9_24
20. Bendall, G., Margot, F.: Greedy type resistance of combinatorial problems. Discret. Optim. **3**, 288–298 (2006)
21. Adenis, P., Mukherjee, K., Ray, A.: State splitting and state merging in probabilistic finite state automata. In: IEEE American Control Conference, pp. 5145–5150 (2011)
22. Lu, G., Miao, H.: An approach to generating test data for EFSM paths considering condition coverage. Electron. Notes Theor. Comput. Sci. **309**, 13–29 (2014)
23. Kalaji, A., Hierons, R., Swift, S.: An integrated search-based approach for automatic testing from extended finite state machine models. Info. Soft. Tech. **53**(12), 1297–1318 (2011)
24. Fleck, M., Troya, J., Kessentini, M., Wimmer, M., Alkhazi, B.: Model transformation modularization as a many-objective optimization problem. IEEE Trans. Softw. Eng. **43**(11), 1009–1032 (2017)

Exploring Evolutionary Search Strategies to Improve Applications' Energy Efficiency

Irene Manotas[1]([⊠]), James Clause[2], and Lori Pollock[2]

[1] IBM Research, Yorktown Heights, NY, USA
irene.manotas@ibm.com
[2] University of Delaware, Newark, DE, USA
{clause,pollock}@udel.edu

Abstract. Energy consumption have become an important non-functional requirement for applications running on battery powered devices through data centers. Despite the increased interest on detecting and understanding what causes an application to be energy inefficient, few works focus on helping developers to automatically make their applications more energy efficient based on developers' design and implementation decisions. This paper explores how search strategies based on genetic algorithms can help developers automatically find an energy efficient version of an application based on transformations corresponding to developers' high level decisions (e.g., selecting API implementations). Our results show how different search strategies can help to improve the energy efficiency for nine Java applications.

1 Introduction

Reducing the energy usage of applications can increase the usability of battery-constrained devices, might decrease the costs of running applications on servers, and in general make software applications both more sustainable and environmentally friendly. Thus, both developers and researchers are motivated to examine the energy consumption of software applications, including the energy effects of developers' decisions, as well as ways to improve applications with regard to energy usage.

Empirical studies that analyze the energy impacts of developers' decisions have focused on the selection of data structures [16], design patterns [25], algorithms [6], refactorings [26], and application programming interfaces (APIs) [18]. More recently, researchers have been building tools that help developers to identify sources of energy inefficiencies in their code [1,12], and on developing strategies to automatically improve the energy usage of applications [2,5,19,27]. For example, Linares-Vásquez et al. proposed an optimization approach to automatically select energy efficient combinations of colors for mobile apps' GUI [19], and Manotas et al. [21] proposed the Software Energy-Efficient Decision Support framework (SEEDS) to automatically transform applications and explore

T. E. Colanzi and P. McMinn (Eds.): SSBSE 2018, LNCS 11036, pp. 278–292, 2018.
https://doi.org/10.1007/978-3-319-99241-9_15

the search space looking for energy efficient versions of applications. Similarly, some researchers proposed the use of metaheuristics, or Evolutionary Computation (EC) techniques [17, 29], to transform and generate source code that makes an application more energy efficient [2, 4, 5, 22, 27].

Although these strategies help developers to analyze applications' energy usage, pinpoint energy-related issues, or propose transformations to applications to improve energy usage, they do not provide ways to automatically analyze and apply combinations of transformations that represent high level decisions made by developers (e.g., selecting an implementation library, refactoring, or algorithm's choice) that make an application more energy efficient. Moreover, most of the existing approaches that apply changes to an application's code to improve its energy usage have been evaluated on a small set of applications' artifacts (e.g., classes from two Collection libraries [4]), or the evaluation have been done with applications that belong to a specific domain only (e.g., applications for the MiniSAT Boolean satisfiability solver [5], concurrent applications [27], or scientific applications using spectral element methods [2]).

To enable the exploration of the energy impacts for large search spaces composed of possible code transformations, we propose to take advantage of metaheuristic evolutionary optimization techniques. Specifically using (GAs) as a metaheuristic-based search strategy to automatically explore software developers' high level decisions that improve an application's energy usage. The proposed search strategies enable a guided examination of a diverse set of code transformations, including combinations of such transformations, to create different application versions. By automatically examining diverse compositions of code transformations, we can help developers to generate energy-efficient versions of their applications, and to understand which decisions, and their interactions, make an application less or more energy efficient without the developers having to exhaustively explore all possible code transformations and their combinations manually. To automatically apply code transformations associated with solutions generated by the metaheuristic-based search approach, we leverage the SEEDS framework [21]. Previous work shows that SEEDS API Implementation Selector (SEEDS$_{api}$), an instantiation of SEEDS, is able to find energy-efficient versions of Java applications, by using a limited exhaustive search strategy. artificial data synthesis. In contrast, this paper evaluates how metaheuristic-based search strategies, based on a (GA), allows SEEDS$_{api}$ to explore more thoroughly and efficiently the search space by considering solutions composed of various combinations of code transformations.

In this paper, we evaluate metaheuristic search strategies based on two different GAs, and compare the results with the limited exhaustive search previously used by SEEDS$_{api}$. We analyzed the performance of the search strategies with nine Java applications. Our results show that metaheuristic search strategies are able to find energy-friendly combinations of code transformations. However, for some applications, the limited search strategy is able to find solutions that are better than those found by search strategies based on GAs, both in energy savings and time required to find a solution. We describe how a developer can take advantage of different search strategies available in SEEDS$_{api}$ and further directions for research.

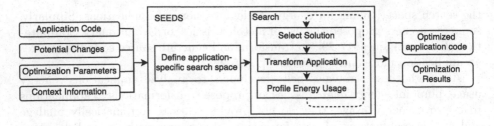

Fig. 1. Overview of the SEEDS framework

2 Background

2.1 SEEDS Framework

SEEDS [21] is a software framework that allows developers to both explore the impact of software developers' decisions on an application's energy usage, and automatically improve an application's energy consumption by applying different types of source-code transformations to an application. Figure 1 shows the main components of the SEEDS framework. SEEDS' inputs include: (1) the application source code, (2) a set of potential changes or transformations, (3) a list of optimization parameters (optional), and (4) the application's context information. The framework is composed of two major building blocks: (1) An *application-specific search space component* that creates different application's versions (i.e., solutions) by applying code transformations to the original application, and compose the search space to be navigated, and (2) a *search component* that defines the search strategy used to navigate the search space of solutions to find an improved version of the original application in terms of its energy usage. The outputs are the improved version of the application along with a list of the application change(s) that have been made to make it more energy efficient.

The SEEDS$_{api}$ Instantiation of SEEDS. SEEDS$_{api}$ is an instantiation of SEEDS that supports software engineers as they make decisions about which library implementations they should use to optimize the overall energy usage of their applications. Choosing a collection implementation is a common decision that is faced by software developers. However, developers commonly choose API implementations based on familiarity or execution time concerns only, which means that applications are unlikely to have optimized their choice of collection implementation to energy usage. The goal of SEEDS$_{api}$ is to improve Java applications by identifying implementations of Java Collections APIs that are more energy efficient, if any, than the implementations currently used by an application. In SEEDS$_{api}$ [21], the application-specific search space is defined as the solutions that result in the ordered combination of all allocation locations of Collection API's instances and the possible changes (i.e., implementations of Collections libraries) that can be applied in each location. As more transformations or allocation locations are found for an application, the search space grows exponentially making it difficult to explore every single solution. The search component in SEEDS$_{api}$ was initially defined with a limited exhaustive search strategy that considered a narrowed size of the search space. Two different configurations of solutions were considered by the limited exhaustive search. The first configuration considered the search space composed by versions of an application that have one single concrete code transformation at one of the different application's change locations. The second solution configuration consisted of the search space composed of versions of an application that have multiple code transformations corresponding to the "energy efficient" transformation for every application's change locations. These configurations resulted in a reduced size of the search space of solutions. However, with the limited exhaustive search it was not possible to analyze how multiple permutations of transformations in different application locations could impact the energy usage of an application, nor whether or not there exist any other optimal configurations of solutions.

2.2 Metaheuristic Optimization

The problem of automatically exploring combinations of possible code transformations have several characteristics: (1) an optimal solution is unknown beforehand, (2) there is no clear way to find an optimal solution, and (3) an exhaustive or brute-force search is very expensive to use because the size of the search space is too large. These characteristics make it ideal for exploring the use of metaheuristic-based optimizations. We chose to apply GAs for improving applications' energy usage because they are popular metaheuristic optimization strategies that, due their intrinsic evolutionary structure, make them suitable for the exploration and evaluation of different compositions of code transformations for an application.

3   Improving Energy Usage of Applications via Genetic Algorithms

This section presents our approach for searching and improving an application's energy usage via GAs. To analyze and identify which combinations of code transformations help to reduce the energy usage of an application, we need to (1) be able to navigate the search space of solutions by using an algorithm that allows us to identify optimal solutions, (2) have a way to automatically apply the code transformations represented by a solution drawn from the search space, and (3) have a way to measure the energy consumption of a solution under analysis. The following subsections describe how we address these challenges by using GAs (Sect. 3.1), the SEEDS$_{api}$ and an energy estimation technique (Sect. 3.2).

3.1   Genetic Algorithms to Navigate an Application's Search Space

The Generational Genetic Algorithm (gGA). The generational Genetic Algorithm (gGA) is an evolutionary algorithm for single objective optimization problems. The gGA finds optimal solutions to a given problem by exploring the

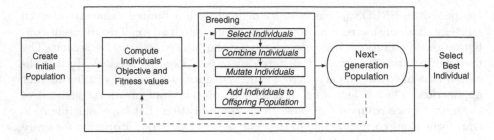

Fig. 2. Generational genetic algorithm.

search space based on ideas similar to those in biological evolution theory [10]. A gGA uses a *generational replacement* mechanism to update the entire population of solutions once per iteration [20]. Figure 2 shows an overview of a gGA algorithm. First, the algorithm constructs an initial population and then iterates over three major steps: (1) compute an objective and a fitness value for all the individuals in the population, (2) use the objective and fitness information of the individuals to breed a new offspring population by using mutation and crossover operators, and (3) join the parents and offspring to form a new next-generation population. The breeding process continues until the desired size of the offspring population has been reached. To avoid the phenomenon where there are no individuals in the population that are getting fitter than previous individuals, we carried forward the best two individuals (i.e., *elite* parents) from the previous population. Thus, the elite parents are selected to survive for the next offspring generation of individuals. Steps 1–3 continue until a given number of generations has been completed. The total number of generations in which populations are being created is restricted by the selected stopping criteria: when a given total number of evaluations of the objective function have occurred, a total number of generations is reached, or when a given objective value or execution time has been reached.

The Non-dominated Sorting Genetic Algorithm II (NSGAII). In some cases, not only the energy but also the execution time of an application wants to be improved, or at least not degraded. To consider both the energy usage and the execution time of solutions, we used a multiobjective evolutionary algorithm, the Non-dominated Sorting Genetic Algorithm II (NSGA-II). Multiobjective optimization algorithms try to find one or multiple "optimal" solutions that can achieve the best optimization with multiple, possibly conflicting, objectives. The goal is to find one or more solutions that belong to the set of optimal values of the problem, called the *pareto optimal* set. The optimal values of the problem, which constitute the *pareto front*, are the collection of objective vectors that cannot be dominated. In a minimization problem, an objective vector v, is considered to be better, or to dominate another objective vector w in the pareto sense, if all the components of v are lower or equal to the components of w, with at least one strictly lower component. Thus, the pareto-optimal set is the collection of solutions from the search space in which the objective vectors belong to the pareto front. We selected NSGA-II because it is an evolutionary algorithm for multiobjective optimization problems that has been shown to be able to find better solutions than other multiobjective evolutionary approaches [9].

GA Parameters. GAs have various parameter settings. Here, we describe how we selected the parameter settings for our problem.

Solution Representation: Each solution (i.e., application version) in the search space is represented as an array of integers. This representation lets us consider all possible configurations of changes in the application's search space. Each index of the array corresponds to a location in the application where changes can be made. Each value assigned to a position in the array identifies one of the possible changes to be made in the application. For instance, for the *Barbecue* application,[1] there exist 10 allocation locations where transformations can be made by swapping Collections implementations. Thus, for the *Barbecue* application the representation of a solution is an array $\mathbf{x}$ of size 10, where $\mathbf{x_i}$ is an integer representing a specific Collection implementation (i.e., ArrayList, LinkedList, etc.) to be used at site i, and transforming the original application to create a solution, $\mathbf{x}$, representing a different version of the *Barbecue* application.

Creation of the Initial Population: For the creation of the initial population, we randomly generated individuals by selecting different transformations for every potential change location of an application. All the transformations to be applied to an application are tested for validation in each of the pre-identified potential change locations of the application. Only transformations that result in an application version that passes all application's test cases are considered as valid changes.

Selection and Genetic Operators: For the selection, crossover, and mutation operators, in both gGA and NSGA-II, we chose the binary tournament selection strategy, the single point crossover, and the simple uniform mutation, respectively. We selected a rate of 1/(number of change sites), and a crossover rate of 0.9. We selected these operators because they are standard operators that support the exploration of a diverse set of solutions from the search space while trying to preserve fit solutions.

Objective Function and Fitness: Lower values of the objective and fitness functions for an individual make an individual more appealing for reproduction and evolution during the execution of the corresponding GA. We selected the objective value for each individual in a population as the Mean Energy Usage (MEU) of the application version represented by the individual ($MEU_{solution}$), divided over the effect size of the individual's energy samples $effectSize_{solution}$. The MEU of an individual is computed in two steps. First, the individual is instantiated, i.e., all transformations indicated by the individual's array are applied to the original application code, and a new version of the application is created. Then, the energy usage of the individual is taken by running the application's test suite using an energy estimation tool as described in Sect. 3.2. The

---

[1] http://barbecue.sourceforge.net/source-repository.html.

energy usage of each individual is taken ten times to be able to compute the statistical significance of the application's energy usage. After all the individuals have been created and their MEU value have been computed for the current population, a statistical analysis test is performed to identify which solutions in the current population are statistically different from the original application. Then, for statistically significant different individuals, we compute their *Cliff's d* [24] *effect size* to account for the significance of the difference in the energy usage. Lastly, for the assignment of an individual fitness value, we used the individual's MEU divided by the MEU of the original application version. A solution with a fitness value less than one means the solution represents an application version that is more energy efficient than the original application. In the next subsection, we describe how the two GAs are implemented and configured.

3.2   Implementation of the Search Strategy in SEEDS$_{api}$

To implement the metaheuristic-based search strategy in SEEDS$_{api}$, we need to implement the selected GA, find a way to evaluate online the energy usage of the solutions generated by the search strategies, and select a measure of effect size that allow us to quantify the magnitude of the difference between the energy usage of an application's solution compared to the original application's version. To implement the two selected GAs in SEEDS$_{api}$, we leveraged the features provided by the JMetal[2] framework. JMetal is a widely adopted metaheuristic framework in Java [11] that provides different metaheuristic algorithms and operators. In JMetal, each GA operator is bound with a variable type (i.e., float, boolean, etc), according to the representation of a solution in the search space.

We used the Running Average Power Limit (RAPL) interface [8] to profile the amount of energy consumed by a given application version (i.e., individual) generated by each GA. We selected RAPL for several reasons: (1) previous studies have verified that RAPL power estimates are fairly accurate [14], (2) RAPL's interface enables us to seamlessly integrate energy estimates into the SEEDS framework, and (3) RAPL's estimation technique allows us to easily obtain the application's energy usage without incurring the extra costs and complexity introduced by external hardware instrumentation techniques.

4   Evaluation

The evaluation of metaheuristic-based search via GAs to find energy efficient versions of applications is driven by the following research questions:

RQ1—Effectiveness. Are GAs an effective approach to improve an application' energy usage by means of introducing code changes in SEEDS$_{api}$?

RQ2—Cost. Can GAs reduce the costs associated with the search of an improved solution in SEEDS$_{api}$?

---

[2] http://jmetal.sourceforge.net.

Table 1. Subject applications.

Application	Version	LoC	# tests	Coverage (%)	# change sites
Barbecue	—	13,610	247	55.9	10
Commons CLI	1.2	8,638	187	96.7	14
Joda-Time	2.1	69,225	197	36.6	16
Gson	2.2.4	29,119	913	86.6	13
Jfreechart	1.0.15	315,787	6,663	67.8	158
Commons Lang	3.1	100,566	2,046	94.9	47
Jdepend	2.9.1	5,865	53	53.2	14
Commons Beanutils	1.8.3	69,355	1,277	71.3	7
Apache-xml-security	1.0	50,412	175	41.9	15

4.1 Experimental Subjects

To evaluate the proposed metaheuristic-based search strategy with SEEDS$_{api}$, we
selected nine Java applications that use the Collections API. We selected these
programs because they have been used in other software engineering research
studies, they are publicly available, and because they are subjects representative
of applications that use the Java Collection Framework (JCF). In addition, these
applications provided a test suite, which both provide an approximation of real
use case scenarios for each application and it is required by SEEDS$_{api}$ to validate
the correctness of the solutions generated by the search strategy.

Table 1 describes the selected subject applications. The first and second
columns, *Application* and *Version*, together identify the application version. The
third column, *LoC*, provides the number of lines of source code. The fourth and
fifth columns, *# Tests* and *Coverage (%)*, report the number of tests in the associated test suite provided with each subject and the percentage of the statements
in the application that are covered by the test suite, respectively. The last column reports the number of possible sites in the application code for the program
changes of interest i.e., potential change locations. We obtained the subjects from
four different public repositories: (1) Software-artifact Infrastructure Repository
(SIR),[3] which provides a variety of open-source projects, (2) SourceForge[4] and,
(3) Github[5], two popular repositories for open-source projects, and (4) Apache
Commons,[6] a collection of reusable components.

4.2 RQ1: Effectiveness

To answer the question *"Are GAs an effective approach to improve applications'
energy usage by means of introducing code changes?"*, we compared the limited

---

[3] http://sir.unl.edu.
[4] https://sourceforge.net.
[5] http://github.com.
[6] http://commons.apache.org.

Table 2. Comparison between limited exhaustive search (LES) and metaheuristic-based search strategies (gGa, NSGA-II)

Application	% Energy savings					
	JCF			ALL		
	LES	gGA	NSGA-II	LES	gGA	NSGA-II
Barbecue	26	23	28	28	23	28
Commons-CLI	6	11	25	6	12	25
Jodatime	7	2	–	8	2	–
Gson	1	14	5	1	14	7
Jfreechart	7	13	–	7	1	3
Commons Lang	3	2	3	3	2	4
Jdepend	2	12	2	2	18	3
C. Beanutils	1	2	1	2	3	2
Apache-xml	3	1	–	4	1	–

exhaustive search against the gGA and NSGA-II algorithms described in Sect. 3 for driving the search for an energy efficient solution in SEEDS$_{api}$.

Table 2 shows the results, average of five runs, of using three search strategies in SEEDS$_{api}$ to find energy efficient solutions of the selected subject applications. The first column, *Application*, presents the name of the application; the second, third and fourth columns show the percentage in energy savings obtained with SEEDS$_{api}$ when using implementations from the JCF library only (*'JCF'*) for the limited exhaustive strategy (*LES*), the search strategy driven by the gGA, and the search strategy driven by the NSGA-II, respectively. For the fifth, sixth, and seventh columns, the results are shown when the implementations used to create the alternative application versions are drawn from all the Collections libraries (*'ALL'*), for the LES, gGA, and NSGA-II search strategies, respectively. A '−' in the table indicates that no better solution than the original application was found by the corresponding search strategy. For the NSGA-II, the best solution in terms of energy usage and execution time was selected. From the results shown in this table, we can see that evolutionary algorithms are indeed able to find improved versions of applications in terms of their energy usage. For instance, for the *Commons-CLI* application, both metaheuristic-based search strategies (i.e., gGA and NSGA-II) found solutions twice to four times more energy efficient than the solutions found for this application when using the limited exhaustive search strategy. For six of the nine applications (e.g., Commons-CLI, Gson, Jfreechart, Commons-lang, Jdepend, and Commons Beanutils), the metaheuristic-based search strategies were able to find better solutions than the solutions found using the limited exhaustive search strategy in SEEDS$_{api}$. For example, the energy savings obtained by the solution found by SEEDS$_{api}$ when using the gGA search strategy is 13% for Jfreechart, compared to a 7% energy savings obtained by the solution found for this application when using the limited exhaustive strategy. Also, for the Gson application, the metaheuristic search using the gGA search strategy found a solution 14 times more energy efficient than the solution found by the limited exhaustive search strategy for this application.

Although the studied GAs were able to find improved solutions of an application, the results also indicate that evolutionary algorithms can sometimes yield other solutions with lower or equal energy savings than solutions found by the limited exhaustive strategy used initially in SEEDS$_{api}$. For instance, for the *Barbecue* application, the best solutions found by the gGA strategy were 3–5% less energy efficient than the solutions found by the limited exhaustive strategy. Similarly, when using the NSGA-II strategy, SEEDS$_{api}$ found a solution with 28% energy savings, which was the same energy savings obtained by the solution found by SEEDS$_{api}$ when using the limited exhaustive search strategy. A similar case occurs for the *Jodatime*, for which only the gGA was able to find an improved application version with 2% energy savings. This could be due to the configuration (e.g., initial population, selected genetic operators, and stop criteria) used for the metaheuristic-based search strategies, which in some cases might not direct the search technique to explore portions of the search space where other better solutions exist for these applications. However, finding a general configuration of the metaheuristic-based search strategies that works best for all subject applications is a complex task requiring the analysis of multiple parameters for the GAs.

From these results, we can see that both limited exhaustive and metaheuristic-based search strategies can be effective strategies to find energy efficient versions of applications within SEEDS$_{api}$. Metaheuristic-based search strategies sometimes find solutions with higher energy savings than those obtained with the limited exhaustive search strategy in SEEDS$_{api}$, but this is not a general rule. For some applications, using the limited exhaustive search strategy can yield better results in terms of the energy savings obtained by the improved application version.

4.3   RQ2: Cost

To answer the question *"Can GAs reduce the costs associated with the search of an improved solution in SEEDS?"*, we analyzed how the cost of using metaheuristic-based search strategies compare to the cost of using the limited exhaustive strategy in SEEDS$_{api}$.

Table 3 shows, in a similar way to Table 2, the costs in terms of the time required for each search strategy to find an improved version of an application. The first column shows the name of the subject application; the second, third and fourth columns show the time in hours required by SEEDS$_{api}$ to obtain an improved version of an application when using implementations from the JCF library only (*'JCF'*) for the limited exhaustive strategy (LES), the search strategy driven by the gGA, and the search strategy driven by the search strategy driven by the, respectively. Columns five to seven, show the costs of obtaining the solutions in SEEDS$_{api}$ when implementations from all the Collections libraries (*'ALL'*) are used to create the alternative application versions for the LES, gGA,

Table 3. Costs for limited exhaustive search (LES) and metaheuristic-based search strategies (gGa, NSGA-II)

Application	Cost					
	JCF			ALL		
	LES	gGA	NSGA-II	LES	gGA	NSGA-II
Barbecue	0.8	2.4	2.3	1.6	5.1	0.9
Commons-CLI	0.6	2	1.3	0.9	2.2	1.2
Jodatime	1.1	1.5	–	4.9	1.6	–
Gson	0.9	1	2.4	2.4	16.7	2.3
Jfreechart	16	7.5	–	20.2	41	5.9
Commons Lang	8	1.2	10.7	26.8	7	20.1
Jdepend	1.2	3.4	2.9	1.5	3.6	3.1
C. Beanutils	3.3	2.1	1.2	3.5	2.3	1.5
Apache-xml	2.2	1.6	–	2.7	1.8	–

and NSGA-II search strategies, respectively. A '–' in the table indicates that no better solution than the original application was found by the corresponding search strategy. For instance, for *Barbecue*, the time required to find an improved version when using the implementations from the JCF only is 0.8 h when using the limited exhaustive search, and 2.4 h when using the gGA search.

From Table 3, we can see that for five out of the nine subjects (*Barbecue, Commons-CLI, Jodatime, Gson, and Jdepend*) the limited exhaustive search takes less time to find an improved application version when compared with the time required by the search strategies using the gGA or the NSGA-II. This can be because the limited search strategy has a set with few application versions to explore, while the metaheuristic-based search strategies have to explore a larger portion of the search space looking for the improved application versions, or also because of the stopping criteria used for the GAs, which in our case was until completing 100 generations. However, in some cases, the metaheuristic-based search strategies are able to find an improved version of an application in about the same or less time than with the limited exhaustive search. This is the case for the *Gson* application, for which the gGA is able to find a solution with better energy savings (i.e., 14% compared to 1% energy savings) than the limited exhaustive search, expending almost the same amount of time (i.e., one hour) when using the implementations from the JCF only. Another example is the *Commons-lang* application, when using the NSGA-II search with the implementations from all the Collections libraries, the time required to find an improved version is about 20.1 h, compared to 26.8 h required by the limited exhaustive search for this application. Metaheuristic-based search strategies sometimes need less time to find an improved version of an application due to the way they navigate the search space, which allows them to find better solutions in less time by considering at every generation, the best solutions to find the improved version of an application.

4.4   Threats to Validity

Threats to construct validity: We evaluated three search strategies in SEEDS by implementing them in one the SEEDS$_{api}$ instantiation. It is possible that other instantiations will not lead to improved energy usage of an application. Although we considered three search strategies, the results show that the evaluated search strategies indeed can find alternative application's versions that are more energy efficient than its original version. *Threats to internal validity:* Confounding variables include the processes and background tasks. Also, the selected Operating System (OS) and garbage collector (GC) selected, along with the temperature of the room where the experiments took place could have an impact. We minimize this threat by deactivating unnecessary processes and services, like the network and OS update manager of the machine that we used for our experiments; we also controlled the selection of the OS and GC, which were the same for all experiments: XUbuntu 12.04, and the default GC for Java. *Threats to external validity:* For our evaluation, we selected nine Java applications, used their associated test suites, and chose six libraries as the source of our considered potential choices. It is possible that conclusions drawn from this set may not generalize to all applications or other languages, libraries, or test suites. To minimize the threat, the applications we considered were selected because they have been used by many researchers and they are representative of applications using the JCF.

5   Related Work

The closest related works to this paper are the works recently presented by Brownlee et al. and Bokhari et al., where approaches based on genetic improvement are used to search and optimize the energy usage of Collection classes and the Rebound Java library, respectively [3,4]. In [4], Brownlee et al. presented an Object-Oriented Genetic Algorithm (OO-GI) to find an energy-efficient implementation for 6 Collection classes in the Guava and Apache Commons Collections Libraries. Similarly, in [3] a deep parameter optimization algorithm based on genetic algorithms is used to toggle an application's parameters and find versions of an application that improve the original version in terms of its energy usage. Although our approach also uses a GA to drive the search for an energy efficient version of an application, our work is different from the existing work in several aspects: (1) the transformations we carried out are based on implementation changes selected by developers instead of general/random lines of code from a program, (2) the optimizations found by our approach are not necessarily target-specific as those based on assembly code, (3) our study involves complete Java programs while previous studies have been applied to isolated classes or to a specific library, and (4) our evaluation includes 9 real applications with various code sizes.

Genetic Improvement (GI), the process of automatically improving a systems behaviour by automatically generating application code, a.k.a. genetic programming (GP), is another area closely related to our work [29]. GI has been used to improve systems' performance [17], and more recently to improve energy usage of systems [5,27]. In [27], the authors use a similar approach to GI where a Genetic Optimization Algorithm (GOA) finds program versions that use less energy than the original program by changing the assembly code of C/C++ programs. Our work is different from those using GI in that we do not use GP (i.e., produce automatically application code) as a way to improve an application's energy usage. Instead of GP, we use evolutionary computation as a mechanism to search for an optimized version of the original application, where variations of an application are created by making changes in the application's bytecode or source code.

Three major approaches to measure the energy consumption of programs are instrumentation of hardware with power meters, estimation models, and simulation of the energy usage for different hardware components [13,28]. Estimation-based approaches have gained more attention lately since they are easy to use and provide good quality approximations close to real measurements [7,8,23]. For instance, Opacitor [7] uses a custom version of the OpenJDK to incorporate the energy model of the Java opcodes created by Hao et al. [15]. Although these tools provide good energy estimates, some of them are not publicly available, their energy models are machine dependent, or they require running additional software that introduce noise to the system. We selected the RAPL energy estimation approach since it provides energy estimates close to the real measurements, it has been widely tested and used in practice [14].

6   Conclusions and Future Work

We have studied two genetic algorithms, gGA and NSGA-II, to drive the search for transformations that make a Java application more energy efficient. Based on our experiments, for large applications, the limited exhaustive search strategy seems to be more adequate for SEEDS$_{api}$ in terms of the time required and energy savings obtained. For small to medium size applications, metaheuristic-based search strategies tend to provide a better energy savings to cost ratio, and therefore might be preferred. These results motivate the instantiation of multiple search strategies in SEEDS$_{api}$ that allow developers to try various search techniques to find an improved energy application version of their applications. In general, users of SEEDS$_{api}$ can decide which search strategy to use based on their energy goals and budget. Future work will include the exploration of different configurations for GAs, other metaheuristic strategies to drive the search, and additional types of code transformations commonly used by developers in mobile and Internet of Things applications.

Acknowledgments. This work is supported in part by National Science Foundation Grant No. 1618161.

References

1. Banerjee, A., Chong, L.K., Chattopadhyay, S., Roychoudhury, A.: Detecting energy bugs and hotspots in mobile apps. In: International Symposium on Foundations of, Software Engineering, pp. 588–598 (2014)
2. Banerjee, T., Ranka, S.: A genetic algorithm based autotuning approach for performance and energy optimization. In: International Green and Sustainable Computing Conference, pp. 1–8. IEEE Computer Society (2015)
3. Bokhari, M.A., Bruce, B.R., Alexander, B., Wagner, M.: Deep parameter optimisation on android smartphones for energy minimisation: a tale of woe and a proof-of-concept. In: Genetic and Evolutionary Computation Conference Companion. ACM (2017)
4. Brownlee, A.E.I., Burles, N., Swan, J.: Search-based energy optimization of some ubiquitous algorithms. IEEE Trans. Emerg. Top. Comput. Intell. **1**(3), 188–201 (2017)
5. Bruce, B.R., Petke, J., Harman, M.: Reducing energy consumption using genetic improvement. In: Conference on Genetic and Evolutionary Computation, pp. 1327–1334. ACM (2015)
6. Bunse, C., Hopfner, H., Roychoudhury, S., Mansour, E.: Choosing the 'Best' sorting algorithm for optimal energy consumption. In: International Conference on Software and Data Technologies, pp. 199–206 (2009)
7. Burles, N., Bowles, E., Brownlee, A.E.I., Kocsis, Z.A., Swan, J., Veerapen, N.: Object-oriented genetic improvement for improved energy consumption in Google Guava. In: Barros, M., Labiche, Y. (eds.) SSBSE 2015. LNCS, vol. 9275, pp. 255–261. Springer, Cham (2015). https://doi.org/10.1007/978-3-319-22183-0_20
8. Counts, T.: Running average power limit. Technical report. Intel Open Source (2012). https://01.org/blogs/tlcounts/2014/running-average-power-limit-E2%80%93-rapl
9. Deb, K., Pratap, A., Agarwal, S., Meyarivan, T.: A fast and elitist multiobjective genetic algorithm: NSGA-II. Trans. Evol. Comp **6**(2), 182–197 (2002)
10. Dreo, J., Siarry, P., Petrowski, A., Taillard, E.: Metaheuristics for Hard Optimization: Methods and Case Studies. Springer, Heidelberg (2006). https://doi.org/10.1007/3-540-30966-7
11. Durillo, J.J., Nebro, A.J.: jMetal: a Java framework for multi-objective optimization. Adv. Eng. Softw. **42**, 760–771 (2011)
12. Guo, C., Zhang, J., Yan, J., Zhang, Z., Zhang, Y.: Characterizing and detecting resource leaks in android applications. In: International Conference on Automated Software Engineering. IEEE Press (2013)
13. Gurumurthi, S., et al.: Using complete machine simulation for software power estimation: the softWatt approach. In: International Symposium on High-Performance Computer, Architecture, pp. 141–151 (2002)
14. Hackenberg, D., Ilsche, T., Schöne, R., Molka, D., Schmidt, M., Nagel, W.E.: Power measurement techniques on standard compute nodes: a quantitative comparison. In: IEEE International Symposium on Performance Analysis of Systems and Software, pp. 194–204 (2013)
15. Hao, S., Li, D., Halfond, W.G.J., Govindan, R.: Estimating mobile application energy consumption using program analysis. In: International Conference on Software Engineering, pp. 92–101 (2013)
16. Hunt, N., Sandhu, P., Ceze, L.: Characterizing the performance and energy efficiency of lock-free data structures. In: Workshop on Interaction between Compilers and Computer Architectures, pp. 63–70 (2011)

17. Langdon, W.B., Harman, M.: Optimizing existing software with genetic programming. IEEE Trans. Evol. Comput. **19**(1), 118–135 (2015)
18. Linares-Vásquez, M., Bavota, G., Bernal-Cárdenas, C., Oliveto, R., Di Penta, M., Poshyvanyk, D.: Mining energy-greedy API usage patterns in Android apps: an empirical study. In: Working Conference on Mining Software Repositories. ACM (2014)
19. Linares-Vásquez, M., Bavota, G., Cárdenas, C.E.B., Oliveto, R., Di Penta, M., Poshyvanyk, D.: Optimizing energy consumption of GUIs in Android apps: a multi-objective approach. In: Joint Meeting on Foundations of Software Engineering. ACM (2015)
20. Luke, S.: Essentials of Metaheuristics, vol. 2. Lulu, Raleigh (2013)
21. Manotas, I., Pollock, L., Clause, J.: Seeds: a software engineer's energy-optimization decision support framework. In: International Conference on Software Engineering. ACM (2014)
22. Morales, R., Saborido, R., Khomh, F., Chicano, F., Antoniol, G.: Earmo: an energy-aware refactoring approach for mobile apps. IEEE Trans. Softw. Eng. 1 (2017)
23. Noureddine, A., Islam, S., Bashroush, R.: Jolinar: analysing the energy footprint of software applications (demo). In: International Symposium on Software Testing and Analysis, pp. 445–448. ACM (2016)
24. Grissom, R.J., Kim, J.J.: Effect Sizes for Research: Univariate and Multivariate Applications, 2nd edn. Taylor and Francis Group, LLC, Routledge (2012)
25. Sahin, C., et al.: Initial explorations on design pattern energy usage. In: International Workshop on Green and Sustainable Software, pp. 55–61 (2012)
26. Sahin, C., Pollock, L., Clause, J.: How do code refactorings affect energy usage? In: International Symposium on Empirical Software Engineering and Measurement. ACM (2014)
27. Schulte, E., Dorn, J., Harding, S., Forrest, S., Weimer, W.: Post-compiler software optimization for reducing energy. In: International Conference on Architectural Support for Programming Languages and Operating Systems. ACM (2014)
28. Singh, D., Peterson, P.A.H., Reiher, P.L., Kaiser, W.J.: The Atom LEAP platform for energy-efficient embedded computing: Architecture, operation, and system implementation (2010). http://lasr.cs.ucla.edu/leap/FrontPage?action=AttachFile&do=get&target=leapwhitepaper.pdf
29. Woodward, J.R., Johnson, C.G., Brownlee, A.E.: GP vs GI: if you can't beat them, join them. In: Genetic and Evolutionary Computation Conference Companion, pp. 1155–1156. ACM (2016)

Optimization Experiments in the Continuous Space

The Limited Growth Optimistic Optimization Algorithm

David Issa Mattos[1]($\boxtimes$) (iD), Erling Mårtensson[2], Jan Bosch[1] (iD),
and Helena Holmström Olsson[3] (iD)

[1] Department of Computer Science and Engineering,
Chalmers University of Technology,
Hörselgången 11, 412 96 Göteborg, Sweden
{davidis, jan.bosch}@chalmers.se
[2] Sony Mobile Communications, Nya Vattentornet, 221 88 Lund, Sweden
erling.martensson@sony.com
[3] Department of Computer Science and Media Technology, Malmö University,
Nordenskiöldsgatan, 211 19 Malmö, Sweden
helena.holmstrom.olsson@mah.se

Abstract. Online controlled experiments are extensively used by web-facing companies to validate and optimize their systems, providing a competitive advantage in their business. As the number of experiments scale, companies aim to invest their experimentation resources in larger feature changes and leave the automated techniques to optimize smaller features. Optimization experiments in the continuous space are encompassed in the many-armed bandits class of problems. Although previous research provides algorithms for solving this class of problems, these algorithms were not implemented in real-world online experimentation problems and do not consider the application constraints, such as time to compute a solution, selection of a best arm and the estimation of the mean-reward function. This work discusses the online experiments in context of the many-armed bandits class of problems and provides three main contributions: (1) an algorithm modification to include online experiments constraints, (2) implementation of this algorithm in an industrial setting in collaboration with Sony Mobile, and (3) statistical evidence that supports the modification of the algorithm for online experiments scenarios. These contributions support the relevance of the LG-HOO algorithm in the context of optimization experiments and show how the algorithm can be used to support continuous optimization of online systems in stochastic scenarios.

Keywords: Online experiments · Multi-armed bandits
Infinitely many-armed bandits · Continuous-space optimization

1 Introduction

Traditional requirements engineering relies on domain experts and market research to model the user behavior and define requirements for their systems. However, research shows that, often as 70–90% of the time, companies can be wrong about their customer

© Springer Nature Switzerland AG 2018
T. E. Colanzi and P. McMinn (Eds.): SSBSE 2018, LNCS 11036, pp. 293–308, 2018.
https://doi.org/10.1007/978-3-319-99241-9_16

preferences [1–3]. In this scenario, several companies are adding on top their requirements engineering practices the usage of post-deployment data to evaluate the user behavior and set prioritization and optimization objectives. One way use post-deployment data in software development is through online controlled experiments with user behavior. Aligned with a set of long-term business goals metrics [4], these companies are running business-driven experiments, such as A/B tests, to validate their business hypotheses [5].

This movement started with web-facing companies such as Microsoft, Google, Facebook, Amazon, LinkedIn, among others [2, 6–9], and they continuously report the competitive advantages that experimentation techniques such as A/B delivers in business-driven experiments [10]. As these companies scale their experimentation infrastructure and organization to keep their competitive edge, they developed sophisticated techniques to run experiments in range of situations that simple A/B experiments face limitations. Some of these techniques are overlapping experiments [6], optimal ramp-up [9], networked A/B testing [11], multi-armed bandits [12], counterfactual analysis [13] and optimization experiments [14, 15]. With the increasing number of experiments being run every year [1, 9], companies are looking for new techniques that can free some of their research and development resources from the lower risk optimization experiments and allow these resources to be employed in experiments that have higher risk and higher potential return on investment and that cannot be managed automatically by a computer.

In this context, bandit algorithms started to be employed by software companies to simplify the experimentation process in some experiments [12]. Bandit problems is a class of problems that deals with the exploration/exploitation dilemma [16]. This work focuses on a subset of bandit problems called the infinitely many-armed bandit problems. This subset investigates the optimization of parameters in a continuous space, in the presence of an unknown mean reward function. This class of problems is particularly important in online controlled experiments, as several user-behavior assumptions are captured in the systems in the form of constants that can be mapped in a continuous space. The most prominent and least restrictive algorithm for the infinitely many-armed bandit problem is the Hierarchical Optimistic Optimization (HOO) algorithm [17, 18]. However, there is no evidence or empirical evaluation of the usage of this algorithm in online experiments. During the implementation of the HOO algorithm in collaboration with Sony Mobile, this algorithm presented limitations some limitations, such as the computation time, the correctness of the output based on different mean-reward distribution functions, the lack of a criterion to select the best arm at any point, and an estimation of the mean-reward.

The contribution of this work is three-fold. First, we provide a modification of the HOO algorithm to overcome the identified online experiments restrictions, improving the correctness of the output, the time to compute, a criterion to select the best arm and an estimation of the mean-reward function. We call this new algorithm as the Limited Growth Hierarchical Optimistic Optimization algorithm (LG-HOO). Second, we present an implementation of LG-HOO in an industrial setting, in collaboration with Sony Mobile. Third, we provide statistical evidence that supports the modification of the algorithm not only in real-world scenario, but also on simulation scenarios.

This paper is organized as follows. Section 2 presents background information in controlled experiments, bandits problems and the infinitely many-armed bandit problem, the HOO algorithm and related work. Section 3 discusses the research process. Section 4 presents the LG-HOO algorithm, results from simulations, and the results of the implementation of the LG-HOO in an industrial context in collaboration with Sony Mobile. Section 5 discuss the results of the LG-HOO and makes a statistical comparison of the LG-HOO algorithm with the HOO. Section 6 concludes and discusses future research directions.

2   Background and Related Work

2.1   Online Controlled Experiments

Controlled experiments are a technique where the users are randomly assigned to two variants of a product: the control (current system) and the treatment (the system with a change X). The change X can be the implementation of a new feature or the parametrization for optimization of existing features. After the change is implemented, the system is instrumented and the user's behavior and the system performance are computed. After a predetermined period of data collection, the computed metrics for all variations of the system (control and treatments) are analyzed. If the two following conditions are true: (1) the assumption that the external factors are spread out evenly between the two variants due to consistent randomization process holds true (quality checks can help assess this assumption) and (2) the only consistent difference between the treatment and the control is the change X; we can establish a causal relationship of the change X and the observed difference in the metrics. Kohavi et al. [19] provide a detailed guide on how to run online controlled experiments in the web. If the experimentation process is used in incremental variations of the system, this becomes an optimization procedure.

2.2   The Multi-armed Bandit, the χ-Bandit Problem, and the HOO

The Multi-armed Bandit Problem
Multi-armed bandit problems are a class of problems that deals with the exploration and exploitation trade-off. The problem statement and its name come from parallel the of the gambler problem facing a row of N slot machines, also called one-armed bandits. The gambler wants to maximize the end reward from the slot machines after a set of plays. Each slot machine/arm has a fixed unknown probability distribution for the reward. The gambler faces the problem of exploiting the arm that provides the largest reward while exploring other arms to make sure he does not miss arms that can provide a better reward. In its simpler formulation, the bandit has limited number of rows to play, the number of arms is finite, the arms are independent of each other, and each arm has a stationary stochastic distribution over time.

The general problem can be formulated as [13]:

$$a = \pi(\delta), \text{ Arm } a \in \{a_1 \ldots a_K\} \tag{1}$$

$$y = r(a, \delta'), \text{ Reward } y \in \mathbb{R} \tag{2}$$

Where a is the arm selected, K is the number of arms, π is the user-defined policy (a selection of actions) function to balance the exploration of arms and the exploitation of the best arm so far, δ and δ' are noise variable (that makes the problem stochastic), y is the measured reward and r is the unknown mean-reward function for the selected arm. Several policies can be formulated in this class of problem, the most used is to minimize the regret. Regret is comparison of the cumulative mean reward of the algorithm and the expected reward of playing the optimal arm.

$$Regret(t) = r(a^*) \cdot t - \sum_{s=1}^{t} \mu(a_s) \tag{3}$$

Where $\mu(a)$ is the mean reward of the arm a over the time and a^* is the arm with the largest mean-reward over time:

$$a^* = \max_{a \in \{a_1 \ldots a_K\}} \mu(a) \tag{4}$$

The multi-armed bandit algorithms are the construction of the user-defined policy π to select the arm.

The χ-Bandit Problem and The Infinitely Many-Armed Bandit Problem

The χ-bandit problem, also known as the continuum-armed bandit problem, is formulated similarly to the multi-armed bandit problem. However, instead of a predefined and finite number of arms (Arm $a \in \{a_1 \ldots a_K\}$), the χ-bandit problem has an infinite number of arms that are drawn from a continuous set (Arm $a \in \chi$, where $\chi \subset \mathbb{R}$). The χ-bandit problem is part of the general problem of the infinitely many-armed bandits (when the number of arms in much greater than the allowed number of plays). Some of the advantages of selecting the arms from a continuous space compared to the discrete many-arms counterpart are: (1) discretization of the space reduces limits the optimization precision to the discretization interval. To obtain a more refined interval it is necessary to add new arms that have lower confidence compared to the existing ones. (2) It is not necessary to discretize and compute the arms prior to the experiment, as well as keeping statistics for them all. (3) infinitely many-armed bandits require less exploration time than finite armed bandits (discretized) in the same conditions [20].

The χ-bandit problem can be represented as finding the arm a^* that minimizes the regret function:

$$a = \pi(\delta), \text{ Arm } a \in \chi, \text{ where } \chi \subset \mathbb{R} \tag{5}$$

$$y = r(a, \delta'), \text{ Reward } y \in \mathbb{R} \tag{6}$$

$$Regret(t) = r(a^*) \cdot t - \sum_{s=1}^{t} \mu(a_s) \tag{7}$$

$$a^* = \arg \min_a Regret(t) \tag{8}$$

The infinitely many-armed bandit problems have been studied in different frameworks, Bayesian, frequentist parametric and frequentist non-parametric settings. The Bayesian problem is to compute the optimal actions efficiently, while the frequentist is to achieve a low rate of regret [21]. A class of algorithms for the frequentist non-parametric setting is the hierarchical optimization. A recent report compares Bayesian and the frequentist non-parametric frameworks concluding that major advantage of a hierarchical optimization algorithms is that they are faster in term of time complexity [18]. In the frequentist non-parametric framework two algorithms stand out, the Bandit Algorithm for Smooth Trees (BAST) and the Hierarchical Optimistic Optimization (HOO) [17]. In this work we use the HOO algorithm, as the BAST algorithm makes strong assumptions on the unknown mean-reward distribution functions that might not be valid in real-world applications [17]. An in-depth discussion and comparison with other algorithms are presented in [18, 21].

The HOO algorithm
The Hierarchical Optimistic Optimization (HOO) algorithm [21] investigates the infinite many-armed bandit problem. This algorithm is classified inside of the hierarchical optimization algorithms in the frequentist non-parametric framework. In this section, we briefly describe the HOO algorithm and its assumptions.

The algorithm makes the stochastic assumption of the mean-reward of any new selected arm. This assumption means that the reward from the new arm is an independent sample from a fixed distribution. The reward is assumed to be in the interval of $y \in [0, 1]$. This assumption is realistic as the reward metric is defined and can be normalized to this range. The other assumption is that the unknown reward function is continuous around the maximum, which is a reasonable assumption in practical problems [21].

The algorithm aims to estimate the underlying unknown reward function f around its maxima while it estimates loosely f in other parts of the space χ. This is implemented using a binary tree in which each arm is associated to a region of the space. The deeper the tree grows the smaller the subset of the space χ that it estimates. The HOO uses an optimistic estimate B, using the upper confidence bound, for each node. The tree is traversed and at each iteration the node of largest bound B, is selected. Based on the reward the tree is updated.

The algorithm starts from the root and selects the child with the largest bound B (ties are broken randomly) until it reaches the leaf. From the traversed path from root to leaf, it randomly selects one node to play. The node statistics are updated and the tree is extended if it is a leaf. The statistics and bounds are computed recursively from the leaf until the root using the formulas below. Below is the notation used in throughout this work (and is the same as the one presented in [21]).

$v((H, I))$ is the value of the node (H, I).

a_{played} is the value of the played arm.

$B_{h,i}$ is the bound for the node i at the height h. The children for this node are $B_{h+1,2i-1}$ and $B_{h+1,2i}$. The root is denoted by the index $(0, 1)$.

n is the current discrete time instance and the mean reward for time is represented by $\widehat{\mu_{h,i}}(n)$.

$T_{h,i}(n)$ is the number of times a node was played until time n.

The bounds are updated according to the formulas below:

$$U_{h,i}(n) = \begin{cases} \widehat{\mu_{h,i}}(n) + \sqrt{\frac{2\ln n}{T_{h,i}(n)}} + v_1\rho^h, & \text{if } T_{h,i}(n) > 0 \\ +\infty, & \text{if } T_{h,i}(n) = 0 \end{cases} \tag{9}$$

$$B_{h,i}(n) = \begin{cases} \min\{U_{h,i}(n), \ \max\{B_{h+1,2i-1}(n), \ B_{h+1,2i}(n)\}\} & \text{if}(h,i) \in \text{Tree}_n \\ +\infty, & \text{otherwise} \end{cases} \tag{10}$$

Apart from the mentioned advantages of χ-armed bandits algorithms in comparison with grid searching, one of the main advantages of this method is the updating of confidence bound of the whole path as a child is selected. Even though a particular node was not played, its confidence bound is updated if any of its descendants are played. This leads to tighter confidence intervals of a whole path. In most grid search and regular multi-armed bandits, the confidence intervals are created and updated only for the discrete played arm.

2.3 Related Work

Optimization in online experiments can be done by using a range of different techniques. The simplest one is conducting sequential A/B/n experiments. This technique has the advantage of having comparable sample sizes for all variations in the statistical analysis at the expense of increase in the regret and the higher sample size for the optimization. Genetic algorithm has also been used in simulation of online experiments. Tamburrelli and Margara [15] proposed an infrastructure and a genetic algorithm to optimize HTML web pages in a large space. However, the proposed solution requires using non-validated assumptions on the hyper-parameters and on the mating strategies. Additionally, the solution requires a large space of unique users that makes it application in real world restricted to very large scale software companies.

Multi-armed bandits algorithms provide a framework for optimization of experiments and it is widely used in industry [14, 22, 23]. Google's Vizier [14] is a tool for black-box optimization that take advantage of multi-armed bandit algorithms. While the paper does not focus on online controlled experiments, it mentions the use of the tool for optimization of web properties such as thumbnail sizes and color scheme. Shang [18] presents an overview of black-box optimization methods using bandits algorithms and Gaussian processes. Mattos et al. [24, 25] presents an architecture framework and architecture decisions to run optimization experiments with a domain specific heuristic for the bandit problem.

3   Research Process

This research was conducted in collaboration with Sony Mobile Communications in Lund, Sweden. Sony Mobile is a subsidiary of Sony Corporation and is a leading global innovator in information technology products for both consumer and professional markets. One of the Sony Mobile's products is transitioning to data-driven development and aims to run experiments continuously throughout its development process. The product consists of a business to business solution, where the user of the software consists of employees of the company that requested the solution. The software development of this product span development for web, mobile, backend systems and distributed embedded hardware. Therefore, the requirements for an experimentation system include the ability of allowing experiments to be run in the variety of supported systems and the capability of supporting both traditional A/B experiments as well as search solutions in a larger or continuous space. An experimentation system (called ACE) that fulfills the requirements was developed following the framework and architecture decisions presented in [24, 25]. A full description of this system is beyond the scope of this paper. During the development of the product several assumptions were made, such as numerical, textual, and GUI constants that has a direct impact in the how the user interact with the system. Some of the numerical assumptions are constants in the real space or in a predetermined range ($x \in \mathbb{R}$ or $x \in [0, 1]$). The development team of this product wants to optimize these constants and to verify these assumptions in based on actual user behavior metrics. The HOO algorithm was selected as the starting point for the optimization search process. The HOO algorithm was implemented in the ACE system and was repeatedly tested and iterated in both simulation and with real users. The results of these iterations were constantly discussed with the product development team and the modifications of this algorithm resulted in the LG-HOO algorithm. The limitations of the HOO algorithm, the changes motivation for the LG-HOO algorithm, and an empirical comparison between both are presented in the Sect. 4.

4   The LG-HOO Algorithm and the Empirical Data

This section presents the modification version of the HOO algorithm [21]. The HOO algorithm was modified to allow its application in online controlled experiments. The LG-HOO follows the same structure as the HOO with the main modifications highlighted below. The growth restrictions motivate the name Limited Growth HOO. The implementation source code, the results for comparison, and the raw data used and the analysis source is available at https://github.com/davidissamattos/LG-HOO.

- A node (arm) is only allowed to grow if it has been played a minimum number of times. This ensures that each arm has a minimum confidence level to ensure the growing in more confident direction. The HOO grows based only on the upper bound of the arm, and this bound can be unrealistic if only one observation has been made, as it grows with $\sqrt{(2 \ln n)/T_{h,\, i}(n)}$. The tradeoff of selecting a minimum growth limit is that it needs a higher number of plays to reach the same level of interval refinements (that is related to the height of the tree). However, as shown later, the minimum growth does not imply that the estimated best arm is further to the theoretical best arm when the underlying function is known.

- The original HOO does not point a method for selecting the best arm, as it is intended to be a continuous process. The algorithm indicates that the highest node on the tree represents the maximum of the underlying function. However, in online experiments, after a period of time the company might want to stop the experiment to save resources, improve performance or make a static decision regarding the change. Given these constraints we defined the process to select the best arm as the node (h, i) with the largest criterion $C_{h,i}$, where

$$
C_{h,i} = \begin{cases} \dfrac{\widehat{\mu_{h,i}}(n)}{\sqrt{\frac{2 \ln n}{T_{h,i}(n)}} + v_1 \rho^h}, & \text{if } T_{h,i}(n) > 0 \\ 0, & \text{if } T_{h,i}(n) = 0 \end{cases} \tag{11}
$$

The idea behind this criterion is to select the node with the largest average while having the lowest bound. This penalizes nodes that have been play few times compared to nodes that have a higher confidence. A downside of this is that it favors nodes that had several plays, and this is usually associated with nodes at lower heights. However, this criterion performs better than the suggested highest height node, when measuring the distance to the theoretical best arm using an absolute Euclidian distance. Note that this criterion does not influence the growth of the tree as it still uses the upper confidence bound to select the best child node.

- The LG-HOO introduces a restriction to the height of the tree. As the tree grows it becomes computationally intensive to update all bounds in a single play iteration. Delays and computational restriction if running in computers with limited resources (such as embedding the algorithm in mobile apps) can significantly impact the user experience. Restricting the tree height puts an upper bound in the computational time, however it limits the precision that the algorithm can reach.

- To facilitates the understanding of the user behavior after running the algorithm for a limited time period, we make an estimation of the underlying mean-reward function using the Savitzky-Golay filter [26] with the decision criterion. Empirically, we determine that a window size of (number of nodes)/2 and a polynomial order equal to the tree's height, to produce good results. The tradeoff of using the Savitzky-Golay smoothing filter is the underestimation of high derivative peaks, leading to a conservative estimation.

- In practice, it often happens that an experiment is coded and then launched without being active (showing for all users the same variation). When the experiment is finally launched several users might be using arms that are not the defined root of the HOO algorithm. Similar situation can also happen in approximation of values by different users/clients. The LG-HOO tries to minimize the number of lost data points by selecting the closest node. If the played arm is closer to the node then its children, the reward is added to the node, otherwise it is discarded. This strategy works under the assumption of continuity of the underlying function while it minimizes the number of discarded data points.

Algorithm 1 represents the full LG-HOO strategy, using the same notation as the HOO, as discussed in the background. This algorithm is implemented in Python 2.7 and is available at https://github.com/davidissamattos/LG-HOO.

Algorithm 1 The LG-HOO algorithm

Input: $\nu_1 > 0$, $\rho \in (0,1)$, minimum growth $\gamma > 0$, tree maximum height σ
Initialization: $\tau = (0,1)$ and $B_{1,2} = B_{2,2} = +\infty$

1: **procedure** SELECT ARM(n)
2:     $(h,i) \leftarrow (0,1)$
3:     $P \leftarrow (h,i)$
4:     **while** $(h,i) \in \tau$ **do**
5:         **if** $B_{h+1,2i-1} > B_{h+1,2i+1}$ **then**
6:             $(h,i) \leftarrow (h+1, 2i-1)$
7:         **else**
8:             **if** $B_{h+1,2i-1} < B_{h+1,2i+1}$ **then** $B_{h+1,2i-1} > B_{h+1,2i}$
9:             **else**
10:                 Z Ber(0.5)
11:                 $(h,i) \leftarrow (h+1, 2i-Z)$
12:         $P \leftarrow P \cup (h,i)$
13:     $(H,I) \leftarrow (h,i)$
14:     Selected arm $\leftarrow U(1, P_{H,I})$
15: **procedure** UPDATE TREE(a_{played}, n, reward Y)
16:     Select the closest arm a_{played} to the node $v((H,I))$
17:     **if** $|a_{\text{played}} - v((H,I))| < \dfrac{|v((H+1,2I)) - v((H+1,2I-1))|}{2}$ **then**
18:         $a_{\text{played}} \leftarrow v((H,I))$
19:     **else**
20:         **break**
21:     **for** all node in $P_{H,I}$ **do**
22:         $T_{h,i} \leftarrow T_{h,i} + 1$
23:         $\hat{\mu}_{h,i} \leftarrow (1 - \dfrac{1}{T_{h,i}})\hat{\mu}_{h,i} + \dfrac{Y}{T_{h,i}}$
24:     **for** all node in τ **do**
25:         $U_{h,i} \leftarrow \hat{\mu}_{h,i} + \sqrt{(2\ln n)/T_{h,i}} + \nu_1\rho^h$
26:     **if** $T_{H,I} > \gamma$ and $H < \sigma$ **then**
27:         $B_{H+1,2I-1} \leftarrow +\infty$
28:         $B_{H+1,2I} \leftarrow +\infty$
29:     **while** node $\neq (0,)$ **do**
30:         $(h,i) \leftarrow$ new leaf
31:         $B_{h,i} \leftarrow \min\{U_{h,i}, \max(B_{h+1,2i-1}, B_{h+1,2i})\}$
32: **procedure** SELECT BEST ARM
33:     $a_{\text{best}} = \max_\tau (\dfrac{\hat{\mu}_{h,i}}{\sqrt{(2\ln n)/T_{h,i}} + \nu_1\rho^h})$
34: **procedure** APPROXIMATION OF THE UNDERLYING FUNCTION
35:     $\hat{f} = \text{Savitzky-Golay}((\dfrac{\hat{\mu}_{h,i}}{\sqrt{(2\ln n)/T_{h,i}} + \nu_1\rho^h}), \text{number of nodes}/2, \max_\tau h)$

The repository presents additional information on the connection of the algorithm with the implemented code. The algorithm is composed of four procedures. The first procedure is the procedure that selects the arm to be played in with the current tree. The second is called after an arm is played and a reward is received, updating and extending the tree. The third selects the best arm, when the optimization process is being finalized. The forth estimates the mean-reward function using the Savitzky-Golay filter.

4.1 The LG-HOO in Simulation

In this subsection, we provide some illustrative pictures of the LG-HOO algorithm in a simulation environment using different mean reward functions. Figure 1 shows the usage of the LG-HOO algorithm in 6 different conditions. The orange line is the true mean-reward function that determines the probability of a Bernoulli distribution $Y = Ber(f(x))$. Where Y is the measure value (0 or 1, click or no click) and $f(x)$ is the mean reward function with variation x. This line can represent a customer profile (that is unknown but we still want to optimize a variation for this function). This profile can be complex as the picture in the left-top corner or simpler such as the picture in left-middle with only three ranges of value. The optimization process consists of finding the variation x that maximizes the mean reward function based only on the stochastic measured Y.

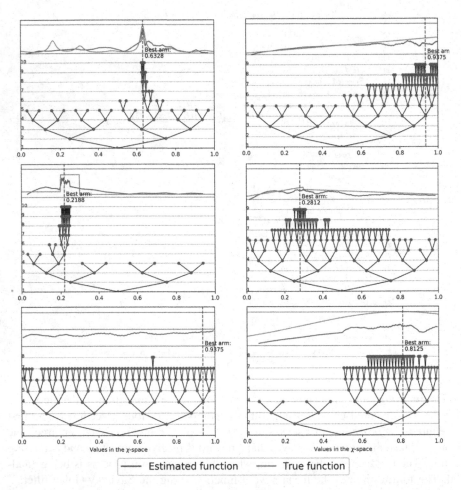

Fig. 1. Simulation results of the LG-HOO algorithm in wide range of different user mean-reward functions. In orange, is the true mean-reward function (unknown to the LG-HOO). In blue, is the estimated mean-reward function. The tree represents the LG-HOO search process at the end of the iteration, and the blue vertical line represents the best arm selection using the proposed selection criterion. The top-left subplot represents the same mean-reward function discussed in the original HOO algorithm [21]. (Color figure online)

These simulations show how the LG-HOO algorithm work and estimate the mean reward function (blue line). All the simulations were conducted considering a total of 10,000 unique interactions (horizon $n = 10,000$), using the minimum growth of 10, maximum tree height limit of 10, $v_1 = 1.0$, and $\rho = 0.5$, which is representative of the amount of data collected in a period of one month of the conducted experiment with Sony Mobile. We can see that with this number of unique interactions we can estimate the parameter that maximizes mean reward function.

4.2   The LG-HOO at Sony Mobile

The LG-HOO was implemented in the context of the product described in Sect. 3. One of the features of the product has an algorithm that estimates the time for launching a notification to users. If the notification arrives too early the users can ignore it and the feature has little value. If it arrives too late it can have a negative impact in the overall user experience. Before the experiment, the feature was using the minimum time scenario (reducing even more the time makes the notification arrives too late). The impact of the notification is measured depending on the action the user takes after receiving the notification. This metric is a stochastic variable that follows a Bernoulli distribution, where 1 (positive value) represents when the user takes an action in time and 0 when the user does not take an action in time (negative). The metric is stochastic because different factors not related to the time of the notification might influence the user action. The team wanted to investigate if a change in the algorithm that modifies the notification time impacts the metric. The hypothesis of this experiment is that adding a constant delay in the algorithm could indicate the extent the algorithm influences the metric and if development effort was needed to improve it. The team also wanted to minimize the regret of too early notifications. Sequential A/B/n experiments would take too long to cover the whole extent of search space while increasing the regret. This scenario sets an appropriate experiment for a continuum-armed bandit algorithm such as the LG-HOO.

The experiment consisted of searching an appropriate delay offset for the notification. The experiment limited the offset in the range of 0 and 600,000 ms (10 min). The users were assigned to a new variation delay every time they launched their mobile applications, and they logged their behavior right after the timeout to complete the action.

The LG-HOO was implemented in the ACE system in Python 2.7. The ACE system is hosted in the Google App Engine Flexible cloud environment[1]. The company application logged data and requested variation arms from the ACE system using POST requests. In case of lost packages or failure in requesting a new variation, the system uses the current variation (offset of zero). The parameters of the LG-HOO in this scenario are: minimum growth of 10, maximum tree height limit of 10, $v_1 = 1.0$, and $\rho = 0.5$. The limit in the tree height restricts the precision of the output of the algorithm in approximately 500 ms, which is considered good level of precision for the application. For this experiment, it was collected data from over 5000 user interactions

---

[1] https://cloud.google.com/appengine/docs/flexible/.

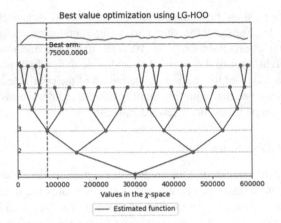

Fig. 2. The LG-HOO used in the Sony Mobile case. This picture provides both the visualization of the search tree, as well as the approximated mean-reward function and the selected best arm.

in the period of 4 weeks. The results and the outputs of the algorithm are shown in Fig. 2. This Figure provides both the visualization of the search tree, as well as the approximated mean-reward function and the selected best arm. The mean-reward function indicates that the offset does not have a large influence in the selected metric for the extent of the whole range of delays, but it still shows that a small delay can improve the concerned metric.

For the team the approximation of the of the mean reward function was important because it maps how the users behave in respect to this modification on the system, and therefore can help decisions such as to modify the feature, try other experiments on the feature or related features or move the development effort to another part of the system.

This section described the LG-HOO algorithm, the modifications, and trade-offs of the LG-HOO. In the simulation subsection, we provide simulation results and evidence of the LG-HOO being applied to different mean-reward functions. The simulation results allowed us to implement the LG-HOO algorithm with confidence in an industrial setting in collaboration with Sony Mobile. As there is no industrial evidence of the use of the HOO algorithm, some of its limitations were unknown prior to this work. The industrial case provides real-world evidence of the use of the LG-HOO in online experiments.

5   Discussion

Prior to launching the algorithm to real users, a comparison between the HOO and the LG-HOO was made and is discussed in this section. The algorithms were compared using the absolute Euclidian distance to the theoretical maximum and the time to compute an algorithm iteration. The first comparison looks at how far the algorithm got from the true value and relates to the following LG-HOO modifications: (1) the selection of the best arm policy modification and (2) the minimum number of times an arm must be played before growing. The second comparison relates to degradation of user experience and performance of the system due to the introduction of delays in the estimation of the next arm to be played.

The algorithms were compared using a Monte Carlo simulation comparing one thousand runs with a horizon of $n = 1000$. At each simulation of the algorithm, it was used a generated random polynomial function as the true mean-reward function $f(x)$. The polynomial functions were generated by: (1) generating a set of 30 random points in the (x, y) plane, (2) fitting a polynomial with random order (ranging between 0 and 10) to these points, and (3) constraining both the space (x) and the mean reward probability (y) between 0 and 1. The user follows a Bernoulli distribution $Bern(f(x))$, where $y = f(x)$, and 1 represents a success. With this method we generate random polynomial functions that are used as the mean reward functions to simulate the user profile for the algorithms. With this method we can simulated both algorithms against the same set of true mean reward functions and compare the LG-HOO and the HOO solutions with the true solution using the absolute Euclidean distance.

The time spent in the calculation for selecting the next arm and the Euclidian distance were done in the same hardware and operational conditions. The data collected from this Monte Carlo simulation, and the conducted analysis is also available at repository. The collected data for the Euclidian distance and the time spent metrics for both algorithms are non-normal, Shapiro-Wilk test with p < 2.2e−16 and by visual inspection. Therefore, we compared the two algorithms metrics using the Mann-Whitney U non-parametric test [27]. We considered as null hypothesis that the respective LG-HOO metric does not differ from the HOO metric. Table 1 provides a summary of the statistical analysis. This statistical analysis provide evidence that the LG-HOO reduces the distance average Euclidian in 14.3% and reduces the spent time in 26%, using a confidence level of 95%. Due to the increased performance of the LG-HOO regarding to the correctness of the output and the computation time, only the LG-HOO algorithm was selected for empirical evaluation in the company case. The data and code to run this statistical analysis is available at the repository.

Table 1. Summary of the statistical analysis to compare the LG-HOO and the HOO algorithms using the Mann-Whitney U test, using a confidence level of 95%

Metric	Algorithm	Mean value	Absolute relative difference	P-value
Euclidian distance	LG-HOO	0.293	14.3%	0.04179
	HOO	0.335		
Time spent (in seconds)	LG-HOO	1.00	26%	<2.2e−16
	HOO	1.26		

6 Conclusion

Optimization procedures associated with bandit algorithms are of great interest to companies running online experiments. A particular case is the optimization of a continuous space in the presence of an unknown mean-reward function. As companies develop their products, several user assumptions are incorporated into constants in their software development. Optimization in this scenario is a subclass of bandit problems called infinitely many-armed bandits. Previous research provides algorithms to solve this problem in the unidimensional space. However, these algorithms do not have empirical evidence or usage in online experiments and have restrictions that prevent their utilization as proposed. This work explores the unidimensional infinitely many-armed bandits problem in collaboration with Sony Mobile Communications.

The contribution of this work is three-fold. First, we present a modification of the Hierarchical Optimistic Optimization algorithm (HOO), called the Limited Growth Hierarchical Optimistic Optimization algorithm (LG-HOO). This modification is intended to overcome the problems associate with implementing the HOO algorithm in real-world online experiments. The modifications and the trade-offs involved with these modifications are presented. Second, the LG-HOO was implemented in collaboration with Sony Mobile. In this scenario, we provide real-world evidence of the usage of this algorithm for optimization of software constants. Third, we provide a statistical comparison between the LG-HOO and the HOO algorithm in simulation. The statistical analysis supports the conclusion that the LG-HOO perform better than the HOO, in the time spent to run and the accuracy of the results. These contributions support the relevance of the LG-HOO algorithm in the context of optimization experiments and show how the algorithm can be used to support continuous optimization of online systems in stochastic scenarios.

This work is the first step in analyzing the usage of infinitely many-armed bandit algorithms in optimization procedures in software development. In future work, we plan to expand the LG-HOO to support multi-dimensional arm space, support a multi-dimensional reward, as these are one of the key aspects that companies want to provide optimization, and validate these extensions in relevant industrial problems.

Acknowledgments. This work was partially supported by the Wallenberg Artificial Intelligence, Autonomous Systems and Software Program (WASP) funded by Knut and Alice Wallenberg Foundation. The authors would also like to thank to all the support provided by the development team at Sony Mobile.

References

1. Kevic, K., Murphy, B., Williams, L., Beckmann, J.: Characterizing experimentation in continuous deployment: a case study on bing. In: Proceedings - 2017 IEEE/ACM 39th International Conference on Software Engineering: Software Engineering in Practice Track, ICSE-SEIP 2017, pp. 123–132 (2017)
2. Fabijan, A., Dmitriev, P., Olsson, H.H., Bosch, J.: The evolution of continuous experimentation in software product development. In: Proceedings of the 39th International Conference on Software Engineering ICSE 2017 (2017)
3. Fabijan, A.: Developing the right features: the role and impact of customer and product data in software product development (2016)
4. Dmitriev, P., Wu, X.: Measuring metrics. In: Proceedings of the 25th ACM International Conference on Information and Knowledge. Management - CIKM 2016, pp. 429–437 (2016)

5. Schermann, G., Cito, J., Leitner, P.: Continuous experimentation - challenges, implementation techniques, and current research. IEEE Softw. **35**, 1 (2018)
6. Tang, D., Agarwal, A., O'Brien, D., Meyer, M.: Overlapping experiment infrastructure. In: Proceedings of the 16th ACM SIGKDD international conference on Knowledge discovery and data mining - KDD 2010, p. 17 (2010)
7. Bakshy, E., Eckles, D., Bernstein, M.S.: Designing and deploying online field experiments. In: Proceedings of the 23rd International Conference on World wide web - WWW 2014, pp. 283–292, September 2014
8. Kohavi, R., Deng, A., Longbotham, R., Xu, Y.: Seven rules of thumb for web site experimenters. In: Proceedings of the 20th ACM SIGKDD International Conference Knowledge Discovery and data Mining, KDD 2014, pp. 1857–1866 (2014)
9. Xu, Y., Duan, W., Huang, S.: SQR: balancing speed, quality and risk in online experiments, no. 1, pp. 1–9, January 2018
10. Fabijan, A., Dmitriev, P., Olsson, H.H., Bosch, J.: The benefits of controlled experimentation at scale. In: Proceedings of the 43rd Euromicro Conference on Software Engineering and Advanced Applications, SEAA 2017, pp. 18–26 (2017)
11. Gui, H., Xu, Y., Bhasin, A., Han, J.: Network A/B testing. In: Proceedings of the 24th International Conference on World Wide Web - WWW 2015, pp. 399–409 (2015)
12. Li, L., Chu, W., Langford, J., Schapire, R.E.: A contextual-bandit approach to personalized news article recommendation. In: WWW 2010, p. 10 (2010)
13. Bottou, L., Peters, J., Quiñonero-Candela, J., Charles, D.X., Chickering, D.M., Portugaly, E., Ray, D., Simard, P., Snelson, E.: Counterfactual reasoning and learning systems. J. Mach. Learn. Res. **14**, 3207–3260 (2013)
14. Golovin, D., Solnik, B., Moitra, S., Kochanski, G., Karro, J., Sculley, D.: Google vizier. In: Proceedings of the 23rd ACM SIGKDD International Conference on Knowledge Discovery and Data Mining - KDD 2017, pp. 1487–1495 (2017)
15. Tamburrelli, G., Margara, A.: Towards automated A/B testing. In: Le Goues, C., Yoo, S. (eds.) SSBSE 2014. LNCS, vol. 8636, pp. 184–198. Springer, Cham (2014). https://doi.org/10.1007/978-3-319-09940-8_13
16. Sutton, R.S., Barto, A.G.: Sutton & Barto Book: Reinforcement Learning: An Introduction. The MIT Press, Cambridge (1998)
17. Burtini, G., Loeppky, J., Lawrence, R.: A survey of online experiment design with the stochastic multi-armed bandit, pp. 1–49, October 2015
18. Shang, X., Kaufmann, E., Valko, M.: Hierarchical Bandits for "Black Box " Optimization, Lille, (2015)
19. Kohavi, R., Longbotham, R., Sommerfield, D., Henne, R.M.: Controlled experiments on the web: survey and practical guide. Data Min. Knowl. Discov. **18**(1), 140–181 (2009)
20. Wang, Y., Audibert, J.-Y., Munos, R.: Algorithms for infinitely many-armed bandits. In: Advances in Neural Information Processing Systems, pp. 1–8 (2008)
21. Bubeck, S., Munos, R., Stoltz, G., Szepesvári, C.: X - Armed Bandits. J. Mach. Learn. Res. **12**, 1655–1695 (2011)
22. Urban, G.L., Liberali, G.G., MacDonald, E., Bordley, R., Hauser, J.R.: Morphing banner advertising. Mark. Sci. **33**(1), 27–46 (2014)
23. Li, L., Chu, W., Langford, J., Schapire, R.E.: A contextual-bandit approach to personalized news article recommendation. In: Proceedings of the 19th International Conference on World Wide Web, 2010, pp. 661–670 (2010)
24. Mattos, D.I., Bosch, J., Olsson, H.H.: Your system gets better every day you use it: towards automated continuous experimentation. In: Proceedings of the 43rd Euromicro Conference on Software Engineering and Advanced Applications (SEAA) (2017)

25. Mattos, D.I., Bosch, J., Olsson, H.H.: More for less: automated experimentation in software-intensive systems. In: Felderer, M., Méndez Fernández, D., Turhan, B., Kalinowski, M., Sarro, F., Winkler, D. (eds.) PROFES 2017. LNCS, vol. 10611, pp. 146–161. Springer, Cham (2017). https://doi.org/10.1007/978-3-319-69926-4_12
26. Savitzky, A., Golay, M.J.E.: Smoothing and differentiation of data by simplified least squares procedures. Anal. Chem. **36**(8), 1627–1639 (1964)
27. Juristo, N., Moreno, A.M.: Basics of Software Engineering Experimentation, vol. 5/6. Springer, Hidelberg (2001). https://doi.org/10.1007/978-1-4757-3304-4

Incremental Control Dependency Frontier Exploration for Many-Criteria Test Case Generation

Annibale Panichella[1]($\boxtimes$), Fitsum Meshesha Kifetew[2], and Paolo Tonella[3]

[1] Delft University of Technology, Delft, The Netherlands
a.panichella@tudelft.nl
[2] Fondazione Bruno Kessler, Trento, Italy
kifetew@fbk.eu
[3] Università della Svizzera Italiana(USI), Lugano, Switzerland
paolo.tonella@gmail.com

Abstract. Several criteria have been proposed over the years for measuring test suite adequacy. Each criterion can be converted into a specific objective function to optimize with search-based techniques in an attempt to generate test suites achieving the highest possible coverage for that criterion. Recent work has tried to optimize for multiple-criteria at once by constructing a single objective function obtained as a weighted sum of the objective functions of the respective criteria. However, this solution suffers the problem of sum scalarization, i.e., differences along the various dimensions being optimized get lost when such dimensions are projected into a single value. Recent advances in SBST formulated coverage as a many-objective optimization problem rather than applying sum scalarization. Starting from this formulation, in this work, we apply many-objective test generation that handles multiple adequacy criteria simultaneously. To scale the approach to the big number of objectives to be optimized at the same time, we adopt an incremental strategy, where only coverage targets in the control dependency frontier are considered until the frontier is expanded by covering a previously uncovered target.

1 Introduction

Various coverage criteria, such as branch or mutation coverage, have been proposed to measure how thoroughly a given test suite exercises the program under test. Correspondingly, automated test case generation has focused on the achievement of these criteria as the objectives of the generation process. While these criteria have been tackled mostly independently from each other, a recent work by Rojas et al. [19] has proposed a test generation approach that optimizes for multiple criteria simultaneously. With this strategy, the individual fitness functions of each criterion are aggregated via weighted sum and optimized using single-objective search algorithms [19]. The resulting test suites are able to detect more faults compared to those generated with a single criterion [11].

© Springer Nature Switzerland AG 2018
T. E. Colanzi and P. McMinn (Eds.): SSBSE 2018, LNCS 11036, pp. 309–324, 2018.
https://doi.org/10.1007/978-3-319-99241-9_17

While the aforementioned studies showed the benefits of focusing on multiple criteria, the weighted sum suffers from well-known theoretical limitations [7]: (i) it is not able to find optimal solutions for *non-convex* problems; (ii) small changes in the weights may lead to completely different solutions; (iii) differences along the various criteria being optimized get lost when they are projected into a single value. Moreover, the weighted sum is based on the assumption that the criteria being summed-up are independent of each other. However, this assumption is not applicable in coverage testing, because of the *subsumption* relationships between coverage targets, due to the control dependencies in the program under test. For example, to cover the lines of code in a basic block, the conditional branch leading to it must be covered first. In turn, the branch condition could be nested inside another conditional statement that controls its execution.

In our recent work [16,17] we applied many-objective algorithms to handle single coverage criterion in which each criterion is handled as a different objective to optimize in a many-objective fashion. To cope with a possibly large number of objectives, coverage targets are selected dynamically by the proposed algorithm, DynaMOSA [17]. This incremental/dynamic search helps achieve higher coverage than sum scalarization when focusing on a single criterion [4,17].

In this paper, we extend the idea of many-objective dynamic test generation to multiple heterogeneous criteria being optimized simultaneously. First, we define an *enhanced control dependency graph* (ECDG), a variant of the classical *control dependency graph* (CDG)[1] enriched with the structural dependencies among coverage targets coming from different coverage criteria (e.g., lines of code, mutants, etc.). Second, we introduce a search algorithm, which we named MC-DynaMOSA, that performs incremental exploration of the control dependency frontier to achieve multiple criteria coverage. In particular, coverage targets are incrementally selected during the search according to their position in the ECDG, where the covered frontier expands over time. The results of our empirical study show that the incremental exploration implemented in MC-DynaMOSA is more effective than (i) using the weighted sum with archiving strategy (MC-WSA), and (ii) handling all coverage criteria as fully independent objectives (MC-MOSA). Effectiveness is measured as the ability of the generated test suites in both (i) achieving higher coverage scores for seven testing criteria and (ii) detecting more faults. Furthermore, our results confirm that combining multiple criteria leads to test suites with superior fault revealing capability.

2   Background and Related Work

Several criteria have been proposed for structural coverage over the years. In this work, we focus on branch, line, method, weak mutation, input, output, and exception coverage [19]. In the context of Search-based Software Testing (SBST), each of these coverage criteria is associated with a fitness function that is used to

---

[1] A control dependency edge between two nodes holds *iff* the latter is not a post-dominator of the former, while it is a post-dominator of all intermediate nodes between the two.

guide the test generation process towards test cases that achieve the maximum possible coverage for that particular criterion.

Branch coverage (BC): is the most widely adopted coverage criterion. The fitness function of a test case t with respect to a branch b is computed by considering the sum of the *approach level (al)* and the normalized *branch distance (bd)* [15]: $f(t, b) = al(t, b) + norm(bd(t, b))$, where $norm$ is a function that normalizes values into the range $[0, 1]$.

Line coverage (LC): is the simplest and most straightforward coverage criterion, which measures coverage of non-comment lines of code in the System Under Test (SUT). The associated fitness function is computed by minimizing the distance to the closest branch on which the line is control dependent.

Weak mutation coverage (WMC): is a coverage criterion based on mutation where a mutant is considered *weakly killed* if for a given test case t, the execution of t on the mutant results in a different internal state than the original program. Differently, from strong mutation coverage, the internal state difference (aka *infection* [21]) may not necessarily propagate to any externally visible difference (e.g., to a return value). Given a mutant μ and a test t, the fitness function for calculating WMC is defined based on a heuristic *infection distance (id)* as follows: $f(t, \mu) = al(t, \mu) + norm(bd(t, \mu)) + norm(id(t, \mu))$, where approach level and branch distance refer to the branch which holds a control dependency on μ, while $id(t, \mu)$ estimates the distance to infecting the mutant state. If the mutation is executed, the minimal state infection distance depends on the mutation operator that was applied and is estimated as the numerical distance from a value that would make the states of mutant and original program differ. If the mutation is not executed, the normalized infection distance is equal to 1 [20].

Input coverage (IC): captures the diversity in the inputs to the SUT used by the test cases. It measures how spread the values are in the SUT input space.

Output coverage (OC): captures the diversity of the values output by methods in the SUT. Ultimately, it measures the uniqueness of the output values produced as a result of executing a test on the SUT.

Exception coverage (EC): measures the number of exceptions triggered by the execution of a test. The more exceptions a test triggers, the higher EC.

Method coverage (MC): requires that every method of the SUT be called, either directly or indirectly, by at least one test case.

When used as components of SBST, not all fitness functions of the various criteria mentioned above provide the same degree of guidance to the search. In fact, in our experience, IC, OC, EC, and MC contribute little or no guidance to the search during test generation. On the other hand, criteria such as BC, LC, and WMC provide strong guidance to the search. The reason for such stronger guidance is that all the mentioned criteria are, directly or indirectly, associated with some underlying branches that must be necessarily covered because they hold a control dependency on the coverage targets.

Multiple Criteria Coverage. The first attempt to combine multiple coverage criteria was proposed by Rojas et al. [19]. The authors aggregated the various coverage criteria using a weighted sum with uniform weights (equal to 1), and have left further investigation of different weight assignments to future work. The approach was implemented in EvoSuite [10], and experimental results on subjects sampled from the SF110 corpus [10] showed that adding a second criterion besides line coverage resulted in 14% increase in test suite size and 20% increase in coverage. On the other hand, using all coverage criteria increased test suite size by 70%, while the coverage of the individual criteria was reduced on average by just 0.4%. Overall, the work provides encouraging evidence that combining multiple coverage criteria during test generation is feasible and beneficial.

After this initial work by Rojas et al., recent work explored, beyond feasibility, fine-grained analysis of combinations of multiple criteria. In particular, Gay [11] explored the ability of test suites, generated via multiple criteria, of exposing known, real-world faults, considering the Defects4J benchmark [12]. Results show that combining multiple criteria could improve fault detection up to 31%.

A recent trend in automated test case generation consists in recasting it as a many-objective optimization problem [2,16,17]. However, none of the existing work on multi-criteria coverage [11,19] takes advantage of the recent, advanced many-objective test generation algorithms. In fact, they aggregate all fitness functions associated with multiple criteria into a single fitness function by means of sum scalarization [6]. This paper presents the first attempt to apply many-objective test generation to multiple coverage criteria, rather than just to the multiple targets that can be found for a single criterion.

Recently, we introduced MOSA (Many-Objective Sorting Algorithm), a many-objective genetic algorithm that considers each coverage target as an independent objective to be optimized [16]. It employs a specialized preference criterion to favor promising individuals in the search. Such a preference criterion helps MOSA focus the search on the most promising individuals, whereas traditional dominance-based ranking would have resulted in a larger number of non-dominated individuals, which are not necessarily useful for covering new targets. Empirical results show that MOSA is indeed superior to state-of-the-art single objective approaches [16]. MOSA was later improved by its successor DynaMOSA [17] with the objective of increasing the efficiency of the test generation process. Indeed, in the presence of a high number of coverage targets, MOSA could suffer from the algorithmic overhead for computing the Pareto fronts. DynaMOSA introduces a smarter approach for dealing with this issue, by dynamically adding new targets to be covered each time a previously uncovered target is reached. DynaMOSA starts with branches that represent method entries, and every time a branch is covered, all targets dependent on the covered branch are added to the set of targets to be covered.

A recent study by Campos et al. [4] empirically explored the performance of various test generation algorithms. They compared variants of traditional Evolutionary Algorithms (EAs), MOSA, DynaMOSA, and Random Search in terms of various coverage metrics. Results showed that EAs, supported by test archives, perform better than random search. Furthermore, many-objective algorithms (MOSA, DynaMOSA) achieve superior performance on branch coverage.

This paper shares with DynaMOSA [4,17] the idea of dynamically updating the coverage targets to be addressed by many-objective optimization. However, DynaMOSA cannot be applied directly to multiple, heterogeneous criteria. In this paper, we extend the idea of dynamic target update to take into account targets of heterogeneous nature (mutants, branches, diversity, etc.). Our intuition is that the benefits brought by considering multiple coverage targets at the same time could be even larger when not only multiple targets but also multiple criteria, which in turn include multiple targets, are considered at the same time.

3   Approach

Our approach relies on control dependency analysis and branch/dependency coverage as the guiding criterion, and exploits this guidance to effectively explore the search space with respect to all the other criteria. Moreover, our approach optimizes for multiple criteria via many-objective optimization, rather than summing up several different fitness functions into a single-objective function.

Problem Formulation. Given a SUT, the multiple criteria test generation problem can be formulated as follows: *Let $B = \alpha \cup \beta \cup \ldots \cup \omega$ be the set of all coverage targets representing different adequacy criteria $\alpha, \beta, \ldots, \omega$ and corresponding fitness functions $f_\alpha, f_\beta, \ldots, f_\omega$. Find a set of test cases $T = \{t_1, \ldots, t_n\}$ that minimize the fitness functions for all targets $\tau_i \in B$.* This formulation gives rise to the many-objective optimization problem for minimizing the following $k_\alpha + k_\beta + \ldots + k_\omega$ objectives:

$$
\begin{cases}
\min O_{\alpha,1}(t) = f_\alpha(\tau_{\alpha,1}, t), \ldots, & \min O_{\alpha,k_\alpha}(t) = f_\alpha(\tau_{\alpha,k_\alpha}, t) \\
\min O_{\beta,1}(t) = f_\beta(\tau_{\beta,1}, t), \ldots, & \min O_{\beta,k_\beta}(t) = f_\beta(\tau_{\beta,k_\beta}, t) \\
\vdots & \\
\min O_{\omega,1}(t) = f_\omega(\tau_{\omega,1}, t), \ldots, & \min O_{\omega,k_\omega}(t) = f_\omega(\tau_{\omega,k_\omega}, t)
\end{cases}
\tag{1}
$$

where $f_\alpha, f_\beta, \ldots, f_\omega$ represent the fitness functions of adequacy criteria $\alpha, \beta, \ldots, \omega$.

Example. To explain our approach, we present a simple example whose code is shown in Fig. 1(a). In the example, three types of coverage targets are indicated: (i) branches $\alpha = \{b_1, b_2, b_3, b_4\}$, (ii) lines $\beta = \{l1, \ldots, l8\}$, and (iii) mutants $\gamma = \{\mu_1, \mu_2\}$. The final set of coverage targets would be: $B = \alpha \cup \beta \cup \gamma = \{l_1, \ldots, l_8, b_1, b_2, b_3, b_4, \mu_1, \mu_2\}$, and the problem consists of finding a set of test cases that achieve full coverage of all targets in B. The control dependency graph (CDG) of the example program is shown in Fig. 1(b). We can see from the CDG that the branches in the sample program are interdependent, with some branches being control dependent on others. For example, branch b_2 can only be executed after branch b_1 has been executed.

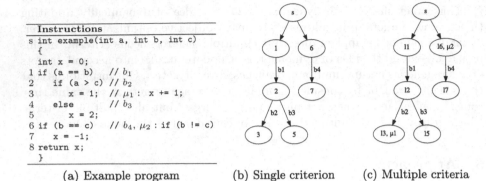

(a) Example program   (b) Single criterion   (c) Multiple criteria

Fig. 1. Code (left), CDG (middle), and ECDG (right) of an example program

---

Algorithm 1: MC-DynaMOSA

Input:
$B = \{\tau_1, \ldots, \tau_m\}$ the set of coverage targets of a program.
$CDG = \langle N, E, s \rangle$: control dependency graph of the program
Result: A test suite T

1 **begin**
2     $\phi \longleftarrow$ EXTEND-CDG(CDG, B)
3     $B^* \longleftarrow$ ENTRY-POINTS (CDG, ϕ, B) //targets without control dependencies
4     $P_t \longleftarrow$ RANDOM-POPULATION(M) // followed by fitness evaluation
5   archive $\longleftarrow$ UPDATE-ARCHIVE($P_t, \emptyset$) // collect tests covering new targets
6     $B^* \longleftarrow$ UPDATE-TARGETS(B^*, CDG, ϕ)
7   **while** not (search_budget_consumed) AND ($B^* \neq \emptyset$) **do**
8        $P_{t+1} \longleftarrow$ EVOLVE(P_t) // crossover, mutation, evaluation, selection
9   archive $\longleftarrow$ UPDATE-ARCHIVE(P_{t+1}, archive)
10        $B^* \longleftarrow$ UPDATE-TARGETS(B^*, CDG, ϕ)
11     $T \longleftarrow$ archive

3.1 MC-DynaMOSA: Many-Criteria Dynamic Many-Objective Optimization with Incremental Frontier Exploration

Our approach, MC-DynaMOSA (Many-Criteria Dynamic Many-objective Sorting Algorithm) hereafter, optimizes for multiple criteria simultaneously by representing the various coverage criteria into an *Enhanced CDG* (ECDG), in such a way that the control dependency based frontier exploration can be performed on multiple criteria using the ECDG as guidance. The high-level algorithm used to build the ECDG is outlined in Algorithm 2: the original CDG is enriched with the coverage targets that are control dependent on each branch. For example, the ECDG for the program in Fig. 1(a) is depicted in Fig. 1(c): the coverage targets related to line, branch, and weak mutation are all represented in the ECDG, as either node or edge labels, because the associated fitness functions can be computed only when executing the frontier node whose outgoing control dependency edge leads to the target. For method, input and output coverage, the corresponding targets are associated with the root branch of the ECDG: if the root branch is covered it implies that the method has been called/covered and therefore it is possible to measure the diversity of both its input and output.

Algorithm 2: EXTEND-CDG

Input:
$G = \langle N, E, s \rangle$: control dependency graph of the program
B: set of all coverage targets
Result:
$\phi : E \to \mathcal{P}(B)$: partial map between edges and targets
1 **begin**
2    $\forall e \in E : \phi(e) \longleftarrow \emptyset$
3   **for** $\tau \in B$ **do**
4      $e \longleftarrow getImmediateControlDependency(\tau)$
5      $\phi(e) \longleftarrow \phi(e) \cup \{\tau\}$

Algorithm 3: UPDATE-TARGETS

Input:
$CDG = \langle N, E, s \rangle$: control dependency graph
$B^* \subseteq B$: current set of targets
$\phi : E \to B$: partial map between edges and targets
Result:
B^*: updated set of current targets
1 **begin**
2   **for** $\tau \in B^*$ **do**
3   **if** τ *is covered* **then**
4        $B^* \longleftarrow B^* - \{\tau\}$
5        $e_\tau \longleftarrow \phi^{-1}(\tau)$
6        $B^* \longleftarrow$ADD-NEXT-TARGETS(B^*, e_τ)

Algorithm 4: ADD-NEXT-TARGETS

Input:
$CDG = \langle N, E, s \rangle$: control dependency graph
$B^* \subseteq B$: current set of targets
Result:
B^*: updated set of current targets
1 **begin**
2   **for** *each* $e_n \in E$ *immediately following* e *in* CDG **do**
3   **for** *each* $\tau \in \phi(e_n)$ **do**
4   **if** τ *is not covered* **then**
5          $B^* \longleftarrow B^* \cup \{\tau\}$
6   **return** B^*

The high-level algorithm of MC-DynaMOSA is shown in Algorithm 1. As outlined in Algorithm 1, MC-DynaMOSA starts (line 2) by building the enhanced CDG using Algorithm 2, which essentially extends the CDG by attaching coverage targets to the edges of the CDG which hold a control dependency over the targets. Once the ECDG is built (i.e., function ϕ has been determined), MC-DynaMOSA computes the initial set of coverage targets from the ECDG by collecting the targets in the initial frontier, i.e., those targets which are not under any control dependency (line 3). It then generates the initial population of individuals (test cases) and evaluates them (line 4). Subsequently, it collects individuals that cover one or more previously uncovered targets (line 5). It then enters an evolutionary loop in which it evolves the individuals by applying genetic operators (crossover, mutation, fitness evaluation, and selection), resulting in the next generation of individuals (line 8). It then collects individuals covering new targets (line 9), and finally updates the current set of targets by removing those covered and adding the targets which have the covered targets as their control dependencies (line 10). This process continues until either the search budget is finished or all targets are covered. Finally, the archive of test cases collected throughout the process is returned as the final solution, i.e., the test suite (line 11).

We now illustrate the MC-DynaMOSA algorithm on the example in Fig. 1(a) whose ECDG is shown in Fig. 1(c). A possible execution trace of MC-DynaMOSA is shown in Table 1. In the beginning, the set of current targets are those with no control dependency (second row in Table 1). When target $b1$ is covered (which also means $l1, l2$ are covered), the set of current targets is updated by removing $b1, l1, l2$ and adding other targets over which $b1$ holds a control dependency according to the ECDG, i.e., $b2, b3$ (third row in Table 1). Similarly, as new

Table 1. A simulation of MC-DynaMOSA on the example

	Current targets	Covered targets
init	$\{l1, l6, \mu2, b1, b4\}$	$\{\}$
b1 covered	$\{b2, b3, \mu2, b4\}$	$\{l1, b1, l2, l6\}$
b4 covered	$\{b2, b3, \mu2\}$	$\{l1, b1, l2, l6, b4, l7\}$
b2 covered	$\{b3, \mu2, \mu1\}$	$\{l1, b1, l2, l6, b4, l7, b2, l3\}$
b3 covered	$\{\mu2, \mu1\}$	$\{l1, b1, l2, l6, b4, l7, b2, l3, b3, l5\}$
$\mu2$ covered	$\{\mu1\}$	$\{l1, b1, l2, l6, b4, l7, b2, l3, b3, l5, \mu2\}$

branches are covered, new targets are added to the set of current targets incrementally following the ECDG. Finally, MC-DynaMOSA may be able to cover all targets or may fail to cover some, as in this case where target $\mu1$ remains uncovered at the end of the process.

4 Empirical Evaluation

To evaluate the performance of MC-DynaMOSA, we conducted an empirical study with a set of non-trivial Java classes selected from different open-source projects.

Research Questions. Our first RQ aims at assessing the benefits (if any) of using incremental many-objective search compared to the weighted-sum:

RQ1: *What is the effectiveness of unified many-objective/multi-criteria coverage compared to the weighted-sum approach?*

Furthermore, we want to investigate how MC-DynaMOSA performs compared with a simple many-objective search that considers all coverage targets related to different coverage criteria as independent search objectives:

RQ2: *What are the benefits of incremental control dependency frontier exploration?*

A key observation in the previous section is that existing coverage criteria can be directly related to branch-coverage (via ECDG) and that control dependency branches can be used to guide multi-criteria coverage. Hence, the next question is whether combining multiple criteria and performing an incremental many-objective search provides any benefits over optimizing just branch coverage:

RQ3: *Is it enough to target all branches in order to achieve high coverage of all the other criteria?*

Moreover, we question whether multi-criteria coverage is associated with higher fault detection than branch coverage alone:

RQ4: *What is the fault detection capability of the final test suites obtained by many-criteria coverage vs branch coverage only?*

In the following, we refer to MC-WSA (Multi-criteria Weighted Sum with Archives) and MC-MOSA (Multi-criteria Many-Objective) as the baselines for RQ1 and RQ2, respectively. For RQ3, we refer to SC-DynaMOSA (Single-Criteria Many-Objective) for the many-objective algorithm (DynaMOSA) that optimizes branch coverage alone.

Benchmark. The benchmark of our study is a set of 180 non-trivial Java classes randomly sampled from the SF110 dataset [10], which contains 110 open-source projects from the SourceForge.net repository. This dataset has been used in recent studies [9,10,17,20] to assess both the efficiency and the effectiveness of test case generation tools.

To form our benchmark, we applied the same selection procedure used in prior studies [17,18], which first measures the McCabe's cyclomatic complexity [14] (CC) to avoid sampling trivial classes. Specifically, we first removed classes from SF110 containing exclusively methods with a CC lower than five [17]. Then, we randomly sampled 180 classes from the resulting pruned SF110 dataset: two classes from the largest projects in SF110 and one class from the remaining projects. The number of coverage targets ranges between 61 (for class SapdbTableList from project db-everywhere) and 4,252 (for class JVCParserTokenManager from project javaviewcontrol); the median number of coverage targets per class is 405. These numbers include all coverage targets from the seven coverage criteria described in Sect. 2, namely *branch, line, weak mutation, input, output, method* and *exception coverage*. The complete list of classes under test (CUTs) in our benchmark is publicly available in FigShare at the following link: https://figshare.com/s/c74652d1fcb79fa853dd.

Implementation. The four test generation strategies—i.e., MC-DynaMOSA, MC-MOSA, MC-WSA, SC-DynaMOSA— were implemented in EvoSuite [8,9]. MC-WSA corresponds to the default strategy in EvoSuite, which evolves test suites using a monotonic genetic algorithm [4] guided by one single fitness function that combines all coverage criteria using a weighted sum. MC-MOSA corresponds to the MOSA algorithm [16], which evolves test cases rather than test suites, targeting all coverage criteria simultaneously. Each coverage criterion corresponds to a different set of search objectives, one objective for each coverage target. Therefore, the set of objectives in MC-MOSA is the union of the sets of objectives from all seven coverage criteria. SC-DynaMOSA considers only branch coverage as testing criterion, but it dynamically updates the set of objectives based on the structural dependencies among branches, i.e., it corresponds to original DynaMOSA [17]. Finally, we implemented MC-DynaMOSA in EvoSuite as described in Sect. 3.1. The implementation is publicly available on GitHub: https://github.com/apanichella/evosuite.

All testing strategies are implemented in the same version of EvoSuite, downloaded from GitHub on October 1st, 2017. Furthermore, all strategies use an *archive* [17,20], to take accidental coverage into account: whenever a test case (or test suite) T satisfies a previously uncovered target, T is stored in the *archive* while the target is removed from the set of objectives [1] or from computation of the weighted sum [4,20]. Therefore, in all testing strategies, the search is focused on the uncovered targets only.

Methodology. For each CUT in our benchmark, we ran each testing strategy 30 times and collected the number and the type of targets covered in each run. This setting led to 30 EvoSuite runs × 4 strategies × 180 CUTs = 21,600 executions in total. In each run, we measured the percentage of covered targets for each coverage criterion as: $Cov(C,T) = \frac{\#Covered(C,T)}{\#Total(C)}$ where $\#Total$ denotes the total number of targets for a given criterion C, while $\#Covered(C,T)$ is the number of targets covered by the generated test suite T. Coverage scores are computed after EvoSuite's post-processing, which minimizes the generated suite T and adds candidate assertions using a mutation-based strategy [10].

Then, we compare each pair of testing strategies by considering the average (arithmetic mean) of each coverage criterion over 30 independent repetitions. Differences (if any) are shown and discussed in terms *percentage points* (*pp*), i.e., the absolute difference between the coverage scores of the test suites generated by the two testing strategies being compared. To assess the statistical significance of such differences, we applied the Wilcoxon rank sum test [5] for each CUTs and for each pair of testing strategies, adopting a significance level $\alpha = 0.05$. The obtained p-values are then adjusted with the Holm-Bonferroni procedure [5] as required when comparing more than two treatments.

We also wanted to assess the ability of the generated test suites to detect faults. To this aim, we applied strong mutation coverage as a proxy for the actual fault detection capability. This is a common practice when assessing software testing tools and approaches since previous studies [13] showed that mutants can be regarded as valid substitutes of real-world faults to assess fault detection rates. In this study, we used the mutation testing engine available in EvoSuite. Strong mutation coverage is computed as the percentage of mutants that are strongly killed by a generated test suite, i.e., the test suite contains a test case that fails when comparing the output of the mutant to the output of the original program. Note that strong mutation is not used in this study as guidance to the search (i.e., as part of a fitness function or of some objectives), so it was possible to use it to assess the fault-detection capability of the suite generated by each testing strategy. It is also worth to remark that strong mutation has never been used in previous studies in combination with other coverage criteria due to its large overhead [4,11,19].

Parameter Setting. Previous studies have shown that default parameters provide acceptable results compared to fine-tuning of the evolutionary parameters [3]. Hence, we adopted default parameter values in EvoSuite [20], as done in previous studies targeting the SF110 dataset [17,19,20]: for all testing strategies, (single and many-objective), genetic algorithms are configured with a population size of 50 test cases/suites; *single-point crossover* with probability $p_c = 0.75$; *mutation* with probability $p_m = 1/n$, where n is the number of statements in a test case (or number of test cases in the test suite for MC-WS); the selection operator is *tournament selection*, the default in EvoSuite. For the search budget, we set the same maximum execution time of three minutes for all testing strategies. The search stopped earlier only when 100% coverage was obtained for all coverage criteria before reaching the search timeout.

5   Experimental Results

Due to the space limits, we report only the average results obtained by each strategy across all CUTs and the number of classes with a statistically significant difference. The detailed results for each class are available at the following link: https://figshare.com/s/b06984aa36bfe2e9d934.

Table 2 summarizes the results of the pairwise comparison for the three multi-criteria testing strategies, i.e., MC-DynaMOSA, MC-WSA, and MC-MOSA. For each strategy, the table reports (i) the mean coverage score obtained for each coverage criterion across all 180 CUTs and (ii) the number of classes in our benchmark in which MC-DynaMOSA is statistically better, worse or equivalent to MC-WSA and MC-MOSA according to the Wilcoxon test. Finally, the last row of the table shows the results (average scores and number of significant data points) for strong mutation.

Results of MC-DynaMOSA vs. MC-WSA (RQ1). For branch coverage, MC-Dyna-MOSA achieved on average $+3pp$ across all CUTs in our benchmark. The former was statistically significantly better than the latter in 82 classes out of 180, while the latter statistically outperformed the former in only 9 classes. Similar results can be observed for *line coverage* and *weak mutation*: in 85 classes and in 82 classes out of 180, MC-DynaMOSA achieved statistically significantly higher line and weak mutation coverage than MC-WSA, respectively. For these cases, the largest difference of $27.94pp$ in line coverage is observed for class TableMeta (project schemaspy); the largest difference in weak mutation is equal to $33.21pp$ and was observed for class Shift (project jiggler). Only in 10 classes (for line coverage) and 12 classes (for weak mutation) out of 180, MC-WSA outperformed MC-DynaMOSA with an average difference of $3.61pp$ and $5.11pp$ for line and weak mutation, respectively. For the remaining criteria—i.e., method, input, output, and exception—MC-DynaMOSA still achieves higher coverage scores than MC-WSA.

Table 2. Comparison between MC-DynaMOSA, MC-MOSA, and MC-WSA on all considered coverage criteria and on strong mutation

Cov. criterion	Average coverage			MC-DynaMOSA vs. MC-MOSA			MC-DynaMOSA vs. MC-WSA		
	MC-DynaMOSA	MC-MOSA	MC-WSA	#Better	#Worse	#No Diff.	#Better	#Worse	#No Diff.
Branch	**0.62**	0.60	0.59	71	5	104	82	9	72
Line	**0.67**	0.65	0.64	62	4	114	85	10	85
Weak mutation	**0.64**	0.63	0.62	57	6	117	81	12	87
Method	**0.97**	0.96	0.96	16	4	160	12	6	162
Input	**0.95**	0.94	0.94	30	4	146	29	14	137
Output	**0.60**	0.59	0.58	39	4	137	39	9	132
Exception	**1.00**	0.99	0.99	13	0	167	16	0	164
Strong mutation	**0.29**	0.27	0.23	55	25	100	97	4	79

However, the number of CUTs with statistically significant difference decreases compared to the previously discussed criteria. In the very large majority of the classes, the two testing strategies turned out to be statistically equivalent. In 6%–21% of the classes, the winner of the comparison is MC-DynaMOSA, while in 3%–7% the winner is MC-WSA. Remarkably, in none of the 180 classes, the test suites generated by MC-WSA could trigger/cover more exceptions than the suites generated by MC-DynaMOSA. In summary, we observed a much larger number of significantly improved cases for branch, line and weak mutation coverage, as compared to the other criteria, when MC-DynaMOSA is used. A possible explanation for this finding is that branch, line and weak-mutation coverage provide stronger guidance, as their associated fitness functions are crafted based on carefully defined, fine-grained heuristics, i.e., approach level [15], branch distance [15] and infection distance [19].

In terms of strong mutation (last row in Table 2), MC-DynaMOSA detects a significantly larger number of faults (strongly killed mutants) than MC-WSA in 97 CUTs out of 180. The opposite is true in only 4 classes. MC-DynaMOSA improved the strong mutation score by $+6pp$ on average. The largest improvement ($+53pp$) is observed for class TableMeta from schemaspy (as for branch coverage).

> *The test suites generated by MC-DynaMOSA achieve higher coverage scores and are able to detect more faults than the suites produced by MC-WS.*

Results of MC-DynaMOSA vs. MC-MOSA (RQ2). As indicated in Table 2, MC-DynaMOSA yielded on average $+2pp$ over MC-MOSA for branch and line coverage, and $+1pp$ for the remaining coverage criteria. In 71 CUTs out of 180, MC-DynaMOSA achieved a significantly higher branch coverage; the opposite is true in only 5 classes. The largest difference ($+23.68pp$) is achieved for class JMCAAnalyzer from project jmca. Instead, in the very few cases where MC-MOSA achieves significantly higher branch coverage, the difference ranges between $0.50pp$ (class ServerGameModel from hft-bomberman) and $6.49pp$ (class SimpleComboBox from caloriecount). The results for the other coverage criteria are in line with those observed for branch coverage. In 62 classes for line coverage and in 57 classes for weak mutation out of 180, MC-DynaMOSA outperformed MC-MOSA. The differences range between $0.10pp$ (class FBProcedureCall from firebird) and $24.15pp$ (class JMCAAnalyzer from jmca) for line coverage and between $0.10pp$ (class AntPathMatcher from jsecurity) and $32.36pp$ (the same class of line and branch coverage) for weak mutation. MC-MOSA achieved higher scores than MC-DynaMOSA in only 4 and 6 classes out of 180, for line coverage ($3.05pp$ on average) and weak mutation ($1.37pp$ on average), respectively. The number of CUTs with statistically significant difference decreases when analyzing method, input, output and exception coverage compared to the other three criteria. Nevertheless, there are many more CUTs where better coverage scores are obtained when running MC-DynaMOSA (6%–21% of the benchmark) than cases where the winner of the comparison is MC-MOSA (2%–3% of the benchmark). In none of the 180 classes, the test suites generated by MC-MOSA covered more exceptions than the tests generated with MC-DynaMOSA.

The values reported in the last row in Table 2 indicate that MC-DynaMOSA detected a significantly larger number of faults (strongly killed mutants) than MC-MOSA in 55 CUTs out of 180. On these cases, the average improvement in strong mutation score is $+8.79pp$, with the maximum of $+39.46pp$ for class HostMonitoringService (project quickserver). On the other hand, MC-MOSA achieved a better mutation score in 25 classes out of 180. However, in these cases the magnitude of the difference is small, being $4.76pp$ on average.

> *The incremental exploration of the control dependency frontier implemented in MC-DynaMOSA leads to larger coverage scores and to a better fault-detection capability than simply targeting all coverage targets as done by MC-MOSA.*

Results of MC-DynaMOSA vs. SC-DynaMOSA (RQ3, RQ4). Table 3 summarizes the results of the comparison of many-objective search with an incremental exploration of the control dependency frontier when handling multiple criteria (MC-DynaMOSA) compared to branch coverage only (SC-DynaMOSA). In 53 classes out of 180, SC-DynaMOSA achieved significantly higher branch coverage than MC-DynaMOSA; on the other hand, the latter outperformed the former in 36 classes. This finding clearly indicates that optimizing many coverage criteria at the same time may lead to lower coverage scores compared to the optimization of each criterion, taken separately from the others (as for branch coverage in this case). For example, branch coverage decreases by $1.65pp$ on average, with a minimum decrement of $1.00pp$ for class jgaapGUI (project jgaap) and a maximum one of $24.66pp$ for class JMCAAnalyzer (project jmca). On the CUTs where MC-DynaMOSA won the comparison, the differences range between $1.40pp$ (class Profile from project jiprof) and $24.71pp$ (class JSJshop from project shop), being $5.63pp$ on average. While we observe that targeting only branches leads to higher branch coverage in around 30% of CUTs, the results are quite different when looking at the other coverage criteria. For example, MC-DynaMOSA statistically outperforms SC-DynaMOSA in 88 CUTs and 107 CUTs for line coverage and weak mutation, respectively. This means that the additional branches covered by SC-DynaMOSA and not by MC-DynaMOSA are associated to basic blocks in the control flow graph with no statements (other than the branch itself) or with no (or very few) weakly killed mutants. Although branches represent the main backbone to build the multi-criteria control dependency graph (and to incrementally explore the frontier), branch coverage is not equivalent to the other criteria.

> *Even though MC-DynaMOSA may lead to lower branch coverage than SC-DynaMOSA, it achieves higher coverage on all other criteria. Therefore, it is not enough to target all branches in order to achieve high coverage of all the other criteria.*

Despite leading to lower branch coverage, MC-DynaMOSA achieved a higher strong mutation score than SC-DynaMOSA in 89 CUTs out of 180. The increment in strong mutation score ranges between $1.11pp$ (class ExportHook from project freemind) and $35.80pp$ (class QuickServerConfig from project quickserver),

Table 3. Comparison between MC-DynaMOSA and SC-DynaMOSA in terms of coverage and strong mutation scores

Coverage criterion	Average coverage		MC-DynaMOSA vs. SC-DynaMOSA		
	MC-DynaMOSA	SC-DynaMOSA	#Better	#Worse	#No Diff.
Branch	0.62	**0.63**	36	53	119
Line	**0.67**	0.65	88	28	64
Weak mutation	**0.64**	0.62	107	19	54
Method	**0.97**	0.90	89	2	89
Input	**0.95**	0.57	146	1	33
Output	**0.60**	0.46	115	5	60
Exception	**1.00**	0.45	137	0	43
Strong mutation	**0.29**	0.26	89	21	70

being $9.62pp$ on average. On the other hand, SC-DynaMOSA outperformed MC-Dyna-MOSA in just 21 CUTs, with an average difference of only $2.93pp$. This finding is particularly remarkable as it shows that a statistically higher branch coverage does not necessarily lead the generated test suites to reveal more faults.

> *Handling many criteria with MC-DynaMOSA increases the fault detection capability of the generated test suites compared to targeting branch coverage alone.*

Threats to Validity. *Construct validity.* All algorithms are implemented in the same tool, minimizing the risk of confounding factors. *Internal validity.* We did 30 independent runs and drew conclusions following statistical significance. We used default parameter values and those used in the respective algorithms. The comparison was based on metrics with respect to the considered criteria, and mutation scores. *External validity.* Enlarging the benchmark (beyond 180 CUTs) in future experiments could increase confidence of the results.

6   Conclusion

Coverage of multiple criteria has been the subject of recent research effort. While targeting multiple criteria simultaneously offers various advantages, it also poses difficulties to the search algorithm as the number of targets to be considered increases. In this paper, we have presented an approach, MC-DynaMOSA, based on incremental frontier exploration for multiple criteria test generation. In particular, we exploit inherent inter-dependencies among the various criteria to establish an enhanced control dependency graph, based on which we explore the coverage targets incrementally. Experimental results on 180 classes showed that MC-DynaMOSA outperforms the state-of-the-art approach for multiple criteria coverage, which is based on sum scalarization, in terms of coverage of the various criteria as well as strong mutation scores. Furthermore, results also showed that covering all branches is not sufficient to achieve higher coverage of the other criteria, even though control dependency branches provide the principal guidance to the search.

Acknowledgement. This work is partially supported by the Italian Ministry of Education, University, and Research (MIUR) with the PRIN project GAUSS (grant no. 2015KWREMX).

References

1. Abreu, R., Zoeteweij, P., Van Gemund, A.J.: An observation-based model for fault localization (2008)
2. Arcuri, A.: Many independent objective (MIO) algorithm for test suite generation. In: Menzies, T., Petke, J. (eds.) SSBSE 2017. LNCS, vol. 10452, pp. 3–17. Springer, Cham (2017). https://doi.org/10.1007/978-3-319-66299-2_1
3. Arcuri, A., Fraser, G.: Parameter tuning or default values? An empirical investigation in search-based software engineering. Empirical Softw. Eng. **18**(3), 594–623 (2013)
4. Campos, J., Ge, Y., Fraser, G., Eler, M., Arcuri, A.: An empirical evaluation of evolutionary algorithms for test suite generation. In: Menzies, T., Petke, J. (eds.) SSBSE 2017. LNCS, vol. 10452, pp. 33–48. Springer, Cham (2017). https://doi.org/10.1007/978-3-319-66299-2_3
5. Conover, W.J.: Practical Nonparametric Statistics, 3rd edn. Wiley, Hoboken (1998)
6. Deb, K., Deb, K.: Multi-objective optimization. In: Burke, E., Kendall, G. (eds.) Search Methodologies. Springer, Boston (2014). https://doi.org/10.1007/978-1-4614-6940-7_15
7. Fonseca, C.M., Fleming, P.J.: An overview of evolutionary algorithms in multiobjective optimization. Evol. Comput. **3**(1), 1–16 (1995)
8. Fraser, G., Arcuri, A.: EvoSuite: automatic test suite generation for object-oriented software. In: Proceedings of the 19th ACM SIGSOFT Symposium and the 13th European Conference on Foundations of Software Engineering, ESEC/FSE 2011, pp. 416–419 (2011)
9. Fraser, G., Arcuri, A.: Whole test suite generation. IEEE Trans. Softw. Eng. **39**(2), 276–291 (2013)
10. Fraser, G., Arcuri, A.: A large-scale evaluation of automated unit test generation using evosuite. ACM Trans. Softw. Eng. Methodol. **24**(2), 8:1–8:42 (2014). https://doi.org/10.1145/2685612
11. Gay, G.: Generating effective test suites by combining coverage criteria. In: Menzies, T., Petke, J. (eds.) SSBSE 2017. LNCS, vol. 10452, pp. 65–82. Springer, Cham (2017). https://doi.org/10.1007/978-3-319-66299-2_5
12. Just, R., Jalali, D., Ernst, M.D.: Defects4j: a database of existing faults to enable controlled testing studies for Java programs. In: International Symposium on Software Testing and Analysis, ISSTA 2014, San Jose, CA, USA, 21–26 July 2014, pp. 437–440 (2014)
13. Just, R., Jalali, D., Inozemtseva, L., Ernst, M.D., Holmes, R., Fraser, G.: Are mutants a valid substitute for real faults in software testing? In: Proceedings of the 22nd ACM SIGSOFT International Symposium on Foundations of Software Engineering, FSE 2014, pp. 654–665. ACM, New York (2014). https://doi.org/10.1145/2635868.2635929

14. McCabe, T.J.: A complexity measure. IEEE Trans. Softw. Eng. **4**, 308–320 (1976)
15. McMinn, P.: Search-based software test data generation: a survey. Softw. Test. Verif. Reliab. **14**(2), 105–156 (2004)
16. Panichella, A., Kifetew, F.M., Tonella, P.: Reformulating branch coverage as a many-objective optimization problem. In: 8th IEEE International Conference on Software Testing, Verification and Validation, ICST, pp. 1–10 (2015)
17. Panichella, A., Kifetew, F.M., Tonella, P.: Automated test case generation as a many-objective optimisation problem with dynamic selection of the targets. IEEE Trans. Softw. Eng. **44**(2), 122–158 (2018). https://doi.org/10.1109/TSE. 2017.2663435
18. Panichella, A., Molina, U.R.: Java unit testing tool competition: fifth round. In: Proceedings of the 10th International Workshop on Search-Based Software Testing, pp. 32–38. IEEE Press (2017)
19. Rojas, J.M., Campos, J., Vivanti, M., Fraser, G., Arcuri, A.: Combining multiple coverage criteria in search-based unit test generation. In: Barros, M., Labiche, Y. (eds.) SSBSE 2015. LNCS, vol. 9275, pp. 93–108. Springer, Cham (2015). https:// doi.org/10.1007/978-3-319-22183-0_7
20. Rojas, J.M., Vivanti, M., Arcuri, A., Fraser, G.: A detailed investigation of the effectiveness of whole test suite generation. Empirical Softw. Eng. **22**(2), 852–893 (2017). https://doi.org/10.1007/s10664-015-9424-2
21. Voas, J.M.: Pie: a dynamic failure-based technique. IEEE Trans. Softw. Eng. **18**(8), 717–727 (1992). https://doi.org/10.1109/32.153381

Single-objective Versus Multi-objectivized Optimization for Evolutionary Crash Reproduction

Mozhan Soltani[(⊠)], Pouria Derakhshanfar, Annibale Panichella[(⊠)],
Xavier Devroey[iD], Andy Zaidman[iD], and Arie van Deursen[iD]

Delft University of Technology, Delft, The Netherlands
{m.soltani,p.derakhshanfar,a.panichella,x.d.m.devroey,a.e.zaidman,
arie.vandeursen}@tudelft.nl

Abstract. EvoCrash is a recent search-based approach to generate a
test case that reproduces reported crashes. The search is guided by a
fitness function that uses a weighted sum scalarization to combine three
different heuristics: (i) code coverage, (ii) crash coverage and (iii) stack
trace similarity. In this study, we propose and investigate two alternatives
to the weighted sum scalarization: (i) the simple sum scalarization and
(ii) the multi-objectivization, which decomposes the fitness function into
several optimization objectives as an attempt to increase test case diversity. We implemented the three alternative optimizations as an extension
of EvoSuite, a popular search-based unit test generator, and applied them
on 33 real-world crashes. Our results indicate that for complex crashes
the weighted sum reduces the test case generation time, compared to the
simple sum, while for simpler crashes the effect is the opposite. Similarly, for complex crashes, multi-objectivization reduces test generation
time compared to optimizing with the weighted sum; we also observe
one crash that can be replicated only by multi-objectivization. Through
our manual analysis, we found out that when optimizing the original
weighted function gets trapped in local optima, optimization for decomposed objectives improves the search for crash reproduction. Generally,
while multi-objectivization is under-explored, our results are promising
and encourage further investigations of the approach.

1 Introduction

Crash reproduction is an important step in debugging field crashes. Therefore,
various automated approaches to crash reproduction [3, 4, 19, 20, 22, 24] have been
proposed in the literature. Among these, EvoCrash [22] is a search-based approach, which applies a Guided Genetic Algorithm (GGA) to generate a crash-
reproducing test. To optimize test generation for crash reproduction, the GGA
uses a weighted-sum scalarized function, which is a sum of three heuristics,
namely: (i) line coverage, (ii) exception coverage, and (iii) stack trace similarity
rate. The function resulting from the sum scalarization is further subject to the

© Springer Nature Switzerland AG 2018
T. E. Colanzi and P. McMinn (Eds.): SSBSE 2018, LNCS 11036, pp. 325–340, 2018.
https://doi.org/10.1007/978-3-319-99241-9_18

constraint that the target exception has to be thrown at the code line reported in the crash stack trace. Depending on how close a generated test case may come to trigger a reported crash, its fitness value may be between 0.0 (i.e., each of the three heuristics evaluates to 0.0), and 6.0 (i.e., none of the heuristics is satisfied by the generated test). Soltani et al. [22] evaluated EvoCrash on 50 real-world crashes and showed that the search-based approach improved over other non-search-based approaches proposed in the related literature [4,19,24].

As any search-based technique, the success of EvoCrash depends on its capability of maintaining a good balance between *exploitation* and *exploration* [6]. The former refers to the ability to visit regions of the search space within the neighborhood of the current solutions (i.e., refining previously generated tests); the latter refers to the ability to generate completely different new test cases. In crash reproduction, the exploitation is guaranteed by the guided genetic operators that focus the search on methods appearing in the crash stack trace [22]. However, such a depth and focused search may lead to a low exploration power. Poor exploration results in low diversity between the generated test cases and, consequently, the search process easily gets trapped in local optima [6].

In this paper, we investigate two strategies to increase the diversity of generated test cases for crash reproduction. While EvoCrash uses one single-objective fitness function to guide the search, prior studies in evolutionary computation showed that relaxing the constraints [5] or multi-objectivizing the fitness function [17] help promoting diversity. Multi-objectivization is the process of (temporarily) decomposing a single-objective fitness function into multiple subobjectives to optimize simultaneously with multi-objective evolutionary algorithms. At the end of the search, the global optimal solution of the single-objective problem is one of the points of the Pareto front generated by the multi-objective algorithms. The decomposed objectives should be as independent of each other as possible to avoid getting trapped in local optima [17].

Therefore, we study whether transforming the original weighted scalarized function in EvoCrash into (i) a simple scalarized function via constraint relaxation, and (ii) multiple decomposed objectives, impacts the crash reproduction rate, and test generation time. EvoCrash [22] relies on EvoSuite [9] for test generation, and as such, we implemented the original weighted function as an extension of EvoSuite. Similarly, we implemented the alternative optimization functions by extending EvoSuite. We evaluated the alternatives on 33 real-world crashes from four open source projects. Our results show that indeed, when crashes are complex and require several generations of test cases, using multiobjectivization reduces the test generation time compared to the weighted scalarized function, and in turn, the weighted scalarized function reduces test generation time compared to the simple scalarized function. Furthermore, we observe that one crash can be fully replicated only by multi-objectivized search and not by the two single-objective strategies. Generally, our results show that problems that are single-objective by nature can benefit from multi-objectivization. We believe that our findings will foster the usage of multi-objectivization in search-based software engineering.

The remainder of the paper is structured as follows: Sect. 2 provides background and related work. Section 3 describes single and multi-objectivization for crash reproduction. Sections 4 and 5 present the evaluation and results, respectively. Discussion follows in Sect. 6. Section 7 concludes.

2   Background and Related Work

Crash reproduction tools aim at generating a test case able to reproduce a given crash based on the information gathered during the crash itself. This *crash reproduction test case* can help developers to identify the fault causing the crash [4]. For Java programs, the available information usually consists of a stack trace, i.e., lists of classes, methods and code lines involved in the crash. For instance, the following stack trace has been generated by the test cases of LANG v9b from the Defects4J [15] dataset:

```
0   java.lang.ArrayIndexOutOfBoundsException:
1       at org.apache.commons.lang3.time.FastDateParser.toArray(FastDateParser
            .java:413)
2       at org.apache.commons.lang3.time.FastDateParser.getDisplayNames(
            FastDateParser.java:381)
3       ...
```

It has a thrown exception (ArrayIndexOutOfBoundsException) and different frames (lines 1 to 3), each one pointing to a method call in the source code.

2.1   Related Work

Over the years, various Java crash replication approaches that use stack traces as input have been developed. RECORE [20] is a search-based approach that in addition to crash stack traces, uses core dumps as input data for automated test generation. MUCRASH [24] applies mutation operators on existing test cases, for classes that are present in a reported stack trace, to trigger the reported crash. While BUGREDUX [14] is based on forward symbolic execution, STAR [4] is a more recent approach that applies optimized backward symbolic execution on the method calls recorded in a stack trace in order to compute the input parameters that trigger the target crash. JCHARMING [19] is also based on using crash stack traces as the only source of information about a reported crash. JCHARMING [19] applies directed model checking to identify the pre-conditions and input parameters that cause the target crash. Finally, CONCRASH [3] is a recent approach that focuses on reproducing concurrency crashes, in particular. CONCRASH applies pruning strategies to iteratively look for test code that triggers the target crash in a thread interleaving.

More recently, Soltani et al. have proposed EVOCRASH [22], an evolutionary search-based tool for crash replication built on top of EVOSUITE [10]. EvoCrash uses a novel Guided Genetic Algorithm (GGA), which focuses the search on the method calls that appear in the crash stack trace rather than maximizing coverage as in classical coverage-oriented GAs. Their empirical evaluation demonstrated that EvoCrash outperforms other existing crash reproduction approaches.

2.2   EvoCrash

To design EvoCrash, Soltani et al. [22] defined a fitness function (*weighted sum fitness function*) and a search algorithm (*guided genetic algorithm*) dedicated to crash reproduction. The fitness function is used to characterize the "quality" of test case generated during each iteration of the guided GA.

Weighted Sum (WS) Fitness Function. The three components of the WS fitness function are: (i) the coverage of the code line (*target statement*) where the exception is thrown, (ii) the target exception has to be thrown, and (iii) the similarity between the generated stack trace (if any) and the original one. Formally, the fitness function for a given test t is defined as [22]:

$$f(t) = \begin{cases} 3 \times d_s(t) + 2 \times max(d_{except}) + max(d_{trace}) & \text{if the line is not reached} \\ 3 \times min(d_s) + 2 \times d_{except}(t) + max(d_{trace}) & \text{if the line is reached} \\ 3 \times min(d_s) + 2 \times min(d_{except}) + d_{trace}(t) & \text{if the exception is thrown} \end{cases}$$
(1)

where $d_s(t) \in [0, 1]$ denotes how far t is from executing the target statement using two well-known heuristics, *approach level* and *branch distance* [21]. The approach level measures the minimum number of control dependencies between the path of the code executed by t and the target statement s. The branch distance scores how close t is to satisfying the branch condition for the branch on which the target statement is directly control dependent [18]. In Eq. 1, $d_{except}(t) \in \{0, 1\}$ is a binary value indicating whether the target exception is thrown (0) or not (1); $d_{trace}(t)$ measures the similarity of the generated stack trace with the expected one based on methods, classes, and line numbers appearing in the stack traces; $max(d_{except})$ and $max(d_{trace})$ denote the maximum possible value for d_{except} and d_{trace}, respectively. Therefore, the last two addends of the fitness function (i.e., d_{except} and d_{trace}) are computed upon the satisfaction of two *constraints*. This is because the target exception has to be thrown in the target line s (first constraint) and the stack trace similarity should be computed only if the target exception is actually thrown (second constraint).

Guided Genetic Algorithm (GGA). EvoCrash (as EvoSuite) generates test cases at the unit level, meaning that test cases are generated by instrumenting and targeting one particular class (the *target class*). Contrary to classical unit test generation, EvoCrash does not seek to maximize coverage by invoking all the methods of the target class, but privileges those involved in the target failure. This is why the GGA algorithm relies on the stack trace to guide the search and reduces the search space at different steps. (i) A *target frame* is selected by the user amongst the different frames of the input stack trace. Usually, the target frame is the last one in the crash trace as it corresponds to the root method call where the exception was thrown. The class appearing in this target frame corresponds to the target class for which a test case will be generated. (ii) The *initial population* of test cases is generated in such a way that the method m of the target frame (the *target method*) is called at least once in each test case [22]: either directly if m is public or protected, or indirectly by calling another method that invokes the target method if m is private. (iii) During the search, dedicated *guided crossover* and *guided mutation* operators [22] ensure that newly generated test cases contain at least one call to the target method. (iv) The search is guided by the WS *fitness function*. (v) Finally, the algorithm stops if the time budget is consumed or when a zero-fitness value is achieved. In this last case, the test case is minimized by a *post-processing* that removes randomly inserted method calls that do not contribute to reproducing the crash.

3 Single-objective and Multi-objectivization for Crash Reproduction

A key limitation of evolutionary algorithms (and metaheuristics in general) is that they may become trapped in local optima due to *diversity loss* [6], a phenomenon in which no modification (with crossover and mutation) of the current best solutions will lead to discovering a better one. This phenomenon is quite common in white-box unit-level test case/suite generation, as shown by previous studies in search-based software testing [1,8,12,16]. Many strategies have been investigated by the evolutionary computation community to alleviate the problem of diversity loss, including (i) combining different types of evolutionary algorithms [6,12], (ii) defining new genetic operators to better promote diversity [6,7,12], (iii) altering the fitness function [6,11,17], and (iv) relaxing the constraints of the problem [5].

In the context of crash replication, most attention has been devoted to improving the genetic operators [21,22] to better focus the search on method calls related to the target crash. However, to the best of our knowledge, no previous study investigated alternative formulations to the fitness function in Eq. 1 and how they are related to diversity and convergence to local optima. The original equation by Soltani et al. [22] (i.e., Eq. 1) combines three different factors into one single scalar value based on some constraints. Given this type of equation, there are two possible alternatives to investigate: (i) relaxing the constraints and (ii) split the fitness function into three search objectives to optimize simultaneously. The next subsections describe these two alternative formulations of the crash replication problem and how they are related to test case diversity.

3.1 Constraints Relaxation

As explained in Sect. 2, the crash replication problem has been implicitly formulated in previous studies as a constraint problem. The constraints are handled using *penalties* [22], i.e., the fitness score of a test case is penalized by adding (or subtracting in case of a maximization problem) a certain scalar value proportional to the number of constraints being violated. For example, in Eq. 1 all test cases that do not cover the target code line are penalized by the two addends $2 \times max(d_{except})$ and $max(d_{trace})$ as there are two violated constraints (i.e., the line to cover and the exception to throw in that line). Instead, tests that cover the target line but that do not trigger the target exception are penalized by the factor $max(d_{trace})$ (only one constraint is violated in this case).

While adding penalties is a well-known strategy to handle constraints in evolutionary algorithms [5], it may lead to diversity loss because any test not satisfying the constraints have very low probability to survive across the generations. For example, let us assume for example that we have two test cases t_1 and t_2 for the example crash reported in Sect. 2. Now, let us assume that both test cases have a distance $d_s = 1.0$ (i.e., none of the two could cover the target line), but the former test could generate an exception while the latter does not. Using Eq. 1, the fitness value for both t_1 and t_2 is $f(t_1) = f(t_2) = 3 \times d_s + 3.0 = 6.0$. However, t_2 should be promoted if it can generate the same target exception of the target crash (although on a different line) and the generated trace is somehow similar to the original one (e.g., some methods are shared).

Therefore, a first alternative to the fitness function in Eq. 1 consists of relaxing the constraints, i.e., removing the penalties. This can be easily implemented with a *Simple Sum Scalarization* (SSS):

$$f(t) = d_s(t) + d_{except}(t) + d_{trace}(t) \qquad (2)$$

where $d_s(t)$, $d_{except}(t) \in \{0, 1\}$, and $d_{trace}(t)$ are the same as in Eq. 1. This relaxed variant—hereafter referred as *simple sum scalarization*— helps increase test case diversity because test cases that lead to better $d_{except}(t)$ or $d_{trace}(t)$ may survive across the GGA generation independently from the value of $d_s(t)$, which was not the case for the weighted sum, thanks to the constraints from Eq. 1. On the other hand, this reformulation may increase the number of local optima; therefore, an empirical evaluation of weighted and simple sum variants to the fitness function is needed.

3.2   Multi-objectivization

Knowles et al. [17] suggested to replace the original single-objective fitness function of a problem with a set of new objectives in an attempt to promote diversity. This process, called *multi-objectivization* (MO), can be performed in two ways [13,17]: (i) by decomposing the single-objective function into multiple subobjectives, or (ii) by adding new objectives in addition to the original function. The multi-objectivized problem can then be solved using a multi-objective evolutionary algorithm, such as NSGA-II [7]. By definition, multi-objectivization preserves the global optimal solution of the single-objective problem that, after problem transformation, becomes a Pareto efficient solution, i.e., one point of the Pareto front generated by multi-objective algorithms.

In our context, applying multi-objectivization is straightforward as the fitness function in Eq. 1 is defined as the weighted sum of three components. Therefore, our multi-objectivized version of the crash replication problem consists of optimizing the following three objectives:

$$\begin{cases} f_1(t) = d_s(t) \\ f_2(t) = d_{except}(t) \\ f_3(t) = d_{trace}(t) \end{cases} \tag{3}$$

Test cases in this three-objectivized formulation are therefore compared (and selected) according to the concept of *dominance* and *Pareto optimality*. A test case t_1 is said to *dominate* another test t_2 ($t_1 \prec_p t_2$ in math notation), iff $f_i(t_1) \le f_i(t_2)$ for all $i \in \{1, 2, 3\}$ and $f_j(t_1) < f_j(t_2)$ for at least one objective f_j. A test case t is said *Pareto optimal* if there does not exist any another test case t_3 such that $t_3 \prec_p t_1$. For instance, for the test cases (i.e., solutions) generated by a multi-objectivized (*Multi-obj.*) search presented in Fig. 1, A, B, and D dominate C, E, and F.

In our problem, there can be multiple non-dominated solutions within the population generated by GGA at a given generation. These non-dominated solutions represent the best trade-offs among the search objectives that have been discovered/generated during the search so far. Diversity is therefore promoted by considering all non-dominated test cases (trade-offs) as equally good according to the *dominance* relation and that are assigned the same probability to survive in the next generations.

It is worth noting that a test case t that replicates the target crash will achieve the score $f_1(t) = f_2(t) = f_3(t) = 0$, which is the optimal value for all objectives. In terms of optimality, t is the global optimum for the original single-objective problem but it is also the single Pareto optimal solution because it dominates all other test cases in the search space. This is exactly the main difference between classical multi-objective search and multi-objectivization: in multi-objective search we are interested in generating a well-distributed set of Pareto optimal solutions (or optimal trade-offs); in multi-objectivization, some trade-offs are generated during the search (and preserved to help diversity), but there is only one optimal test case, i.e., the one reproducing the target crash.[1]

Non-dominated Sorting Genetic Algorithm II. To solve our multi-objectivized problem, we use NSGA-II [7], which is a well-known multi-objective genetic algorithm (GA) that provides well-distributed Pareto fronts and good performance when dealing with up to three objectives [7]. As any genetic algorithm, NSGA-II evolves an initial population of test cases using crossover and mutation; however, differently from other GAs, the selection is performed using tournament selection and based on the *dominance* relation and the *crowding distance*. The former plays a role during the *non-dominated sorting* procedure,

---

[1] Note that there might exist multiple tests that can replicate the target crash; however, these tests are *coincident points* as they will all have a zero-value for all objectives.

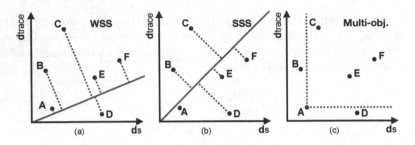

Fig. 1. A graphical interpretation of different fitness functions (Color figure online)

where solutions are ranked in non-dominance fronts according to their dominance relation; non-dominated solutions have the highest probability to survive and to be selected for reproduction. The crowding distance is further used to promote the more diverse test cases within the same non-dominance front.

In this paper, we implemented a *guided* variant of NSGA-II, where its genetic operators are replaced with the *guided crossover* and *guided mutation* implemented in GGA. We used these operators (i) to focus the search on the method call appearing in the target trace and (ii) to guarantee a fair comparison with GGA by adopting the same operators.

3.3   Graphical Interpretation

Figure 1 shows commonalities and differences among the tree alternative formulations of the crash reproduction problem (see Sects. 3.1 and 3.2). For simplicity, let us focus on only two objectives (d_s and d_{trace}) and let us assume that we have a set of generated tests which are shown as points in the bi-dimensional space delimited by the two objectives. As shown in Fig. 1(c), points (test cases) in multi-objectivization are compared in terms of non-dominance. In the example, the tests A, B, and D are non-dominated tests and all of them are assigned to the first non-dominance front in NSGA-II, i.e., they have the same probability of being selected. On the other hand, sum scalarization (either simple or weighted) projects all point to one single vector, i.e., the blue lines in Figs. 1(a) and (b). With weighted sum scalarization (WSS), the vector of the aggregated fitness function is inclined to the d_s axis due to the higher weight of the line coverage penalty. In contrast, the vector obtained with simple sum scalarization (SSS) is the bisector of the first quadrant, i.e., both objectives share the same weights. While in both Fig. 1(a) and (b), the best solution (point A) is the one closer to the origin of the axes, the order of the solutions (and their selection probability) can vary. For instance, we can see in the Figure that case C is a better choice than case D in the weighted sum because it has a lower value for d_s. But, case D is better than C in the simple sum. These differences in the selection procedure may lead the search toward exploring/exploiting different regions of the search space (Table 1).

Table 1. Crashes used in the study.

Exception type	Defects4J	XWiki
NullPointerException (NPE)	9	9
ArrayIndexOutOfBoundsExceptions (AIOOBE)	7	0
ClassCastException (CCE)	2	3

4 Empirical Evaluation

We conducted an empirical evaluation to assess the impact of the single objective or multi objectivization fitness functions, answering the following research questions:

RQ$_1$: *How does crash reproduction with simple sum scalarization compare to crash reproduction using weighted sum scalarization?*

RQ$_2$: *How does crash reproduction with a multi-objectivized optimization function compare to crash reproduction using weighted sum scalarization?*

Comparisons for **RQ$_1$** and **RQ$_2$** are done by considering the number of crashes reproduced (*crash coverage rate*) and the time taken by EvoCrash to generate a crash reproducing test case (*test generation time*).

4.1 Setup

To perform our evaluation, we randomly selected 33 crashes from five open source projects: 18 crashes from four projects contained in Defects4J [15], which is a well-known collection of bugs from popular libraries; and 12 crashes from XWiki,[2] a web application project developed by our industrial partner.

We execute the EvoSuite extensions, with the three approaches (weighted sum, simple sum, and multi-objectivization), on 23 virtual machines. Each machine has 8 CPU-cores, 32 GB of memory, and a 1TB shared hard drive. All of them run CentOs Linux release 7.4.1708 as operating system, with Open-JDK version 1.8.0-151.

For each crash c, we run each approach in order to generate a test case that reproduces c and targeting each frame one by one, starting from the highest one (the last one in the stack frame). As soon as one of the approaches is able to generate a test case for the given frame (k), we stop the execution and do not try to generate test cases for the lower frames ($<k$). To address the random nature of the evaluated search approaches, we execute each approach 15 times on each frame for a total number of 12,022 executions independent runs.

Parameter Settings. We use the default parameter configurations from Evo-Suite with functional mocking to minimize the risk of environmental interactions and increase the coverage [2]. We set the search budget to 10 minutes, which is double of the maximal amount reported by Soltani et al. [22].

---

[2] http://www.xwiki.org/.

4.2   Analysis

Since the crash coverage data is a binary distribution (i.e., a crash is reproduced or not), we use the Odds Ratio (OR) to measure the impact of the single or multi-objectivization on the *crash coverage* rate. A value of OR > 1 for comparing a pair of factors (A, B) indicates that the coverage rate increases when factor A is applied, while a value of OR < 1 indicates the opposite. A value of OR $= 1$ indicates that there is no difference between A and B. In addition, we use Fisher's exact test, with $\alpha = 0.05$ for Type I errors to assess the significance of the results. A p-value < 0.05 indicates the observed impact on the coverage rate is statistically significant, while a value of p-value > 0.05 indicates the opposite.

Furthermore, we use the Vargha-Delaney $\hat{A}_{12}$ statistic [23] to assess the effect size of the differences between the two sum scalarization approaches or between weighted sum and multi-objectivization for *test generation time*. A value of $\hat{A}_{12} < 0.5$ for a pair of factors (A, B) indicates that A reduces the test generation time, while a value of $\hat{A}_{12} > 0.5$ indicates that B reduces the generation time. If $\hat{A}_{12} = 0.5$, there is no difference between A and B on generation time. To check whether the observed impacts are statistically significant, we used the non-parametric Wilcoxon Rank Sum test, with $\alpha = 0.05$ for Type I error. P-values smaller than 0.05 indicate that the observed difference in the test generation time is statistically significant.

5   Results

In this section, we present the results of the experiments. Thereby, we answer the two research questions on comparing simple and weighted sum aggregation functions as well as weighted sum and multi-objectivization for crash reproduction.

Results (RQ1). Table 2 presents the crash reproduction results for the 33 crashes used in the experiment. As the table shows, 21 cases were reproduced using the original weighted sum scalarized function, while 20 cases were reproduced using simple sum scalarization. Thus, MATH-32b is only reproduced by the weighted sum approach. Both optimization approaches reproduced the crashes at the same frame level.

As Table 3 shows, we do not observe any statistically significant impact on the crash reproduction rate, comparing weighted and simple sum scalarization. However, for one case, XWIKI-13031, the odds ratio measure is 6.5, which indicates that the rate of crash reproduction using the weighted scalarized function is 6.5 times larger than the reproduction rate of using the simple scalarized function. In this case, the p value is 0.1, therefore we cannot draw a statistically significant conclusion.

For four cases, we see a significant impact on the test generation time. Based on our manual analysis, we observe that when a crash (XWIKI-13031) is complex, i.e., it takes several generations to produce a crash reproducing test case, weighted sum reduces execution time. However, when a crash, e.g., XWIKI-13377, is easy to reproduce, then weighted sum takes longer to find a crash reproducing test.

Table 2. Experiment results for Multi-objectivized (Multi-obj.), Weighted (WSS) and Simple Sum (SSS) Scalarization. "-" indicates that the optimization approach did not reproduce the crash. Bold cases represent the crashes only reproduced by some of the approaches, not all. **Rep., T.,** and **SD** indicate reproduction rate, average execution time, and standard deviation, respectively.

Crash ID	Exception	Frame	Multi-obj.			WSS			SSS		
			Rep.	$\overline{T}$	SD	Rep.	$\overline{T}$	SD	Rep.	$\overline{T}$	SD
CHART-4b	NPE	6	15	16.5	1.4	15	16.6	1.4	15	14.8	1.3
LANG-12b	AIOOBE	2	15	2.5	0.3	15	2.5	0.5	15	2.4	0.5
LANG-33b	NPE	1	15	1.7	0.0	15	1.0	0.2	15	1.0	0.0
LANG-39b	NPE	2	15	2.7	1.0	15	1.1	0.5	15	1.6	1.2
LANG-47b	NPE	1	15	3.4	1.3	15	2.1	1.1	15	1.0	0.7
LANG-57b	NPE	1	11	1.1	0.0	9	185.0	288.0	12	86.1	218.1
LANG-9b	AIOOBE	-	-			-			-		
MATH-100b	AIOOBE	1	15	8.4	13.4	15	7.2	1.7	15	8.2	7.3
MATH-32b	**CCE**	**1**	**15**	**3.9**	**0.9**	**15**	**5.3**	**2.5**	-		
MATH-4b	NPE	3	15	27.3	49.2	14	21.7	16.1	14	62.0	150.0
MATH-70b	NPE	3	15	1.7	0.2	15	1.1	0.3	15	1.0	0.0
MATH-79b	NPE	1	15	1.7	0.1	15	1.0	0.2	15	1.0	0.0
MATH-81b	AIOOBE	6	9	82.0	63.0	11	180.7	230.5	15	115.0	114.0
MATH-98b	AIOOBE	1	15	7.7	5.3	14	9.5	5.7	15	9.9	9.7
MOCKITO-12b	CCE	-	-			-			-		
MOCKITO-34b	AIOOBE	-	-			-			-		
MOCKITO-36b	NPE	1	15	10.9	6.9	15	9.2	7.5	15	13.7	11.3
MOCKITO-38b	NPE	-	-			-			-		
MOCKITO-3b	AIOOBE	-	-			-			-		
XRENDERING-418	NPE	-	-			-			-		
XWIKI-12482	NPE	-	-			-			-		
XWIKI-12584	CCE	-	-			-			-		
XWIKI-13031	CCE	3	15	25.8	17.4	15	47.2	67.0	10	249.0	175.0
XWIKI-13096	NPE	-	-			-			-		
XWIKI-13303	NPE	-	-			-			-		
XWIKI-13316	NPE	2	15	37.9	47.7	15	16.6	34.6	15	31.3	86.8
XWIKI-13377	CCE	1	15	10.7	8.6	15	11.8	7.7	15	4.8	3.9
XWIKI-13616	NPE	3	15	4.1	0.1	15	4.0	0.0	15	4.0	0.0
XWIKI-14227	NPE	-	-			-			-		
XWIKI-14319	NPE	1	15	87.0	21.2	15	89.4	17.5	15	87.8	15.2
XWIKI-14475	**NPE**	**1**	**15**	**117.1**	**53.6**	-			-		
XWIKI-13916	CCE	1	15	59.7	19.8	14	65.0	13.6	15	57.6	13.8
XWIKI-14612	NPE	1	15	8.9	2.0	15	8.7	1.8	15	8.5	2.4

Results (RQ2). Table 2 shows that 22 cases were reproduced using decomposed crash optimization objectives, while 21 cases were reproduced by the original weighted sum function. XWIKI-14475 is reproduced by the multi-objectivized approach only.

As Table 3 shows, in most cases, we do not observe any impact on the rate of crash coverage. However, for MATH-81b and LANG-57b, the odds ratio measures are 4.8 and 1.7 respectively, which indicates that the rate of crash reproduction using multi-objectivized optimization is 4.8 times and 1.7 times higher than

Table 3. Comparing coverage rate and test generation time between the optimization approaches, for cases where both optimization approaches in each pair reproduces the crash. P-values for both Wilcoxon tests and odds ratios are reported. Effect sizes and p-values of the comparisons are in bold when the p-values are lower than 0.05.

Crash ID	Exception	Fr.	Multi-weighted				Weighted-simple			
			$\hat{A}_{12}$	p	OR	p	$\hat{A}_{12}$	p	OR	p
CHART-4b	NPE	6	0.3	0.30	0.0	1.0	**0.8**	**<0.01**	0.0	1.00
LANG-12b	AIOOBE	2	0.5	0.50	0.0	1.0	0.4	0.70	0.0	1.00
LANG-33b	NPE	1	**0.9**	**<0.01**	0.0	1.0	0.5	0.30	0.0	1.00
LANG-39b	NPE	2	**0.9**	**<0.01**	0.0	1.0	0.4	0.10	0.0	1.00
LANG-47b	NPE	1	**0.9**	**<0.01**	0.0	1.0	0.4	0.70	0.0	1.00
LANG-57b	NPE	1	0.6	0.20	1.7	0.6	0.5	0.60	0.3	0.40
MATH-100b	AIOOBE	1	**0.1**	**<0.01**	0.0	1.0	0.5	0.40	0.0	1.00
MATH-32b	CCE	2	**0.3**	**<0.01**	0.0	0.5	0.4	0.50	0.0	1.00
MATH-4b	NPE	3	**0.4**	**0.04**	1.0	1.0	0.4	0.70	1.0	1.00
MATH-70b	NPE	3	**0.8**	**<0.01**	0.0	1.0	0.5	0.10	0.0	1.00
MATH-81b	AIOOBE	6	0.5	0.60	4.8	0.3	0.5	0.50	0.0	0.09
MATH-98b	AIOOBE	1	**0.3**	**<0.01**	0.0	1.0	0.6	0.20	0.0	1.00
MOCKITO-36b	NPE	1	0.2	0.60	0.0	1.0	0.3	0.30	Inf	1.00
XWIKI-13031	CCE	3	**0.3**	**0.03**	Inf	1.0	**0.1**	**<0.01**	6.5	0.10
XWIKI-13316	NPE	2	0.6	0.09	0.0	1.0	0.6	0.10	0.0	1.00
XWIKI-13377	CCE	1	0.6	0.50	0.0	1.0	**0.7**	**0.01**	0.0	1.00
XWIKI-13616	NPE	3	**0.5**	**<0.01**	0.0	1.0	**0.5**	**<0.01**	0.0	1.00
XWIKI-14319	NPE	1	**0.4**	**<0.01**	0.0	1.0	0.5	0.70	0.0	1.00
XWIKI-13916	CCE	1	0.3	0.60	0.0	1.0	0.6	0.08	0.0	1.00
XWIKI-14612	NPE	1	0.5	0.40	0.0	1.0	0.4	0.70	0.0	1.00

the rate of reproduction using the weighted sum function. For these cases, the p-values are 0.3 and 0.6 respectively, therefore, we cannot draw a statistically significant conclusion yet.

Moreover, as Table 3 shows, for six cases, namely: MATH-100b, MATH-32b, MATH-4b, MATH-98b, XWIKI-13031, and XWIKI-14319, we observe that using multi-objectivization reduces the time for test generation (as $\hat{A}_{12}$ measures are lower than 0.5). For all these cases, the p values are lower than 0.05, which indicates the observed impacts are statistically significant. On the other hand, for four other cases, namely: LANG-33b, LANG-39b, LANG-47b, and MATH-70b, we observe an opposite trend, i.e., the weighted sum achieves a lower test generation time (as the $\hat{A}_{12}$ measures are larger than 0.5). Based on our manual analysis, as also indicated by the average execution time values reported in Table 2, when a crash is complex and the search requires several generations (e.g., XWIKI-13031), multi-objectivization reduces the execution time. On the other hand, when a crash is easy to be reproduced and a few generations of test cases quickly converge to a global optimum, then using the weighted sum approach is more efficient.

6 Discussion

As Table 3 shows, for only one case, XWIKI-13031, the weighted sum is more efficient than the simple sum, while for two other cases, XWIKI-13377 and CHART-4b, the simple sum is more efficient. From our manual analysis of these cases, we see that when the target line is covered in a few seconds (when initializing the first population), the simple sum is more efficient than the weighted sum. However, when more search iterations (generations) are needed to find a test that reaches the target line, like for XWIKI-13031, the weighted sum is much faster. As indicated in Sect. 3, while using weights in single-objective optimization may reduce the likelihood of getting stuck in local optima, it may accept solutions that trigger the target exception but not at the target code line. Therefore, a possible explanation for these cases is that while maintaining diversity improves efficiency to a small degree, relaxing the constraints may penalize the exploitation. In practice, since it is not possible to know *a priori* when getting stuck in local optima occurs, using weighted sum (that provides more guidance, thanks to the constraints it takes into account) seems a more reliable approach, which might be few seconds less efficient compared to simple sum (in some cases).

As Knowles et al. [17] discussed, when applying multi-objectivization, for a successful search, it is important to derive independent objectives. In our multi-objectivization approach, as presented in Sect. 3, we decompose the three heuristics in the original scalarized function into three optimization objectives. However, these objectives are not entirely independent of each other; line coverage is interrelated to the stack trace similarity. Thus, if the target line is not covered, the stack trace similarity will never converge to 0.0. This can be one possible explanation for why when the target frame is one, single-objective optimization performed better for most cases in our experiments. The fewer frames to reproduce, the stronger the interrelation between the two objectives is.

Furthermore, we observe that when a crash is complex and requires several generations to be reproduced, the multi-objectivized approach performs more efficiently than single-objective optimization. On the other hand, when crashes can be reproduced in few generations (i.e., the target line is covered by the initial population of GAs and evolution is mostly needed for triggering the same crash), then the single-objective approach is more efficient. This is due to the cost of the fast non-domination sorting algorithm in NSGA-II [7], whose computational complexity is $\mathcal{O}(MN^2)$, where M is the number of objectives and N is the population size. Instead, the computational complexity of the selection in a single-objective GA is $\mathcal{O}(M)$, where N is the population size. Thus, sorting/selecting individuals is computationally more expensive in NSGA-II and it is worthwhile only when converging to 0.0 requires effective exploration through the enhanced diversity in NSGA-II.

Insights. From our results and discussion, we formulate the following insights: (i) **prefer multi-objectivization**, as it substantially reduces the execution time for complex crashes (up to three minutes) and the time loss for simple crashes is small (few seconds on average); furthermore, it allows to reproduce one additional crash that weighted sum could not reproduce; (ii) Alternatively, use a **hybrid search** that switches from weighted sum to multi-objectivized search when the execution time is above a certain threshold (20 seconds in our case) or if the target code line is not covered within the first few generations; and finally, (iii) Avoid **simple sum scalarization** as it may get stuck into local optima (multi-objectivization).

Threats to Validity. We randomly selected 33 crashes from five different open source projects for our evaluation. Those crashes come from Defects4J, a collection of defects from popular libraries, and from the issue tracker of our industrial partner, ensuring diversity in the considered projects. In addition, the selected crashes contain three types of commonly occurring exceptions. While we did not analyze the exception types, they may be a factor that impacts the test generation time and crash reproduction rate. Finally, our extension to EvoSuite may contain unknown defects. To mitigate this risk, in addition to testing the extensions, the first three authors reviewed the artifacts independently.

7   Conclusion

Crash reproduction is an important step in the process of debugging field crashes that are reported by end users. Several automated approaches to crash reproduction have been proposed in the literature to help developers debug field crashes. EvoCrash is a recent approach which applies a Guided Genetic Algorithm (GGA) to generate a crash reproducing test case. GGA uses a weighted scalarized function to optimize test generation for crash reproduction. In this study, we apply the GGA approach as an extension of EvoSuite and show that using a weighted sum scalarization fitness function improves test generation compared to a simple sum scalarization fitness function when reproducing complex crashes. Moreover, we also investigate the impact of decomposing the scalarized function into multiple optimization functions. Similarly, compared to using the weighted scalarized function, we observe that applying multi-objectivization improves the test generation time when reproducing complex crashes requiring several generations of test case evolution.

In general, we believe that multi-objectivization is under-explored to tackle (by-nature-)single-objective problems in search-based software testing. Our results on multi-objectivization by decomposition of the fitness function for crash reproduction are promising. This calls for the application of this technique to other (by-nature-) single-objective search-based problems.

References

1. Albunian, N.M.: Diversity in search-based unit test suite generation. In: Menzies, T., Petke, J. (eds.) SSBSE 2017. LNCS, vol. 10452, pp. 183–189. Springer, Cham (2017). https://doi.org/10.1007/978-3-319-66299-2_17
2. Arcuri, A., Fraser, G., Just, R.: Private API access and functional mocking in automated unit test generation. In: Proceedings of International Conference on Software Testing, Verification and Validation (ICST), pp. 126–137. IEEE (2017)
3. Bianchi, F.A., Pezzè, M., Terragni, V.: Reproducing concurrency failures from crash stacks. In: Proceedings of the Joint Meeting on Foundations of Software Engineering (FSE), pp. 705–716. ACM (2017)
4. Chen, N., Kim, S.: STAR: stack trace based automatic crash reproduction via symbolic execution. IEEE Trans. Softw. Eng. **41**(2), 198–220 (2015)
5. Coello Coello, C.A.: Constraint-handling techniques used with evolutionary algorithms. In: Proceedings of the Genetic and Evolutionary Computation Conference Companion (GECCO Companion), pp. 563–587. ACM (2016)
6. Črepinšek, M., Liu, S.H., Mernik, M.: Exploration and exploitation in evolutionary algorithms: a survey. ACM Comput. Surv. (CSUR) **45**(3), 35 (2013)
7. Deb, K., Pratap, A., Agarwal, S., Meyarivan, T.: A fast and elitist multiobjective genetic algorithm: NSGA-II. TEVC **6**(2), 182–197 (2002)
8. Feldt, R., Torkar, R., Gorschek, T., Afzal, W.: Searching for cognitively diverse tests: towards universal test diversity metrics. In: Proceedings of International Conference on Software Testing Verification and Validation Workshops (ICSTW), pp. 178–186. IEEE (2008)
9. Fraser, G., Arcuri, A.: Whole test suite generation. IEEE Trans. Softw. Eng. **39**(2), 276–291 (2013)
10. Fraser, G., Arcuri, A.: A large-scale evaluation of automated unit test generation using evosuite. TOSEM **24**(2), 8 (2014)
11. Goldberg, D.E., Richardson, J.: Genetic algorithms with sharing for multimodal function optimization. In: Proceedings of International Conference on Genetic Algorithms and Their Application, pp. 41–49. Lawrence Erlbaum Associates Inc. (1987)
12. Harman, M., McMinn, P.: A theoretical & empirical analysis of evolutionary testing and hill climbing for structural test data generation. In: Proceedings of the 2007 International Symposium on Software Testing and Analysis, pp. 73–83. ACM (2007)
13. Jähne, M., Li, X., Branke, J.: Evolutionary algorithms and multi-objectivization for the travelling salesman problem. In: Proceedings of the 11th Annual Conference on Genetic and Evolutionary Computation, pp. 595–602. ACM (2009)
14. Jin, W., Orso, A.: Bugredux: reproducing field failures for in-house debugging. In: Proceedings of International Conference on Software Engineering (ICSE), pp. 474–484. IEEE Press (2012)
15. Just, R., Jalali, D., Ernst, M.D.: Defects4J: a database of existing faults to enable controlled testing studies for Java programs. In: Proceedings of the International Symposium on Software Testing and Analysis (ISSTA), pp. 437–440. ACM (2014)
16. Kifetew, F.M., Panichella, A., De Lucia, A., Oliveto, R., Tonella, P.: Orthogonal exploration of the search space in evolutionary test case generation. In: Proceedings of International Symposium on Software Testing and Analysis (ISSTA), pp. 257–267. ACM (2013)

17. Knowles, J.D., Watson, R.A., Corne, D.W.: Reducing local optima in single-objective problems by multi-objectivization. In: Zitzler, E., Thiele, L., Deb, K., Coello Coello, C.A., Corne, D. (eds.) EMO 2001. LNCS, vol. 1993, pp. 269–283. Springer, Heidelberg (2001). https://doi.org/10.1007/3-540-44719-9_19

18. McMinn, P.: Search-based software test data generation: a survey. Softw. Test. Verification Reliab. **14**(2), 105–156 (2004)

19. Nayrolles, M., Hamou-Lhadj, A., Tahar, S., Larsson, A.: A bug reproduction approach based on directed model checking and crash traces. J. Softw.: Evol. Process **29**(3), e1789 (2017)

20. Rößler, J., Zeller, A., Fraser, G., Zamfir, C., Candea, G.: Reconstructing core dumps. In: Proceedings of International Conference on Software Testing, Verification and Validation (ICST), pp. 114–123. IEEE (2013)

21. Soltani, M., Panichella, A., van Deursen, A.: Evolutionary testing for crash reproduction. In: Proceedings of the 9th International Workshop on Search-Based Software Testing - SBST 2016, pp. 1–4 (2016)

22. Soltani, M., Panichella, A., van Deursen, A.: A guided genetic algorithm for automated crash reproduction. In: International Conference on Software Engineering (ICSE), pp. 209–220. IEEE, May 2017

23. Vargha, A., Delaney, H.D.: A critique and improvement of the CL common language effect size statistics of McGraw and Wong. J. Educ. Behav. Stat. **25**(2), 101–132 (2000)

24. Xuan, J., Xie, X., Monperrus, M.: Crash reproduction via test case mutation: let existing test cases help. In: Proceedings of the Joint Meeting on Foundations of Software Engineering (ESEC/FSE), pp. 910–913. ACM (2015)

Hot off the Press Papers

A New Approach for Search Space Reduction and Seeding by Analysis of the Clauses

Atieh Monemi Bidgoli$^{(\boxtimes)}$ (iD) and Hassan Haghighi$^{(\boxtimes)}$ (iD)

Department of Computer Science and Engineering, Shahid Beheshti University, G.C., Tehran, Iran
monemiatieh@gmail.com, h_haghighi@sbu.ac.ir

Abstract. The search space of potential inputs of a program is very large, even for the very small one, while this size is a key determining factor affecting the performance of any search-based test data generation approach. However, despite the large volume of work on search-based test data generation, the literature contains little work that concerns this problem. In this paper, by analysis of the clauses of the program, in addition to proposing a new search space reduction strategy, a new seeding approach is introduced.

Keywords: Search-based software testing · Test data generation
Input domain reduction · Search space reduction · Seeding

1 Introduction

Search-based software testing is an important research topic in automatic test data generation. Search-based test data generation reformulates testing targets as fitness functions, so that, test data generation can be automated by some chosen search-based optimization algorithm. The optimization algorithm searches the space of potential inputs to reach the target. Structural-oriented test data generators attempt to cover certain structural elements in the program and typically use an abstract representation of the program such as a Control Flow Graph (CFG). The CFG of a program is a directed graph that represents the control structure of the program.

In the structural testing, the potential inputs are very large, even for the very small program, while this size is a key determining factor affecting the performance of any search-based test data generation approach. Although search-based software testing has received a great deal of attention, there has been little work investigating this concern. The authors of [4,5] seek to address this problem by an approach to remove the domain of irrelevant input variables. Irrelevant input variables are input variables that do not influence whether a target structure will be executed or not.

Removing the irrelevant input variables raises the question whether it is necessary to search all the domain of relevant variables. In other words, could

© Springer Nature Switzerland AG 2018
T. E. Colanzi and P. McMinn (Eds.): SSBSE 2018, LNCS 11036, pp. 343–348, 2018.
https://doi.org/10.1007/978-3-319-99241-9_19

we have a strategy to select a subset of it with the condition that the structural targets will be found within that? Consider a well-known triangle type program, it has three input variables, instead of searching in all the domains of input variables, from INT_MIN to INT_MAX, it could be done in a subset of it (e.g., [1000,2000]). In practice, the one that is familiar with the logic of the program knows how to select a subset of search space such that all the targets will be found within that. However, could we have an approach to do this search space reduction automatically? In this paper, based on the clauses[1] of the program, an approach is proposed to indirectly approximate the reduced search space and do input domain reduction automatically.

In addition, to more enhance the performance of test data generation techniques, a new seeding (i.e., initialization of individuals) strategy is proposed based on the calculated values during search space reduction procedure. Studies show that providing domain knowledge improves the performance of test data generation techniques [2,7].

The underlying idea behind the proposed approach is that there is no need to investigate all the input domain of the program. Input variables of a program have a relation with each other and a special combination of them causes reaching a specific structure. By obtaining the relation between input parameters through the clauses of the program, we could reduce the domain based on. The clauses of the program are the place that the variables and the combination of them are checked to choose an appropriate branch. Therefore, per each clause, we calculate values for involved input variables such that changing one of the values makes the different evaluation for the clause, i.e., from True to False or vice versa. It must be noted that this is not Dynamic Domain Reduction (DDR) proposed by Offutt and Pan [6]: "It takes an initial set of values for each input, and dynamically pushes the values through the control-flow graph of the program, modifying the sets of values as branches in the program are taken. The result is usually a set of values for each input parameter that has the property that any choice from the sets will cause the path to be traversed."

Their approach works dynamically but the proposed approach does a static preprocessing before starting the search. DDR tries to find an exact value such that reach the target, our approach tries to approximately minimize the search space. Our approach considers every clause separately, while in DDR all clauses[2] are considered respectively.

2   The Proposed Approach

Since the search space in the numerical programs is made of the domains of input variables, all the clauses of the program must only involve input variables. The clauses are initially expressed in terms of program variables; since each of these program variables can be ultimately expressed in terms of input variables using assignment statements along the control path, it is possible to re-express the

---

[1] A clause is a predicate that does not have any logical operator.

[2] They used the word constraint instead.

```
For each clause C that only involves input variables of the program,
     Gain clause C' for clause C by the replacement of its relational
          operator with the equality operator
     Find a value per each input variable that will satisfy C'
End For
```

Fig. 1. Analysis of the clauses of the program

Table 1. Some examples of satisfaction values

	Clause C	Clause C'	Satisfaction values		
			a	b	c
1	$a > 50$	$a = 50$	50		
2	$a < b$	$a = b$	20	20	
3	$a + b > c$	$a + b = c$	50	50	100
4	$b \times b - 4 \times a \times c > 0$	$b \times b - 4 \times a \times c = 0$	4	4	1
5	$b \neq c$	$b = c$		150	150

clauses in terms of only the input variables. The approach applies a simplified version of symbolic evaluation to rewrite the clauses to be in terms of input variables. In this step, we might have more than one modified version of a clause based on the number of paths exist in the program. In our approach, only basis paths are considered for converting non-input variables to input variables.

(a)   (b)

Fig. 2. (a) Satisfaction values for the clause $a < b$ (b) A sample partitioned search space based on the clauses $a > b$ and $a > 50$

In the next step (Fig. 1), each clause is modified by replacing its relational operator (i.e., $\leq, \geq, \neq, =, <, >$) with the equality $(=)$ operator. The values that satisfy the resulting clause are calculated. For a simple clause like xRc or xRy, where both x and y are variables, c a constant and R a relational operator, a sample value for each input variable must be chosen to satisfy it. One variable is considered as dependent variables and its value is calculated based on the value of the other independent variables. For independent variables, a sample value must be selected from a preset domain. For a more complicated clause (i.e., non-linear), by putting right side of the clause to the left side, the function $F = 0$ is gained. Based on its type, analytically or numerically the root of the function F is calculated. Although there might be too many values that satisfy a clause, only one of them is used in the proposed approach. The root might be an approximate one if the numerical approach is used.

Consider the clause $a > 50$ in Table 1, the calculated value for this clause is $a = 50$. Therefore, the domain of variable a, based on value $a = 50$, is divided into two parts; the values in one part make the clause evaluated to $True$ and the values in the other part make it evaluated to $False$. Hence, we can divide the domain of variable a into two parts, one of which satisfies the true case and the other one satisfies the false case. In the case of $a < b$, with $a = 20$ and $b = 20$ as satisfaction values, the input domain of variables a and b is separately divided into two parts, and therefore, we have 2×2 combination of parts (i.e., partition) in the whole search space. Values in one of these four partitions make the clause evaluated to $True$ and values in one partition make it evaluated to $False$. Fig. 2 illustrate these examples. Table 1 shows satisfaction values for some more examples.

Seeding: The satisfaction values calculated in the Fig. 1 are used in the initialization of individuals to improve the performance of search based test data generation approach. Consider a program only has the five clauses presented in Table 1, and (a, b, c) are the parameters of it, the inputs in the following set should be used in the initialization of individuals: {(50, -, -), (20, 20, -), (50, 50, 100), (4, 4, 1), (-, 150, 150)}. The symbol "-" means that we could choose any value for the corresponding variable.

Search Space Reduction: If X be the set of obtained values for variable x, we could consider the range $[(min/1000) * 1000, ((max/1000) + 1) * 1000]$ as the domain of variable x, such that, min is the minimum value in the set X and max is the maximum value in the set X. For example, the calculated values for variable "income" in the program "compute tax" are {8350, 11950, 16700, 33950, 45500, 67900, 68525, 82250, 83500, 104425, 117450, 137050, 171550, 186475, 186500, 190200, 208850, 372950, 380000}, so the domain for the variable "income" can be set as [8000, 381000]. For another example, the reduced input domain for variables a, b and c in Table 1 is [0, 1000].

3   Preliminary Result

To see the effect of search space reduction and seeding on the performance of Genetic Algorithm (GA), we ran three different algorithms, GA, GA-R, and GA-R-S (R stands for Reduction and S stands for Seeding). GA ran on the whole search space. In GA-R, GA ran in the reduced search space. In GA-R-S, in addition to searching in a reduced search, the initialization was done based on the proposed approach.

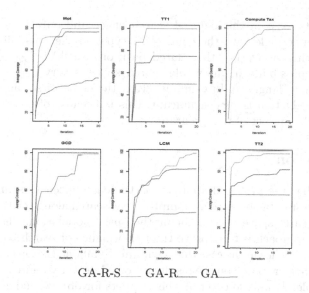

GA-R-S ___ GA-R___ GA___

Fig. 3. The average coverage of three algorithms on six different benchmarks

To perform the experiments, the average coverage is used as the evaluation metric. Average coverage denotes the average percentage of covered branches in repeated runs. It is calculated in each iteration. We selected a set of benchmark programs. Most of these programs are commonly used in the structural testing literature. TT1 and TT2 are two different algorithms for calculating the type of triangle. GCD and LCM find greatest common divisor and least common multiplier respectively. Compute Tax is an algorithm for computing tax amount. Mot is the synthesis of while, for and if. Of course, these are relatively small programs, but our approach right now is designed to work on the program units, not integrated software systems. Before conducting the experiments, the parameters of the algorithm had to be initialized. The number of population was set as 30. The number of iterations (i.e., generations) was 20. The crossover rate and the mutation rate were set as 0.8 and 0.03. All input variables are encoded as binary codes and "single point crossover" is the type of crossover. The fitness function is branch coverage with whole test suite generation strategy [3]. The range [0, 1000)] is considered as the preset domain for finding satisfaction values (Fig. 3).

For each program, experiments were repeated 50 times with different random seeds to take into account the stochastic nature of meta-heuristic algorithms. The statistical analysis was done just for the iteration equal to 10 (as the midpoint), but, for the sake of page limitation, we can not show that.

As expected the results, in most cases with high statistical confidence, manifest the positive effect of reduction and seeding in the performance of test data generation. Consider TT1, the search space is reduced for each input variable such that each one has 1000 different values. Thus, only $1000 \times 1000 \times 1000$

different inputs exist in this reduced search space and only 1000 inputs exist that make the triangle with the equilateral type, so the possibility of finding test data for this target (i.e., the related path or branch) is $\frac{1000}{1000 \times 1000 \times 1000}$. In contrast, this possibility in the whole search space is very high depending on the programming language. In Compute Tax, the effect of seeding compare to search space reduction is very significant, this is because of equality operators that exist in the clauses of this program.

4   Conclusion

We can say that the proposed approach is the customized version of DDR for search based test data generation to improve the search along the two directions: reducing the search space and enhancing the initial population. The final goal of the proposed approach is to improve the performance of search based test data generation approaches in the case that Dynamic Symbolic Execution (DSE) tools like Pex work better. Based on the results reported in [1] EvoSuite is the only tool which is completely able to cover all the snippets for objects and generics and it reaches high coverage on the majority of the code snippets. However, EvoSuite's limit is solving complex constraints and mathematical problems (in contrast, it is the power of Pex). Based on the way that Pex works based on, it seems that the proposed approach could be a solution to the mentioned limitation. We obtain promising results in the simple benchmarks and we hope that the preliminary results could serve as actionable feedback to tool developers.

References

1. Cseppento, L., Micskei, Z.: Evaluating symbolic execution-based test tools. In: 2015 IEEE 8th International Conference on Software Testing, Verification and Validation (ICST), pp. 1–10. IEEE (2015)
2. Fraser, G., Arcuri, A.: The seed is strong: seeding strategies in search-based software testing. In: 2012 IEEE Fifth International Conference on Software Testing, Verification and Validation (ICST), pp. 121–130. IEEE (2012)
3. Fraser, G., Arcuri, A.: Whole test suite generation. IEEE Trans. Softw. Eng. **39**(2), 276–291 (2013)
4. Harman, M., Hassoun, Y., Lakhotia, K., McMinn, P., Wegener, J.: The impact of input domain reduction on search-based test data generation. In: Proceedings of the 6th Joint Meeting of the European Software Engineering Conference and the ACM SIGSOFT Symposium on the Foundations of Software Engineering, pp. 155–164. ACM (2007)
5. McMinn, P., Harman, M., Lakhotia, K., Hassoun, Y., Wegener, J.: Input domain reduction through irrelevant variable removal and its effect on local, global, and hybrid search-based structural test data generation. IEEE Trans. Softw. Eng. **38**(2), 453–477 (2012)
6. Offutt, A.J., Jin, Z., Pan, J.: The dynamic domain reduction procedure for test data generation. Softw. Pract. Exp. **29**(2), 167–93 (1999)
7. Rojas, J.M., Fraser, G., Arcuri, A.: Seeding strategies in search-based unit test generation. Softw Test. Verif. Reliab. **26**(5), 366–401 (2016)

Learning Fault Localisation for both Humans and Machines Using Multi-objective GP

Kabdo Choi[(✉)], Jeongju Sohn, and Shin Yoo

Korea Advanced Institute of Science and Technology, Daejeon, Republic of Korea
{cyron1259,kasio555,shin.yoo}@kaist.ac.kr

Abstract. Genetic Programming has been successfully applied to fault localisation to learn ranking models that place the faulty program element as near the top as possible. However, it is also known that, when localisation results are used by Automatic Program Repair (APR) techniques, higher rankings of faulty program elements do not necessarily result in better repair effectiveness. Since APR techniques tend to use localisation scores as weights for program mutation, lower scores for non-faulty program elements are as important as high scores for faulty program elements. We formulate a multi-objective version of GP based fault localisation to learn ranking models that not only aim to place the faulty program element higher in the ranking, but also aim to assign as low scores as possible to non-faulty program elements. The results show minor improvements in the suspiciousness score distribution. However, surprisingly, the multi-objective formulation also results in more accurate fault localisation *ranking-wise*, placing 155 out of 386 faulty methods at the top, compared to 135 placed at the top by the single objective formulation.

Keywords: Fault localisation · Multi-objective evolutionary algorithm

1 Introduction

Genetic Programming has been successfully applied to fault localisation [9], initially to learn individual Spectrum-Based Fault Localisation (SBFL) risk evaluation formulæ [11] and subsequently to learn more complicated ranking models that take multiple SBFL formulæ as well as code and change metrics as input and produce rankings of program elements [7].

Increasingly, fault localisation techniques are being used by Automated Program Repair techniques, such as GenProg [8]: suspiciousness scores, i.e., the scores used for rankings, are often used as weights to determine parts of the program under repair that need to be patched. Noting this, Qi et al. evaluated fault localisation techniques using success rates of APR techniques as the effectiveness measure [6] and reported an interesting finding: SBFL formulas proven

© Springer Nature Switzerland AG 2018
T. E. Colanzi and P. McMinn (Eds.): SSBSE 2018, LNCS 11036, pp. 349–355, 2018.
https://doi.org/10.1007/978-3-319-99241-9_20

to produce better ranking than others [10] turned out to be less effective than formulæ they dominate when used with APR.

Inspired by Qi et al., we formulate a multi-objective learning to rank problem for fault localisation, aiming to evolve a ranking model that assigns not only higher scores (and, therefore, rankings) to faulty program elements, but also lower scores to non-faulty program elements. Thus, we aim to maintain better *rankings* for humans, while producing better *distributions* for APR techniques.

2   Locality Information Loss as Fitness Function

We extend FLUCCS [7], a GP based fault localisation technique, to have multiple objectives. The primary fitness function of FLUCCS is average ranking of the first faulty program elements computed against the faults in the training data as the fitness function. This section explains how we convert the distribution of suspiciousness scores into a secondary fitness function.

2.1   Locality Information Loss (LIL)

LIL is an evaluation metric for fault localization based on information theory [4]. Essentially, LIL treats the distribution of suspiciousness scores as a probability distribution, and computes the cross-entropy between the ground truth and the given score distribution using Kullback-Leibler divergence. The score distribution for the ground truth is give $\mathcal{L}(s_i) = 1$ if the program element s_i belongs to the set of faulty elements, S_f, and $0 < \epsilon \ll 1$ otherwise. LIL converts both the ground truth distribution, $\mathcal{L}$, and the given suspiciousness score distribution, τ, into probability distribution using linear normalisation, i.e., $P_\tau(s_i) = \frac{\tau(s_i)}{\sum_{i=1}^{n} \tau(s_i)} (1 \leq i \leq n)$. Finally, LIL itself is computed as the Kullbeck-Leibler divergence between two distributions: $D_{KL}(P_\mathcal{L}||P_\tau) = \sum_i P_\mathcal{L}(s_i) \ln \frac{P_\mathcal{L}(s_i)}{P_\tau(s_i)}$.

2.2   Weighted Locality Information Loss (wLIL)

After initial investigation, we learnt that LIL in its basic form is not suitable as a fitness function. As the number of program elements grows, the faulty program elements, of which there are only a few, have decreasing impact on the final LIL score. Reducing the suspiciousness scores for all program elements becomes a more effective strategy for GP to learn, damaging the ranking based fitness.

To counter this, we introduce wLIL, defined as $|S_f| \frac{|S \setminus S_f|}{|S|} P_\mathcal{L}(s_{f_m}) \ln \frac{P_\mathcal{L}(s_{f_m})}{P_\tau(s_{f_m})} +$ $\sum_{s_i \notin S_f} \frac{|S_f|}{|S|} P_\mathcal{L}(s_i) \ln \frac{P_\mathcal{L}(s_i)}{P_\tau(s_i)}$ (S is the set of all program elements, and s_{f_m} is the faulty element with maximum suspiciousness score). We use s_{f_m} as a substitute for $s_i \in S_f$ to boost the impact of faulty elements over the total score.

3   Experimental Setup

This section presents our research questions and the experimental set-up.

3.1   Research Questions

We investigate the following research questions to evaluate the effectiveness of the multi-objective version of FLUCCS, $\mathbb{F}_{MO}$, which uses NSGA-II [1] to implement multi-objective GP.

> **RQ1. Ranking Effectiveness:** how effective is $\mathbb{F}_{MO}$ at ranking the faulty program elements higher than non-faulty elements?
>
> **RQ2. Distribution Effectiveness:** how effective is $\mathbb{F}_{MO}$ at producing distributions of suspiciousness scores that resembles the ground truth?

Intuitively, RQ1 evaluates $\mathbb{F}_{MO}$ from the human perspective by checking the ranking of the faulty program elements, while RQ2 evaluates $\mathbb{F}_{MO}$ from the machine (i.e., APR) perspective. We use the original FLUCCS as the single objective baseline, $\mathbb{F}_{SO}$. To answer RQ1, we adopt the widely used evaluation metrics, $acc@n$ and wef, to compare $\mathbb{F}_{MO}$ and $\mathbb{F}_{SO}$: $acc@n$ counts the number of faults that have been ranked within the top n places by ranking models, whereas wef is the number of non-faulty program elements ranked higher than the first faulty program elements[1]. To answer RQ2, we measure the ratio between the highest suspiciousness scores of faulty and non-faulty program elements: casually, the higher the ratio is, the more *obvious* the faulty program elements appears to APR techniques. We report these ratios because wLIL values are hard to interpret intuitively.

3.2   Subject Programs

We use real world faults from `Defects4J` [3], the same benchmark that has been used in our previous work [7]. From the 395 faults provided by `Defects4J` 1.1.0, we use 386 faults, excluding 9 faults that we could not reproduce in the method level localisation experiments. Table 1 contains the details of subjects and faults.

Table 1. Subject software systems and their faults

Project	# faults	Loc	# Methods	# Test cases
Commons lang	63	9059–11490	1953–2408	1540–2295
Commons math	105	4726–41344	1049–6668	817–4429
Joda-time	26	12732–13270	3628–3802	3749–4041
Closure compiler	131	30438–50523	4848–8880	2595–8443
Jfreechart	25	41075–51523	6578–8281	1586–2193
Mockito	36	2110–4385	747–1476	695–1399

---

[1] Note that our primary fitness function is essentially the mean wef computed for faults in the training data-set.

3.3 Configuration

Both $\mathbb{F}_{MO}$ and $\mathbb{F}_{SO}$ are implemented using DEAP 1.2.2 [2], a Python evolutionary computation framework. We use tree-based GP, with single-point cross over with rate 1.0 and subtree mutation with rate 0.1; each GP individual describes a candidate ranking model. The population size is 40, and the maximum and minimum tree depth are eight and one respectively. The stopping criterion is after 100 generations. We use six GP operators: addition, subtraction, multiplication, safe division, negation, and safe square root. Both $\mathbb{F}_{MO}$ and $\mathbb{F}_{SO}$ use the same set of features and constant values as the previous work [7]. All experiments were performed on Ubuntu 16.04.4 LTS.

To avoid overfitting, we adopt ten-fold cross validation: 386 faults have been divided into 10 folds, each consisting of 35 to 39 faults. Each fold is used as the test data set to validate the ranking models trained with the remaining folds. We repeat GP ten times for each fold: for $\mathbb{F}_{MO}$, from each run in a fold, we first choose the ranking model with the best ranking fitness on the final Pareto-front to represent the run. Subsequently, we choose the ranking models with median and minimum ranking fitness ($\mathbb{F}_{MO}^{med}$ and $\mathbb{F}_{MO}^{min}$) among the ten representatives. For $\mathbb{F}_{SO}$, we simply choose the best individual from each run in a fold as the representative, and subsequently choose ones with median and minimum ranking fitness ($\mathbb{F}_{SO}^{med}$ and $\mathbb{F}_{SO}^{min}$) among the ten representatives. Finally, all faults are localised by $\mathbb{F}_{MO}^{med}$, $\mathbb{F}_{MO}^{min}$, $\mathbb{F}_{SO}^{med}$, and $\mathbb{F}_{SO}^{min}$ trained in their corresponding folds.

Ranking models generated by both $\mathbb{F}_{MO}$ and $\mathbb{F}_{SO}$ are essentially a large expressions that produce suspiciousness scores. When raking program elements using these scores, it is possible for ties to take place. We use the maximum tie-breaking rule, which assigns the lowest rank to all of the tied elements.

Table 2. Ranking Effectiveness of Single and Multi-objective FLUCCS

Config.	Subject	Flt.	acc				wef		Config.	Subject	Flt.	acc				wef	
			@1	@3	@5	@10	mean	σ				@1	@3	@5	@10	mean	σ
$\mathbb{F}_{SO}^{med}$	Chart	25	15	18	20	22	6.6400	20.0497	$\mathbb{F}_{MO}^{med}$	Chart	25	17	20	23	24	1.3600	3.0447
	Clos.	131	34	66	81	92	29.9008	101.3193		Clos.	131	37	66	83	97	33.3282	118.3868
	Lang	63	27	44	49	54	2.8571	4.5595		Lang	63	36	48	54	61	2.5556	9.0374
	Math	105	42	56	58	70	46.2857	305.3330		Math	105	45	60	67	76	107.1143	674.0247
	Mock.	36	10	19	21	28	9.2500	22.5085		Mock.	36	9	17	21	28	15.5833	54.0896
	Time	26	7	13	15	19	133.6538	636.7294		Time	26	11	16	17	19	253.0385	854.3380
Overall		386	135	216	244	285	33.5000	239.1826	Overall		386	155	227	265	305	59.4508	426.7188
$\mathbb{F}_{SO}^{min}$	Chart	25	16	20	23	23	1.8400	4.3237	$\mathbb{F}_{MO}^{min}$	Chart	25	15	20	23	23	1.9600	4.7873
	Clos.	131	25	61	74	92	33.5191	113.6997		Clos.	131	38	66	79	95	31.6336	103.2980
	Lang	63	34	42	48	55	2.8571	4.4645		Lang	63	34	46	53	59	33.5555	247.6137
	Math	105	49	62	65	76	57.8571	454.5908		Math	105	39	55	60	68	64.9714	480.6590
	Mock.	36	9	17	22	29	10.0555	21.7496		Mock.	36	8	18	21	27	49.8611	212.5439
	Time	26	10	16	18	19	89.5769	379.9093		Time	26	8	17	18	20	142.1538	636.0536
Overall		386	143	218	250	294	34.6710	266.4820	Overall		386	142	222	254	292	48.2383	329.9654

4   Results

Table 2 shows the results of ranking models generated by $\mathbb{F}_{MO}$ and $\mathbb{F}_{SO}$. Median fitness models perform better, $\mathbb{F}_{SO}^{med}$ and $\mathbb{F}_{MO}^{med}$ localising 35% and 40% of the total faults at the top of ranking respectively. Both $\mathbb{F}_{SO}^{min}$ and $\mathbb{F}_{MO}^{min}$ places approximately 37% of the faults at the top in comparison. Within top 10, 73% and 76% of the faults are localized by $\mathbb{F}_{SO}^{med}$ and $\mathbb{F}_{SO}^{min}$, respectively; $\mathbb{F}_{MO}^{med}$ and $\mathbb{F}_{MO}^{min}$ place 79% and 75.6% within top 10.

Most notably, $\mathbb{F}_{MO}^{med}$ ranking models performs either better or almost equally well according to $acc@1$, when compared to $\mathbb{F}_{SO}^{med}$ counterparts. We interpret this as a similar phenomenon to that reported by Praditwong et al. [5] in software remodularisation: formulating the same problem in a multi-objective fashion contributes to better fitness than in the single objective formulation. While the results call for a closer analysis, we cautiously posit that this improvement is due to the increased diversity during the multi-objective evolution. Interestingly, in terms of wef, $\mathbb{F}_{SO}$ tends to outperform $\mathbb{F}_{MO}$, which is as expected because $\mathbb{F}_{SO}$ can focus on improving wef alone whereas $\mathbb{F}_{MO}$ has to maintain Pareto-optimal populations. To answer RQ1: $\mathbb{F}_{MO}$ can rank as effectively as $\mathbb{F}_{SO}$.

To evaluate the distribution effectiveness, we report the ratio between the maximum score among faulty elements, v_f, and the maximum score among non-faulty elements, v_n. For both ratios $\frac{v_f}{v_n}$ and $\frac{v_n}{v_f}$, we count the number of faults for which the ratio exceeded $n = 1, 2, 5, 10$. The results are shown in Table 3 and Fig. 1. $\mathbb{F}_{MO}$ localise more faults with higher ratios up to $n = 2$, but fail to localise more faults with ratios higher than five. However, also note that the number of faults whose $\frac{v_n}{v_f}$ is greater than 10, i.e., the number of faults that are extremely difficult to localise, has been decreased by $\mathbb{F}_{MO}$ ranking models: from 110 to 103 by $\mathbb{F}_{MO}^{med}$, and from 111 to 101 by $\mathbb{F}_{MO}^{min}$, respectively. We suspect that the secondary objective, wLIL, encouraged the faulty program elements to be assigned with higher scores. To answer RQ2: $\mathbb{F}_{MO}$ does produce better distributions, but its effect is limited.

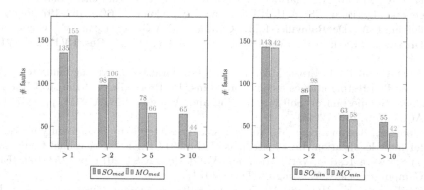

Fig. 1. Histograms of $\frac{v_f}{v_n}$ ratios achieved by $\mathbb{F}_{MO}$ and $\mathbb{F}_{SO}$

Table 3. Effectiveness of Single and Multi-objective FLUCCS

Config.	Subject	Flt.	v_f/v_n >1	>2	>5	>10	v_n/v_f ≥1	≥2	≥5	≥10	Config.	Subject	Flt.	v_f/v_n >1	>2	>5	>10	v_n/v_f ≥1	≥2	≥5	≥10
F_{SO}^{med}	Chart	25	15	12	12	6	10	7	3	3	F_{MO}^{med}	Chart	25	17	13	11	4	8	7	6	4
	Clos.	131	34	24	17	15	97	74	58	50		Clos.	131	37	26	12	8	94	81	61	50
	Lang	63	27	24	21	20	36	23	19	15		Lang	63	36	29	20	18	27	19	11	7
	Math	105	42	25	20	19	63	45	30	26		Math	105	45	28	17	10	60	48	34	23
	Mock.	36	10	7	5	3	26	19	15	12		Mock.	36	9	5	2	2	27	22	12	10
	Time	26	7	6	3	2	19	11	4	4		Time	26	11	5	4	2	15	13	9	9
Overall		386	135	98	78	65	251	179	129	110	Overall		386	155	106	66	44	231	190	133	103
F_{SO}^{min}	Chart	25	16	13	11	8	9	6	6	6	F_{MO}^{min}	Chart	25	15	9	5	2	10	8	7	2
	Clos.	131	25	18	14	14	106	64	51	45		Clos.	131	38	28	13	10	93	75	60	49
	Lang	63	34	16	15	13	29	20	19	16		Lang	63	34	26	22	17	29	19	10	8
	Math	105	49	27	18	15	56	41	32	28		Math	105	39	23	13	8	66	49	37	25
	Mock.	36	9	5	2	2	27	13	10	7		Mock.	36	8	6	1	1	28	22	14	9
	Time	26	10	7	3	3	16	10	10	9		Time	26	8	6	4	4	18	15	10	8
Overall		386	143	86	63	55	243	154	128	111	Overall		386	142	98	58	42	244	188	138	101

5   Conclusion

We report the first attempt to evolve ranking models for fault localisation that is useful for both humans and machines using multi-objective GP. The results suggest that the added diversity produces better rankings.

Acknowledgements. This research was supported by the Korean MSIT(Ministry of Science and ICT), under the National Program for Excellence in SW (2016-0-00018), supervised by the IITP(Institute for Information & communications Technology Promotion).

References

1. Deb, K., Pratap, A., Agarwal, S., Meyarivan, T.: A fast and elitist multiobjective genetic algorithm: NSGA-II. IEEE Trans. Evol. Comput. **6**(2), 182–197 (2002)
2. Fortin, F.A., De Rainville, F.M., Gardner, M.A.G., Parizeau, M., Gagné, C.: DEAP: evolutionary algorithms made easy. J. Mach. Learn. Res. **13**(1), 2171–2175 (2012)
3. Just, R., Jalali, D., Ernst, M.D.: Defects4J: a database of existing faults to enable controlled testing studies for java programs. In: Proceedings of the 2014 International Symposium on Software Testing and Analysis, ISSTA 2014, pp. 437–440. ACM, New York (2014)
4. Moon, S., Kim, Y., Kim, M., Yoo, S.: Ask the mutants: mutating faulty programs for fault localization. In: Proceedings of the 2014 IEEE International Conference on Software Testing, Verification, and Validation, ICST 2014, pp. 153–162. IEEE Computer Society, Washington, D.C. (2014)
5. Praditwong, K., Harman, M., Yao, X.: Software module clustering as a multi-objective search problem. IEEE Trans. Softw. Eng. **37**(2), 264–282 (2010)

6. Qi, Y., Mao, X., Lei, Y., Wang, C.: Using automated program repair for evaluating the effectiveness of fault localization techniques. In: Proceedings of the 2013 International Symposium on Software Testing and Analysis, ISSTA 2013, pp. 191–201. ACM, New York (2013)

7. Sohn, J., Yoo, S.: FLUCCS: using code and change metrics to improve fault localization. In: Proceedings of the 26th International Symposium on Software Testing and Analysis, ISSTA 2017, pp. 273–283. ACM (2017)

8. Weimer, W., Nguyen, T., Goues, C.L., Forrest, S.: Automatically finding patches using genetic programming. In: Proceedings of the 31st IEEE International Conference on Software Engineering (ICSE 2009), pp. 364–374, 16–24 May 2009

9. Wong, W.E., Gao, R., Li, Y., Abreu, R., Wotawa, F.: A survey on software fault localization. IEEE Trans. Softw. Eng. **42**(8), 707 (2016)

10. Xie, X., Chen, T.Y., Kuo, F.C., Xu, B.: A theoretical analysis of the risk evaluation formulas for spectrum-based fault localization. ACM Trans. Softw. Eng. Methodol. **22**(4), 31:1–31:40 (2013)

11. Yoo, S.: Evolving human competitive spectra-based fault localisation techniques. In: Fraser, G., Teixeira de Souza, J. (eds.) SSBSE 2012. LNCS, vol. 7515, pp. 244–258. Springer, Heidelberg (2012). https://doi.org/10.1007/978-3-642-33119-0_18

Mapping Class Dependencies
for Fun and Profit

Allen Kanapala[1] and Gregory Gay[2($\boxtimes$)]

[1] University of South Carolina Salkehatchie, Allendale, SC, USA
kanapalaa@acm.org
[2] University of South Carolina, Columbia, SC, USA
greg@greggay.com

Abstract. Classes depend on other classes to perform certain tasks. By *mapping* these dependencies, we may be able to improve software quality. We have developed a prototype framework for generating optimized groupings of classes coupled to targets of interest. From a pilot study investigating the value of coupling information in test generation, we have seen that coupled classes generally have minimal impact on results. However, we found 23 cases where the inclusion of coupled classes improves test suite efficacy, with an average improvement of 120.26% in the likelihood of fault detection. Seven faults were detected only through the inclusion of coupled classes. These results offer lessons on how coupling information could improve automated test generation.

Keywords: Coupling · Search-based software engineering
Software testing

1 Introduction

In complex systems, *coupled* classes depend on other classes to perform certain tasks [6]. By *mapping* and grouping these dependencies, we may be able to offer valuable information that can improve software quality.

Automated test generation can be performed to control testing costs. However, a question remains—which classes should be targeted for generation? Often, only the classes that are known to be faulty are targeted. However, a class that is coupled to a faulty class may still exhibit unexpected behavior. By generating tests for coupled classes, we may be able to detect faults that would otherwise be missed.

We have developed a prototype framework to investigate the effect of coupling in test generation. The framework maps the dependencies between Java classes into a directed graph. This graph can then be used to generate small, dense groupings of classes centered around selected targets. To understand whether test generation is more effective when including coupled classes, we have performed

T. E. Colanzi and P. McMinn (Eds.): SSBSE 2018, LNCS 11036, pp. 356–362, 2018.
https://doi.org/10.1007/978-3-319-99241-9_21

a pilot case study. Using 588 real faults from 14 Java projects, we have identified groupings of classes, generated test suites for these groupings and the faulty classes alone, and assessed whether the inclusion of coupled classes improves the likelihood of fault detection.

Overall, there is only an average improvement of 3.79% in the likelihood of fault detection when incorporating coupled classes. However, when these additional classes have *any* impact, there is an average improvement of 120.26% and seven additional faults were detected only through coupling. The inclusion of coupled classes could yield significant efficacy improvements if we can identify in advance where they would be useful, and improve coverage of dependencies. In addition, our optimization process often yields unnecessarily large groupings.

We hypothesize that the ability to map and optimize groups of coupled classes could benefit many areas of software engineering research—particularly when automating tasks. Our framework has offered promising preliminary results. We will further explore how coupling information could improve automated software engineering.

2   Coupling Mapping Framework

We have developed a framework that maps class dependencies into a directed graph[1]. We then use this graph to optimize small, highly-interconnected groupings of classes coupled to designated targets using a simple genetic algorithm. The following basic process is used to generate groupings:

1. This framework first maps dependencies between classes. In this case, we consider dependencies to be either method calls or variable references to another class.
2. A directed graph is created, where each class is a node, and each edge indicates a dependency. Any classes that have no dependencies and are not the target of a dependency will be filtered out from consideration at this stage. If no classes are coupled to a changed class, the changed class will still be added to the target list.
3. We generate a population of 1,000 groupings, formed by randomly selecting classes.
4. Each grouping is scored using the fitness function described below, and a new population is formed through retention of best solutions (by default, 10%), mutation (20%), crossover (20%), and further random generation (50%).
5. Evolution continues until the time budget is exhausted—by default, five minutes[2].
6. The best grouping is returned. The changed classes are added to that grouping.

---

[1] Available from https://github.com/Greg4cr/Coupling-Mapping.
[2] Experimentation suggested that convergence was often reached before that time.

The fitness function used to score groupings is:

$$F_G = \sqrt{\overline{size}^2 + (\overline{coverage} - 1)^2 + \overline{avg(distance)}^2} \qquad (1)$$

That is, we prioritize groupings that are closer to a *sweet spot* of fewer classes (*size*), where the chosen classes are coupled to a large number of other classes (*coverage*), and where more classes are either coupled directly to the changed classes or through a small number of indirect dependency links (average *distance*). This should result in a relatively small grouping of classes that are densely coupled to each other and other classes. $\bar{x}$ is a normalized value $0 \leq \frac{x - min(x)}{max(x) - min(x)} \leq 1$. Scores range from $0 \leq F_G \leq \sqrt{3}$ and lower scores are better.

3   Case Study

Traditionally, in unit test generation research, tests are generated solely for the classes we know to contain faults. However, other classes may depend on the faulty classes, and by targeting these coupled classes, we may be more likely to detect faults. We wish to examine whether we could use knowledge of class dependencies to enhance test generation. Specifically, we wish to address: (1) *Can the inclusion of coupled classes improve the efficacy and reliability of test suite generation?* (2) *Are the groupings produced by our framework small enough to be of practical use?*

We have performed the following experiment: (1) We have gathered 588 real faults, from 14 Java projects. (2) For each fault we generate 10 groupings of coupled classes. (3) For each fault, we generate 10 suites per grouping (and for the set of faulty classes) using the non-faulty version of each class. We allow a two-minute generation budget per targeted class. (4) For each fault, we measure the proportion of test suites that detect the fault to the total number generated.

Defects4J is an extensible database of real faults extracted from Java projects [4][3]. Currently, it consists of 597 faults from 15 projects. For each fault, Defects4J provides access to the faulty and fixed versions of the code, developer-written test cases that expose the faults, and a list of classes and lines of code modified by the patch that fixes the fault. The Guava project was omitted from this study, as its code uses features not supported by our framework. We have used the remaining 588 faults for this study.

EvoSuite applies a genetic algorithm in order to evolve test suites over several generations, forming a new population by retaining, mutating, and combining the strongest solutions [7]. It is actively maintained and has been successfully applied to the Defects4J dataset [2]. In this study, we used EvoSuite version 1.0.5.

Tests are generated from the fixed version of each class and applied to the faulty version in order to eliminate the oracle problem. Tests are generated targeting Branch Coverage, and EvoSuite is allowed two minutes per class—a time

---

[3] Available from http://defects4j.org.

chosen to fit within the strict time constraints of the continuous integration (CI) process that testing is commonly performed as part of. In the CI process, changed code is built, verified, and deployed. As this process may be performed multiple times per day, test generation and execution must take place on a limited time scale. As results may vary, we generate 10 groupings of classes per fault, and we perform 10 test generation trials for each fault, grouping, and budget. Generation tools may generate flaky (unstable) tests [2]. We automatically remove non-compiling test cases. Then, each test is executed on the fixed CUT five times. If results are inconsistent, the test case is removed. On average, less than 1% of tests are removed from each suite.

4   Results and Discussion

In Table 1, we compare the average likelihood of detection between the normal case—where only the faulty classes are targeted—and when we generate for a set of targets including coupled classes. From this table, we can see that there is often *some* improvement, but the overall effect is minimal. The inclusion of coupled classes fails to improve results for six systems. For the others, we see average improvements of up to 13.36%. Overall, the average improvement from including coupled classes is only 3.79%.

To understand when coupled classes can benefit generation, we can filter out situations where their inclusion does not improve results. Table 2 lists the average likelihood of detection for the 23 faults where the inclusion of coupled classes had an impact. These filtered results show that when additional classes have *any* impact, it is a major one. In such cases, the likelihood of detection improves by an average of 120.26%. In fact, seven new faults were *only* detected by including coupled classes.

Table 1. Average likelihood of detection when only changed classes are targeted and when coupled classes are included, omitting systems with no observed differences.

Project	Detection likelihood (changed-only)	Detection likelihood (with coupled)
Chart	40.00%	42.58%
Closure	4.10%	5.10%
CommonsCodec	31.36%	35.55%
CommonsCSV	55.00%	58.50%
Jsoup	19.80%	21.70%
Lang	35.20%	35.50%
Math	28.68%	29.29%
Time	34.40%	35.90%
Overall	22.69%	23.55%

Table 2. Average likelihood of detection–omitting cases where coupled classes have no effect.

Project	Detection likelihood (changed-only)	Detection likelihood (with coupled)
Chart	15.00%	27.50%
Closure	30.00%	62.50%
CommonsCodec	13.33%	44.00%
CommonsCSV	30.00%	51.00%
Jsoup	15.00%	27.80%
Lang	10.00%	30.00%
Math	6.67%	28.33%
Time	25.00%	44.00%
Overall	18.26%	40.22%

While the addition of classes can be very powerful, it is also very expensive given that—by default—the same amount of time is devoted to generating test cases for each class. Our results illustrate that we should not generate tests for such classes if there is a low likelihood they will help detect faults. **To decide when to add additional targets, we must understand when their inclusion will be helpful.**

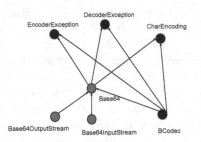

Fig. 1. Partial visualization of coupling. Relevant classes are colored red. (Color figure online)

Figure 1 depicts a selection of classes in the CommonsCodec project. Three faults—centering around the `Base64` class (faults 12, 15, and 20[4])—see improved efficacy from the inclusion of coupled classes `Base64Input Stream` and `Base64OutputStream`. Tests generated solely to target `Base64` are able to detect all three faults, but not reliably. The incorporation of these two coupled classes greatly increases the likelihood of detection. Class—`BCodec`—is also coupled to `Base64`, but does not contribute to efficacy.

These three examples are interesting because the two additional classes are not just coupled through in-code dependencies, but all three are linked by a common conceptual purpose—encoding binary data by treating it numerically and translating it into a base 64 representation. One option for incorporating coupled classes would be to periodically present human developers with coupling information and ask them to filter groupings. Each time that any class in that grouping is altered, those coupled classes could be included in generation.

Of course, not all situations where coupling assists are as straightforward as the CommonsCodec example. For instance, consider fault 31 for the Math system[5]. Generated tests never detect the issue when targeting faulty class `ContinuedFraction`. Instead, the fault is only detected when tests are generated for `Gamma` (coupled to `Continued Fraction`) and `GammaDistribution` (coupled to `Gamma`). The reason the coupled classes are useful is likely because they provide guidance to the generator in how to make use of `ContinuedFraction`. Exposing the fault requires setting up a series of values and calling `ContinuedFraction.evaluate(...)` on those values. By attaining coverage of `Gamma`, EvoSuite is able to set up and execute the functionality of `ContinuedFraction`. Without that guidance, it struggles.

While only a small number of classes are coupled to `Continued Fraction`, there is not a common conceptual connection like with the CommonsCodec example above. In retrospect, we can explain these situations. However, more research is needed to recognize patterns in when the inclusion of coupled classes is beneficial. Further, asking developers to name useful couplings creates addi-

---

[4] https://github.com/Greg4cr/defects4j/blob/master/framework/projects/CommonsCodec/patches/[12/15/20].src.patch.

[5] https://github.com/rjust/defects4j/blob/master/framework/projects/Math/patches/31.src.patch.

tional maintenance effort, and may not offer sufficient benefit for the time and knowledge required. Therefore, we also need further research into automated means to suggest and prune couplings.

We should also endeavor to make the inclusion of coupled classes more useful by focusing on increased coverage of those dependencies. **The efficacy of generation—when coupled classes are included as targets—may be improved if coverage is ensured of references to changed classes.**

Test generation for each class is an entirely independent process. While the attained Branch Coverage may be relatively high for each targeted class, we have no guarantee that dependencies *between classes* are covered. Steps could be taken to improve coverage of such dependencies by considering coverage of dependencies between classes. Jin and Offutt have proposed coverage criteria for integration testing that could be used to ensure class dependencies are covered [3]. These forms of "Coupling Coverage" could be used to prioritize suites that attain a higher coverage of the specific code segments that require data or functionality from a changed class.

Recent work has found that combinations of coverage criteria can be more effective than individual criteria [2]. For example, combining Branch and Exception Coverage yields test suites that both cover the code and force the program into unusual configurations. "Coupling Coverage" metrics could be thought of as another situationally-appropriate orthogonal criterion. Rather than generating tests using Branch Coverage alone, the generator could combine Branch and "Coupling Coverage" when targeting coupled classes—potentially creating suites that are especially effective at exploiting dependencies between classes, and in turn, at detecting faults.

Table 3. Average number of classes in the groupings.

	Number of classes
Chart	18.63
Closure	73.92
CommonsCLI	1.91
CommonsCodec	3.51
CommonsCSV	3.40
CommonsJXPath	20.80
JacksonCore	5.03
JacksonDatabind	34.96
JacksonXML	2.80
Jsoup	26.34
Lang	7.12
Math	12.64
Mockito	34.43
Time	52.87

Regardless of the use, our framework is intended to produce small, effective groups of coupled classes. The size of that group must be small enough to be of practical use. In Table 3, we list the average grouping size for each system. In many cases, we can see that these groupings are larger than would be practical. We used them for this case study, as they are useful for understanding the benefits of such information. **However, we must refine the optimization process to further limit grouping size.**

We found that, in situations where coupling affects the results, only a small number of classes are useful, and they are closely linked to the target classes. Therefore, these groupings could be easily pruned down to a more appropriate size. We will reformulate our fitness function to further constrain grouping size.

5   Related Work

Coupling between classes is a well-established area of research [6]. Similar search-based techniques have been used to suggest refactorings. The CCDA algorithm uses a graph structure and a genetic algorithm to restructure packages based on class dependencies [5]. However, we are aware of no other use of such techniques to optimize groupings for test generation. Past work on integration testing has suggested ways to better ensure that class dependencies are tested [1,3], but has largely not addressed the question of *which* classes to test. In addition, we are not focused purely on integration testing, but a broader set of scenarios.

6   Conclusions

We have developed a framework to optimize groupings of classes. The results of a pilot study on the applicability of coupling to test generation show potential benefits from generating tests for coupled classes and offer new research challenges.

References

1. Alexander, R.T., Offutt, A.J.: Criteria for testing polymorphic relationships. In: Proceedings of 11th International Symposium on Software Reliability Engineering, pp. 15–23 (2000)
2. Gay, G.: Generating effective test suites by combining coverage criteria. In: Menzies, T., Petke, J. (eds.) SSBSE 2017. LNCS, vol. 10452, pp. 65–82. Springer, Cham (2017). https://doi.org/10.1007/978-3-319-66299-2_5
3. Jin, Z., Offutt, A.J.: Coupling-based criteria for integration testing. Softw. Test. Verif. Reliab. 8(3), 133–154 (1998). https://onlinelibrary.wiley.com
4. Just, R., Jalali, D., Ernst, M.D.: Defects4J: a database of existing faults to enable controlled testing studies for Java programs. In: Proceedings of the 2014 International Symposium on Software Testing and Analysis, ISSTA 2014, pp. 437–440. ACM, New York (2014). https://doi.org/10.1145/2610384.2628055
5. Pan, W., Jiang, B., Xu, Y.: Refactoring packages of objectoriented software using genetic algorithm based community detection technique. Int. J. Comput. Appl. Technol. 48(3), 185–194 (2013). https://doi.org/10.1504/IJCAT.2013.056914
6. Poshyvanyk, D., Marcus, A.: The conceptual coupling metrics for object-oriented systems. In: 22nd IEEE International Conference on Software Maintenance, pp. 469–478, September 2006
7. Rojas, J.M., Campos, J., Vivanti, M., Fraser, G., Arcuri, A.: Combining multiple coverage criteria in search-based unit test generation. In: Barros, M., Labiche, Y. (eds.) SSBSE 2015. LNCS, vol. 9275, pp. 93–108. Springer, Cham (2015). https://doi.org/10.1007/978-3-319-22183-0_7

Evolving Better Software Parameters

William B. Langdon$^{(\boxtimes)}$ and Justyna Petke

CREST, Computer Science, UCL, London WC1E 6BT, UK
w.langdon@cs.ucl.ac.uk
http://www.cs.ucl.ac.uk/staff/W.Langdon,
http://www.cs.ucl.ac.uk/staff/J.Petke,
http://crest.cs.ucl.ac.uk

Abstract. Genetic improvement might be widely used to adapt existing numerical values within programs. Applying GI to embedded parameters in computer code can create new functionality. For example, CMA-ES can evolve 1024 real numbers in a GNU C library square root to implement a cube root routine for C.

Keywords: Genetic improvement · SBSE · GGGP
Software maintenance of empirical constants · Data transplantation
glibc · sqrt · cbrt

1 Literature on Maintaining Numbers Within Code

Many programs contain embedded parameters. Typically these are numeric values (often float or double, but also integers, e.g. the GNU C library contains more than a million integer constants, see Fig. 1, also [1]). In many cases these parameters relate to the software itself or to simple facts which are unlikely to change during the program's lifetime or period of active use. However, many others aught to be updated. This maintenance problem has been known for a long time (Martin and Osborne [2, Sect. 6.8, p. 24, Hard Coded Parameters Which Are Subject To Change]).

Parameters may relate to heuristics within the code, which the developer chose before contact with real users. Their values perhaps should have been updated shortly after first release, or values (e.g. those relating to memory or array sizes) may need updating due to operating on new hardware, as well as to changes in patterns of use. Other parameters can relate to the problem itself. For example, chemical reaction rate constants in ozone layer simulations [3]. In some cases the exact numerical values are critical [3]. Some physical values are known with very high precision, but for others the state of scientific knowledge can improve over the operational life of the program. For example, the ViennaRNA package [4] contains more than 50 000 binding energy values. These are derived from scientific measurements of RNA molecules. Even so, during the relatively short life of this suite of C programs, knowledge has moved on and various newer versions of these parameters are available. Recently [5], we showed genetic

© Springer Nature Switzerland AG 2018
T. E. Colanzi and P. McMinn (Eds.): SSBSE 2018, LNCS 11036, pp. 363–369, 2018.
https://doi.org/10.1007/978-3-319-99241-9_22

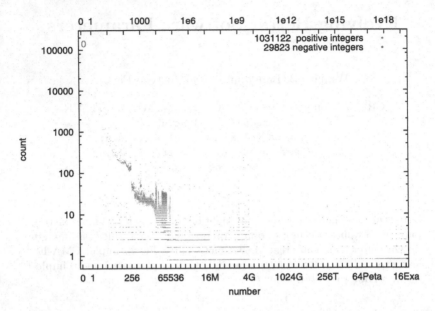

Fig. 1. The GNU C library version 2.27 (excluding test suite) contains 1 202 711 integer constants. Zero is the most common, occurring a total of 141,874 times, followed by 1 (19 203) and −1 (6 479). Every integer between −28 and 40 956 occurs at least once.

improvement could be used to adapt these 50 000 int values. (The GI values have been distributed with ViennaRNA since version 2.4.5).

As computing is now mature, maintaining software has become the dominant cost. Marounek [6, p. 51] quotes figures of more than 90% of total cost. Moreover, software maintenance routinely requires highly skilled experts [7, p. 65]. Yet a forthcoming survey [8] starts by saying "a relatively small amount [of SBSE research] is related to software maintenance", whilst [9] does not give a break down of the SBSE literature on software maintenance. Indeed it appears that maintaining embedded constants within existing packages has received little attention so far. For example, [10] considers the maintenance impact of names given to constants in Java source code, but not how to maintain their values. Similarly, [11] consider how to hide constant values, but not how to update them.

There is some research on parameter tuning. For example, ParamILS[1] or irace[2] tools. However, there is scarcely any on updating parameters in the code that are not specifically exposed to the user for tuning. The deep parameter tuning work by Wu et al. [12] being the first known example, where they optimised for runtime and memory consumption. Unlike Wu et al. [12], we focus on adapting numerical values only. Previous work on evolving new features using GI dealt with transplantation of portions of one program to another [13], or evolving functionality separately and then adding them to existing code using

---

[1] http://www.cs.ubc.ca/labs/beta/Projects/ParamILS/.

[2] http://iridia.ulb.ac.be/irace/.

automated software transplantation [14] (so-called 'grow-and-graft'). Our approach does not require additional code, just changes within the existing code base.

In the next section we continue exploring automated parameter tuning by taking existing code which relies on $\approx$1 thousand embedded constants from the GNU C library to create a function, cbrt, which is not implemented by the library. Section 2.3 shows its accuracy is typically better than $2 \ 10^{-16}$ and not worse than 10^{-15}. (I.e. typically within one bit in the IEEE 754 double precision representation.) Finally, in Sect. 3, we suggest there is a great need for research into both automated data update and data transplantation.

2 Example of Automated Parameter Tuning for Evolving New Functionality

We use an existing implementation of the square root function and use genetic improvement to evolve a cube root function. This is achieved by mutating the constant values in the chosen code for square root.

The current release of the GNU C library (glibc-2.27, 1 Feb 2018, 851 080 lines of non-test code) was downloaded from https://www.gnu.org/s/libc/. It contains multiple implementations of the square root function (sqrt). One (../powerpc/fpu) which uses table lookup [15] was selected for use as a model for a table-based version of the cube root function (cbrt).

2.1 Manual Changes

We are primarily concerned with adjusting data values. However, a few changes to the existing powerPC sqrt code were made by hand so that it could support cbrt. Whilst in [5] no code changes were needed, we envision that such changes may be required. For cbrt: (1) Various powerPC optimisations were disabled. (2) Replaced the trap for negative numbers by returning $-\sqrt[3]{-x}$ if x is negative. (3) Division of the exponent part of double precision numbers by three is rather more tricky than division by two. Keeping track of the remainder required the multiplication or division by $\sqrt[3]{2}$ or $\sqrt[3]{2^2}$ (Sect. 2.3). The existing constants CBRT2 and SQR_CBRT2 were used. (4) sysdeps/powerpc/fpu/e_sqrt.c uses a right shift to do two operations. Firstly to divide the exponent by two. And secondly to combine the least significant bit of the exponent with the top eight bits of the fractional part, forming a nine bit index into the table. Effectively mapping numbers in the range 0.5 to 2 onto the table. The more tricky division by three led to the decision to exclude the exponent and to just use the top nine bits of the fractional part as the table index. So numbers in the range 1 to 2 are mapped onto the table, see also Fig. 2. (5) The constant almost_half was replaced by new constant almost_third = 0.3333333333333334.

2.2   Automatic Changes to Data Table Using CMA-ES

The _t_sqrt table contains 512 pairs of floats. The top 256 correspond to numbers in the range 1 to 2. These were used as start points when evolving the 512 pairs of floats in the new table _t_cbrt.

The Covariance Matrix Adaptation Evolution Strategy algorithm (CMA-ES [16]) was downloaded from https://github.com/cma-es/c-cmaes/archive/master.zip. It was set up to fill the table of floats one pair at a time. Each pair being initially set to either the corresponding pair of values in _t_sqrt or the mean of two adjacent pairs. The initial mutation step sizes used by CMA-ES were set (pairwise) to 3.0 times the standard deviation calculated from the 512 pairs of numbers in _t_sqrt.

CMA-ES Parameters. The CMA-ES defaults (cmaes_initials.par) were used, except: the problem size (N 2), the initial values and mutation sizes are loaded from _t_sqrt (see previous section) and various small values concerned with run termination were set to zero (stopFitness, stopTolFun, stopTolFunHist, stopTolX). The initial seed used for pseudo random numbers was also set externally.

Fitness Function. Each time CMA-ES proposes a pair $(N = 2)$ of double values, they are converted into floats and loaded into _t_cbrt at the location that CMA-ES is currently trying to optimise. The fitness function uses three fixed test double values in the range 1.0 to 2.0. These are: the lowest value for the _t_cbrt entry, the mid point and the top most value. The cbrt function is called (using the updated _t_cbrt) for each and a sub-fitness value calculated with each of the three returned doubles. The sub-fitnesses are combined by adding them.

Each sub-fitness takes the output of cbrt, cubes it and takes the absolute difference between this and the corresponding test value. If they are the same, the sub-fitness is 0, otherwise it is positive. Since when cbrt is working well, the differences are very small, they are re-scaled for CMA-ES. If the absolute difference is less than one, its log is taken, otherwise the absolute value is used. However, in both cases, to prevent the sub-fitness being negative, log of the smallest feasible non-zero difference DBL_EPSILON is subtracted.

CMA-ES will stop when the difference on all three test points is zero.

Restart Strategy. When CMA-ES failed to find a pair of values for which all three test cases pass, it was run again with the same initial starting position and mutation size, but a new pseudo random number seed. Mostly CMA-ES found a suitable pair in one run, but in 107 of 512 cases it was run more than once. (In no case was CMS-ES run more than 4 times on a particular pair.)

2.3   Testing the Evolved cbrt Function

The pairs of float values found by CMA-ES, called sg, sy in the system, are shown in Fig. 2. The glibc-2.27 powerPC IEEE754 table-based double sqrt function

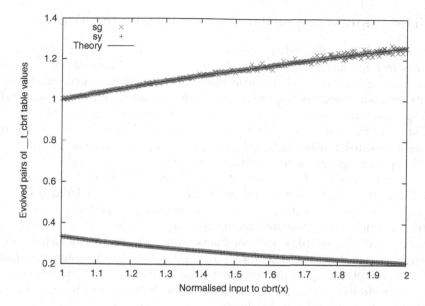

Fig. 2. 512 (*sg, sy*) pairs of numbers found by CMA-ES for _t_cbrt. Horizontal axis is the normalised argument of cbrt which corresponds to each pair in _t_cbrt.

claims to produce answers within one bit of the correct solution. On 1 536 tests of large integers ($\approx 10^{16}$) designed to test each of the 512 bins 3 times (min, max and a randomly chosen point) the largest discrepancy between (cbrt(x)**3) and x was three (i.e. 6.66 10^{-16}). In all tests, including those described in the rest of this section, this only arose when the exponent part of the double was not a multiple of 3. This requires the cbrt code to do an extra multiply or divide by $\sqrt[3]{2}$ or $\sqrt[3]{2}$ (i.e. CBRT2 or SQR_CBRT2, see Sect. 2.1), apparently resulting in additional loss of precision.

As well as ad-hoc testing, and the large positive integer tests mentioned in the previous paragraph, cbrt was tested with 5 120 random numbers uniformly distributed between 1 and 2 (the largest deviation was two[3] 5 120 random scientific notation numbers and 5 120 random 64 bit patterns. Half the random scientific notation numbers were negative and half positive. Half were smaller than one and half larger. The exponent was chosen uniformly at random from the range 0 to |308|. In one case a random 64 bit pattern corresponded to NAN (Not-A-Number) and cbrt correctly returned NAN. In most cases cbrt returned a double, which when cubed was its input or within one bit of it. In some cases the cubed answer was two from the input. The maximum deviation was 3.

---

[3] 2 at the least significant part of IEEE754 double precision corresponds to 4.44 10^{-16}.

3   The Importance of Automated Parameter Tuning

Section 1 has briefly covered the existing literature. It makes clear that, apart from our own recent work [5], the problem of automatic update of values embedded in existing software has been little studied. By page 2 it showed that the cost of software maintenance is staggering, yet there is little research on automatically adjusting software parameters, not exposed to the user for modification.

Currently the task of keeping constants embedded in existing software up-to-date is labour-intensive and so there is great scope for automation.

Even parameters given by scientific measurement can be subject to change in just a few years [5]. Andronescu et al. [17] had tried to update parameters in RNAfold using constraint optimization. Nevertheless, our GI did better [5]. Section 2 expands this to the related task of creating new system software from existing functions via automated parameter tuning. In Sect. 2 we use CMA-ES to automatically adapt 1024 float constants, giving rise to cbrt, which does not currently exist in the C run time library. In addition to $\sqrt[3]{x}$, this framework could be readily adapted to provide new maths double functions [18] where there is an objective function, e.g. the inverse operation. It could also be used to port existing functions to different hardware.

Previously [5] we have demonstrated using SBSE to adapt 50 000 parameters to new scientific knowledge may be possible. Section 2 showed in less than five minutes it can adapt more than a thousand continuous values. We have used extensive testing to show the correctness of the automatically transplanted data. Additionally, e.g. following [15], it may be feasible to verify our GI cbrt.

These very early experiments hint, in a world addicted to software, both automated data maintenance and data transplantation could be vital new areas for search based software engineering.

Code. See http://www.cs.ucl.ac.uk/staff/W.Langdon/ftp/gp-code/gi_cbrt.tar.gz.

Acknowledgements. My thanks to our EuroGP [5] anonymous reviewers.

References

1. Langdon, W.B., Petke, J.: Software is not fragile. In: Parrend, P., Bourgine, P., Collet, P. (eds.) First Complex Systems Digital Campus World E-Conference 2015. SPC, pp. 203–211. Springer, Cham (2017). https://doi.org/10.1007/978-3-319-45901-1_24. http://www.cs.bham.ac.uk/~wbl/biblio/gp-html/langdon_2015_csdc.html
2. Martin, R.J., Osborne, W.M.: Guidance on software maintenance. NBS Special Publication 500–106, National Bureau of Standards, USA (1983). http://nvlpubs.nist.gov/nistpubs/Legacy/SP/nbsspecialpublication500-106.pdf
3. Cao, L., Sihler, H., Platt, U., Gutheil, E.: Numerical analysis of the chemical kinetic mechanisms of ozone depletion and halogen release in the polar troposphere. Atmos. Chem. Phys. **14**(7), 3771–3787 (2014). https://doi.org/10.5194/acp-14-3771-2014

4. Lorenz, R., et al.: ViennaRNA package 2.0. AMB **6**(1) (2011). https://doi.org/10. 1186/1748-7188-6-26

5. Langdon, W.B., Petke, J., Lorenz, R.: Evolving better RNAfold structure prediction. In: Castelli, M., Sekanina, L., Zhang, M., Cagnoni, S., García-Sánchez, P. (eds.) EuroGP 2018. LNCS, vol. 10781, pp. 220–236. Springer, Cham (2018). https://doi.org/10.1007/978-3-319-77553-1_14. http://www.cs.bham.ac.uk/~wbl/ biblio/gp-html/langdon_2018_EuroGP.html

6. Marounek, P.: Simplified approach to effort estimation in software maintenance. J. Syst. Integr. **3**(3) (2012). https://doi.org/10.20470/jsi.v3i3.123

7. Dehaghani, S.M.H., Hajrahimi, N.: Which factors affect software projects maintenance cost more? Acta Informatica Medica **21**(1), 63–66 (2013). https://doi.org/ 10.5455/AIM.2012.21.63-66

8. Mohan, M., Greer, D.: A survey of search-based refactoring for software maintenance. J. Softw. Eng. Res. Dev. **6**(1) (2018). https://doi.org/10.1186/s40411-018-0046-4

9. de Freitas, F.G., de Souza, J.T.: Ten years of search based software engineering: a bibliometric analysis. In: Cohen, M.B., Ó Cinnéide, M. (eds.) SSBSE 2011. LNCS, vol. 6956, pp. 18–32. Springer, Heidelberg (2011). https://doi.org/10.1007/978-3-642-23716-4_5

10. Butler, S.: Analysing Java Identifier Names. Ph.D. thesis, Open University, UK. http://oro.open.ac.uk/46653/

11. Tiella, R., Ceccato, M.: Automatic generation of opaque constants based on the K-clique problem for resilient data obfuscation. In: SANER 2017, pp. 182–192 (2017). https://doi.org/10.1109/SANER.2017.7884620

12. Wu, F., Weimer, W., Harman, M., Jia, Y., Krinke, J.: Deep parameter optimisation. In: Silva, S., et al. (eds.) GECCO, pp. 1375–1382. ACM, Madrid (2015). http:// www.cs.bham.ac.uk/~wbl/biblio/gp-html/Wu_2015_GECCO.html

13. Marginean, A., Barr, E.T., Harman, M., Jia, Y.: Automated transplantation of call graph and layout features into kate. In: Barros, M., Labiche, Y. (eds.) SSBSE 2015. LNCS, vol. 9275, pp. 262–268. Springer, Cham (2015). https://doi.org/ 10.1007/978-3-319-22183-0_21. http://www.cs.bham.ac.uk/~wbl/biblio/gp-html/ Marginean_2015_SSBSE.html

14. Langdon, W.B., Harman, M.: Grow and graft a better CUDA pknotsRG for RNA pseudoknot free energy calculation. In: Langdon, W.B., et al. (eds.) Genetic Improvement 2015 Workshop, pp. 805–810. ACM, Madrid (2015). http://www.cs. bham.ac.uk/~wbl/biblio/gp-html/langdon_2015_gi_pknots.html

15. Markstein, P.W.: Computation of elementary functions on the IBM RISC System/6000 processor. IBM J. Res. Dev. **34**(1), 111–119 (1990). https://doi.org/10. 1147/rd.341.0111

16. Hansen, N., Ostermeier, A.: Completely derandomized self-adaptation in evolution strategies. Evol. Comput. **9**(2), 159–195 (2001). https://doi.org/10.1162/ 106365601750190398

17. Andronescu, M., Condon, A., Hoos, H.H., Mathews, D.H., Murphy, K.P.: Efficient parameter estimation for RNA secondary structure prediction. Bioinformatics **23**(13), i19–i28 (2007). https://doi.org/10.1093/bioinformatics/btm223

18. Langdon, W.B.: Evolving square root into binary logarithm. Technical report RN/18/05, University College, London, London, UK (2018). http://www.cs.bham. ac.uk/~wbl/biblio/gp-html/langdon_RN1805.html

On the Placebo Effect in Interactive SBSE: A Preliminary Study

Jerffeson Souza[1]([✉]), Allysson Allex Araújo[2], Italo Yeltsin[1],
Raphael Saraiva[1], and Pamella Soares[1]

[1] Optimization in Software Engineering Group,
State University of Ceará, Fortaleza, Brazil
jerffeson.souza@uece.br
[2] Optimization in Software Engineering Group,
Federal University of Ceará, Crateús, Brazil
http://goes.uece.br

Abstract. Search Based Software Engineering approaches have proven to be feasible and promising in tackling a number of software engineering problems. More recently, researchers have been considering the challenges and opportunities related to involving users' expertise in the resolution process, among other reasons, to deal with the mistrust or misunderstanding of fully automated optimisation approaches. This paper presents a preliminary study concerned at assessing the users' subjective perception when his/her preferences are considered in an Interactive SBSE approach. Regarding the evaluation, we conducted a placebo-controlled study with 12 software engineering practitioners by simulating a Next Release Problem scenario. The results indicate that most (68%) of the gain achieved by the interactive approach could be attributed to being the placebo effect, that is, refers strictly to the fact that the user felt part of the optimisation process. In addition, there was an important increased confidence in the results, even in the placebo group.

Keywords: Interactive optimisation · Human aspects
Placebo effect · Search Based Software Engineering

1 Introduction

Search Based Software Engineering (SBSE) has proven to be feasible and promising in tackling a number of software engineering problems [1]. More recently, several studies have been investigating the idea of involving the Decision Maker (DM) in SBSE applications to engender his/her engagement, confidence and acceptance [2]. The subfield of SBSE specifically concerned to the usage of interactive optimisation is called Interactive SBSE [3]. In favor of this subjective model enrichment, Meignan *et al.* [4] expose that the mistrust or misunderstanding of automated optimisation systems by users constitutes one major obstacle to the effective use of advanced optimisation methods. This argument seems

© Springer Nature Switzerland AG 2018
T. E. Colanzi and P. McMinn (Eds.): SSBSE 2018, LNCS 11036, pp. 370–376, 2018.
https://doi.org/10.1007/978-3-319-99241-9_23

to be reasonable since the DM tends to have more confidence and present less resistance to the final results when he/she feels involved throughout the solution construction [5]. In fact, trust in automation has been the focus of substantial research over the past several decades addressing different fields of research [6].

In this sense, it has been argued over the years that cooperative and human aspects of software development have become crucial in order to comprehend how methods and tools are used [7]. In his seminal paper about the future of SBSE, Harman [8] highlights that automated search techniques have to effectively work with the human and thereby better encapsulate his/her assumptions and intuition. Even though SBSE results have been shown to be generally promising, we assume that they tend to be more acceptable by the DM when he/she collaborates and feels part of the process.

This preliminary study explores the research gap concerned to the comprehension of the DM's subjective perception when his/her preferences are considered in a SBSE approach. Regarding the evaluation, we conducted a "placebo-controlled" study with software engineering practitioners by simulating a Next Release Problem (NRP) scenario based on the interactive approach proposed by Araújo et al. [9]. This study mainly attempts to measure the placebo effect of having the DM participate in the SBSE process, that is, how much of the positive effect obtained by considering the DM's preference may be assigned simply to having the human added to the search process.

2   Experimental Study

As discussed above, we have simulated a scenario in which the NRP is solved by using the interactive approach proposed by Araújo et al. [9]. In summary, the NRP consists of selecting which requirements will be implemented in the next software release [10]. In this context, Araújo et al. [9]'s architecture is based on the usage of an interactive genetic algorithm alongside a machine learning model. The preferences are gathered through a subjective evaluation provided by the DM to each solution (a possible release) during a number of generations, while a machine learning model learns his/her evaluation profile. This Subjective

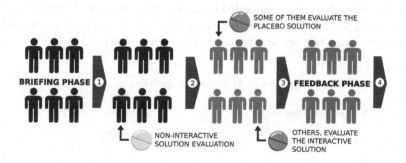

Fig. 1. Research experiment design

Evaluation (*SE*) follows a scale ranging from very unsatisfactory (1) to very satisfactory (100). After a number of subjective evaluations, the learning model replaces the DM and evaluates the remainder of the solutions.

As we can see in the Fig. 1, our experiment follows the design of a placebo-controlled study and consists of four major phases as explained below.

In the 1st phase, named *Briefing Phase*, each participant was separately briefed to perform the DM role in a scenario in which his/her company have to develop a word processor software. We have also provided details about the approach and the tool usability, including how their preferences are captured through a *SE* to each solution as much as he/she be comfortable to evaluate. Based on real-world data [11], we presented the requirements specification which contains the requirement descriptions, budget, importance values given by the clients to each requirement as well as the relevance of each client.

After concluding the *Briefing Phase*, the 2nd phase was initiated, where each participant provided a *SE* to the solution generated by the canonical genetic algorithm, that we named *non-interactive solution*. After collected this *SE*, it was conducted the 3rd phase concerned to the evaluation of the *interactive* and *placebo* solutions. The participants were unknowingly divided into two groups: (i) the ones (5) which preferences were properly considered throughout the optimisation process (**non-placebo group**) and (ii) the ones (7) which preferences were gathered but, in fact, not considered in the optimisation process, i.e., the **placebo group**. Subsequently, it was required to the members of each group a *SE* about the final solution generated by the tool. Finally, in the *Feedbacks Phase*, we asked each participant about how they classify their experience of selecting requirements using the non-interactive (2nd phase) and interactive (3rd phase) approaches. Their answers followed a five-level Likert scale ranging from very unsatisfactory to very satisfactory. We also asked about their confidence at using the non-interactive and interactive approaches at their work. Their answers followed a five-level Likert scale from "definitely no" to "definitely yes".

We have visited a Software Engineering specialisation course inviting for volunteers, from which 12 of the students shown to be available to the experiment. They have worked on software development industry for 7.2 years in average, having the least experienced participant worked for 2 years and the most experienced one for 20. Regarding their experience with release planning process, on a five-level scale, 2 of them responded to have low experience, 5 medium experience and 5 alleged to have high experience. In addition, we have developed two novel metrics to clarify our analyses. They are formalised in the Table 1:

Table 1. Proposed metrics

Subjective Factor (SF)	Placebo Factor (PF)
$SF(NI_S, I_S) = \dfrac{SE(I_S) - SE(NI_S)}{SE(NI_S)}$	$PF(P, NP) = \dfrac{\overline{SF_P}}{\overline{SF_{NP}}}$

The **Subjective Factor** (SF) indicates the relative gain in SE when compared an interactive solution (I_S) to the non-interactive (NI_S). For instance, if a solution with human intervention has a $SE(I_S) = 80$, while the non-interactive solution has a $SE(NI_S) = 40$, the gain in SF achieved by I_S over NI_S is 100%. Additionally, the **Placebo Factor** (PF) indicates how much the SE given by the DM is explained by the placebo effect, in our case, the feeling of being part of the optimisation process. To measure this, we calculated the SF average of the placebo group $(\overline{SF}_P)$ over the SF average of the non-placebo group $(\overline{SF}_{NP})$. For example, considering that placebo group has a $\overline{SF}_P = 60\%$ and the non-placebo reached a $\overline{SF}_{NP} = 80\%$, we may conclude that 75% (PF) of the SF gain is explained by the placebo effect.

To this empirical study, we defined the following three research questions: **RQ$_1$**: there is a relative gain of SE between the interactive solution over the non-interactive one?; **RQ$_2$**: how much of this gain may be explained by the placebo effect?; **RQ$_3$**: how the participants classified their experience and confidence using both non-interactive and interactive approaches?

3 Preliminary Results and Analyses

Figure 3 depicts the SE values assigned by each participant from placebo and non-placebo groups to the interactive and non-interactive solutions. In the non-placebo group (Fig. 2b), we have accounted that the majority of the participants (60%) has preferred the interactive solution over the non-interactive one. The remainder have been divided between those that did not perceive difference between the solutions (20%) and the ones who preferred the non-interactive (20%). This behaviour is quite similar for the placebo group (Fig. 2a) since 57.14% have preferred the interactive solution, 28.57% did not perceive the difference and 14.28% have opted to the non-interactive solution. We also assume that this option by the non-interactive solution, although using an interactive approach, may be explained by the inefficiency of the proposal to reach the DM

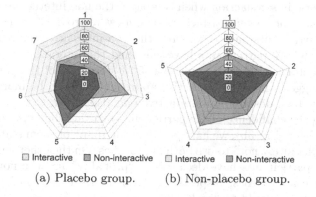

(a) Placebo group.   (b) Non-placebo group.

Fig. 2. SE values assigned by each participant from each group.

preferences in certain circumstances. To measure the relative gain between both solutions (non-interactive and interactive), we used the SF metric. In average, the SF gain achieved by the non-placebo group was 69.09%, while in the placebo one was 47.04%. Therefore, answering **RQ₁**, there was, in fact, a relative gain of SE by the interactive solution over the non-interactive in both groups.

Since we have confirmed the SE gain between both solutions, we may analyse how much of this gain is explained by the placebo effect by measuring the PF metric. Of the SF achieved, on average, by the placebo group (47.04%) over the non-placebo group (69.09%), there was a PF of 68%. Therefore, answering **RQ₂**, given all the subjective gain related to the DM interaction, 68% refers strictly to the fact that he/she felt part of the resolution process.

Finally, we analysed the answers provided by the participants during the *Feedbacks Phase* to answer **RQ₃**. Figure 3 shows the percentage of answers made by both groups about the experience of selecting requirements (Fig. 3a) and their confidence (Fig. 3b), respectively for the interactive (outer circle) and non-interactive (inner circle) approaches.

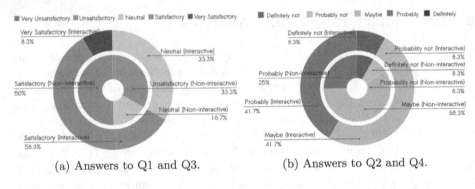

(a) Answers to Q1 and Q3.   (b) Answers to Q2 and Q4.

Fig. 3. Answers provided by the participants during the *Feedbacks Phase*.

Concerning to the experience of selecting requirements (Fig. 3a), it was identified an increase in satisfaction when compared the non-interactive to the interactive approach, since no unsatisfactory answers were provided to the second one. 50% of the participants have considered the non-interactive approach as satisfactory, while 66.6% participants have classified the interactive as satisfactory or very satisfactory, even considering that 50% were part of the placebo group. The results suggest that the interactive approach seems to be more acceptable by the participants, despite non-interactive one also shown to be valuable.

Regarding the confidence of the participants at using the approaches in their work environment (Fig. 3b), we have noticed that 16.6% of them stated to "probably not" or "definitely not" to use both approaches. On the other hand, 25% and 41.7% of the participants have declared to "probably" use the non-interactive and interactive approaches, respectively. Even more interesting, 80% of these participants who declared to "probably" use the interactive approach are members of the placebo group. Ultimately, these results contribute to enlight the studies in favour of preference-based approaches since they reinforce the argument that the DM tends to have more confidence in the final results when he/she feels involved throughout the solution construction [5].

4   Final Considerations and Future Research Works

Preference-based approaches have been recurrently investigated under the SBSE context. These strategies are based on the valuable synergy which can be exploited between human-cooperation and artificial intelligence techniques.

In this sense, this work intends to be a preliminary study about the research gap concerned to the comprehension of the DM's subjective perception when he/she feels part and collaborates to the resolution process in an SBSE approach. To that, we have conducted a placebo-controlled study with 12 SE practitioners which used an interactive architecture to solve an NRP scenario. Overall, our initial findings are shown to be promising. Firstly, we demonstrated to definitely have an increase in the subjective evaluation when compared an interactive to the non-interactive solution. Then, we verified that almost 68% of this gain refers only to the fact of the DM felt part of the process (placebo effect). Lastly, according to the feedback of the participants, the interactive approach seems to be more acceptable, despite of non-interactive one also shown to be valuable.

As a preliminary work, there are several limitations and threats to the validity of the results, in special the small number of subjects. However, we consider that conducting these experiments was essential to motivate our and others future works, which will/should at least consider more human subjects and other SBSE problems. In addition, we aim to expand and evaluate other human and cooperative aspects involved in Interactive SBSE.

References

1. Harman, M., McMinn, P., de Souza, J.T., Yoo, S.: Search based software engineering: techniques, taxonomy, tutorial. In: Meyer, B., Nordio, M. (eds.) LASER 2008-2010. LNCS, vol. 7007, pp. 1–59. Springer, Heidelberg (2012). https://doi.org/10.1007/978-3-642-25231-0_1
2. Ferreira, T.N., Vergilio, S.R., de Souza, J.T.: Incorporating user preferences in search-based software engineering: a systematic mapping study. Inf. Softw. Technol. **90**, 55–69 (2017)
3. Ramirez, A., Romero, J.R., Simons, C.: A systematic review of interaction in search-based software engineering. IEEE Trans. Softw. Eng. (TSE) (2018)
4. Meignan, D., Knust, S., Frayret, J.-M., Pesant, G., Gaud, N.: A review and taxonomy of interactive optimization methods in operations research. ACM Trans. Interact. Intell. Syst. **5**(3), 17:1–17:43 (2015)
5. Miettinen, K.: Nonlinear Multiobjective Optimization. International Series in Operations Research and Management Science. Springer, Heidelberg (1999). https://doi.org/10.1007/978-1-4615-5563-6
6. Hoff, K., Bashir, M.: Trust in automation: integrating empirical evidence on factors that influence trust. Hum. Factors **57**(3), 407–434 (2015)

7. Prikladnicki, R., Dittrich, Y., Sharp, H., De Souza, C., Cataldo, M., Hoda, R.: Cooperative and human aspects of software engineering. ACM SIGSOFT Softw. Eng. Notes **38**(5), 34–37 (2013)
8. Harman, M.: The current state and future of search based software engineering. In: 2007 Future of Software Engineering. IEEE Computer Society (2007)
9. Araújo, A.A., Paixao, M., Yeltsin, I., Dantas, A., Souza, J.: An architecture based on interactive optimization and machine learning applied to the next release problem. Autom. Softw. Eng. **24**, 623–671 (2017)
10. Baker, P., Harman, M., Steinhofel, K., Skaliotis, A.: Search based approaches to component selection and prioritization for the next release problem. In: 22nd IEEE International Conference on Software Maintenance 2006. ICSM 2006. pp. 176–185. IEEE (2006)
11. Karim, M.R., Ruhe, G.: Bi-objective genetic search for release planning in support of themes. In: Le Goues, C., Yoo, S. (eds.) SSBSE 2014. LNCS, vol. 8636, pp. 123–137. Springer, Cham (2014). https://doi.org/10.1007/978-3-319-09940-8_9

EvoIsolator: Evolving Program Slices
for Hardware Isolation Based Security

Mengmei Ye$^{(\boxtimes)}$, Myra B. Cohen, Witawas Srisa-an, and Sheng Wei

Department of Computer Science and Engineering,
University of Nebraska-Lincoln, Lincoln, NE 68588-0115, USA
{mye,myra,witty,swei}@cse.unl.edu

Abstract. To provide strong security support for today's applications, microprocessor manufacturers have introduced hardware isolation, an on-chip mechanism that provides secure accesses to sensitive data. Currently, hardware isolation is still difficult to use by software developers because the process to identify access points to sensitive data is error-prone and can lead to under and over protection of sensitive data. Under protection can lead to security vulnerabilities. Over protection can lead to an increased attack surface and excessive communication overhead. In this paper we describe EVOISOLATOR, a search-based framework to (i) automatically generate executable minimal slices that include all access points to a set of specified sensitive data; and (ii) automatically optimize (for small code block size and low communication overhead) the code modules for hardware isolation. We demonstrate, through a small feasibility study, the potential impact of our proposed code optimizer.

Keywords: Software transplantation · Genetic algorithms
Hardware security

1 Introduction

Hardware isolation is growing as a way for software developers to secure sensitive program calculations and data. For instance, customized secure chips are being used to store fingerprints and payment data on mobile phones. Isolation must include not only the data, but the code that accesses that data to avoid leakage of sensitive information. One popular isolation technique that we will work with in this paper is the ARM TrustZone [1]. Sensitive data and associated program code are stored in the *secure world* while the rest of the code is placed in the *normal world*. Code in the secure world can access data in both environments, while the normal world cannot directly query the secure world.

While this type of isolation provides stronger security than traditional software only approaches, there are some potential pitfalls. A bug in the secure world can cause significant harm by leaking or corrupting sensitive information. This argues for placing only a limited amount of (well tested) code into the secure world. There is also communication overhead between the secure and normal

© Springer Nature Switzerland AG 2018
T. E. Colanzi and P. McMinn (Eds.): SSBSE 2018, LNCS 11036, pp. 377–382, 2018.
https://doi.org/10.1007/978-3-319-99241-9_24

worlds. This suggests that different slices of code, and different code interleavings can impact the performance of such an architecture.

Recently we developed TZSlicer [2], a technique that uses slicing and a taint analysis to carve a program for use in hardware isolation. TZSlicer, while a good first step, over approximates the amount of the code that needs to be isolated in the secure world. We also found the need to add optimizations. For example, statements that do not access sensitive data might be interwoven with statements that do. This will lead to the inclusion of statements that do not access sensitive data into the secure world. On the other hand, if we separate the sensitive and non-sensitive statements into their respective spaces, it will result in fewer statements in the secure world but may also incur a significantly higher communication overhead. It is desirable to develop an optimization approach, which can reorder the statements to achieve security-aware program slicing with low communication overhead.

In this paper we present our vision of a more flexible framework for hardware isolation, using a search-based approach [3,4] that can balance different objectives. Our framework applies evolutionary algorithms in two phases. First, we propose to create a secure slice and synthesize it into the secure world. We view this as a type of software transplantation (where we remove code from the normal world and place it into the secure world) [4,5]. Our goal is to include the smallest slice that passes a security test suite. Second, we use another evolutionary algorithm (a genetic algorithm) to re-order and optimize the synthesized code within the secure world, with the goal of reducing communication overhead. We call our framework EVOISOLATOR. To the best of our knowledge, this is the first search-based approach to hardware isolation for program security.

While our vision is not yet fully implemented, we present our idea and motivating examples in this paper, along with a feasibility study to demonstrate how the second part of the framework, the optimization to reduce communication overhead, can improve performance.

2   Background and Motivation

ARM TrustZone. The ARM TrustZone mechanism is a widely used security platform to prevent against threat models such as information leakage attacks [1,6]. The secure world and the normal world in the TrustZone framework are separated by a bus-level hardware isolation interface. The communication between the secure and normal worlds is conducted by a secure monitor in the secure world. In addition, there are secure apps used to execute the sensitive programs and a secure memory space to store the sensitive information. The normal world contains a normal app to execute non-sensitive programs and a shared memory space to store information that both the secure and normal apps can access.

In our hardware isolation framework based on TrustZone [1], the normal app first sends a request to the secure world and provides input data for the shared memory. Then, the secure monitor issues a secure monitor call (SMC) to switch the CPU mode from the normal to the secure world. The secure app conducts computations for each request after reading the input data stored in the shared memory and writes the end results to the shared memory for the normal app to access prior to switching the CPU mode back to the normal world. Note that resources stored in the secure world are treated as a part of the trusted computing base (TCB), and any faults or security vulnerabilities in the secure world can compromise the entire system [7].

TZSlicer. TZSlicer [2] uses a dynamic taint analysis to slice a small part of the program into the TrustZone framework that meets the security requirements and maintains the original program functionality. The developer provides an original program, the input data, and the tainted (secure) variables to TZSlicer. Then, TZSlicer generates a system dependency graph (SDG) [8] and extracts the propagation flow for the sensitive computations. It then slices the program, synthesizes the secure and normal slices, and deploys them into the TrustZone system. TZSlicer then attempts to optimize the slices using loop unrolling and variable renaming. However, the applicability and the room for optimization by adopting these simple strategies are limited [2]. We believe search-based techniques can help develop more applicable and effective optimization strategies including code reordering, demonstrated in this work.

3   EvoIsolator

Figure 1 shows our vision of EVOISOLATOR. It has two primary optimization steps. First, it determines and synthesizes the slice (TZSurgeon). Then, it optimizes that slice for performance (TZOptimizer). EVOISOLATOR starts with the original program and a set of sensitive variables. It generates random initial secure and normal slices that pass a security test suite. It then transplants the sensitive computations into the secure world and the remaining non-sensitive computations into the normal world using genetic programming to find the best code configuration. In TZOptimizer it reorders the code to reduce communication overhead.

The EVOISOLATOR chromosome includes both secure and normal code blocks. The code blocks are split by the TrustZone SMC. A test suite used for fitness contains input-output pairs designed to detect information leakage and other traditional bugs. A second fitness function is added in TZOptimizer for reordering which counts the number of switches between the secure and normal worlds.

Fitness Function. We present a prototype fitness function for TZOptimizer:

$$f = \begin{cases} -1000 & \text{if the program does not compile} \\ w_1 * P_{IO} - w_2 * S & \text{if the program successfully compiles} \end{cases}$$

P_{IO} indicates the number of the input-output pairs that pass the test suite, and S indicates the number of world switches. w_1 and w_2 indicate the weights for P_{IO} and S, respectively. We leave normalization and tuning as future work.

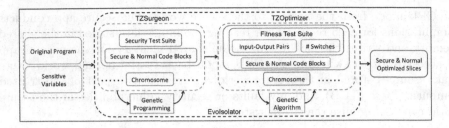

Fig. 1. System architecture and workflow of EVOISOLATOR

4   Feasibility Study

To evaluate the feasibility of EVOISOLATOR, we implemented a version of the second phase, TZOptimizer, using TZSlicer as input. We leave TZSurgeon as future work. We demonstrate our approach with an example (Fig. 2(a)).

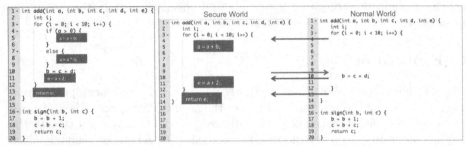

(a) Original Example   (b) Secure and Normal Slices

Fig. 2. Preparation for EvoIsolator (Color figure online)

4.1   Setup

This example contains the *add* and *sign* functions. The variable *a* in the *add* function is the secure (tainted variable). TZSlicer treats the lines 5, 8, 11, and 13 as sensitive computations (shown with the red text boxes). TZSlicer partitions the program as is seen in Fig. 2(b), placing the lines 5, 11, and 13 from the original program into the secure world and removing the redundant/non-executed code (e.g., line 8). The arrows indicate the world switching flow.

Fig. 3. Sliced example

Using the secure and normal slices generated by TZSlicer, EVOISOLATOR moves the slices to the secure and normal code blocks. To generate the fitness test suite, the code blocks are merged into a sliced program that is executable in a regular C environment (shown in Fig. 3). The *SMC* lines in the sliced program count the number of world switches in each loop iteration. In all, there are 31 switches in the initial sliced example.

TZOptimizer then tries to optimize solutions that pass all the test cases and achieves the minimum number of world switches. Figure 4 shows one of the crossover operations and one of the mutation operations for this phase. In Fig. 4(a), assume that TZOptimizer randomly picks two secure slices from the two chromosomes. By randomly selecting a crossover point, it swaps the code blocks in the chromosome parents and generates the offspring. In Fig. 4(b), assume that the mutation point is a line of the sensitive computation. TZOptimizer splits the target code block to two code blocks.

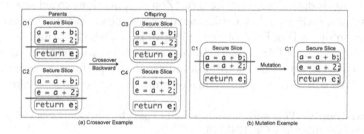

Fig. 4. Crossover and mutation examples

4.2   Evaluation

We built a version of TZOptimizer as a genetic algorithm in Python. We first generate 50 test cases (input-output pairs) based on the original program. Then, we input the secure and normal slices generated by TZSlicer to the TZOptimizer part of EvoIsolator. We use a population size of 12 based on some initial experiments. We set $w_1 = 10$ and $w_2 = 1/50$ for the weights in the fitness function. After executing multiple runs, EvoIsolator outputs two solutions, which reduce the original 31 switches (from TZSlicer) to 21 switches as is shown in Fig. 5. Solution 1 moves the line $e = a + 2$ backward and still keeps this line within the loop computation. In addition, EvoIsolator detects that it is unnecessary to place this line inside of the loop. Therefore, the second solution moves this line forward to the outside of the loop, which further reduces the resource usage during the computation and improves the efficiency of the program execution.

We ran the program 100 times to understand if it converges on a solution each time. We found that the number of generations to find this solution was usually less than 3, and in all cases we found a better solution. While this is a simple example we believe this can scale to larger programs.

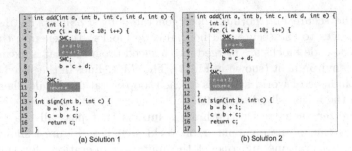

(a) Solution 1   (b) Solution 2

Fig. 5. Optimized example generated by EvoIsolator

5 Conclusions and Future Work

In this paper we proposed a search-based framework for hardware isolation, EVOISOLATOR. It optimizes slices for TrustZone applications to achieve the security of data and code with low communication overhead. We performed a feasibility study on phase II of EvoIsolator (TZOptimizer), which optimizes programs generated by Phase I (TZSurgeon). In future work we will implement the full-fledged EVOISOLATOR, tune the fitness function, and perform a comprehensive evaluation. We will also explore the use of multi-objective optimization.

Acknowledgments. This work was supported in part by National Science Foundation Grants CNS-1750867 and CCF-1745775.

References

1. ARM security technology: building a secure system using TrustZone technology. http://infocenter.arm.com/help/index.jsp?topic=/com.arm.doc.prd29-genc-009492c/index.html
2. Ye, M., Sherman, J., Srisa-an, W., Wei, S.: TZSlicer: security-aware dynamic program slicing for hardware isolation. In: HOST (2018)
3. Mark Harman, S., Mansouri, A., Zhang, Y.: Search-based software engineering: trends, techniques and applications. ACM Comput. Surv. **45**(1), 11:1–11:61 (2012)
4. Petke, J., Haraldsson, S.O., Harman, M., Langdon, W.B., White, D.R., Woodward, J.R.: Genetic improvement of software: a comprehensive survey. IEEE Trans. Evol. Comput. **22**(3), 415–432 (2018)
5. Petke, J., Harman, M., Langdon, W.B., Weimer, W.: Specialising software for different downstream applications using genetic improvement and code transplantation. IEEE Trans. Softw. Eng. **44**, 574–594 (2017)
6. Hu, N., Ye, M., Wei, S.: Surviving information leakage hardware Trojan attacks using hardware isolation. IEEE TETC (2017)
7. Schuster, F., et al.: VC3: trustworthy data analytics in the cloud using SGX. In: S&P, pp. 38–54 (2015)
8. Horwitz, S., Reps, T., Binkley, D.: Interprocedural slicing using dependence graphs. In: PLDI, pp. 35–46 (1988)

Challenge Paper

Detecting Real Faults in the Gson Library Through Search-Based Unit Test Generation

Gregory Gay[⊠]

University of South Carolina, Columbia, SC, USA
greg@greggay.com

Abstract. An important benchmark for test generation tools is their ability to detect *real faults*. We have identified 16 real faults in Gson—a Java library for manipulating JSON data—and added them to the Defects4J fault database. Tests generated using the EvoSuite framework are able to detect seven faults. Analysis of the remaining faults offers lessons in how to improve generation. We offer these faults to the community to assist future research.

Keywords: Search-based test generation
Automated test generation · Software faults

1   Introduction

Automation of unit test creation can assist in controlling the cost of testing. One promising form of automated generation is *search-based* generation. Given a measurable testing goal, powerful optimization algorithms can select test inputs meeting that goal [6].

To impact practice, automated generation techniques must be effective at detecting the complex faults that manifest in real-world software projects [2]. "Detecting faults" is not a goal that can be measured. Instead, search-based generation relies on *fitness functions*—based on coverage of code structures, synthetic faults, and other targeted aspects—that are believed to increase the probability of fault detection. It is important to identify which functions produce tests that detect real faults.

By offering case examples, fault databases—such as Defects4J [5]—allow us to explore questions like those above. The Google Gson library[1] offers an excellent opportunity for expanding Defects4J. Gson is an open-source library for serializing and deserializing JSON input that is an essential tool of Java and Android development and is one of the most popular Java libraries [4].

This work is supported by National Science Foundation grant CCF-1657299.

[1] https://github.com/google/gson.

T. E. Colanzi and P. McMinn (Eds.): SSBSE 2018, LNCS 11036, pp. 385–391, 2018.
https://doi.org/10.1007/978-3-319-99241-9_25

Gson serves as an interesting benchmark because much of its functionality is related to the parsing of JSON input and creation and manipulation of complex objects. Manipulation of complex input and non-primitive objects is challenging for automated generation. Gson is also a mature project. Its faults will generally be more complex than the simple syntactic mistakes modeled by mutation testing [2]. Rather, detecting faults will require specific, contextual, combinations of input and method calls. By studying these faults, we may be able to learn lessons that will improve test generation tools.

We have identified 16 real faults in the Gson project, and added them to Defects4J. We generated test suites using the EvoSuite framework [6]—focusing on eight fitness functions and three combinations of functions—and assessed the ability of these suites to detect the faults. Ultimately, EvoSuite is able to detect seven faults. Some of the issues preventing detection include a need for stronger coverage criteria, the need for specific data types or values as input, and faults that only emerge through class interactions—requiring system testing to detect. We offer these faults and this analysis to the community to assist future research and improve test generation efforts.

2   Study

In this study, we have extracted faults from the Gson project, gathering faulty and fixed versions of the code and developer-written test cases that expose each fault. For each fault, we have generated tests for each affected class-under-test (CUT) with the EvoSuite framework [6]—using eight fitness functions and three combinations of functions—and assessed the efficacy of generated suites. We wish to answer the following research questions: (1) *can suites optimizing any function detect the extracted faults?*, (2) *which fitness function or combination of functions generates suites with the highest overall likelihood of fault detection?* and (3), *what factors prevented fault detection?*

In order to answer these questions, we have performed the following experiment:

1. **Extracted Faults:** We have identified 16 real faults in the Gson project, and added them to the Defects4J fault database (See Sect. 2.1).
2. **Generated Test Cases:** For each fault, we generated 10 suites per fitness function and combination of functions, using the fixed version of each CUT. We repeat this step with a two-minute and a ten-minute search budget per CUT (See Sect. 2.2).
3. **Removed Non-Compiling Tests:** Any tests that do not compile, or that return inconsistent results, are automatically removed (See Sect. 2.2).
4. **Assessed Fault-finding Efficacy:** For each budget, function, and fault, we measure the likelihood of fault detection. For each undetected fault, we examined gathered data and the source code to identify possible detection-preventing factors.

2.1 Fault Extraction

Defects4J is an extensible database of real faults extracted from Java projects [5]. Currently, the core dataset consists of 395 faults from six projects, with an experimental release containing 597 faults from fifteen projects[2]. For each fault, Defects4J provides access to the faulty and fixed versions of the code, developer-written test cases that expose each fault, and a list of classes and lines of code modified to fix the fault.

We have added Gson to Defects4J. This process consisted of developing build scripts that would compile and execute all tested project versions, extracting candidate faults using Gson's version control and issue tracking systems, ensuring that each candidate could be reliable reproduced, and minimizing the "patch" used to distinguish fixed and faulty classes until it only contains fault-related code. Following this process, we extracted 16 faults from a pool of 132 candidate faults that met all requirements.

Each fault is required to meet three properties. First, the fault must be related to the source code. The "fixed" version must be explicitly labeled as a fix to an issue[3], and changes imposed by the fix must be to source code, not to other project artifacts such as the build system. Second, the fault must be reproducible—at least one test must pass on the fixed version and fail on the faulty version. Third, the fix to the fault must be isolated from unrelated code changes such as refactoring.

The faults used in this study can be accessed through the experimental version of Defects4J[4]. Additional data about each fault can be found at http://greggay.com/data/gson/GsonFaults.csv, including commit IDs, fault descriptions, and a list of triggering tests. We plan to add additional faults and improvements in the future.

2.2 Test Generation and Removal

EvoSuite applies a genetic algorithm in order to evolve test suites over several generations, forming a new population by retaining, mutating, and combining the strongest solutions [6]. In this study, we used EvoSuite version 1.0.5 with eight fitness functions: Branch Coverage, Direct Branch Coverage, Line Coverage, Exception Coverage, Method Coverage, Method (Top-Level, No Exception) Coverage, Output Coverage, and Weak Mutation Coverage. Rojas et al. provide a primer on each [6]. We have also used three combinations of fitness functions: all eight of the above, Branch/Exception Coverage, and Branch/Exception/Method Coverage. The first is EvoSuite's default configuration, and the other two were found to be generally effective at detecting faults [3]. When a combination is used to generate tests, the individual fitness functions are calculated and added to obtain a single fitness score.

---

[2] Core: http://defects4j.org; Experimental: http://github.com/Greg4cr/defects4j.

[3] The commit message for the "fixed" version must reference either a reported issue or a pull request that describes and fixes a fault (that is, it must not add new functionality).

[4] These faults will be migrated into the core dataset following additional testing and study.

Tests are generated from the fixed version of the system and applied to the faulty version in order to eliminate the oracle problem. Given the potential difficulty in achieving coverage over Gson classes, two search budgets were used—two and ten minutes, a typical and an extended budget [2]. As results may vary, we performed 10 trials for each fault, fitness function, and budget. Generation tools may generate flaky (unstable) tests [2]. We automatically remove non-compiling test cases. Then, each test is executed on the fixed CUT five times. If results are inconsistent, the test case is removed. On average, less than 1% of tests are removed from each suite.

3   Results and Discussion

In Table 1, we list—for each search budget and fitness function—the likelihood of fault detection (the proportion of suites that detected the fault). Seven of the sixteen faults were detected. EvoSuite failed to generate test suites for Fault 12. At the two minute budget, the most effective fitness function is a combination of Branch/Exception/Method Coverage, with an average likelihood of fault detection of 40.67%—closely followed by the Branch/Exception combination and Branch Coverage alone. At the ten minute budget, these three configurations perform equally, with an average detection likelihood of 46.00%. Unlike in other Defects4J systems [3], Exception Coverage does not add significant value. Specialized metrics, like Output Coverage, also do not seem to have much situational applicability.

Table 1. Likelihood of fault detection for each fitness function (two-minute/ten-minute budget). (D)BC = (Direct) Branch Coverage, EC = Exception Coverage, LC = Line Coverage, M(TLNE)C = Method (Top-Level, No Exception) Coverage, OC = Output Coverage, WMC = Weak Mutation Coverage, C-All = combination of all criteria, C-BE = combination of BC/EC, C-BEM = combination of BC/EC/MC. Undetected faults (1, 4, 5, 7, 9, 11, 14, and 15) are omitted.

Fault	Budget	BC	DBC	EC	LC	MC	M(TLNE)	OC	WMC	C-All	C-BE	C-BEM
2	2 m	100.00%	100.00%	70.00%	70.00%	-	-	-	100.00%	100.00%	100.00%	100.00%
	10 m	100.00%	100.00%	40.00%	90.00%	-	-	-	100.00%	100.00%	100.00%	100.00%
3	2 m	70.00%	60.00%	-	80.00%	-	-	-	60.00%	30.00%	90.00%	70.00%
	10 m	100.00%	80.00%	-	100.00%	-	-	-	100.00%	70.00%	90.00%	100.00%
6	2 m	100.00%	100.00%	100.00%	100.00%	100.00%	100.00%	100.00%	100.00%	100.00%	100.00%	100.00%
	10 m	100.00%	100.00%	100.00%	100.00%	100.00%	100.00%	100.00%	100.00%	100.00%	100.00%	100.00%
8	2 m	20.00	30.00%	-	50.00%	-	-	-	10.00%	10.00%	10.00%	40.00%
	10 m	90.00%	60.00%	-	100.00%	-	-	-	80.00%	80.00%	100.00%	90.00%
10	2 m	100.00%	100.00%	30.00%	100.00%	20.00%	10.00%	40.00%	50.00%	100.00%	100.00%	100.00%
	10 m	100.00%	100.00%	10.00%	100.00%	30.00%	10.00%	40.00%	70.00%	100.00%	100.00%	100.00%
13	2 m	100.00%	100.00%	20.00%	30.00%	100.00%	100.00%	-	90.00%	100.00%	100.00%	100.00%
	10 m	100.00%	100.00%	10.00%	-	100.00%	100.00%	-	100.00%	100.00%	100.00%	100.00%
16	2 m	100.00%	100.00%	60.00%	100.00%	40.00%	10.00%	-	40.00%	100.00%	100.00%	100.00%
	10 m	100.00%	100.00%	30.00%	100.00%	-	30.00%	30.00%	10.00%	100.00%	100.00%	100.00%
Average	2 m	39.33%	39.33%	18.67%	35.33%	17.33%	14.67%	9.33%	30.00%	36.00%	40.00%	40.67%
	10 m	46.00%	42.67%	12.67%	39.33%	15.33%	16.00%	11.33%	37.33%	43.33%	46.00%	46.00%

Fault 6 was detected the most reliably, regardless of search budget or fitness function. This fault updates Gson to be compliant with the 2014 JSON RFC 7159 standard, and adds a leniency check to enable backwards compatibility[5]. Compliance checks are spread throughout the code, resulting in fault detection if even a small amount of coverage is attained. Fault 13[6], dealing with an index out of bounds error, is a classic example of what automated generation excels at. The fix adds boundary checks, which are efficiently covered by Branch Coverage—ensuring differing output between versions.

Fault 8[7] was detected the least reliably. This fault causes issues with deserializing map structures when a key is an unquoted long or integer. The generated tests arguably expose the fault—they produce differing behavior and result in the same exception as the human-written test cases. Yet, these failing tests also point out an issue with test suite generation. The test cases fail in the same manner as the human-written cases, but not for the same reason. The failing tests pass strings to methods meant to handle long or integer values and expect a `NumberFormatException`—which is not thrown by the faulty version. The exception thrown instead—a complaint about a string—makes sense, given the input used. Rather than helping a human tester identify actual issues, these test cases only show that the two versions of the code behave differently.

EvoSuite failed to detect the other eight faults. Therefore, our next step was to examine these faults to identify factors preventing detection. These factors include:

Stronger Adequacy Criteria are Required: Fault 14[8] causes all instances of -0 ("negative 0") to be converted to 0. Catching this fault would require the generation framework to produce -0 as input—an unlikely choice. However, the test generator could be guided towards this input. The fixed version of the class has a complex `if-condition` that includes this corner case. Branch Coverage simply requires the full predicate to evaluate to `true` and `false`, so coverage can be achieved without -0 input. However, a stronger criterion such as Modified Condition/Decision Coverage [1] would require -0 to attain full coverage.

Specific Data Types are Required as Input: Fault 9[9] causes an error when Gson attempts to initialize an interface or abstract class. This fault can only be detected if a test case attempts to instantiate either type of object. Most generation frameworks will not attempt this, and the feedback provided by criteria like Branch Coverage is not sufficient to suggest such an action.

---

[5] https://github.com/google/gson/commit/af68d70cd55826fa7149effd7397d64667ca264c.

[6] https://github.com/google/gson/commit/9e6f2bab20257b6823a5b753739f047d79e9dcbd.

[7] https://github.com/google/gson/commit/2b08c88c09d14e0b1a68a982bab0bb18206df76b.

[8] https://github.com/google/gson/commit/9a2421997e83ec803c88ea370a2d102052699d3b.

[9] https://github.com/google/gson/commit/0f66f4fac441f7d7d7bc4afc907454f3fe4c0faa.

Fault Emerges Through Class Interactions and System Testing: Fault 1^{10} causes Gson to fail to serialize or deserialize a class when its super class has a type parameter. Like Fault 9, this is a case where tests would need to attempt to generate a highly specific object. In addition, the developer-written test exposing this fault is a *system-level* test, not a unit test—working through Gson's top-level serialization and deserialization functions. It is possible that unit testing could expose the fault, but this is code that—like Fault 9 above—that would be hard to cover. System testing is more likely to expose the fault, but external context would still be needed to guide data type selection.

By default, Gson converts application classes to JSON using its built-in type adapters. If Gson's default JSON conversion isn't appropriate for a type, users can specify their own adapter using an annotation. Fault 5^{11} deals with ensuring that custom type adapters safely handle null objects. However, performing unit testing of the modified class will not expose the fault. Rather, one needs to define a type adapter for a null class, then use Gson's top-level API. Fault 7^{12} modifies the same class, fixing a null pointer exception when a null object is returned instead of a proper `TypeAdapter`. A similar scenario exists for Fault 11^{13}, where custom adapters are ignored for primitive fields. In all three cases—as long as the right input is chosen—system testing will expose this fault while unit testing may not be able to replicate the same example. However, system testing alone will still not be sufficient. Each of these scenarios requires external context to create the specific conditions called for to detect the fault.

Gson is a complex system designed to be accessed through a simple API. Human-written tests tend to use that API, even when testing specific classes. Unit test generation may not be suited to detecting some of the faults that emerge from this type of system, and even if it can, the generated test suites may not be easily understood by human developers. Many of the most mature test generation approaches are based on unit testing, and more work clearly needs to be conducted in the system testing realm.

Regardless of the form of testing, better means are needed of extracting *context* from the system and its associated artifacts. Automation requires information to guide test creation. Often, this is some form of code coverage. However, code coverage doesn't provide the same type of information developers use during test creation, and many of the studied faults were detected by *almost any* coverage criterion or *no* criterion. Rather, information from the project is needed to guide input generation. Methods of gleaning that information, either through seeding from existing test cases or data mining of project elements, may assist in improving the efficacy of test generation. Approaches to mining of requirements information or bug reports, for instance, might suggest using particular data types or values as input.

---

[10] https://github.com/google/gson/commit/c6a4f55d1a9b191dbbd958c366091e567191ccab.

[11] https://github.com/google/gson/commit/57b08bbc31421653481762507cc88ee3eb373563.

[12] https://github.com/google/gson/commit/dea305503ad8827121e8212248c271f1f2f90048.

[13] https://github.com/google/gson/commit/bb451eac43313ae08b30ac0916718ca00c39656d.

4   Conclusion

Testing costs can be reduced through automated unit test generation. An important benchmark for such tools is their ability to detect *real faults*. We have identified 16 real faults in Gson, and added them to Defects4J. We generated test suites and found that EvoSuite is able to detect seven faults. Some of the issues preventing fault detection include a lack of fitness functions for stronger coverage criteria, the need for specific data types or values as input, and faults that only emerge through class interactions—requiring system testing rather than unit testing to detect. We offer these faults to the community to assist future research.

References

1. Chilenski, J.: An investigation of three forms of the modified condition decision coverage (MCDC) criterion. Technical report DOT/FAA/AR-01/18, Office of Aviation Research, Washington, D.C., April 2001
2. Gay, G.: The fitness function for the job: search-based generation of test suites that detect real faults. In: Proceedings of the International Conference on Software Testing ICST 2017. IEEE (2017)
3. Gay, G.: Generating effective test suites by combining coverage criteria. In: Menzies, T., Petke, J. (eds.) SSBSE 2017. LNCS, vol. 10452, pp. 65–82. Springer, Cham (2017). https://doi.org/10.1007/978-3-319-66299-2_5
4. Idan, H.: The top 100 java libraries in 2017 - based on 259,885 source files (2017). https://blog.takipi.com/the-top-100-Java-libraries-in-2017-based-on-259885-source-files/
5. Just, R., Jalali, D., Ernst, M.D.: Defects4J: a database of existing faults to enable controlled testing studies for Java programs. In: Proceedings of the 2014 International Symposium on Software Testing and Analysis ISSTA 2014, pp. 437–440. ACM, New York (2014). https://doi.org/10.1145/2610384.2628055
6. Rojas, J.M., Campos, J., Vivanti, M., Fraser, G., Arcuri, A.: Combining multiple coverage criteria in search-based unit test generation. In: Barros, M., Labiche, Y. (eds.) SSBSE 2015. LNCS, vol. 9275, pp. 93–108. Springer, Cham (2015). https://doi.org/10.1007/978-3-319-22183-0_7

Author Index

Printed in the United States
By Bookmasters

Printed in the United States
By Bookmasters